THE EEA AND THE EFTA COURT

The EEA Agreement extends the free movement of persons, goods, services and capital to the EEA/EFTA States: Iceland, Liechtenstein and Norway. It provides for equal conditions of competition and abolishes discrimination on grounds of nationality in all 31 EEA States. The successful operation of the EEA depends upon a two-pillar system of supervision involving the European Commission and the EFTA Surveillance Authority. A two-pillar structure has also been established in respect of judicial control with the EFTA Court operating in parallel to the Court of Justice of the European Union.

The EFTA Court, which celebrates its 20th anniversary in 2014, has jurisdiction with regard to EFTA States which are parties to the EEA Agreement. The jurisdiction of the EFTA Court accordingly corresponds to the jurisdiction of the Court of Justice of the European Union over EU Member States in matters of EEA law.

The EEA and the EFTA Court

Decentred Integration

To Mark the 20th Anniversary of the EFTA Court

Edited by the EFTA Court

Editorial Committee
Carl Baudenbacher, President of the EFTA Court
Philipp Speitler, Legal Secretary, EFTA Court
Bryndís Pálmarsdóttir, Senior Officer, EFTA Court

·HART·
PUBLISHING
OXFORD AND PORTLAND, OREGON
2014

Published in the United Kingdom by Hart Publishing Ltd
16C Worcester Place, Oxford, OX1 2JW
Telephone: +44 (0)1865 517530
Fax: +44 (0)1865 510710
E-mail: mail@hartpub.co.uk
Website: http://www.hartpub.co.uk

Published in North America (US and Canada) by
Hart Publishing
c/o International Specialized Book Services
920 NE 58th Avenue, Suite 300
Portland, OR 97213-3786
USA
Tel: +1 503 287 3093 or toll-free: (1) 800 944 6190
Fax: +1 503 280 8832
E-mail: orders@isbs.com
Website: http://www.isbs.com

Hart Publishing is an imprint of Bloomsbury Publishing plc.

British Library Cataloguing in Publication Data
Data Available

ISBN: 978-1-84946-626-4

Typeset by Compuscript Ltd, Shannon
Printed and bound in Great Britain by
CPI Group (UK) Ltd, Croydon CR0 4YY

Foreword

The EFTA Court turned twenty on 1 January 2014. Since 1 July 1995, the Court has consisted of three judges nominated by Iceland, Liechtenstein and Norway, appointed by common accord of the governments. In addition, there are six ad hoc judges who are called upon to sit if a regular judge is prevented from so doing. But there is no Advocate General. Three judges are not many, but they are enough for a court of law to function. One must not overlook that US Federal Appellate Courts almost always sit in a bench of three judges and that the WTO Appellate Body decides in a three-members panel. Indeed, to be three has certain advantages. A small court tends to be fast and efficient. Moreover, as Lord Denning reportedly said when he was asked why he moved back from the House of Lords to the Court of Appeal where cases are normally heard by three judges: 'You only have to convince one.'

When the EFTA Court was set up, the ECJ's biggest worry was that homogeneity could not be preserved. After 20 years, it is safe to say that this fear has not materialised, quite the contrary! Landmarks on the road to homogeneity were the recognition of EEA State liability in E-9/97 *Sveinbjörnsdóttir* and subsequent cases, of quasi-direct effect and quasi-primacy in E-1/01 *Einarsson* and E-1/94 *Restamark*, of conform interpretation in E-1/07 *Criminal proceedings against A*, and of fundamental rights in E-8/97 *TV 1000*, E-2/03 *Ásgeirsson* and E-15/10 *Norway Post*. The Court has also recognised other general principles of EEA law. An important tool of homogeneity is the right of participation of the European Commission and of the Governments of the EU Member States' in proceedings before the Court and the respective competences of the EFTA Surveillance Authority and of the EEA/EFTA States in proceedings before the EU courts. The EU courts themselves have made essential contributions to the preservation of homogeneity, in particular in T-115/94 *Opel Austria*, C-140/97 *Rechberger*, C-452/01 *Ospelt* and C-286/02 *Bellio Fratelli*.

Homogeneity could, however, not have been achieved if the governments and the courts of the EEA/EFTA States had not loyally implemented the Court's judgments. Some rare exceptions confirm the rule. Another matter is whether there is reciprocity with regard to access to the EU courts. The Court made clear in E-18/11 *Irish Bank* and subsequent cases that the absence of a written obligation on the EEA/EFTA States' courts of last resort does not mean that those courts are absolutely free to determine whether or not to refer.

In the 20 years of its existence, the Court has registered more than 200 cases, among them 94 references from national courts. Most of the controversial cases have involved novel legal questions which had not been addressed by the ECJ. We at the Court have the feeling that this input into the European jurisprudence is appreciated on the other side of Avenue Kennedy. The ECJ, its Advocates General and the General Court have in almost 100 cases made over 150 references to EFTA Court case law. As ECJ President Vassilios Skouris writes in his contribution to this commemorative book: 'The long lasting dialogue between the EFTA Court and the CJEU has allowed the flow of information in both directions. The symbiotic nature of the relationship has contributed to the successful development of the EEA Single Market. Both courts stand as examples for each other thus depicting mutual respect, strengthening the rules of homogeneity and representing a high level of appreciation. Cooperation between the two was built on strong foundations which have stood the test of time.'

The contributions to the present book are divided into the following Parts: The EFTA Court's Role in the Judicial Architecture of the EEA; Decentred Integration; General Principles and Fundamental Rights in EEA Law; EEA Business and Economic Law; Actors in the EEA; and A Look from the Outside. The authors are drawn from all branches of the legal profession, private practice, the judiciary, government and administration, and academia. The variety of the topics reflects the wide scope of the EEA Agreement, the only association treaty ever concluded by the European Union to permit associated States to have their own surveillance authority and their own court.

One of the features of European integration is the phenomenon of different speeds. The EEA Agreement is a key component of this concept. For the foreseeable future, the EEA Agreement and thereby the EFTA Court will continue to function. Others may or may not join the EFTA pillar. The model is there. For the three present Member States it has proven to be beneficial.

Carl Baudenbacher

Contents

II. Decentred Integration

IV. EEA Business and Economic Law

List of Contributors

Cand Jur Knut Almestad is Ambassador and former President of the EFTA Surveillance Authority

Kristinn F Árnason is Secretary-General, EFTA

Éric Barbier de La Serre is a Partner at Jones Day and a Member of the Paris, Brussels and New York Bars

Professor Catherine Barnard, LLM is Professor of European Union Law and Employment Law, University of Cambridge and Fellow of Trinity College

Lic iur Andreas Batliner is President of the Administrative Court of the Principality of Liechtenstein (Verwaltungsgerichtshof des Fürstentums Liechtenstein)

Professor Dr Dr hc Carl Baudenbacher is President, EFTA Court

Dr Georges Baur is Assistant Secretary-General, EFTA

Xavier Bettel is Prime Minister of Luxembourg

Dr Henrik Bull is Justice at the Supreme Court of Norway and former Judge at the EFTA Court

Professor Dr Davíð Thór Björgvinsson is Professor of law at iCourts, University of Copenhagen, Faculty of law and at University of Iceland and former Judge at the European Court of Human Rights

Professor Damian Chalmers is Professor at the Department of Law of London School of Economics and Political Science

Arild O Eidesen is President/Chief Judge at Haalogaland Court of Appeal, the Regional Court of Appeal of North Norway, and Chair of the board of the Law Faculty of The University of Tromsø; He is former President of the Norwegian Association of Judges

Professor Ian S Forrester, QC, LLD, is a Partner at White & Case, Brussels and Honorary Professor at the University of Glasgow

Professor Dr Halvard Haukeland Fredriksen is Professor of EU/EEA law at the Faculty of Law, University of Bergen and an associate of Bergen Centre for Competition Law and Economics (BECCLE)

Professor Dr Hans Petter Graver is Professor and Dean of the Faculty of Law at University of Oslo

Professor Dr Dr Yoichi Ito is Professor of European Law at the University of Tokyo

Marc Jaeger is President of the General Court of the European Union

Martin Johansson, LLM, **Diplôme de Hautes Études Européenne**, is a Partner at Advokatfirman Vinge and a Member of The Swedish Bar Association. He is former Legal Secretary at the EU Court of Justice and the EFTA Court, as well as Officer at the Legal Affairs Department of the EFTA Secretariat

Heikki Kanninen is former Assistant Registrar of the EFTA Court and Vice-President of the General Court of the European Union

Professor Dr Christian Kohler is Professor at the Europa-Institut, University of Saarbrücken and former Director General at the Court of Justice of the European Union

Professor Dr Juliane Kokott, LLM (Am Univ), SJD (Harvard) is Advocate General at the Court of Justice of the European Union

Dr Daniel Dittert is Legal Secretary at the Court of Justice of the European Union

Carl Lebeck, LLM is Associate Professor of Law at University College, Lillehammer

Professor Dr Koen Lenaerts, LLM is Vice-President of the Court of Justice of the European Union and Professor of European Union Law, Leuven University

Skúli Magnússon is Judge at Reykjavik District Court of and Docent at the University of Iceland, Faculty of Law

Professor Dr Paolo Mengozzi is Advocate General at the Court of Justice of the European Union

Eric Morgan de Rivery is a Partner at Jones Day (Paris) and a Member of the Paris and Brussels Bars

Alexandre Fall is a trainee at Jones Day (Paris)

Thomas Nordby, Supreme Court Lawyer, is Partner at Arntzen de Besche and Head of the Dispute Resolution and Litigation Group, Oslo

Dr Sven Norberg is former Judge of the EFTA Court and former Director of the EU Commission and Director of Legal Affairs, EFTA

Professor Fergal O' Regan is Head of Unit at the European Ombudsman and Visiting Professor at the College of Europe, Bruges

Dr Romina Polley, LLM is Partner at Cleary Gottlieb Steen & Hamilton LLP, Cologne and Member of the Executive—MBL—HSG faculty at the University of St Gallen

Georges Ravarani is President of the 'Cour Administrative' and Vice-President of the Constitutional Court, Luxembourg and Guest Professor at the Faculty of Law at the University of Luxembourg

Dr Viviane Reding is former Vice-President of the European Commission and EU Commissioner for Justice, Fundamental Rights and Citizenship and Member of the European Parliament

Professor Dr Dr hc Allan Rosas is Judge at the Court of Justice of the European Union and Senior Fellow of the University of Turku as well as Visiting Professor at the College of Europe and University of Helsinki

Professor Dr Alexander Rust, LLM is Professor at the Institute for Austrian and International Tax Law at Vienna University of Economics and Business

Markús Sigurbjörnsson is President of the Supreme Court of Iceland

Oda Helen Sletnes is President of the EFTA Surveillance Authority

Professor Dr Vassilios Skouris is President of the Court of Justice of the European Union

Takao Suami is Professor of Law at Waseda Law School, Tokyo

Professor Dr Christa Tobler, LLM is Professor at the 'Europainstitute'/Institute for European Global Studies, University of Basel and at the University of Leiden

Dr Prince Nikolaus von Liechtenstein is former EEA Chief Negotiator for Liechtenstein and Ambassador to the European Union

Nils Wahl is Advocate General at the Court of Justice of the European Union

Part I

The EFTA Court's Role in the Judicial Architecture of the EEA

A

The Two EEA Courts

1

The Role of the Court of Justice of the European Union in the Development of the EEA Single Market

Advancement through Collaboration between the EFTA Court and the CJEU

VASSILIOS SKOURIS

I. INTRODUCTION

I
N WRITING ON the occasion of the twentieth anniversary of the EFTA Court
I risk repeating what I said 10 years ago concerning the role and extraordinary collaboration of our respective courts. But I will take that risk, since the
basic thread of this chapter is the confirmation of an efficient and complementary approach to the role supranational jurisdictions can play towards European
integration.

First it is important to frame the overall context. The Agreement on the
European Economic Area (EEA), which was concluded in 1992 and entered into
force in 1994, extends the internal market established within the European Union
to the EFTA states of Iceland, Liechtenstein and Norway. Even if the arrangement
appears to encompass two distinct single markets, in reality we are considering a
unique market with two sets of slightly different integration mechanisms, the EU
one applying more tightly amongst EU Member States.[1] The two-pillar approach
which underpins the functioning of the EEA is an ingenious stratagem in the
development of the EEA Single Market. Since EEA law draws from its EU counterpart, they are both largely identical in substance and thus corresponding institutions become a prominent lever for the advancement of European integration.

In particular, the relationship between the CJEU and the EFTA Court, coupled
with a number of their common characteristics, underlines their role as central

---

[1] See below n 30.

factors contributing to the successful development of the EEA Single Market. Even if the initial idea of a reinforced collaboration in the form of a Court of combined EC/EFTA participation was rejected by ECJ Opinion 1/91,[2] since the inception of the EFTA Court a constant judicial dialogue has been established with the CJEU, particularly in the fields of free movement of goods, labour law, monopolies, IP law, insurance law, state aid, food law[3] and free movement of capital.[4] This dialogue is more than a simple academic conversation practised on the occasion of conferences and the celebration of anniversaries; it proves to be a fruitful exchange of information, ideas and a cross-dependency of sources. It comprises a broad spectrum of communication, ranging from explicit and implicit references to the direct use of the Opinions of the Advocates General of the CJEU.

The last two decades, marked by the existence of the EFTA Court, have signified the successful evolvement of the EEA Single Market. A careful analysis indicates that the aforementioned judicial dialogue has strengthened the efforts for the uniform application of the common rules in all EEA States—both EFTA and EU. I would take a particular pride in suggesting that the role of the CJEU has been and is bound to continue to be that of a communicative and supporting collaborator.

II. CJEU AND EFTA COURT COMMONALITIES

There are a number of obvious specificities and commonalities between the EFTA Court and the CJEU which contribute to the successful cooperation between the two institutions. Such cooperation takes place mainly on a direct twofold unilateral level, comforted by the fact that both institutions have similar areas of competence within their respective legal orders. Quite symbolically the seat of both courts is in Luxembourg. Their rules of procedure stem also from a common matrix. However, the collaboration success goes beyond these points. There have been consistent efforts to maintain a high level of mutual understanding thus allowing homogeneity, coherence and the advancement of case law. And the result of this collaboration was gradually decanted via preliminary rulings and the collaboration of national courts towards the national legal orders.

---

[2] C Baudenbacher, 'The EFTA Court and Court of Justice of the European Union: Coming in Parts But Winning Together' in A Rosas, E Levits and Y Bot (eds), *The Court of Justice and the Construction of Europe: Analyses and Perspectives on Sixty Years of Case Law* (The Hague/Berlin, Asser Press/Springer, 2013).
[3] Eg Judgment of 23 September 2003, Case C-192/01 *Commission v Denmark*, ECR, EU:C:2003:492, and Case E-3/00 *Kellogg's* [2001].
[4] Eg Case E-22/13 *Íslandsbanki* [2000].

III. THE HOMOGENEITY OBJECTIVE[5]

The purpose of judicial homogeneity is the golden thread that runs through the relationship between the two courts. It has been rightly summed up as follows: two courts and two separate legal orders, but law that is essentially identical in substance.[6] All three EEA jurisdictions (the CJEU, the General Court and the EFTA Court) have not only stressed the need for uniform interpretation of EU and EEA law, but have vigorously endeavoured to preserve it. The EEA Single Market can only function in an accurate manner if there is a regulatory playing field for citizens and business operators.[7]

As evidenced in Article 6 of the EEA Agreement and Article 3 paragraph 2 of the Surveillance and Court Agreement, the EFTA Court is bound to follow the relevant case law of the CJEU for the period prior to the signing of EEA Agreement (2 May 1992) and, on the other hand, it is required to pay due account to the principles laid down by the relevant rulings of the CJEU after this date.

It can certainly be argued that a requirement to follow a precedent is not the same as the requirement to pay due account to a precedent. Nevertheless, it does not appear that the EFTA Court has treated the CJEU case law differently depending on when the pertinent judgments were rendered. The reason for this ought to be twofold. First, constantly evolving case law on a particular legal issue of the EU or EEA often does not derive from one judgment only, but rather from a series of judgments rendered over a long period of time. Second, one has to take into account the fact that the contexts in which the CJEU and the EFTA Court are interpreting identical provisions are not the same. Thus, the limits between being bound by precedent and having to take due account of a precedent automatically become blurred. Conversely, there are instances after the advent of the EEA where the CJEU case law was not considered by the EFTA Court as binding in the EEA context.[8]

The provisions of the Agreement on the EEA imposing a certain stance on the EFTA Court may arguably appear to be one-sided and to force obligations exclusively on the EFTA Court. This has probably led to misinterpretations about the relationship between the two courts, even reaching the conclusion that the interpretation of EEA law rests firmly with the CJEU.[9] However, it must be emphasised that although the exclusive burden on the EFTA Court may be the case in theory,

---

[5] Recital 15 to the EEA Agreement, Art 6 EEA and Art 3(2) SCA.

[6] C Baudenbacher, 'The EFTA Court, the ECJ, and the Latter's Advocates General—a Tale of Judicial Dialogue' in A Arnull, P Eeckhout and T Tridimas (eds), *Continuity and Change in EU Law, Essays in Honour of Sir Francis Jacobs* (Oxford, Oxford University Press, 2008).

[7] Recital 4 of the Preamble to the EEA Agreement.

[8] C Baudenbacher, 'The goal of homogeneous interpretation of the law in the European Economic Area—Two courts and two separate legal orders, but law that is essentially identical in substance' in *The European Legal Forum*, Issue 1-2008, p I-23.

[9] H Haukeland Fredriksen, 'One market, two courts: legal pluralism vs homogeneity in the European Economic Area' (2010) *Nordic Journal of International Law* 79, 4, p 499.

in practice the said provisions have proved to offer an adequate framework and eventually achieve a stable and harmonious coexistence between the two courts. As a matter of fact, avoiding conflicting judgments and developing coherent case law are tasks that require constant cooperation and vigilance from all the institutions involved. The day-to-day practice of the CJEU and the EFTA Court is a vivid example of this.

Many would agree that the EFTA Court strictly respects the obligations imposed upon it by the Agreement and respects the precedence of the CJEU. It must, however, be acknowledged that the EFTA Court has gone beyond this. Although its obligations with regard to respecting the case law of the CJEU only concerned either the rules of the EEA Agreement, or EU law provisions which find their identical counterpart within the EEA context, the EFTA Court was inspired by the fundamental doctrines which underpin Union law, as developed in the CJEU case law within its corresponding domain of competence. The case law on the general prohibition to discriminate, fundamental freedoms, the principle of proportionality, fundamental notions of competition and State aid rules were taken over by the EFTA Court.[10] The celebrated *Sveinbjornsdóttir*[11] judgment depicts the EFTA Court's recognition of the fact that the EEA Agreement is a *sui generis* international treaty which contains a distinct legal order.

On the other hand, although precedence does not oblige the CJEU to follow or pay due account to the case law of the EFTA Court, ignoring it would risk being detrimental and would trump the principal objective of homogeneity according to the EEA Agreement. Therefore, the CJEU has not turned a blind eye to the case law of the EFTA Court and has effectively taken it into account, expressly and impliedly. A notable example is the case of *EFTA Surveillance Authority v Norway*,[12] which had a positive influence on the CJEU decision in the case of *Commission v Denmark*.[13] In the first decade, the CJEU was faced with situations such as the one portrayed in the latter case, in which the Member States could prevent the production and marketing of enriched foodstuffs on the basis of public health concerns.[14] In reaching its decision to consolidate a balance in the free movement of goods and public health concerns, the CJEU cited the former case six times. Similarly with an explicit mention of the need of uniform interpretation in Case C-471/04 *Keller Holding*[15] the CJEU sought inspiration from the *EFTA Surveillance Authority v Iceland*.

---

[10]   Above n 8, p I-23.
[11]   Case E-7/07 *Sveinbjornsdóttir* [1998] EFTA Ct Rep 127.
[12]   Case E-3/00 *EFTA Surveillance Authority v Norway* [2000–01] EFTA Ct Rep 73.
[13]   *Commission v Denmark*, EU:C:2003:492.
[14]   The Commission sought from the Court a declaration that, by applying an administrative practice which entailed that rich foodstuffs lawfully produced or marketed in other Member States may be marketed in Denmark only if it were shown that such enrichment with nutrients met a need in the Danish population, the Kingdom of Denmark had failed to fulfil its obligations under Article 28 of the EC Treaty.
[15]   Judgment of 23 February 2006, C-471/04 *Keller Holding*, ECR, EU:C:2006:143.

Doctrine has focused on occasions where the CJEU did not follow related EFTA case law. For instance in *Silhouette*[16] the CJEU did not refer to the EFTA Court's ruling in *Maglite*.[17] Advocate General Jacobs explained in his Opinion that the jurisprudence of the CJEU with regard to the functioning of trademarks was developed in the context of the EU rather than the world market, therefore justifying the result reached. The judgment reached was centred on the need to secure the functioning of the internal market.

Nevertheless, homogeneity has continued to develop and this is due to the fact that the perceptions on both sides did not end with simply paying due account. What was also evidently required was taking into consideration objectives of the EEA Agreement, and this was portrayed in the case of *Ospelt*.[18] The issue in this case was whether EEA States were 'third countries' within the meaning of Article 73c of the EC Treaty and whether such restrictions on the free movement of capital could be imposed on transactions involving nationals of EEA States. The CJEU first considered that:

> One of the principal aims of the EEA Agreement is to provide for the fullest possible realization of the free movement of goods, persons, services and capital within the whole European Economic Area, so that the internal market established within the European Union is extended to the EFTA States. From that angle, several provisions of the above-mentioned Agreement are intended to ensure as uniform an interpretation as possible thereof throughout the EEA. It is for the Court, in that context, to ensure that the rules of the EEA Agreement which are identical in substance to those of the Treaty are interpreted uniformly with the Member States.[19]

The CJEU further stated:

> [I]t would run counter to that objective as to uniformity of application of the rules relating to free movement of capital within the EEA for a State such as the Republic of Austria, which is a party to that Agreement, which entered into force on 1 January 1994, to be able, after its accession to the European Union on 1 January 1995, to maintain legislation which restricts that freedom vis-à-vis another State party to that Agreement by basing itself on Article 73c of the Treaty.

Therefore, it is evident that both the CJEU and the EFTA Court have gone to great lengths in order to achieve homogeneity and to ensure the efficient coexistence of EEA and EU law.[20]

---

[16] Judgment of 16 July 1998, C-355/96 *Silhouette International Schmied*, ECR, EU:C:1998:374 (regarding the exhaustion of trademarks under Directive 89/104/EEC).

[17] Case E-2/97 *Maglite* [1997] EFTA Ct Rep 127.

[18] Judgment of 23 September 2003, C-452/01 *Ospelt and Schlössle Weissenberg*, ECR, EU:C:2003:493.

[19] ibid, point 29.

[20] Reference to the case of *Ospelt* was made in Case E-16/11 *EFTA Court ESA v Iceland* [2003].

IV. THE JUDICIAL DIALOGUE BETWEEN THE TWO COURTS

As previously stated, there is no formal provision establishing a day-to-day collaboration between the CJEU and the EFTA Court in the form of a procedural link
that forces them to synchronise their working or to consult each other during the
procedural stage of cases. In an attempt to fulfil and maintain the goal of homogeneity, another form of judicial dialogue has been the key strategy. According to
the case of *Bellio*,[21] both courts have to be credited with this achievement:

> [B]oth the Court and the EFTA Court have recognized the need to ensure that the rules
> of the EEA Agreement which are identical in substance to those of the Treaty are inter-
> preted uniformly.[22]

The approach was confirmed in the case of *Fokus Bank*,[23] which made reference
to *Bellio*.

V. THE CJEU'S CONTRIBUTION TO THE JUDICIAL
DIALOGUE AND THE EEA SINGLE MARKET

In my view the CJEU has contributed significantly to the development of the EEA
Single Market via the judicial dialogue between the two courts since it did haul
inspiration into the EFTA Court's reasoning. In numerous cases, the CJEU has
referred to the EFTA Court case law as leading authority. A prominent example is
Mattel Scandinavia and Lego Norge,[24] whereby the EFTA Court held that Articles
2(2) and 16 of the Television Directive 89/552/EEC must be interpreted as avert-
ing an EEA State from applying a general ban on television advertising aimed
at children if the latter is part of a television programme which is accredited in
another EEA State. The judgment of the CJEU in the case of *De Agostini and
TV- Shop I Sverige*[25] fully affirmed the stance previously taken by the EFTA Court.

A further prominent example is evidenced in the influence of the *Kellogg's*
judgment of the EFTA Court on the case law of the CJEU. Although the CJEU
rejected the position of the Danish government in *Commission v Denmark*,[26] it
had acknowledged the precautionary principle established in *Kellogg's* and thus
formulated similar requirements for its application as the EFTA Court had held
in *Kellogg's*.

It has also been noted that EFTA Court case law may be cited in a CJEU
case as a supporting argument rather than a leading authority. For instance, in

---

[21] Judgment of 1 April 2004, C-286/02 *Bellio F.lli*, ECR, EU:C:2004:212.
[22] ibid, point 34.
[23] Case E-1/04 *Fokus Bank* [2004].
[24] Joined Cases E-8/94 and E-9/94.
[25] Judgment of 9 July 1997, C-34/95 to C-36/95 *De Agostini and TV-Shop*, ECR, EU:C:1997:344.
[26] *Commission v Denmark*, EU:C:2003:492.

Sveinbjörnsdótt [27] the EFTA Court ruled that the principle of State liability was an inherent part of EEA law despite the resistance of the governments of Iceland, Norway and Sweden. Consequently, the CJEU took care to avoid a gap in the EEA system of protection of individual rights. The significance of this case is evidenced by the fact that the CJEU subsequently referred to it in the *Rechberger* judgment.[28] More recently in Case C-277/12 the CJEU referred to the EFTA Court judgment of *Nguyen*[29] concerning the definition of 'personal injuries'.

Nonetheless one should also focus on direct jurisprudential contributions. In the first place there are numerous cases lodged before the CJEU where the EFTA Surveillance Authority submitted observations which were taken into account in the Court's reasoning. Furthermore the CJEU has contributed to the advancement of the wider Single Market with its case law in references for preliminary rulings. The CJEU had the task of confirming the unison of the EEA Market and the definition of its outer boundaries in a good number of cases[30] referred to it for preliminary rulings in areas of goods imported or being placed in the market in the EEA or the approximation of laws in trademarks. Very recently a similar approach was adopted, albeit by an order, in *Astrazeneca*.[31] The order was issued on 14 November 2013 on the basis of Article 99 of the Rules of Procedure, as the CJEU considered that the answer to the question referred for a preliminary ruling could be clearly deduced from existing case law, in particular from its judgment in *Novartis and Others*,[32] and it ruled that, in the context of the European Economic Area (EEA), Article 13(1) of Regulation (EC) No 469/2009 of the European Parliament and of the Council of 6 May 2009 concerning the supplementary protection certificate for medicinal products must be interpreted as meaning that an administrative authorisation issued for a medicinal product by the Swiss authorities, which is automatically recognised in Liechtenstein, must be regarded as the first authorisation to place that medicinal product on the EEA market.

Additionally, the CJEU has gone to great lengths not only to reconsider its case law in view of a specific judgment of the EFTA Court, but also to clarify it in the light of the EFTA Court's overall judicial interpretation. Case C-13/95 *Suzen*,[33] which dealt with the succession of contracts, is such an example.

Equally in Case C-284/06, upon reference by the German Supreme Fiscal Court concerning compatibility of a national rule to provide for divergent set-off arrangements vis-à-vis Articles 56, 58 and 43 EC and in view of substantive

---

[27] Case E-7/07 [1998] EFTA Ct Rep 127.

[28] Judgment of 15 June 1999, C-140/97 *Rechberger and Others*, ECR, EU:C:1999:306.

[29] Case E-8/07 [2008] EFTA Ct Rep 224, paras 26 and 27.

[30] Judgments in Cases C-173/98, ECR, EU:C:1999:173; C-300/98 and C-392/98, ECR, EU:C:2000:378; C-414/99 to C-416/99, ECR, EU:C:2001:617; C-244/00, ECR, EU:C:2003:204; C-16/03, ECR, EU:C:2004:759; C-405/03, ECR, EU:C:2005:616; C-479/04, ECR, EU:C:2006:549; C-324/08, ECR, EU:C:2009:633; C-436/08 and C-437/08, ECR, EU:C:2011:61; C-558/08, ECR, EU:C:2010:416; C-127/09, ECR, EU:C:2010:313; C-324/09, ECR, EU:C:2011:474; C-661/11, ECR, EU:C:2013:577.

[31] Order of 14 November 2013 C-617/12 *Astrazeneca*, ECR, EU:C:2013:761.

[32] Judgment of 21 April 2005, C-207/03 and C-252/03 *Novartis and Others*, ECR, EU:C:2005:245.

[33] Judgment of 11 March 1997, C-13/95 *Süzen*, ECR, EU:C:1997:141.

references by the German Court to the EFTA Court's judgment in *Fokus Bank*, the CJEU offered the clarification requested.[34]

VI. THE CASE LAW OF THE EFTA COURT

The EFTA Court's clear and concise judgments are playing a leading role in strengthening the judicial dialogue between the European Courts and helping to create a seamless body of European law on judicial review, which applies to judgments of national courts in all States that are members of the Council of Europe, as well as to the EU and EFTA Courts.[35]

Subsequent to the unambiguous understanding in legal scholarship, the case law of the EFTA Court has made an imperative contribution to the smooth development of the EEA and for safeguarding its homogeneity.[36] EFTA Court judgments are clear, straightforward and authoritative.

The judgments that the EFTA Court has delivered since its foundation have been of consistent and reliable quality and have provided considerable insight. It has earned its respected standing for judicial clarification and discussion.

VII. THE PARTICULAR ADDED VALUE OF THE ROLE OF ADVOCATE GENERAL

Of particular interest is the attention reserved by the EFTA Court to the role of Advocate General of the CJEU. Despite the absence of a similar institution in the EFTA Court[37]—or maybe specifically for that reason—Advocates General seem nevertheless to influence the workings of this parallel jurisdiction but also to be influenced by developments on the EFTA side. As a matter of principle, Advocates General take into consideration each source of information which will assist them in their duty as outlined in Article 222(2) EC. This undoubtedly includes the case law of the EFTA Court, thus Opinions of Advocates General are a noteworthy gateway for EFTA Court case law into the CJEU's jurisprudence.[38] A number of cases depict this assertion, such as *De Agostini/ TV- shop i Sverige*[39] whereby

---

[34] Judgment of 26 June 2008, C-284/06 *Finanzamt Hamburg-Am Tierpark v Burda Verlagsbeteiligungen*, ECR, EU:C:2008:365.

[35] J Lang, 'Judicial review of competition decisions under the European Convention on Human Rights and the importance of the EFTA Court: the *Norway Post* judgment' (2012) 4 *European Law Review* 464.

[36] R Wolfrum, *Max Planck Encyclopedia of International Law* (Oxford, Oxford University Press, 2013).

[37] C Baudenbacher, 'The EFTA Court's relationship with the Advocates General of the European Court of Justice' in V Kronenberger, M-T d'Alessio and V Placco (eds), *Mélanges en l'honneur de Paolo Mengozzi* (Brussels, Bruylant, 2013) 341.

[38] ibid, p 369.

[39] Joined cases *De Agostini and TV-Shop*, EU:C:1997:344.

Advocate General Jacobs advocated that transfrontier advertising directed at children falls within the scope of the TV Directive. He also mentioned that the EFTA Court had reached the same conclusion in *Mattel Scandinavia/Lego Norge.*[40] In the case of *GEMO*,[41] Advocate General Jacobs also referred to the EFTA Court's judgment in *Husbanken II*[42] regarding the issue of state aid approach and whether financial compensation granted by a Member State to an undertaking providing a public service should be granted state aid.[43]

Further, in the well-known case of *Ospelt*, Advocate General Geelhoed disallowed the attempt of the Austrian government to compare Article 40 EEA to Article 67 EEC in its pre-Maastricht version and referred to the decision of the EFTA Court in *Islandsbanki*; it was asserted that the requirements for free movement of capital in the EEA Agreement have direct effect.[44] Hence, EEA judicial dialogue in this instance was evidently crucial for safeguarding the identity of the rules on free movement of capital.

Advocate General Sharpston advocated in *Boehringer Ingelheim II*[45] that the precise style of re-boxing which affects merely the outer packaging would not prejudice the guarantee of origin, and the concept of the condition of the goods being compromised in Article 7(2) of the Trade Marks Directive should not be interpreted broadly. In the Advocate General's reasoning, she positively cited passages from the EFTA Court's *Paranova v Merck* judgment.[46]

On occasions, Advocates General have been willing to enter into practical discussions with the EFTA Court such as in the previously mentioned case of *De Agostini* whereby Francis Jacobs stated:

> In an area where laws have already been harmonized, it is difficult to see any rationale for the view that those laws may be invoked against broadcasts in respect of which the Television Directive guarantees freedom of reception and retransmission. Moreover ... the result of such a view would be both unsatisfactory and anomalous, requiring individual broadcasts to be conceptually dismantled in order to determine which fragments were within the scope of that directive and which were not.[47]

More recently Advocate General Kokott in her Opinion of 30 January 2014 in Case C-557/12[48] reinforced a series of arguments by quoting the EFTA Court's judgment in Case E-14/11 *DB Schenker* concerning the importance of the private enforcement of competition law in the public interest. On the same date Advocate

---

[40] Joined Cases E-8/94 and E-9/94.

[41] Judgment of 20 November 2003, C-126/01 *GEMO*, ECR, EU:C:2003:622.

[42] Case E-7/97 *Norwegian Bankers' Association v EFTA Surveillance Authority* [1999] EFTA Ct Rep 1.

[43] Opinion of 30 April 2002 C-126/01*GEMO*, ECR, EU:C:2002:273; references to Case E-4/97 *Husbanken II* [1999] EFTA Ct Rep [1999] 1, fn 64, 77.

[44] Opinion in C-452/01 *Ospelt and Schlössle Weissenberg*, ECR, EU:C:2003:232; reference to Case E-1/00 *Íslandsbanki* [2000–01] EFTA Ct Rep 8, fn 32.

[45] Opinion in C-348/04 *Boehringer Ingelheim*, ECLI:EU:C:2007:235.

[46] ibid, points 49–55; references to Case E-3/02 *Merck v Paranova* [2003] EFTA Ct Rep 101.

[47] Opinion in *De Agostini and TV-Shop*, EU:C:1996:333, point 85.

[48] Opinion in C-557/12 *KONE and Others*, ECR, EU:C:2014:45.

General Mengozzi handed down an Opinion in *MasterCard and Others v Commission*,[49] on an appeal against the judgment of the General Court of 24 May 2012 in Case T-111/08. In support of his view that it is the CJEU's intention to reduce as much as possible the margin of discretion on the extent of judicial review of Commission decisions imposing penalties for infringement of Article 81 EC he invoked the EFTA Court in Case E-15/10 *Posten Norge AS*, where similar solutions were retained.

It should be further noted that there have been instances, on the one hand, whereby the EFTA Court has referred to Opinions of Advocates General independently of whether a CJEU judgment had been handed down, such as the Joined Cases E-5/04, E-6/04 and E-7/04 *Fesil and Finnfjord and Others v EFTA Surveillance Authority* (2005). On the other hand, the EFTA Court has made reference to Opinions of Advocates General notwithstanding existing CJEU case law, as was done in Case E-1/02 *University of Oslo*.

Attention was also drawn to Case E-8/00 *Norwegian Federation of Trade Unions and Others v Norwegian Association of Local and Regional Authorities and Others* as it further demonstrates the effective dialogue. In this case, the EFTA Court referred to Advocate General Jacobs' Opinion verbatim but nevertheless followed an alternative authority to that of the CJEU.

VIII. CONCLUSIONS

We may say with confidence that expectations of reciprocity have largely been fulfilled. The courts in both EEA pillars have made momentous determinations to safeguard a homogenous development of case law. From its very beginning,[50] the EFTA Court highlighted the importance of the objective of the Contracting Parties to create a dynamic and homogenously regulated EEA.[51] The long-lasting dialogue between the EFTA Court and the CJEU has allowed the flow of information in both directions. 'Ignoring EFTA Court precedents would simply be incompatible with the overriding objective of the EEA Agreement, which is homogeneity.'[52]

The symbiotic nature of the relationship has contributed to the successful development of the EEA Single Market. Both courts stand as examples for each other thus depicting mutual respect, strengthening the rules of homogeneity and representing a high level of appreciation. Cooperation between the two was built on strong foundations which have stood the test of time.

---

[49]   Opinion in C-382/12 P *MasterCard and Others v Commission*, ECR, EU:C:2014:42.

[50]   Case E-1/94 *Restamark*.

[51]   V Kronenberger, 'Does the EFTA Court interpret the EEA Agreement as if it were the EC Treaty? Some Questions Raised by the *Restamark* Judgment' (1996) 45 *Intl & Comp LQ* 198, 207.

[52]   V Skouris, 'The ECJ and the EFTA Court under the EEA Agreement' in C Baudenbacher, P Tresselt and T Örlygsson (eds), *The EFTA Court Ten Years On* (Oxford, Hart Publishing, 2005).

2

The EFTA Court's Early Days

HEIKKI KANNINEN

I. THE FIRST CASES

THE VERY FIRST case was brought before the EFTA Court on 27 April 1994.[1] Such an event merited a celebration for the staff of the new court. It is not pleasant for any court to be congested with too many cases and to have a large backlog. However, a court with no cases is even less pleasant. It is the cases that are brought before it that bring the court to life and give it its 'raison d'être'. The EFTA Court came into official existence on 1 January 1994, when the Agreement on the European Economic Area (EEA Agreement) and the Agreement on the Establishment of a Surveillance Authority and a Court of Justice (the Surveillance and Court Agreement) came into force. After four months of waiting and an even longer preparation time it was now time to hear the first case. The EFTA Court was ready for it. The whole court attacked its first jurisdictional challenge with enthusiasm. After the energy devoted to setting up the court, especially on the administrative side, the serious business was now about to start.

For a new court, the first cases are particularly important to establish its legitimacy, its credibility and its authority. The competence with which the court is invested by treaties and other legal means is not enough. A court makes its name by the quality of its judgments and the conduct of its proceedings. As the president of the EFTA Court, Carl Baudenbacher, has noted, a small court in particular can feel itself weakened by certain remarks or the behaviour of certain parties or the public.[2] For a small and totally new court, it is therefore particularly important from the start to show that it meets expectations.[3]

Fortunately for the EFTA Court the first case was not just any case. It consisted of important questions from the point of view of both procedural and substantive

---

[1] Case E-1/94 *Restamark* [1994–1995] EFTA Ct Rep 15.

[2] C Baudenbacher, *The EFTA Court in Action*, Five lectures, p 96.

[3] The early stages of the Civil Service Tribunal of the European Union confirmed that in the beginning a new court, in the eyes of its clients, passes through a kind of probationary period in which it sometimes 'tested' by the parties.

law. It was also important for the country from which the case originated, Finland. In this sense it was an ideal case to start with. In the words of Carl Baudenbacher, 'it was a beautiful case'.[4]

This first case (*Restamark*) raised a serious problem of admissibility. The request for an advisory opinion was sent by the Tullilautakunta, an appeal body linked to the Finnish customs administration. The question was whether this body was a 'court or tribunal' within the meaning of Article 34 of the Surveillance and Court Agreement. The Finnish Government, the Norwegian Government and the EFTA Surveillance Authority were of the opinion that the request for an advisory opinion should be declared inadmissible. The applicant before the Tullilautakunta, Ravintoloitsijain Liiton Kustannus Oy Restamark, considered that the Tullilautakunta falls within the concept of court or tribunal. The EC Commission was of the opinion that, where there is a genuine doubt whether a body requesting the EFTA Court to give an advisory opinion is a court or a tribunal, the EFTA Court should resolve in favour of considering it as a court or tribunal.[5]

The EFTA Court was not in a very comfortable situation. The Court had received its first case, a very important one, but was it admissible? Was the new court to begin its work by declaring this case inadmissible? Or, as the first president of the EFTA Court, Leif Sevón, put it: 'Avoiding work, one might say'.[6] The job of the EFTA Court was not necessarily made easier by the fact that it could not ignore the jurisprudence of the Court of Justice of the European Communities regarding the interpretation of Article 177 of the Treaty establishing the European Economic Community. In its *Restamark* judgment, the EFTA Court states that 'the reasoning which has led the EC Court of Justice to its interpretations of the same expression [court or tribunal] in Article 177 EC is relevant in this context'.

Finally, in its judgment of 16 December the EFTA Court declared the case as admissible. To reach that conclusion, the EFTA Court had to give a broad interpretation to the expression 'court or tribunal'. As Carl Baudenbacher observed, the EFTA Court 'wanted to give individuals and economic operators broad access to justice'.[7]

The *Restamark* judgment did not remain an isolated decision on that procedural issue. The EFTA Court confirmed its approach in its judgment of 16 June 1995 in Joined Cases E-8/94 and E-9/94 *Fordbrukerombudet v Mattel Scandinavia A/S, Lego Norge A/S*.[8] It seems that this interpretation has become established case law of the EFTA Court.[9] More importantly, it appears that later case law of the EC (EU) Court of Justice shows that there are no fundamental divergences between

---

[4] Baudenbacher, above n 2, p 20.
[5] Case E-1/94 *Restamark* [1994–1995] EFTA Ct Rep 15, para 9.
[6] L Sevón, 'The EFTA Court—Ten Years On' in C Baudenbacher, P Tresselt and T Orlygsson (eds), *The EFTA Court. Ten Years On* (Oxford, Hart Publishing, 2005) 186.
[7] Baudenbacher, above n 2, p 20.
[8] [1994–1995] EFTA Ct Rep 113, para 15.
[9] See, eg, Case E-4/04 *Pedicel AS v Sosial- og helsedirektoratet* [2005] EFTA Ct Rep 1.

these two courts on that issue.[10] The Tullilautakunta was the first Finnish body to seek a preliminary ruling from the EC Court of Justice. The reference for a preliminary ruling was sent to the Court on 10 April 1996 and it concerned the taxation of imported electricity.[11] However, the EC Court of Justice never had the occasion to pronounce on the quality of the Tullilautakunta as a court or tribunal since the reference for a preliminary ruling was withdrawn.[12]

As the first case before the EFTA Court was admissible, the Court could answer the questions of the Tullilautakunta. It was no surprise that the case concerned the compatibility of the Finnish state monopoly for the importation of alcohol. In many of the EFTA States, the importation and sale of alcohol had been strictly regulated. Questions would necessarily arise on the compatibility of these regulations with the principle of the free movement of goods. The *Restamark* case concerned 120 bottles of Italian red wine imported from Italy and 60 bottles of whisky imported from Germany only days after the entry into force of the EEA Agreement. The Finnish authorities, invoking the State import monopoly, refused to place the bottles in free circulation in Finland.

In its judgment, the EFTA Court decided that a national measure that grants a state monopoly the exclusive right to import alcoholic beverages or stipulates an import licence, even if the latter is granted automatically, was incompatible with the EEA Agreement.

The *Restamark* judgment was also important as regards the nature of the EEA law and its effects on the legal orders of the EEA Member States. In its answer to one of the questions from the Tullilautakunta, the EFTA Court found that implemented provisions of the EEA agreement may have a direct effect on the national legal order and that was the case with Article 16 of the EEA Agreement, which provides that the Contracting Parties to that agreement must ensure that any State monopoly of a commercial character be adjusted so that no discrimination regarding the conditions under which goods are produced and marketed will exist between nationals of EU Member States and EFTA States.

The *Restamark* case largely occupied the judicial activities of the EFTA Court in 1994. The handling of this important case provided a good basis for the future work and legitimacy of the EFTA Court.

The Court's second case came only one day after the *Restamark* case, on 28 April 1994. Two cases in two days! That case was an action for annulment of a decision of the EFTA Surveillance Authority. The EFTA Court has jurisdiction for direct actions initiated by an EFTA State or a natural or legal person. Article 36 of the Surveillance and Court Agreement determines the conditions for initiating these actions. That provision corresponds to a large extent to Article 263 of the Treaty on the Functioning of the European Union.

---

[10] See Baudenbacher, above n 2, p 20.
[11] Case C-115/96 *Outokumpu Oy*.
[12] Order of the President of the EC Court of Justice of 24 September 1996.

In the action for annulment, the EFTA Court can be compared to the General Court of the European Union. Indeed, in its judgment in the second case, the EFTA Court took into account the relevant case law of the Court of First Instance of the European Communities.[13]

The second case was also important. It gave the EFTA Court the opportunity to decide on certain significant issues in the action for annulment. The first question was whether a letter, in which the EFTA Surveillance Authority rejected a complaint from a Scottish salmon growers' association demanding an investigation into alleged state aid, was a reviewable act. The second question concerned the *locus standi* to bring an action for annulment by a legal person. Finally, the obligation to state the reasons for a decision of the EFTA Surveillance Authority was examined by the EFTA Court. On that point, the EFTA Court found that the challenged decision was not adequately reasoned.

The EFTA Court was lucky to receive rather quickly two cases on the two main types of action, the request for an advisory opinion and the action for annulment. It took longer for the EFTA Court to receive the first action for failure of a Contracting Party to fulfil its obligations.[14]

In the first year, 1994, 10 cases in total were brought before the EFTA Court. It is true that six of them were concluded by an order of the Court or the President of the Court.[15] The two last cases introduced in 1994 were requests for an advisory opinion from the Marketsrådet (Norway).[16] In these cases the EFTA Court was asked to give an interpretation of provisions of Council Directive 89/552/EC on the coordination of certain provisions laid down by law, regulation or administrative action in Member States concerning the pursuit of television broadcasting activities. The two cases were joined and decided by a judgment on 16 June 1995.

The last case handled by the initial composition of the EFTA Court was Case E-1/95 where the judgment was rendered on 20 June 1995.[17] The case was a request for an advisory opinion by a Swedish court of first instance. The question

[13] Case E-2/94 *Scottish Salmon Growers Association* [1994–1995] EFTA Ct Rep 59, para 13.

[14] Case E-7/97 *EFTA Surveillance Authority v Norway* [1998] EFTA Ct Rep 62.

[15] Case E-3/94 *Alexander Flander Friedmann ea v Austria* [1994–1995] EFTA Ct Rep 83 was declared inadmissible because of lack of jurisdiction. Case E-4/94 *Konsumentombudsmannen v De Agostini (Svenska) Förlag AB* [1994–1995] EFTA Ct Rep 89 was removed from the register since the request for an advisory opinion was withdrawn. Case E-5/94 *Konsumentombudsmannen v TV-shop I Sverige AB* [1994–1995] EFTA Ct Rep 93 was removed from the register for the same reason. Case E-6/94 *Reinhard Helmes v the EFTA Surveillance Authority and Sweden* [1994–1995] EFTA Ct Rep 97 was declared inadmissible since the applicant was not represented by a lawyer. An application for revision of the order in Case E-6/94 was dismissed as inadmissible, Case E-6/94 Rev [1994–1995] EFTA Ct Rep 103. In Case E-7/94 *Data Delecta Aktiebolag and Ronnie Forsberg v MSL Dynamics Ltd* [1994–1995] EFTA Ct Rep 109, the Swedish Supreme Court had requested an advisory opinion but in February 1995 the Supreme Court decided to withdraw its request and instead to request the Court of Justice of the European Communities to give a preliminary ruling on a similar question (Case C-43/95 *Data Delecta Aktiebolag and Ronnie Forsberg v MSL Dynamics Ltd* [1996] ECR I-4661).

[16] Joined Cases E-8/94 and E-9/94 *Forbrukerombudet v Mattel Scandinavia A/S and Lego Norge A/S* [1994–1995] EFTA Ct Rep 113.

[17] Case E-1/95 *Ulf Samuelsson v Svenska staten* [1994–1995] EFTA Ct Rep 145.

referred to the EFTA Court concerned the interpretation of Council Directive 80/987/EEC on the approximation of the laws of the Member States relating to the protection of employees in the event of the insolvency of their employer. In its judgment, the EFTA Court also had to pronounce on the admissibility of the request since the Swedish Government submitted that an answer could not be used for the solution in the case before the national court. The EFTA Court noted that it is primarily a matter for the national court to decide whether it is necessary to request an advisory opinion from it.

All the initial cases and decisions taken in them show that, on the one hand, the EFTA Court had quickly become one whose usefulness was recognised and, on the other, that cases were varied and could be of not inconsiderable interest. The EFTA Court was not a paper tiger.

II. THE PAINFUL ESTABLISHMENT OF THE EFTA COURT

Until August 1996, the EFTA Court was located in Geneva, more precisely in Petit-Lancy, in a building which it also shared with a bank. However, there was almost no contact with the bank and its staff. For example, there was an unsuccessful attempt to use the bank's canteen—doubtless prevented by banking secrecy.

It was certainly a little bit strange that the EFTA Court had its headquarters in Switzerland—a country which was not a party to the EEA agreement. On the other hand it could be said that it is not uninteresting to locate the court of an international organisation in a neutral country. The real reason for the headquarters of the EFTA Court being there can be explained by its difficult birth. Since September 1996, the EFTA Court has had its headquarters in Luxembourg.

Initially the EEA Contracting Parties had envisaged establishing an EEA Court with members from the EC Court of Justice and the EFTA States. This solution was, however, rejected by the EC Court of Justice in its Opinion 1/91.[18] This meant that a new organisational structure had to be found among the EFTA States. The establishment of a court of justice, whose competence would extend only to the EFTA States, was prepared by the Preparatory Committee for the EFTA Court, Leif Sevón being its chairman. The new structure was approved by the EC Court of Justice in its Opinion 1/92.[19]

The Preparatory Committee for the EFTA Court also had to recruit the personnel for the EFTA Court. The judges were to be appointed by the common accord of the Governments of the EFTA States.

When everything seemed to be clear for the entry into force of the EEA Agreement and of the Surveillance and Court Agreement in 1993, there was a further complication. Following the outcome of the Swiss referendum on 6 December 1992, Switzerland remained outside the EEA. This postponed the entry

---

[18] Opinion 1/91 [1991] ECR I-6097.
[19] Opinion 1/92 [1992] ECR I-2821.

into force to 1 January 1994. Even if Switzerland did not become a member of the EEA Agreement and of the Surveillance and Court Agreement and, consequently, could not have a judge at the EFTA Court, the seat of the new court was not changed. The preparatory work in Geneva was well advanced and a decision to move the seat would have considerably complicated the start of the EFTA Court. In addition, the fact that the EFTA Court could get administrative help and advice from the EFTA Secretariat, also situated in Geneva, was of great benefit during the first few months.

The first five judges from the EFTA States which had ratified the Surveillance and Court Agreement, that is Austria, Finland, Iceland, Norway and Sweden, were appointed on 16 June 1993. But they had to wait until 1 January 1994 before coming to Geneva. However, most staff members were already in place in autumn 1993. The inaugural session of the EFTA Court took place at its premises on 4 January 1994, where the five judges took the oath, elected Leif Sevón president of the Court and appointed Karin Hökborg as Registrar.

The jurisdiction of the EFTA Court was largely copied from that of the EC Court of Justice. The EFTA Court is a kind of EC Court of Justice in miniature. The main difference was the replacement of the preliminary ruling procedure by the advisory opinion procedure. To some extent even for the organisation of the EFTA Court the choice was to use the model of the EC Court of Justice. This especially concerned the judicial personnel. As at the EU Court of Justice, each judge of the EFTA Court has his own cabinet, consisting of one legal secretary and one assistant.

The EFTA Court occupied two floors in its premises in Geneva. The upper floor was for the cabinets (in total 15 people). The lower floor was occupied by the administrative personnel, the Registrar, the Assistant Registrar, the administrative officials, the librarian, the research lawyers and the caretakers (in total 12 people). Fortunately, this separation into two sections did not create a wall between them. There were only 27 of us. This meant that everybody had to be ready and able to carry out many tasks and help each other. This necessarily created a good team spirit.

The EFTA Court was small but it had to act autonomously both judicially and administratively. It could not rely on the support of another body. In any case, a dependence on an external body would not have been appropriate to the requirement of independence of a court of justice. That is why the Court had to manage its personnel and financial tasks on its own. Even if the Court was not overloaded with judicial cases, its personnel was already fully occupied in the first months of 1994 in getting it established. Some of the administrative personnel had started even earlier, in autumn 1993.

The main link to the EFTA States was the ESA/Court Committee which was composed of representatives of all participating states. One of its tasks was to draw up the annual budget.

From the point of view of the administrative organisation, the biggest difference with the EC Courts in Luxembourg was (and remains) the different language regimes. In the EFTA Court, this regime is much simpler than before the EU Courts in Luxembourg. English is the only official and working language in the EFTA Court. Therefore, the need for translators and interpreters in the EFTA Court was very limited. Translation work would occur mainly in advisory opinion procedures where the national court is entitled to make its request in the language of the case and the parties to the main proceedings may submit documents in that language. The EFTA Court recruited as legal editor a British lawyer whose task was mainly to check the English of the judgments.

To have English as the only working language had the advantages of simplifying everything, speeding up the procedure and putting staff on an equal basis, as English was not the official language of any of the five EFTA Member States. It was quite natural to have English as the common language. English had already been the working language of the EFTA Secretariat and of the EEA negotiations.[20]

The rules of procedure of the EFTA Court had already been prepared before the EEA Agreement and the Surveillance and Court Agreement entered into force. They were largely modelled on the Rules of Procedure of the EC Court of Justice. They were able to be adopted by the EFTA Court quickly and approved by the EFTA Member States in January and February 1994. They were translated into Finnish, German, Icelandic, Norwegian and Swedish by the personnel of the EFTA Court.

A number of other legal instruments had also to be drawn up by the EFTA Court during the first months of 1994 since it could not rely on an existing structure. Thus the Court had to work out its Staff Regulations and Rules as well the Financial Regulations and Rules. In addition, a Staff Insurance Scheme for the EFTA Court and EFTA Surveillance Authority was set up.

It has already been mentioned that the EFTA Secretariat provided much help and advice during the period when the Court was being set up. As the EC Court of Justice was the model for the EFTA Court, it also gave support, for example, in the setting up of the registry of the EFTA Court. To that effect the assistance of the Registrar of the Court of First Instance of the EC, Hans Jung, was particularly valuable.

The establishment of the EFTA Court was completed by the end of the first half of 1994. The Court was set up, it had its first cases and the personnel were fully occupied. Everything was ready to conduct normal activities of an international court. However, it became clear rather quickly that there might soon be big changes. Four of the five EFTA Member States were on the point of leaving the EFTA structure. On 24 June 1994 these countries signed a treaty on their accession to the European Union on 1 January 1995. To give effect to this accession, each country had decided to organise a referendum. A period of uncertainty started.

---

[20] Report of the EFTA Court 1994–1995, p 6; S Norberg (1994) 31 *Common Market Law Review* 1147–1156, p 1149.

As the first Swedish judge at EFTA Court has said, the Court was faced with building up its own activities and planning to wind them up at the same time.[21]

III. DOWNSIZING AND CONTINUATION

The second half of 1994 was difficult for the EFTA Court. If the four candidate States for the European Union should actually leave the EFTA structure, what would remain of the EFTA Court with just one member, Iceland? The thinking was that it would be the end of the EFTA Court. The judges and other staff of the EFTA Court were of course also asking themselves what their future would be. Mentally, people began preparing for their departure. At the same time, they had to carry on working on cases.

While the Austrians held their referendum in June 1994, the Finns and the Swedes did so in October and the Norwegians only on 28 November 1994. The dice were cast. The surprise was that Norway once again said 'No' to accession. So finally two founding members of the EFTA Court remained. As Liechtenstein became a party to the EEA Agreement and the Surveillance and Court Agreement on 1 May 1995, the EFTA Court could continue to work with three Member States.

The departure of one Member State and, even more so, that of three, raised the question of how to conclude pending cases, in particular those concerning the departing Member State. For this reason, in September 1994 the five EFTA States concluded an Agreement on Transitional Arrangements for a Period after the Accession of Certain EFTA States to the European Union. This agreement made it possible for the EFTA Court in its original composition to pronounce two judgments on 16 June 1994 (Joined Cases E-8/94 and E-9/94) and on 20 June 1995 (Case E-1/95).

For many of us who were working at the EFTA Court, the European Union presented a new and attractive challenge, something that we had wanted and expected. Nonetheless there was also a feeling that we had to leave what we had built too quickly. Living and working in Geneva was nonetheless very pleasant. Our departure from the EFTA Court was fortunately not the end of the EFTA Court. It had a life after us. We can only be happy about this success, which has already lasted for more than 20 years.

---

[21] Norberg, above n 20, p 1156.

3

The Style of the EFTA Court

I. A FIRST ENCOUNTER

L AWYERS WHO HAVE the honourable challenge of pleading before one of
the three European Union Courts will often spend the night in the hotel
across the road from the Courts (née Holiday Inn and having undergone
several incarnations and face-lifts since then). Usually a fitful night is followed by
the not very welcoming security precautions at the door of the Court of Justice.
Hours of preparation for 20 minutes of speech before the Court of Justice may
elicit nothing in intellectual challenge other than polite silence from the bench.

By contrast, my first argument before the EFTA Court, in the *Bellona* case,[1]
took place in the Salle Flamande of the Cercle Municipal, off the bustling public
square in the middle of Luxembourg city. A band played outside (coincidentally,
one presumes, not at the expense of the Court), and law students were served
croissants and coffee as they waited for the argument to start. I changed into the
court dress of a Scot (adapted to mark the death of Her Britannic Majesty Queen
Anne in 1715, and changed only moderately since then) in the hallway, facilities
in rented accommodation for the wig-wearing exotic not being a judicial priority, one imagines. During the robing process, one of the judges passed the clients
on the stairway and commented that they had picked counsel well. (Never trust
judicial flattery: we were deemed inadmissible.) But the experience was civilised,
demanding, and there was vigorous debate between counsel and the bench.

Was this a metaphor, the lively Place d'Armes in the middle of a city, as opposed
to the Kirchberg with its monstrously long, cold, intimidating black stone

* Thanks are expressed to Nuno Calaim Lourenço, Jerome Dickinson, Fabian Lutz, Martin
Möllman, Sophie Sählin and others unnamed, for valuable ideas. The opinions expressed are wholly
personal.
[1] Case E-2/02, *Technologien Bau- und Wirtschaftsberatung GmbH and Bellona Foundation v ESA*,
EFTA Ct Rep [2003] 52.

staircase, one of the most painfully unwelcoming means of access to a supreme court that I know? Yes, to some extent.

II. EARLY CHOICES

Twenty years ago, the judges of the EFTA Court had to decide whether they should follow closely the approach of the European Community Courts to competence and procedure. Some judges of these Courts encouraged their prospective judicial brethren (no sistren then or since) to seize the opportunity not to be 'too continental', to be pragmatic and direct, and to get to the problem directly. Easy to say, difficult to practise. Relevant to these discussions was the fact that the European Court of Justice and the Court of First Instance had laid down a body of European law: the new EFTA Court could not become something so totally new that it was shockingly different. On the other hand, whereas the ECJ was an accepted necessity for the EC world, the auspices for the EFTA Court were not unanimously enthusiastic. The EFTA had existed for decades without needing a court. And the Court's experience has indeed confirmed the potential for constitutional dissent about its role. Even though there was no malign sorceress at the baptismal party,[2] one EFTA government has made no secret of its opposition to judicial meddling in the affairs of robust independent states. Indeed, the members of the EFTA were by definition dissenters, candidate passengers who had elected not to board the Community train bound for European Union.[3]

An early question for the EFTA judges to address was whether to follow (and if so, how closely) the style of the other European Courts. The aspiration of the early judges, sitting in Geneva, with Austria, Sweden, Finland, Iceland and Norway as Member States, was to be both dynamic and homogeneous. But the political evolutions of the European adventure altered the Court's constituency. Thus in 1960, the EFTA consisted of Austria, Denmark, Norway, Portugal, Sweden, Switzerland and the United Kingdom, joined by Finland in 1961, Iceland in 1970 and Liechtenstein in 1991; but by 1995, the EFTA Territory had shrunk to two maritime countries—Norway and Iceland—and two land-locked Alpine countries—Switzerland and the principality of Liechtenstein. Whereas the six founding Member States of the EC were contiguous and had the potential to be, if not rivals, economic partners, Liechtenstein and Iceland are very differently placed.

Like the inevitable wasps that arrive at a picnic, clever lawyers will discover unimagined questions if given a few hours of library time. So the EFTA Court could not hope for a carefree ride, welcomed by governments which it would

---

[2] In Tchaikovsky's ballet 'Sleeping Beauty', the dark force who arrived uninvited and grumpily and who placed a curse was named Carabosse, not a Norwegian sounding name. Indeed, the uneasy atmosphere at the creation of the EFTA Court could instead be attributed to the hostile terms of Opinion 1/91 of the European Court of Justice, referred to below.

[3] The satirical magazine *Private Eye* referred to Worshippers of the Single European Light-bulb.

annoy by disagreeing with their policies or actions, but who would accept with moderate good grace unwelcome judgments. Likewise, it could not refrain from addressing and answering questions put by national courts, convinced by clever lawyers that there are Treaty-based doubts.

Judges are easy targets for political criticism, as they usually do not answer back. 'Amazing order by Euro-Court', or 'Judge frees terrorist' usually reflect less dramatic news than the headline might suggest.[4] Indeed, the EFTA Court judges (President Carl Baudenbacher, Judge Per Christiansen and Judge Páll Hreinsson) do not convey the physical appearance of being messianic power-hungry zealots. All three live in Luxembourg and might be called relatively stateless. The President has lived in Texas, but he eschews snakeskin boots, guns at the hip, the death penalty and other indicia of eccentric independence. Sven Norberg, Leif Sevón, Bjørn Haug, Thór Vilhjálmsson and the other diplomats, teachers and officials are well-recognised jurists who have served on the EFTA Court.

Most of the 11 judges who have served the EFTA Court since 1994 have had academic experience, and the others have been very senior diplomats or officials (not so many judges). President Baudenbacher has written many books and articles on European and international law covering a wide range of issues from competition law to intellectual property law. The members of the Court write prudently, legally and diplomatically, and their personal conduct matches that restraint. That said, there have been occasions when their judgment has displeased a country, or the ESA, or several countries.[5]

III. THE MELANCHOLY BIRTH

The ECJ rejected the establishment of an EEA-wide judiciary in an Opinion about which I (and others) felt rather puzzled, in that the tone of the Opinion sounded positively hostile to the judicial cooperation which we now regard as natural. It revealed the European Court's initial suspicions towards integrating EFTA country judges in a grand European judicial project.[6] The ECJ feared a threat to the integrity of the European Union if all EFTA States were to send judges to sit

---

[4] My mentor, Sir David Edward, habitually an elegant figure, was once depicted in a British newspaper looking like a *sans-abri*, presumably to suggest the unreliability of his court, and was reproached in the article for working more than the Working Time Directive contemplated.

[5] Of the extensive literature on Norwegian reluctance to give deference to the EFTA Court, see H Haukeland Fredriksen, 'The Troubled Relationship between the Supreme Court of Norway and the EFTA Court—Recent Developments' in Müller-Graff and Mestad (eds), *Europe and its European relations* (Bergen Open Research Archive, UiB publications, 2014) as a good recent account of the constitutional problem.

[6] Opinion 1/91 of the ECJ on the Draft agreement between the European Community and the countries of the European Free Trade Association relating to the creation of the European Economic Area [1991] ECR I-6079. Under the draft agreement, the envisaged EEA judiciary would have comprised ECJ and EFTA judges.

together with the judges from the EC/EU. The idea of a plenum with five ECJ judges and three EEA judges was not welcomed in the Court's Opinion.

> Consequently, the agreement's objective of ensuring homogeneity of the law throughout the EEA will determine not only the interpretation of the rules of the agreement itself but also the interpretation of the corresponding rules of Community law.
>
> It follows that in so far as it conditions the future interpretation of the Community rules on free movement and competition the machinery of courts provided for in the agreement conflicts with Article 164 of the EEC Treaty and, more generally, with the very foundations of the Community.
>
> The threat posed by the court system set up by the agreement to the autonomy of the Community legal order is not reduced by the fact that Articles 95 and 101 of the agreement seek to create organic links between the EEA Court and the Court of Justice …
>
> On the contrary, it is to be feared that the application of those provisions will accentuate the general problems arising from the court system to be set up by the agreement.[7]
>
> …
>
> In those circumstances, it will be very difficult, if not impossible, for those judges, when sitting in the Court of Justice, to tackle questions with completely open minds where they have taken part in determining those questions as members of the EEA Court.[8]

These bleak words about judges working together may be contrasted with the current cordiality. It was against this background (or despite it) that the principle of homogeneity, which is at the heart of the EEA Agreement, was formulated.[9] Thus although EEA law and the law of the EC (now the EU) were separate legal orders, and although the EFTA and the EU were constitutionally significantly different, there was a powerful policy consideration in favour of consistency in the applicable European law rules. There would also be constitutional arguments in favour of maintaining differences between the two regimes.

The EFTA Member States have agreed to accept the *acquis communautaire*. EFTA States may sometimes feel politically irritated that, although they have not endorsed an agenda in favour of an ever closer union with the EU, they are bound by a set of rules which evolve regularly, which they are obliged to apply, but which they have not drafted or amended. Worse, the EFTA Court elected to create a *Francovich* rule on the basis that homogeneity would be enhanced if EFTA citizens had direct claims against their states where national legislation failed to deliver the benefits intended by the EU legislator. Some of the judicial steps were bold. For example, though EFTA citizens have quite limited EU Treaty rights, they can nonetheless invoke the principle of state liability against the state in case of breach of duty. Thus the EFTA Court has adopted what we might call quasi-direct effect, quasi-primacy and state liability. There has also been what is called a useful

---

[7] Opinion 1/91, paras 45–48.
[8] Opinion 1/91, para 52.
[9] Art 6 of the EEA Agreement.

EFTA Court dialogue with the EU Courts. Indeed there are dozens of references in EU law to EFTA precedents, as well as even more references in EFTA judgments, from the very first case on,[10] to EU judgments.[11] Both the EU and EFTA Courts have recognised the importance of the EEA homogeneity objective.[12] The EU Courts take account of and regularly refer to EFTA Court case law. Likewise some national supreme courts. The European Commission is a regular intervener in EFTA Court cases, the ESA a less frequent intervener before the ECJ.

While it is usually the ECJ that attracts media attention (often erroneous, or at least exaggerated), the EFTA Court has its moments in the limelight. Sometimes, the EFTA Court encounters the question after the ECJ, sometimes before. In *Philip Morris*, the EFTA Court was the first international court to examine the legality of a visual ban on tobacco products at points of sale with trade rules.[13] The case received widespread media attention, notably from the mainstream press.[14] In *GEMO*, Advocate General Jacobs agreed with the EFTA Court's so-called 'state aid approach' in *Husbanken II*, in which a state guarantee granted by Norway to its State Housing Bank to provide a service of general economic interest was deemed to constitute state aid.[15] *Television Without Frontiers* was another relative first, as were cases about the precautionary principle, transfer of undertakings, and insurance.

The EFTA Court has the great advantage of smallness and of using only one language. It was born after the most interventionist phase of the ECJ had come to an end. When one discusses style, one is necessarily comparing aesthetics, tone, crispness and other not easily quantifiable factors. So my remarks are anecdotal, impressionistic and unscientific. My guess at the start of preparing this chapter was that the style of the EFTA Court would be perceptibly, though not radically, different from that of the other EU Courts. The differences would be: speedier (easy if there are only three judges and one language), somewhat shorter (compare

---

[10] Of many examples, see the opinions of Advocate General Kokott in Case C-681/11 *Schenker & Co AG and Others*, 28 February 2013; Advocate General Mischo in Case 192/01 *Commission v Denmark* [2003] ECR I-9693; Advocate General Maduro in Case C-434/04 *Ahokainen and Leppik* [2006] ECR I-9171; Advocate General Jacobs in Case C-126/01 *Ministre de l'Économie, des Finances et de l'Industrie v GEMO SA* [2003] ECR I-13769; Advocate Jacobs Geelhoed in Case C-452/01 *Ospelt and Schlössle Weissenberg* [2003] ECR I-9743; and Advocate General Sharpston in Case C-384/04 *Federation of Technological Industries and Others* [2006] ECR I-4191.

[11] Case E-1/94 *Restamark* [1994–1995] EFTA Ct Rep 15, paras 32 *et seq* noted that individuals and economic operators must be entitled to invoke and claim nationally EEA rights if unconditional and sufficiently precise; Case E-1/01 *Einarsson* [2002] EFTA Ct Rep 1, on primacy of EEA law; Case E-9/97 *Sveinbjörnsdóttir* [1998] EFTA Ct Rep 95, paras 44–60 on state liability.

[12] Case T-115/94 *Opel Arstial* [1997] ECR II-00039, paras 104–110; Case C-452/01 *Margarethe Ospelt and Schlössle Weissenberg Familienstiftung* [2003] ECR I-09743, para 29.

[13] Case E-16/10 *Philip Morris Norway AS and Staten/Helse-og omsorgsdepartementet* [2011] EFTA Ct Rep 330; see also Alberto Alemanno, '*Philip Morris v Norway*: EFTA Court upheld visual display bans of tobacco products with a precautionary twist', 16 September 2011.

[14] Stephanie Bodoni, 'Philip Morris Must Show Norway Tobacco Display Ban Is Unfounded', Bloomberg News, 12 September 2011.

[15] Opinion of Advocate General Jacobs in *GEMO*, cited above n 10.

Posten Norge[16] and *Post Danmark*[17]), and more internally consistent (see *Lelos v GSK Greece*[18] as a judgment written by multiple hands). Let us consider if these first impressions are confirmed by examples.

IV. THE SINGLE MARKET: A MAGNIFICENT OBSESSION?

It is appropriate to begin with the model against which the easiest comparison can be made: the European Court of Justice itself. There was a time when judgments of the ECJ traced out a fearless, confident line in which problems of disparity between regulators were resolved by endorsing whatever would enhance market integration. The Commission was given considerably more generous latitude than the Member States. If a disparity emerged between how a Member State and the Commission assessed a particular question, the Court was likely to endorse the Commission's approach. In matters like food recipe law, the Member State posture was sometimes frivolous, though solemnly defended in emotionally rich terms ('beer is liquid bread on which our country's working men depend for their strength and selling as beer any less noble liquid than Real Beer will weaken our men'). Controversies over inconsistent national rules on croissants, feta, hams, wine, boudin sausage, cheese and other comestibles came to the Court's attention, until in *Cassis de Dijon*[19] it robustly adopted something close to full faith and credit: if it can be sold in that Member State, it should be sold in this Member State unless exigent circumstances can be shown to exist.

There was in those days a period when the ECJ produced quirky gems: short, pithy, and flavourful. The ECJ's '*Sunday Trading*' cases were a summer flowering of litigious and judicial creativity. (One ECJ judge told me that he was advised to render a draft more antiseptic, less coloured.) The ECJ was accepting many cases which were remotely and tangentially linked to market integration. Under the Court's broad interpretation of national rules which hindered trade between Member States, blocking the sale of goods on the English Sabbath could indeed (coincidentally and unintentionally) hinder the sale of imported goods. There were numerous clever challenges to local English trading rules, with some success for the creative lawyers involved. Then the music stopped, and the ECJ ultimately decided that national trading rules imposing shop closures on Sundays did not hinder intra-EU trade as these applied equally and non-discriminatorily to domestic products and imports from other EU Member States.[20]

---

[16] Case E-15/10 *Posten Norge v EFTA Surveillance Authority* [2012] EFTA Ct Rep 246.
[17] Case C-209/10 *Post Danmark A/S v Konkurrencerådet*, judgment of 27 March 2012, published electronically.
[18] Joined Cases C-468/06 to C-478/06 *Lelos kai Sia EE v GlaxoSmithKline* [2008] ECR I-7139.
[19] Case 120/78 *Rewe-Zentral AG v Bundesmonopolverwaltung für Branntwein* [1979] ECR 649.
[20] Case C-169/91 *Stoke-on-Trent* [1992] ECR I-6653; Joined Cases C-69/93 and C-258/93 *Punto Casa and PPV* [1994] ECR I-2355.

The political context of today's European Union is hugely different from that before 1972 and the first enlargement from six to nine Member States. In its early days, the Court had the advantage of small size, light case-load, the rather warm support of the lawyers who regularly appeared before it, and a certain vision of the legal future. (At my first argument, counsel were invited to pre-lunch drinks with the judges.) As the EU has swollen to 28 members, the savour of its judgments has diminished. That is a matter of regret, but not of criticism. The judgments of the EFTA Court have never been exuberant, but they have remained intelligible and unconvoluted.

There is a great difference between a court of three, using one language (English, which is grammatically tolerant of stretching and of novel structuring), with a moderate case-load, and a court with 38 members (judges and advocates general) and 23 official languages of which French (grammatically rather more conservative) is the working language. It is easier for a small monolingual court which is not much in the public eye to reach consensus, remain consistent, and identify sensitivities, questions best postponed, and intelligent solutions.

V. UNWELCOME PERSONS

Sometimes, the underlying choices are genuinely delicate, and the jurisprudence is not consistent. Creating order out of miscellaneous and contrasting precedents calls for skill. The delicacy of the choices to be made is illustrated by several cases about the right to reside, in particular circumstances, of foreign individuals who were lawful but unwelcome.

Mrs van Duyn, a Dutch citizen, was an active member of the Church of Scientology, which was regarded by the UK authorities as a lawful but socially undesirable cult. She was denied permission to live in the United Kingdom to work as a Scientologist, and challenged the immigration officer's decision as being an unjustified restriction on the free movement of workers.[21] The UK government invoked public policy for the restriction. The ECJ found that Mrs van Duyn's personal conduct did not in itself need to be unlawful. The United Kingdom was allowed to exclude her from entering the country. But then came *Adoui v Belgian State*,[22] in which two French nationals, delicately referred to in the European Court Reports as 'waitresses' who attracted customers by sitting in the windows of establishments in the red-light area of the city of Liège, were threatened with deportation. Prostitution was not illegal in Belgium. They prevailed on the grounds that French citizens could be deported only if Belgian citizens, who could not be deported, were equally liable to repressive penalties intended to combat the same conduct.

---

[21] Case 41/74 *Van Duyn v Home Office* [1974] ECR 1337.
[22] Joined Cases 115 and 116/81 [1982] ECR 1665.

The EFTA incarnation of the problem of the lawful but unwelcome foreigner was Jan Anfinn Wahl,[23] a Norwegian citizen who was refused admission to Iceland on the grounds of his membership of the Hells Angels motorcycling fraternity. He was a university student (albeit an elderly one, in his mid-thirties), had no criminal record, and wanted to go sight-seeing in Iceland as well as to make contact with prospective members of the Hells Angels club. But Hells Angels paraphernalia were found in his luggage, and he was refused permission to enter Iceland. It emerged that Iceland's law enforcers had 'been taking measures over a considerable period to prevent the national motorcycle club in question from becoming a charter of the Hells Angels, inter alia, by repeatedly denying foreign members of Hells Angels entry on arrival to Iceland by reference to public policy and public security'.[24] Thus they wanted to prevent 'a national motorcycle club acceding to become a full charter member of an international motorcycle club associated with organised crime ... Furthermore, it appears from the reference that the national motorcycle club needed the support of an established charter of Hells Angels in order to become a full charter itself and, for that reason, the measures in question could only target foreigners. Since there was no such charter in Iceland, the support of a foreign member was a prerequisite.'[25]

One can readily see the different points of view. Norway and Iceland fiercely opposed limitations on their power to control social turbulence and potential criminality. The European Commission reminded the Court of the need to respect the principle of proportionality.[26] The ESA submitted that a person may be a threat despite not having a criminal record. But the man was not a criminal, and what was wrong with motorcycle enthusiasts getting together? Why assume they would break the law?

The EFTA Court produced an adroit and elegant conclusion, which called for 'specificity, precision and clarity'; then demanded a danger assessment based on the individual's personal conduct, and further stipulated that the controversial conduct should 'represent a genuine, present and sufficiently serious threat to one of the fundamental interests of society'. It was for the national court to apply those liberal-sounding but actually fairly cautious notions to the situation of Mr Wahl.

Even though the Court may have had a view about whether he should be allowed to travel the road of Iceland, it left the crucial determination to be made locally. In the famous *Bosman* case,[27] the ECJ had to decide on supposed tensions between national and European football rules and the Treaty's rules on free movement of workers.[28] The Court found that the duty of the acquiring club to make a

[23] Case E-15/12 *Jan Anfinn Wahl v the Icelandic State* ('*Hells Angels*') [2013] EFTA Ct Rep 534.
[24] ibid, para 102.
[25] ibid, paras 106–107.
[26] See some examples cited in *Hells Angels*: Case 36/75 *Roland Rutili v Minister of the Interior* [1975] ECR 1219; Case 30/77 *Régina v Pierre Bouchereau* [1977] ECR 1999.
[27] ibid, paras 114 and 137.
[28] Case C-415/93 *Union Royale Belge des Sociétés de Football Association v Bosman* [1995] ECR I-4921.

payment to the former club of the young player in recognition of the former club's contribution to his professional development was factually unacceptable (rather than leaving it to the national court to check whether the practice did in fact have the alleged negative consequences). The ECJ erred there—I submit—by making factual conclusions which the national court was better equipped to make. In a hotly contentious, facts-rich case, it is wise, as the EFTA Court did in the *Hells Angels* case, to trust the local judge to decide the facts prudently and accurately.

VI. CONTROVERSIAL MATTERS: GAMBLING, TRADE UNION PRIVILEGES AND BANKING REGULATION

Governments, for good reasons, strictly regulate the activity of gambling. There are risks of addiction and risks of corruption, as well as the potential for raising large sums of revenue for the state. Commonly, the national measures regulate on a national basis and limit or forbid gambling equipment or services from other countries. The Norwegian authorities indeed voiced reluctance to contemplate that a national rule might be overruled on grounds of incompatibility with EEA law, but the crisis evaporated. Later on, however, in *STX*,[29] the question arose of whether workers in a shipyard should receive compensation for expenses incurred when detached to work away from home, not an obviously politically sensitive topic. After consulting the EFTA Court,[30] the Norwegian appellate court found against the employer on the basis of the European Directive,[31] but its decision was then appealed to Norway's Supreme Court, the Høyesterett. There the idea was discussed of circumventing the problem by having the employees hired locally in Norway rather than transferring them. The Høyesterett criticised the EFTA Court's decision, and was in its turn the object of a critique by President Baudenbacher,[32] who concluded by saying approximately 'This is not what EEA law is about'.[33] He noted that the same court[34] had in the earlier case accepted the authority of the EFTA Court as regards the regulation of gaming machines. Thus the EFTA Court has well demonstrated its political readiness to displease governments, a crucial marker of true constitutional independence.

Another occasion when a judgment displeased governments was *Icesave*, concerning Iceland's possible liabilities for lost deposits in Icesave accounts in the aftermath of the economic crisis of 2008.[35] Under Directive 94/19/EC, EEA States are required to put in place deposit-guarantee schemes to cover a minimum

---

[29] Norges Høyesterett, Rt 2012 s 1447, *STX and Others v Staten v/Tariffnemnda*.

[30] Case E-2/11 *STX Norway Offshore AS m fl v Staten v/Tariffnemnda* [2012] EFTA Ct Rep p 4.

[31] Directive 96/71/EC of the European Parliament and of the Council of 16 December 1996 concerning the posting of workers in the framework of the provision of services [1997] OJ L 18/1.

[32] C Baudenbacher, 'EFTA-domstolen og dens samhandling med de norske domstolene' (2013) 52 *LOV OG RETT* 8, 515–534.

[33] 'Det er ikke dette EOS-retten handler om.' ibid, p 525.

[34] Norges Høyesterett, Rt 2005 s 1320, *Norsk Lotteri- og Automatbransjeforbund v Staten v/Kultur- og kirkedepartmentet*.

[35] Case E-16/11 *EFTA Surveillance Authority v Iceland* [2013] EFTA Ct Rep 4.

amount of the deposits of depositors in case of bank failures. This is intended to protect depositors as well as to prevent panic, calm investor agitation, and avert runs on banks. Iceland had not paid the UK and Dutch depositors of one of its failing banks, Landsbanki, within the three-month time limit set by the Directive. By a Reasoned Opinion, the ESA commenced proceedings before the EFTA Court against Iceland, alleging failure to guarantee the deposits and to respect the Directive. At the heart of the dispute was the ESA's claim that the Directive imposed a strict '*obligation of result*' on EEA States in the event that deposit-guarantee schemes fail. Iceland argued instead that its obligations were limited to creating and ensuring the maintenance of a deposit-guarantee scheme, but not to pay compensation as a last resort no matter what the circumstances.[36]

It was evident that the political stakes were high, and that the ESA as well as two heavyweight countries were of one mind. But the EFTA Court demurred. Instead of deciding between Iceland ('small democracy, financial ruin, no one could escape the crisis') and the UK and the Netherlands ('Iceland created or tolerated a lax unsustainable banking environment'), the Court followed a procedurally narrow approach, examining the merits of the reproaches of the Reasoned Opinion. It did not explore more widely the other contentions advanced by Iceland's critics. While there were indeed potent arguments that Iceland's tolerant banking regulations had provoked a preventable flood of deposits on unsustainable terms, the Court confined its analysis to the Reasoned Opinion and did not consider the wider range of regulatory criticisms relating to subsequently arising obligations which might have been made but did not figure in the Reasoned Opinion.

Iceland had set up a deposit-guarantee scheme.[37] There was no obligation on EEA States to compensate deposits in all circumstances, but only to make arrangements towards a harmonised minimum level of protection.[38] These could therefore not be expected to fill in the void of failing banks in the face of a systemic crisis of the magnitude encountered. Any suggestion to the contrary would cause moral hazard by having the effect of encouraging unsound management of credit institutions.[39] The EFTA Court acknowledged that under the new Directive 2009/14, which provides for much stricter requirements, a different conclusion would probably have been reached. The outcome would probably have been different in the EU.[40]

VII. THE PRECAUTIONARY PRINCIPLE

I will add one case where I enthusiastically endorse the Court's approach to that slippery and woolly minded doctrine, the precautionary principle. To save the

---

[36] ibid, paras 96–97 and paras 102–103.
[37] ibid, paras 130–131, 133.
[38] ibid, paras 134–135 and 144.
[39] ibid, para 167.
[40] See R Milne, 'Iceland triumphs in Icesave court battle', *Financial Times*, 28 January 2013.

health of Norway's child-bearing and elderly citizens, cornflakes with added iron or vitamins were banned.[41] Norway forbade the sale of cornflakes enriched with iron or vitamins, mainly on the ground that there was no need to deliver extra iron to the population, that there was a problem of excess iron in the bodies of some Norwegians, that scientific enquiry was ongoing, that Norway's endorsement of adding iron to cheese and whey should not change the result for cornflakes, and that the ban was both necessary and proportionate. Judge-Rapporteur Baudenbacher's Report for the Hearing is 35 pages long, sober and detailed. It deserves reading as an example of how to record neutrally a variety of different opinions, some of them extravagant, respectfully but accurately.

In a short judgment, the Court disagreed with Norway. When the case arose, the government's policy on iron fortification was inconsistent, in that some 'fortified' products (cheese and whey, for example) were sold as a matter of government policy. Moreover, no comprehensive risk assessment had been conducted. The argument that if cornflakes could be 'fortified' other products could not be refused by the authorities as candidates for 'fortification' was rejected as 'floodgates' fears. Most importantly, the judgment noted that the principal justification for the measures was a supposed lack of need in the Norwegian population, rather than danger to the public health.

The Judgment and the Report for the Hearing are admirably lucid, easy to follow, and concrete. The Court declined to accept the precautionary principle as a justification to use a hypothesis to ban something which is probably harmless but might not be. The ECJ went roughly the same way in a Danish case about ill-justified prohibitions on vitamin additives to cranberry juice.[42] The difficult choices for a court confronted with a confident state scientist who says his country is correct, and a hugely eminent expert in the specific area of health who says the fears are absurdly exaggerated, are noted in a lengthy article in honour of David Edward on the topic of the precautionary principle and the risks of its regular invocation as an excuse to avoid political criticism.[43] I there regretted that the Court of First Instance was less confident in *Pfizer Animal Health v Council*[44] than was the EFTA Court in *ESA v Norway*.

VIII. TRADEMARKS AND REPACKAGING

As to trademark exhaustion, the EFTA Court had to consider whether grey imports into Norway of portable torches made in the United States could be blocked on trademark grounds in the *Maglite* case.[45] The dispute was classic: the

[41] Case C-3/00 *EFTA Surveillance Authority v Kingdom of Norway* [2000–2001] EFTA Ct Rep 73.
[42] Case C-192/01 *Commission v Kingdom of Denmark* [2003] ECR I-9693.
[43] I Forrester, 'The Dangers of Too Much Precaution', *A True European: Essays for Judge David Edward* (Oxford, Hart Publishing, 2003).
[44] Case T-13/99 *Pfizer Animal Health* [2002] ECR II-3305.
[45] Case E-2/97 *Mag Instrument Inc v California Trading Company Norway* [1997] EFTA Ct Rep 127.

local distributor argued that his effort had created demand and the parallel importer was an illegitimate free-rider who should not be allowed to use the brand name. The selling of trademarked products was a breach of the trademark rights of Maglite and its corporate family. Several EU governments agreed, invoking the risk that if international exhaustion existed, some EFTA countries would have parallel imports and others would not: free movement of goods would be compromised. The EFTA Court disagreed: since the EEA Agreement did not create a customs union but only a free trade area, with no common external trade policy, it was for the EFTA States to reach their own individual conclusions as to which trademark regime would apply.

Courts should be embarrassed about having to make U-turns, but not too embarrassed. The ECJ has corrected its route on a few occasions. Courts very properly are reluctant to change their mind, but very properly do so occasionally. In the words of Advocate General Lagrange in the famous *Da Costa*[46] case, one of the longest analyses in the Court's reports about the role of previous jurisprudence and the desirability of departing therefrom in appropriate circumstances:

> … the Court of Justice should, in this as in all other matters, remain free when giving its future judgments. However important the judgment which it is led to give on some point may be, whatever may be the abstract character which the interpretation of some provision of the Treaty may present—or appear to present—the golden rule of res judicata should be preserved: it is from the moral authority of its decisions, and not from the legal authority of res judicata, that a jurisdiction like ours should derive its force. Clearly no one will expect that, having given a leading judgment, such as the judgment in Case 26/62, the Court will depart from it in another action without strong reasons, but it should retain the legal right to do so. The rule that res judicata binds only the particular case is a wise rule; rather than enabling the court to shelter formally behind a previous judgment, as one shelters behind a law or regulation, it obliges it unceasingly to retain awareness of its responsibility, that is, to confront the realities of the situation with the legal rule in each action, which can lead it in appropriate cases to recognize its errors in the light of new facts, of new arguments or even of a spontaneous rethinking, or more frequently to alter its point of view subtly without changing it fundamentally, thus being party in the light of experience and the evolution of legal theories and economic, social or other phenomena, to what is called the evolution of case law.[47]

Ten years later, the EFTA Court had to take account of the fact that the ECJ, in its *Silhouette*[48] and *Sebago*[49] judgments, had decided the trademark holders had the right to invoke before the EU Courts their rights to prevent the importation of non-spurious (genuine but unwelcome) merchandise from third countries into the EU. The EFTA Court adroitly noted that there were 'weighty arguments' in favour of both approaches, and concluded that 'the differences between the EEA

---

[46] Joined Cases 28, 29 and 30/62 *Da Costa v Nederlandse Belastingadministratie* [1963] ECR 31.
[47] ibid, pp 42–43.
[48] Case C-355/96 *Silhouette International Schmied v Hartlauer Handelsgesellschaft* [1998] ECR I-4799.
[49] Case C-173/98 *Sebago and Maison Dubois* [1999] ECR I-4103.

Agreement and the EC Treaty with regard to trade relations with third countries do not constitute compelling grounds for divergent interpretations of Article 7(1) of the Trade Mark Directive in EEA law and EC law.'[50] As a result, grey imports of trademarked goods from third countries can be blocked consistently throughout the EEA. This was a good choice. I regret that the Court was less bold in another trademark case, *Paranova*.[51]

IX. *PARANOVA*: AN OPPORTUNITY FOR INDEPENDENT THOUGHT WASTED

The current state of EU trademark law as to pharmaceutical law is fuelling curious and quite artificial patterns of commerce which might trouble patients if they knew about them. Wholesalers of pharmaceutical drugs in Europe have achieved the right to buy and take delivery of large volumes of boxes of drugs from the patentee or its affiliates, unwrap and discard the original packaging of each bottle or blister, repackage the drug in a new packet bearing the trade dress of the wholesaler, and bearing the manufacturer's name and trademark, and resell such repackaged products in competition with the un-manipulated goods being resold in the manufacturer's trade dress. Such manipulations have been authorised by the European Court of Justice in a series of judgments for the policy goal of easing barriers to trade between Member States. Such lawful manipulations of trade-marked products are unique in the world.[52]

The pharmaceutical manufacturers made a number of predictable arguments about different sell-by dates, light-sensitive products, out-of-date products, opportunities for counterfeit medicines to enter the supply chain and so on, but these arguments were rejected. To take one case as an example, the ECJ said: 'It is not possible for each hypothetical risk of isolated error to suffice to confer on the trade mark owner the right to oppose any repackaging of pharmaceutical products in new external packaging.'[53] It is intriguing to observe that the ECJ was quite categorical in rejecting the complaints of manufacturers of highly dangerous products about possible confusions or errors in the dispensing of those products to the public. But those factors assume that there is no trademark consideration worth protecting, and that market integration of pharmaceuticals (uniquely) justifies permitting the repackaging of drugs in such a manner as to allow the repackager both to build his own reputation and affix the patentee's trademark. Paradoxically, one may assume that producers of less toxic consumer products such as tennis balls, razor blades or other trademarked items have today virtually

---

[50] Joined Cases E-9/07 and E 10/07 *L'Oréal Norge AS, L'Oréal SA v Per Aarskog AS, Nille AS, Smart Club AS* [2008] EFTA Ct Rep 259, para 37.

[51] Case E-3/02 *Paranova AS v Merck & Co, Inc and Others* (2003).

[52] I Forrester, 'The EFTA Court confronts re-labelling' (2003) 7–8 *European Law Reporter* 278.

[53] Joined Cases C-427-93, C-429/93 and C-436/93 *Bristol-Myers Squibb v Paranova* [1996] ECR I-3457, para 63.

no concern that a parallel trader would repackage or re-label their goods in order to facilitate resale in another Member State, because such an exercise would not be worth the money and would be a clear breach of trademark rights.

Good law drafted to remedy wrongs in one industry can be bad law when applied to another industry. Would one want to tolerate the re-labelling and repackaging of whisky, cola, film, sun-cream, golf balls and other products to assist traders who identify price discrepancies and hope to boost their own name by referring to the famous brand? Should it be permissible for Marks & Spencer to sell 'Marks & Spencer Coca Cola' in bottles designed to promote Marks & Spencer products? Or for Carrefour to sell 'Carrefour Uncle Ben's Rice'?

When judges endeavour to remedy a wrong and have to make new law, the outcome of well-intentioned judicial generosity can be hazardous. Whenever a judgment is written to give comfort to the morally superior party whose claim is weak in legal or technical terms, or in principle, there is a risk of broken crockery, broken because of the unforeseeable consequences (sometimes foretold but not believably foretold). To take again the example of football, the ECJ was so keen to help Mr Bosman, who had unquestionably been badly treated, that it rewrote Article 48.[54] Article 48 had hitherto been regarded as an obligation on Member States, so that it covered private action, not based on nationality, taken by an association governed by private law. The consequences have been bad for football and bad for most footballers, though excellent for the richest clubs and players.

One function of trademarks is to make money. Some are very valuable. Taking away from the pharmaceutical rightholder the sole right to affix his mark is a massive encroachment, a European first which does no particular good to European industry, consumers or health ministries, although it has helped parallel traders.

X. DELAY AND VOLUME OF CASE-LOAD

Courts are sometimes slow, but sometimes they try to speed up. The account of a case from the year 1310 states thus:

> And after the inquest was sworn, they could not agree.
>
> STANTON J. Good people, you cannot agree?
>
> STANTON J., to John Allen [apparently the marshal]: Go and put them in a house until Monday, and let them not eat or drink.
>
> On that commandment John put them in a house without [food or drink]. At length on the same day about vesper-time they agreed. And John went to Sir Hervey and told him that they agreed. Then STANTON J., gave them leave to eat.[55]

Seven hundred years later, delay is still a judicial anxiety.

---

[54] *Bosman*, above n 28.
[55] *Walding v Fairfax* (1310) YB Mich 4 Edw II, 22 SS 188.

The EFTA Court has an enviable record of delivering judgment within reasonable periods of time. There are influencing factors: the Court's monolingual practice, its size, limited geographic reach and lesser workload compared to EU Courts. A closer look reveals that while these may all have an effect, recent figures indicate that, in relative terms, the EFTA Court has arguably more cases than the ECJ. For instance, there were 631 new cases for the ECJ in 2010, which represents 1.26 cases per million inhabitants.[56] For the same year, there were 18 new cases for the EFTA Court, which represents 3.6 cases per million inhabitants. Thus, the EFTA Court hears approximately three times as many cases as the ECJ per million inhabitants. There is no evidence to suggest that such a high yield has had any negative repercussions on the quality of the EFTA Court's judgments. To the contrary, their lightness of style is a merit, although it is also a natural consequence of small size and only one language.

XI. DUE PROCESS IN COMPETITION CASES

The emergence of European competition law as world leader in creativity and severity of financial penalty has rekindled an old debate about the procedures by which cases are decided by the European Commission and reviewed on appeal. Thus far, there have been very few judicial setbacks for the Commission's practices and its choices of level of fines. The advent of the direct applicability of the ECHR (at some date) and the arrival of the Charter of Fundamental Rights (now) have increased interest in the constitutional propriety of the EU's arrangements for detecting and condemning economic crimes. The ECtHR has recognised that the 'criminal charge' under Article 6 of the ECHR has expanded beyond the traditional categories of criminal law to potentially include competition law.[57] The ECtHR's judgment in *Menarini*[58] confirmed that a fine imposed by the Italian competition authority, because of its seriousness, amounted to a criminal sanction within the meaning of Article 6 ECHR.[59] However, the imposition of such a sanction by an agency could be lawful as long as the decision was subject to a full review by a court having 'full jurisdiction'.[60]

Both the EU and EFTA administrative regimes opt for an administrative model with a strong authority to enforce competition law. There is an extensive body of literature on the topic of how the processes by which competition cases are decided by the European Commission match the requirements of the ECHR.[61]

---

[56] See Note by the EFTA Court on the Norwegian Official Reports NOU 2012:2 'Outside and Inside, Norway's Agreements with the European Union', 27 January 2012: http://www.eftacourt.int/fileadmin/user_upload/Files/News/2012/2012_A_Note.pdf.

[57] *Jussila v Finland*, ECtHR (Application No 73053/01), 23 November 2006, para 43.

[58] *A Menarini Diagnostics SRL v Italy*, ECtHR (Application No 43509/08), 27 September 2011.

[59] ibid, para 44.

[60] ibid, para 59.

[61] See, among many, F Montag, 'The Case for a Radical Reform of the Infringement Procedure under Regulation 17' [1996] 8 ECLR 428, at 430; J Schwarze and R Bechtold, *Deficiencies in European*

I have argued that the current inquisitorial regime is inadequate in that the investigators are attributed decision-making and punishing functions, there is no hearing by a decision-maker, and the decision on guilt or innocence of an economic crime is taken by a political body; and I have separately argued that deferential judicial review by the EU Courts has exacerbated the underlying problem. It is 30 years since the Commission lost an abuse of dominance case in Luxembourg.[62]

It is my anecdotal impression that the ESA's competition enforcement uses a lighter touch, and is less prescriptive, than its EU counterpart. It follows from the nature of the EEA Agreement itself that both legal orders are broadly based on an administrative model under which the enforcing authority investigates, prosecutes, and decides in competition cases. The Commission and the ESA each have similar powers to sanction competition law infringements by fines and behavioural remedies. In addition, the basic competition provisions which both authorities enforce (ie Articles 101/102 TFEU, and 53/54 EEA Agreement) are broad in language, which makes them subject to evolution and changes in policy. The words of the two Treaties are substantially identical.[63]

Fines imposed by the European Commission have reached heights which are by any standard astonishing. They are heavy (tens of millions of euros may be deemed low; hundreds of millions are deemed normal; over a billion is unusual), and may exceed any other financial penalty for any offence in any democracy in the world. The severity of its interlocutory penalties is also striking.[64] According to the ESA's own statistics, competition-related fines were approximately €30 million in 2012.[65] Commission statistics for that same year reveal that, for cartel cases alone, fines reached €1.87 billion.[66] While it is true that part of this may be attributed to the reduced geographic scope of the EFTA countries and the lower turnover of targeted companies, the difference is substantial.

Community Competition Law: Critical analysis of current practice and proposal for change (Gleiss Lutz, 2008); D Slater, S Thomas and D Waelbroeck, 'Competition law proceedings before the European Commission and the right to a fair trial: no need for reform?', *Global Competition Law Centre Working Paper 04/08*; A Andreangeli et al, 'Enforcement by the Commission: The Decisional and Enforcement Structure in Antitrust Cases and the Commission's Fining System' in Merola and Waelbroeck (eds), *Towards an optimal enforcement of competition rules in Europe* (Brussels, Bruylant, 2010); F Castillo de la Torre, 'Evidence, Proof and Judicial Review in Cartel Cases' (2009) *World Competition* 32, 1; CD Ehlermann and M Marquis (eds), *European Competition Law Annual 2009: Evaluation of Evidence and its Judicial Review in Competition Cases* (Oxford, Hart Publishing, 2010); WPJ Wils, 'The Increased Level of EU Antitrust Fines, Judicial Review, and the European Convention on Human Rights' (2010) *World Competition: Law and Economics Review* 33, 1.

[62] On this issue, see D Geradin and N Petit, 'Judicial Review in European Union Competition Law: A Quantitative and Qualitative Assessment', Tilburg Law and Economics Center (TILEC), Discussion Paper No 2011-008 (October 2010).

[63] See, eg, the recent *Euribor/Libor* case, where fines imposed on banks amounted to €1.7 billion; the *TV and computer monitor tubes* case, where the fine totalled €1.47 billion; and finally the *Car glass cartel* case, where the Commission imposed a €1.35 billion fine on producers.

[64] Cases COMP/39388 and COMP/39389—*E.ON* (2008): huge fines for possibly disturbing a possibly out-of-date adhesive seal, which was neither photographed nor preserved *in situ*.

[65] EFTA Surveillance Authority, Annual Report 2012.

[66] See Cartel Statistics, DG COMP website.

On the specific issue of fines, the EU Courts have often done no more than verify whether these were consistent with the Commission's applicable Fining Guidelines. But that should be the beginning of the process of judicial review, not the end. Unlimited jurisdiction supposes consideration of whether the fine actually imposed is fair, proportionate and just. That the Commission has followed its own guidelines should not confer immunity from judicial scrutiny.

XII. A WELCOME DISSENT? THE PROBLEM OF LIGHT JUDICIAL REVIEW

It is difficult to avoid the conclusion that the judicial review of European Commission action, especially in competition cases, has been inconsistent. Sometimes the Court has gone deeply into the facts and has indeed substituted its own conclusions for those of the authority (see, for example, the early case of *Geitling*);[67] sometimes it has elected, after reflection, to agree with a conclusion reached by the Commission (*Remia/Nutricia*);[68] frequently it has endorsed light judicial review in the sense of deferring to the Commission's assessment of complex economic matters; in one case[69] it extended that deference to technical matters; and in several cases it endorsed fines on the same deferential basis, verifying if they were lawful, not whether they were just. In *Chalkor*,[70] the ECJ was asked to rule on the scope of the judicial review by the EU General Court on an appeal from a Commission decision imposing a fine. Faced with the language in the judgment under appeal of 'light judicial review', the ECJ ruled that the General Court could not refrain from reviewing the Commission's assessment of complex economic data. Not only should the evidence relied on be 'factually accurate, reliable and consistent', it should also support the Commission's assessment and the conclusions.[71] The position has improved with *Chalkor*, but it remains the case that most practitioners regard judicial review in competition matters as unpredictable. The underlying decisions are hundreds of pages long, there may well be tens of thousands of pages in the administrative file, and the relevant standard is legality, not full merits review. So diligent judges must naturally find it difficult to be confident that the authority slipped into illegality.

On some occasions in competition matters, the EU Courts have expressed themselves admirably: 'the essential function of evidence … is to establish convincingly the merits of a … decision'.[72] On other occasions, there has been

---

[67] Joined Cases 36, 37, 38 and 40/59 *Geitling Ruhrkohlen Verkaufsgesellchaft mbH and others v High Authority* [1960] ECR 423. (The author is indebted to Michel Waelbroeck for drawing this case to his attention.)

[68] Case 42/84 *Remia BV v Commission* [1985] ECR 2545.

[69] Case T-201/04 *Microsoft Corp v Commission* [2007] ECR II-3601.

[70] Case C-389/10 P *KME v Commission* [2011] ECR I-0000, nyr; C-386/10 P *Chalkor v Commission* [2011] ECR I-000, nyr.

[71] *KME*, above n 70, para 121.

[72] Case C-12/03 P *Commission v Tetra Laval* [2005] ECR-I 987, para 41.

embarrassingly deferential approval. In *Wieland-Werke* the Court stated: 'In areas such as determination of the amount of a fine imposed pursuant to Article 15(2) of Regulation No 17, where the Commission has a discretion, for example, as regards the amount of increase for the purposes of deterrence, review of the legality of those assessments is limited to determining the absence of manifest error of assessment.'[73] The Court here appears to start from a presumption that the Commission enjoys a 'discretion' with which the Court will be reluctant to interfere 'in absence of manifest error of assessment'. The ECJ has regularly used language such as 'The Court cannot substitute, on grounds of fairness, its assessment for that of the Court of First Instance'. Such abstention from the merits is not, I submit, constitutionally appropriate these days.

XIII. THE *POSTEN NORGE* CASE

Three cheers, therefore, for the EFTA Court's rejection in *Posten Norge*[74] of the light judicial review weed which has crept into the EU garden: 'The submission that the Court may intervene only if it considers a complex assessment to be manifestly wrong must be rejected.'[75]

The EFTA Court mentioned in its judgment the ECtHR's *Menarini* judgment (about full merits review being available on appeal) and its *Jussila* judgment (about stigma). It did not question the administrative enforcement model but instead focused on the scope of judicial review. It found that the fine imposed on *Posten Norge* was 'substantial' and the stigma attached to being condemned 'not negligible'.[76] In the process, the EFTA Court disagreed that the review of complex economic assessments by the ESA would have to be based only on whether they were 'manifestly wrong' and went further than the ECJ in *KME* by not accepting that ESA was entitled to a substantial amount of discretion in complex economic assessments.[77] In its view, there was 'no doubt' *Posten Norge* had been abusive.[78]

The *Post Danmark* Case in the EU Courts In *Post Danmark*,[79] a reference, the ECJ followed the EFTA Court's lead in a case which also concerned an alleged abuse of dominance by a postal service. The problem and the facts were not dissimilar. More specifically, the incumbent postal service provider, Post Danmark, had a pricing system which made the life of competitors difficult. The ECJ chose

---

[73] Case T-116/04 *Wieland-Werke v Commission* [2009], ECR II-1087, paras 32–33. See also Case T-241/01 *Scandinavian Airlines System v Commission* [2005] ECR II-2917, para 79 cited in *Wieland-Werke* ('It next has to be examined whether the Commission's assessment of the seriousness of the infringements, having regard to the three factors of their nature, the extent of the geographic market concerned and their actual impact on the market, is vitiated by obvious error').

[74] Case E-15/10, *Posten Norge v EFTA Surveillance Authority* (2012).

[75] ibid, para 102.

[76] ibid, para 90.

[77] ibid, para 102.

[78] ibid, para 180.

[79] Case C-209/10 *Post Danmark A/S v Konkurrencerådet* [2012] ECR I-0000, nyr.

to assess this pricing system by adopting the 'As-Efficient-Competitor' test.[80] Thus it may be legal for a dominant player to charge prices which a competitor cannot match, provided that an equally efficient competitor could do so. It is probably fair to say that the ESA's approach to discounts and rebates can be more comfortably reconciled with the Commission's modern effect-based approach to exclusionary conduct under Article 102 TFEU[81] than the actual practice of the Commission and the ECJ, since both of them are hampered by the court's old case law which makes little commercial sense in today's world.

XIV. RIGOUR TOWARDS THE PUBLIC AUTHORITY

My impression is that the ESA may have a harder job than the Commission in defending its cases in court. In *Norwegian Bankers' Association v EFTA Surveillance Authority (Husbanken II)*, the ESA had found that a state guarantee for Husbanken (the Norwegian State Housing Bank) constituted state aid under Article 61(1) of the EEA Agreement, which was justified under Article 59(2) thereof on services of general economic interest grounds.[82] On appeal, the EFTA Court essentially agreed with the above but annulled the ESA's decision on the grounds that it had not considered 'to the extent necessary' several factors: the relevant market, whether there were alternative means less distortive of competition, a cost and benefits analysis of state aid, and the proportionality test.[83] The EFTA Court evidently did not give the ESA an easy ride.

Of course every case is different, and it is difficult to generalise; it is also true that Commission officials and lawyers as well as ESA lawyers feel frequently that the Court has been too intrusive. Judges in both the EU and EFTA Courts are probably equally guided by a sense of smell, a judicial instinct that something is not right.

XV. THE GOAL OF HOMOGENEITY BETWEEN THE TWO REGIMES

In the recent case of *Irish Bank Resolution Corp*, the EFTA Court attempted to push the boundaries of the duty of loyal cooperation under Article 3 EEA even further.[84] Article 34 of the EFTA Surveillance and Court Agreement (SCA) does not have a preliminary reference procedure and instead provides for an 'advisory opinion' procedure. The national courts of the EFTA States are neither obliged to

---

[80] ibid, para 38.
[81] Guidance on the Commission's enforcement priorities in applying Art 102 TFEU to abusive exclusionary conduct by dominant undertakings (2009).
[82] Case E-4/97 *Norwegian Bankers' Association v EFTA Surveillance Authority* [1999] EFTA Ct Rep 1, paras 9–10.
[83] ibid, paras 67–70.
[84] See Case E-18/11 *Irish Bank Resolution Corporation Ltd* [2012] EFTA Ct Rep p 592.

refer questions for interpretation of EEA law nor bound to follow the EFTA Court ruling. But that is not the end of the matter.

While the EFTA Court recognised that there were differences between Article 267 TFEU on the procedure for a preliminary reference and Article 34 SCA based on 'less far-reaching' depth of integration considerations, it also strongly hinted that the national courts of EFTA States were less free than they might have hoped to disregard their duty of loyalty under Article 3 EEA:

> At the same time, courts against whose decisions there is no judicial remedy under national law will take due account of the fact that they are bound to fulfil their duty of loyalty under Article 3 EEA. The Court notes in this context that EFTA citizens and economic operators benefit from the obligation of courts of the EU Member States against whose decision there is no judicial remedy under national law to make a reference to the ECJ (see Case C-452/01 *Ospelt and Schlössle Weissenberg* [1993] ECR I-9743).[85]

In other words, the national courts of the EFTA States may be bound by what we might call a strong moral duty to refer. Indeed, other observers have been quick to compare this development to a small step towards a preliminary reference procedure for EEA EFTA countries.[86] This assessment is further supported by the findings in *Jonsson*, where it was held that if the legal situation lacks clarity, then a reference is appropriate since by that means 'unnecessary mistakes in the interpretation and application of EEA law are avoided and the coherence and reciprocity in relation to rights of EEA citizens, including EFTA nationals, in the EU are ensured'.[87]

In a recent interpretation order, the EFTA Court speaks of 'the different legal situation concerning courts against whose decisions there is no remedy under national law'.[88]

XVI. CONCLUSION

Lord Justice Megarry said that 'One of the important duties of the courts is to send away defeated litigants who feel no justifiable sense of injustice in the judicial process'.[89] By that standard, the EFTA Court does rather well. The processes it uses convey a readiness to listen, to engage in public, and to be independent.

No one reading the exchanges between Judge Baudenbacher and Norwegian critics[90] could doubt that the Court is independent. Equally, the tone of the

---

[85] ibid, para 58.
[86] See 'Case E-18/11: Small steps towards a preliminary reference procedure for the EEA EFTA countries?', *European Law Blog*, 16 January 2013.
[87] Case E-3/12 *Staten v/Arbeidsdepartmentet v Stig Jonsson* [2013] EFTA Ct Rep 136, para 60.
[88] Case E-2/12 *HOB-vín ehf and The State Alcohol and Tobacco Company of Iceland (ÁTVR)* [2013] EFTA Ct Rep 1092, para 11.
[89] RE Megarry, 'Temptations of the Bench' (1978) 12 *Univ Brit Colum L Rev* 145 at 151, 152.
[90] See Baudenbacher, above n 32, as well as the perceptive comments of H Haukeland Fredriksen in 'The two EEA Courts—a Norwegian perspective' in EFTA Court (ed), *Judicial Protection in the European Economic Area* (Stuttgart, German Law Publishers, 2012) 187–210.

Court's pronouncements on whether the ESA has done its job appear neither sceptical nor deferential. Those are all merits.

Its judgments are easy to read, and not too long. They seem to be little burdened by the repetition of familiar mantras taken from previous judgments. They have conclusions which are rather clear. The layout is largely familiar to those who are accustomed to the judgments of the three EU Courts.

It is astonishing that, despite the antipathy of a number of legal and political figures to such creativity, the EFTA Court has been able to endow the EFTA regime with constitutional judicial principles matching those of the EU. Homogeneity lives.

Lord Denning, an icon of judicial robustness combined with the common touch, spent much of his career in the Court of Appeal, below the House of Lords. He noted wryly that the House of Lords had the position of being the examiner of the Court of Appeal and that his court had no choice but to accept that when the House of Lords took a different view:

> We did our best, but recently our papers were marked by the House of Lords …[91] They only gave us about 50 per cent. The House of Lords are fortunate in that there is no one to examine them or mark their papers. If there were, I do not suppose they would get any higher marks than we.[92]

Lord Denning perhaps underestimated the European Court of Justice, which certainly today is a powerful source of authority to which even the House of Lords must defer; and teachers of law as well as writers of articles have no inhibitions about offering alternative views about any judgment, even from a supreme court. But in any event, it is a rare honour for a practitioner to be asked to mark the exam paper of a court. I would award the birthday court an honourable pass.

---

[91] Citing *Bremer Handelsgesellschaft mbH v Vanden (Avenne-)Izegem PVBA* [1978] 2 Lloyd's Rep 109.
[92] *Bremer Handelsgesellschaft mbH v C Mackprang Jr* [1979] 1 Lloyd's Rep 221 at 222.

4

European Courts in Dialogue

JULIANE KOKOTT AND
DANIEL DITTERT*

I. INTRODUCTION

OVER THE PAST decades, European law[1] has developed into a complex multi-level system (or *Mehrebenensystem*, to use a well-known German term) in which the legal rules applicable to citizens and undertakings no longer emanate exclusively from the national legislatures. Various international organisations have seen the light of the day, many of which have created autonomous legal systems whose rules often co-exist with those enshrined in the national legal systems and are highly relevant for people's everyday life.

All those rules are liable to be applied not only by a large number of domestic courts and tribunals across Europe, but also by several judicial institutions at the supranational level. Strictly speaking, of course, most of the judges involved have very specific and clearly circumscribed competences. As a consequence, they will not necessarily deal with the exact same cases, or if they do, they will look at those cases from different angles. Nevertheless, all the judicial bodies involved may sooner or later be faced with the same legal issues, or at least with very similar ones. This has become particularly clear in recent years during the financial crisis,[2] but it does

* Juliane Kokott is Advocate General at the Court of Justice of the European Union; Daniel Dittert is legal secretary at the Court. Both are expressing their personal opinions in this chapter, which expands on a speech given by Juliane Kokott, with the support of Daniel Dittert, on the occasion of the twentieth anniversary of the EFTA Court in Luxembourg on 20 June 2014.
    [1] We have deliberately chosen to refer to 'European law' in the broad sense, without restricting the scope of our thoughts to the law of the European Union (EU) or the law of the European Economic Area (EEA).
    [2] Different aspects of the financial crisis have been dealt with by courts and tribunals across Europe, eg in Portugal, Romania and Ireland; as far as the European Union level is concerned, see ECJ, *Pringle* (C-370/12, ECLI:EU:C:2012:756), as well as pending case *Gauweiler and Others* (C-62/14).

not end there: issues such as age discrimination,[3] gambling[4] or practical problems related to the private enforcement of competition rules,[5] to name but a few, have kept numerous courts and tribunals in Europe busy over the past few years.

A constructive dialogue among those various judicial institutions can help them ensure a minimum of coherence between their respective approaches and, most importantly, produce the best possible solutions for citizens and businesses all over Europe. On top of that, such dialogue may also be a way for numerous courts and tribunals in Europe to save precious resources, preventing them from having to 'reinvent the wheel', while the case law of their counterparts in other jurisdictions may already contain useful indications and sources of inspiration.

One can distinguish two basic forms of judicial dialogue: the informal type (II) and the formal type (III). For the past 20 years, the EFTA Court has been a champion of both, in particular under the steady leadership of its President Carl Baudenbacher.

II. INFORMAL TYPES OF JUDICIAL DIALOGUE

To begin with, it is important to mention the many shades of judicial dialogue which take place outside of any specific procedural framework and which could therefore be characterised as 'informal'.

For instance, judges may meet their counterparts from other jurisdictions at conferences, anniversaries[6] or during official visits paid by the members of one institution to those of another.[7] They may also publish articles in law journals or discuss certain issues of mutual interest within specialised networks uniting their various judicial institutions.[8] All these occasions can give rise to highly fruitful exchanges on issues of practical relevance to Europe's common legal order.

---

[3] ECJ, *Prigge and Others* (C-447/09, ECLI:EU:C:2011:573); BAG (Bundesarbeitsgericht—German Federal Labour Court), 11 March 1998, Case 7 AZR 700/96; BAG, 18 January 2012, Case 7 AZR 112/08; BVerfG (Bundesverfassungsgericht—German Constitutional Court), 25 November 2004, Case 1 BvR 2459/04.

[4] See, among many others: ECJ, *Winner Wetten* (C-409/06, ECLI:EU:C:2010:503); BVerfG, 28 March 2006, Case 1 BvR 1054/01.

[5] See, eg, EFTA Court, *DB Schenker v ESA* (E-14/11, 2012 EFTA Ct Rep 1178); ECJ, *Donau Chemie and Others* (C-536/11, ECLI:EU:C:2013:366), and *EnBW v Commission* (C-365/12 P, ECLI:EU:C:2014:112).

[6] In recent years, among many other conferences, one may think of those held in Luxembourg on the occasion of the fiftieth anniversary of the Court of Justice of the European Union (2002), the fiftieth anniversary of the ECJ judgment in Case *van Gend en Loos* (2013), and of the twentieth anniversary of the EFTA Court (2014).

[7] For instance, the members of the Court of Justice of the European Union regularly meet their counterparts from the supreme courts of various EU Member States as well as those of the European Court of Human Rights in Strasbourg.

[8] See, eg, the Network of the Presidents of the Supreme Judicial Courts of the EU, the Association of the Councils of State and Supreme Administrative Jurisdictions of the European Union, the Association of European Administrative Judges, the European Judicial Network, the European Judges and Prosecutors Association, the European Judicial Network in Civil and Commercial Matters, and the Association of European Competition Law Judges.

But there are more 'serious' types of informal judicial dialogue which go well beyond such purely academic or sociable exchanges at the fringes of judicial activities. In particular, modern judicial institutions in Europe need to be careful observers of each other's jurisprudence and should recognise, wherever possible, the usefulness of the judgments pronounced by their respective counterparts as a source of inspiration and authority.

One very early example of such interaction in the case law of European courts was, without any doubt, the informal judicial dialogue engaged between the Court of Justice of the European Union (ECJ)[9] and the German Constitutional Court about the protection of fundamental rights. It cannot be denied that, from the 1970s until the mid-1990s, the '*Solange*' case law[10] of the Bundesverfassungsgericht strongly increased the awareness of the ECJ for the protection of fundamental rights. Today, by contrast, it appears that the Luxembourg jurisprudence has become at least as efficient in protecting fundamental rights as that practised in Karlsruhe,[11] if not a bit more progressive on certain issues, namely discrimination cases.[12]

Moving then to the European level, the relationship between the ECJ and the EFTA Court has evolved over time to become a landmark example of informal judicial dialogue.[13] It is true that the partnership between these two Luxembourg-based supranational jurisdictions needs to be, by definition, a very close one, given that they share a common mission—protecting and developing the European internal market established by the EEA Agreement—and apply two sets of rules which are particularly similar, if not identical: the EU's rules on its internal market on the one hand, and the EEA Agreement's provisions on the other.[14] However, that in itself does not suffice to explain the huge success of the judicial dialogue in which the ECJ and the EFTA Court are engaged. Indeed, there appears to be a common awareness among the members of both institutions that the jurisprudence of their respective counterparts on the other side of Luxembourg's

---

[9] At the time: Court of Justice of the European Communities.

[10] See, in particular, the judgments of the German Constitutional Court in BVerfGE 37 p 271 (*Solange I*), BVerfGE 73 p 339 (*Solange II*), and BVerfGE 89 p 155 (*Maastricht*).

[11] Most notably, both the ECJ and the German Constitutional Court seem to be sharing the same views as to the fundamental rights problems arising from the European system of retention of data generated or processed in connection with the provision of electronic communications services; see ECJ, *Digital Rights Ireland and Others* (C-293/12 and C-594/12, ECLI:EU:C:2014:238) on the one hand, and BVerfGE 125 p 260 on the other.

[12] One may point, in particular, to the Bundesverfassungsgericht's initial hesitations as regards the principle of non-discrimination on the grounds of sexual orientation (for details see below nn 26–28).

[13] For details *cf*, among many others, C Baudenbacher, The Judicial Dimension of the European Neighbourhood Policy, EU Diplomacy Paper no 08/2013 (published by the College of Europe, Bruges), pp 10ff.

[14] Pursuant to Art 6 of the EEA Agreement, '[w]ithout prejudice to future developments of case law, the provisions of this Agreement, in so far as they are identical in substance to corresponding rules of the Treaty establishing the European Economic Community and the Treaty establishing the European Coal and Steel Community and to acts adopted in application of these two Treaties, shall, in their implementation and application, be interpreted in conformity with the relevant rulings of the Court of Justice of the European Communities given prior to the date of signature of this Agreement'.

Boulevard Kennedy contains a very useful source of inspiration. From the outset, that awareness had been particularly strong among the judges of the EFTA Court and among the Advocates General of the ECJ, but the judges of the ECJ, who might have been a little bit more hesitant in the early years, have long since followed suit. As the ECJ's President stated at the EFTA Court's tenth anniversary: 'ignoring EFTA Court precedents would simply be incompatible with the overriding objective of the EEA Agreement, which is homogeneity'.[15]

Among the many positive examples of fruitful judicial dialogue between the ECJ and the EFTA Court, we should like to single out the EFTA Court's jurisprudence on the precautionary principle in the field of food safety[16] which was quoted and built upon by the ECJ in its own case law.[17] In a similar way, the EFTA Court's judgments in the field of free movement of persons, services and capital has guided the ECJ more than once.[18] Obviously, it does not come as a surprise that the EFTA Court's case law provides a particularly interesting source of inspiration for other judicial institutions in Europe, despite its relatively small number of judgments handed down per year: that case law is of the highest quality and can draw upon a particularly thorough and well-reflected reasoning.

For its part, the ECJ has had occasion to interpret certain provisions of the EU Treaties and of the EEA Agreement in its judgments which do provide guidance to the EFTA Court whenever similar questions arise before it. Naturally, the ECJ's case law with relevance for the EFTA Court mainly deals with European internal market and competition rules,[19] but it can also include rulings which concern the more 'institutional' aspects of the functioning of the EEA. One such institutional aspect was clarified by the ECJ in 2013; it concerns the value of regulations[20] adopted by the EU institutions where such regulations have been designated to form part of the 'EEA acquis' in the Annexes of the EEA Agreement. Do such regulations nevertheless need to be transposed into the domestic legal systems of the EFTA countries? The ECJ's answer is 'no'; it ruled that EU regulations 'are "as such" to be made part of the internal legal order of the EEA Contracting Parties, that is to say, without any implementing measures being required for that purpose'.[21]

---

[15] V Skouris, 'The CJEU and the EFTA Court under the EEA Agreement: A Paradigm for International Cooperation between Judicial Institutions' in C Baudenbacher, P Tresselt and T Örlygsson (eds), *The EFTA Court Ten Years On* (Oxford, Hart Publishing, 2005) pp 123, 125.

[16] EFTA Court, *ESA v Norway* (*Kellogg's*, E-3/00, 2000-2001 EFTA Ct Rep 73).

[17] ECJ, *Commission v Denmark* (C-192/01, ECLI:EU:C:2003:492 paras 47, 49–53), *Bellio F.lli* (C-286/02, ECLI:EU:C:2004:212 paras 34, 57–60) and *Commission v Netherlands* (C-41/02, ECLI:EU:C:2004:762 para 62).

[18] See, eg, ECJ, *De Agostini and TV-Shop* (C-34/95 to C-36/95, ECLI:EU:C:1997:344 para 37), and *Fidium Finanz* (C-452/04, ECLI:EU:C:2006:631 para 34).

[19] See, among many others, ECJ, *Ospelt and Schlössle Weissenberg* (C-452/01, ECLI:EU:C:2003:493 para 29), *Commission v Netherlands* (C-521/07, ECLI:EU:C:2009:360 para 32), and pending case *Fonnship and Svenska Transportarbetareförbundet* (C-83/13).

[20] Within the meaning of Art 288(2) TFEU.

[21] ECJ, *United Kingdom v Council* (C-431/11, ECLI:EU:C:2013:589 para 54), and Opinion *United Kingdom v Council* (C-431/11, ECLI:EU:C:2013:187 para 42).

It is interesting to note that the informal kind of judicial dialogue in which the ECJ and the EFTA Court are respectively engaged is not confined to the bilateral relationship between these two institutions. Indeed, both the ECJ and the EFTA Court regularly follow the case law of another important supranational judicial institution in Europe: the European Court of Human Rights (ECtHR) based in Strasbourg.[22] The same is true for national courts and tribunals which equally apply the Strasbourg jurisprudence on a regular basis wherever fundamental rights issues are raised before them. Thanks to the Human Rights Court, there appears to be a growing degree of convergence today on issues which might have given rise to diverging solutions in the past.[23] Overall, it is fair to say that the judgments and decisions of the ECtHR are nowadays commonly recognised as being one of the most important frameworks of reference as far as the protection of fundamental rights is concerned, thus establishing a minimum standard to be respected all over Europe. This had already been true before the entry into force of the Treaty of Lisbon,[24] but the direct link established by that Treaty between the Charter of Fundamental Rights of the European Union—see, in particular, Article 52(3) of the Charter—on the one hand and the European Convention on Human Rights (ECHR) on the other has certainly reinforced that tendency.[25]

Last but not least, there also appears to be a growing awareness among national courts and tribunals—even the highest and traditionally slightly reluctant ones— of new trends initiated, at the supranational level, by the ECJ. In this respect, we are thinking, in particular, of the most recent case law of the German Constitutional Court as regards the principle of non-discrimination on the grounds of sexual orientation. After some initial hesitation,[26] the Bundesverfassungsgericht now

---

[22] As regards the reception of the ECtHR's case law by the EFTA Court *cf*, among many others, *Ásgeirsson* (E-2/03, 2003 EFTA Ct Rep 285, para 23), *Posten Norge v ESA* (E-15/10, 2012 EFTA Ct Rep 246, paras 88ff), and *Irish Bank* (E-18/11, 2012 EFTA Ct Rep 592, paras 63f).

[23] As regards the protection of business premises against searches, see ECJ, *Roquette Frères* (C-94/00, ECLI:EU:C:2002:603 para 29); in that judgment, the ECJ applied the Strasbourg case law (in particular, ECtHR, *Société Colas Est and Others v France*, Reports of Judgments and Decisions 2002-III, Application no 37971/97 and *Niemietz v Germany* Series A no 251-B, Application no 13710/88), thus going beyond its previous jurisprudence (see ECJ, *Hoechst v Commission*, 46/87 and 227/88, ECLI:EU:C:1989:337). Similarly, there seems to be a great deal of convergence between the ECJ, the EFTA Court and the ECtHR as far as 'full jurisdiction' within the meaning of Art 6(1) ECHR is concerned: see, on the one hand, ECtHR, *A Menarini Diagnostics SRL v Italy*, 27 September 2011, Application no 43509/08, and on the other hand, EFTA Court, *Posten Norge v ESA* (E-15/10, 2012 EFTA Ct Rep 246, paras 84ff), as well as ECJ, *Chalkor v Commission* (C-386/10 P, ECLI:EU:C:2011:815 paras 63–67), *Otis and Others* (C-199/11, ECLI:EU:C:2012:684 paras 62–63), and *Schindler Holding and Others v Commission* (C-501/11 P, ECLI:EU:C:2013:522 paras 33–38).

[24] See, among many others, ECJ, *Parliament v Council* (C-540/03, ECLI:EU:C:2006:429 para 54), and *Ordre des barreaux francophones et germanophone and Others* (C-305/05, ECLI:EU:C:2007:383 para 31).

[25] See, eg, ECJ, *NS* (C-411/10 and C-493/10, ECLI:EU:C:2011:865 para 88), *Schecke and Eifert* (C-92/09 and C-93/09, ECLI:EU:C:2010:662 para 52 and 59), and *Digital Rights Ireland and Others* (C-293/12 and C-594/12, ECLI:EU:C:2014 paras 35, 47, 54 and 55).

[26] BVerfG, 20 September 2007, 2 BvR 855/06; BVerfG, 8 November 2007, 2 BvR 2334/06 and others; BVerfG, 6 May 2008, 2 BvR 1830/06.

seems to be following the example set by the ECJ[27] in such anti-discrimination cases.[28]

Admittedly, all of the aforementioned types of informal judicial dialogue do not necessarily guarantee that similar legal issues will always be resolved in exactly the same way across Europe. Different approaches may still continue to manifest themselves, in particular where highly ideological questions, choices of society, cultural issues or matters of national identity are concerned.[29] That notwithstanding, the awareness of the problems involved can only be enhanced by the various forms of informal judicial dialogue, just as the chances of homogeneity can only be improved, for the benefit of citizens and businesses all over Europe.

III. FORMALISED TYPES OF JUDICIAL DIALOGUE

Beyond the aforementioned informal types of judicial dialogue, one should not forget the existence of various formalised types of judicial dialogue between European courts and tribunals. Such formal dialogue can be initiated wherever a dedicated procedural framework unites two or more judicial bodies, normally in the form of a preliminary ruling procedure.

There do exist certain examples of such preliminary ruling procedures at the national level in countries such as Germany[30] and Italy,[31] with France[32] having followed more recently. But the most well-known ones are without any doubt the preliminary ruling procedures currently in force at the European level, providing the courts and tribunals of the EU and EEA Member States with privileged access to truly supranational judicial institutions. Indeed, both the ECJ and the EFTA Court are at the centre of their respective preliminary rulings systems, with the ECJ being in charge of the judicial dialogue with the courts and tribunals of the EU Member States,[33] while the EFTA Court can be addressed by those of Norway, Iceland and Liechtenstein.[34]

---

[27] ECJ, *Maruko* (C-267/06, ECLI:EU:C:2008:179), *Römer* (C-147/08, ECLI:EU:C:2011:286), and *Asociaţia Accept* (C-81/12, ECLI:EU:C:2013:275).

[28] BVerfG, 7 July 2009, 1 BvR 1164/07; BVerfG, 19 February 2013, 1 BvL 1/11; BVerfG, 7 May 2013, 2 BvR 909/06 and Others.

[29] See, eg, the diverging approaches of the ECtHR and of the German Constitutional Court as regards religious symbols in classrooms (BVerfG, 16 May 1995, Case 1 BvR 1078/91; ECtHR, *Lautsi and Others v Italy*, Reports of Judgments and Decisions 2011, Application no 30814/06) or the right balance between freedom of the press and protection of privacy in the so-called *Caroline* cases (BVerfG, 15 December 1999, Case 1 BvR 653/96; BVerfG, 8 December 2011, Case 1 BvR 927/08; ECtHR, *von Hannover v Germany*, Reports of Judgments and Decisions 2004-VI, Application no 59320/00).

[30] Art 100 of the German Constitution (*Grundgesetz*).

[31] Arts 134 and 137 of the Italian Constitution, read together with Art 1 of the *Legge Costituzionale* No 1/48.

[32] *Questions prioritaires de constitutionnalité* pursuant to Art 61-1 of the French Constitution.

[33] Arts 19(3)(b) TEU and 267 TFEU.

[34] Art 34 of the Agreement between the EFTA States on the Establishment of a Surveillance Authority and a Court of Justice.

Such preliminary ruling procedures are one of the most striking characteristics of highly developed supranational systems. It therefore comes as no surprise that they exist both in the EU and in the EFTA pillars of the EEA, given that these two international organisations represent the most integrated associations of independent states in Europe, and probably worldwide. As far as the EU is concerned, the preliminary ruling procedure has been a highly efficient tool whenever it comes to guaranteeing uniform interpretation and application of European law in the EU Member States, and it is fair to say that the development of EU law as a whole would have been profoundly different had the ECJ not had the opportunity of handing down large numbers of preliminary rulings in the last six decades. The most distinct features of EU law, such as direct effect,[35] primacy,[36] state responsibility[37] and the protection of fundamental rights,[38] have all been recognised by the ECJ as part of its formal dialogue with national judges, in the framework of the preliminary ruling procedure established by the Treaties of Rome. Admittedly, this appears to be a little bit less the case as far as the EFTA Court is concerned; nevertheless, some important cases dealt with by the EFTA Court were also referred to it by national judges from the EFTA Member States.[39]

While the origins of the success of the preliminary ruling procedure in the EU date a long way back to the early 1960s, one can observe that the dialogue between European and national judges has steadily intensified ever since. On the one hand, in quantitative terms, the sheer number of cases referred to the European level by national judges has constantly increased, with new entries now reaching a level of more than 400 cases per year at the ECJ, thus giving the European judges more and more opportunities to strengthen their dialogue with their national counterparts. On the other hand, that judicial dialogue has also increased in qualitative terms, given that even the highest courts of the big EU Member States—which had long been rather reluctant to refer cases to Luxembourg—have in recent years accepted to do so. In this regard the landmark cases which have quite recently been referred to the ECJ by the constitutional courts of Italy,[40] Spain,[41] France[42] and Germany[43] are particularly noteworthy.

---

[35] ECJ, *van Gend & Loos* (26/62, ECLI:EU:C:1963:1).

[36] ECJ, *Costa v ENEL* (6/64, ECLI:EU:C:1964:66).

[37] ECJ, *Francovich and Others* (C-6/90 and C-9/90, ECLI:EU:C:1991:428), and *Brasserie du Pêcheur and Factortame* (C-46/93 and C-48/93, ECLI:EU:C:1996:79).

[38] ECJ, *Internationale Handelsgesellschaft* (11/70, ECLI:EU:C:1970:114), and *Nold v Commission* (4/73, ECLI:EU:C:1974:51).

[39] The very first judgment handed down by the EFTA Court in *Restamark* (E-1/94, 1994 EFTA Ct Rep 15) was an advisory opinion under the EFTA preliminary ruling procedure. Moreover, some of the basic legal principles relevant to the EFTA pillar of the EEA were also developed under that procedure; see, among others, EFTA Court, *Sveinbjörnsdóttir* (E-7/97, 1998 EFTA Ct Rep 95), *Einarsson* (E-1/01, 2002 EFTA Ct Rep 1), and *Karlsson* (E-4/01, 2002 EFTA Ct Rep 240).

[40] ECJ, *Presidente del Consiglio dei Ministri* (C-169/08, ECLI:EU:C:2009:709).

[41] ECJ, *Melloni* (C-399/11, ECLI:EU:C:2013:107).

[42] ECJ, *F* (C-168/13 PPU, ECLI:EU:C:2013:358).

[43] ECJ, pending case *Gauweiler and Others* (C-62/14).

Quite naturally, the enormous success of preliminary ruling procedures both at the national level and at the EU/EEA level pushed other jurisdictions to follow suit. Most interestingly, the Council of Europe decided to create its own layout for a formalised judicial dialogue between the ECtHR and the highest courts of the contracting parties to the European Convention of Human Rights. Who knows, maybe one day that type of procedure will even set the framework for a formal judicial dialogue between the Strasbourg Court on the one hand and its two Luxembourg-based counterparts on the other. Admittedly, neither the ECJ nor the EFTA Court are qualified to refer cases to the ECtHR as things currently stand. Referrals by the ECJ might, however, become possible should the EU ratify not only the ECHR as such, but also Additional Protocol No 16.[44] As far as the EFTA Court is concerned, it should not be excluded from the outset that this institution may also get authorisation to refer cases to the Strasbourg Court; after all, it is a common judicial body of three contracting parties of the Convention. Why should Norway, Iceland and Liechtenstein not jointly designate the EFTA Court as a jurisdiction within the meaning of Article 10 of Additional Protocol No 16 when ratifying that text?

Independently of Additional Protocol No 16, another type of formalised judicial dialogue is already foreseen between the ECtHR and the ECJ in the framework of the European Union's accession to the European Convention of Human Rights. In fact, the draft accession agreement provides for a designated mechanism of 'prior involvement' of the EU judges where they have not yet assessed the compatibility of EU law with the Convention.[45]

Needless to say, not all of the aforementioned types of formal judicial dialogue are functioning in the same way. The technical details are largely dependent on the degree of integration achieved in each judicial system. There can be a number of fundamental differences: for instance, in certain types of preliminary ruling procedures, references are obligatory,[46] whereas in others, they are a mere faculty;[47] similarly, in some types of procedure, the preliminary ruling may consist of a

---

[44] Council of Europe, Protocol No 16 to the Convention for the Protection of Human Rights and Fundamental Freedoms (CETS No 214), open for signature since 2 October 2013.

[45] Art 3(6) of the Draft revised agreement on the accession of the European Union to the Convention for the Protection of Human Rights and Fundamental Freedoms, accessible on the website of the Council of Europe as Appendix I to the Final report to the CDDH, presented in Strasbourg on 10 June 2013, Doc no 47+1(2013)008 rev2.

[46] This is the case within the European Union whenever domestic courts or tribunals of last resort are confronted with questions of EU law on which the outcome of their respective cases depends; see Art 267(3) TFEU.

[47] This is normally the case within the European Union as far as lower instance national courts or tribunals are concerned; see Art 267(2) TFEU. In the framework of the ECHR, Additional Protocol No 16 provides for voluntary referrals only; see Art 1(1) of that Protocol. Finally, as regards the EFTA pillar of the EEA, the EFTA Court's case law is beginning to slightly tighten the rules as far as courts and tribunals of last resort from Norway, Iceland or Liechtenstein are concerned; see, among others, *Irish Bank* (E-18/11, 2012 EFTA Ct Rep 592 paras 57ff).

purely advisory opinion,[48] whereas it does take the form of a binding judgment in others,[49] thereby establishing some degree of hierarchy between the judge asking the question and the institution answering it.

The practical consequences of such differences must not be underestimated, but they should not be overstated either. For the most striking common feature of all such procedures is that they present a unique opportunity of judicial dialogue between judges from different legal and cultural backgrounds, with a view to finding widely accepted solutions for common legal problems. That does not mean that preliminary reference proceedings can or even should be conceived as a means of achieving full harmonisation of each and every aspect of law across the European continent. Rather, the central judicial instances of each system—be it the ECJ, the EFTA Court or the ECtHR—will always have to strike the right balance between uniformity and diversity. In our view, that can best be achieved by a certain degree of judicial self-restraint on the part of the European judges, who should leave a decent margin of appreciation to their national counterparts, where appropriate,[50] while the national judges will in turn have to make all reasonable efforts to bring their respective domestic laws and jurisprudence in line with the prescriptions of higher-ranking rules that were agreed upon by numerous countries at the European level—be it in the framework of the EU, of EFTA or of the Council of Europe.

IV. FINAL REMARKS

To multi-level legal systems such as Europe's, which are not structured in a purely hierarchical way, an intensified judicial dialogue between domestic and supranational courts and tribunals is of utmost importance. At the end of the day, only such dialogue can ensure that the rule of law is strengthened and that a basic degree of homogeneity and coherence in the case law of judicial bodies across Europe may be achieved and preserved. One can only encourage the judges involved, be it in domestic courts and tribunals or in our supranational European judicial bodies, to be as proactive as possible in this respect. After all, only those who do participate in judicial dialogue will be able to influence things and will

---

[48] This is likely to be the case with advisory opinions under Art 5 of Additional Protocol No 16 to the ECHR. By contrast, it is submitted that advisory opinions of the EFTA Court could hardly be totally ignored by the domestic courts and tribunals of Norway, Iceland and Liechtenstein, given their duty of loyalty pursuant to Art 3 of the EEA Agreement.

[49] Art 91 of the Rules of Procedure of the Court of Justice of the European Union; see also ECJ, *Benedetti* (52/76, ECLI:EU:C:1977:16 para 26), *Wünsche* (69/85, ECLI:EU:C:1986:104 paras 13–15), and *Elchinov* (C-173/09, ECLI:EU:C:2010:581 paras 29, 30).

[50] See, among many others, ECJ, *Omega* (C-36/02, ECLI:EU:C:2004:614 paras 31–40), and *Blanco Pérez and Chao Gómez* (C-570/07 and C-571/07, ECLI:EU:C:2010:300 paras 44, 68 and 106).

set the scene for the debate.[51] All the others are going to get marginalised sooner or later.

In order to further facilitate the different types of judicial dialogue which are currently in practice, one of the main challenges in the years to come will be transparency. It is going to be indispensable to make the case law of the various jurisdictions in Europe more readily accessible and visible to users working in different legal systems and, in particular, in different languages. For instance, there will no doubt be a need for more powerful research facilities and more efficient databases which should, moreover, be interconnected wherever possible.

Last but not least, judicial dialogue should not be confined to the relationship between European courts. In some areas of law, it can be extremely useful to extend judicial dialogue beyond the outer borders of Europe and reach across continents to include other jurisdictions all over the world.[52]

---

[51] A Tizzano, 'Der italienische Verfassungsgerichtshof (Corte costituzionale) und der Gerichtshof der Europäischen Union' (2010) *Europäische Grundrechte-Zeitschrift (EuGRZ)* p 1 (in particular pp 10–12); T von Danwitz, 'Kooperation der Gerichtsbarkeiten in Europa' (2010) *Zeitschrift für Rechtspolitik (ZRP)* pp 143, 145; J Kokott and C Sobotta, 'Das BVerwG und das europäische Umweltrecht' (special edition 2013, Festheft 60 Jahre Bundesverwaltungsgericht), *Neue Zeitschrift für Verwaltungsrecht (NVwZ)* pp 48, 52.

[52] See, eg, Opinion *Association belge des Consommateurs Test-Achats and Others* (C-236/09, ECLI:EU:C:2010:564 para 70), and Opinion *Akzo Nobel Chemicals and Akcros Chemicals v Commission* (C-550/07 P, ECLI:EU:C:2010:229 fn 87).

5

The Advocates General and the EFTA Court

PAOLO MENGOZZI

I. INTRODUCTION

THE NECESSITY TO ensure an homogeneous European Economic Area (EEA) has triggered a regular and often intensive dialogue between the judicial institutions of the two pillars of the EEA Agreement, namely the Court of Justice of the European Union (the EU Court) and the EFTA Court.

As far as the Advocates General of the EU Court are concerned, this dialogue, at least formally speaking, is even younger than the celebrated twentieth anniversary of the EFTA Court. Indeed, the first occurrence of an EFTA Court judgment in an Advocate General's Opinion dates back to 1996,[1] whereas the first time the EFTA Court ever referred to such an Opinion dates from 2002.[2]

This brief contribution on the occasion of the EFTA Court's twentieth anniversary will focus on two aspects in relation to the Advocates General of the EU Court. First, it will discuss the relationship between the advisory opinions the EFTA Court delivers in the exercise of the competence granted by the Agreement between the EFTA States on the Establishment of a Surveillance Authority and a Court of Justice (Surveillance and Court Agreement)[3] and the Opinions of the Advocates General of the EU Court. Second, as this chapter is the fruit of the thoughts of an Advocate General, it will dwell on the existing degree of parallelism between the judgments delivered by the EFTA Court and Advocates General's Opinions, as well as the attention they pay to each other on the basis of recent examples.

---

[1] See the Opinion of Advocate General Lenz delivered on 30 April 1996 in Case C-222/94 *Commission v United Kingdom* [1996] ECR I-4025 with reference to EFTA Court Joined Cases E-8/94 and E-9/94 *Mattel Scandinavia and Lego Norge* [1994–1995] EFTA Ct Rep 113.

[2] EFTA Court, Case E-8/00 *Norwegian Federation of Trade Unions and others v Norwegian Association of Local Regional Authorities and others* [2002] EFTA Ct Rep 114, para 35 with reference to Advocate General Jacobs' Opinion in Case C-67/96 *Albany* [1999] ECR I-5751, para 109 concerning the application of EU competition law rules to collective agreements.

[3] OJEC L 34 of 31 December 1994, pp 1–83.

II. ADVISORY OPINIONS OF THE EFTA COURT AND OPINIONS
OF THE ADVOCATES GENERAL

In a fairly recent article, it has been suggested that both EFTA Court's rulings
and Advocates General's Opinions constitute 'advisory opinions'.[4] This qualification is no doubt evocative of the phase following the delivery of these legal texts
within the two different legal systems which foresee them. In the case of an EU
Advocate General's Opinion, the EU Court is free to follow or to disregard it; as
far as an EFTA Court's advisory opinion is concerned, the Surveillance and Court
Agreement indicates that the EFTA Court's judgment does not bind the referring
court of the EFTA Member State, nor does it bind the national judges of the other
EFTA Member States. However, such a qualification is not suitable to grant EFTA
Court's advisory opinions and Advocates General's Opinions a common nature.
The Advocates General's Opinions are, in fact, part of a single procedure which
leads to a judgment that is the result of a collective reflection of a Chamber's
judges. The fact that Advocates General's Opinions are inserted in this context,
on one hand, excludes that their qualification as 'a sort of parallel ruling'[5] since
they entertain an 'organic and functional link'[6] with the judgments delivered by
the EU Court. In addition, because the EU Court often quotes certain paragraphs
of Opinions in its judgments, these paragraphs, if not entirely reproduced by the
Court, may form an integral part of the reasoning of its judgments.[7] The 'organic
and functional link' between Opinions and the judgments is now expressed in
Article 252 TFEU, according to which 'the Court of Justice shall be *assisted* by …
Advocates General'[8] in the exercise of its function of ensuring, according
to Article 19 TEU, 'that in the interpretation and application of the Treaties the
law is observed'. On the other hand, as it transpires from what the EU Court stated
in the *Emesa Sugar* order,[9] the fact that the Advocate General's Opinion 'opens the

---

[4] E Sharpston and M-J Clifton, 'The Two EEA Courts—Unequal Balance or Fruitful Partnership?'
in EFTA Court (ed), *Judicial Protection in the European Economic Area* (2012) 181.

[5] P Biavati and F Carpi, *Diritto processuale comunitario*, Milano 2006, p 100. For a similar thesis
see Gori, P, 'L'avvocato generale della Corte di giustizia delle Comunità europee' in *Studi in onore di
°Riccardo Monaco*, Milano 1977, reminded by Borraccetti, M, *L'avvocato generale nella giurisdizione
dell'Unione europea*, Napoli 2011. For a qualification of the Advocate General as a 'sort of "amicus
curiae"' see U Villani, *Istituzioni di Diritto dell'Unione europea*, Bari, 2013, p 187.

[6] JA Carillo Salcedo, 'La figùra del abogado general en las comunidades supranacionales europeas:
naturaleza juridica y function' in *Revista española de derecho internacional* 1959, p 119; A Tizzano,
Trattato istitutivo della CEE, a cura di Quadri-Monaco-Trabucchi, Milano 1965.

[7] See, among numerous examples, Case C-299/02 *Commission v The Netherlands* [2004] ECR
I-9761, para 23 in which the Court refers to paras 51 to 59 of the Opinion delivered in that case by
Advocate General Léger, himself referring to the International Tribunal for the Law of the Sea (ITLOS)
judgment of 1 July 1999, '*M/V Saiga*' case No 2, *Saint Vincent and Grenadines v Guinea*, Reports of
Judgments, Opinions and Orders, vol 3, 1999. See, also in respect of the EFTA Court, Court of Justice,
Case C-537/03 *Katja Candolin* [2005] ECR I-5745, para 22 where the Court quoted paragraphs of the
Opinion of Advocate General Gelhoed which made reference to Case E-1/99 *Finanger* [1999] EFTA
Ct Rep 119.

[8] Emphasis added.

[9] Court of Justice, Case C-17/98 *Emesa Sugar*, ECR [2000] I-665.

stage of deliberation by the Court' does not mean that it is 'an opinion addressed to the judges or to the parties which stems from an authority outside the Court ... [r]ather, it constitutes the individual reasoned opinion, expressed in open court, of a Member of the Court of Justice itself'.[10] The Advocate General thus takes part, publicly and individually, in the process by which the Court reaches its judgment, and therefore in carrying out the judicial function entrusted to it.

As to the advisory opinions delivered by the EFTA Court at the request of the national courts of the three EFTA States, one must stress that they are adopted by a Court which has the same characteristics as those of a judicial body. In fact, the EFTA Court a) has a legal origin since it was constituted on the basis of an international agreement among States, b) respects the adversarial principle between the parties in the proceedings, c) applies the rule of law and d) is independent in respect to the parties in the proceedings.

In addition, the EFTA Court must not satisfy the condition of the compulsory nature of its jurisdiction. The Court of Justice, since its judgment in the *Vaassen-Göbbels*[11] case, has considered this condition as relevant for the qualification of a Member State's body as a 'court' for the purposes of Article 267 TFEU. In the framework of EU law, the EU Court has interpreted this condition in the sense that the parties in the main proceedings cannot choose to avoid the jurisdiction of the national court, which is decided by virtue of law. Nevertheless, this does not mean that the national court in question shall be obliged to refer a preliminary ruling to the EU Court on the interpretation of EU law.

Moreover, the fact that, according to the Surveillance and Court Agreement, EFTA Court advisory opinions do not expressly bind the national courts of the EFTA States does not exclude that they are generally followed by the referring courts and by the other EFTA States' courts.

In this regard, it is worth mentioning the *Finanger II* case, in which the Norwegian Supreme Court, despite its refusal since 2002 to refer cases to the EFTA Court, has followed the advisory opinion delivered in *Sveinbjörnsdóttir*[12] at the request of an Icelandic court concerning the responsibility of an EFTA State for violation of EEA law. Against this background, and despite their formal qualification, both the Opinions of Advocates General and advisory opinions of the EFTA Court appear *de facto* more binding than one may at first sight think.

III. THE DIALOGUE BETWEEN THE EFTA COURT AND EU ADVOCATES GENERAL

The attention that the EFTA Court's judgments and Advocates General's Opinions give to each other was clearly illustrated by the President of the EFTA

---

[10] ibid, para 14.
[11] Court of Justice, Case 61/65 *Vaassen-Göbbels* [1966] ECR [1966] 261 (special English edition).
[12] EFTA Court, Case E-9/97 *Sveinbjörnsdóttir* [1998] EFTA Ct Rep 95.

Court, Carl Baudenbacher, in a recent essay.[13] The same attention has of course continued since the publication of that essay. I will therefore confine myself to the most recent examples. Hence, as far as references by Advocates General's Opinions to EFTA Court's judgments are concerned, I would like to draw attention to Advocate General Kokott's Opinion in the *Schenker* case[14] and to my Opinion in the *MasterCard* case.[15] In respect of references by the EFTA Court to the EU Advocates Generals' Opinions, I will take into consideration the Order of the President of the EFTA Court in the *Schenker v EFTA Surveillance Authority* case,[16] as well as the EFTA Court's advisory opinion in *Koch v Swiss Life*.[17]

A. Recent References by Advocates General's Opinions to the EFTA Court's Judgments

As well as cases where they refer to the EFTA Court's judgments when the EEA Agreement is concerned,[18] in general, Advocates General may touch on those judgments when they wish to corroborate their position or when they wish to propose to the EU Court a development of EU law that does not find explicit support in the latter case law. The two recent examples mentioned above will illustrate this tendency.

In the *Schenker* preliminary ruling referred to by the EU Court, one of the issues raised was whether the competition authorities (including national courts) of a Member State were allowed under (EC) Regulation No 1/2003 to find an infringement of EU competition law committed by an undertaking without imposing a fine. In her Opinion in the case, Advocate General Kokott considered that 'it certainly cannot be inferred from the silence in Article 5 of Regulation No 1/2003 that the national authorities would be prohibited from merely finding the existence of an infringement without imposing penalties'.[19] However, one might have wondered whether the principle of effectiveness, that is the effective enforcement of EU antitrust law, would not be jeopardised if no penalties are imposed on the undertakings infringing EU competition law. Advocate General Kokott rejected this by stressing that 'the declaration of the infringement acts as a deterrent to other undertakings and boosts the confidence of all market operators in

---

[13] C Baudenbacher, 'The EFTA Court's relationship with the Advocates General of the European Court of Justice' in *De Rome à Lisbonne: les juridictions de l'Union à la croisée des chemins—Mélanges en l'honneur de Paolo Mengozzi* (Bruxelles, Bruylant, 2013).
[14] Court of Justice, Case C-681/11 *Schenker & Co and others* [2013] nyr (Opinion delivered on 28 February 2013).
[15] Court of Justice, C-382/12 P *MasterCard*, case pending (Opinion delivered on 30 January 2014).
[16] EFTA Court, Case E-14/11 *DB Schenker v EFTA Surveillance Authority* [2012] EFTA Ct Rep 1178.
[17] EFTA Court, Case E-11/12 *Koch and others v Swiss Life*, nyr.
[18] See, eg, this author's Opinion in Court of Justice, C-83/13 *Fonnship*, delivered on 1 April 2014, case pending.
[19] C-681/11 *Schenker & Co and others*, above n 14, Advocate General's Opinion, para 107.

the power of the competition rules in the European internal market'.[20] In addition, she emphasised that such declaration 'also makes it considerably easier for undertakings and consumers which suffer damage as a result of a cartel to make civil claims against the participants in the cartel'.[21] In this context, she referred to the EFTA Court's judgment in the *Schenker v EFTA Surveillance Authority* case where the EFTA Court indicated the importance of private enforcement of competition law and stressed that it is in the public interest. By making that reference she clearly intended to signal to the EU Court that her position was also supported by the other Court sitting in Kirchberg.

References to the EFTA Court's judgments may sometimes be made by Advocates General in order to support their proposals to develop EU law.[22] This is, for example, the case in the Opinion I recently delivered in the *MasterCard* case. This case, which is still pending at the time of writing, concerns an appeal against the General Court's judgment which had confirmed a decision in which the Commission had considered that the MasterCard decisions of setting multilateral fallback interchange fees (MIF) to be paid by the acquiring banks to the issuing banks for any transaction carried out by MasterCard or Maestro branded payment cards are decisions of an association of undertakings within the meaning of Article 81(1) EC in that they amount in fact to setting a minimum price for the merchant service charges (MSC).

Among their different arguments, the appellants claimed the review carried out by the General Court in evaluating the Commission's analysis of the objective necessity of the MIF was insufficient. They deemed that, in considering the entry into force of the EU Charter of Fundamental Rights and the ECHR's case law, such a review should have been absolute. In this way, the issue of the Commission's margin of discretion with regard to economic matters, in particular concerning its decisions to inflict fines on undertakings infringing competition law rules, arose once more.

In my Opinion, I began by stressing that, in the last few years, the attitude of Union judges has progressively changed, in respect of their previous position in

---

[20] ibid, para 114 (Opinion).

[21] ibid.

[22] Of course, this trend is not new and is also endorsed by the EU Courts themselves. As a meaningful example one can mention the Court of First Instance (now General Court) judgment in *Salzgitter v Commission* (Court of First Instance, Case T-308/00 *Salzgitter v Commission* [2004] ECR II-1933) in which this author was reporting judge. In this case the Court of First Instance had to decide whether a tax measure fostering investments in a geographically limited area within a Member State had a selective nature and therefore had to be qualified as state aid. This was not easy, in particular because there was no precedent in the EU Court's case law. In this context, the Court of First Instance solved the problem by stating, with specific reference to the EFTA Court's *Norway v EFTA Surveillance Authority* (Case E-6/98 [1999] EFTA Ct Rep 74) that '[i]t does not matter that the selective nature of the measure flows, for example, from a sectorial criterion or, as in the present case, from a criterion relating to geographic location in a defined part of the territory of a Member State. What matters, however, for a measure to be found to be State aid, is that the recipient undertakings belong to a specific category determined by the application, in law or in fact, of the criterion established by the measure in question' (Case T-308/00 *Salzgitter v Commission* [2004] ECR II-1933, para 38).

which they considered that their review should have been limited to 'verifying whether the rules on procedure and on the statement of reasons have been complied with, whether the facts have been accurately stated and whether there has been any manifest error of appraisal or misuse of powers'.[23] I then recalled that, in *KME and others v Commission*,[24] the EU Court had held that 'whilst, in areas giving rise to complex economic assessments, the Commission has a margin of discretion with regard to economic matters',[25] the Union judges must carry out the review of legality incumbent upon them on the basis of the evidence adduced by the applicant in support of the pleas in law put forward and they cannot, in carrying out that review, use the Commission's margin of discretion 'as a basis for dispensing with the conduct of an in-depth review of the law and of the facts'.[26]

I emphasised that '[t]he precise scope of that dictum, which has in itself the potential to neutralise *de facto* the very principle of the recognition of a margin of economic assessment to the Commission, is not yet clear'.[27] I went on to deem that it is reasonable to deduce, from the absolute character of that *dictum*, the objective pursued by the Court to reduce as much as possible the deference it gives to the Commission's margin of discretion when carrying out its judicial review of decisions imposing fines for infringement of competition law. The EFTA Court's judgment E-15/10, *Posten Norge AS v EFTA Surveillance Authority*[28] of 18 April 2012 corroborated my idea of considering that such a deduction was reasonable. In this judgment, basing itself on *KME and others v Commission*, the EFTA Court pointed out that 'the Court must be able to quash in all respects, on questions of fact and of law, the challenged decision'.[29]

As, at the time of writing, *MasterCard* is still pending, it remains to be seen whether the EU Court will follow my Opinion and will quote *Posten Norge v EFTA Surveillance Authority*.

Just as Advocate General Kokott found confirmation of what she held in her Opinion in the EFTA Court's case law, that same case law, as far as my Opinion is concerned, corroborated the deductions I came to from the most recent EU Court case law. This may be seen as a cross-fertilisation of the judicial dialogue between the two judicial institutions of the EEA Agreement.

B. Recent References by the EFTA Court to Advocates General's Opinions

In one of his articles concerning the dialogue between the EFTA Court and Advocates General, President Baudenbacher pointed out that the most interesting

---

[23] C-382/12 P *MasterCard*, above n 15, para 118 of author's Opinion.
[24] Court of Justice, C-389/10 P *KME Germany v Commission* [2011] ECR I-13125.
[25] C-382/12 P *MasterCard*, above n 15, para 119 of author's Opinion.
[26] ibid.
[27] ibid, para 119 and fn 101.
[28] EFTA Court, Case E-15/10 *Posten Norge v EFTA Surveillance Authority* [2012] EFTA Ct Rep 246.
[29] ibid, para 100.

occasions when the EFTA Court makes references to the Opinions of Advocates General are cases where there is no case law of the EU Court or where the EFTA Court wishes to pursue another line of argument than that of the EU Court's judgments.[30] The references to Advocates General's Opinions should also be understood in the light of the fact that the EFTA Court has still no such figure.[31]

In the wake of President Baudenbacher's most recent essay, cited above, it is quite interesting to perceive the homogeneity of attitude between the EFTA Court and the EU Advocates General, including, as we will see, cross-references. In fact, such a situation occurred in the EFTA Court's President's Order of 30 April 2013 in *Schenker and others v EFTA Surveillance Authority*[32] (E-4/13). In this case, the EFTA Court was requested to annul an ESA decision denying, for a second time, access to inspection documents ESA seized at Norway Post's premises in order to provide evidence for Schenker's follow-on damages claim against Norway Post in Norwegian courts for alleged abuse of dominant position according to Article 54 EEA. The applicants asked the EFTA Court to grant an expedited procedure since the Norwegian courts had suspended the national proceedings opened by the claim whilst waiting for the evidence which would have been supplied once the access to the documents requested to ESA had been given. To support the request for an expedited procedure, the applicants invoked a 'fundamental right to an effective remedy ... within a reasonable time'.[33] The President of the EFTA Court rejected this request. Nevertheless, in his reasoning he took the opportunity to affirm, in principle, the possibility to use the expedited procedure in cases concerning private enforcement of competition law.

He recalled that the EFTA Court in *Schenker* (E-14/11)[34] 'has recognised the importance of private enforcement of competition law as having the ability to make a significant contribution to the maintenance of effective competition in the EEA'.[35]

In this regard, he also pointed out that, in the same case, the EFTA Court admitted that, while pursuing his private interest, a plaintiff in proceedings for private enforcement of competition law contributes at the same time to the protection of public interest and thereby also benefits consumers. He reinforced this statement by reference to footnote 78 in the Opinion of Advocate General Kokott in the

---

[30] See C Baudenbacher, *The EFTA Court, the ECJ and the Latter's Advocates General—A Tale of Judicial Dialogue* in Arnull, Eeckhout and Tridimas (eds), *Continuity and Change in the EU Law, Essays in Honour of Sir Francis Jacobs* (Oxford, Oxford University Press, 2008) 115–116.

[31] In this respect, it is worth noting that in December 2011 the EFTA Court proposed amendments to the SCA, among which was the creation of the position of an Advocate General to assist it either permanently or in exceptionally important cases. However, this proposal has not been accepted by the EFTA States.

[32] EFTA Court, Case E-4/13 *Schenker and others v EFTA Surveillance Authority* (Order of the President).

[33] ibid, para 8.

[34] EFTA Court, Case E-14/11 *DB Schenker v EFTA Surveillance Authority* [2012] EFTA Ct Rep 1178.

[35] Case E-4/13 *Schenker and others v EFTA Surveillance Authority*, above n 32, para 26.

Schenker case[36] discussed above. Curiously enough, that footnote quotes the EFTA Court's judgment in *DB Schenker*. Such cross-references, albeit unusual, illustrate to what extent the dialogue between the EFTA Court and the Court of Justice's Advocates General can go.

In its advisory opinion in case E-11/12, *Koch and Swiss Life*[37] the EFTA Court also drew interesting procedural consequences, in particular, from the statements made by Advocate General Kokott in her Opinion in the *United Kingdom v Council*[38] case.

In *Koch and Swiss Life*, the EFTA Court was requested by the Liechtenstein Princely Court to interpret, among others, Directives 92/96/EEC and 2002/83/EC, which were incorporated into the EEA Agreement by an EEA Joint Committee decision. Those Directives oblige assurance undertakings to provide policy holders, before the contract is concluded, with clear and accurate information as listed in the Annexes of those Directives.

In a situation where an assurance undertaking allegedly failed to satisfy its obligation to inform the policy holder, the referring court asked 'whether a national rule which provides for an administrative complaint procedure, which is only subject to a regulatory sanction such as the imposition of a fine [or] withdrawal of license … may constitute a sufficient remedy for the purposes'[39] of those Directives (and not whether such national rule could, more generally, be consistent with EU/EEA law).

First, the EFTA Court noted that neither Directive requires the EEA States to introduce sanctions for the situation where, in its relations with a consumer, an assurance undertaking infringes a rule of national contract law.[40] Therefore, the EFTA Court rightly deduced that compensation for pecuniary loss is governed by national law.

As ESA observed during the proceedings before the EFTA Court, the question referred had consequently to be answered in light of the principles of equivalence and effectiveness as established by the Court of Justice under EU law.[41]

The EFTA Court agreed to answer the question taking into account these two principles and going beyond its wording.

It started by referring to the right to equal treatment enjoyed by nationals under both EU and EFTA pillars of the EEA. In particular, it cited the Opinion of Advocate General Kokott in the *United Kingdom v Council* case, which concerned

---

[36] Court of Justice, Case C-681/11 *Schenker and others*, nyr (Opinion delivered on 28 February 2013).
[37] EFTA Court, Case E-11/12 *Koch and others v Swiss Life*, nyr.
[38] Court of Justice, Case C-431/11 *United Kingdom v Council*, nyr (Opinion delivered on 21 March 2013).
[39] Case E-11/12, *Koch and others v Swiss Life*, above n 37, para 111.
[40] ibid, para 113.
[41] According to the Court of Justice's case law the principle of equivalence means that national procedural rules governing actions for safeguarding rights under EU law are no less favourable than those governing similar domestic actions. As far as the principle of effectiveness is concerned such national procedural rules must not render practically impossible or excessively difficult the exercise of rights conferred by EU law (see, in particular, Court of Justice, C-432/05 *Unibet* [2007] ECR I-2271, para 43).

the extension of substantial social rights conferred on EU citizens under Regulation (EC) 883/2004[42] to nationals of the three EFTA States. In her Opinion, she had stressed that, in order to achieve the aims of the EEA Agreement, which is to create equal conditions of competition with the same rules in a homogeneous economic area, the principle of equality must be applied. This reference to the principle of equality was made as far as substantial—but not procedural—rights are concerned.

Nevertheless, in *Koch v Swiss Life*, the EFTA Court drew, in particular from Advocate General Kokott's Opinion, the conclusion that the procedural 'principle of equivalence extends the general principle of equality to the law of remedies',[43] because that principle requires national rules 'to be applied without distinction, whether the infringement alleged is of EEA law or national law'.[44] Therefore, 'national procedural law must remain neutral in relation to the origin of the rights invoked'.[45]

One may note that the EFTA Court succeeded in deducing from a substantial right to equal treatment within the EEA, as emphasised by Advocate General Kokott in her Opinion, the procedural principle of equivalence, which also enabled the EFTA Court to escape the bottleneck where it would have been confined if it had simply answered the question as referred by the national court. In so doing it seized the opportunity to reinforce the protection of consumers in Liechtenstein as well as in the EEA.

IV. CONCLUSION

As illustrated in this brief chapter, the dialogue between the EU Advocates General and the EFTA Court takes different forms. It enables the Advocates General to reinforce their proposals to the EU Court whenever necessary, including outside the strict application of the EEA Agreement. In my experience, the EFTA Court's rulings, including its advisory opinions, often serve as valid precedents for the judgments delivered by the EU Court.

---

[42] Regulation (EC) No 883/2004 of the European Parliament and of the Council of 29 April 2004 on the coordination of social security systems (Text with relevance for the EEA and for Switzerland), OJ L 166, 30.4.2004, p 1.

[43] Case E-11/12 *Koch and others v Swiss Life*, above n 37, para 123.

[44] ibid, para 122.

[45] ibid, para 123.

6

The Immoral Choice—How Judges Participate in the Transformation of Rule of Law to Legal Evil

HANS PETTER GRAVER

I. INTRODUCTION

T HE EFTA COURT is part of an international legal structure that was established after the experiences of authoritarianism and war in Europe in the twentieth century. The day-to-day workings of the Court may perhaps not reflect this. But it is a lesson from a not-too-distant past that judges, even in our western legal culture, may contribute to and participate in atrocities and oppressive measures. When Chief Superintendent of the Police in occupied Oslo in August 1943, Gunnar Eilifsen refused to carry out orders to arrest three women for refusing to assemble for work duty under the Nazi authorities. Reichskommissar Terboven decided that it was necessary to set an example, and demanded of the collaborationist Norwegian authorities that Eilifsen be sentenced to death. To accommodate this, Minister-President Quisling signed a law that retroactively made it possible to punish Eilifsen's offence by death, and established a special court to try Eilifsen. The Court returned with a 2–1 vote for the death penalty. Eilifsen was not pardoned, and the execution took place later on the same night. One of the judges was subsequently liquidated by the Norwegian resistance in a raid in 1944. After the war, a second was sentenced to prison for having served on the collaborationist Supreme Court. He had voted against sentencing Eilifsen to death. The third judge was convicted of manslaughter for his participation in the sentencing of Eilifsen.

We expect judges to be the protectors of individual rights and the rule of law. Our western legal tradition has common roots and a history where law at different points in time has been invoked to protect the dissident and the heretic against the prevailing political and moral forces of society.[1] The ideology of law as something

---

[1] See HJ Berman, *Law and Revolution: The Formation of the Western Legal Tradition* (Cambridge, Mass, Harvard University Press, 1983) 43.

autonomous dedicated to protecting more general values such as justice, equality and the rule of law binds judges together across time and space. In cases where the executive and legislative powers of a state attack these basic values of our society, we want the courts to exercise their powers of review to uphold these rights.

We like to think of judges as taking heroic stances against authoritarian rulers, like the case in present-day Hungary where the constitutional court has been providing checks and balances between the different state organs. In fact, under many conditions judges, together with other members of the legal profession, mobilise in protection of basic legal freedoms. The exceptions to this are in situations of widespread public fears about internal disorder or threats to domestic security, when an otherwise liberal legal complex tends to support oppression by the executive.[2] In many recent examples of authoritarian rule in countries within our western legal tradition, the courts have failed to offer such protection. This was the case, for instance, in Chile, which was a military usurpation of judicial power with the complicity of the legal establishment.[3] The South African judges brought up in the liberal tradition of English common law did not stop apartheid and the repression that the regime employed to safeguard its existence. On the contrary, the South African Truth and Reconciliation Commission concluded that 'part of the reason for the longevity of apartheid was the superficial adherence to "rule by law" by the National Party, whose leaders craved the aura of legitimacy that "the law" bestowed on their harsh injustice'.[4] This legitimacy was willingly offered by the courts. The judges of Nazi Germany were deeply involved both in the transformation of Germany into a totalitarian state based on a racial ideology and in the oppression of Jews and any opposition to the regime. In the words of US prosecutor Telford Taylor in his opening statement of the trial against the leaders of the Nazi legal system, the defendants:

> [L]eaders of the German judicial system, consciously and deliberately suppressed the law, engaged in an unholy masquerade of brutish tyranny disguised as justice, and converted the German judicial system to an engine of despotism, conquest, pillage, and slaughter.[5]

These are but examples of a pattern. Judges in other Latin American states such as Argentina and Brazil supported dictatorship and judges in the occupied nations of Western Europe during the Second World War helped to uphold and enforce measures in the interests of the German occupying authorities. Even after the war, judges in the liberated countries departed from basic principles such as the

---

[2] See Terence C Halliday, Karpik, Lucien and Feeley, Malcolm M, 'The Legal Complex in Struggles for Political Liberalism' in Halliday, Terence, C, Karpik, Lucien and Feeley, Malcolm M, *Fighting for Political Freedom Comparative Studies of the Legal Complex and Political Liberalism*, (Oxford and Portland, Oregon, Hart Publishing,g 2007), pp 32–33.

[3] AW Pereira, *Political (In)justice, Authoritarianism and the Rule of Law in Brazil, Chile and Argentina* (Pittsburgh, University of Pittsburgh Press, 2005), Kindle edition, location 2293.

[4] Report vol 4 from the South African Truth and Reconciliation Commission, 1998, p 101.

[5] *Trials of War Criminals before the Nuremberg Military Tribunals, vol III, the Justice Case*, Washington 1951, p 31.

non-retroactivity of criminal legislation and the requirement of individual guilt in order to punish collaborators.

Politics, social forces and class interests go a long way to explaining judicial behaviour and support for ruling elites. But politics and psychology are interwoven, according to Jonathan Glover in his moral history of the twentieth century.[6] This is because both authoritarian rulers, schemes and institutions set up to avoid authoritarianism need the support of the officials and of the public for their policies and measures to take effect. The climate of public opinion can make a difference as to whether a disaster is unfolded or avoided.

Judges across many different settings have something in common when the state attacks basic values of the western legal tradition and calls upon the judges to join this attack against the tradition. There are some common dilemmas facing a judge in the situation where positive law contradicts standards of justice, equality and the rule of law. The answers to these dilemmas will vary with place and time, but the types of reason the judge must consider to take a sound and defensible course of action are the same in all situations.

Disregarding the question of whether the immoral law is 'law' or not and the question of the duty to follow the law, the judge is also a human being, an individual and a member of society. As such, he has moral responsibilities. In oppressive situations, he is faced with the question, as Hannah Arendt puts it, of asking himself to what extent he is able to live with himself after having committed certain deeds.[7] Many seek to hide behind the law and to regard themselves in the mirror as an upholder of law and justice and live well with this, even if upholding law and justice means participating in the oppression of other human beings. In fact, many judges believe that by applying the law they are defending the rule of law, even under the most oppressive circumstances. In his great apology of the German judges under the Nazi period, Hubert Schorn writes about 'those judges who performed their work by following their conscience and who saw upholding the law in a courageous and upraised way as their highest duty'.[8] There is no reason to doubt that this expresses the self-understanding of many judges in authoritarian settings. Nevertheless, the consequences of their performance may be horrendous and far removed from any reasonable understanding of the rule of law.

Why do judges so easily give up on the rule of law? Should an honest judge resign or should he stay in office? Are there ways to make the judge better equipped to defend the rule of law? These are the questions addressed in this chapter.

---

[6] Jonathan Glover, *Humanity a Moral History of the 20th Century*, 2nd edn (New Haven, Yale University Press, 2012) p 401.

[7] H Arendt, *Responsibility and Judgment* (New York, Schocken Books, 2003) 44.

[8] Hubert Schorn, *Der Richter im Dritten Reich Geschichte und Dokumente*, (Frankfurt am Main, Vittorio Klostermann, 1959) 4.

II. OBEDIENCE TO AUTHORITY

Obedience to the law is a central value to most judges. A common reason given by judges for their cooperation is the authority of the law and the duty of judges to uphold it. Law is compelling as far as it is positively given, and it is not the role of the judge to substitute their personal views for that of the legislator.

The judge in any legal order is expected to apply the law, not to create or modify it. Despite theoretical differences at the conceptual and philosophical level between positivists, realists and adherents of natural law, there is no legal theory that rejects the authority of the legislator as such. No legal order proclaims that natural law or personal preferences of the judge are the sole or even the primary basis for judicial decision making. Natural lawyers do not deny the authority of positive law but discuss its limits; realists do not refute the existence of legislation as a motivating factor for the judge, but discuss its effectiveness.

Certainly judges as part of their role expectation are disposed to observe legislation and adhere to the authority of the legislator. The authority of the legislator is to lawyers mostly an effect of formal requirements—those who legally hold the position of legislator have the authority to legislate. We see from experience that the judiciary seldom questions the authority of the legislator once formal requirements are met. Judges seem indisposed to enter into substantive issues regarding the legitimacy of the legislator, questions like whether the elections were fair, whether the electorate is representative of the people or whether there really are grounds for enacting emergency powers. This even holds in many cases when the illegitimacy of the legislator is obvious. In his study of all post-colonial common law cases dealing with the aftermath of coups d'état up to 1994, Tayyab Mahmud concludes that 'most courts have opted for the worst choice, namely, validation and legitimation of extra-constitutional usurpation'.[9]

Obedience to authority is often confused with legal positivism. Historical experiences show that these are two different things. Obedience to the Führer and not adherence to positive law was the prevailing legal ideology during Nazi Germany.

Illustrating the point of obedience to authority and the position as a judge is the case of Lothar Kreyssig.[10] Kreyssig was appointed as a judge in 1928 and was regarded by his superiors as a very competent and able jurist and judge. After the Nazi takeover, he repeatedly came into the sights of the Nazis due to his refusal to partake in political formalities. He left the room during the uncovering of a portrait of Adolf Hitler, he 'only moved his lips slightly' during a triple 'Heil' and he omitted attending political training sessions. Above all, being active in the

---

[9] T Mahmud, 'Jurisprudence of Successful Treason: Coup d'Etat and Common Law' (1994) 27 *Cornell International Law Journal* 49–140, at 138–139.

[10] For his career as a judge based on his file in the Nazi Ministry of Justice, see L Gruchmann, 'Ein unbequemer Amtsrichter im Dritten Reich aus den Personalakten des Dr Lothar Kreyssig' in Hans-Joachim Döring (Hrsg), *Lothar Kreyssig Aufsätze, Autobiographie und Dokumente* (Leipzig, Evangelische Verlagsanstalt, 2011).

evangelical church he sided with the church in its conflict with the Nazi regime. Several complaints to the Ministry of Justice to have him removed as a judge were not supported. The ministry did not find sufficient grounds to remove a competent judge, and did not want to escalate the conflict with the church by removing one of its prominent supporters. After having bought a farm, Kreyssig applied for, and was granted, transfer to an unimportant county court in a rural area in Brandenburg. From there, he continued being reported to the ministry for political activities—distributing political leaflets in support of the church.

The issue that has made him known, and which eventually led to his being pensioned off, was his activities in relation to the euthanasia programme against the mentally ill. As a judge, he was the custodian of several people who due to mental illness could not take care of their own affairs. He discovered that persons under his custody were transferred to an institution where they were killed. On this basis, he wrote a letter protesting to the president of the regional court. He was asked to recall this 'improper' document, but refused. The letter was then reported by the president to the Ministry of Justice.

To the ministry, Kreyssig wrote that he did not protest solely on religious grounds but also because of the consequences that the euthanasia programme would have for the concept of justice of the German people.

'In the name of the terrible slogan "law is what serves the people", not yet contradicted by any of the guardians of justice in Germany, whole sections of society have been excluded from the law like for instance in the concentration camps and now also in our institutions for health and care,' Kreyssig wrote. He admitted that the judicial role as custodian did not give him a legal right to intervene. But he saw it as his judicial duty to engage himself on the side of law and justice and to ask for a resolution from the Ministry of Justice.

After several meetings with Roland Freisler in the ministry, where no legal grounds for the killings could be demonstrated, the ministry itself being kept in the dark, Kreyssig issued orders to several institutions forbidding them to end the lives of persons under the custody of the Regional Court of Brandenburg. Again he was called to the ministry, this time to meet with the minister in person. He was given the option to recall his orders. But even after having been shown a photocopy of the secret order by the Führer, Kreyssig was unconvinced that the euthanasia programme was legal. The minister then made clear to him that it was impossible for him to continue as a judge if he could not accept the will of the Führer as the ultimate source of law. A few days later, Kreyssig wrote to the ministry stating that he could not for his conscience withdraw his order, and he asked to be relieved of his duties as a judge.

The story of Kreyssig shows how obedience is demanded not as a duty to obey the law, but a duty to obey authority, disregarding its legal status and accordance with the law. Legal positivism was not the dominating theory or method in Germany before the Nazi rule, and certainly not during it.

Stanley Milgram distinguished between 'binding factors' and 'adjustments in the subject's thinking' in explaining the subject obedience in his study of authority.[11] The binding factors lock the subject into the situation and include politeness, a desire to honour the initial promise to contribute to the experiment and the awkwardness of withdrawal. Adjustments in thinking help the subject maintain his relationship with the experimenter, while at the same time reducing the strain brought about by the experimental conflict.

The binding factors operating on the judge are obvious. On the one hand, we have the commitments stemming from the judicial role and the perceived legal and professional duty to uphold the law. As long as he stays on the bench, the judge perceives this duty. The awkwardness of withdrawal from a collective or a group is thoroughly examined in other studies that show that people go to extremes in order not to break out into nonconformity. Group pressure operates through a basic identification among the members of the group and a strong urge not to separate oneself.[12]

Adjustments in a judge's thinking are evident in the emphasis on the binding effect of the law and stating that the law leaves no choice to the judge. Also, the strong drive to separate the legal from morality and human consequences of the application of the law can help the judge to overcome the cognitive conflict that exists between his application of oppressive law and his rule of law ideals.

The American legal scholar Robert M Cover studied anti-slavery and the judicial process in the United States in the nineteenth century.[13] He found that liberal judges committed to anti-slavery upheld legislation designed to protect the rights of the slaveholders. He launched the idea that the psychological theory of cognitive dissonance could offer an explanation for this judicial behaviour. Anti-slavery judges faced with legal rules compelling them to find in favour of slavery must have experienced strong conflicts between their ethical beliefs in the evil of slavery and their loyalty to the law and their judicial role. Cover points out that a judge caught in this way between law and morality has the option to apply the law against his morality, to disregard the law and follow his morality, to resign or to state that the law is not what he honestly believes it to be.[14] None of these options is psychologically attractive, and most people will seek to find some compromise. Cover's dissonance hypothesis predicts in this situation that the judges who were the most troubled by results that favoured slavery would be most likely to exhibit some behaviour that reduced this dissonance. This dissonance could be reduced by elevating the formal status of the law, by a retreat to a mechanical formalism in the application of the law and by ascribing responsibility for the result elsewhere than to the personal choice of the judge.[15]

---

[11]   Stanley Milgram, *Obedience to Authority* (New York, Perennial Classics, 1974) with a foreword by Jerome S Bruner (New York, 2004) 17.

[12]   Christopher R Browning, *Ordinary Men Reserve Police Battalion 101 and the Final Solution in Poland*, (New York, Harper Perennial, 1998) 71.

[13]   RM Cover, *Justice Accused: Antislavery and the Judicial Process* (New Haven, Yale University Press, 1975).

[14]   ibid, p 6.

[15]   ibid, p 229.

III. MORAL BLINDNESS

Adherence to authority may be part of an explanation, but it can only be part. After all, not all judges participate in the oppression of authoritarian regimes. Judges have both independence and a choice in determining the law and applying it. Why do they not do more to avoid obvious departures from the rule of law? One explanation could be that they develop a 'moral blindness' which prevents them from relating to the consequences of oppressive measures.

Moral blindness is cultivated by distance. The distance may be psychological, institutional or physical. Psychological distance is created by tribal thinking and by dehumanisation of the victims of our actions. These are well-known factors in explaining how people can commit evil deeds on others. We see them in action in the racial jurisprudence of Nazi Germany and of apartheid. We also see them when people brought to trial are defined as anti-social enemies in a 'war' to defend national security. Institutional distance is created by thinking about people in abstract categories, as holders of rights or duties, as offenders and defendants, instead of as whole persons. This distance is inherent and necessary to legal thinking. It is worth thinking about the dangers it entails in fostering moral blindness in situations where the law turns oppressive. Physical distance weakens sympathy. A special form of physical distance is the one where atrocities take place in unreal and distant settings. As Glover points out, sympathy can be weakened by a sense of unreality.[16] Auschwitz was, as he points out, 'another planet', which made it possible to think 'this is not really happening'. This effect could contribute to the moral blindness of the SS Judge Konrad Morgen, who went to the eastern front and the extermination camps and witnessed the extermination of Jews, and at the same time took up prosecution of persons involved in the killings for corruption and transgression of orders.

In their study of this judge, Pauer Studer and Velleman cite his self-understanding as a 'fanatic for justice', and ask in what sense Konrad Morgen could be characterised as a fanatic for justice:

> Though not fanatical about the Party or the SS, Morgen belonged to both and was at home in their culture, with all its appalling features. As German forces were ghettoizing, deporting, and shooting Jews in Cracow, he was busy prosecuting embezzlers. He enjoyed a daily steam bath and massage in Buchenwald, while underfed prisoners were sleeping on wooden shelves four-high. After viewing the gas chambers of Auschwitz, he could still be shocked by SS-men fraternizing with Jewish girls. He condoned hard treatment of subject peoples in the East. He referred to mass execution by shooting as "the old, tried method"—whatever that may have meant. When he returned to Cracow at the end of 1944, he was gratified to hear that his reputation as a hanging judge (Blutrichter) had preceded him, striking fear into the hearts of prisoners.[17]

---

[16] Glover, pp 407–408.
[17] Herlinde Pauer-Studer and J David Velleman 'A Fanatic for Justice: The Case of SS-Judge Konrad Morgen' (forthcoming) 157.

Morgen was appalled by the killings and bent on doing something about them, but his ground for concern was a worry that participation in the gassings would make SS members unfit for service as citizens and soldiers.

> He deplored the concentration-camp system not in principle but for its corrupting effects on individuals who went on to commit individual crimes. Even in the case of crime, he was more sensitive to the viciousness of criminals than to the suffering of their victims. His moral sentiments were strong, but their range was narrow. Perhaps he would have been equal to the moral challenges of other times, but for his own times, his moral range was certainly inadequate.[18]

How can we explain such a warped sense of morality and justice? Harald Welzer speaks of the three circles of the process that drives people to abandon their moral ideals and inhibitions against committing atrocities.[19] The first is a societal process where the lines of conflict and division between 'friend' and 'enemy' are established. The employment of lethal means against the enemy in the persecution of Jews and communists during the eastern campaign of the German army in 1941 changed the prohibition against murder to an obligation to kill. The second circle consists of the social situation of the actor and his interpretation of this situation. The third, the innermost circle, is the actor's own perception of the options that are open to him. These are largely influenced by psychological binding factors and factors adjusting the actor's thinking. By this, we see that the participation of judges in oppression is the result of the interplay between changes in the political and social situation of the society, the professional and personal interests of the judge relating to this situation and psychological factors operating on the individual judge.

Such binding factors may influence a judge's thinking to such an extent that he does not see the unreasonableness or injustice in oppressive measures. The South African judges extended the apartheid laws of racist South Africa in much the same way as the Nazi judges extended the discrimination of the Jews. In a case from 1934, the court had to decide whether an instruction by the Postmaster General to divide the post office in Transvaal into one section for Europeans only and one for non-Europeans was legal.[20] The relevant legislation did not authorise such discrimination, so it was not an issue of giving effect to an Act by the legislator. The crucial issue of the case was whether the fundamental principle of equality before the law required that racial discrimination could only be implemented by express provision of Parliament, or whether discrimination between races was a sensible and rational measure that in itself could not be seen as unreasonable.

The Postmaster General was empowered to establish, maintain and abolish post offices, and to supervise and control their services; also to 'issue such instructions

---

[18] ibid, p 158.
[19] Harald Welzer Täter, *Wie aus ganz normalen Menschen Massenmörder werden* (Frankfurt am Main, Fischer Taschenbuch Verlag, 2007), Kindle edition, location 160.
[20] *Minister of Post and Telegraphs v Rasool*, 1934 AD 167.

as he may deem necessary for the conduct and guidance of officers in carrying out the provisions of the Act'. Prior to this order, there was a separate room for natives. The order resulted in people of Indian origin being barred from the European counter and obliged to go to the non-European room. The lower courts found the instructions to be invalid as effecting discrimination based on race or colour.

Justice Stratford of the Appellate Division took as a legal starting-point that 'an enabling Act must not be construed to confer the power to do unreasonable things unless such latter power is specifically given'. When it came to dividing the community into white and coloured, he could not see that in itself as unreasonable, 'for such conclusion runs counter to accepted principle and good sense'. Justice De Villiers distinguished between discrimination on gratuitous grounds and discrimination for which 'reasons may be conceived upon which such discriminations might justify and reasonably be made', and placed discrimination based upon race and colour in the latter category. In his opinion, discrimination between Europeans and non-Europeans was not per se unreasonable as long as it did not entail differences in rights, duties, privileges or treatment.

Acceptance of authoritarian measures is not limited to situations with tyrannical regimes. The courts of liberal democracies also have a record of such acceptance. Many liberal states from the 1920s onwards, and up to as late as the 1970s, went quite a long way based on perceptions of eugenics in repressive means against people who were perceived as mentally degenerate. For instance, in Sweden it is estimated that as many as 21,000 people were forcibly sterilised, most of them between 1935 and 1955.[21] Not all those who supported measures such as enforced sterilisation were motivated by a desire to protect the race from inferior genetic material; many of the supporters were motivated by social policy reasons, to protect against crime and anti-social behaviour, and even to prevent new individuals being born into social misery and poverty. The oppressive measures were generally accepted and enforced by the judiciary.

In 1927, the United States Supreme Court decided the first case on enforced sterilisation. Carrie Buck was a 'feeble-minded' institutionalised daughter of a 'feeble-minded' mother in the same institution who had given birth to an 'illegitimate feeble-minded child'. The authorities held that Carrie Buck was 'the probable potential parent of a socially inadequate offspring, likewise afflicted', and 'that she may be sexually sterilised without detriment to her general health and that her welfare and that of society will be promoted by her sterilization'. In his Opinion for the Court, the famous justice Oliver Wendell Holmes wrote:

> We have seen more than once that the public welfare may call upon the best citizens for their lives. It would be strange if it could not call upon those who already sap the strength of the State for these lesser sacrifices, often not felt to be such by those concerned, in order to prevent our being swamped with incompetence. It is better for the entire world, if instead of waiting to execute degenerate offspring for crime, or to let

---

[21] SOU 2000:20 Steriliseringsfrågan, Stockholm, 2000, p 33.

them starve for their imbecility, society can prevent those who are manifestly unfit from continuing their kind … Three generations of imbeciles are enough.[22]

IV. THE LESSER EVIL

Judges may moderate the excesses of a regime and do justice in individual cases. They may even stem oppressive trends in the beginning and prevent society from developing into a society of oppression. Such contributions will often entail compromises. A judge is, after all, an administrator and executor of the legal policy of the regime he serves. Should contributing to a lesser harm to avoid the greater harm be a recommended way of thinking when a lawyer is asked to contribute to harm and unjustness?

After the Second World War, when the extent of the involvement of the courts in the Nazi oppression was revealed, many German judges sought the lesser evil argument as a defence. Judges in Germany were aware of the 'dual state' and that the Gestapo in many cases were ready to intervene against any person, without any legal guarantees, for political ends, and place a person who had been acquitted in a concentration camp. Hubert Schorn writes that judges in some cases chose to imprison a person even if they believed that the legal grounds were insufficient, in order to prevent the defendant from being apprehended by the Gestapo and sent to a camp.[23] The judges of South Africa during apartheid defended themselves along the same lines.[24]

The 'lesser evil' is obviously a valid argument under ordinary circumstances. We have the accepted reservations to individual rights that are recognised even within modern human rights instruments as 'necessary in a democratic society'. As Chief Justice Rehnquist says, citing Judge Learned Hand: 'A society in which men recognise no check upon their freedom soon becomes a society where freedom is the possession of a savage few.'[25] And many a judge who finds himself in a situation where he must inflict pain by his judgment will comfort himself that the result is to the greater good. When is reference to proportionality and the greater good disallowed? This is the critical question that the 'good' judge must ask himself.

Hannah Arendt is clear on her warning against the lesser evil thinking:

Politically, the weakness of the argument has always been that those who choose the lesser evil forget very quickly that they chose evil … If we look at the techniques of totalitarian government, it is obvious that the argument of 'lesser evil'—far from being

---

[22] *Buck v Bell, Superintendent of State Colony for Epileptics and Feeble Minded*, 271 US 200 1927.

[23] Schorn, pp 32–33.

[24] See the submission to the South African Truth and Reconciliation Commission by the following members of the Supreme Court of Appeal: Mr Justice JW Smalberger, Mr Justice CT Howie, Mr Justice RM Marais, and Mr Justice DG Scott (1998) 115 *S African Law Journal* 44.

[25] Rehnquist, William H, *All Laws but One Civil Liberties in Wartime*, (New York, Vintage books, 1998) Kindle edition, location 3620.

raised only from the outside by those who do not belong to the ruling elite—is one of the mechanisms built into the machinery of terror and criminality. Acceptance of lesser evils is consciously used in conditioning the government officials as well as the population at large to the acceptance of evil as such.[26]

In the case against Wilhelm Stuckart, State Secretary and responsible for the preparation of the anti-Jewish legislation at the Ministry of the Interior, the Military Tribunal in the Ministries Case stated: 'In justice to the defendant it should be said that we are convinced that for a long time he courageously fought the measures against the Mischlings and attempted to intervene in favour of mixed marriages.'[27] Nevertheless, the Tribunal found him guilty with the following words:

> [T]he skill, learning, and legal knowledge of Stuckart was placed at the disposal of those who originated the plan of extermination. The fact that his conscience may have been troubled and the fact that he saw not only the wrong but the folly of the proposals with respect to Mischlings, cannot excuse or condone what he did.[28]

When situations are as extreme as in Nazi Germany, 'the lesser evil' seems an obviously invalid excuse for collaboration in the evil policies of oppression. However, refusal to play the tune of the regime, even when it is oppressive, does not always lead to the best results. History shows that critical judges may push the regime to cover its oppression under extra-legal schemes, and employ police, military and death squads far outside of public view and the jurisdiction of the courts. Under the military dictatorship in Brazil, the Brazilian Supreme Court refused to implement the most repressive measures of the regime and invalidated them on natural law grounds. As a result, the regime circumvented the law with extra-legal terror, in addition to establishing special military courts to deal with political opponents. According to observers, the military courts with their positivist and cooperative attitude to the laws of the regime saved more lives than the Supreme Court did with its resistance.[29] Should the results decide?

The German jurists failed to stem the Holocaust and terror—although some Jews were saved as a result of being processed by the legal system. The law also contributed to saving Jews because of their being married to German spouses and holding persons with mixed ancestry outside the extermination programme. The South African judges did not stop apartheid and the repression of the regime to safeguard its existence. On the contrary, the South African Truth and Reconciliation Commission concluded that 'part of the reason for the longevity of apartheid was the superficial adherence to "rule by law" by the National Party, whose leaders craved the aura of legitimacy that "the law" bestowed on their harsh injustice'.[30] But the persons charged under security or racial laws did welcome

---

[26] H Arendt, above n 7, p 35.
[27] *Trials of War Criminals before the Nuremberg Military Tribunals, vol. XII, the Ministries Case,* Washington 1951, p 641.
[28] The Ministries Case vol XIV p 646.
[29] Osiel, below n 33, p 542.
[30] Report vol 4 from the South African Truth and Reconciliation Commission, 1998, p 101.

judicial assistance and did not reject the help of lawyers on the grounds that it legitimated the oppression. The Brazilian military courts did save lives, with an acquittal rate of 70 per cent.[31] Should they be condemned for the 30 per cent that were convicted according to repressive laws or praised for their acquittals?

The answer is all the more difficult because the interests and values that have to be considered are incommensurable. Consider the anti-slavery judges of the US of the 1830s to 1850s who upheld the fugitive slave laws against their own convictions of the meaning of liberty and its application to all regardless of race. They did not choose between liberty and slavery, but between liberty and an ordered federation of the US, between liberty and fidelity to public trust, and between liberty and the adherence to public undertakings of nationhood. The issue for these judges was whether the moral values served by anti-slavery outweighed interests and values served by slavery.[32]

V. RESISTANCE TO THE RULE OF LAW

Experience shows that legal safeguards are not enough to guard against oppressive measures from authoritarian rulers. Such safeguards are often disregarded, not only by the executive power, but also by the courts that should enforce them. Judges are put in a difficult situation when the legislative and executive powers of the state employ legal means to undermine the rule of law. They have to choose between adherence to the law and respect for values inherent in their legal ideology of the rule of law. Like most others, judges often chose obedience over following their own values under such circumstances. In addition judges are subject to the same tendency to moral blindness as others when moral panic takes hold over society. To this comes the difficult question of the lesser evil. Even morally conscious judges can have a hard time deciding whether their contribution in enforcing tyrannical measures after all may prevent the regime from employing even worse means of oppression.

How can we provide safeguards to prevent judges from contributing to evil policies? Since the causes of authoritarian policies are both political and psychological, the safeguards must be political, psychological and ethical. Particularly during social unrest or when society is under threat we need robust institutions and policies to prevent and control the power of the state. But we also need awareness at the psychological level. Is it possible to equip the judiciary with a moral compass to prevent them from departing from the rule of law and the basic requirements of justice? Many have sought recourse in legal theory and a correct methodological approach to law. If only judges approach the law in a correct way, they will be able to uphold the ideals of the rule of law against an oppressive legislator.

---

[31] Osiel, below n 33, p 538.
[32] Cover, above n 13, pp 197–198.

Experience shows that this is not feasible. In fact, both formal and substantive approaches to interpretation of statutes may be employed in order to temper the oppressive legislator and to correct popular ideas and values.[33] The Prussian Administrative Appeals Court applied a formal approach against oppressive measures of the Nazi regime in the 1930s.[34] By refusing to reinterpret provisions for the protection of individuals that were not explicitly repealed by the Nazis, the Court sought to maintain judicial control with the police. Once these provisions were overridden in clear terms by the Nazi legislator, this defence line fell. As Marc Osiel points out, 'the more willing rulers are to enact their most repressive policies into positive law, the less legal positivism can provide a professional rationale for judicial resistance'.[35]

South African judges of opposition employed on the other hand what David Dyzenhaus labels the common law approach, where statutes and precedents are interpreted in accordance with the rule and reason of the common law, including principles of equality before the law, due process and habeas corpus.[36] Based as it is in common law with its doctrine of parliamentary sovereignty, this approach must also give way to the plain terms of legislation. It is unthinkable that judges, by employing pertinent methods of interpretation, can function consistently as a power contrary to the policy of the ruling power and the dominant societal values in the end and maintain their position as judges of the regime.

Marc Osiel concludes in his study of judges in Argentina and Brazil that legal theories rarely impel the judge to resistance. They merely provide him with alternative rhetorical forms, which the judge can apply in support or in opposition to a regime.[37] Vivian Grosswald Curran observes that German and French lawyers came to similar results regarding the reinterpretation of the law to accommodate the racial category of Jewishness, despite divergent and even contradictory interpretative methods. Where the German judges used the established method of reasoning with general clauses, the French, in contrast, used their established method of avoiding reference to general legal principles.[38] A similar conclusion is drawn by Bernd Rüthers in his thorough study of German private law in the Nazi years. Substantial parts of the judicial practice during the Nazi period are impeccable from the point of view of the legal methodology employed. For this reason,

---

[33] See the analysis of MJ Osiel on pp 489–510 in 'Dialogue with Dictators: Judicial Resistance in Argentina and Brazil' (1995) 20 *Law and Social Inquiry* 481–560 on how positivism, naturalism and realism all can be employed both to support and to resist authoritarian measures.

[34] See Ernst Fraenkel, *The Dual State A Contribution to the Theory of Dictatorship* (New York, Oxford University Press, 1941) 75.

[35] Osiel, above n 33, p 544.

[36] David Dyzenhaus, *Hard Cases in Wicked Legal Systems Pathologies of Legality*, 2nd edn (Oxford, Oxford University Press, 2010) 53.

[37] Osiel, above n 33, p 484.

[38] Curran, Vivian Grosswald, 'Law's Past and Europe's Future' (2005) 6 *German Law Journal* 483–512.

the search for a legal methodology that might protect the legal order from being misused for authoritarian purposes is bound to fail.[39] In his opinion,

> a legal theory that is reduced to questions of methodology and social engineering is like a navigator who commands excellent instruments and methods of calculation, but lacks trustworthy points to navigate from such as stars, lighthouses and radio beacons.[40]

Protection must be sought not at the level of legal theory or law. When the regime turns evil, judges are compelled to follow the authority of the law that is inherent in their role as judges. To the extent they try to temper the excesses of the law and to balance this with their loyalty as judges to the regime, they are forced into the destructive calculus of the lesser evil. Instead, they must step outside their role as judges and ask themselves, as Hannah Arendt observes in her essay on personal responsibility under dictatorship, what the limits are to the consent that they give to oppression.[41]

Judges are, like other people, subject to negative situational forces. As we have seen, the force of authority, moral blindness induced by following the law and the destructive calculus of the lesser evil allow judges to depart from values of justice and the rule of law that they are otherwise committed to. In order to protect themselves from the development that most judges tend to undergo, the people on the bench must learn to prevent or combat negative situational forces and to resist influences that they do not want or need.

Philip Zimbardo, who has researched how good people turn evil, suggests making use of the same personal and situational factors that turn people to evil to induce them to do good.[42] He suggests employing the 'foot-in-the-door' approach that often leads people to lower their moral guard towards strengthening their moral resistance. Judges could employ this tactic in curbing authoritarian measures little by little. Writing to the judges of apartheid, Professor John Dugard wrote: 'There is still some room for the judicial advancement of human rights in the interstices of the apartheid legal order, particularly in the interpretation of statutes, the development of the common law, and the review of administrative action and subordinate legislation.'[43] He appealed to the judges to use this room, arguing that this would not be to act in accordance with their oath of office and not a misconstruction of the law. In this way, judges could learn by experience that resistance is possible, and that they have a measure of independence as long as the regime employs the legal system to maintain legitimacy through legality. Instead of employing their legal reasoning in order to assist the regime in giving their policies legal effect, they should enhance the difficulties.

---

[39] Bernd Rüthers, *Die unbegrenzte Auslegung: Zum Wandel der Privatrechtsordnung im Nationalsozialismus* 7 Ausg (Tübingen, Mohr Siebeck, 2012) 444.

[40] ibid, p 526.

[41] H Arendt, above n 7, p 46.

[42] Philip Zimbardo, *The Lucifer Effect Understanding How Good People Turn Evil* (New York, Random House, 2007) 450.

[43] J Dugard, 'Should Judges Resign?—A reply to Professor Wacks' (1984) 101 *South African Law Journal* 286–294, at 291.

If more courts in Germany had followed the example of the Prussian administrative court in trying to curtail the prerogative state, the dual state may not have been allowed to develop in the way it did with unlimited powers to the security police and the SS. It could have been in the power of the judiciary to prevent Nazi Germany from sliding all the way down the slope to totalitarianism. This could even more be the case of the transformation of the Nazi racial ideology into law. This was, as we have seen, largely the work of the judiciary in rulings giving effect to the anti-Jewish policies of the Nazi Party. This happened in Germany and in France. In both cases, judges had witnessed the removal of their Jewish colleagues from the bench without issuing protests. In Belgium, where the judges protested against the purge of their Jewish colleagues, the courts never engaged in transforming racism into law.

As Zimbardo points out, social models are important in this respect. The 'common law' judges of South Africa were important even though they did not succeed in stemming the regime. They provided a model showing that an alternative jurisprudence was and is possible. They also provided a beacon of hope for the oppressed and the people brought to trial for political offences. Lothar Kreyssig's brave orders to institutions forbidding them to end the lives of persons under the custody of his Court may or may not have contributed to the end of the Nazi programme of euthanasia. But it definitely serves as an inspiration to future generations of judges showing both that such actions are possible for a judge even under such circumstances as totalitarian Germany at the end of the 1930s, and not least that totalitarian governments may be reluctant to meet such judicial actions with the usual terror of the regime. Based on Zimbardo's 'Ten-step program to resist unwanted influences'[44] we may point to some factors that judges faced with the task of applying authoritarian measures ought to consider.

VI. THE PROTECTION OF INTERNATIONAL COURTS

Experience shows that authoritarian regimes are often a passing phenomenon. This has been the case in all regimes that we have studied here, and it was the case of the regimes in central and Eastern Europe under the dominance of the Soviet Union. It is therefore important that judges balance their time perspective and situate their position both in relation to their own past, and in the future to come. When applying the laws of the time they should ask how the application of these laws accords with the ideals of justice and the rule of law of former times. They should also consider times to come and how the future when the authoritarian rule is brought to an end will regard the measures that they enforce. Studies show that in some cases the percentage of anti-government judicial rulings increases once it becomes likely that regime change will occur. Judges may in such cases want to secure their own situation by distancing themselves from the government.

---

[44] Zimbardo, pp 451–456.

Such strategic defections of judges show that judges are able to look beyond mere loyalty to the regime and adherence with its policy and combine this with their judicial role.[45] The challenge is for the judge to take into account the demise of the authoritarian policies before it is obvious to everyone.

In particular, judges should be alert to sacrificing individual liberties for the promise of security. The sacrifices are always real and lead to the implementation of authoritarian measures. Security is often a distant illusion consisting of a threat that is never realised or a future goal that is realised in ways that are difficult to predict and monitor. In his powerful speech in the Belmarsh case, Lord Bingham underlined that protective measures against possible terrorist acts should not go beyond what is strictly required by the exigencies of the situation and that it is for the state to prove that that is so.[46] It is the role of the courts to ensure that the requirements of proportionality are met. The judge should not ask, 'Could even harsher means have been employed but for the judicial review?', but instead ask, 'Has the government proved that the harsh means are necessary, that they will be effective and that no lesser means will be equally effective?'

The difficult task is, of course, for the judge to distinguish between just measures and unjust measures. The positive law gives no answer to this since the question is precisely the limits of the authority of the positive law. The judge must set his own limits based on his own moral intuitions and conscience. But he may take assistance from the ideology and the principles of the rule of law, protection of fundamental individual rights and the requirements of a minimum of proportionality between the act to be judged and the consequences to be measured out. Assistance may also be taken from the case law of criminal proceedings against judges by international tribunals and national cases of restorative justice. This jurisprudence is not extensive, and the requirements that can be extracted from them regarding judicial standards are very basic.[47] But they point in the right direction: There is a limit to what laws a judge can uphold as a judge without the risk of facing criminal sanctions by successor courts. Once this is realised, judges will see that they are personally responsible for what many would like to ascribe to the responsibility of the law and the lawmakers.

The realisation that the judge personally holds responsibility, morally and even legally, for his judicial practice is important, because it is the first step in accepting that the judge is personally accountable for rulings and their consequences. Judges, not laws, put men in prison. Obeying the authority of the law always entails consenting to it. People conform more to antisocial groups when they displace responsibility to the others, to the collective or to the institution. This also

---

[45] G Helmke, 'The Logic of Strategic Defection: Court–Executive Relations in Argentina Under Dictatorship and Democracy' (2002) 96 *American Political Science Review* 291–303, at 296.

[46] *A (FC) and others (FC) (Appellants) v Secretary of State for the Home Department (Respondent), X (FC) and another (FC) (Appellants) v Secretary of State for the Home Department (Respondent)* [2004] UKHL 56.

[47] See for an overview and analysis Hans Petter Graver, *Judges against Justice On Judges When the Rule of Law is Under Attack*, (Heidelberg, Springer, 2015) 189–201.

holds for judges. The blame put on positivism is an illustration of this. Blaming positivism and the law is a way of reducing the personal responsibility of the individual judge. In order to offer resistance it is important for judges to remind themselves that they have a choice when applying the law. When a given piece of legislation manifestly challenges basic notions of justice, equality or the rule of law, there is always a balancing to be performed. The outcome of this balancing is always the responsibility of the individual judge. This is precisely what is inherent in the notion of judicial independence. As long as there is a minimum adherence to the independence of the judiciary, the judge cannot displace his personal responsibility.

In the situation today, national judges have the international regimes for protection of human rights as positive legal sources to employ against oppressive measures of national law. This is first and foremost a role of international human rights courts, but the EU law and the Court of Justice have been following suit. For the EFTA States, the EFTA Court may be an important part of this picture. International law represents standards for the evaluation of national measures. The interpretation and application of these standards is, in many instances, guided by the case law of international courts and tribunals. The laws and practices of national authorities are monitored and evaluated by independent international authorities and courts.

Independently of the national legislator and ruler, international norms can be held to be binding as positive law on national judges. This was the approach taken by the Nuremberg tribunals after World War II and was followed by the German Supreme Court after the breakdown of the German Democratic Republic and the reuniting of Germany. International human rights regimes work on the legal orders of participating states in two ways. On the one hand, they constitute an authoritative body of law which has legally binding force. On the other hand, this body of law forms a basis for which international pressure can be applied on a violating state by other states. Both these ways can contribute to preventing states from serious violations of individual rights through their municipal law.

Hopefully, the force of international law and of international monitoring regimes will make the participation of national judges in oppression and evil less likely. Regardless of the quantitative effects of human rights standards, international norms will represent a contradictory body of law when the legislator enacts oppressive laws. In this respect, they will increase the cross-pressure facing the judge. This is, on the other hand, nothing entirely new. In the cases that we have seen before the establishment of the international human rights regime, judges were also under cross-pressure when an authoritarian regime developed in a society that was formally based on a liberal constitution and the rule of law. The German judges did not lack standards of protection of the rule of law, but they failed to employ them. The South African judges had standards in common law, which they failed to bring into effect. The Chilean Junta even went through the proceedings of ratification of the International Covenant on Civil and Political Rights at the same time as they perpetrated their terror against political opponents at home.

Even though the existence of norms with the force of positive law prohibiting oppressive and authoritarian measures is nothing new, there are important differences in the situation as it has developed since the turn of the millennium. Whereas the international norms in the twentieth century for the most part were very general and abstract in nature, there exists today a vast body of case law giving specific guidance to their interpretation and implementation in practice. There are also well-functioning international institutions that contribute to their enforcement. The role of the European Commission in the French measures against the Roma in 2009 is a notable example of this.[48] The engagement with Hungary by the European Commission and the Council of Europe is another example.

Institutions are important in that they represent an addition to the mere normative force of an argument. Judges who can invoke the international regime for the protection of human rights against oppressive measures of their regime have a much firmer basis for their resistance than their colleagues of the past. The one important difference today is that judges now have the instruments to oppose an authoritarian ruler. These instruments are available even to a positivistic-minded judge. Therefore, a judge does not have to appear 'political' to go against the regime. He can base his opposition in specific norms of positive law, based on traditional legal sources such as enacted norms and case law. Familiarity with international legal norms, respect for its legal authority, as well as awareness of the dangers entailed in the situation of a judge when the legislator wages war on the rule of law, may contribute to the important maintenance of the spirit of liberty in the heart of the judge.

---

[48] See Korando, Andrew M, 'Roma go Home: The Plight of European Roma' (2012) 30 *Law and Inequality* 125–147.

Part I

The EFTA Court's Role in the Judicial Architecture of the EEA

B
Access to Justice

7

The Content of Requests for Preliminary Rulings to the European Court of Justice and the EFTA Court—What are the Minimum Requirements?

ALLAN ROSAS

I. INTRODUCTION

THE QUESTION OF the admissibility of requests for preliminary rulings under Article 267 of the Treaty on the Functioning of the European Union (TFEU) and the scope of the competence of the European Court of Justice (ECJ) to answer the questions raised has given rise to an extensive case law and literature.[1] The discussion has focused above all upon the basic condition expressed in Article 267 that the request be made by a 'court or tribunal' and on problems relating to the distinction between Union law and national law (the Court[2] not being competent to interpret national law). Less attention has been paid to the conditions a request for a preliminary ruling has to fulfil in terms of content in order to be admissible. When is the request sufficiently comprehensive, detailed

---

[1] As to literature, suffice it to mention here the collection of articles by A Barav, *Études sur le renvoi préjudicial dans le droit de léUnion européenne* (Bruxelles, Bruylant, 2011) as well as some general works on the preliminary rulings procedure, C Naomé, *Le renvoi prejudicial en droit européen: Guide pratique*, 2e édition (Bruxelles, Larcier, 2010) 85–133, 297–309; M Broberg and N Fenger, *Preliminary References to the European Court of Justice*, 2nd edn (Oxford, Oxford University Press, 2014) 59–157, 295–321; G Vandersanden, *La procédure préjudicielle devant la Court de justice de l'Union européenne* (Bruxelles, Bruylant, 2011) 13–77.

[2] All requests for preliminary rulings are considered by the ECJ. According to Art 256(3) TFEU, the General Court (formerly the Court of First Instance) could be given jurisdiction to hear and determine questions referred for a preliminary ruling 'in specific areas laid down by the Statute'. No such amendment has been introduced to the Statute of the Court (Protocol No 3 annexed to the Treaties), nor is it envisaged to propose such an amendment in the foreseeable future, given the fact that the General Court is facing a much more serious backlog of cases than the ECJ: see, in this respect, Court of Justice of the European Union, *Annual Report 2013* (Luxembourg, Publications Office of the European Union, 2014), 83, 174.

and precise in order to enable an answer based on a sufficient understanding of the legal questions involved?

The latter question has been considered recently by the Court itself in the context of its work on a recast of its Rules of Procedure, which entered into force on 1 November 2012,[3] and during the first year of application of these Rules. This consideration takes place against the backdrop of the ever-increasing number of references for a preliminary ruling which has been noticeable during the last few years. In 2003, 210 such references were made. In 2008, they had increased to 288 and the corresponding figure for 2013 was 450. Imposing some basic requirements on the request as conditions for its admissibility may not in itself limit the number of requests. This is because a decision declaring a request inadmissible does not prevent the national court from coming back to the ECJ with a further request,[4] which, whether it does or does not fulfil the threshold for admissibility, requires in any case new consideration by the ECJ. But insisting on some minimum requirements may above all contribute to improving the quality of the procedure before the ECJ and also enabling the Court to distinguish between 'easy' cases and cases which require more profound consideration—which in turn may help to expedite the procedures before the Court and increase the 'productivity' of the Court further.[5]

This chapter will focus on the requirements applicable to the content of a request for a preliminary ruling in order for the request to be considered admissible, taking into account notably Article 94 of the new Rules of Procedure and the 'Recommendations to national courts and tribunals relating to the initiation of preliminary ruling proceedings' which the Court updated in October 2012 with a view to reflecting the innovations introduced by the new Rules of Procedure.[6]

As this is a tribute to the EFTA Court, a 'sister court' of the ECJ, the chapter will also make some comparisons with corresponding issues arising in the context of the advisory opinions which the EFTA Court is called upon to give when requested to do so by a national court or tribunal of a State party to the Agreement on the European Economic Area (EEA), in accordance with Article 34

---

[3] Rules of Procedure of the Court of Justice [2012] OJ L265/1. See, eg, M-A Gaudissart, 'La refonte du règlement de procédure de la Cour de justice' (2012) *Cahiers de droit européen* 603; JA Gutiérrez-Fons, 'Le nouveau règlement de procédure de la Cour de justice au regard du contentieux de l'Union européenne' in S Mathieu (ed), *Contentieux de l'Union européenne: Questions choisies* (Bruxelles, Larcier, 2014) 41. The present author is the chairman of the Court's permanent Committee on Rules of Procedure, which prepared the groundwork for the new text, established by the Court of Justice on 25 September 2012, after having obtained the Council's approval on 24 September.

[4] *Cf* Art 104(2) of the Rules of Procedure, which refers to the possibility of a second referral made to the ECJ by a national court or tribunal.

[5] In this respect, it is notable that over a 10-year period the Court has managed to reduce the duration of the procedure from on average 25.5 months in 2003 to months in 2013. In view of the ever-increasing number of preliminary references per year (see above), the average length of procedures will again start to increase, unless the Court finds new ways of combatting this problem.

[6] The Recommendations as adapted were published a few days after the entry into force of the new Rules of Procedure [2012] OJ C338/1.

of the Agreement between the EFTA States on the Establishment of a Surveillance Authority and a Court of Justice.[7]

II. THE SCOPE OF THE COURT'S JURISDICTION

The national courts of the EU Member States are not just national courts. Article 19 of the Treaty on European Union (TEU), as modified by the Treaty of Lisbon, which sets out the main ingredients of the judicial architecture of the Union, not only refers to the ECJ, the General Court and the possibility of establishing specialised courts[8] but also provides that the Member States 'shall provide remedies sufficient to ensure effective legal protection in the fields covered by Union law'. More specific provisions on effective judicial protection both at Union and national level are contained in the Charter of Fundamental Rights of the European Union and its Article 47 in particular.[9] In Opinion 1/09 relating to a draft agreement on a European and Community patents judicial system,[10] the ECJ, citing Article 19(1) TEU, emphasised that both the Court of Justice and the courts and tribunals of the Member States are the guardians of the EU legal order and that they 'fulfil a duty entrusted to them both' of ensuring that in the interpretation and application of the Treaties, the law is observed. The national courts are 'closely involved in the correct application and uniform interpretation of European Union law and also in the protection of individual rights conferred by that legal order'.[11]

The main provision in primary law laying down the framework for cooperation between the ECJ and the national courts is, of course, Article 267 TFEU, which provides that a national court or tribunal may, 'if it considers that a decision on [a] question [relating to the interpretation of the Treaties or the validity and

---

[7] For the text of the EEA Agreement see, eg, [1994] OJ L1/3, and for the Agreement on the Establishment of a Surveillance Authority and a Court of Justice, [1994] OJ L344/3. Art 107 of the EEA Agreement and Protocol No 34 to the Agreement enable an EEA State to allow a court or tribunal to ask the ECJ to decide on the interpretation of an EEA rule but this possibility has never been used. That is why the new Rules of Procedure of the ECJ do not contain a provision corresponding to Art 123g of the previous Rules of Procedure, see E Sharpston and M-J Clifton, 'The Two EEA Courts: Unequal Balance or Fruitful Partnership?' in EFTA Court (ed), *Judicial Protection in the European Economic Area* (Stuttgart, German Law Publishers, 2012) 170 at 175 fn 23.

[8] The only specialised court established so far under Art 257 TFEU is the EU Civil Service Tribunal; see Annex I to the Statute of the Court of Justice of the European Union (Protocol No 3 annexed to the TEU and the TFEU).

[9] According to Art 6(1) TEU, as amended by the Treaty of Lisbon, the Charter, as adapted at Strasbourg on 12 December 2007, 'shall have the same legal value as the Treaties'. For the text of the Charter, see [2010] OJ C83/389. Art 6(1) TEU and Art 52(7) of the Charter refer to explanations which have been drawn up as a way of providing guidance in the interpretation of the Charter and which shall be given 'due regard' by the Union and national courts. For the text of these explanations see [2007] OJ C303/17.

[10] Opinion 1/09 of 8 March 2011, *The Draft Agreement on the European and Community Patents Court* [2011] ECR I-1137.

[11] Paras 69 and 84–85 of Opinion 1/09.

interpretation of legislation and other secondary law] *is necessary* to enable it to give judgment', request the Court to give a ruling thereon (emphasis added).

This formula may be seen in the context of the definition of the scope of the ECJ's jurisdiction as set out at the beginning of Article 267: apart from questions concerning the validity of secondary law, the Court shall have jurisdiction to give rulings concerning the 'interpretation' of the Treaties and of secondary law. The provision thus does *not* refer to the 'application' of the law and the Court has held that when interpreting the Treaty, it 'limits itself to deducing the meaning of the Community rules from the wording and spirit of the Treaty, it being left to the national court to apply in the particular case the rules which are thus interpreted'.[12] That said, the distinction between 'application' and 'interpretation' is not always easy to uphold and an Advocate General of the Court has even suggested that 'when a provision is applied its interpretation and application are interwoven and merge'.[13]

A more obvious limitation of the ECJ's jurisdiction consists of the fact that it is limited to interpreting, and in the case of secondary law, assessing the validity of, Union law, not national law. This limitation has not prevented the Court from heeding a request for the interpretation of a rule of Union law even if the applicability of Union law in the national litigation in question does not follow from Union law itself.[14] This has occurred mainly in the following two types of situation: 1) the request for a preliminary ruling has mentioned the fact that national law refers to Union law in a way which calls for an interpretation of the latter in order to arrive at the correct interpretation of the former;[15] 2) a national constitutional principle instructs national courts to extend the protection offered by Union law to purely internal situations not covered by Union law so as to avoid that people in the former situations be treated less favourably than those who can invoke Union law directly.[16]

The Court has not been very strict in this regard, however, and sometimes the mere fact that a reply 'might be useful' to the national court in the event that its national law required that its own nationals not be given less favourable treatment than nationals of other Member States has satisfied the Court that it should give a

---

[12] Joined Cases 28-30/72 *Da Costa* [1963] ECR (English special edition, p 31). See also, eg, Case C-390/88 *Shipping and Forwarding Enterprise Safe BV* [1990] ECR I-285, paras 10–13, and the case law cited in Broberg and Fenger, above n 1, 154–155. For a recent judgment referring to the distinction between application and interpretation see Joined Cases C-162/12 and C-163/12 *Airport Shuttle Express and Others*, judgment of 13 February 2014, para 31.

[13] Opinion of Advocate General Capotorti of 13 July 1982 in Case 283/81 *CILFIT* [1982] ECR 3415. See also the Opinion of Advocate General Jacobs of 10 July 1997 in Case C-338/95 *Wiener* [1997] ECR I-6495 and Broberg and Fenger, above n 1, 154–155.

[14] See generally, eg, V Kronenberger, 'Actualité du renvoi préjudiciel, de la procédure préjudicielle d'urgence et de la procédure accélérée—Quo vadis?' in Mathieu, above n 3, 397 at 401–412.

[15] See, eg, Joined Cases C-297/88 and C-197/89 *Dzodzi* [1990] ECR I-3763; Case C-28/95 *Leur-Bloem* [1997] ECR I-4161. See also Naomé, above n 1, 124–126.

[16] See, eg, Case C-448/98 *Guimont* [2000] ECR I-10663; Case C-380/05 *Centro Europa* [2008] ECR I-349. See also Naomé, above n 1, 121.

ruling.[17] Moreover, there are some cases where the Court seems to have answered the questions put by the national judge simply by assuming that the interpretation of Union law given would be relevant in a cross-border situation, despite the fact that there was nothing in the national litigation that suggested such cross-border elements.[18] As noted by an Advocate General of the Court, in preliminary ruling cases involving situations of national rather than Union law, 'the Court has adopted a variety of approaches'.[19]

In this context, it should be recalled that the Charter of Fundamental Rights, according to its Article 51(1), is addressed to the Member States, and thus applicable at national level 'only when they are implementing Union law'. This clause has already given rise to an extensive case law as well as academic writings.[20] Whilst the ECJ has declined to give a restrictive interpretation of what constitutes 'implementing' (Union law),[21] there is already by now a string of judgments and reasoned orders where the Court denies competence to apply the Charter as the situation was not considered to fall within the scope of application of Union law (that is, to constitute implementation of this law in the sense of Article 51(1) of the Charter).[22]

The above situations are normally treated by the Court as questions of competence. It may also declare a request non-admissible if it is not satisfied that a ruling is necessary or possible. Whilst the Court, in a spirit of cooperation, regards itself in principle obliged to answer questions referred under Article 267 TFEU, it considers itself competent to verify the necessity of the request.[23] In this regard, the Court verifies that the request relates to an actual case (an action) pending before the national court, including that the case is not fictitious.[24] It may also declare a request non-admissible if it sees no usefulness or relevance of the questions referred for the case before the national court or if the problem raised by it is of a hypothetical nature[25] or it considers the request so lacking in relevant

---

[17] See, eg, Case C-6/01 *Anomar and Others* [2003] ECR I-8621, para 41.

[18] See, eg, Joined Cases C-570/07 and C-572/07 *Blanco Pérez and Chao Gómez* [2010] ECR I-4629, para 40 and the case law cited; Joined Cases C-159/12 to 161/212 *Venturini*, judgment of 5 December 2013, paras 25–26, see also paras 27–28.

[19] Opinion of Jääskinen AG of 11 March 2010, para 29, in Case C-393/08 *Sbarigia* [2010] ECR I-6337. See also the Opinion of Wahl AG of 5 September, paras 16–71 in Joined Cases C-159/12 to C-161/12 *Venturini*, above n 18. See further Kronenberger, above n 14, 407–408, 409–410, 411–412.

[20] See, eg, A Rosas, 'The Applicability of the EU Charter of Fundamental Rights at National Level' (2013) 13 *European Yearbook on Human Rights* 97.

[21] See, in particular, Case C-617/10 *Åkerberg Fransson*, judgment of 26 February 2013, paras 16–31.

[22] For two recent examples see Case C-206/13 *Siragusa*, judgment of 6 March 2014; Case C-265/13 *Torralbo Marcos*, judgment of 27 March 2014.

[23] See, eg, Case C-428/06 *UGT-Rioja et al* [2008] ECR I-6747, para 40. See also Naomé, above n 1, 107.

[24] See, in particular, Case 104/79 *Foglia/Novello* [1980] ECR 745.

[25] An example of a refusal to reply to a hypothetical question is offered by Case C-83/91 *Meilicke* [1992] ECR I-4871. For a recent example see Case C-82/13 *Societá cooperative Madonna dei miracoli*, Order of the Court of 7 October 2013, paras 12, 14. See generally Naomé, above n 1, 115–122, who points out (at 118) that there is in the case law of the Court some overlap between non-relevant and hypothetical questions.

information that it becomes more or less impossible to understand what is being requested.[26] Such an outcome does not necessarily apply to all the questions referred by the national court.

This is not the place to enter into a discussion as to the precise limits of the Court's jurisdiction in these and similar situations. What is of primary interest here is to consider what implications such problems of competence and jurisdiction may have for the requirements imposed by Article 267 TFEU and Article 94 of the Rules of Procedure as to the content of the request for a preliminary ruling. It is to this question that we shall now turn.

III. THE REQUEST FOR A PRELIMINARY RULING: MINIMUM REQUIREMENTS

Before the adoption of the new Rules of Procedure of 2012, the only legally binding provision setting out conditions for a request for a preliminary ruling was what has become Article 267 TFEU. Apart from the condition that, in the view of the national court, a decision on the interpretation and, as the case may be, validity of acts of Union law 'is necessary to enable it to give judgment', there were no explicit requirements on the content of the request itself. True, some guidelines in this regard were provided in an Information Note on references from national courts for a preliminary ruling,[27] but as the title suggests, these guidelines were not legally binding.

Article 94, entitled 'Content of the request for a preliminary ruling', of the new Rules of Procedure is designed to remedy this situation. Article 94 provides that in addition to the text of the actual questions referred to the Court for a ruling, the request 'shall contain' some information relating to the factual situation with which the national judge is faced, the national law applicable in the main proceedings (including, where appropriate, the relevant national case law) as well as the reasons which prompted the referring court to inquire about the interpretation or validity of Union law and the relationship between the relevant provisions of Union law and the national legislation applicable to the main proceedings.

It is obvious that this information is of considerable importance for the Court in considering whether it is competent to give a ruling and whether the request should be declared admissible. Subparagraph c) of Article 94, concerning the

---

[26] See, eg, Case 190/02 *Viacom Outdoor*, Order of the Court of 8 October 2002, where the Court stated, inter alia, that '[i]n the absence of sufficient particulars, it is not possible to discern the specific problem of interpretation which might be raised in relation to each of the provisions of Community law in respect of which the national court seeks an interpretation' (para 22) and the follow-up Case C-134/03 *Viacom Outdoor*, judgment of 17 February 2005, [2005] ECR I-1167, para 31, where it is observed that the order for reference 'does not contain sufficient information' about certain relevant elements of fact and national law.

[27] [2011] OJ C160/1. See also Broberg and Fenger, above n 1, 296–323, which contains a detailed discussion on the form and content of a reference.

need to explain the reasons which prompted the national court to refer the case to the ECJ and the relationship between the relevant provisions of Union law and of national law, is particularly important with respect to questions relating to the competence of the Court (above all, whether the case raises a point of Union law or not[28]). For the question of admissibility, for instance whether there is a real case or whether the litigation is fictitious, an explanation of the facts of the case and of relevant national law may be equally relevant (despite the fact that the Court is not competent to establish the facts, or to rule on the correct interpretation of national law).

The Recommendations to national courts and tribunals in relation to the initiation of preliminary rulings proceedings,[29] which replace the previous Information Note on the same subject,[30] underline the nature of the decision of the national court as a 'document which will serve as the basis of the proceedings before the Court' and that it 'must contain such information as will enable the Court to give a reply which is of assistance to the referring court or tribunal'.[31] The request must on the one hand be succinct but on the other 'sufficiently complete and must contain all the relevant information to give the Court … a clear understanding of the factual and legal context of the main proceedings'.[32]

After having repeated the above requirements set out in Article 94 of the Rules of Procedure, the Recommendations state that the relevant Union law 'should be identified as accurately as possible' in the request, which should include, if need be, a brief summary of the relevant arguments of the parties to the main proceedings. An example of a situation where it is particularly important that the relevant Union law be identified as accurately as possible is a situation which raises doubts about the applicability of the Charter of Fundamental Rights, in other words whether a rule of Union law other than a provision of the Charter can be identified which, apart from concerns for its validity, should be either applied or interpreted in the case in question.[33]

The ECJ, in its recent case law, has started to refer to Article 94 of the Rules of Procedure notably in determining whether the request for a preliminary ruling should be declared inadmissible. This has been done by recalling first the case law of the Court concerning the admissibility of such requests and then adding that the requirements following from this case law are now expressed in Article 94 of the Rules of Procedure,[34] or by taking Article 94 as the point of departure for

---

[28] This includes the question as to whether there is a provision of Union law other than the Charter of Fundamental Rights which is relevant (given that the Charter can never be applied on a stand-alone basis, see above n 20).

[29] See above n 6.

[30] See above n 27.

[31] Recommendations to national courts and tribunals, para 20.

[32] ibid, para 21.

[33] See Rosas, above n 20, 105–110, 111–112.

[34] Case C-257/13 *Mlamali*, Order of the Court of 14 November 2013, para 22; Case C-550/13 *Grimal*, Order of the Court of 19 March 2014, para 16. These Orders of the Court are not available in English. See also Case C-368/12 *Adiamix*, Order of the Court of 18 April 2013, para 22, where the

an examination of whether the content of the request is sufficient to enable the Court to give a ruling.[35] In other decisions, the Court has simply recalled its case law without referring explicitly to Article 94, which is partly explained by the fact that the order for reference had been made before the entry into force of the new Rules of Procedure on 1 November 2012.[36] At least in one case, the Court has also referred to Article 94 in determining whether the Court was competent to give a ruling on a question relating to the applicability of the Charter of Fundamental Rights under its Article 51.[37]

The current workload of the ECJ, and the increasing number of references for preliminary rulings referred to above in particular, seem to call for a somewhat stricter approach to the questions of competence and admissibility than was necessary in the old days of considerably fewer such requests. True, Article 101 of the Rules of Procedure provides the Court with the possibility to request clarification from the referring court within a time limit prescribed by the Court. This possibility is rarely used. This is partly because experience shows that the deficiencies of orders for reference are not always fully rectified through this procedure, partly because the procedure is time-consuming and may also cause procedural problems for the national judge (how to treat the request without infringing the procedural rights of the parties to the main proceedings).

Article 94 of the new Rules of Procedure offers an opportunity and a more explicit legal basis for insisting on some minimum requirements for the orders for reference as formulated by national courts. Such an approach would contribute to encouraging the national courts to provide a satisfactory account of the legal and factual aspects of the case and thus help both the interested parties, including the national governments and the Commission, and the ECJ to have a solid basis for an examination of the questions referred. This, again, could enhance the quality of this examination and at the same time even help to shorten the duration of the proceedings before the ECJ.

IV. THE ADMISSIBILITY OF REQUESTS FOR ADVISORY OPINIONS (EFTA COURT)

According to Article 34 of the Agreement between the EFTA States on the Establishment of a Surveillance Authority and a Court of Justice (SCA), the EFTA Court 'shall have jurisdiction to give advisory opinions on the interpretation of the EEA Agreement'. While the decisions of the EFTA Court thus are referred to

---

Court referred to the Information Note on references from national courts for a preliminary ruling (which preceded the Recommendations issued in 2012), see above nn 27, 29 and 30.

[35] Case C-560/11 *Debiasi*, Order of the Court of 13 December 2012, para 24, not available in English.
[36] See, eg, Case C-79/12 *SC Mora IPR SRL*, judgment of 21 February 2013; Case C-234/12 *Sky Italia*, judgment of 18 July 2013; Case C-514/12 *Zentralbetriebsrat der gemeinnützigen Salzburger Landeskliniken Betriebs*, judgment of 5 December 2013.
[37] Case C-206/13 *Siragusa*, above n 22, para 19.

as 'advisory opinions' in Article 34 SCA, the difference between them and the preliminary rulings given by the ECJ should not be overstated, as failure to follow an advisory opinion, termed 'judgment' by the EFTA Court itself (apart from a short period in the mid-1990s), may raise questions as to whether the EFTA State party to the EEA Agreement is complying with its obligations under the Agreement.[38]

The fact that Article 34 SCA provides for a right but, even with respect to courts of last instance, no obligation to request an advisory opinion may be of greater significance and partly explain why the number of such requests has remained relatively modest (in the period 1994–2013, fewer than 100 altogether), as compared with the ECJ, despite the fact that none of the three EFTA States which are parties to the EEA (Iceland, Liechtenstein and Norway) has made use of the possibility provided for in Article 34(3) SCA to limit the right to request advisory opinions to courts and tribunals 'against whose decisions there is no judicial remedy under national law'.[39] On the other hand the small number of EEA States and the limited size of their population (Iceland has around 325,000, Liechtenstein 37,000 and Norway 5.1 million inhabitants) makes it understandable that the number of requests for advisory opinions is not very high.

Concerning the question of admissibility, the EFTA Court, to quote its President, has been 'quite liberal when giving judgment on the admissibility of a request for a preliminary ruling'.[40] He added as a rhetorical question that '[i]f you are not overloaded, and we are not, then why should we throw out cases if the situation is not crystal clear?'[41] It should be added that the Rules of Procedure of the EFTA Court do not contain any provision corresponding to Article 94 of the Rules of Procedure of the ECJ and listing some minimum requirements for the request for a ruling itself.[42]

In one of its first cases, the EFTA Court stated that 'it is for the national court to assess whether an interpretation of the EEA Agreement is necessary for it to give judgment'.[43] The Court in this context relied on the case law of the ECJ and added, as a caveat, that according to this ECJ case law, it is not for the Court to give opinions on general and hypothetical questions (but as to the case at issue, the EFTA Court stated categorically that the question referred was not hypothetical).[44]

---

[38] See, eg, C Baudenbacher, *The EFTA Court in Action: Five Lectures*, 22–23; J Temple Lang, 'The Duty of National Courts to Provide Access to Justice in the EEA' in EFTA Court, above n 7, 100 at 114–115; Sharpston and Clifton, above n 7, 173–174.

[39] There is a trend in legal literature, however, to consider that given the general obligations contained in the EEA Agreement, the right to refer at least in some cases becomes an obligation to refer; see, eg, S Magnusson, 'On the Authority of Advisory Opinions' (2010) 13 *Europarättslig tidskrift* 528; Baudenbacher, above n 38, 22; C Baudenbacher, 'Some Thoughts on the EFTA Court's Phases of Life' in EFTA Court, above n 7, 24–25.

[40] Baudenbacher, above n 38, 20.

[41] ibid, 21.

[42] See Chapter 7 (advisory opinions) of the Rules of Procedure of the EFTA Court, published on its website, www.eftacourt.int.

[43] Case E-1/95 *Samuelsson* [1994–1995] EFTA Ct Rep, 145, para 13.

[44] ibid, paras 15–16.

In some later judgments, the Court has observed that questions concerning EEA law 'enjoy a presumption of relevance'.[45] The Court has also stated that the presumption of relevance cannot be rebutted simply because the facts ('the accuracy of which is not a matter for the Court to determine') are contested before the national court.[46]

It is especially the problem of hypothetical questions which has given rise to a certain number of further decisions. Most of them have concluded that a certain question the admissibility of which had been contested was after all admissible.[47] Such a conclusion is normally reached after having stated the general approach of the EFTA Court to these matters.[48]

It follows that questions concerning EEA law enjoy a presumption of relevance. Thus, the Court may refuse to rule on a question referred by a national court only here it is quite obvious that the interpretation of EEA law that is sought is unrelated to the facts of the main action or its purpose, where the problem is hypothetical, or where the Court does not have before it the factual or legal material necessary to give a useful answer to the questions submitted to it.

In at least two cases, the EFTA Court has concluded that certain questions (but not the request as a whole) were inadmissible because of their hypothetical nature, in one of the cases referring to the lack of information in the national court's order for reference.[49] The requirement, cited above, that the Court should have before it 'the factual or legal material necessary to give a useful answer to the questions submitted to it' has led the Court to explain that its purpose is, 'first, to enable the Court to arrive at an interpretation of EEA law which may be of use to the national court, and second, to give the governments of the Contracting Parties and other interested parties the opportunity to submit observations pursuant to Article 20 of the Statute of the Court'.[50] In the case cited, the Court arrived at the conclusion that the factual and legal circumstances of the case were sufficiently explained in the request.[51]

There are also some cases in which the EFTA Court has dealt with the question of its jurisdiction in terms of competence. For instance, it has stated that the task of the Court 'is to interpret provisions of EEA law' and that it is not its role 'to

---

[45]   See, eg, Case E-17/11 *Aresbank* [2012] EFTA Ct Rep, 916, para 44.

[46]   Case E-19/11 *Vín Tríó* [2012] EFTA Ct Rep, 974, para 27.

[47]   See Case E-1/95 *Samuelsson*, above n 43, paras 12–18; Case E-5/96 *Nille* [1997] EFTA Ct Rep, 30, paras 10–14; Case E-2/03 *Ákæruvaldið* [2003] EFTA Ct Rep, 185, paras 19–24; Case E-10/04 *Piazza* [2005] EFTA Ct Rep, 76, paras 20–24; Case E-13/11 *Granville* [2012] EFTA Ct Rep, 400, paras 16–24 (in *Granville*, however, it does not seem to be clear on what ground exactly the Court concludes that the request is admissible).

[48]   See, eg, Case E-13/11 *Granville*, above n 47, para 20.

[49]   Case E-6/96 *Wilhelmsen* [1997] EFTA Ct Rep, 53, paras 34–40 ('The Court notes that it is not apparent from the request why the national court would need an answer to questions 3 and 4 to give judgment in the case pending before it', para 39); Case E-11/12 *Koch et al* [2013] EFTA Ct Rep, 272, paras 50–56.

[50]   Case E-10/04 *Piazza*, above n 47, para 18.

[51]   Case E-10/04 *Piazza*, above n 47, para 19. See also Case E-6/96 *Wilhelmsen*, above n 49.

interpret provisions of national law or to ascertain to what extent provisions of EEA law have been transposed into national law'.[52] In another case it was asserted that the Court had no jurisdiction to interpret a free trade agreement which did not form part of EEA law. The Court accepted that 'as a point of departure' it has no jurisdiction (as the agreement was an international agreement other than the EEA Agreement) but continued with a more subtle reasoning concerning the relevance concerning certain clauses connecting both sets of law (and finally arriving at the result that there was no need to answer the relevant questions.[53] In yet another case, the Court examined whether there was a problem of admissibility with respect to the application, in a purely internal situation, of domestic legislation borrowing concepts from EEA law and arrived at the conclusion that the questions were admissible, as it was in the interest of EEA to forestall future differences of interpretation.[54]

The case law of the EFTA Court thus shows a number of similarities with ECJ case law as far as the scope of the Court's jurisdiction is concerned. In particular, the Court has had occasion to examine whether questions are hypothetical and thus should be declared inadmissible, concluding in the majority of cases in favour of admissibility. There are fewer cases where the EFTA Court has examined the request for a preliminary ruling with a view to determining whether its content fulfils the minimum requirements with respect to factual and/or legal material and there appears to be no case where the Court has declared explicitly that it is not competent, for instance, because the questions posed did not concern EEA law. There are thus some differences between the case law of the EFTA Court and that of the ECJ, the latter concluding quite often that it is not competent to give a ruling. To the extent that the ECJ, in the light also of Article 94 of its Rules of Procedure, may become somewhat more restrictive vis-à-vis requests for preliminary rulings which are scant on relevant factual and legal information, the differences in approach between the two Courts might be accentuated. On the other hand, one cannot exclude that the increasing number of cases brought before the EFTA Court will at least in the long run call for a somewhat stricter approach to the question of admissibility.

Be that as it may, the procedural challenges facing the EFTA Court and the ECJ with respect to requests for preliminary rulings show many similarities and parallels and so the two Courts, as is even more so the case with respect to issues of substantive law, can only benefit from learning of their respective case law and experiences.

---

[52] Case E-2/95 *Eidesund* [1995–1996] EFTA Ct Rep, 1, para 14.
[53] Case E-2/03 *Ákæruvaldið*, above n 47, paras 25–37.
[54] Case E-17/11 *Aresbank*, above n 45, paras 42–46, notably para 45.

8

Practical Issues Regarding the Application of EEA Law through the Eyes of a National Judge

ANDREAS BATLINER

THE AGREEMENT ON the European Economic Area (EEA Agreement) of 2 May 1992 entered into force in Liechtenstein on 1 May 1995. Since that date, Liechtenstein authorities and courts have been under an obligation to observe and apply EEA law. This raises many practical questions, some of which will be discussed below with reference to the practice of the Liechtenstein Administrative Court (Verwaltungsgerichtshof—VGH)[1] from the perspective of a national judge.[2]

The judge has the task of determining the relevant facts and the law applicable to the particular case, and then applying the law to the factual situation underlying the proceedings. The interpretation of the law plays a crucial role here. Some practical examples will give an insight into the influence that European law may have on the application of law.

I. TRANSPOSED DIRECTIVES

National legislation implementing an EU directive is to be interpreted within the meaning of that directive.

The Administrative Court interpreted the law on public procurement in line with Council Directive 92/50/EEC of 18 June 1992 on the coordination of procedures for the award of public service contracts. It thereby classified the

---

[1] The Administrative Court or Verwaltungsgerichtshof (VGH) is the highest administrative court of the Principality of Liechtenstein. Until 14 September 2003 it was called the Verwaltungsbeschwerdeinstanz (VBI).

[2] See also A Batliner, 'Die Anwendung des EWR-Rechts durch liechtensteinische Gerichte— Erfahrungen eines Richters' in *Liechtensteinische Juristenzeitung (LJZ)* 2004, 139.

Liechtenstein Postal Corporation as a public authority despite it being established in accordance with private law.[3]

In its judgment of 25 August 2011, the Administrative Court interpreted the Act on the Free Movement of EEA and Swiss Nationals within the meaning of Directive 2004/38/EC of the European Parliament and of the Council of 29 April 2004 on the right of citizens of the Union and their family members to move and reside freely within the territory of the Member States. The Court recognised that an EEA national who has a permanent residence permit in Liechtenstein may even bring his spouse if both are dependent on social welfare.[4] The Administrative Court based this finding on the opinion it had obtained from the EFTA Court.[5]

II. AUTONOMOUS LAWS

Even those national laws that are not based on European law are to be interpreted within the meaning of European law, in particular within the meaning of the EEA Agreement.

With its decision of 17 September 1997 the Verwaltungsbeschwerdeinstanz (VBI) recognised that the employment status of teachers was to be interpreted within the meaning of Article 4 of the EEA Agreement and that therefore the provisions of the Teachers Service Act concerning foreign teachers should cover only those foreign teachers who were not nationals of an EEA Member State.[6]

In its judgment of 18 February 2013 the Administrative Court interpreted the gambling law within the meaning of the case law of the European Court of Justice[7] (ECJ) and recognised that with the award of a service concession (the concession for the operation of a casino), the principle of equality, the prohibition of discrimination on grounds of nationality and the principle of transparency must be observed.[8]

In cases where national law is not applied in line with European law, the state is liable for the resultant damage. In one case the Liechtenstein authorities refused to issue an approval for an Austrian doctor to practise in Liechtenstein. On appeal, the Administrative Court requested an advisory opinion from the EFTA Court on the question of whether the single practice rule contained in national law was compatible with the EEA Agreement. The EFTA Court replied in the negative.[9] Accordingly, on 19 September 2001 the Administrative Court

---

[3] VBI 2001/53, *Liechtensteinische Entscheidungssammlung (LES)* 2002, 78.
[4] VGH 2010/108, www.gerichtsentscheidungen.li.
[5] Case E-4/11 *Arnulf Clauder*.
[6] VBI 1997/17, *LES* 1998, 207.
[7] European Court of Justice (ECJ) Joined Cases C-72/10 and C-77/10 *Costa and Cifone*; ECJ Case C-64/08 *Engelmann*.
[8] VGH 2012/030a; see also Case E-24/13 *Casino Admiral AG v Wolfgang Egger*.
[9] Case E-6/00 *Dr Jürgen Tschannett*; see also Case E-4/00 *Dr Johann Brändle* and Case E-5/00 *Dr Josef Mangold*.

decided not to apply the single practice rule.[10] Because of the delay in issuing its approval in Liechtenstein the doctor was thus entitled to damages from the State of Liechtenstein. He was able to enforce these damages based on the national Office Liability Act, whereby the Office Liability Act was also to be interpreted according to European law.[11]

III. NON-TRANSPOSED DIRECTIVES

A directive that has not yet been transposed into national law is directly applicable and takes precedence over national law, as long as the relevant criteria developed by the ECJ are met. In its judgment of 9 February 2006, the Administrative Court recognised that Council Directive 76/207/EEC (the Equal Treatment Directive) and Directive 97/81/EC on part-time work took precedence over a provision in the national Remuneration Act. The reasoning was as follows: on the basis of the Member States' obligations in Protocol 35 to the EEA Agreement to take the necessary measures at national level to ensure the primacy of EEA law over national law, EEA law is directly applicable, even when there is contradictory national law. In assessing this direct effect, it does not matter if a directive has not yet been implemented in the EEA Agreement in its original version, but has only become EEA law by a decision of the Joint Committee based on approval by parliament.[12]

IV. LACK OF NATIONAL LAWS

The EEA Agreement requires that EEA law take effect at national level and that it be enforced. However, if national law does not provide an option to help give effect to EEA law, the national court is faced with a particular challenge. The Administrative Court had to take one such decision in its judgment of 8 November 2013.[13] After the entry into force of the EEA Agreement, the Liechtenstein legislators introduced a tax privilege for captive insurance companies. Years later, the EFTA Surveillance Authority[14] and the EFTA Court[15] found this tax privilege to be unlawful State aid within the meaning of Article 61 paragraph 1 of the EEA Agreement. Liechtenstein was therefore required to recover this State aid or to impose the appropriate supplementary taxation. The problem was, however,

---

[10] VBI 2000/12; see also VBI 2000/54, *LES* 2002, 75.

[11] Staatsgerichtshof (StGH) 2007/15, www.gerichtsentscheidungen.li; StGH 2008/87, www.gerichtsentscheidungen.li; OGH CO.2004.2, www.gerichtsentscheidungen.li; C Baudenbacher, 'Das Vorabentscheidungsverfahren im EFTA-Pfeiler des EWR' in Hubertus Schumacher and Wigbert Zimmermann (eds), '*90 Jahre Fürstlicher Oberster Gerichtshof*', *Festschrift für Gert Delle Karth* (Vienna, Jan Sramek Verlag, 2013) 1, 11ff.

[12] VGH 2005/94, *LES* 2006, 300 (abstract 2).

[13] VGH 2013/093, currently pending at the Staatsgerichtshof at StGH 2013/196.

[14] EFTA Surveillance Authority (ESA) no 97/10/COL of 24 March 2010.

[15] Case E-4/10, E-6/10, E-7/10 *The Principality of Liechtenstein et al v EFTA Surveillance Authority*.

that over the previous few years procedural and substantive final decisions of the Liechtenstein Tax Administration had been issued, and Liechtenstein law did not foresee any possibility of amending these decisions retroactively. The Administrative Court opined that the absence of a scheme allowing for the 'recovery' of unlawful aid in cases where a taxpayer's final assessment is changed due to a breach of the prohibition of State aid under European law was tantamount to making the recovery prescribed by European law virtually impossible. One could argue that, in view of the principle of effectiveness (*effet utile*) and the primacy of European law over national law, a national procedural rule providing for the retroactive amendment of final tax assessments for special cases should also be applied in the present case. One would arrive at the same result on the basis that the absence of a specific operating procedure for the recovery of illegal aid constitutes a real gap in the law. Indeed, while the authority would have a duty to act (recovery of unlawful aid), it would not have any procedural provisions to base itself on. Such an unplanned and thus unintentional legal lacuna would need to be filled by the competent court by relying on analogies.

V. THE FATE OF LAWS THAT ARE INCOMPATIBLE WITH EUROPEAN LAW

National legal norms that are incompatible with European law are to be interpreted in conformity with European law or disregarded. The primacy of European law is to be observed.[16] Removal by the legislature or the Constitutional Court (Staatsgerichtshof—StGH) is not necessary.[17]

VI. DECISION-MAKING POWERS

Finally, there is also the question of who decides on the application of EEA law.

Liechtenstein follows a monistic approach. EEA law is therefore an integral part of the Liechtenstein legal system[18] and is to be directly applied by each national authority and each appellate authority. This of course also applies to the Administrative Court as the highest court of appeal in administrative matters. If the Administrative Court is in doubt about how a European legal norm should be applied, it may obtain assistance from two different courts. In accordance with the Agreement between the EFTA States on the Establishment of a Surveillance Authority and a Court of 2 May 1992, it may first ask the EFTA Court for an advisory opinion. Second, it may apply for judicial review by the Liechtenstein

---

[16] VGH 2005/94, LES 2006, 300; VGH 2013/093.

[17] P Bussjäger, 'Rechtsfragen des Vorrangs und der Anwendbarkeit von EWR-Recht in Liechtenstein' in *LJZ* 2006, 140 (144f).

[18] StGH 1995/14, LES 1996, 119; P Bussjäger, above n 17, 140ff.

Constitutional Court. The Constitutional Court sees itself competent to examine whether national legal standards are in conformity with EEA law and also applies this competence in practice.[19] It is, however, open to doubt whether in practice it makes sense to apply for judicial review before the Constitutional Court rather than to seek an opinion before the EFTA Court. Legal certainty and legal peace can be established only when the highest court decides on a contentious issue.[20] In European legal issues it is not the Constitutional Court, however, but the EFTA Court that is the highest competent court for Liechtenstein.

If the Administrative Court knows how to interpret a provision of EEA law, it performs the interpretation itself. The fact that there is a chance that the Administrative Court may also make mistakes in this is in the very nature of the matter and unfortunately a reality.[21]

---

[19] StGH 2006/94, www.gerichtsentscheidungen.li; StGH 2008/92, www.gerichtsentscheidungen.li.

[20] A Batliner, in Klaus Tschütscher and Carl Baudenbacher (eds), *20 Jahre Unterzeichnung des EWR-Abkommens—Ein Vierakter mit Original-Darstellern* (Schaan, Regierung des Fürstentums Liechtenstein, 2012) 53.

[21] This happened in the question of export of the Liechtenstein *Hilflosenentschädigung* (helplessness allowance): VBI 2002/125, in contrast see Case E-5/06 *EFTA Surveillance Authority v The Principality of Liechtenstein*; Baudenbacher, above n 11, 11f.

9

'To Refer or Not to Refer?'

MARKÚS SIGURBJÖRNSSON

I. INTRODUCTION

W HEN ONE REFLECTS on the question of when to request an advisory opinion of the EFTA Court, from the Icelandic point of view, with regard to a legal action being processed before the national courts of law, one should at the outset take into account the fact that the Icelandic Legislative Act of 1994 on Obtaining an Advisory Opinion of the EFTA Court on the Interpretation of the EEA Agreement (the Act of 1994) aligns with paragraph 3 of Article 34 of the Agreement on the Establishment of a Surveillance Authority and a Court of Justice (SCA). Therein, the Icelandic legislator granted the Supreme Court and the District Courts, both judicial instances of our two-tiered system of general courts, the right to request an advisory opinion, as well as to the Labour Court, which is the only Icelandic court of special jurisdiction apart from the Court of Impeachment. These courts have the power to decide upon requesting an advisory opinion, either upon motion by the parties to the litigation or at their own initiative, and their power applies irrespective of the type of proceeding involved, whether it be a civil lawsuit, a criminal action or a case conducted pursuant to an extraordinary procedure, such as a dispute concerning an enforcement action, a legal injunction, the recognition of a claim in bankruptcy proceedings or the winding-up of a financial institution. The Act also provides that a summary appeal may be made to the Supreme Court from the rulings on this issue in the District Courts, whether the decision there has been to the effect of requesting an advisory opinion or rejecting a motion thereof. It follows that the Supreme Court has the final say in the matter of whether an advisory opinion should be requested, what issues should be addressed by the request, and how the questions to the EFTA Court should be formulated.

In venturing to examine more closely what may determine whether an advisory opinion will be sought, it is something of an obstacle that the Supreme Court has not laid down for itself a comprehensive policy in this matter, whether at a formal or informal level, and I very much doubt that this has been carried any further within the District Courts. However, certain fundamental factors stand out very clearly in this respect, and I propose to deal briefly with three such factors before proceeding further.

II. WHEN DO THE ICELANDIC COURTS REQUEST
AN ADVISORY OPINION?

First, the wording of the Act of 1994 is perfectly clear on the point that the national courts are empowered to request an advisory opinion on matters relating to the interpretation of the EEA Agreement, but they are not obliged to do so. In this, the Act is in harmony with the wording of paragraph 2 of Article 34 of the SCA. While it is true that the Act does not explicitly refer to the further basic point stated in para 2 of Article 34, the actual practice in Iceland indicates beyond doubt that it was assumed that the position must be such that the national court will request an advisory opinion when it considers it necessary in order to be able give judgment in a case, as this view has been cited on multiple occasions in decisions of the Icelandic courts. An overview of Icelandic judicial practice in this respect will reveal that this point is in fact one of the primary considerations in assessing whether to request an advisory opinion.

Second, it is necessary to recall that Iceland is among those States adhering to the principle of duality between national and international law. Among other matters, it follows that rules of international law, including the EEA Agreement and its complementary materials, do not automatically form an integral part of national law, but will need to be incorporated into Icelandic legislation. As is well known, the features intended to deal with this situation, which persists both in Iceland and Norway, included the adoption of Protocol 35 to the EEA Agreement. The Protocol states, in essence, that in the event of conflict between implemented EEA rules and other statutory provisions, the EEA States undertake to introduce a statutory provision to the effect that EEA rules do prevail in such cases. In response to this Protocol, the Icelandic Act of 1993 on the Agreement of the European Economic Area ('the Act of 1993') laid down in its Article 3 a rule stating that national laws and regulations should, in so far as appropriate, be construed in conformity with the EEA Agreement. This statutory provision obviously embodies a meaning differing from that of Protocol 35, as it makes no mention of priority of an EEA rule in the event of a conflict, but solely indicates that an attempt must be made to resolve the issue of such conflict by interpreting the national statute so as to harmonise with the EEA rule. This necessarily must at all times be subject to the limitation of the actual words of the national statute being of such content as to allow room for an interpretation to this effect, and experience has shown that this cannot be achieved in every instance. The fact is, however, that it was not possible to proceed any further within the framework imposed by the Icelandic Constitution. The Constitution neither contemplates that the sovereignty of the Republic may be limited by a transfer of legislative power to international institutions, nor that national legislation, which is based on international commitments such as those of the EEA Agreement, may, by reason of this alone, acquire a higher status than other ordinary legislation. In other words, the Constitution does not envisage that a problem of conflict among provisions of ordinary legislation be solved by other means than the application of recognised principles of legal interpretation, and does not concede to the legislator a power or margin for giving a specific ordinary statute once and for all a status of priority over other ordinary laws. This position has in certain instances undeniably been of influence in the assessment of whether to request an advisory opinion, to which I will return later on.

Third, it must be observed that the Icelandic rules of legal procedure may have an effect in the matter of assessing whether an advisory opinion should be sought in connection with a civil action. In Iceland, a principle of control by the litigating parties over the scope of a civil action does apply, from which it follows that at least one of them must be contending for his part, directly or indirectly, that rules of the EEA Agreement may have an influence to some effect upon the outcome of the case in order for that question to be raised for consideration. An Icelandic court cannot decide of its own accord to let EEA rules govern the outcome of the case if no argument to such effect is being advanced by the respective parties. In such circumstances it follows *eo ipso* that an advisory opinion would not be obtained, and also would not be necessary to enable the court to render judgment in the case. It must be noted at the same time that procedural rules will only have this effect in civil lawsuits and not in criminal cases, over which the parties do not have similar control.

III. THE CASE LAW OF THE SUPREME COURT OF ICELAND FROM 1994 TO 2014

Having mentioned these basic background elements, it will be appropriate to refer briefly to statistical information. In reviewing the number of cases where the courts of Iceland have submitted requests for an advisory opinion, it must be kept in mind that the total number of inhabitants of the country is only approximately 325,000. The figures here involved must be evaluated accordingly with specific regard to the limited size of the community and therewith of the judicial system, although the number of cases before the courts from time to time certainly is much greater than might be expected, judging by the number of inhabitants alone. Over the period since the EFTA Court commenced its activity, it appears, as far as may be ascertained, that a total of 27 requests for an advisory opinion have in fact been received from the Icelandic courts as per 1 May 2014, with four of these presumably awaiting resolution before the EFTA Court. Out of these 27 instances, the EFTA Court did receive 11 requests for an advisory opinion directly from the District Courts, and up to now four of the cases there involved have been dealt with on the merits by the Supreme Court after being decided in the lower court following receipt of the advisory opinion. In 10 further instances, a District Court had pronounced a ruling for requesting an advisory opinion which was subsequently referred to the Supreme Court by summary appeal and was affirmed there with or without alteration, while in one case the District Court had denied a motion for requesting an opinion by a ruling that was challenged with the result of its findings being reversed by the

Supreme Court. In all of these 22 instances it appears that the litigating parties, one or both, had made a claim for an advisory opinion to be requested, but this by no means excludes the alternative of the issue having been raised with the parties by the District Court judge in some of the instances and the parties subsequently formulating a claim on that account. Lastly, in five instances the Supreme Court has itself requested an advisory opinion, three of which were at its own initiative.

These 27 instances where an opinion has been requested of course merely represent one side of the story, since it must also be relevant in this context to evaluate how often this has not been done. That question is not easy to answer, seeing that this presumably would be very difficult to determine with any certainty as far as the District Courts are concerned. However, reviewing the cases brought before the Supreme Court may indicate the general practice in this respect. An examination of these cases reveals that in 16 instances, rulings of District Courts denying a motion for requesting an advisory opinion have been challenged and brought before the Supreme Court and have there been affirmed. In four additional instances, rulings to the effect of requesting an advisory opinion have been challenged and reversed by the Supreme Court. A record has not specifically been kept of the number of instances where a motion for requesting an advisory opinion has been set forth and rejected during the processing of a case before the Supreme Court, but I believe it may safely be asserted that these are relatively few.

Now a question arises as to how often issues relating to EEA rules are specifically put to the test in cases brought before the Supreme Court. In the time that has passed since 1994, it seems that only 19 such cases were brought before the Supreme Court without an advisory opinion being procured, in two of which a motion for seeking an opinion had previously been denied, and which accordingly are included in the figures already given so that in fact these instances number 17 in total. To sum up, it thus may be said that over a period of 20 years, the Supreme Court has received a total of 64 cases where EEA rules have been put to the test in one way or another. In 17 cases, that is 26.5% of these instances, it appears that no question was raised by the parties as to whether an advisory opinion should be requested, whereas a motion for request was denied in 20 cases or 31.3% of the instances, and granted in 27 cases or 42.2% of said instances.

IV. THE DECIDING FACTORS FOR THE ICELANDIC COURTS

To conclude, I wish to try to extract in summary fashion the material factors which appear to have the greatest weight according to Icelandic judicial practice with respect to the issue of whether an advisory opinion should be requested from the EFTA Court. For simplification, it is tempting to explain the instances where this has been done by the mere assertion that the thing does speak for itself: that the issue has arisen by virtue of a case calling for interpretation of an Icelandic legal rule which has come to exist by reason of the introduction of an EEA rule, and that the courts have found it necessary to obtain an opinion for the purpose of interpreting the EEA rule and thereby the Icelandic legal rule in order to be able to give judgment in the respective case, as is indeed provided for in paragraph 2 of Article 34 of the SCA. Subsequently, the question arises as to what may have been the cause in 37 instances where an advisory opinion was not requested. First, it should be noted that in 17 of these instances, no motion for making a request was advanced by the parties to the case. In one instance, it was expressly stated in the District Court judgment that an opinion had not been sought in the case because no demand to that effect was made by the parties, while this in itself should not have been of decisive influence, whether according to the Icelandic Act of 1994 or paragraph 2 of Article 34 of the SCA. The reality, however, is that judges of civil cases, at least in the District Courts, are likely to refrain from exercising their power to request an opinion in their own capacity if the parties do not respond to such an idea in a positive manner. In that regard it will no doubt be of material significance that costs will be incurred in the procurement of an advisory opinion. This aspect should, however, not have too strong an influence in those cases where a judge wishes to seek an opinion of his own accord, seeing that the Act of 1994 does provide that litigating parties, who have not requested an opinion, should be granted legal aid from the State Treasury in respect of the cost of its procurement. A further matter of consequence for the parties, which may possibly weigh more heavily in actual practice, is that the request for an opinion may delay the pursuit of a case by up to a year, which can be of some effect under prevailing standards in Iceland, where people have become used to the concept that it generally need not take more than two years to complete the process of a lawsuit through the two-tiered court system.

Reflecting upon Icelandic judicial practice and aside from the aforementioned considerations, the most common reasons for not requesting an advisory opinion, highlighted either expressly in a court's decision or inherent in its findings, are as follows: first, when it is found evident upon proper assessment that EEA rules will be of no material relevance to the resolution of a case, either because the issues in dispute clearly do not fall within the scope of any such rule, or because other legal aspects obviously will have the effect of enabling a conclusion to be reached without an EEA rule being put to the test. This patently has, either alone or together with other considerations, governed the result in 10 out of the 20 instances where the courts have rejected the demand of a party for requesting an advisory opinion. Second, the demand for seeking an advisory opinion in four of these 20 instances was rejected by reference either to the existence of clear precedent from the EFTA Court or the European Court of Justice concerning the interpretation of the pertinent EEA rule, or to the fact of an advisory opinion of the EFTA Court on the same issue being awaited in another pending case. Third, the position in three of these 20 instances was that even though the interpretation of EEA rules potentially applicable could be regarded as a matter of some doubt, a corresponding doubt did not surround the Icelandic legal rules applicable to the same matter, and the divergence between the national law and the EEA rules was found to be such as to afford no room for a solution by means of interpretation of the national rule as contemplated in the aforesaid Article 3 of the Icelandic Act of 1993. Finally, it may be noted that in three of the said instances, a motion for requesting an advisory opinion was denied due to the fact that the party raising the motion did not present arguments which could have provided grounds for applying EEA rules, even though they possibly might otherwise have been of relevance.

In several of these 20 instances, elements other than those specifically referred to in the foregoing also may have been underlying factors leading to the result that an advisory opinion was not requested. Thus in seven instances, the reason given for the result included, beside other factors, a reference to the ground that an established judicial practice concerning the resolution of the issue at hand already did exist on the basis of precedent for the interpretation of Icelandic laws, in respect to which an advisory opinion could not make any difference.

V. FINAL REMARKS

Following this overview of statistical information, there is reason to emphasise that the information relates in comprehensive manner to a period of about 20 years, and that the incidence of references from the Icelandic courts to the EFTA Court naturally has been subject to fluctuations within this period. The greatest fluctuation has been experienced in the period since 2008, which was obviously initiated by the collapse of the Icelandic banking system and the cases necessarily coming to be handled within the Icelandic judicial system in consequence thereof. The number of requests from Iceland for an advisory opinion has increased in a proportionately large extent over this latter period. This trend may of course be traced to the fact that the issues arising in the cases regarding the financial meltdown revolve around Icelandic statutory provisions introduced on account of parallel EEA rules to a greater extent than is usually the case. The proportion of the instances where an advisory opinion has been requested, out of the total number of cases where EEA rules may potentially come into play, has neither risen nor fallen by reason of these consequences of the economic collapse, but the number of relevant cases has increased as such, with the number of advisory opinions having increased in proportion therewith.

There is fair reason to raise the question whether the situation in Iceland may develop to some other effect over the coming years, when the tide of court cases connected with the economic collapse will have ebbed away. Presumably, this will lead to a decrease in the number of requests for an advisory opinion, but it may very well be argued that the proportion of requests actually made out of the number of cases potentially calling for the interpretation of EEA rules will, nevertheless, come to be higher than in the years leading up to 2008. In this respect it is likely to be of material significance not only that over this challenging period of time, Icelandic judges have come to acquire a greater familiarity with assessing whether specific cases do call for attention of the EFTA Court and, subsequently, making use of advisory opinions. Furthermore, the experience gained by the Icelandic courts from this interaction with the EFTA Court has provided an incentive towards increasing it further still.

10

'To Refer or Not to Refer?' Confession of a National Judge

GEORGES RAVARANI

A NATIONAL JUDGE of an EU Member State is in permanent contact with EU law. Many areas of national law are inspired or even copied from EU directives, not to mention EU regulations. In administrative law, the influence of the EU is particularly strong. One has only to think of immigration law, procurement law, environmental law, even fiscal law.

It is especially in these highly technical economic areas that a judge trying to apply and to construe law has to deal not only with national law, but also with EU law.

Luxembourg courts have a long-standing tradition of admitting the superiority of international treaties that have been regularly approved by the national legislator. Since a judgment by the Court of Cassation of 1950,[1] Luxembourg courts consider the relevant provisions as if they were domestic law of a superior essence and regularly set aside national law if they consider it contrary to international law. It was therefore no revolution in the Luxembourg legal system when the EU treaties were adopted and EU law introduced. Its superiority was immediately recognised by the national courts and the examples of setting aside national law as being contrary to EU law are countless.

However, admitting the superiority of international law is one thing, construing it is another.

Trying to apply and to construe national law in a consistent way is not an easy thing. Each country has established at the top of its judicial hierarchy a supreme judicial body responsible for a consistent interpretation and application of the law. Concerning EU law, it is obvious that national courts, even on top of the hierarchy, can simply not do the job. What if the French *Cour de cassation* and the German *Bundesgerichtshof* differ concerning the meaning of the same provision?

---

[1] Court of Cassation 8 June 1950, Pasicrisie luxembourgeoise vol 15, p 41. The Council of State, supreme administrative court until 1996, adopted the same solution shortly afterwards; see CE 28 July 1951, Pasicrisie luxembourgeoise vol 15, p 263.

The obligation to refer to the supra-national Court of Justice of the European Union (ECJ) aims to prevent such situations.

However, if every pleading, every affirmation, each question about EU law ended up in front of the ECJ, this Court would be flooded with all sorts of questions, many of them not only being duplications of similar questions, but even being plainly trivial. There intervenes a very important aspect of EU law. In fact, the ECJ is not the only 'European' court, but each national court, from the first to the last instance, is a European court insofar as it almost daily applies and also construes European law.

As pleading advocates very often make things more difficult than they are and like to delay matters by asking the national court to submit a specific problem to the ECJ for a preliminary ruling, the national judge is quite often confronted with the question: to refer or not to refer?

The problems that may occur will be addressed in two stages: (I) what are the theoretical, practical and psychological hurdles the national judge then has to face, and (II) what if he wrongfully refrains from referring?

I. AN OBLIGATION TO REFER?

Everyone knows that if a question of interpretation of EU law arises before a national judge, a lower court may, and a last instance court must, refer to the ECJ, according to the criteria listed in the *CILFIT* judgment of the ECJ issued in 1982.[2]

Yet, the judge first has to clear some psychological hurdles: the most obvious and the least avowable is the fear of exposing himself: it is not easy to know your national law, but which national judge can boast of being a genuine specialist in EU law? He very often simply does not know whether the question is relevant enough, if it is material, or if it has already been answered by a former judgment of the ECJ. It is indeed not exactly refreshing to learn some time after he has asked a certain question that it has already been clearly answered by the ECJ. Nor is it comfortable if the Court of Justice declares a question inadmissible.

So the national judge has to show some courage to step outside the comfort of his own court and to address such a prestigious court as the ECJ.

He also sometimes has to show the courage *not* to refer a certain question. What if there is a question about what is the tariff classification of nightdresses if there is already a solution for pyjamas? This has also to be seen in the context of permanent complaints from the ECJ about overloading and the never-ending discussion of establishing filters.

By the way, the question of overloading risks becoming much more alarming in the near future as a consequence of the entering into force of the Charter of Fundamental Rights, which risks triggering an avalanche of questions. Besides

---

[2] Case C-283/81 *Srl CILFIT and Lanificio di Gavardo SpA v Ministry of Health* [1982] ECR-3415.

the risk of overloading the ECJ, there is another aspect that could lead a national judge to take the decision not to refer a question on fundamental rights: first, whereas economic, environmental and other topics are highly technical and a national judge is very often more than glad to benefit from the expertise of the European judges, fundamental rights are historically part of the core business, of the daily dealings, of each national judge. How often should he abandon the solution of matters that belong to his noblest responsibilities to international judges? Moreover, there has been an international court dealing with human rights since 1953, controlling and federating national case law on matters of human rights. The system established by the European Convention on Human Rights is of a fundamentally different nature: it allows the national judge to give a solution and exercises a control *a posteriori* whereas the ECJ exercises an *a priori* competence. The questions generated by the double competence of two international courts and two different control systems are multiple and complex. For example, has the national judge really to refer if he can rely on a well-established case law of the Strasbourg judges on a provision with the same content? Indeed, most of the fundamental rights of the Charter can also be found in the European Convention on Human Rights. On the other hand, what happens if a national court refers to the ECJ, complies with the given solution in its subsequent judgment and if the same national judgment is attacked in Strasbourg and the judges of the European Court of Human Rights (ECtHR) detect a violation of the Convention? It is really astonishing, at the very least, that we are now confronted with overlapping competences of two international courts in almost identical matters, yet without clear solutions. This triggers many problems that could probably have been easily avoided when the Charter was elaborated and implemented.

Another aspect should not be neglected in this respect: whereas the *a posteriori* control by the ECHR takes into account the concrete facts of the case, the *a priori* answers in the same area by the ECJ risk not being really helpful as too theoretical.

A concrete example taken from Luxembourg case law illustrates this concern. It does not precisely deal with the Charter but with the Council Directive 2004/83/EC of 29 April 2004 on minimum standards for the qualification and status of third-country nationals or stateless persons as refugees or as persons who otherwise need international protection and the content of the protection granted,[3] but both instruments deal with fundamental rights that also fall under the protection of the European Convention on Human Rights. The Luxembourg *Cour administrative*[4] was faced with a request for asylum by an Algerian national who claimed to be homosexual. He referred to the judgment rendered by the ECJ on 7 November 2013[5] in which the Court held that Article 10(1)(d) of Directive

---

[3] OJ L 304, p 12.
[4] Since 1997, the *Cour administrative* is the supreme administrative court of the Grand-Duchy of Luxembourg.
[5] Joint Cases C-199/12 to C-201/12 *Asiel v X, Y* and *Z v Minister voor Immigratie en Asiel*, judgment of 7 November 2013, nyr, paras 49, 61 and 76.

2004/83/EC must be interpreted as meaning that the existence of criminal laws which specifically target homosexuals supports the finding that those persons must be regarded as forming a particular social group; that Article 9(1), read together with Article 9(2)(c), must be interpreted as meaning that the criminalisation of homosexual acts *per se* does not constitute an act of persecution but that a term of imprisonment which sanctions homosexual acts and which is actually applied in the country of origin which adopted such legislation must be regarded as being a punishment which is disproportionate or discriminatory and thus constitutes an act of persecution, and finally that Article 10(1)(d), read together with Article 2(c), must be interpreted as meaning that only homosexual acts which are criminal in accordance with the national law of the Member States are excluded from its scope. The ECJ stresses that when assessing an application for refugee status, the competent authorities cannot reasonably expect, in order to avoid the risk of persecution, the applicant for asylum to conceal his homosexuality in his country of origin or to exercise reserve in the expression of his sexual orientation.

Articles 333 and 338 of the Algerian penal code specifically punish homosexual acts by imprisonment. The asylum seeker adduced evidence that in his country of origin, in 2010, an imam and his friend had been sentenced to two years' imprisonment for a homosexual relationship and that two young homosexuals who had announced on Facebook their intention to marry, asking the Algerian authorities to follow the example of the French movement of 'marriage for everybody', had been placed in provisional detention.

In its order of 6 February 2014,[6] the *Cour administrative* underlined that it is true that the ECJ poses no restriction on the ostentatious or provocative character of the behaviour that may give rise to a repressive attitude of the government, posing as the sole criterion the effective implementation of prison sentences against homosexuals because of their sexual orientation. The court, however, stressed that in order to be considered as sufficiently reasonable grounds for granting refugee status, criminalisation should not touch only particularly exposed people on whom the authorities attempt to set a public example, but should be applied indiscriminately and generally to all persons in the situation described. It found that deciding otherwise, and not to consider specifically what are the *effective and concrete* risks of imprisonment and ill-treatment by the authorities faced by people who claim to be homosexual, could lead to reverse discriminatory treatment of heterosexuals who cannot refer to the mere fact of belonging to a certain ethnic or social minority group to qualify almost automatically for refugee status in the Member State of their choice, but must also establish that they have, because of belonging to such a group, suffered persecution or have real and concrete reasons to fear suffering if they return to their country of origin.

The administrative court held that the claimant had not established that the Algerian authorities apply imprisonment of homosexuals as a general rule.

---

[6] *Cour administrative*, 6 February 2014, no 33641C, available on www.jurad.etat.lu.

There is a scarcely hidden unhappiness about the ECJ's judgment: the national judges have difficulty in accepting that the problem of the ostentatious behaviour of homosexuals is resolved in a few lines only whereas this aspect, according to the *Cour administrative*, represents a core problem: on the one hand, in most countries homosexuals can live a quiet life so long as they do not publicise their sexual orientation too much, and in the other, accepting the open claim to be homosexual as an automatic asylum claim is, bluntly, somewhat unrealistic: it is simply too easy to play the comedy in the Member State where the request for asylum is introduced and to put the national authorities before a true problem of numbers of people entitled to claim refugee status (one cannot, for obvious reasons, ask for evidence that in the country of origin the asylum seeker has effectively had homosexual activities). The problem is similar with persecution for religious motives. According to a ruling of the ECJ, the authorities cannot reasonably expect people not to manifest their religious practices externally.[7]

The underlying problem is the theoretical, *a priori* approach and solution of human rights problems by the ECJ, whereas the ECtHR exercises a very effective, concrete *a posteriori* control that takes into account all the relevant facts of the specific case.

If the judge actually decides to refer a question to the ECJ, he has to draft the question in a way acceptable to the ECJ. It is true that the ECJ tries not to be too demanding with national courts as far as this aspect is concerned, but there have been rejections. Moreover the ECJ from time to time issues a *vademecum* with indications how to formulate questions and how to draft the referring judgment. There again, there is the fear that the national judge will not comply with the requirements and thus expose himself to criticisms.

Another aspect is that, despite the substantial efforts of the ECJ to shorten proceedings, the total duration of the proceedings is seriously extended. This has to be seen in the context of the requirement of Article 6 of the European Convention on Human Rights to issue judgments within a reasonable time.

So the balance between taking one's own responsibilities and shifting into unacceptable autonomy, between a certain degree of confidence of the ECJ into national courts and the exercise of an absolute control of the EU case law, will always be difficult to find.

Sometimes the national judge simply does not see or accept that there is an unsolved question of EU law. This can be qualified as a minor offence.

What, however, if the judge clearly sees that there is such a question but dislikes the look of the solution he will have to accept from the ECJ? There are indeed, from time to time, very important issues where the national courts do not like to lose control of the case, be it for political or economic or whatever reasons. Then

---

[7] Joint Cases C-71/11 and C-91/11 *Bundesrepublik Deutschland v Y and Z*, judgment of 5 September 2012, nyr.

the temptation or even the pressure to see an *acte clair* where in fact there is only darkness is very strong.

Two examples from relatively recent Luxembourg cases illustrate this. The issue was precisely the economic, financial consequences of a certain potential ruling by the ECJ.

(1)   Before the *Cour administrative*, there was the problem of subsidies that, by a national law, are granted to firms that hire unemployed workers over the age of 45 years, and which can only be claimed by firms for workers who are registered with the Luxembourg employment agency and not for workers registered with foreign labour offices, irrespective their place of residence.

By order of 14 July 2011,[8] the court referred the question of the compatibility of this provision with Articles 21 and 45 of the Treaty of the Functioning of the EU to the ECJ.

The ECJ ruled on 13 December 2012.[9] It found that the national regulation was contrary to EU law. In a subsequent order of 22 January 2013,[10] the *Cour administrative* set aside the national law.

The supremacy of EU law was thus plainly assured.

(2)   The Luxembourg Court of Cassation was faced with a related problem with much more far-reaching implications. A German citizen living in Luxembourg had lost his job with a Luxembourg firm and had been granted unemployment compensation. At a certain moment, the agency notified the German citizen that it had found out that he had moved to Germany and, as the said aid was conditional on his residence in Luxembourg territory, he was no longer entitled to benefit from the aid in question. He challenged the decision and lost in the two first instances. In the cassation procedure, the advocate general, after a thorough analysis of recent EU case law, especially recent developments concerning atypical EU workers, asked the court to refer the question to the ECJ. In its order, issued months after the pleadings, the Court of Cassation rejected the appeal by referring to older ECJ judgments concerning atypical workers and without losing a single word about the recent developments in that area.[11]

It is absolutely clear that this order is politically motivated, against the background that in a country of 500,000 inhabitants there is a group of 150,000 workers living in France, Belgium and Germany coming to work in Luxembourg each day and who could potentially be compensated by the Luxembourg labour agency if they

---

[8]   *Cour administrative*, 14 July 2011, no 27203C, available on www.jurad.etat.lu.
[9]   Case C-379/11 *Caves Krier Frères Sàrl v Directeur de l'Administration de l'emploi*, judgment of 13 December 2012, para 55.
[10]   *Cour administrative*, 22 January 2013, no 27303C, available on www.jurad.etat.lu.
[11]   Court of Cassation, 12 February 2009, no 9/09, no 2590 of the registry.

lost their job, which could seriously endanger the ability of the Grand-Duchy to finance the compensation system.

The difference between the case before the *Cour administrative* and the Court of cassation is obvious: if there is a ruling by the ECJ that the system, whereby an unemployed person over the age of 45 years must be registered with the national employment agency and reside on Luxembourg territory in order to be hired by a Luxembourg firm, is declared contrary to EU law, the whole law on subsidies, including for domestic workers, will probably have to be abolished. What to do, however, if the system of unemployment compensation is no longer reserved for workers residing in the country? There is no way out and the system would financially collapse. So, in the case that the Court of Cassation had to deal with, the EU law was simply too dangerous to be applied.

This leads us to the second question: may a national court, in its discretion and despite an obvious problem of application and interpretation of EU law, refrain from referring to the ECJ?

II. LIABILITY FOR NOT REFERRING?

A court is clearly not allowed to refrain, in its discretion, from referring to the ECJ if there is a question of EU law to be construed. Doing so triggers the liability of the Member State whose courts disregard EU law. This flows from the famous *Köbler* judgment of the ECJ from 30 September 2003[12] where the ECJ held that individuals have, under certain circumstances (as in the *Francovich* judgment[13]) a right to compensation if a national court has, by manifestly disregarding or wrongly applying EU law, caused a personal loss to the said party.

So, in theory, a national court cannot bluntly set aside EU law or construe it in an obviously wrongful way without being made liable for the loss caused, at least indirectly via the liability of the State—a court being an emanation of the State.

The *Köbler* judgment goes a long way in setting aside the fictitious invariable truth in the protection of a national court order by the *res judicata* rule, even if the national judgment is final and emanates from a supreme or last instance court.

The impact of the *Köbler* case is far from being theoretical. The Luxembourg Court of Appeal was recently seized with such a liability case. In a very complicated labour law case, a German citizen claimed that German law was applicable, but the Luxembourg courts, up to the Court of Cassation, had held that Luxembourg law was applicable. The German worker then claimed that by way of obvious violation of the Rome Convention on contractual obligations[14]—in the

---

[12] Case C-224/01 *Gerhard Köbler v Republik Österreich* [2003] ECR I-10239.
[13] Joined Cases C-6/90 and C-9/90 *Andrea Francovich and Danila Bonifaci and others v Italian Republic* [1991] ECR I-5357.
[14] Convention 80/934/ECC on the law applicable to contractual obligations opened for signature in Rome on 19 June 1980, OJ L 266, p 1.

meantime replaced by the Rome I Regulation[15] (which is not exactly EU law, but that is to be interpreted in a consistent way by the ECJ, the national courts being obliged to refer if there is a problem of interpretation[16])—the Luxembourg courts had caused him a loss and he sued the Luxembourg State for damages. In the first instance the district court thoroughly examined and appreciated the findings of the Court of Cassation (one has to remember that a lower court appreciates the findings of the highest court) but found that the said court had not misapplied the relevant Regulation. In the appeal proceedings, the Court of Appeal dealt at length with setting aside *res judicata* issues and showed all the problems this could generate. The Court of Appeal finally found that the question of the applicability of German or Luxembourg law was not obvious and in the context of State liability for wrongly applying EU law, it referred the relevant question to the ECJ.[17] The ECJ rendered its judgment on 15 March 2011.[18] It stated that it flows from the Rome Convention that if a worker fulfils his obligations in more than one contracting State, the law applicable to his employment contract is the law of the State where he carries out most of his obligations towards his employer. In the subsequent judgment of 21 March 2012,[19] the Court of Appeal, applying this criterion, found that German law was applicable. So, clearly, all the former courts, including the Court of Cassation, had been wrong in declaring Luxembourg law applicable to the employment contract. However, by way of very complicated reasoning that cannot be detailed here, the court held that the initial claim for compensation for illegal termination of the employment contract was time-barred and, consequently, it was ultimately not the wrongful application of the Luxembourg law that was at the origin of the failure of his lawsuit. It consequently dismissed the claim for damages based on a violation, by Luxembourg courts, of EU law, ultimately for a lack of causation. The German citizen has now the theoretical possibility to launch a new liability claim against the State, challenging the findings of this new judgment.

This shows that the bottom line is that there are two fundamental problems with the *Köbler* system:

1)   First, what if in a liability case based on *Köbler*, a party loses because in a so-called final judgment, the highest court finds that there has been no violation of EU law? He can challenge—without being prevented from doing so by *res judicata*—in a new claim the judgment that dismissed his claim, and so on. It is a vicious circle, but only in one direction: the final point is only reached

---

[15] Regulation (EC) No 593/2008 of the European Parliament and of the Council of 17 June 2008 on the law applicable to contractual obligations (Rome I), OJ L 177, p 6.

[16] The Court of Appeal raised the question whether the Rome Convention was, in respect of the *Köbler* case, to be considered as EU law and stated that it was rather private international law, but examined nevertheless the former findings of the Court of Cassation.

[17] Court of Appeal, 13 January 2010, no 33827 of the registry.

[18] Case C-29/10 *Heiko Kölzsch v État du Grand Duchy of Luxemburg* [2011] ECR I-1595.

[19] No 33827(bis) of the registry.

once he finds a court that finally accepts his claim. Because then the State cannot sue for compensation because of a wrongful functioning of the courts. The State would have to direct its claim against itself.

2) Second, and more fundamentally, the ECJ is a toothless tiger; it is unable to directly sanction Member States for a wrongful application of EU law by national courts in individual cases. The final word remains with the national courts that have to decide, in a liability case, whether their fellow national courts obviously violated EU law. If they find that there was no such violation, *Köbler* will remain largely ineffective.

So, in some sense, the whole system of reference to the ECJ is based on the willingness of the national courts to play the game.

11

Efficient Judicial Protection of EEA Rights in the EFTA Pillar—Different Role for the National Judge?

SKÚLI MAGNÚSSON

I. A 'COHERENT SYSTEM OF JUDICIAL PROTECTION' IN THE EEA?

IT IS DEBATABLE to what extent the drafters of the Treaties founding the European Communities intended Community law to form a 'coherent and complete system of judicial protection of individuals and economic operators inspired by the Rule of Law'—even to what extent such conception was inherent to the 'New Legal Order of International Law' affirmed in *Van Gend en Loos* and subsequent case law.[1] However, when negotiations on the European Economic Area were concluded in 1991, the ECJ had, by then, firmly established the Communities as a legal order based on the Rule of Law where neither the Member States nor the Community institutions could avoid review under the Communities' 'Constitutional Charter'.[2] This, in turn, underpinned the judicial development of the *principle of effective judicial protection* which has now been codified by recent Treaty amendments.[3]

The EU system of judicial protection has been depicted as one of *interlocking jurisdictions* of the ECJ on the one hand, and the national courts of the Member States on the other.[4] Although judicial review can take place directly before the ECJ, requirements concerning *locus standi* will in many cases preclude a direct

---

[1] Nevertheless, in Case C-26/62 *Van Gend en Loos* [1963] ECR 1 the ECJ stressed that 'the States have acknowledged that Community law has an authority which can be invoked by their nationals before those courts and tribunals' referring to the preliminary reference procedure the object of which 'is to secure uniform interpretation of the Treaty by national courts and tribunals'.

[2] *Cf* in particular Case C-294/83 *Parti écologiste 'Les Verts' v European Parliament* [1986] ECR 1339.

[3] *Cf* Art 19(2) TEU and Art 47 of the Charter of Fundamental Rights, which provides for the right to an effective remedy and to a fair trial. Furthermore, Art 2 TEU refers to the rule of law. This codification must be seen in light of the judicial development of the principle of effective judicial protection; *cf* particular discussion in Case 432/05 *Unibet* [2007] ECR I-2271, para 36ff.

[4] *Cf* K Lenaerts, 'The Rule of Law and the Coherence of the Judicial System of the European Union' (2007) 44 *Common Market Law Review* 1625–1658. See also P Lasok, T Millett, *Judicial Control in the EU* [Richmond Law & Tax 2004], pp 164–167 and DWK Anderson, *References to the European Court* [London, Sweet & Maxwell 2002], pp 20–26.

action by a private party. Hence, if the system is to live up to expectations with regard to 'completeness', an action should, in these circumstances, be possible before the courts of a Member State. If, on the other hand, 'coherence' is to be achieved, these courts should refer relevant questions of EU law to the ECJ during some stage of the proceedings.

In the overall picture of the EU judicial mechanism which emerges, each and every judge of the Member States who potentially deals with and applies EU law is considered a member of an EU judiciary without which the ECJ would be unable to carry out its principal function, namely to ensure that in the interpretation and application of the Treaties the law is observed (*cf* Article 19 para 1 TEU). Another, less attractive aspect of the 'interlocking jurisdictions' is the tendency to consider the preliminary reference procedure the main access to justice for private parties which, in turn, advocates for a strict interpretation with regard to *locus standi* in direct actions.[5] Whatever one may think of the merits of this case law, it underscores the role of the national judge as a key actor in enforcing rights under EU law.[6]

This element of the EU legal order raises a question of principle concerning judicial protection in the EFTA pillar of the European Economic Area. Can we assume that there is also a 'coherent and complete system of judicial protection of individuals and economic operators inspired by the Rule of Law' under EEA law? However, this also raises more specific questions concerning the role of the national judge as regards the judicial protection of EEA rights and her relations with the EFTA Court, whose 20th anniversary we now celebrate. Although touching upon the principle of effective judicial protection, my focus in this chapter is these latter questions.

II. JUDICIAL PROTECTION OF EEA RIGHTS—PROCEDURAL HOMOGENEITY

The Preamble to the EEA Agreement refers to the 'role of individuals through the exercise of their rights and through the judicial defence of these rights'. It also emphasises the objective of arriving at and maintaining a uniform interpretation of the EEA and parallel provisions of EU law as well as the achievement of the 'equal treatment of individuals and economic operators as regards the four freedoms and the conditions of competition'. Lastly, the Preamble refers generally to human rights, one of which is generally considered to be the right to fair procedure, *cf* in particular Article 6 ECHR.[7]

---

[5] *Cf* Case C-25/62 *Plauman* [1963] ECR 95. For a restatement of *Plauman*, *cf Inuit Tapiriit Kanatami*, judgment of 3 October 2013 in Case C-583/11, published electronically, at para 71.

[6] See, eg, discussion in Case C-210/06 *Cartesio* [2008] ECR I-09641 on the role of the national judge where it was concluded that Art 267 TFEU precludes national rules which permit a higher court, upon a procedural appeal, to vary an order for reference by a lower court or to set it aside. In his Opinion in the case, Advocate-General Maduro considered that an opposite conclusion would undermine the principle of each and any national court of a Member State being equally a court of the EU (*cf* para 20 of the Opinion).

[7] 1st, 8th and 15th recitals of the Preamble to the EEA Agreement. The EFTA Court has referred to Art 6 ECHR in relation to fundamental rights on various occasion; see, eg, Case E-2/03 *Ásgeirsson* [2003] EFTA Ct Rep 185.

It is submitted on this basis that the EEA Agreement is founded on the presumption that the enforcement of EEA rules, including at the judicial level in the EFTA States, should not only be adequate but also comparable to what is the case within the EU. In this sense, the principle of homogeneity exceeds the boundaries of the substantive provisions of the EEA. This rationale is, for instance, well demonstrated in *DB Schenker I* where the EFTA Court stated that the objective of establishing a dynamic and homogeneous European Economic Area could only be achieved 'if EFTA and EU citizens and economic operators, relying upon EEA law, enjoy the same rights in both the EU and EFTA pillars of the EEA'.[8] In recent case law, the EFTA Court has referred to this aspect of the EEA Agreement as *procedural homogeneity*.[9] In *Posten Norge* it was recalled that this principle serves to ensure equal access to justice for individuals and economic operators throughout the EEA.[10] Moreover, in *HOB-vín III* the Court stipulated that homogeneity cannot be limited to the interpretation of provisions whose wording is identical in substance to parallel provisions of EU law.[11]

In this regard, it is important to note that procedural homogeneity does not mean that the effects and enforcement of EEA rules will always be identical to EU law in each and every case. Thus, differences in the text of the EEA Agreement, or its implicit premises, can result in different conclusions.[12] But procedural homogeneity does imply that, other things being equal, the EEA EFTA States should, by and large, live up to the same standards as the Union pillar with regard to the enforcement and effectiveness of rules, protection of rights, workings of the institutions, etc. This, in turn, may, perhaps surprisingly, necessitate a different interpretation of EEA rules in certain cases if substantive equality between those operating in the EFTA pillar and the EU pillar is to be achieved.[13]

---

[8] *Cf* Case E-14/11 *Schenker North* [2012] EFTA Ct Rep p 1178, para 118. Similarly, in *European Banking Federations*, the EFTA Court had stated that 'in the interest of equal treatment and foreseeability' for parties appearing before the ECJ, the CFI and the EFTA Court a provision on costs should be interpreted and applied in the same way unless specific circumstances would justify different treatment (order of the EFTA Court in Case E-9/04 *The Bankers' and Securities' Dealers Association of Iceland v EFTA Surveillance Authority* [2007] EFTA Ct Rep 74, para 16).

[9] *Cf* Case E-18/10 *ESA v Norway* [2011] EFTA Ct Rep 202, para 26 and Case E-15/10 *Posten Norge* [2012] EFTA Ct Rep 246, para 109. Analysing this principle prior to EFTA Court case law in a paper published in 2010, I used the term *institutional homogeneity* ('On the Authority of Advisory opinions' (2010) 13 *Europarättslig tidskrift* 3, pp 528–551). See, for further discussion, R Spanó, 'Doing Justice in the EEA—The Concept of Procedural Homogeneity' in EFTA Court (ed), *Judicial Protection in the European Economic Area* (Stuttgart, German Law Publishers, 2012), pp 151–160.

[10] *Cf Posten Norge*, para 109, above n 9.

[11] See order of the Court 31 October 2013 in Case E-2/12, para 9.

[12] The EEA is based on the premise that it is does not entail transfer of legislative powers which prevents the applicability of the principles of direct effect and supremacy. If there was ever any ambiguity concerning this, the issue was clarified in Case E-1/07 *Criminal Proceedings Against A* [2007] EFTA Ct Rep 246, para 40).

[13] On this basis I have been critical of the view that there exists a parallel between EU law and EEA law with respect to the substance of State liability and its material conditions. See S Magnússon and Ó Ísberg Hannesson, 'State Liability in EEA Law: Towards Parallelism or Homogeneity?' [2013] 38 *European Law Review*, Issue 2.

Irrespective of procedural homogeneity, the EEA Agreement, in its own right, aims to ensure the judicial protection of individual rights under EEA law. Thus, in its case law, the EFTA Court has held (without referring to EU law) that the provisions of the EEA Agreement are, to a large extent, 'intended for the benefit of individuals and economic operators' and that the proper functioning of the EEA is 'dependent on those individuals and economic operators being able to rely on their rights before the national courts of the EFTA/EEA States'.[14] Furthermore, the EFTA Court has described the EEA as a legal order 'characterised by the protection of the rights of individuals and economic operators and by an institutional framework providing for effective surveillance and judicial review'.[15] In *Posten Norge* the Court completed this train of thought and confirmed *effective judicial protection* as a principle generally applicable to the EEA Agreement.[16]

III. EFTA COURT PRELIMINARY REFERENCE PROCEDURE—CHOICE OR NECESSITY?

While rights under EU law are, to a great extent, enforced before national courts, Article 267(3) TFEU ensures that questions of EU law are resolved by the ECJ by making a reference to the ECJ obligatory when such questions are raised in a case pending before a court or tribunal of last resort. At first sight, a similar system would seem necessary for the EFTA pillar in order to preserve homogeneity of EEA law and avoiding lack of equality and reciprocity vis-à-vis the EU pillar. Furthermore, as will be discussed below, considerations of effective judicial protection advocate for access to a Court which is competent to give a final ruling on rights and obligations under EEA law.

In spite of the apparent importance of preliminary references for homogeneity and the protection of individual rights, the EEA Agreement, by its Article 107, merely provides for 'the possibility for an EFTA State to allow a court or tribunal to ask the [ECJ] to decide on the interpretation of an EEA rule'. Hence, it could be argued that the drafters of the EEA Agreement envisaged that the ECJ would be giving preliminary rulings to the national courts of the EFTA States ensuring the ECJ as the sole 'guardian of uniform interpretation' of EU law (as well as EEA law).[17] Hence, without dwelling on the issue, I would argue that it was somewhat contrary to the spirit of this provision that the EEA EFTA States decided to establish

---

[14] *Cf* eg Case E-9/97 *Sveinbjörnsdóttir* [1998] EFTA Ct Rep 95 and *Ásgeirsson*, above n 7.

[15] *Ásgeirsson*, above n 7, para 28.

[16] Above n 9. The case concerned direct action proceedings by the state-owned Norwegian Post Service before the EFTA Court and therefore did not touch directly upon any potential requirements flowing from effective judicial protection with regard to national court proceedings. It may be added that, in its reasoning, the Court also referred to Art 47 of the EU Charter of Fundamental Rights; a reference not entirely without a precedent (see Case E-4/11 *Arnulf Clauder* [2011] EFTA Ct Rep 216 at para 49).

[17] The ECJ's discussion of Art 107 EEA in Opinion No 1/92 of 10 April 1992 seems to be based on this understanding of the Agreement.

their own preliminary reference procedure before the EFTA Court.[18] On the other hand, the EFTA Court advisory opinion procedure pursuant to Article 34 SCA was clearly established using the ECJ preliminary reference procedure as a model or, if one prefers, 'inspiration'.[19]

Now, if it is agreed that the EEA EFTA States have an obligation to ensure the proper enforcement of EEA rules and effective judicial protection of EEA rights, it simply cannot follow that these States enjoy an unlimited discretion as to *whether* and *how* they establish, implement and apply a preliminary reference procedure in the EFTA pillar. This follows from the simple fact that without such viable procedure in the EFTA pillar, the homogeneous interpretation and application of EEA rules by national courts obviously cannot be ensured which, in turn, would call into question the very tenets of the Agreement. Total absence of a preliminary reference procedure would also mean that individuals and economic operators in the EFTA pillar lacked access to either of the two European Courts competent to rule on their rights and obligations under EEA law. That state of affairs would clearly be unacceptable with regard to effective judicial protection. Lastly, absence of a preliminary reference procedure in the EFTA pillar would mean an imbalance and lack of equality and reciprocity between the EFTA pillar and the EU pillar.

For these reasons, I have argued that a preliminary reference procedure of some sort is a necessity for the EFTA pillar—a necessity that follows from the general principles and aims of the EEA. Therefore the procedure set up by Article 34 SCA cannot be considered a simple creation of the EFTA States the existence or substance of which is entirely up to their liking. The EEA EFTA States, do, of course, retain the possibility of activating Article 107 EEA and allow their courts to make references for a preliminary ruling to the ECJ (instead of the EFTA Court). It would even be thinkable that these EFTA States would have opted for a radically different approach with regard to the enforcement of EEA rules and the judicial protection of individual rights by creating an entirely different surveillance system. However, if these alternatives are considered undesirable—or even impossible due to constitutional constraints of the EFTA States—it is submitted that a preliminary reference procedure that effectively ensures homogeneity and judicial protection *must be* established in the EFTA pillar.

This assumption may appear ambitious given the fact that nowhere in the EEA Agreement is there a mention of an obligation to this effect. But the alternative, namely that no access to the European Courts through national court procedures is compatible with the EEA Agreement, simply refutes the very essence of the Agreement.

---

[18] By this, I am obviously not implying that this arrangement was not without consent from the EU side.

[19] 'When drafting Art 34 SCA, the EFTA States were inspired by Art 267 TFEU' (Case E-18/11 *Irish Bank* [2012] EFTA Ct Rep 592, para 57).

IV. WHETHER TO REFER—FULL DISCRETION?

It may be thought superfluous, even inappropriate, to discuss at length an obligation incumbent on the EEA EFTA States to submit their courts to a preliminary
reference procedure—after all these States *have established* such procedure by
Article 34 SCA, noted above. However, such a potential obligation has various implications for the implementation and application of Article 34 SCA by
national courts. This is, in particular, due to the fact that, unlike Article 267
TFEU, this provision entails no obligation incumbent on national courts to refer
questions concerning EEA law to the EFTA Court at any stage in the national
proceedings.

It may be noted that the EFTA Court preliminary reference procedure has,
from the outset, been conceived to fullfil similar general functions as the EU preliminary reference procedure, namely to establish cooperation between the EFTA
Court and the national judiciary in order to ensure uniform interpretation by
providing assistance to the courts and tribunals which have to apply provisions
of the EEA Agreement.[20] However, during the first years of the EEA Agreement, it
was assumed by many scholars, albeit without much reflection, that it was entirely
optional for national courts whether or not to refer questions to the EFTA Court
under Article 34 SCA. This assumption was obviously based on a simple reading
of the text of Article 34 SCA without any attention being given to the context.

In a paper published in 2010, I highlighted that the EFTA Court preliminary
reference procedure does not exist in a legal vacuum and argued that a purely
textual interpretation of Article 34 SCA was manifestly insufficient—in fact misleading.[21] In this regard, I also pointed out that national courts are, as agents of
the State, under an obligation to take all appropriate measures to ensure the fulfilment of the Agreement pursuant to the *principle of loyal cooperation, cf* Article
3(1) EEA.[22] It was my conclusion that a contention to the effect that national
courts of the EFTA States were never under any obligation to refer questions for
an advisory opinion seemed unsubstantiated, although widely accepted in Iceland
and Norway at the time.

Since the publication of my paper in 2010 there has been considerable development in the academic debate about the nature of the preliminary reference
procedure. Thus, a number of academics and legal practitioners have concurred
with me that national courts cannot be considered to enjoy full discretion with
regard to this matter.[23] Most importantly, the EFTA Court has discussed the issue
in some detail in recent case law.

---

[20] *Cf* Case E-1/94 *Restamark* [1994–1995] EFTA Ct Rep 15, para 26.
[21] *Cf* 'On the Authority of Advisory opinions', above n 9.
[22] For a fresh and thorough analysis of this issue, see J Temple Lang, 'The Duty of National Courts
to Provide Access to Justice in the EEA' in EFTA Court (ed), *Judicial Protection in the European
Economic Area*, above n 9.
[23] Reference is made to the contributions of John Temple Lang, Siri Teigum and Martin Johansson
in a conference organised by the EFTA Court in Luxembourg on 17 June 2011. Their conference

In *Irish Bank* the Court carefully pointed out that Article 34 SCA contained no obligation on national courts of last resort to make a reference to the EFTA Court. However, the Court stated (using 'pseudo-empirical' vocabulary!) that these courts 'will take due account of the fact that they are bound to fulfil their duty of loyalty under Article 3 EEA'.[24] Furthermore, the Court noted that EFTA citizens and economic operators benefit from the obligation of courts of last resort of the EU Member States to make a reference to the ECJ.[25] This obiter dicta of the Court can be interpreted as a statement of procedural homogeneity whereby the EFTA Court preliminary reference procedure must live up to the same basic functions as the procedure set up in the EU pursuant to Article 267 TFEU.

The EFTA Court's position was to some extent clarified in *Jonsson* where it held that it was 'important that ... questions are referred to the Court under the procedure provided for in Article 34 of the Agreement between the EFTA States on the Establishment of a Surveillance Authority if the legal situation lacks clarity'. Echoing the spirit of cooperation underlying the preliminary reference procedure, it was added that thereby 'unnecessary mistakes in the interpretation and application of EEA law are avoided and the coherence and reciprocity in relation to rights of EEA citizens, including EFTA nationals, in the EU are ensured'.[26] Clearly the Court avoids referring to an 'obligation' in its reasoning in these cases. However, by referring to Article 3 SCA it is made clear that 'whether or not to refer' is not purely optional for the national courts.[27]

In various meetings with national judges during my time as the Registrar of the EFTA Court, I observed that speaking of an 'obligation' incumbent on national courts sometimes seemed to raise somewhat the temperature in the room. Similarly, given the fact that Article 34 SCA only contains a permission to refer for the national judge and contains no outright obligation, I have been accused of giving the EEA Agreement a dramatically different meaning from what was intended by its makers and, thus, becoming guilty of advocating for judicial activism. So, let us pause for a moment and consider the alternative—that there is literally no obligation incumbent on national courts to refer questions of EEA law to the EFTA Court. Let us, furthermore, presume that in a certain EEA EFTA State the courts have the formal or informal policy *never to refer* such questions. It seems that in this imaginary EEA EFTA State, individuals and legal entities have, in fact, no access to a European Court competent to give a final ruling on their rights and obligations under EEA law. Hence, their substantive EEA rights are

---

papers are published in EFTA Court (ed), *Judicial Protection in the European Economic Area*, above n 9. I also refer to a paper published in Icelandic by M Einarsdóttir, 'Ráðgefandi álit EFTA-dómstólsins: raunveruleg áhrif í íslenskum rétti' [2012] 62 *Tímarit lögfræðinga* 2, pp 135–156.

[24] Case E-18/11 [2012] EFTA Ct Rep 592, para 57.
[25] ibid, para 58.
[26] Case E-3/12, *Staten v/Arbeidsdepartementet v Stig Arne Jonsson*, EFTA Ct. Rep. 2013 136 nyr, para 60.
[27] *Cf* also Order of the Court in *Hob vín III*, para 11, where the Court notes 'the different legal situation concerning courts against whose decisions there is no remedy under national law'.

subjected to the final and exclusive interpretation of the Supreme Court of the
EEA EFTA State in question. By refusing to cooperate with the EFTA Court, this
Supreme Court in fact claims authority with regard to the interpretation of EEA
law—authority on par with the ECJ and the EFTA Court. Now, is it really legal
activism to argue that such fragmentation and renationalisation of EEA law is
profoundly incompatible with the principles of the EEA Agreement?

V. ECJ OR THE EFTA COURT?

Irrespective of how the question raised in the last section is answered, it might be
argued that the situation of the national judge is in any case dramatically different in the EFTA pillar compared to the EU, insofar that it is the ECJ and not the
EFTA Court that holds the reins in the interpretation of EEA law. This would be
due to the fact that the EFTA Court basically copies ECJ case law when striving for
judicial homogeneity.[28] However, since the national judge in the EFTA State does
not have any direct access to the ECJ, the judge will have no choice but to base
her interpretation of EEA law directly on her own reading of ECJ case law. Hence,
with or without an advisory opinion under the belt, the national judge must base
her interpretation directly on ECJ case law.[29] Although, perhaps, informative as
to the state of EEA law and helpful for the pleadings of the case, a referral to the
EFTA Court will at best only serve a secondary function.I would argue that this
line of thinking is flawed in more than one way. First, it presumes that there is
always a straightforward answer to questions of EEA law which would allow the
EFTA Court to 'copy' ECJ case law and present the national judge with an answer.
However, this beats the very logic of the preliminary reference procedure. This
procedure is, evidently, only intended for genuine legal questions of EEA law. If
the answer to a question can clearly be deduced from ECJ case law (or EFTA Court
case law for that matter), the question should not be referred to EFTA Court at
all.[30] Second, the argument misses out the fact that questions of EEA law do not
always relate to EU law.

---

[28] Joint Cases E-9/07 and E-10/07 *L'Oreal* [2008] EFTA Ct Rep p 259, where the EFTA Court
reversed its case law with reference to later ECJ case law, would probably be referred to as the basis
for this argument. I discuss this case and its implications in detail in 'Judicial Homogeneity in the
European Economic Area and the Authority of the EFTA Court [...]' [2011] 80 *Nordic Journal of
International Law* 507–534 at 518.

[29] See 'Judicial Homogeneity in the European Economic Area and the Authority of the EFTA Court
[...]', above n 29. In this paper I discuss the arguments of Halvard Haukeland Fredriksen submitted
in a paper published in English as 'One Market Two Courts: Legal Pluralism vs Homogeneity in the
European Economic Area' (2010) 79 *Nordic Journal of International Law* 4, pp 481–499.

[30] Similarly, according to Art 97(3) of the Rules of Procedure, a question which is manifestly identical to a question upon which the EFTA Court has already 'ruled or given an opinion' may simply be
answered with reference to the earlier judgment. In this chapter it is however superflous to dwell upon
acte clair and the *CILFIT* case law of the ECJ.

Some of the cases which come before the EFTA Court concern EEA EFTA specific elements with no clear analogy to the EU. Examples are questions concerning the effects of EEA law in the EEA EFTA States, State liability as well as the EFTA institutions and their procedures. In these cases, EU law may, clearly, be of relevance. However, this relevance may be only one factor of several.[31] In other cases the EFTA Court is confronted with problems that would only exceptionally appear before the ECJ, such as questions concerning fundamental rights within the EEA legal order, certain principles of EEA law or the scope of EEA rules.[32] Third and most fundamentally, however, the view presented wrongly presumes that since the EFTA Court has committed itself to judicial homogeneity it equals the Court having subjected itself to the ECJ and lacks independent authority with regard to the interpretation of EEA law.

It follows from the text of the EEA Agreement that the ECJ and the EFTA Court are juxtaposed judicial institutions and hierarchically equal within the EEA legal order. This means—irrespective of any requirements of substantive and procedural provisions—that both Courts have the legal competence to give *final rulings* on the interpretation of the EEA Agreement. It is indeed for this reason that the possibility of conflicting case law between the two Courts is specifically addressed by Article 105(2–3) EEA. It is true that the EFTA Court may decide to align its case law with the ECJ or even reverse it in the interest of homogeneity. It is, however, the EFTA Court and not the ECJ that has the final say as to whether this will be the conclusion in a given case.[33] Hence, if there is any doubt as to the EFTA Court's position (that is, whether or not it will preserve judicial homogeneity by aligning itself to ECJ case law), a national judge should make an order for reference to the EFTA Court to have this clarified in order to avoid 'unnecessary mistakes in the interpretation and application of EEA law'.[34]

At the end of the day it is the EFTA Court, and not the ECJ, who gives a final ruling on whether the EEA EFTA States have complied with their obligations under the EEA Agreement.[35] In the unlikely situation of an open conflict between the ECJ and the EFTA Court, it is the latter that decides on the interpretation of the EEA Agreement vis-à-vis the EEA EFTA States. Hence, it is clear enough which

---

[31] Eg the question whether EEA EFTA State liability is subject to identical conditions as EU State liability, *cf* above n 13.

[32] *Cf*, eg, *L'Oreal*, above n 29, where the EFTA Court essentially had to decide whether elements pertaining to the EEA Agreement (ie the absence of Customs Union) made the principle of European wide pre-emption of trade mark rights inapplicable.

[33] *Cf L'Oreal*, above n 29.

[34] It may be mentioned that the EFTA Surveillance Authority has stated verbally that if a supreme court of an EFTA State rejects a request to make a reference to the EFTA Court in a high-profile case, the Authority may bring an action of infringement against the EFTA State concerned. *Cf* C Baudenbacher, 'How far from Bosphorus is the European Economic Agreement?' in *Human Rights, Democracy and the Rule of Law, Liber amicorum Luzius Wildhaber* (Dike/Nomos, 2007), p 80.

[35] The President of the Liechtenstein Supreme Administrative Court has recently stressed the same point. See A Batliner in K Tschütscher and C Baudenbacher (ed), *20 Jahre Unterzeichung des EWR-Abkommens—Ein Vierakter mit Original-Darstellern*, Schann 2012, p 55.

one of the two EEA Courts the national courts of the EEA EFTA States have to follow in such pathological circumstances. At present, however, these speculations seem to have little actual relevance and full discussion of different case scenarios of conflicts between the EFTA Court and the ECJ essentially would divert me to another issue I do not intend to consider, namely the complex relationship between the ECJ and the EFTA Court.

If it is admitted that there is an obligation incumbent on national courts of the EEA EFTA States to make preliminary references to the EFTA Court, a question arises as to the exact nature of this obligation. So far, the EFTA Court has not expressed itself in any detail on this issue. However, the Court's reasoning, in particular its reference to 'reciprocity', would suggest that this obligation will in any case not exceed what follows from Article 267 TFEU. If this is accepted, the obligation in question is clearly limited to courts of last instance under similar parameters as would apply under Article 267 TFEU.[36] Furthermore, it can be recalled that in *Irish Bank* the EFTA Court cited the ECtHR in *Ullens de Schooten and Rezabek v Belgium* to the effect that a decision by a court of last resort not to make a reference must be reasoned: Article 6(1) ECHR.[37]

VI. NO OBLIGATION TO COMPLY?

There is little dispute about the preliminary rulings of the ECJ being 'binding' upon the referring court whereas the rulings of the EFTA Court are defined as 'advisory' by Article 34 SCA. However, the semantic label 'advisory opinion' says little about the nature of the judicial act in question.[38]

Let me first consider, for comparison, what happens, or is likely to happen, if a national court of one of the EU Member States does not follow a (binding) preliminary ruling of the ECJ. Although Article 267 TFEU is directly applicable and binding upon the national judge, the party to the proceedings will clearly be unable to base any rights directly on the preliminary ruling. In short, the preliminary ruling does not carry with it any direct effect.[39] Hence, if the preliminary ruling is not implemented by the national court's decision, it is plainly and simply without any

---

[36] I do not discuss the the the relations between the advisory opinion procedure and State liability due to judicial acts. However, neglecting to refer a genuine EEA question to the EFTA Court is, no doubt, a relevant factor in this assessment. On the ECJ's *Köbler* case law and its applicability to the EEA, see H Haukeland Fredriksen, above n 30, p 485–509. The reservation to be made to Fredriksen's analysis is that the general question as to whether the same exact conditions for state liability apply in the EEA EFTA as in the EU, has not been fully settled, cf above n 13.

[37] Judgement 20 September 2011 in Cases Nos 3989/07 and 38353/07.

[38] There is, for instance, little doubt that an opinion delivered by the ECJ pursuant to Art 218(11) TFEU is binding in spite of the connotation 'Opinion'. *Cf* eg remarks in Opinion No 1/91, para 61.

[39] This characteristic implies that the preliminary ruling system does not, strictly speaking, entail a transfer of judicial powers, ie the ultimate authority to rule on legal rights and obligations within the national jurisdiction remains vested in the national judiciary. It is therefore difficult to see that a fully fledged preliminary reference procedure would constitute constitutional issues with regard to sovereignty.

legal effect in the domestic legal order.[40] From the viewpoint of EU law, the party's rights have been violated and there is a presumption of a breach by the Member State. However, presuming that national remedies have been pre-empted, the party's sole recourse is a complaint to the Commission which may (or may not) take the matter up and initiate infringement proceedings against the Member State. If the infringement proceedings result in a direct action by the Commission (or, in theory, by another Member State) before the ECJ, it is, undeniably, quite likely that the ECJ will refer to its previous preliminary ruling when deciding the case. However, this is not a logical necessity. On the other hand, if the Commission were not to act in spite of a complaint, it would, generally, not be possible for the party to bring a case against the Commission for a failure to act.[41]

Now, what happens, or is likely to happen, in the EFTA pillar? If a national court does not follow an advisory opinion, it has *not* contradicted a formally binding judicial act. But it has contradicted an interpretation delivered by the judicial institution which is competent to give a final ruling on the EFTA States' obligations under the EEA Agreement, within the framework of direct action proceedings. True enough, the party can base no rights directly on the advisory opinion. But with that, we find ourselves in the same situation as with the 'binding' preliminary ruling. Just as there, the party must content itself with complaining to the competent surveillance organisation, in this case the EFTA Surveillance Authority (ESA). If infringement proceedings by ESA (or, in theory, by another EEA EFTA state) result in a direct action before the EFTA Court, the EFTA Court will most probably refer to its advisory opinion when determining whether the State has violated its obligations.[42] If ESA chooses not to act in spite of a complaint, similar rules on *locus standi* apply to an action for failure to act as in the EU.

So, where is the difference between preliminary rulings and advisory opinions when it comes to tangible consequences of a non-following by a national court? It is true that in the EU pillar, the Member State could ultimately be ordered to pay a penalty by the ECJ. This, however, does not affect the analogy between the two procedures; in both cases the consequences of non-compliance are limited to an

---

[40] The possibility of liability proceedings against the State, or even a direct action, does not necessarily endow the preliminary ruling with a direct effect. The preliminary ruling may be given importance in a subsequent case concerning State liability. However, the outcome of a liability case is also, ultimately, subject to the national court's assessment of several factors. In any event, the situation with regard to State liability is, by and large, the same under EEA law as under EU law.

[41] The Commission is not considered to be under an obligation to act upon a complaint concerning a Member State's alleged infringement to EU law but this would be a prerequisite for standing of a non-privileged applicant. See further K Lenaerts, D Arts and I Maselis, *Procedural Law of the European Union* (London, Sweet & Maxwell 2006) 330–331.

[42] The EFTA Court has, by now, a firmly established practice of referring to and following its own case law as a rule. Although there are exceptions (as I believe is the case with all courts of last resort, even the most conservative ones!), it would be far-fetched to infer that the case law of the Court, including advisory opinions, carries no normative force and, accordingly, no power of predictability. I discuss this in 'Judicial Homogeneity in the European Economic Area and the Authority of the EFTA Court […]', above n 30.

action against the respective Member State and there is no immediate direct effect within the domestic legal order.

If, on the other hand, the preliminary reference procedure is considered through the prism of the aims and principles of the EEA, the same conclusion emerges. Not following an advisory opinion entails a possible fragmentation of EEA law and risks violating the rights of individuals and economic operators under the Agreement. In this respect it should be noted that advisory opinions are treated as conclusive with regard to the questions answered in a certain case by the EFTA Court itself, as well as others concerned.[43] If the same question were to be referred to the EFTA Court again in the same proceedings, it would be dismissed: *cf*, for example, *CIBA*.[44] Similarly, according to Article 97(3) of the Rules of Procedure, a question which is manifestly identical to a question upon which the EFTA Court has already 'ruled or given an opinion' may simply be answered with reference to the earlier judgment in an order. Hence, as far as any preliminary ruling can be said to have *res judicata*, the effects of advisory opinions of the EFTA Court are comparable to preliminary rulings of the ECJ.

It is true that the EEA Agreement is generally not intended to entail transfer of judicial powers to the EEA EFTA institutions. However, stating that a national court has an obligation to request and follow the interpretation of EEA law given by the EFTA Court does not equal the EFTA Court having obtained the power to carry out judicial functions within that State's territory. That competence continues to be exclusively vested in the national court, which has the final say on the substance of the rights and obligations of individuals and legal entities within the States' geographical and material jurisdiction. Hence, although national courts are—under EEA law—obliged to comply with an advisory opinion, no sovereign powers have been limited or transferred. This, of course, is only a restatement of the simplistic truth that sovereignty does not preclude submitting the interpretation of an international norm, binding upon the State under international law, to an international court.

To my knowledge, there is no example of a national judge going openly against an advisory opinion of the EFTA Court in the proceedings where that opinion was obtained. It should be noted that by this it is not implied that EEA law has always prevailed in the final outcome of the case before the national court.[45] Furthermore, by this it is not claimed that national courts have in all cases treated the rulings of the EFTA Court as binding precedents in other cases. However, the

---

[43] ibid.

[44] Case E-6/01 [2002] EFTA Ct Rep 281, paras 21–23.

[45] It may be the case that national law does not allow the national judge to decide a case according to EEA law. This, however, does not equal non-compliance with an advisory opinion. It may also be the case that for some reason the advisory opinion is not relevant for the final outcome of the case; compare Case E-4/01 *Karlsson* [2002] EFTA Ct Rep 240 and the Icelandic Supreme Court Decision in the case of 18 January 2007, Case 417/2006. The Supreme Court concluded, without refuting the EFTA Court's conclusion concerning State liability, that the applicant had not been successful in demonstrating any damage.

case law of the EFTA Court, and its value as a source of EEA law, is not dealt with in this chapter.[46]

VII. MORE HORIZONTAL JUDICIAL RELATIONS IN THE EFTA PILLAR?

In *Irish Bank,* the EFTA Court stated that the wording of Article 34 SCA reflects the fact that the depth of integration under the EEA Agreement is less far-reaching than that under the EU treaties.[47] This remark may refer to the fact that Article 34 SCA does not refer to any outright obligation incumbent upon national courts, neither with regard to referral, nor compliance with an advisory opinion. However, since both these aspects of Article 34 SCA have to be qualified, it is somewhat difficult to grasp what the Court is really getting at here. Furthermore, in spite of less far-reaching integration, namely the lack of direct effect and supremacy of EEA rules, a preliminary reference system is clearly needed in view of the aims and principles of the EEA Agreement. All in all, the implications of 'less far-reaching integration' for the preliminary reference system remain questionable in my view.[48]

Perhaps more importantly, in *Irish Bank* the EFTA Court also stated that 'the relationship between the Court and the national courts of last resort is, in this respect, more partner-like'. This statement holds true, insofar it is on the basis of the principle of primacy that a ruling of the ECJ is to affect rights and obligations directly within the national legal order. Since primacy is not recognised in EEA law, the EFTA Court does not assume this role of the ECJ. Furthermore, the EFTA Court does not—not formally in any case—rule on the validity of the Acts contained in the Annexes of the EEA Agreement. It therefore does not assume the constitutional role of the ECJ, so to speak. In this way, the EFTA Court and the national courts may be considered as more juxtaposed judicial institutions compared to the EU.

Although the *dicta* concerning the 'partner-like relationship' with national courts may, perhaps, have the flavour of public relations tactics rather than the statement of a legal norm, it can nevertheless also be understood as a more serious recognition of 'pluralism' in the judicial development of EEA law. Without tempting to dig into this subject, I take the term 'legal pluralism' to refer to the fact that the sources (or factors) that are subject to legal interpretation and hence judicial development cannot be accounted for in a simple hierarchical manner, but must

---

[46] See 'Judicial Homogeneity in the European Economic Area and the Authority of the EFTA Court [...]', above n 30.

[47] Above n 24.

[48] Nevertheless, the judgment in *Irish Bank* indicates that the ECJ's reasoning in Case C-210/06 *Cartesio* [2008] ECR I-09641 is inapplicable in the interpretation of Art 34 SCA. This goes contrary to my arguments in 'On the Authority of Advisory opinions'. *Cf* above n 9.

be seen in the context of normative interaction and, in some instances, conflict.[49] Legal pluralism, however, implicitly carries with it a normative theory, according to which a Court, although sitting atop the ladder, *should* be conscientious of this fact and, therefore, be ready give attention—and accord a place in its reasoning— to 'non-pedigree' sources, such as arguments put forward by national courts.

In this regard, it should be noted that the EFTA Court is, in a certain way, born into a context of 'legal pluralism' inasmuch as it was destined from the outset to interact with the ECJ in a variety of ways.[50] The ECJ has shown a certain willingness to engage in judicial dialogue with the EFTA Court by referring to the case law of the latter. Without dwelling on the relations between the two courts, it may therefore not be surprising that the EFTA Court has an understanding for judicial dialogue with the national courts of the EFTA States and, therefore, describes the preliminary reference procedure as 'partner-like' in nature. In this relation, it can also be recalled that the EFTA Court has, in some cases, highlighted specific observations and opinions submitted by the referring judge.[51] Similarly, the Court's Registry strives to keep national judges informed about the proceedings in Luxembourg and shows interest in the final outcome of the case before the national court. Furthermore, in my experience, the members of the EFTA Court view it as an important part of their duties to follow legal debates in the EFTA States and exchange their views with the legal communities in these countries. In the long run, this has a potential impact on the workings of the Court and its relations with the national judges.

VIII. THE ROLE OF THE NATIONAL JUDGE—DIFFERENT OR THE SAME?

In a nutshell, the EEA Agreement may be described as an attempt to create an arrangement by which the EFTA States—who did not accept the 'new legal order of international law' but nevertheless wanted to become full members of the Internal Market—were to both have their cake and eat it! The built-in tension resulting from this compromise was, to a considerable extent, left unresolved by the text of the EEA Agreement and it was thus handed over to the judiciary to deal with—in particular, the EFTA Court, which was charged with judicial authority vis-à-vis the EEA EFTA States. Hence, when interpreting the EEA Agreement, the EFTA Court had, from the very outset, to strike a balance between, on the one hand, the demand for a fully fledged homogeneity and, on the other, the premise

---

[49] See, further, M Poires Maduro, 'Contrapunctual Law: Europe's Constitutional Pluralism in Action' in N Walker (ed), *Sovereignty in Transition* (Oxford, Hart Publishing, 2003) 501–537. For a discussion of a pluralist conception of the law in the EFTA States, *cf* Ó Ísberg Hannesson, 'Giving Effect to EEA Law—The Role of the Icelandic National Courts and the EFTA Court in the European Judicial Dialogue' in *The authority of European law: exploring primacy of EU law and effect of EEA law from European and Icelandic perspectives* (Reykjavik, University of Iceland, 2012).

[50] For a discussion, see M Elvira Méndez-Pinedo, *EC and EEA Law—A Comparative Study of the Effectiveness of European Law* (Groningen, Europa Law Publishing, 2009), Ch 11.

[51] See for repeated references to the referring court's observations Case E-11/12 *Beatrix Koch* [2013] EFTA Ct Rep 272.

of non-interference with the legislative, executive and judicial powers of the EEA EFTA States. This element is sometimes left unmentioned when the EFTA Court is criticised for having either reached too far in its interpretation of the Agreement or not far enough.

As is reflected by the case law of the EFTA Court, the balance has over the years swung between these two poles of 'interpretative gravity'.[52] The Contracting Parties have, of course, at all times remained free to step into the judicial development of the EEA by amending the Agreement. To my knowledge, however, there have never been any serious suggestions to this effect, not even in governmental circles of the two remaining Nordic EFTA States. In this sense, the principles developed by EFTA Court case law constitute, by now, a *de facto* recognised EEA 'acquis'.

In its case law, the EFTA Court preliminary reference procedure has from the very beginning been assigned similar functions as the EU procedure. Furthermore, in recent case law the EFTA Court has put the procedure in perspective with considerations of procedural homogeneity and effective judicial protection. At the same time, the EFTA Court has also, in the interest of procedural homogeneity, continued to follow the ECJ *Plaumann* case law and kept direct access to the Court strict notwithstanding some pressure to the contrary.[53] It follows from all this that the role of the national judge in an EEA EFTA State is, by and large, comparable to what would be the case in an EU State. Thus, a great deal of responsibility for judicial protection under EEA law is placed on the national judiciary which, in turn, has to cooperate with the EFTA Court through the preliminary reference procedure when it is confronted with genuine and relevant questions of EEA law.

In spite of possible divergences compared to the EU, the elements noted above imply an aspiration for a 'coherent and complete system of judicial protection of individuals and economic operators inspired by the Rule of Law' on a par with the EU. However, this coherence and completeness cannot be achieved without the principle of loyal cooperation pursuant to Article 3 EEA being observed. This, in turn, means that national courts of last resort may be under an obligation to make a referral to the EFTA Court and subsequently to comply with an advisory opinion when applying EEA law.

At the same time, the relationship between the EFTA Court and the national courts of the EEA EFTA States needs careful attention. From the viewpoint of some, it would, perhaps, have been preferable to base these relations entirely on the spirit of free cooperation with no reference to any obligation at all! Although such a view would, in my opinion, be utopian and bound to fall short of the aims

---

[52] The interconnection between these two poles should also not be overlooked. Thus, the rejection of the principles of direct effect and supremacy fits the EEA premise of 'no limitation of sovereignty' well, but it raises the question of how to ensure the adequate effects and enforcement of EEA rules; the recognition of the principle of State liability enhances fully fledged homogeneity but it still falls short of placing the EEA on an equal footing with the EU, etc.

[53] *Cf* in particular Case E-2/02 *Bellona* [2003] EFTA Ct Rep 52 and Case E-5/07 *Private Barnehagers* [2008] EFTA Ct Rep 62.

of the EEA Agreement in the long run, I stress that the relations between the EFTA Court and the national courts cannot be understood only through legal dogmatics (as in this chapter). In this regard, it may be recalled that the EFTA Court has put forward proposals for institutional amendments with the aim of enhancing its credibility vis-à-vis the national judiciary.[54] Although these proposals, which envisaged the possibility of assembling an 'EFTA Court of five', only had very modest implications for the Court's budget, the endeavour sadly turned out to be unsuccessful.

Thus, at present, it seems that the EFTA Court cannot look to the Governments of the EEA EFTA States for any help in reinforcing credibility and enhancing relations with the national courts. Similarly, the EFTA Surveillance Authority has not been willing to take up issues concerning attitudes of certain national courts. Seen in this context, the EFTA Court does well in encouraging 'partner-like cooperation' with the national courts through formal and informal means. Whatever is the conclusion on the legal authority of the EFTA Court and its case law, the increasing number of references from national judges over the recent years, suggests that the Court has in any case been successful in establishing an 'authority of persuasion' by its 20 years in action.

[54] These reforms, presented in 2011, which had the main aim of making it possible to call in supplementary judges in cases of importance in order to have a 'Court of five', are discussed in the Norwegian Governmental Report: 'Innenfor og utenfor', NOU 2012:2, Ch 10.6.5. The need for the 'EFTA Court of five' is rather obvious to most, in particular when considering the composition of the ECJ and the highest courts of the EFTA States. Until this day, however, no real effort has been taken by the three EEA EFTA States with a view to strengthen the credibility of the EFTA Court by institutional amendments.

12

The Norwegian Experience of the EEA Judiciary

ARILD O EIDESEN

I. INTRODUCTION

THE WIDE TOPIC was suggested to me and, rather fired my imagination. I shall, however, limit myself to giving a personal and impressionistic sketch mainly related to the Norwegian interaction with the EFTA Court, based on my experience as a socially engaged and politically interested Norwegian citizen and judge in a court of second instance.

This chapter will move from a short general assessment (II) to some comments *'sui generis'* on Norway (III); it will then continue with some remarks on the concrete interactions between the EFTA Court and the Norwegian courts (IV), and conclude with some observations on the development of the interactions including the evolvement of the EFTA Court as an institution (V).

II. SHORT GENERAL ASSESSMENT

The successful operation of the European Economic Area (EEA) depends upon uniform interpretation and application of the common rules in all EEA States. To this end, the EFTA States are monitored by the EFTA Surveillance Authority (ESA). The EFTA Court has jurisdiction with regard to the EFTA States, according to the Agreement between the EFTA States on the Establishment of a Surveillance Authority and a Court of Justice (SCA).

Norway signed the Agreement on the European Economic Area (the EEA Agreement) on 2 May 1992. The Agreement linked Norway to the European integration process in a new way. Since then, Norway has become increasingly closely tied to the European Union (EU).[1]

---

[1] Norwegian Ministry of Foreign Affairs, Official Norwegian Reports NOU 2012:2, *Outside and Inside, Norway's agreements with the European Union*, p 5.

When the EEA Agreement was signed, few thought it would still shape Norway's relations with the EU more than 20 years later.[2] But in 1994, a second national referendum—the first was held in 1972—determined that Norway should not join the EU, and since then the EEA Agreement has been the main foundation for Norway's connection to the EU. In the following years, through the EEA Agreement and other agreements with the EU, Norway has incorporated approximately three-quarters of all EU legislative acts into Norwegian legislation and has implemented them more effectively than many of the EU Member States.[3]

In 2010 the Norwegian Government appointed a broad-based independent committee to undertake a comprehensive and thorough review of the political, legal, administrative, economic and other social consequences of the EEA Agreement and other arrangements between Norway and the EU.[4] The 900-page report is, aptly, called *Outside and Inside. Norway's agreements with the European Union.*[5] In this chapter, I rely heavily upon this report.

Chapter 10, 'Compliance and control', examines the control measures taken to ensure compliance with EU/EEA obligations in public administration and Norwegian courts. It also discusses the control exercised by ESA and the EFTA Court.[6]

The main story according to the committee is that the implementation of, and compliance with, the EEA Agreement is, by and large, a success, and that there are few conflicts relative to the scope of obligations adopted as a consequence of the EEA Agreement. The committee considers striking the extent to which the Norwegian legislature, administrative authorities and courts, as well as civil society, have proved capable of incorporating rules and regulations, as well as political signals and guidelines, designed by an organisation where Norway is not a member and is not represented.

A substantial part of the verification of Norway's compliance with EU/EEA law is based on internal Norwegian control. To my knowledge, many investigations by ESA have so far been conducted and have led to the outcome that Norwegian actions and decisions were correct. Norway has won some of the relatively few court cases, but has also lost major cases.[7]

In Norway, it is widely accepted that the Norwegian society has benefited from the EEA Agreement and the associated agreements, in spite of the democratic deficit. As for today, there is no common call for fundamental changes in the EEA Agreement or in Norway's interaction with the EU.

Regarding the EFTA Court, the official position of the Norwegian authorities is that the Court is well functioning according to its purposes and design, and well

[2] ibid, p 6.
[3] ibid, p 9.
[4] ibid, p 3.
[5] *Cf* n 1.
[6] *Outside and Inside, Norway's agreements with the European Union*, p 14.
[7] *Cf* Case E-2/06 *EFTA Surveillance Authority v The Kingdom of Norway* [2007] EFTA Ct Rep 164; Case E-3/06 *Ladbrokes Ltd v The Government of Norway, Ministry of Culture and Church Affairs and Ministry of Agriculture and Food* [2007] EFTA Ct Rep 86.

capable of fulfilling its intent and obligations. The Court has integrity and enjoys trust and recognition.

The EFTA Court has, however, been comparatively little known in Norway, even among practising lawyers. Personally, I used not to give much thought to the EFTA Court as such, even when applying decisions handed down by the Court.

The EFTA Court is also limited by having jurisdiction over only three small countries, two of which are very small, and by *de facto* having to shadow the dynamic development in the much larger ECJ.

III. NORWAY '*SUI GENERIS*'

All national experiences are different from one another and in Norway we tend to see ours as unique.

Norway is a comparatively young nation state. As a Norwegian, I can affirm that, to some extent, we take pride in seeing Norway as the land apart, and speak of ourselves as 'the odd country out'. At the same time Norway is a small, export-dependent country, which has learnt, through necessity, and particularly after World War II, that it must participate in international organisations and dispute settlement bodies in order to safeguard its independence and prosperity.

Such an international participation was, however, reached through a hefty internal debate, and a limitation of the sovereignty releases.

In 1967, a well-known Norwegian professor of history, Sverre Steen,[8] gave a series of 14 lectures on national radio under the collective title *Langsomt ble landet vårt eget* ('Slowly, the land became our own'). The series and the ensuing book were widely popular.

In 1972, a majority of 53.5 per cent of the participating voters voted against Norway entering the European Community (EC), following intense national debate.

In 1994, 52.2 per cent voted against entering the EU, although Finland and Sweden joined the EU in the same year, and Denmark had already joined the EC in 1972. The national debate was less divisive, but national sovereignty was still a central issue in the discussions.

As for today, polls show considerably less support for the EU, and there is also some scepticism about the EEA agreement.

In 2002, Inge Lorange Backer, professor at the University of Oslo,[9] wrote an article entitled 'Is Norway still an independent state?'[10] He analysed the concept of independence as defined in Section 1 of the Norwegian Constitution, discussed how and to what extent bodies outside the state could exercise legislative authority

---

[8] Sverre Steen (1 August 1898—23 June 1983) was a Norwegian historian and a professor at the University of Oslo.

[9] Inge Lorange Backer is professor at the Department of Public Law at the Faculty of Law at the University of Oslo.

[10] I Lorange Backer, *Er Norge fortsatt en selvstendig stat?* in P Lødrup, S Tjomsland, G Aasland and M Aarbakke (eds), *Festskrift til Carsten Smith til 70-årsdagen 13 juli 2002* (Oslo, Universitetsforlaget, 2002) pp 43–58 (Festschrift to Carsten Smith, former Supreme Court Chief Justice of Norway).

with direct effect on Norwegian citizens, how executive authority was transferred to other states or international bodies, and how judicial authority was transferred and to what effect. One of his conclusions was that, through a dynamic and integrating interpretation of the EEA Agreement, the EFTA Court has contributed to giving accepted obligations new and unforeseen consequences, thereby entering the domain of the national legislative authority. He concluded by affirming that, though still being an independent state, Norway was not as independent as it was throughout most of the twentieth century. According to him, what was lost in independence, however, could be won back to some extent, influencing other states in fields which were meaningful to the country itself.

In 2014 Norway celebrated the 200th anniversary of its Constitution, adopted on 17 May 1814. The *Storting* (Parliament) has initiated attempts to modernise this fundamental law, but at the time of writing it seems unlikely that major changes will be enacted. One reason which is strongly expressed is the fear that the proposals will transfer more power from the *Storting* to judicial bodies, inside and outside of Norway.

IV. THE CONCRETE INTERACTIONS BETWEEN THE EFTA COURT AND NORWEGIAN COURTS

Norway is deeply rooted in political and constitutional concerns. Following the national referendums of 1972 and 1994, the EEA Agreement should not establish and should not develop into a supranational legal system comparable to the EU. The EEA Agreement was meant to extend the internal market to the EEA States without forcing them to surrender legislative, administrative or judicial sovereignty.

As discussed by Backer and shown by the scope of incorporation of EU legislative acts, this initial idea does not match reality. The EEA Agreement, the EFTA Court, and thereby EU law, have deeply affected Norwegian domestic legislation.

As already indicated, however, it should be noted that the Norwegian singularity plays a key role in understanding the Norwegian approach to the EEA and its interpretation of the commitments under the SCA.

In the above-mentioned report, the committee quotes a study prepared for it by Halvard Haukeland Fredriksen, professor at the University of Bergen.[11] The study seems to suggest that Norwegian courts do their utmost to enforce EEA legal rights and obligations, and in the vast majority of cases succeed in their efforts. The study also observes that Norwegian courts apply not only EEA law in cases

---

[11] Halvard Haukeland Fredriksen is professor at the University of Bergen, member of the Research group for Competition and Market Law and of the research group for Legal Culture. Professor Fredriksen elaborated the study *EU/EØS-rett i norske domstoler*, 2011, Europautredningen, rapport no 3.

falling within the framework of the EEA Agreement, but also refer and apply EU law to a quite significant degree, although they are not obliged to do so.

The disputed areas in the interaction between the EFTA Court and Norwegian courts concern the requests for advisory opinions on the interpretation of the EEA Agreement, namely when to ask and how to use the consequent answers.

The right to request an advisory opinion is incorporated into the EEA system by Article 34 SCA, which establishes the competence of the EFTA Court, and is not directly applicable by Norwegian courts. The related procedure was implemented by section 51a of the *domstolloven* (Administration of Courts Act).

Article 34 SCA differs from Article 267 of the Treaty on the Functioning of the European Union (TFEU) in two important ways. Unlike in the EU, where Article 267(3) TFEU obliges national courts of last instance, against whose decisions there is no judicial remedy, to refer questions concerning the interpretation of the EU Treaties and the validity and interpretation of acts of the institutions, bodies, offices or agencies of the EU to the ECJ, Article 34 SCA as such imposes no corresponding obligation on the national courts of the EFTA States. Moreover, the answers provided by the EFTA Court are merely advisory opinions on the interpretation of the EEA Agreement, and not binding judgments.

In the above-mentioned Report, the committee, in Chapter 10.4.1, states that the only difference between the Norwegian courts' handling of cases concerning EU/EEA law and of cases under ordinary Norwegian law is that Norwegian courts, when dealing with EU/EEA law cases, 'have a right (but not a duty) to obtain an advisory opinion from the EFTA Court regarding the interpretation of EU/EEA law, if the Norwegian court in question finds it appropriate'.

In Chapter 10.4.3, this concept is expounded upon and strengthened, observing that '[t]he possibility of asking questions according to Article 34 SCA is only a right for courts in the EFTA States, never a duty'. Considering the clear and unambiguous wording of Article 34 SCA and the established case law from national courts in the EFTA States, the committee holds that it is legally impossible to support an argument for a different interpretation of the article.

The EFTA Court answers to questions that are submitted through advisory opinions, not binding judgments. This deliberate nonconformity with the referral procedure under EU law is connected to constitutional concerns of the EFTA States and the very construction of the EEA Agreement as an international instrument.

The Norwegian Supreme Court has ruled on several occasions on the understanding of Article 34 SCA, the latest case being HR-2013-496-A (the *STX Norway* case).[12]

---

[12] The decision is analysed by EFTA Court President Carl Baudenbacher and Norwegian Supreme Court Justice Arnfinn Bårdsen in the Norwegian law journal *Lov og Rett* (2013) 515, 535. The articles are based on lectures given at the seminar 'The interaction between the Supreme Court of Norway, the European Court of Human Rights and the EFTA Court', organised by Hålogaland Court of Appeal and the Faculty of Law at the University of Tromsø, 19 April 2013.

In the plenary case HR-2000-49-A (*Finanger*), the Supreme Court stated unanimously that:

> [t]he EFTA Court's opinion is of an advisory nature; *cf* Article 34 [SCA] between EFTA and the Norwegian State. This means that the Supreme Court has the authority and duty to consider independently whether and to what extent the Supreme Court's decision should be based on this opinion. Nevertheless, I find that significant importance must be attributed to the opinion. This follows in my view from the fact that the EFTA States, in accordance with Article 108(2) of the EEA Agreement, upon entering into the [SCA] found reason to establish this Court, one of the reasons being the need to reach and maintain uniformity in the interpretation and application of the EEA Agreement.

In the *STX Norway* case, the Supreme Court, sitting in ordinary chamber of five judges, concluded that:

> [t]he Supreme Court shall not accept the EFTA Court's opinion without due examination; it has the authority as well as the duty to consider independently whether and to what extent this is warranted. In this light, I cannot see that the Supreme Court is formally prevented from relying on a different opinion. However, because significant importance must obviously be attributed to the opinion, special reasons would be required for the Supreme Court to diverge.

Which the Supreme Court proceeded to do.

In the lecture in Tromsø and the ensuing article in *Lov og rett*,[13] one of the conclusions of Justice Bårdsen was that:

> it would certainly be mistaken to derive from *STX* that the Supreme Court as such has any kind of agenda as to minimising the EFTA Court's position within the EEA Treaty, or that there is an ongoing struggle for judicial supremacy in the EFTA pillar of the EEA Treaty. Even in the future the interplay and dialogue of our two courts must be based on the joint understanding that nobody would gain from challenging the fine-tuned judicial architecture established by the EEA Treaty and the SCA.

Seen from my vantage point, this is also the prevailing opinion among Norwegian practitioners and theoreticians.

V. FUTURE INTERACTION AND DEVELOPMENTS

The European Convention on Human Rights and also the European Court of Human Rights had existed more than 30 years before the Convention came to be common ground for argument in a substantial number of Norwegian court cases. In my opinion, the EEA Agreement and the EFTA Court are still newcomers in comparison, and alas not quite as essential in nature.

---

[13] Above n 12.

The number of EU/EEA cases to come before Norwegian courts is a consequence of private parties and lawyers knowing and invoking EU/EEA law, because they see the necessity and the advantage of such a reliance. The number of such cases before Norwegian courts is steadily increasing, and there seem to be a process of growing awareness and sense of importance regarding the issues involved.

The number of cases before the EFTA Court is also increasing, apparently at an accelerating pace. The importance of the decisions is more recognised. Cases like E-10/11 and E-11/11 *Hurtigruten*[14] certainly contributed to raising the awareness of the importance of the EFTA Court in Norway. This enhanced attention may also lead to more requests for advisory opinions.

For my part, as a judge in a court of second instance, bound to follow the precedents of the Supreme Court, I also believe that the development of the body of law stands to gain by a process where cases start in courts of first instance, proceed to courts of second instance, and are finally decided by the Supreme Court, based also on considered analyses by previous courts. I can envisage cases where this underlying premise may have effect on my ability to see the need for an advisory opinion from the EFTA Court, which is the deciding court in a system already characterised by democratic deficit.

In my opinion, the scope of the EFTA Court will always to some extent be limited by it being an international court with a rather narrow base. Norway has not indicated a will to accept institutional growth by incorporating a number of small states into the EFTA pillar. As for Switzerland, it remains to be seen what will happen.

Regardless of this, it has been suggested that with three judges, the EFTA Court is small when the number of cases and the importance of cases increase. I am therefore in favour of (at least) appointing two judges to strengthen the composition of the Court.

Law used to be an identifiably national subject, and international law a specialist subject for those with special interests. National law was based on national traditions and could be interpreted based on common national assumptions. This scenario has changed. An increasing part of national law is created by international institutions. The body of law is internationalised, and so is the interpretation and application of law.

In this regard, I am at times concerned about inherent differences between a body of law restricted to the handling of cases in the light of free flow of services, and a more comprehensive body of law serving the complexities of the Norwegian welfare model. Internationalisation must affect the way we think about and approach the creation and interpretation of law, and pose challenges of political as well as legal concern. The EFTA Court and Norwegian courts should face these challenges together.

---

[14] Joined Cases E-10/11 and E-11/11 *Hurtigruten ASA, The Kingdom of Norway v ESA* [2012] EFTA Ct Rep 758.

My overall conclusion is that time and increased interaction will lead to better understanding, growth and closer cooperation. To this effect, I commend the will of the EFTA Court to initiate and participate in legal dialogue concerning the EEA Agreement and the SCA, in cooperation with courts and law faculties in the EFTA States. In my experience, this will constructively contribute to the development of the EFTA Court and its authority in the EFTA States. The Norwegian experience illustrates in particular the need for such a dialogue.

13

The Role of Individual Lawyers in EEA Law

THOMAS NORDBY

I. THE TIDE

T
O REWRITE THE famous words of Lord Denning, EEA law has flown into the Norwegian legal order like a tidal wave, and the tide is not turning. During the past 20 years, Norway has implemented more than 8,000 EU Directives and Regulations, and taken on board the acquis communautaire from the European Court of Justice, the EFTA Court, the European Commission and the EFTA Surveillance Authority.

It is hardly possible to apply law in Norway without directly or indirectly knowing the fundamentals of EEA law. National law and EEA law are not two separate legal orders. EEA law forms a part of national law.

II. THE ROLE OF INDIVIDUAL LAWYERS

The role of individual lawyers in EEA law is as difficult as it is simple; one has to understand the EEA legal method.

Lawyers obviously play different roles depending on their place in the legal profession and the nature of their law practice or activity. The Council of the Bars and Law Societies of Europe (CCBE) addresses the role of lawyers this way:

> In a society founded on respect for the rule of law the lawyer fulfils a special role. His duties do not begin and end with the faithful performance of what he is instructed to do so far as the law permits. A lawyer must serve the interests of justice as well as those whose rights and liberties he is trusted to assert and defend and it is his duty not only to plead his client's cause but to be his adviser.[1]

Lawyers are essential to the dynamic capacity of a legal system and the rule of law because they are the carriers of legal human capital—the raw material on

---

[1] Code of conduct for lawyers in the European Union, preamble (2002).

which a legal system draws in the process of interpreting, implementing and adapting legality (based in statutory rules or otherwise) to local and changing conditions.

Expertise developed by a lawyer prosecuting or defending an antitrust case—about the pro- and anti-competitive effects of vertical restraints or the cost of precautionary technology, for example—are shared initially with the court and the lawyer's law firm colleagues, and in time, potentially, throughout the legal profession more generally through the publication of decisions, legal writing, conferences and so on. Such expertise ultimately has the effect of influencing the capacity of future lawyers and courts (and legislators and legal commentators) to assess the application of antitrust or tort law in related circumstances.

As every experienced lawyer and their clients know, these legal functions depend on far more than mere knowledge of 'the rules'. They require knowledge of complex environments and relationships. They require, too, complex knowledge of the way other lawyers and judges interpret these environments and the package of legal materials that might be relevant to the enforcement of a set of rules or the resolution of a dispute under the provisions of a set of rules. As every experienced law professor knows too, the challenge of legal education often involves getting students to realise that it's not (just) about knowing the rules, it's about becoming a member of legal culture and developing judgment within that culture: assessing what arguments and strategies are possible, which arguments and strategies are strong and which are weak and how those assessments depend on the subtleties (and vagaries) of facts and the possibilities of proof. As a consequence, the rule of law depends on more than a well-schooled legal profession.

So, is there any difference between the EEA lawyer and other lawyers? The fact is that EEA law has over the past 20 years been a relevant part of almost any lawyer's practice. Knowledge of fundamental EEA law has to be a part of the practice of any commercial lawyer today.

However, deep legal expertise and experience of how to handle EEA law cases is a profession for the individual lawyer in EEA law. The individual lawyer in EEA law plays a critical part in this dynamic aspect and development of the rule of EEA law, applying the EEA legal method.

In contrast to the European Community, the EEA Agreement was constructed as a regular agreement under international law. Formally, the EEA Agreement is therefore an international legal treaty. In practice, however, the EEA Agreement has an impact on Norwegian law that goes beyond what one sees for other international legal agreements that Norway is a part of. In case of conflict between Norwegian regulations and provisions arising from EEA law, the EEA will apply over the Norwegian legislation. Whether EEA law has been circumvented must be assessed based on EEA law.

When the EEA agreement was new, it was debated whether the agreement could be characterised differently from an ordinary international treaty and whether it could be seen to include general principles not entailed by its express provisions.[2] Many of these questions may now be regarded as settled by the jurisprudence of the EFTA Court and by the Norwegian Supreme Court in *Finanger*. In this case, the Court stated that the principle of loyalty in Article 3 of the EEA Agreement is applicable to the courts and that Norwegian courts should use the principle of presumption in a way 'not less far-reaching' than the community interpretation obligation.[3] The majority of the Supreme Court Judges in the *Finanger* case rejected the claim to give the directive direct effect contrary to the express wording of a Norwegian statute. But it is important to note that the issue was one of horizontal effect between two private parties, which does not fall under the obligation to give direct effect in Community law. Even under these circumstances a large minority was of the opinion that the directive should prevail over national law, and the majority made it part of their reasoning that the facts were not a case of giving an individual rights in a claim against the state.

Some Norwegian scholars question the legality of this supranational level of the EEA agreement. However, for practising lawyers this has resulted in a wide range of cases raising the question of breach of EEA law in the form of non-implementation of EEA law obligations in Norwegian law or inadequate adaptation of general Norwegian legislation.

One of many interesting examples is the question of the legality of the Norwegian watercrafts regulation, prohibiting almost all use of personal watercraft, as an unlawful restriction pursuant to Article 11 of the EEA Agreement. The Supreme Court was resistant to analogical application of EEA law to the detriment of Norwegian legislation in its judgment of Rt-2004, p 834. Since, in preparation for the appeal to the Supreme Court, it became known that the current watercraft originated outside the European Economic Area, the Supreme Court decided to reverse its decision to address the questions concerning the prohibition on the use of personal watercraft. Later, the EFTA Surveillance Authority, based on a complaint, turned down the Norwegian scheme. It was later changed and is today harmonised with the obligations under EEA law. This case, as one of many examples, illustrates the very role of the EEA lawyers.

III. THE IMPACT OF THE EUROPEAN COURTS

The idea behind the EEA is to give the EFTA Member States the free trade advantages of EU membership without making them part of the EU political system. All the rules of EU law regarding free movement of goods (but only as regards

---

[2] See, eg, chapters by Peter Christian Müller-Graff and Fredrik Sejersted in Müller-Graff and Selvig (eds), *The European Economic Area—Norway's Basic Status in the Legal Construction of Europe* (Berlin/Oslo, Berliner Wissenschafts-Verlag, 1997).

[3] HP Graver, *The Effects of EFTA Court Jurisprudence on the Legal Orders of the EFTA States*, ARENA Working Papers WP 04/18.

products originating in the Member States), persons, services and capital apply—with only slight modifications—to the EFTA countries, as do the rules of EU law relating to competition and state aid.

In its Opinion 1/91, the ECJ held that the EEA Agreement (as it then stood) was not compatible with the EEC Treaty. It gave four grounds. As these all involved the judicial provisions of the Agreement, it should be explained that, in its original form, the EEA Agreement provided for the setting up of an EEA Court, to which each EFTA country would nominate one judge. When sitting in plenary session, it would have been composed of eight judges, five from the European Court together with three EFTA judges. There was also to have been an EEA Court of First Instance, consisting of five judges (two from the European Court and three EFTA judges). It was provided that, when interpreting the EEA Agreement and legislation applying under it, the EEA Court would be bound by decisions of the European Court made prior to the signing of the EEA Agreement.

After the European Court's negative opinion in the first EEA case, it was necessary to renegotiate the Agreement, something about which the EFTA countries were not very happy. A number of amendments were made.

The purpose of the EEA Agreement is to guarantee, in all 30 EEA States, the free movement of goods, people, services and capital—'the four freedoms'. As a result of the agreement, EC law on the four freedoms is incorporated into the domestic law of the participating EFTA States. The Agreement seeks to guarantee equal conditions of competition, and equal rights to participate in the internal market for citizens and economic operators in the EEA. It also provides for co-operation across the EEA in other important areas such as research and development, education, social policy, the environment, consumer protection, tourism and culture. The very idea is to develop one Internal Market.

It is my opinion that the question of how the EEA Agreement shall be interpreted should be based on a realistic assessment of who actually determines the interpretation of the agreement, of which the case law from the European Courts forms a fundamental pillar for EEA legal development and understanding. The understanding of EEA law is equivalent to the understanding of the legal method of the European Courts.

The ECJ and the EFTA Court have a role other than to determine specific litigation effective only for the parties involved. They have, as their main role, to ensure EEA-wide homogeneity and thus the function of the EEA legal order: see, *inter alia*, the principles set out in Article 106 EEA.

The functioning of the EFTA Court is set out in the Agreement between the EFTA States on the Establishment of a Surveillance Authority and a Court of Justice (SCA), in Protocol 5 to that agreement containing the Statute of the EFTA Court, as well as in Protocol 7 on the legal capacity, privileges and immunities of the EFTA Court. In addition, according to Article 43, paragraph 2 of the SCA, the Court shall adopt its rules of procedure to be approved by the Governments of the EFTA States by common accord.

In the context of EEA law, it is clear that Court case law cannot be used as a verification criterion for what the European pillar of the Community shall be considered as applicable EEA law. When the European Court in 1991 rejected the original proposal for a joint EEA court, it was claimed that having a duty to take 'due account' of another court's interpretation of EEA law would be incompatible with EU Court sovereignty over EU law. Although recent practice indicates that the European Court nevertheless considers Court practice as a relevant source of law, it is clear enough that the European pillar is the European Court that has the final say in the interpretation of EEA law.

In *Finanger I*, the Norwegian Supreme Court stated that Norwegian courts have 'authority and duty' to decide whether and to what extent a preliminary opinion of the Court shall be taken into account.[4] In my view, it is in principle impossible to see the Court practice as anything other than the authoritative expression of the EEA law obligations.

Under Article 3 of the EEA Agreement and Article 2 of the SCA, which are identical, the Contracting Parties and the EFTA States, and thereunder the national courts, are under an obligation to take all appropriate measures to ensure fulfilment of the obligations arising under the Agreements. Moreover, they shall facilitate cooperation within the framework of the Agreements.

Thus, efforts to derive a unified EEA legal interpretation theory rests on the perception that the principle is only one correct solution to the EEA interpretation of legal issues, regardless of where in the EEA the question should arise. Some find it therefore problematic when the Supreme Court has repeatedly stated that the Norwegian courts must ascribe the Court's opinion as holding 'significant weight' when the content of our EEA law obligations should be defined.[5]

The EEA Agreement and the SCA Agreement contain two possibilities for assistance to national courts in the administration of justice. First, under Article 1 of Protocol 34 to the EEA Agreement, the EFTA States may permit their courts to request that the ECJ decide on a question of interpretation of provisions of the EEA Agreement, which are identical in substance to provisions of the Treaties establishing the European Communities, or of acts adopted pursuant to these treaties. An EFTA State which intends to make use of this possibility shall under Article 2 of the Protocol notify the Depository of the EEA Agreement and the European Court of Justice how and to what extent the Protocol will apply to its courts and tribunals. The EFTA States thus have discretion as to the courts which would be entitled to seek a decision.

Since reference is made in the Protocol to a decision by the ECJ, an interpretation by that court would be binding on the requesting court. In light of this fact, and the views held by the EFTA States during the negotiations, it is unlikely that any of the EFTA States could avail themselves of this possibility, since such a possibility would require constitutional amendments even in States where seeking an advisory opinion would not be so required.

---

[4] Rt-2000 s 1811 P, p 1820.
[5] H Haukeland Fredriksen, *Hvem avgjør tolkningen av EØS-avtalen?—noen betraktninger om størrelsen «gjeldende EØS-rett»*, Tidsskrift for Rettsvitenskap 02/2010.

The other possibility follows from Article 34 SCA. Under that provision the EFTA Court shall have jurisdiction to give advisory opinions on the interpretation of the EEA Agreement. An EFTA State may in its internal legislation limit the right to request such an opinion to courts and tribunals against whose decisions there is no judicial remedy under national law.

This possibility differs from the preliminary rulings under the EEC Treaty in three respects. First, no obligation to seek an advisory opinion is established. Second, an opinion may be sought only on the interpretation of the EEA Agreement, not on the validity of acts of the bodies established under the Agreement. Third, the response by the EFTA Court is not binding on the requesting court.

In my view, the advisory opinions procedure is of crucial assistance to national courts. The courts would otherwise be faced with the task of deciding matters concerning the interpretation of the EEA Agreement. Such matters may arise occasionally before courts which do not have a clear view of the Agreement and the methods for its interpretation. The need for assistance may be particularly great at the outset. Upon entry into force of the EEA Agreement and the agreements between the EFTA States, the national courts were faced with some 14,000 pages of new rules and a considerable number of amendments to existing legislation. Today, Norway has implemented some 80,000 pages. The national courts, and in particular the Supreme Court in Norway, should in my view use the advisory opinions procedure more actively.

EU law is dynamic, and the European Court of Justice and the EFTA Court play an active role in its development through their case law. To ensure the homogeneity of legislation, EEA law should as a general rule be developed correspondingly. When the EFTA Court and the European Court of Justice make statements concerning the interpretation of EEA legislation they influence the development of EEA law. In the same way, decisions taken by the EFTA Surveillance Authority may have implications for how EEA legislation is applied in practice. Thus, the decisions of the courts and the Authority may affect the development of Norwegian law in areas that fall within the scope of the EEA Agreement.

Under the EEA Agreement, it is the task of the EFTA Surveillance Authority to ensure that the participating EFTA states respect their obligations under the Agreement. The Authority can do this on its own initiative or on the basis of complaints from private parties.

There have been disagreements between the EFTA Surveillance Authority and Norway on the interpretation of the EEA Agreement in a number of individual cases. In some of these the Authority's position has been upheld, while in others Norway's views have won acceptance. From the perspective of the private lawyer to an affected enterprise, experience shows that close dialogue with the Authority is important if Norway is to gain acceptance for its position. This should be initiated before any formal case is brought, to ensure that Norway is aware of the Authority's assessments at an early stage. In order to safeguard Norwegian interests, it is also important that the Authority receives all relevant information as early as possible and that Norway's point of view is supported by sound, consistent arguments. It is crucial that there is close coordination between the relevant ministries in processes relating to the EFTA Surveillance Authority.

There have historically been few cases referred from the Norwegian Supreme Court. Dr Halvard Haukeland Fredriksen found that applications to make a reference to the EFTA Court are in most cases firmly opposed by the Norwegian State Attorney for Civil Affairs.[6] Supreme Court Judge Henrik Bull has even asked the question whether the Government hopes that Norwegian judges may be more inclined to rule in its favour than the judges of the EFTA Court.[7] But however reluctant the Norwegian state may be to get cases referred, there are ways that lead to Brussels and Luxembourg without going through a Norwegian court.

Considering the objective of establishing a dynamic and homogeneous European Economic Area, the fact that Norwegian courts are reluctant to refer cases is in fact problematic, in particular for private operators leaning on the fundamental EEA law rights.

IV. THE ROLE OF THE SURVEILLANCE AUTHORITY

The best way to initiate a process on the EEA level is by a meeting with the EFTA Surveillance Authority. We often see that clients are well served by getting to meet with the Authority and discuss their concerns without this leading to a formal complaint.

Starting a discussion with the Authority does not mean that there has to be a formal infringement proceeding opened against an EFTA State. However, it gives the parties in question the opportunity to inform the Authority about the case at hand and their concerns. As an individual lawyer one still has a lot of the control over the situation and one may use this advantage to proceed with the case. And one does not get a discussion as to whether the question at hand shall be forwarded to the EFTA Court.

Following registration of a complaint by the Authority, an official reference number is assigned. After a thorough assessment of the complaint, the Authority will decide whether or not further action should be taken. The Authority endeavours to reach a decision on the substance of a complaint (either to open infringement proceedings or to close the case) within a year of registration of the complaint. If the Authority considers that an infringement of EEA law has been committed, it will issue a letter of formal notice to the EFTA State concerned, requesting it to submit observations by a specified date.

---

[6] H Haukeland Fredriksen, 'The Two EEA Courts—a Norwegian Perspective' in EFTA Court (ed), *Judicial Protection in the European Economic Area* (Stuttgart, German Law Publishers, 2012) 187, 205.
[7] 'European Law and Norwegian Courts' in Müller-Graff and Selvig (eds), *The Approach to European Law in Germany and Norway* (Berlin, Berliner Wissenschafts-Verlag, 2004) 95, 113.

By making an official complaint one opens a formal and open proceeding. This might be an advantage in many cases. However, as an individual lawyer one does see that the Authority is in charge, and oneself is a requisite. By that meaning that one are reduced to a position where one have to accept that the Authority are in charge of the development of the process. This is of course just partly right, because if one brings a case before the national court one may not influence the speed of the process. However, one is still in the front seat. When the Authority takes the lead one have to sit in the back seat of the car and try to be involved in the Authority's choice of route. One may of course secure one's clients interest by supplying the Authority with arguments. But in the end it is the Authority themselves that are in charge and that takes the steps they find necessary. This might not always be a disadvantage, but the Authority has control of the situation and how they will proceed is often uncertain.

If the EFTA State fails to comply with the reasoned opinion, the Authority may decide to bring the case before the EFTA Court. So, despite the fact that there have been few questions referred from the Norwegian Courts during the last 20 years, the EEA lawyers have found other ways to get their cases before the EFTA Court.

The jurisdiction of the court is defined in Article 31(2) SCA, which states that if a State concerned does not comply with a reasoned opinion of the EFTA Surveillance Authority, the latter may bring the matter before the EFTA Court, and in Article 32 that the EFTA Court shall have jurisdiction in actions concerning the settlement of disputes between two or more EFTA States regarding the interpretation or application of the EEA Agreement, the Agreement on a Standing Committee of the EFTA States or the Surveillance and Court Agreement itself. Article 35 states that the EFTA Court shall have unlimited jurisdiction in regard to penalties imposed by the EFTA Surveillance Authority and Article 36 and 37 that the EFTA Court shall have jurisdiction in actions brought by an EFTA State or any natural or legal person against a decision of the EFTA Surveillance Authority or a failure on the part of the Authority to act in infringement of its obligations under the agreement.

The EFTA Court plays an important role in keeping, *inter alia*, the homogeneity principle and continuous cooperation and legitimate development in its judgments.

The EFTA Court was set up to adjudicate in four types of direct actions: infringement actions brought by the Authority against an EEA State, settlement of disputes between the Authority and the EEA States, actions against the Surveillance Authority, and actions for annulment of decisions taken by the Surveillance Authority.[8] The role of the individual EEA lawyer is normally most important in the actions for annulment of decisions taken by the Authority, as it is in fact here that the private lawyer may have an active role. In the other cases the

---

[8] David Thór Björgvinsson, 'Application of Article 34 of the ESA/Court Agreement by Icelandic Courts' in M Monti and others (eds), *Economic Law and Justice in Times of Globalisation—Festschrift for Carl Baudenbacher* (Baden-Baden, Nomos, 2007) p 37.

role of the private lawyer is minor, but not without force. Representing an intervening part may be of importance for the individual to protect one's interests.

V. 'THE FLOOR IS YOURS'

Looking back 20 years, the EEA lawyer has a role today which was lacking, or even rejected, at the moment of the Agreement's inception. The Agreement was created as an instrument under international law, and as a clear alternative to the supranational arrangement of the then European Communities. Basic elements of community law as a legal order, the subjects of which comprise not only Member States but also their nationals, with main characteristics such as the overall aim of integration, direct effect, state liability and the obligatory leading interpretive role of the ECJ, did not form part of the agreement.

To those of you who are heading for the ultimate challenge as an EEA lawyer, pleading a case before the EFTA Court, I would very much like to share a checklist which I have noted from my experience, both as a research lawyer at the Court and later as a lawyer pleading before the Court:

— Above all: client expectations
  — The uncommon procedure
  — What will the EFTA Court's ruling imply?
— Preparation, preparation, preparation
  — Start early
  — Strategy—alliances?
  — Evidence, arguments, case law
— It is mainly a written procedure
  — Advisory Opinions: one written shot
  — Direct actions: two written shots
— The EFTA Court knows EEA law better than you. Don't present general assessments. Choose your arguments carefully. Stick to the crux of the matter.
— The EFTA Court does not only deal with law. Think carefully whether you should present evidence and have it translated into English.
— Time allocation oral observations
  — Short, unfamiliar, must be to the point
  — Do not repeat the written observations
  — Use your time to underline and contradict
— Language issues in the AO's proceedings
— Decide early whether you would write your observations in English or your mother tongue. I would recommend English.
— Answers questions from the Court directly if you are able to.

* * *

Finally—to the EFTA Court and all EEA lawyers: happy anniversary! We've got at least 20 more to go!

14

Reciprocity, Homogeneity and Loyal Cooperation: Dealing with Recalcitrant National Courts?

CATHERINE BARNARD*

I. INTRODUCTION

IN ITS 20 years of existence, the EFTA Court has decided over 180 cases, most the result of references from the national courts of Norway, Iceland and Liechtenstein. Some national courts have been more willing than others to refer cases. The EU system has experienced this as well. But in both systems the reference procedure has been the lynchpin for the development of the EEA and EU acquis; for the acquis to be applied correctly the national courts must follow the advisory opinions (EFTA Court) or preliminary rulings (CJEU) of the relevant courts.

The EEA agreement alluded to two principles—homogeneity and reciprocity—which would oil the wheels of the reference process. The third principle, the duty of loyal cooperation, is more explicitly articulated. The aim of this chapter is to use the preliminary reference procedure as a prism through which to examine the operation of these three principles. In particular, it will focus on the *STX* case,[1] a case referred to the EFTA Court by the Norwegian Court of Appeal but finally decided by the Norwegian Supreme Court, a case which demonstrated the Supreme Court's discomfort with aspects of the EFTA Court's advisory opinion in *STX,* and its determination to plough its own furrow. At first sight, this looks like a serious challenge to the authority of the EFTA Court and a breach, at a minimum, of the principles of homogeneity and the duty of loyal cooperation. However, this chapter will argue that the *STX* case should not be seen as a crisis but, in a maturing system, as an opportunity for both courts to understand the different perspectives of the two systems and to engage in a constructive dialogue to resolve the difficulties.

---

* I am grateful to an anonymous referee for his comments.
[1] Case E-2/11 *STX Norway and Others*, judgment of 23 January 2012 [2012] EFTA Ct Rep 4; *STX a O v Tariffnemda*, judgment of the Supreme Court of Norway of 5 March 2013, Rt-2013, 258.

The chapter will be structured as follows. First, it will briefly examine the three constitutional principles of EEA law, homogeneity, reciprocity and the duty of loyal cooperation (II), before considering the application of those principles in the context of the advisory opinion procedure (III). It will then examine the *STX* decision to see what it tells us about the operation of those principles and the current state of the relations between Norway and the EFTA Court (IV). Section V concludes.

II. HOMOGENEITY, RECIPROCITY AND LOYAL COOPERATION: THE THREE PILLARS OF EEA LAW

A. Introduction

The important fourth recital of the EEA agreement says:

> CONSIDERING the objective of establishing a dynamic and *homogeneous* European Economic Area, based on common rules and equal conditions of competition and providing for the adequate means of enforcement including at the judicial level, and achieved on the basis of equality and *reciprocity* and of an overall balance of benefits, rights and obligations for the Contracting Parties; (emphasis added)

This contains the kernel of what have become two key principles of EEA law: *homogeneity*, designed to deliver a single EU- and EEA-wide market, and *reciprocity*, designed to ensure that the protection enjoyed by EEA citizens in EU states applies equally to EU nationals in EEA states. The *duty of loyal cooperation*, already well known in EU law, is also explicitly recognised in the EEA Agreement, most notably in Article 3 EEA and Article 2 SCA. We shall briefly consider these three principles in turn.

B. The Principle of Homogeneity

The principle of homogeneity has attracted more legal attention than its brethren. The first reference to the principle is found in the fourth recital of the EEA agreement (cited above). The fifteenth recital of the EEA Agreement also talks of 'the objective of the Contracting Parties is to arrive at, and maintain, a uniform interpretation and application of this Agreement and those provisions of Community legislation which are substantially reproduced in this Agreement and to arrive at an equal treatment of individuals and economic operators as regards the four freedoms and the conditions of competition'. This provision links the principle of homogeneity with the uniform application of EEA law.[2]

---

[2] See further http://www.efta.int/sites/default/files/documents/eea/seminars/eea-s13/EFTA_ Seminar_-_Presentation_-_Speitler.pdf.

The specific instantiation of the principle of homogeneity can be found in Article 6 EEA:[3]

> Without prejudice to future developments of case law, the provisions of this Agreement, in so far as they are identical in substance to corresponding rules of the Treaty establishing the European Economic Community and the Treaty establishing the European Coal and Steel Community and to acts adopted in application of these two Treaties, shall, in their implementation and application, be interpreted in conformity with the relevant rulings of the Court of Justice of the European Communities given prior to the date of signature of this Agreement.

This suggests a priority for the case law of the Court of Justice in the hierarchy of legal orders, albeit, as former CJEU Judge Timmermans has portrayed it, homogeneity does not need to be slavish. It can be creative.[4]

The EEA Agreement also contains a section entitled 'Homogeneity'. This establishes administrative tools to ensure the Contracting Parties arrive at 'as uniform an interpretation as possible of the provisions of the Agreement and those provisions of Community legislation which are substantially reproduced in the Agreement'.[5] Article 105 EEA sets up the EEA Joint Committee which is to keep under constant review the development of the case law of the CJEU and the EFTA Court, while Article 106 EEA provides for the establishment of a system for the exchange of information concerning judgments by the EFTA Court, the EU Courts and the courts of last instance of the EFTA States. This system has not yet been set up.

Thus, given the commonality of the rules on the internal market in the TEU/TFEU and EEA agreements, the homogeneity rule is intended to avoid a race to the bottom and forum shopping between systems by requiring the EFTA Court to follow relevant CJEU case law and to ensure the two treaties are interpreted in the same way.[6] This obligation was emphasised by the EFTA Court in its first ever judgment: in *Restamark*[7] the EFTA Court said that the main focus of the EEA Agreement was not on alleged differences between EU and EEA law, but on homogeneity.

Despite the emphasis on homogeneity between EEA and EU law in the EEA Agreement, there is no written provision obliging the CJEU to take into account

---

[3] See also Art 3(2) of the Surveillance and Court Agreement (SCA), which provides: 'In the interpretation and application of the EEA Agreement and this Agreement, the EFTA Surveillance Authority and the EFTA Court shall pay due account to the principles laid down by the relevant rulings by the Court of Justice of the European Communities given after the date of signature of the EEA Agreement and which concern the interpretation of that Agreement or of such rules of the Treaty establishing the European Economic Community and the Treaty establishing the European Coal and Steel Community in so far as they are identical in substance to the provisions of the EEA Agreement or to the provisions of Protocols 1 to 4 and the provisions of the acts corresponding to those listed in Annexes I and II to the present Agreement.'

[4] See C Timmermans, 'Creative Homogeneity' in M Johansson, N Wahl and U Bernitz (eds), *Liber amicorum in Honour of Sven Norberg: A European for all Seasons* (Brussels, Bruylant, 2006) 471–484.

[5] Art 105(1) EEA.

[6] See further H Haukeland Fredriksen, 'Bridging the Widening Gap between the EU Treaties and the Agreement on the European Economic Area' (2012) 18 *European Law Journal* 868.

[7] Case E-1/94 *Ravintoloitsijain Liiton Kustannus Oy Restamark* [1994–95] EFTA Ct Rep 15, paras 32–35.

relevant EFTA Court case law.[8] However, in practice the Court of Justice makes good use of the EFTA Court's jurisprudence.[9] Thus, despite the one-sided nature of the homogeneity rules on paper, they have largely been superseded by a 'unique judicial dialogue' in practice.[10]

Carl Baudenbacher, President of the EFTA Court, identifies three dimensions to judicial homogeneity. First, there is *substantive homogeneity.* This requires the homogeneous interpretation of the substantive rules of EEA law. As he points out, although governments often argue that due to alleged differences in goal and context, the EEA Agreement must be interpreted in a less integrationist, and therefore more government-friendly way, than the EU Treaties, all claims to that effect have been rejected by the Court.[11]

Second, there is *homogeneity with regard to effect.* Despite claims that there cannot be direct effect or supremacy of EEA law, or state liability because these are the constitutional principles of EU law, the EFTA Court has created equivalent principles which take due account of the architectural differences between the EU and the EEA.[12] However, the outcome is that a homogeneous and dynamic EEA is ensured ('obligation de résultat').

Third, there is *procedural homogeneity.*[13] The EFTA Court has held that although it is not required to follow the reasoning of the CJEU when interpreting the main part of the Surveillance and Court Agreement (SCA) which applies to the EFTA states only, the reasoning which led the CJEU to its interpretations of expressions in Union law is relevant when those expressions are identical in substance to those which fall to be interpreted by the Court.[14]

C. The Principle of Reciprocity

The principle of reciprocity is less fully articulated than the principle of homogeneity. However, some of its content can be gleaned from the case law and from the literature. In essence, it requires that the rights conferred by the EEA Agreement should be the same for EU nationals in the EEA/EFTA pillar as for EEA/EFTA nationals in the EU pillar. The principle of reciprocity therefore amounts to an 'obligation de résultat'.

---

[8]   www.eftacourt.int/fileadmin/user_upload/Files/News/2009/15_Years_EFTA_Court.pdf.

[9]   See, eg, AG Kokott's Opinion in Case C-681/11 of 28 February 2013 quoting the Court's judgment in E-14/11 *DB Schenker* as regards the importance of private enforcement in competition law.

[10]   See Case C-300/10 *Marques Almeida*, Opinion of Advocate General Trstenjak, ECLI:EU:C:2012:414, Fn 25.

[11]   In Case E-2/06 *Norwegian Waterfalls* the Court held that there is a presumption that identically worded provisions in EEA law are to be interpreted in the same way as in EU law.

[12]   In Case E-1/94 *Restamark* [1994–95] EFTA Ct Rep 15 the EFTA Court found that the provisions of the EEA Agreement have quasi-direct effect, ie once they have been implemented into the legal orders of the EFTA States they may be invoked by citizens and economic operators before the national courts (and the EFTA Court). In Case E-1/01 *Einarsson* [2002] EFTA Ct Rep 1 the Court recognised the quasi-primacy of EEA law. Most importantly, the Court held in Case E-9/97 *Sveinbjörnsdóttir* [1998] EFTA Ct Rep 95 that full state liability applies in EEA law.

[13]   See, in particular, Case E-18/10 *ESA v Norway* [2011] EFTA Ct Rep 202.

[14]   Case E-2/02 *Technologien Bau- und Wirtschaftsberatung GmbH and Bellona Foundation v ESA* [2003] EFTA Ct Rep 52.

The principle of reciprocity has a substantive and a procedural dimension. The substantive dimension concerns the content of rights. As Advocate General Kokott put it in *UK v Council*,[15] the contested decision on social security regulates not only the social rights of *third-country nationals*—Norwegians, Icelanders and Liechtensteiners—in the Union, but also, conversely, regulates the social rights of *Union citizens* in the three EFTA States concerned. She continued: 'Consequently, by virtue of the amendment to the EEA Agreement intended by the contested decision, not only does a Norwegian national, to name one example, benefit from the coordination of social security systems under Regulation No 883/2004 within the territory of the European Union, but also a Union citizen in Norway.'

The procedural dimension of reciprocity requires equal treatment in access to the courts, especially in the context of the Article 34 SCA reference procedure (ie EU citizens should enjoy the same rights in EEA states in respect of access to justice as EEA citizens enjoy before the courts in EU states). We shall return to this point below.

D. Duty of Loyal Cooperation

The duty of loyal cooperation, found originally in Article 5 EEC[16] and now Article 4(3) TEU, has proved a crucial tool for the Court of Justice. It has used Article 4(3) TEU to impose extensive obligations, primarily on the Member States but also on the EU institutions. In particular, it has used Article 4(3) TEU to help justify the development of state liability.[17]

Article 3 EEA contains an equivalent provision which directly mirrors Article 4(3) TEU:[18]

> The Contracting Parties shall take all appropriate measures, whether general or particular, to ensure fulfilment of the obligations arising out of this Agreement.
>
> They shall abstain from any measure which could jeopardize the attainment of the objectives of this Agreement.
>
> Moreover, they shall facilitate cooperation within the framework of this Agreement.

John Temple Lang provides a comprehensive overview of instances where the duty of loyal cooperation has been used both by the CJEU and the EFTA Court. In

---

[15] Case C-431/11 *UK v Council*, ECLI:EU:C:2013:187, para 42.

[16] Member States shall take all appropriate measures, whether general or particular, to ensure fulfilment of the obligations arising out of this Treaty or resulting from action taken by the institutions of the Community. They shall facilitate the achievement of the Community's tasks.
  They shall abstain from any measure which could jeopardise the attainment of the objections of this Treaty.

[17] See, eg, Joined Cases C-6/90 and C-9/90 *Francovich v Italy* [1991] ECR I-5357, para 36: 'A further basis for the obligation of Member States to make good such loss and damage is to be found in Article [4(3) TEU], under which the Member States are required to take all appropriate measures, whether general or particular, to ensure fulfilment of their obligations under [Union] law.'

[18] Case E-1/04 *Fokus Bank* [2004] EFTA Ct Rep 11, para 41. Art 2 SCA contains an equivalent provision to Art 3 EEA.

particular, he notes that the Articles impose both positive duties (to take measures to promote Treaty objectives) and negative duties (to avoid measures that would interfere with Treaty objectives or measures or with the operation of EU policies).[19]

III. THE REFERENCE PROCEDURE

A. Introduction

Having briefly examined the three guiding principles of EEA law, we turn now to consider how these principles can, and should, apply in the vexed context of references to the EFTA Court. Article 34 SCA provides:[20]

> The EFTA Court shall have jurisdiction to give advisory opinions on the interpretation of the EEA Agreement.
>
> Where such a question is raised before any court or tribunal in an EFTA State, that court or tribunal *may*, if it considers it necessary to enable it to give judgment, request the EFTA Court to give such an opinion.
>
> An EFTA State may in its internal legislation limit the right to request such an advisory opinion to courts and tribunals against whose decisions there is no judicial remedy under national law.

While modelled on the Article 267 TFEU preliminary reference procedure in the EU, Article 34 SCA contains one major difference: there is no obligation to refer by the national courts against whose decision there is no judicial remedy. As we shall see, this has become a matter of heated debate in the EEA.

In this section we shall look at two issues: first, the nature of the duty to refer and whether courts from the EEA states are actually making references; and second, if references are being made, what happens when those references return to the national courts.

B. Making a Reference

i. *The Situation of Courts of Last Resort*

In *Restamark* the EFTA Court said:[21]

> The purpose of Article 34 of the Surveillance and Court Agreement is to establish co-operation between the EFTA Court and the courts and tribunals in the EFTA States. It is

---

[19] 'The Duty of National Courts to Provide Access to Justice in the EEA' in EFTA Court (ed), *Judicial Protection in the European Economic Area* (Stuttgart, German Law Publishers, 2012) 111.

[20] http://www.efta.int/media/documents/legal-texts/the-surveillance-and-court-agreement/agreement-annexes-and-protocols/Surveillance-and-Court-Agreement-consolidated.pdf.

[21] Para 25.

intended as a means of ensuring a uniform interpretation of the EEA Agreement and to provide assistance to the courts and tribunals in the EFTA States in cases in which they have to apply provisions of the EEA Agreement.

Thus, the EFTA Court recognises that Article 34 SCA provides an important vehicle for ensuring the homogeneity of EEA law.

However, the absence of an obligation on courts of last resort to make a reference is a major hurdle standing in the way of uniformity. The reason for this lacuna, as the EFTA Court explained in *Irish Bank*,[22] is that 'the depth of integration under the EEA Agreement is less far-reaching that under the EU treaties'. However, it also means that the 'relationship between the Court and the national courts of last resort is, in this respect, more partner-like'.

That said, the EFTA Court has tried to shape an obligation on courts of last resort to refer. In *Jonsson*,[23] for example, the EFTA Court said that it is important that questions are referred to the Court under the Article 34 SCA procedure 'if the legal situation lacks clarity', thereby avoiding 'unnecessary mistakes in the interpretation and application of EEA law' and ensuring 'the coherence and reciprocity in relation to rights of EEA citizens, including EFTA nationals, in the EU'.[24] Speaking extra-judicially,[25] Professor Baudenbacher observed that in *Jonsson* the EFTA Court reminded the courts of last resort of the EEA States that when deciding whether to make a reference, they could not limit themselves to applying Article 34 SCA. They also had to fulfil their duty of loyalty under Article 3 EEA, and they had to take due account of the fact that EFTA citizens and economic operators benefit from the obligation of respective courts of the EU Member States to make a reference to the CJEU. He added that national supreme courts had to take into account the fact that if they refused a motion for reference, this might fall foul of the standards of Article 6(1) ECHR. He concluded: 'This means that national courts of last resort are in certain cases obliged to make a reference. The Court expects this obligation to be respected and, if necessary, enforced.'

Thus Professor Baudenbacher invokes two of the three key principles discussed above to justify extending an obligation to refer to courts of last resort: the duty of loyal cooperation and the principle of reciprocity. In respect of reciprocity, the argument runs as follows: since EEA nationals can enforce their rights in courts of EU Member States,[26] the courts of last resort in those states are subject to the

---

[22] Case E-18/11 *Irish Bank Resolution Corporation Ltd v Kaupthing Bank hf*, judgment of 28 Sept 2012, para 57.

[23] Case E-3/12 *Jonsson*, judgment of 20 March 2013, para 60.

[24] The point in *Jonsson* was emphasised in Case E-2/12 *INT*, http://www.eftacourt.int/uploads/tx_nvcases/2_12_INT_Order_of_the_Court.pdf): 'for the *different legal situation* concerning courts against whose decisions there is no remedy under national law, see paragraphs 57 to 58, and Case E-3/12 *Jonsson*, judgment of 20 March 2013, not yet reported, paragraph 60'.

[25] http://www.eftacourt.int/fileadmin/user_upload/Files/News/2013/24.06.13_President_Baudenbacher_-EFTA_Ministerial_2013_Oral_Statement.pdf.

[26] See, eg, Case C-452/01 *Margarethe Ospelt v Schlössle Weissenberg Familienstiftung* [2003] ECR I-9743.

duty to refer under Article 267 TFEU. The principle of reciprocity would therefore suggest that EU nationals—and consequently EEA nationals—suing in courts in EEA states should also benefit from an obligation on the courts of last resort to refer. This would comply with the principle of reciprocity while also ensuring the necessary uniform—and homogenous—application of EU and EEA law.

ii. The Willingness of Courts to Refer

As in the EU, some courts are more willing to refer than others;[27] and, as in the EU, some courts of last resort are reluctant to refer. While Iceland's Supreme Court has adopted a more EEA-friendly referral policy and Liechtenstein has sent a record number of cases per capita,[28] the Norwegian courts have been less willing to play ball. According to the 2011 Fredriksen Report on EEA law in Norwegian courts, all Norwegian courts generally hold back from making references, often without adequate reasons, but the problem has been particularly acute in the case of the Norwegian Supreme Court. It has made only four references to the EFTA Court in 20 years and two of those were withdrawn. So it has received replies from the EFTA Court in only two cases, *Finanger (No 1)*[29] and *Paranova*,[30] with the last reference being made in 2002.

Various explanations have been offered by Baudenbacher as to why references are not being made.[31] Most relevant for the argument that follows are:

— since the EFTA Court's rulings are advisory 'only', there is little to be gained from them because they lack legally binding effect;
— only the CJEU is entitled to make certain decisions;
— a national supreme court is in a better position to decide certain sensitive cases;
— the EFTA Court is a judicial activist;
— the EFTA Court is 'more Catholic than the Pope', ie the EFTA court is tougher on the EEA states than the CJEU is on the EU States;
— delay and costs speak against referring cases.

The last point about delay and costs is particularly relevant for the Norwegian courts: as Fredriksen points out, Norwegian courts take great pride in their status as the most efficient courts in Europe and a delay of eight months while the

---

[27] See generally M Broberg and N Fenger, 'Variations in Member States' Preliminary References to the Court of Justice—Are Structural Factors (Part of) the Explanation? (2013) 13 *European Law Journal* 488.
[28] http://www.eftacourt.int/fileadmin/user_upload/Files/News/2012/CB_The_EFTA_Judicial_System_-reaches_the_Age_of_Majority_final.pdf.
[29] Rt-2000, p 1811.
[30] *Paranova* Rt-2004, p 904.
[31] C Baudenbacher, 'The EFTA judicial system reaches the age of majority: accomplishments and problems', speech given at the EEA Seminar of the EFTA Secretariat of 19 January 2012 in Brussels http://www.eftacourt.int/fileadmin/user_upload/Files/News/2012/CB_The_EFTA_Judicial_System_reaches_the_Age_of_Majority_final.pdf.

EFTA Court considers the case, although far better than the CJEU's average of 16 months, still postpones the delivery of justice. As to the first charge, on the futility of 'advisory opinions', Baudenbacher refutes this. He says: 'From a sociological standpoint ... the EFTA Court's opinions are hardly weaker than preliminary rulings rendered by the Court of Justice of the European [Union]. If the national court were to disregard the EFTA Court's opinion, it would bring the respective EFTA State into a situation of breach of the EEA Agreement. In view of this *sui generis* nature, the EFTA Court decided to call its decisions rendered under Article 34 SCA "judgments" in the rubrum and "advisory opinions" in the operative part.'[32] Further, it is now recognised that although the national courts are not under a legal obligation to comply with decisions of the EFTA Court, in practice they usually do.[33]

We shall return to consider the other criticisms of the reference procedure and the EFTA Court below.

C. Bringing the References back Home

In the EU, where there is an obligation for the referring court to comply with the Court of Justice's ruling, national courts 'faithfully carry out rulings of the Court of Justice'[34]—academic commentators are in agreement on this. The recent book by Edwards and Lane expresses the common view:[35]

> Yet in virtually all cases the national courts apply the rulings without a murmur. The rare exception may be taken as a shot across the Court's bow, an occasional warning of the limits of its jurisdiction and a reassertion of that of the national court.

The position in the EEA is somewhat different. In *Finanger (No 1)*[36] the Norwegian Supreme Court (full court) emphasised that the opinions of the EFTA Court under Article 34 SCA were of an advisory character only and that it was for the Supreme Court to decide for itself whether and to what extent they were to be followed. The Supreme Court held that the case law of the EFTA Court was to be accorded 'significant weight' by Norwegian courts when interpreting the EEA Agreement.[37] Yet, according to Fredriksen, the Norwegian courts, including the Supreme Court, apply CJEU decisions in the same way as the courts of the

---

[32] C Baudenbacher, *Legal Framework and Case Law*, 3rd edn, p 10.

[33] HP Graver, 'The Effects of EFTA Court Jurisprudence on the Legal Orders of the EFTA States' ARENA WP 04/18, http://www.sv.uio.no/arena/english/research/publications/arena-publications/workingpapers/working-papers2004/wp04_18.pdf.

[34] T Millett in *Vaughan and Robertson Law of the EU*, 2008, para 361.

[35] *Edward and Lane on European Union Law* (Cheltenham, Edward Elgar, 2013), 270.

[36] Rt-2000, p 1811.

[37] Subsequent approval of these statements is found in, eg, *Paranova* Rt-2004, p 904, para 67, *Finanger (No 2)* Rt-2005, p 1365, para 52, *Gaming Machines* Rt-2007, p 1003, para 79 and *Pedicel* Rt-2009, p 839, para 7. This is taken from Fredriksen, above n 6.

EU Member States and CJEU case law is de facto followed as binding authority.[38] Fredriksen continues that generally, the Norwegian Supreme Court considers that its track record in the field of EEA law is a fine one and that, essentially, what matters to economic operators doing business in Norway is that their EEA rights are adequately protected, not in which court judicial protection is offered.[39] We shall test this assertion by considering the *STX* litigation.

IV. THE *STX* CASE

A. The Decision

STX concerned Regulations issued by the Norwegian Tariff Board based on the Norwegian Engineering Industry's collective agreement for the maritime construction industry 2008–2010 (technically termed 'extension of collective agreement').[40] The collective agreement contained various provisions on rates of minimum hourly pay, working hours, allowances for posting, and compensation for expenses incurred for travel, board and lodging. The question raised by various shipyard-owners, including STX, was whether the Regulations were compatible with the Posted Workers Directive 96/71 (PWD) and Article 36 EEA (the equivalent to Article 56 TFEU) on free movement of services. The Oslo District Court found against the employers, who appealed to the Court of Appeal, which decided to obtain an advisory opinion from the EFTA Court. When the case returned to the Court of Appeal, it dismissed the employers' appeal; the employers appealed this decision to the Norwegian Supreme Court, which also dismissed the appeal.

STX raised three questions on the meaning of pay in Article 3(1)(c) PWD. In order to give context to the discussion in sections B and C below, I will briefly consider the EFTA Court's answers to these three questions and the Norwegian Supreme Court's response to those answers. Unfortunately this turns on a reading of the technical provisions of Article 3(1) PWD, and Article 3(1)(c) PWD in particular. The Article provides:

> Member States shall ensure that, whatever the law applicable to the employment relationship, the undertakings referred to in Article 1(1) guarantee workers posted to their territory the terms and conditions of employment covering the following matters:
>
> ...
>
> (c) the minimum rates of pay, including overtime rates; this point does not apply to supplementary occupational retirement pension schemes.

---

[38] https://bora.uib.no/bitstream/handle/1956/7862/The%20two%20EEA%20Courts. pdf?sequence=1, 4.
[39] ibid, 21.
[40] This section is taken from C Barnard, 'More posting' (2014) 43 *Industrial Law Journal* 194.

Article 3(1) second indent says: 'For the purposes of this directive, the concept of minimum rates of pay referred to in paragraph 1(c) is defined by the national law and/or practice of the Member State to whose territory the worker is posted.' This suggests that the Directive allows the host state a free hand to determine what constitutes pay. As we shall see, the reality is not as simple as that.

The first question in *STX* was whether overtime rates constituted pay and were thus applicable to posted workers. The EFTA Court said that overtime rates were specifically allowed in Article 3(1)(c) PWD but the rates had to be limited to minimum rates of pay for work outside maximum normal working hours, and set out in a clear and accessible manner.[41] The Norwegian Supreme Court broadly agreed and said that the Norwegian Regulations clearly showed the basis on which the overtime premia should be calculated and were necessary, suitable and proportionate.[42] Presumably, with its reference to the proportionality principle the Supreme Court thought it was applying the test under Article 36 EEA, although this is not made clear. The provision on overtime rates could therefore be applied to posted workers.

The second issue concerned a posting allowance for assignments requiring overnight stays. This posting allowance constituted about 20 per cent of the hourly rate. The EFTA Court said that it was for the Member States to define minimum rates of pay. This could include a posting allowance, provided it was (i) a minimum;[43] (ii) it was expressly stated and transparent, referring to Article 4(3) PWD; (iii) it applied in a general and equal manner to all similar undertakings; and (iv) it was not contrary to Article 36 EEA.[44] The EFTA Court said that if the national court found that the requirement for the service provider to pay a posting allowance breached Article 36 EEA, it could be justified provided it was genuinely intended to protect posted workers and the rules did not deter employers from other Member States offering their services in Norway because of the costs involved.[45]

The Supreme Court, *obiter*, rejected, as a matter of principle, the need for a further examination of the posting allowance rule with Article 36 EEA.[46] However, presumably in order to try to comply with the instructions of the EFTA Court, the Supreme Court said there was no need to conclude on this matter, as the allowance was nevertheless justifiable under Article 36 EEA. It found that the compensation for the inconvenience of living away from home was a measure that genuinely protected workers,[47] and that there was no evidence that the rule weakened job opportunities for posted workers.[48] It also found that the posting

---

[41] Paras 56–57.
[42] Para 135.
[43] Para 72.
[44] Para 74–78.
[45] Paras 84–85.
[46] Paras 96–103.
[47] Para 109.
[48] Para 112.

allowance was proportionate, albeit following a fairly perfunctory review.[49] Thus, this provision too could be applied to posted workers.

The third issue was whether expenses for travel, board and lodging were covered by the term 'pay'. The EFTA Court said that the compensation was not pay because the amount varied depending on the costs involved.[50] It also thought that the compensation was not covered by the other heads of Article 3(1)(a)–(g) PWD[51] nor, following *Luxembourg*[52] which gave a highly restrictive reading of the term public policy, would it be covered by the public policy provisions of Article 3(10),[53] although it left the national court to make the final decision on this point. Thus, the EFTA Court indicated that it thought that this provision of the collective agreement could not be applied to posted workers.

The Norwegian Supreme Court took a different approach. Relying on both Article 3(1), second indent, and Article 3(7), second paragraph of the PWD,[54] it said, again *obiter*, that travel expenses were pay; if not and workers had to meet the costs themselves, the workers' pay would be reduced.[55] However, the Supreme Court did not find it necessary to conclude on this point, since it said that the compensation could be justified on the basis of public policy under Article 3(10) due to the importance of paying expenses to 'the stability of the Norwegian working life model'.[56]

B. Observations

The most striking feature of this case is the express disagreement between the EFTA Court and the Supreme Court on the third issue, namely whether the travel expenses were pay and, even if they were not, whether they could be justified on public policy grounds under Article 3(10) PWD. This suggests a degree of antagonism between the two courts and a fundamental disagreement as to their roles in the EEA system and their understanding of EU/EEA law. However, the picture is actually more complex than this.

---

[49] Para 116.
[50] *Cf* Art 3(7), second paragraph, which the Court did not expressly refer to in its findings.
[51] Para 97.
[52] Case C-319/06 *Commission v Luxembourg* [2008] ECR I-4323, noted by C Barnard (2009) 38 *Industrial Law Journal* 122.
[53] Para 101.
[54] Art 3(7), second paragraph, adds: 'Allowances specific to the posting shall be considered to be part of the minimum wage, unless they are paid in reimbursement of expenditure actually incurred on account of the posting, such as expenditure on travel, board and lodging.'
[55] Para 154.
[56] Paras 155, 170. *Cf* Case E-12/10 *ESA v Iceland* [2011] EFTA Ct Rep 117, where the EFTA Court found that Iceland had failed to make out a public policy defence due to the fact that there were only nine posted workers in Iceland in 2010 and so it was difficult to see how the requirements in the Icelandic Act could be considered 'crucial to Iceland's social order' (para 59).

i. The EFTA Court's Judgment

The EFTA Court's judgment itself closely mirrors the Court of Justice's *Laval*[57] line of case law. The *Laval* case law has been highly controversial but in essence the CJEU, reading the Posted Workers Directive in the light of its free movement of services legal basis, allowed host states (1) to apply their labour law rules to posted workers, but only in the areas listed in Articles 3(1)(a)–(g) PWD, and (2) only if those laws complied exactly with the terms of the directive. Allowing host states to apply any labour law rules to posted workers was already a derogation from the principle of home state control embodied in Article 56 TFEU (Article 36 EEA). Therefore, for the Court, any derogations from Article 3(1) (namely Article 3(7), the so-called minimum standards clause, and Article 3(10), the public policy provision), as derogations to derogations, had to be even more narrowly construed.

The EFTA Court respected this understanding in its interpretation of, for example, Article 3(10) PWD. Substantive homogeneity was preserved. *STX* therefore seems to support Fredriksen's view that the EFTA Court consistently (and commendably) has let the objective of a homogeneous EEA prevail over any temptation it may have had to pursue its own interpretation of the EEA Agreement. He concludes that the result is 'the de facto acknowledgment of the [CJEU] as the supreme authority on the interpretation of (substantive) EEA law'.[58] Therefore, rather than describing the EFTA Court as 'more catholic than the Pope', which, as we saw above, has been alleged by some commentators, it is more accurate to say that the EFTA Court is a good and obedient student of EU law.

However, the questions referred in *STX* also forced the EFTA Court to consider matters to which the CJEU has not yet turned its attention: in particular, the precise nature of the relationship between the Posted Workers Directive and Article 36 EEA, especially in the context of meaning of pay in the second indent of Article 3(1) PWD. In a ground-breaking decision, the EFTA Court said that where the PWD leaves matters to national law (eg determining the content of the host state rules which are to apply to posted workers), that national law must be compatible with Article 36 EEA/56 TFEU. Specifically, it said at paragraphs 31 and 74:

> [T]he Directive does not harmonise the material content of those mandatory rules for minimum protection. Accordingly, the content of these rules may be freely defined by the EEA States, in compliance with the EEA Agreement and the general principles of EEA law (see *ESA v Iceland*, ... paragraph 45, and, for comparison, *Laval* ... paragraph 60).
>
> ...
>
> In exercising the discretion accorded to them to define the *content of mandatory rules for minimum protection* for the purposes of Article 3(1) of the Directive, EEA States are

---

[57] Case C-341/05 *Laval un Partneri Ltd* [2007] ECR I-11767.
[58] https://bora.uib.no/bitstream/handle/1956/7862/The%20two%20EEA%20Courts. pdf?sequence=1, 17.

obliged, furthermore, to respect the EEA Agreement, in particular, in the present case, Article 36 EEA. Therefore, even if the national court finds that the remuneration which forms the subject of Question 1(b) satisfies the specific requirements of the Directive with regard to minimum rates and other criteria, this question must also be examined with regard to the provisions of the Directive interpreted in the light of Article 36 EEA, and, where appropriate, with regard to the latter provision itself.

This is an innovative and sophisticated approach. The EFTA Court recognises the complex nature of the PWD: that it contains an element of exhaustive harmonisation (concerning which rules apply—home or host state) but that it also contains provisions which refer back to national law and it is this national law, particularly in respect of pay, which needs to be judged with reference to Article 36 EEA. While there are problems with this approach,[59] it is probably the least bad in the circumstances. This is not judicial activism, as also alleged against the EFTA Court; it is the EFTA Court engaging in difficult but necessary decision making.

The decision on how and when Article 36 EEA is to be applied is perhaps expressed more opaquely in paragraphs 31 and 74 of *STX* than might have been desirable, and it may be for this reason that the Norwegian Supreme Court struggled in deciding when, precisely, to apply Article 36 EEA in conjunction with the Directive. Leaving aside the question on the scope of Article 3(10) PWD to which we return below, the striking feature of the Norwegian Supreme Court's decision in *STX* is the lengths to which it goes to apply the EFTA Court's decision even when it firmly believes it is not obliged to do so.[60]

ii. The Judgment of the Norwegian Supreme Court

As regards the Norwegian Supreme Court's decision in *STX*, at first sight it looks like the Norwegian Supreme Court's disagreement with the EFTA Court on the third question risks jeopardising the principles of homogeneity and uniformity of EEA law, the duty of loyal cooperation and ultimately reciprocity. I am not so sure. In order to explain, some context is necessary. Matters of pay are highly sensitive; this is underlined by the exclusion of EU competence in respect of pay under Article 153(5) TFEU. It is also reflected in the fact that Article 3(1) second indent appears to insist that the concept of minimum rates of pay referred to in Article 3(1)(c) is defined by the national law and/or practice of the Member State to whose territory the worker is posted. This appears to send a strong message to the national courts that what constitutes pay should be decided by the national systems and adjudicated by the national courts. While the EFTA Court's sophisticated analysis (in paragraphs 31 and 74 cited above) casts doubt on this, for national courts the position is more straightforward: they should determine what constitutes pay. So from this point of view, there may be some salience in the

---

[59] See the discussion in C Barnard, 'Posting Matters' (2014) 11 *Arbeidsrett* 1.
[60] Para 17.

argument discussed above (as to why references are not being made to the EFTA Court) that 'A national supreme court is in a better position to decide certain sensitive cases'.

In respect of the disagreement over the scope of application of the Article 3(10) public policy derogation, as we have seen, the EFTA Court followed the Court of Justice's decision in *Luxembourg* to the letter. The problem is that many people think that the CJEU in *Luxembourg* went too far when it insisted that 'while the Member States are still, in principle, free to determine the requirements of public policy in the light of national needs, the notion of public policy in the [Union] context ... may be relied on only if there is a genuine and sufficiently serious threat to a fundamental interest of society'.[61] This test for public policy in *Luxembourg* replicates the well-known test for public policy used by the Court in the context of free movement of persons to consider whether a Member State is justified in deporting a migrant.[62] With the exception of laws against slavery,[63] it is difficult to see how states can argue that any labour laws, however fundamental to the system of employment protection, satisfy this extraordinarily high standard.[64] The Court of Justice's interpretation risked de facto killing Article 3(10).

The Norwegian Supreme Court has injected a new lease of life into Article 3(10). As we have seen, it said that the compensation could be justified on the basis of public policy under Article 3(10), due to the importance of paying expenses to 'the stability of the Norwegian working life model',[65] relying on evidence produced by the Norwegian government to support its assertion of the precarity of the Norwegian social model if expenses were not reimbursed.[66] While it seems somewhat surprising that the Norwegian social model really is so fragile, the Supreme Court's decision constitutes a sensible recalibration of the decision in *Luxembourg*.

---

[61] Para 50. In support, it cited Declaration No 10 on Art 3(10) PWD recorded in the Council minutes, which provides that the expression 'public policy provisions' should be construed as covering 'those *mandatory* rules from which there can be no derogation and which, by their nature and objective, meet the imperative requirements of the public interest. These may include, in particular, the prohibition of forced labour or the involvement of public authorities in monitoring compliance with legislation on working conditions' (para 33, emphasis added).

[62] Case 30/77 *Bouchereau* [1977] ECR 1999, now enshrined in Article 27 of the Citizens Rights Directive 2004/38.

[63] Referred to in Declaration No 10 considered above n 61.

[64] The group of experts advising the Commission thought that public policy provisions would cover fundamental rights and freedoms such as freedom of association and collective bargaining, prohibition of forced labour, the principle of non-discrimination and elimination of exploitative forms of child labour, data protection and the right to privacy, but there is no evidence that the Commission agreed with this (COM(2003) 458, 14.

[65] Paras 155, 170. *Cf ESA v Iceland* where the EFTA Court found that Iceland had failed to make out a public policy defence due to the fact that there were only nine posted workers in Iceland in 2010 and so it was difficult to see how the requirements in the Icelandic Act could be considered 'crucial to Iceland's social order' (para 59).

[66] Paras 159–170. The trade unions had produced statistics to demonstrate the consequences of a two-tier model developing if expenses were not reimbursed. By contrast the employers and the employers' association emphasised the rude health of the Norwegian social model (paras 26, 31–33).

The Supreme Court could, of course, have asked for further clarification in respect of the interpretation of pay and the meaning of Article 3(10) PWD but it may well be that, in addition to its general reluctance to refer, the Supreme Court asked itself, as Fredriksen says in a different context, 'how much there really is to gain from a preliminary reference to the EFTA Court and if the advantages outweigh the delay, work and cost entailed'.[67]

Finally, the EFTA Court and the Supreme Court inevitably approach social issues from different perspectives. As I have argued elsewhere,[68] the CJEU and the EFTA Court are expressly mandated by the Treaties to look at the economic context of cross-border migration and attempt to balance that with labour rights. While national courts, respecting their obligations under EU and EEA law, should do this too, it is easy to understand why national courts, at one stage removed from the process of interpreting EU Treaties (and with greater familiarity and confidence in their own systems), tend to default to a more familiar labour/social law position, which is about protecting the weak. Thus for the Norwegian Supreme Court posted *workers* are workers and thus weak and so need protection by Norwegian law/collective agreements; as *posted* workers they are weaker still and all the more in need of protection. This is reflected in the Supreme Court's observation that:[69]

> Section 1 of the Norwegian General Application Act incorporates the need for protection of foreign workers on an equal footing with Norwegian workers. In other words, it is inherent in the consideration for equality of treatment that posted workers have a need for social protection.

And the economic narrative of the CJEU/EFTA Court is not necessarily attractive to national courts. The effect of the European Court's rulings in *Laval* and *STX* is that Swedish/Norwegian workers are expected to incur a sacrifice (loss of their jobs to cheaper competition from the east) simply because they are part of a more wealthy economy: they are making a sacrifice 'for the sake of belonging to a "bigger" transnational regime'.[70] And they do this based presumably on some deep-seated sense of solidarity between members of that transnational regime. In other words, Norwegian/Swedish workers must make a sacrifice for the benefit of unknown workers from other Member States in the EU-8. Such a requirement is anathema to nationalist logic[71] and one that *national* courts find hard to stomach.

---

[67] He also notes that it is possible that the Norwegian legislator's emphasis on proportionality as a general principle of civil procedure in the new 2005 Dispute Act has led Norwegian courts to think twice before requesting an advisory opinion from the EFTA Court: According to Section 1-1, the procedure and the costs involved shall be 'reasonably proportionate to the importance of the case'. If not read in an EEA-friendly manner, this principle could be understood as raising the threshold for a reference in cases where the value of the subject matter of the action is rather low (as, eg, in most consumer protection cases) (https://bora.uib.no/bitstream/handle/1956/7862/The%20two%20EEA%20Courts.pdf?sequence=1, 17).

[68] Barnard, above n 59.

[69] Para 126.

[70] A Somek, 'The Social Question in a Transnational Context' (2011) LEQS Paper No 39/2011, 31.

[71] ibid, 30.

C. Crisis, what Crisis?

The Supreme Court's refusal to follow the EFTA Court's decision on the third point in *STX* did come as something of a shock; generally EU and EFTA courts do follow the rulings of the EFTA Court/CJEU. The fact that there are only a handful of cases where this does not happen bears testimony to the success of the reference system in both the EU and EEA.

Is this a crisis for the EFTA Court system? Some suggest it might be and it might force the CJEU to do a '*Polydor*'[72] on at least part of the EEA agreement (that is, given the differences between the EEA's approach and the EU's approach, the EU and EEA provisions are interpreted differently). I am less apocalyptic. As I have indicated above, there are good reasons why the Supreme Court decided as it did.[73] Moreover, a '*Polydor*' could only be done if the EFTA Court itself violates the principles of homogeneity and reciprocity or if the EFTA Surveillance Authority fails to enforce the EFTA Court's judgments in a systematic way. There is no evidence of this happening.

The reluctance of the Norwegian Supreme Court to make references means that the EFTA Court cannot respond to the issue directly but it has found other ways to express its dissatisfaction with the actions of the Supreme Court: through indirect criticism in *Jonsson*,[74] and through direct criticism in various speeches made extra-judicially.[75] BUSINESSEUROPE has now made a complaint to the EFTA Surveillance Authority about the Norwegian Supreme Court's decision, criticising in particular the Supreme Court's generous approach to public policy.[76]

However, there is another way of looking at this situation: as indicated above, the Norwegian Court had legitimate reasons for doing what it did. Although its actions appear to contravene the principles of homogeneity, reciprocity and the duty of loyal cooperation, these are *principles*, not mandatory *rules*. Where there are legitimate reasons for acting in the way it did, the EFTA Court needs to listen, particularly if, as the EFTA Court said in *Irish Bank*,[77] the relationship between the EFTA Court and the national courts of last resort is more 'partner-like'. As we know from the case law of the Court of Justice, the duty of loyal cooperation also

---

[72] Case C-270/80 *Polydor v Harlequin Record Shops* [1982] ECR 329.

[73] It was subsequently revealed that the employers had attempted to avoid the application of the clauses in the collective agreement by establishing an entity in Norway which would allow local recruitment of the same workers: C Baudenbacher, 'The EFTA Court and its interaction with the Norwegian Courts'.

[74] Case E-3/12.

[75] See, eg, the speech given by Prof Baudenbacher, President of the EFTA Court, 'The EFTA Court and its interaction with the Norwegian Courts', speech at the conference *International courts and their importance for the Norwegian Legal Order*, Tromsø 19 April 2013. The intensity of the dialogue between the EFTA Court and the Norwegian Supreme Court has increased markedly in recent months (email on file with author).

[76] Complaint dated 21 October 2013.

[77] Case E-18/11 *Irish Bank Resolution Corporation Ltd v Kaupthing Bank hf*, judgment of 28 September 2012, para 57.

applies to the EU institutions. The duty should apply equally to the EFTA institutions; they should take the Supreme Court's concerns about the interpretation of the Posted Workers' Directive seriously. Using Edwards and Lane's language, the Supreme Court's decision in *STX* (and its refusal to refer) is a (loud) shot across the EFTA Court's bows. Yes, an Article 34 SCA reference would have allowed it to engage more positively with the EFTA Court, especially in areas of EEA law which have not been settled by the Luxembourg courts, but we have also seen that there are reasons as to why this has not occurred.

V. CONCLUSIONS

This chapter has considered how the key principles of homogeneity, reciprocity and the duty of loyal cooperation have influenced, and should influence, the interpretation of Article 34 SCA on references to the EFTA Court. This is not a dry, abstract question but one of practical—and constitutional—significance. In the EU, Article 267 TFEU preliminary references have profoundly shaped EU law; references to the EFTA Court have the capacity to do the same.

Refusal to refer by national courts, or the refusal by national courts to respect the rulings/advisory opinions of the Court, have the capacity to affect profoundly the uniformity and evolution of EU/EEA law. But national courts refusing to engage, or to engage only reluctantly, may have their reasons in special circumstances, as was the case with the Norwegian Supreme Court in *STX*. In these circumstances their concerns deserve respect as one manifestation of the duty of loyal cooperation.

15

Preliminary Rulings in the EEA— Bridging (Institutional) Homogeneity and Procedural Autonomy by Exchange of Information

GEORGES BAUR[*]

I. INTRODUCTION

A. Jurisprudence in the EEA: A Blurred Picture

IN THE 20 years of its existence, much has already been written on the subject of preliminary rulings in the European Economic Area (EEA)[1] and more is to be expected. The interest in this issue is likely to be triggered by the question

[*] I am grateful for the support provided by my colleagues in the EEA Coordination Division, Jacqueline Breidlid, Gunnþóra Elín Erlingsdóttir and Thomas Tzieropoulos, who read the text and helped improve it. I also thank Juliet Reynolds for her copy-editing work. Any errors which remain and all opinions expressed herein are entirely mine and do not engage anyone else.

[1] To name but a few: C Baudenbacher, 'Das Vorabentscheidungsverfahren im EFTA-Pfeiler des EWR' in H Schumacher and W Zimmermann (eds), *90 Jahre Fürstlicher Oberster Gerichtshof, Festschrift für Gert Delle Karth* (Vienna, Jan Sramek Verlag, 2013) 1–22; A Batliner, 'Die Anwendung des EWR-Rechts durch liechtensteinische Gerichte—Erfahrungen eines Richters' in [2004] *LJZ* 139; DT Björgvinsson, 'Application of Article 34 of the ESA/Court Agreement by the Icelandic Courts' in *Economic Law and Justice in Times of Globalisation, Festschrift for Carl Baudenbacher* (Baden-Baden/ Bern/Vienna, Nomos/Stämpfli/Verlag Österreich, 2007) 37–50; M Broberg and N Fenger, *Preliminary References to the European Court of Justice*, 2nd edn (Oxford, Oxford University Press, 2014) 10–16; N Fenger, M Sánchez Rydelski and T van Stiphout, *European Free Trade Association (EFTA) and European Economic Area (EEA)*, 2nd edn (Alphen aan den Rijn, Wolters Kluwer, 2012) 156–162; H Haukeland Fredriksen, *Europäische Vorlageverfahren und nationales Zivilprozessrecht* (Tübingen, Mohr Siebeck, 2009) *passim*; HP Graver, 'The EFTA Court and the Court of Justice of the EC: Legal Homogeneity at Stake?' in P-C Müller-Graff and E Selvig (eds), *EEA-EU Relations* (Berlin, Berlin Verlag Arno Spitz, 1999) 48–52; P Hreinsson, 'The Interaction between Icelandic Courts and the EFTA Court' in EFTA Court (ed), *Judicial Protection in the European Economic Area* (Stuttgart, German Law Publishers, 2012) 90–99; S Magnusson, 'On the Authority of Advisory Opinions: Reflections on the Functions and the Normativity of Advisory Opinions of the EFTA Court' (2010) *Europarättslig Tidskrift* 528–551; T Örlygsson, 'Iceland and the EFTA Court' in *Economic Law and Justice in Times of Globalisation, Festschrift for Carl Baudenbacher* (Baden-Baden/Bern/Vienna, Nomos/Stämpfli/Verlag Österreich, 2007) 225–242 at 231; M Walser, 'Liechtenstein vor den EWR-Gerichten' [2011] *JUS & NEWS* 285–318.

of how similar, comparable or distinct the preliminary reference systems are in both the European Union (EU) and the EFTA pillars of the EEA. In order not to simply repeat what has already been written we will, therefore, after briefly introducing the general notions of the issue, move on to describe the current state of play in the reality of the EFTA States' side of the EEA as it has developed over the last 20 years. In doing so, we will refer back to the roots of the Agreement and, for that matter, try to compare the current practice in the EEA EFTA countries with the original agreement. It would be tempting to dig a bit deeper into the differences between the legal concepts of the EEA Agreement and the EU Treaties, but that would not be possible to the desired extent in the space available.

We shall in this chapter scrutinise the relationship between national courts and the EFTA Court with respect to the homogeneity principle and the national reservations with the inherent tension that characterises the EEA Agreement throughout. This tension is characteristic of the Agreement, and inherent by virtue of its aim to achieve a common market, but without supranational elements. First of all it needs to be recalled that this Agreement aims to give the EFTA States' citizens and enterprises rights and obligations with regard to the Internal Market.[2] It was certainly not intended merely to protect the States' interests above all else, as one nowadays might sometimes get the impression. By expressly mentioning 'the important role that individuals will play in the European Economic Area through the exercise of the rights conferred on them by this Agreement and through the judicial defence of these rights'[3] the parties clearly moved away from a classical international law agreement that only imposes rights and obligations upon States. Perhaps they did not go as far as to create a 'new order of international law' as in the EU,[4] but the EEA Agreement is described by the EFTA Court as an 'international treaty *sui generis* which contains a distinct legal order of its own'.[5]

B. The Tension between Two Poles and Choices to be Made

Needless to say, 'homogeneity' is the key principle in the EEA Agreement. The first reference to 'homogeneity' is, apart from the fourth recital of the preamble, already to be found in the first paragraph of the first Article of the EEA Agreement. The importance of that notion is, whether expressly or impliedly, also reflected in, among others, Articles 3, 6, 7 and 105 EEA. These provisions all address substantive homogeneity, that is, the aim to ensure, as far as possible, that

---

[2] S Norberg, 'The European Economic Space—Legal and institutional issues' in *EFTA Bulletin* 3/90, 9.

[3] Eighth recital of the preamble to the EEA Agreement; see also S Norberg, 'EEA Judicial Mechanism 20 Years On', in P Cardonnel, A Rosas and N Wahl (eds), *Constitutionalising the EU Judicial System, Essays in Honour of Pernilla Lindh* (Oxford, Hart Publishing, 2012) 75.

[4] *Cf* Case 26/62 *Van Gend & Loos* [1963] ECR 1, 25.

[5] Case E-9/97 *Erla Maria Sveinbjörnsdóttir v Iceland* [1998] EFTA Ct Rep 95, para 59.

the same rules, including procedural rules of the Courts, are applied throughout the EEA. This seems to be undisputed.

However, the procedural autonomy of the national courts[6] of the EEA EFTA States evidently creates a tension with the objective of homogeneity in the EEA. Reconciling these two goals thus implies that there are *choices* to be made between upholding national sovereignty and the guarantee of homogeneous rules.[7] This, for example, already becomes evident in the very first phase of the taking over of an EU legal act into the EEA. The whole structure of the EEA decision-making procedure suggests that, in principle, every outcome is possible: inclusion of new EU legislation, possibly with adaptations to the specific situation of one or more EEA EFTA States, recognition of equivalent national legislation and exclusion of new legislation from the annexes to the EEA Agreement.[8] Hence and again, *choices* have to be made as to which of the above outcomes will prevail.

From this follows the question of what principles will guide the Contracting Parties in their choices and of the nature of the arguments supporting these choices. Answering the latter first: notwithstanding its *sui generis* nature due to the *de facto* supranational elements , it is evident from the very nature of the EEA Agreement as an international treaty that choices will not only be made based on legal considerations[9] but also on political ones,[10] as will be shown below. This may, in principle, also be the case in the EU, but to a much lesser degree due to its clearly more integrated structure. Such decisions will unavoidably oscillate between the principles enshrined in the EEA Agreement, namely homogeneity[11] and

---

[6] Fredriksen, above n 1, 88.

[7] For this thought I am indebted to Thomas Tzieropoulos.

[8] There is no clear legal basis for this, but the EFTA Court argued that according to Art 102(3) EEA 'the Contracting Parties shall make all efforts to agree on matters relevant to the EEA Agreement. Moreover, Art 102(4) envisages that in the event an agreement cannot be reached, the EEA Joint Committee shall take any decision necessary to maintain the good functioning of the EEA Agreement' (Case E-6/01 *CIBA v Norway* [2002] EFTA Ct Rep 281, para 31). As this includes 'tak[ing] notice of the equivalence of legislation' (Art 102(4) first sentence *in fine*), hence no decision on the taking over at all, the Court applies the interpretative instrument of *a maiore ad minus*.

[9] See, eg, with regard to the scope of the EEA Agreement when incorporating Directive 2004/38/EC of the European Parliament and of the Council of 29 April 2004 on the right of citizens of the Union and their family members to move and reside freely within the territory of the Member States (etc), the Decision of the EEA Joint Committee (No 158/2007 of 7 December 2007) explicitly states: 'The Directive shall apply, as appropriate, to the fields covered by this Annex' (JCD 158/2007 Art 1(1)(a)) with the reasoning that, 'the concept of "Union Citizenship" is not included in the Agreement' (recital 8), 'immigration policy is not part of the Agreement' (recital 9) and 'the Agreement does not apply to third country nationals' (recital 10).

[10] See, eg, with regard to Norway's long-standing refusal to agree to integrating the Third Postal Directive (2008/6/EC of the European Parliament and of the Council of 20 February 2008 amending Directive 97/67/EC with regard to the full accomplishment of the internal market of Community postal services [OJ L 52, 3 of 27.02.2008]) into the EEA Agreement, AG Bersagel, 'Norway's Planned Reservation of the Third European Postal Directive and the Future of the European Economic Agreement' in *European Union Law Working Papers No 5* (Stanford/Vienna, Stanford Law School, 2012) 10 or the decision of the Norwegian Supreme Court in *STX* (Norges Høyesterett, Rt 2012 1447; see further II.C).

[11] See, eg, Arts 3, 6, 7 and 105 EEA.

national sovereignty.[12] Evidently this creates a huge tension as the two principles are difficult to reconcile.[13] In comparison, in the EU this tension has been lifted by gradually replacing the intergovernmental liens by conferring respective national powers to common (supranational) institutions, and that autonomous legal order being guided, among others, by the principles of supremacy and direct effect.[14] All of this is caused by the fundamental objective whereas a common market craves common rules. In the EU, the balance was tilted towards identical rules, which implied that sovereignty had to give way a little—this was the birth of direct effect and supremacy. In contrast, in the EEA the balance tilts in the other direction, that is, towards safeguarding national sovereignty. Hence, the birth of the homogeneity principle, which assumes that rules will be of the same kind and achieve the same purpose, but are not necessarily perfectly identical.

The question is, then, whether the homogeneity principle mentioned above extends to the institutions to secure it. Skúli Magnússon suggests that there are indeed also provisions that aim to achieve 'institutional homogeneity', as 'the enforcement of EEA rules, including at the judicial level in the EFTA States, should not only be adequate but also comparable to what is the case within the EU'.[15] He highlights three elements of this institutional homogeneity: first, he mentions 'the fact that the EFTA institutions are, in important aspects, modelled on the respective EU institutions'.[16] Second, the EFTA Court refers in its case law to the relevance of the reasoning of the Court of Justice of the European Union (CJEU) 'when interpreting various *procedural provisions* identical or comparable to those found in EU law'.[17] It should be mentioned that, according to Article 108(1) EEA, the EFTA Court and the Surveillance Authority adopt rules of procedure in many respects identical to those of the CJEU and the Commission. See, for example, Protocol 1 to the EEA Agreement or the Surveillance and Court Agreement. These only have effect, however, in the EFTA pillar of the EEA. Third, he mentions the EFTA Court's case law on the effect of EEA rules, pointing particularly to that on state liability.[18]

The two first elements are of relevance when assessing the character of the preliminary reference procedure in the EEA while the third element is important

---

[12] See, eg, the last recital of the Preamble to the EEA Agreement: '… does not restrict the decision making autonomy or the treaty-making power'.

[13] Fenger, Sánchez Rydelski and van Stiphout, above n 1, 63; how strong this tension is can be shown by the degree of inconsistent decisions made, eg with respect to whether or not an EU legal act is to be seen as EEA-relevant and if so, which adoptions are to be inserted into a JCD by which the legal act is incorporated into the EEA; *cf* Protocol 1 on horizontal adaptations.

[14] See Case 6/64 *Costa v ENEL* [1964] ECJ 1251, 1269–1271; it cannot be discussed here whether, and to what degree ('quasi-direct effect'), such principles apply in the EEA. *Cf,* however, Magnússon, above n 1.

[15] Magnússon, above n 1, 533.

[16] ibid.

[17] ibid, 533–534, italics in the original.

[18] ibid, 534, referring to Case E-9/97 *Sveinbjörnsdóttir*, above n 5, 95.

with regard to the consequences that a violation of duties by an EEA EFTA State might have in this context.

In any case it needs to be kept in mind that the EFTA pillar of the EEA does not—at least formally—provide for a supranational legal order binding the national courts in a coherent manner.[19] This, on the one hand, places the centre of gravity of EEA jurisprudence on the EFTA States' courts and, on the other, calls for even more intense cooperation between the courts. The parties to the EEA Agreement were well aware of this. In Article 106 EEA they therefore sketched a system for the exchange of information on EEA-related jurisprudence. As we will see, however, this was never put in place.

II. PRELIMINARY REFERENCE IN THE EFTA PILLAR: ADVISORY OPINIONS

A. General

The preliminary reference procedure is, generally speaking, probably the most important legal instrument for legal integration.[20] This was clearly the case in the EU ('clé de l'intégration juridique'). In the EEA its success and effectiveness depend in both pillars on close cooperation between the courts.[21] The preliminary reference procedure for national courts of the EFTA States to request advisory opinions as provided for in Article 34 of the Surveillance and Court Agreement (SCA) is such a result of institutional homogeneity. This provision was modelled after Article 177 of the Treaty establishing the European Community (TEC) (now Article 267 of the Treaty on the Functioning of the European Union (TFEU)). It should be noted, though, that in accordance with the two-pillar structure the jurisdiction of the EFTA Court only covers the EEA EFTA States; if a question of EEA law arises before a national court in an EU Member State, that court must use the procedure in Article 267 TFEU, and satisfy its conditions to request the CJEU to give the necessary interpretation of the relevant EEA provision.

As we shall see, there are quite some differences as to how the EFTA States' courts applied Article 34 SCA in the 20 years since its entry into force. However, differentiated application of law within a legal set-up that is nevertheless deemed to lead to homogenous interpretation is problematic. From that point of view certain practices at national level seem to be at least questionable. Some are

---

[19] For the 'cadre supranational de justification de la magistrature du juge national' see F Niang, 'La fonction européenne du juge national' (Geneva/Zurich/Basel, Schulthess, 2013) 31 et seq.

[20] C Schreuer, 'Diversity and Harmonization of Treaty Interpretation in Investment Arbitration' in M Fitzmaurice, OA Elias and P Merkouris (eds), *Treaty Interpretation and the Vienna Convention on the Law of Treaties: 30 years on* (Leiden/Boston, Nijhoff, 2010) 129–151, 150.

[21] See O Jacot-Guillarmod, 'Le juge national face au droit européen' (Basel and Frankfurt am Main/Brussels, Helbing & Lichtenhahn/Bruylant, 1993) 181: 'Un dialogue privilégié entre le juge national et le juge communautaire'.

based on procedural norms, some mere reality of law, and some on national legal theory. Critics see this as an attempt to regain control over elements of the EEA Agreement that, in their view, elude the control of the national jurisdiction.[22] We shall therefore also examine the reality of such allegations and, if they are justified, how this might jeopardise the homogeneous application of law in the EEA.

In any case, however, the procedural provisions aiming to give effect to European law, be it that of the EU or the EEA, and especially the preliminary reference procedures, are highly dependent on the well-established and equally well functioning discourse of national and supranational courts. Given the less mandatory character of EEA procedures, that willingness to cooperate is of fundamental importance as the success of homogeneous application of law depends on it.

B. Preliminary Reference Request

i. Who May Submit a Request?

Article 34 para 3 SCA allows the EEA EFTA States to restrict the right to submit requests for advisory opinions to 'courts and tribunals against whose decisions there is no judicial remedy under national law'. None of the current EEA EFTA States[23] has made use of this possibility and imposed such a restriction for only high or even last instance courts to submit.

Iceland, however, has introduced a procedure that might be seen as a filter. Although there is no formal restriction for any court to refer, decisions to do so are subject to an appeal system.[24] In practice, nearly every referral must be approved by the Icelandic Supreme Court. This raises the question of whether there is a difference between a formal restriction of the right to submit to courts of last instance, which is explicitly permitted pursuant to Article 34 SCA, and the restriction in substance to have lower courts' referrals reviewed by the Supreme Court upon appeal. One could now argue that as there is the possibility to restrict the right to refer to courts of last instance, an appeal system would *a maiore ad minus* be covered.[25]

As regards the EU, the jurisprudence of the CJEU strongly opposes this: the most topical case to date is quite certainly *Cartesio*.[26] According to the CJEU, the competence conferred to the referring court by Article 234 TEC (now Article 267

---

[22] C Baudenbacher, 'EFTA-domstolene og dens samhandling med de norske domstolene' (2013) *LoR*, 519.

[23] Only the former EEA EFTA State Austria had introduced such a restriction (EWR-Bundesverfassungsgesetz, BGBl 115/1993 Art 6).

[24] Act No 21/1994 on Advisory Opinions from the EFTA Court.

[25] See that line of argument in Case E-6/01 *CIBA v Norway* [2002] EFTA Ct Rep 281, para 31, where the Court applies this interpretative instrument, but in another context.

[26] Case C-210/06 *Cartesio* [2008] ECR I-9641; cf Case 166/73 *Rheinmühlen Düsseldorf* [1974] ECR I-33; see also Case E-18/11 *Irish Bank Resolution Corporation Ltd v Kaupthing Bank hf* [2012] EFTA Ct Rep 592, para 57.

TFEU) cannot be superseded by that of the appellate court. It remains in the sole competence of the referring court to decide whether 'to maintain the reference for a preliminary ruling, or to amend it or to withdraw it'.[27] This would clearly raise questions with regard to the case *Gunnar V Engilbertsson v Íslandsbanki*,[28] pending before the EFTA Court, in which the Icelandic Supreme Court altered the questions intended for referral by the Reykjavík District Court.[29] With this procedure, which was already criticised by others,[30] it remains *inter alia* unclear how many cases will end up not being referred, either because referral is refused or altered by the Supreme Court or because an inferior instance court might not dare to refer to the EFTA Court.[31]

Similarly, the discussion in Liechtenstein about the so-called 'constitutional review procedure' (*Normenkontrollverfahren*) might, if it ever became jurisprudence in EEA-related matters, also lead to a 'filter effect'. Since the entry into force of the EEA Agreement for Liechtenstein in 1995, the Administrative Court (*Verwaltungsgerichtshof*) had developed a very EEA-friendly attitude. It not only accepted supremacy and direct effect, at least in the national context, but also quite regularly asked the EFTA Court for advisory opinions.[32] As in Germany and Austria, the Principality of Liechtenstein has a fully fledged constitutional court with the competence to examine the constitutionality of laws, regulations and international treaties.[33] This procedure not only contains a formal element of prior referral to the Supreme Court, but also a material element, as the Supreme Court will have to deal with the matter at hand to decide if it will allow it to be referred to the EFTA Court and in which form. The aim of this constitutional review is to maintain the coherence of the legal order and legal certainty. However, according to Herbert Wille, an unlimited right to submit to the EFTA Court endangers the monopoly held by the Liechtenstein Constitutional Court with regard to the constitutional review. Wille therefore holds the view that the practice of the Liechtenstein Administrative Court to refer to the EFTA Court whenever there is a question of EEA law constitutes a violation of the Constitution.[34]

As for the judicial review procedure, which can limit the immediate impact of European legislation in the EU Member States, this was clarified by the ECJ. An

---

[27] ibid, para 96.

[28] Case E-25/13 *Gunnar V Engilbertsson v Íslandsbanki h*, nyr.

[29] It seems worth noting that the EFTA Court has accepted this. See also report for the hearing, Case E-25/13, paras 46–47. See also Örlygsson, above n 1, 232.

[30] See Björgvinsson, above n 1, 50; C Baudenbacher, 'Some thoughts on the EFTA Court's Phases of Life' in EFTA Court (ed), *Judicial Protection in the European Economic Area* (Stuttgart, German Law Publishers, 2012), 26.

[31] According to Hreinsson, above n 1, 91, 'out of fifteen cases that have ended up at the EFTA Court from Iceland, nine have had to pass the muster of the Supreme Court' (as at mid-2011).

[32] See, eg, VGH 2005/94, Decision of 9 February 2006 [2006] LES 300.

[33] Arts 18–22 StGHG (Act on the Constitutional Court [*Staatsgerichtshof*]; LGBl 2004 Nr 32; LR 173.10).

[34] H Wille, 'Das EWR-Abkommen und das Verfassungs- und Verwaltungsrecht' in T Bruha, Z Pállinger and R Quaderer (eds), *Liechtenstein—10 Jahre im EWR* (Schaan, Liechtensteinische Akademische Gesellschaft, 2005) 132.

Italian court invited the ECJ to take a position with regard to the conflict between the principle of direct effect of Community law and subsequent national legislation. In this case an additional problem arose that with regard to such conflicts the Italian Constitution in its Article 11 provides for a procedure on the control of norms by the Constitutional Court. The ECJ ruled that such a rule had no validity, because '*any provision of a national legal system and any legislative, administrative or judicial practice which might impair the effectiveness of Community law by withholding from the national court having jurisdiction to apply such law the power to do everything necessary at the moment of its application to set aside national legislative provisions which might prevent Community rules from having full force and effect are incompatible with those requirements ...*' and it went on to say that '*This would be the case ... if the solution of the conflict were to be reserved for an authority with a discretion of its own, other than the court called upon*'.[35]

If requests of the Liechtenstein Administrative Court to the EFTA Court for an advisory opinion were conditional upon prior blessing by the Constitutional Court according to the Act on the Constitutional Court, similar reservations, as they were invoked in *Simmenthal II*,[36] would apply with regard to Liechtenstein as a party to the EEA Agreement. This view is, in essence, rather based on arguments of legal peace and legal certainty and, without referring to *Simmenthal II*, shared by the President of the Liechtenstein Administrative Court when he contests the Constitutional Court's claim of competence 'to examine whether national legal standards are in conformity with EEA law'.[37]

In the same vein, the Constitutional Court of the Czech Republic also responded recently to the conferral of such a competence to its own 'benefit' by stating that this would be contravening Community law. It based its decision on the *Simmenthal II* jurisprudence.[38]

Even without referring to the disputed argument of (quasi-)direct effect in the EEA,[39] it seems quite clear that there are limits to the procedural autonomy of the EEA EFTA States' courts. These are seen as the principles of effectiveness and equivalence based on Article 3 EEA and Article 2 SCA.[40] It would, hence, be quite unacceptable for the EEA EFTA States to obstruct the rights of citizens by imposing obstacles.[41]

---

[35] Case C-106/77 *Simmenthal II* [1978] ECR p 643 (nos 22 and 23).

[36] ibid, p 629.

[37] A Batliner, 'Practical Issues Regarding the Application of EEA Law through the Eyes of a National Judge', Ch 8 in this volume, 'VI Decision-making Powers'.

[38] Ústavní soud, Decision of 2.12.2008, Pl ÚS 12/08, URL http://www.usoud.cz/en/-decisions/?tx_ttnews%5Btt_news%5D=483&cHash=6b8830d1a16e4ba14dcbc3b678bb7bb2 (English), visited on 3.04.2014.

[39] See n 14.

[40] H Haukeland Fredriksen, *Europäische Vorlageverfahren und nationales Zivilprozessrecht* (Tübingen, Mohr Siebeck, 2009) 89, referring to A Robberstad, 'Norske dommeres plikt til å veilede om EØS-retten' (2002) *LoR* 201.

[41] Case E-1/04 *Fokus Bank* [2004] EFTA Ct Rep 11, para 41.

ii. Obligation to Submit?

There are some differences between Article 34 SCA and Article 267 TFEU, of which we will evoke just two.[42] The first difference in Article 267 TFEU is that Article 34 SCA does not provide for any mandatory references for national courts or tribunals whose decisions are final. This view is based on the 'clear wording of Article 34 SCA'.[43] It has, however, been argued that it follows from the principles of judicial protection and loyalty laid down in Article 3 EEA that national courts of last instance are not free to decide whether or not to refer, but that criteria similar to those found in Article 267(3) TFEU should apply by analogy to the national courts in the EFTA countries.[44] This view is, in the opinion of others, untenable.[45]

However, the EFTA Court in recent decisions followed a line that clearly suggests, at least in certain cases, that there is a *de facto* duty to submit. In this view the duty to loyalty according to Article 3 EEA outweighs the explicit wording of Article 34 SCA.[46]

The President of the EFTA Court has, on several occasions, criticised Norway's unwillingness to refer to the EFTA Court.[47] Indeed, Iceland's figures of referral to the EFTA Court are still, relatively and notwithstanding the Icelandic appeal system with regard to preliminary references, higher than those of Norway. So the question arises as to why this might be the case, despite Norway not having any restrictions with regard to preliminary references. The alleged unwillingness to submit,[48] perhaps partly due to an attitude of renationalisation,[49] seems to be only part of the truth.[50] And the same happens within the EU.[51] There also seem to be

---

[42] The third difference being that the jurisdiction of the EFTA Court under Art 34 SCA *a priori* does not extend to the validity of secondary acts of EU law as in Art 267 TFEU. *Cf* Fenger, Sánchez Rydelski and van Stiphout, above n 1, 158.

[43] Art 34(2): '[...] may [...] request'; see Fenger, Sánchez Rydelski and van Stiphout, above n 1, 156, 157 at fn 345.

[44] Baudenbacher, above n 30, 15, speaks of '*persuasive authority*' while Magnússon, above n 1, 540, contends that there is an implied duty to refer.

[45] Fenger, Sánchez Rydelski and van Stiphout, above n 1, 157; H Wille, 'Das EWR-Abkommen und das Verfassungs- und Verwaltungsrecht' in T Bruha, Z Pallinger and R Quaderer (eds), *Liechtenstein—10 Jahre im EWR* (Schaan, Liechtensteinische Akademische Gesellschaft, 2005) 132.

[46] Case E-18/11 *Irish Bank Resolution Corporation Ltd v Kaupthing Bank hf* [2012] EFTA Ct Rep 592, para 58 (et seq); Case E-3/12 *Jonsson* [2013] EFTA Ct Rep 136, para 60; Case E-2/12 and also indirectly in *HOB-vín ehf v The State Alcohol and Tobacco Company of Iceland (ÁTVR)* [2013] EFTA Ct Rep 816, para 122; see also G Baur, 'Kohärente Interpretationsmethoden als Instrument europarechts-konformer Rechtsanwendung—eine rechtspolitische Skizze' in Liechtenstein-Institut (ed), *25 Jahre Liechtenstein-Institut (1986-2011)* (Schaan, Verlag der Liechtensteinischen Akademischen Gesellschaft (Liechtenstein Politische Schriften, Bd 50), 2011) 47, 63.

[47] Baudenbacher, above n 22, 518, 532, 533.

[48] See the Norwegian State Attorney's position referred to in H Haukeland Fredriksen, 'The Two EEA Courts—a Norwegian Perspective' in EFTA Court (ed), *Judicial Protection in the European Economic Area* (Stuttgart, German Law Publishers, 2012) 205.

[49] C Kohler, 'Homogeneity or Renationalisation in the European Judicial Area? Comments on a Recent Judgment of the Norwegian Supreme Court', this volume.

[50] Fredriksen, *Vorlageverfahren*, above n 1, 188.

[51] U Bernitz, 'Preliminary References and Swedish Courts: What Explains the Continuing Restrictive Attitude?' in P Cardonnel, A Rosas and N Wahl (eds), *Constitutionalising the EU Judicial*

very practical grounds, such as the Norwegian Courts struggling with their case load and parties being unwilling to wait longer due to an additional procedural step when referring to the EFTA Court.[52] However, if these were relevant grounds and it was therefore left to the absolute discretion of the EFTA States' courts whether to submit or not, the instruments to secure the homogenous interpretation of EEA law would lose their entire justification. This would increase the tendency towards the development of 'several EEA laws', following a certain notion of 'the two EEA Courts'.[53]

It is interesting to note that until recently the (upper) Liechtenstein civil (and criminal) courts' practice—contrary to the very EEA-friendly attitude of the Liechtenstein Administrative Court[54]—essentially followed the same line as the Norwegian courts.[55]

In a recent decision, however, the Liechtenstein Constitutional Court adopted a more factual view that no longer argued about whether or not there was a duty to refer. It simply stated that it would refer ('*legt dem EFTA-Gerichtshof [...] vor*') if the law lacked clarity and if the respective question on EEA law was relevant to the decision. The Liechtenstein Constitutional Court therefore simply applies a test to establish whether these two criteria are met and, in the affirmative, submits a respective preliminary request to the EFTA Court.[56]

The consequences of non-referral will be dealt with under Part III. It may, however, not be forgotten that there is also a fundamental rights aspect to a refusal to refer: Article 6 of the European Convention on Human Rights (ECHR)—which, according to the EFTA Court, is part of the EEA legal order[57]—requires that a

---

System, Essays in Honour of Pernilla Lindh (Oxford, Hart Publishing, 2012), 177–187; Fredriksen, *Vorlageverfahren*, above n 1, 188.

[52] Supreme Judge Henrik Bull in a comment in the EFTA Court Spring Conference 2013 on 21 June 2013 referred to such facts as Norway missing an administrative courts system, oral proceedings judges' unwillingness to break off in between or the parties' reluctance to prolong procedures or incur additional costs.

[53] See the understanding by some in Norway referred to in Fredriksen, above n 48, 204; *cf*, however, A Batliner, 'Erfolgsmodell EWR' in Regierung des Fürstentums Liechtenstein/EFTA-Gerichtshof (eds), *20 Jahre Unterzeichnung des EWR-Abkommens—Ein Vierakter mit Original-Darstellern*, 53, who contends from a Liechtenstein perspective that there is only one last instance in EEA matters: the EFTA Court.

[54] See A Batliner, above, n 1; A Batliner, above n 37 and jurisprudence referred to therein.

[55] OG (Liechtenstein High Court), Decision of 27.5.2010, Cg.2009.407; see also Case E-5/10 *Dr Kottke v Präsidial Anstalt und Sweetyle Stiftung*, report for the hearing; OGH (Liechtenstein Supreme Court) Decision of 7.5.2010, CO.2004.2, where reference to the EFTA Court was refused because questions were answered in favour of the claimant (81); however, reference was made directly to relevant case law of the ECJ (66 et seq).

[56] Decision of 7.4.2014, StGH 2013/127, 26. The Constitutional Court had to decide on an appeal against a decision of the Liechtenstein Supreme Court not to refer. It held that while the law was indeed unclear, the question at stake was not relevant to the decision of this case. For the relevance test it referred to Case C-283/81 *C.I.L.F.I.T.*, ECR [1982] I-3415.

[57] JT Lang, 'The Duty of National Courts to Provide Access to Justice in the EEA' in EFTA Court (ed), *Judicial Protection in the European Economic Area* (Stuttgart, German Law Publishers, 2012) 101; see also M Schmauch, 'The Preliminary Ruling Procedure and the Right to a Fair Trial—Strasbourg Demands Reasoned Decisions from National Courts when They Refuse to Refer a Case to the ECJ' in [2012] *ELR* 362, 366.

refusal to refer be justified, the reason essentially being that EFTA States' citizens' access to justice is at stake.[58]

iii. Obligation to Follow?

The second difference between Article 267 TFEU and Article 34 SCA is that, according to the latter's wording, the rulings of the EFTA Court are merely advisory to the national courts. The EFTA States did not want to give the EFTA Court the competence to give binding interpretations of the Agreement for constitutional reasons. In the relevant literature it is, however, contended that, although formally of importance, the practical implications of this difference to the EU legal system should not be overestimated. A national court that has requested an advisory opinion would surely be reluctant to disregard that opinion and it would require quite detailed and compelling motives to do so. It has also been argued that if a referring court should disregard an opinion of the EFTA Court, for example if part of an EFTA State's legislation was found to be incompatible with EEA law that would amount to a violation of the EEA Agreement by that EFTA State.[59] Given that the national court has no obligation to follow the advisory opinion of the EFTA Court, this may appear to be a logical twist.

   Here it is argued, however, that the national court, by arriving at another result than that of the EFTA Court, had applied the EEA Agreement incorrectly, rather than refusing to follow the EFTA Court's decision. In consequence, the EFTA Surveillance Authority could bring an infringement case against the state concerned for having failed to fulfil its obligation to apply EEA law properly. Faced with that case again, but through an infringement procedure according to Article 31 para 2 SCA, the EFTA Court would most likely maintain the view that it held in the preliminary advisory opinion and decide in favour of the Authority. This could also result in state liability.[60]

   A case which—at this point in time—has the potential for such a development is the prominent Norwegian case *STX Norway*, which caused quite some upheaval.[61] This was not least due to very political aspects, *inter alia* a discussion on 'social dumping'. This case concerned certain clauses in the collective agreement of the maritime construction industry against the background of Directive 96/71/EC[62] (the 'Posting of Workers Directive'). These clauses obliged the employers to pay posted workers a 20 per cent salary supplement for work assignments requiring overnight stays as well as compensation for expenses (travel, board and lodging) for such assignments. Upon reference by the Borgarting Lagmansrett, the EFTA

---

[58] Case E-2/02 *TBW and Bellona v EFTA Surveillance Authority* [2003] EFTA Ct Rep 52, para 37; Case E-2/03 *Ásgeirsson* [2003] EFTA Ct Rep 185, para 23; Case E-4/11, *Arnulf Clauder* [2011] EFTA Ct Rep 216, para 48.

[59] Fenger, Sánchez Rydelski and van Stiphout, above n 1, 157.

[60] See III.B.

[61] Norges Høyesterett, Rt 2012, 1447.

[62] Directive 96/71/EC of the European Parliament and of the Council of 16 December 1996 concerning the posting of workers in the framework of the provision of services, OJ L 018 of 21.1.1997, 1–6.

Court gave its judgment in the case, essentially confirming the view that the two clauses went against the Directive.[63] The referring court and ultimately the Supreme Court, however, found the clauses to be justified on grounds of public policy and disregarded the EFTA Court's ruling.[64] As it made clear in its subsequent ruling in *Jonsson*,[65] which was partly seen as an undue revengeful comment,[66] the EFTA Court regarded the Norwegian Supreme Court's ruling as being erroneous.

Whatever the correct reasoning might have been, there is a need for a 'last instance on EEA law'[67] because there obviously is a necessity for conform interpretation to safeguard homogeneity. What makes the situation difficult in the EEA is that the national courts do not always interpret their cases in conformity with EEA law, or that their interpretation is sometimes not very accurate. Should homogeneity be seen as being systematically jeopardised, here by jurisprudence, this might have consequences, which we will discuss under III.A.

III. POSSIBLE CONSEQUENCES

A. *'Polydor'* Jurisprudence

Should the EFTA States' national jurisprudence be seen as systematically jeopardising the homogeneity principle, this could, ultimately, lead to the application of the *Polydor* doctrine by the CJEU.[68] This doctrine refers to the Court's jurisprudence in relation to texts of free trade agreements with third countries that are identically or similarly worded to provisions of EU law. The CJEU decided that such provisions were to be interpreted in a differentiated way, taking into account the purpose and the context of the respective agreement.[69] Should this happen in the context of the EEA, individuals and enterprises from the EEA EFTA States would no longer be able to enjoy the same rights and freedoms conferred by the EEA Agreement as EU citizens.

The CJEU already demonstrated what this would look like in the 'small Polydor'[70] case, *Rimbaud*. In that case, dealing with higher taxes applied by France on real estate held through legal entities in countries (here Liechtenstein)

---

[63] Case E-2/11, *STX Norway* [2012] EFTA Ct Rep 4.

[64] Baudenbacher, above n 22, 524–529.

[65] Case E-3/12, *Jonsson* [2013] EFTA Ct Rep 136, para 56; see also Baudenbacher, above n 22, 525–528.

[66] Eg, Professor Finn Arnesen in a comment at the EFTA Court Spring Conference 2013 on 21 June 2013.

[67] See A Batliner, above n 53, 53.

[68] Case 270/80 *Polydor Ltd and RSO Records Inc v Harlequin Record Shops and Simons Records Ltd* [1982] ECR 329; confirmed in Case C-541/08 *Christian Grimme v Deutsche Angestellten-Krankenkasse* [2009] ECR I-1077 and Case C-541/08 *Fokus Invest AG v FIAG* [2010] ECR I-1025.

[69] *Cf* Art 31 of the Vienna Convention on the Law of Treaties; see further C Tobler, 'Die EuGH-Entscheidung *Grimme*—Die Wiederkehr von *Polydor* und die Grenze des bilateralen Rechts' in *Jahrbuch für Europarecht 2009/2010* (Bern/Zürich, Stämpfli/Schulthess, 2010) 369–384.

[70] Baudenbacher, above n 22, 531.

with which France had no tax or administrative agreements, the CJEU justified a deviation from the free movement of capital and non-discrimination principles. A similar case, this time with respect to Luxembourg,[71] which also did not exchange information on tax matters, had been decided differently. Comparing the two cases, the CJEU stressed the lack of a comparable 'regulatory framework'.[72] The relevance of *Rimbaud* for the whole of the EEA of course also depends on whether the focus is rather on the free movement of capital or tax policy which is not covered by the EEA Agreement.

B. State Liability

As is widely known, state liability for breach of obligations under the EEA Agreement was established by the EFTA Court in its landmark case, *Sveinbjörnsdóttir*.[73] Again, we cannot discuss the problems this raises with regard to a theoretically different legal basis in the EEA Agreement compared to the EU and its links with (quasi-) direct effect etc; nor can we discuss the importance that it is to be given compared to in the EU.[74] It is nevertheless clear that state liability is *inter alia* seen as a compensatory instrument for the very lack of direct effect and supremacy in the EEA context.[75] The EFTA Court set, here with respect to the incorrect implementation of a directive, three conditions that must be met, thereby following the CJEU's jurisprudence established in *Francovich*[76] and *Brasserie du Pêcheur*.[77] First, the directive is intended to confer rights to individuals. Second, there must be a serious enough breach. Third, there needs to be a causal link between breach and loss or damage. This was later extended, in *Karlsson*,[78] to, more broadly, the adoption of legislative or administrative acts in breach of EEA law, as well as to failure to act. It thus widely aligned state liability with the level available to injured parties in the EU.[79]

With regard to Norway, where the principle of state liability as established by the EFTA Court had been accepted in the widely quoted *Finanger* case, the Supreme Court decided that the conditions were the same in both the EU and the

---

[71] Case C-451/05 *Européenne et Luxembourgeoise d'investissements SA (ELISA) v Directeur général des impôts and Ministère public* [2007] ECR I-8251.

[72] Case C-72/09 *Établissements Rimbaud SA v Directeur général des impôts, Directeur des services fiscaux d'Aix-en-Provence* [2010] ECR I-10659, paras 45–52 ; see also G Baur and C Tobler, 'Zwischen Skylla und Charybdis—oder die Schweiz vor der Wahl zwischen bilateralem Weg und EWR?' in *Schweizerisches Jahrbuch für Europarecht 2010/2011* (Bern/Zürich, Stämpfli/Schulthess) 524–528.

[73] Case E-9/97 *Sveinbjörnsdóttir*, above n 5, para 95.

[74] C Baudenbacher, 'The Implementation of Decisions of the ECJ and of the EFTA Court in Member States' Domestic Legal Orders' in [2005] *Texas International Law Journal* 40:383, 414.

[75] SI Gisladóttir, 'The Saga of Þór Kolbeinsson', Master's thesis (Reykjavík: Faculty of Law, University of Iceland School of Social Sciences, 2012) 87.

[76] Joined Cases C-6/90 and C-9/90 *Francovich et al* [1991] ECR I-5357.

[77] Joined Cases C-46/93 and C-48/93 *Brasserie du Pêcheur and Factortame* [1996] ECR I-1029.

[78] Case E-4/01 *Karlsson v Iceland* [2002] EFTA Ct Rep 240, para 32; see also Case E-2/12 *HOB-Vín III* [2012] EFTA Ct Rep 1092, para 121.

[79] Fenger, Sánchez Rydelski and van Stiphout, above n 1, 80.

EEA. The threshold was thus neither higher nor lower; the latter not sitting 'well with the case law of the EFTA Court'.[80]

In Liechtenstein, the difference between the approach of the Administrative Court and the Supreme Court (in civil and criminal matters) when referring to the EFTA Court became apparent in the 'Tschanett Saga'[81] with respect to a case that ultimately led to a state liability procedure. The Austrian physician, Dr Tschanett, was denied a concession to practice in Liechtenstein based on the *Single Practice Rule*. The administrative appeal procedure ultimately led to a decision of the Administrative Court that the licence had been denied wrongly, based on an advisory opinion of the EFTA Court.[82] Based on the EFTA Court's state liability jurisprudence, Tschanett then claimed 1.15 million Swiss francs in losses. While the High Court ruled that the claim was justified, the Supreme Court denied the responsibility of the Liechtenstein Government because it was not known that the Single Practice Rule was incompatible with EEA law.[83] This decision was remanded by the Constitutional Court. Nevertheless, the Supreme Court again dismissed the claim, this time arguing that the violation of EEA law was not serious enough. The plaintiff's application for referral to the EFTA Court was dismissed on the grounds that the Constitutional Court had ordered the Supreme Court to answer the questions at hand and not the EFTA Court.[84] The plaintiff appealed to the EFTA Surveillance Authority, but to no avail. After the Constitutional Court had also suspended that second decision, the Supreme Court decided a third time, now in favour of the plaintiff.[85] This time the Liechtenstein Supreme Court followed the Norwegian Supreme Court and applied the *acte clair* doctrine, as the Norwegian Supreme Court had in *Finanger*.[86]

Finally, we should mention a comparable Icelandic case, given its several runs through the instances, called the 'Saga of Þór Kolbeinsson'.[87] The plaintiff claimed compensation from his employer for injuries suffered in an accident at work. This claim was dismissed by the Supreme Court. Subsequently a claim was lodged for compensation from the Icelandic State based on it having failed to fulfil its obligation under EEA law to implement certain directives on safety at work. The EFTA Court, in its advisory opinion, decided that 'an EEA State may be held liable'.[88] The EFTA Court stated that 'save in exceptional cases it was not compatible with

---

[80]   Baudenbacher, above n 22, 531, referring to Norges Høyesterett, Rt 2010, 1500 para 91 and Rt 2012, 1793 para 40.

[81]   C Baudenbacher, 'Das Vorabentscheidungsverfahren im EFTA-Pfeiler des EWR' in H Schumacher and W Zimmermann (eds), *Festschrift für Gert Delle Karth* (Vienna, Jan Sramek Verlag, 2013), 12.

[82]   Case E-5/06 *ESA v Liechtenstein* [2007] EFTA Ct Rep 296.

[83]   OGH CO.2004.2-25 of 7.12.2006, see (2007) *JUS & NEWS* 137; see also the critical comment by Bernhard Hofstötter, 'Rechtsfehlerhafte Abweisung einer EWR-Staatshaftungsklage als judikatives Unrecht?' (Urteil des Obersten Gerichtshofs vom 7. Dezember 2006 (CO.2004.2-25)), in (2007) *JUS & NEWS* 33–35.

[84]   OGH CO.2004.2-38 of 5.7.2008.

[85]   OGH CO.2004.2-46 of 7.5.2010.

[86]   Norges Høyesterett, Rt 2005 1365.

[87]   Gisladóttir, above n 74, *passim*.

[88]   Case E-2/10 *Kolbeinsson* [2010] EFTA Ct Rep 234, para 85.

Council Directive 89/391/EEC ... to hold a worker liable under national tort law for all, or the greater share, of losses suffered."[89] However, it was left to the national court to assess whether, under national case law on state liability, the conditions had been met in this case. Subsequently the Supreme Court of Iceland confirmed the position of the District Court and again dismissed the claim on the grounds that the breach was not sufficiently serious.[90]

The national courts' jurisprudence referred to in the cases above shows the extent to which the application of EEA law lacks coherence, even though (or because?) with regard to state liability it is left for national courts to decide on whether conditions for liability, and often also transparency, are fulfilled.

IV. COOPERATION

On a more positive note, the successful functioning of an agreement strongly depends on the mutual trust of the parties involved. This is also the case with regard to the EEA. In the beginning there was some reluctance on the part of the EU in this respect.[91] This now seems to have gone and the functioning of EEA EFTA jurisprudence at the level of the EFTA Court seems to be undisputed.[92] Little, however, is known about the national courts' jurisprudence with regard to the EEA, mainly if we look at the level of communication between them. Given the proclaimed importance of the national courts, especially in the EEA context, their jurisprudence lacks visibility beyond the national boundaries. As has been shown in chapter II it also seems evident that there is a lot of questionable practice if checked against the background of what is commonly perceived as convened in the EEA Agreement and the SCA. One problem seems to be the lack of information.

Much has been written about the cooperation between courts, their dialogue, etc. However, in reality, dialogue takes place mainly between the CJEU and the EFTA Court, the latter 'going first' in some cases and also having its decisions respected and taken into account by the former. The development mentioned last was not expected at the time of the EEA's inception.[93] Then there is some exchange through 'academic' means (articles, seminars, etc). But real dialogue between the national courts and the EFTA Court, except for the immediate contact already immanent in the preliminary reference procedure or references to the EFTA Court's jurisprudence (or the CJEU's) in their rulings, is not evident. However, as the parties to the EEA Agreement were well aware, the less coherent

---

[89] ibid, Opinion Answer 1.

[90] Case No 532/2012 *Þór Kolbeinsson v íslenska ríkið*, Supreme Court of Iceland, 21 February 2013.

[91] Opinion 1/91 [1991] ECR I-6079; C Baudenbacher, 'Was ist aus dem Gutachten des EuGH 1/91 geworden?' in G Baur (ed), *Europäer—Botschafter—Mensch, Liber amicorum für Prinz Nikolaus von Liechtenstein* (Schaan, Liechtenstein Verlag, 2007) 79–107.

[92] A review of the functioning of the European Economic Area, [EU] Commission Staff Working Document (SWD[2012] 425 final of 7.12.2012), 4.

[93] See also Fredriksen, above n 39, 188, especially fn 9 thereto.

structure of the judicial set-up in the EEA called for a proper exchange of interpretations in order to have a transparent overview of the decisions of the different
courts involved. This is foreseen in Article 106 EEA, which calls for the parties
to establish 'a system of exchange of information concerning judgments by the
EFTA Court, the Court of Justice of the European Communities and the Court
of First Instance of the European Communities and the Courts of last instance of
the EFTA States'. [94]

What did the parties mean by this? Such a system should provide for (a) the
transmission of relevant judgments to the Registrar of the CJEU; (b) the classification, translation and creation of abstracts; and (c) the communication of
relevant documents to the competent authorities designated by the contracting
parties.[95] Preparatory material to the EEA Agreement is equally clear on this issue:
it is evident from earlier sources[96] that this system should be designed according
to the example of Article 2 of Protocol 2 to the Lugano Convention,[97] which contains such a provision on the exchange of information.

To our knowledge, such a system has never been established, although the
wording is unambiguous: 'shall be set up'. Information obtained suggests that the
Registrar of the then ECJ did once look into the matter but did not pursue it, as
a decision to establish such a system should have been taken by the EEA Joint
Committee. Why this never happened is, at this point in time, mere speculation:
the drop-out of Switzerland in 1992; the accession of Austria, Finland and Sweden
to the EC; the deferral of Liechtenstein's accession until 1 May 1995; never the
time to really deal with this; or was it simply forgotten?

A better overview of the case law in EEA matters would, first, help national
courts to apply the law and, especially with regard to the preliminary reference
procedure, provide orientation to the national courts in charge of submitting
their respective questions primarily to the EFTA Court. Second, it would help
the EFTA Court identify where national courts might need guidance.[98] Third,
and most importantly, it would help to secure more homogenous case law of the
national courts. That this is currently not the case can be demonstrated, in addition to the cases quoted previously, by the fact that, for example, the delicate issues
of direct effect and supremacy in the EEA are decided in opposite manners if one
compares Nordic and Liechtenstein[99] case law. This may well be justified by the

---

[94] Art 106 EEA, first sentence.

[95] Art 106 EEA (a) to (c).

[96] Botschaft zur Genehmigung des Abkommens über den Europäischen Wirtschaftsraum vom 18.
Mai 1992, BBl 1992 IV 1 (Swiss Government Bill on the EEA Agreement, special print, volume I), 480;
see also S Norberg, K Hökborg, M Johansson D Eliasson and L Dedichen, *The European Economic
Area—EEA Law—A Commentary on the EEA Agreement* (Stockholm, Fritzes, 1992) 193.

[97] Convention on jurisdiction and the enforcement of judgments in civil and commercial matters, done at Lugano on 16 September 1988 (88/592/EEC), OJ of 25.11.1988, nr L 319, 9; see also
T Schmidt-Parzefall, *Die Auslegung des Parallelübereinkommens von Lugano* (Tübingen, Mohr Siebeck,
1995) 57 et seq.

[98] See Case E-18/11 *Irish Bank Resolution Corporation Ltd v Kaupthing Bank hf*, [2012] EFTA Ct
Rep 592, para 56.

[99] In the affirmative, eg, VGH 2005/94, para 21 et seq, based on Art 7 EEA and Protocol 35.

different international law systems (monistic versus dualistic). It cannot, however, be the result wished for by 'the objective of the Contracting Parties to arrive at as uniform an interpretation as possible'.[100]

V. CONCLUSION

We have tried to show how difficult it is to develop, first, a clear doctrine for dealing with the decisions imposed on those having to interpret the EEA Agreement against the background of the tension between homogeneity and national competence. Hence, choices need to be made. It is contended herein that homogeneity trumps national competence when interpreting the EEA Agreement. Given the wording of the EEA Agreement it would, however, be too easy to simply refer to the institutional set-up of the EU and the CJEU's respective case law. The role of the national courts is not to be underestimated. As in the EEA Agreement the relation between the EFTA Court and the national courts is more 'partner-like',[101] homogeneity as the central principle of this Agreement is all the more important.

We did not aim to describe the content of this principle, but to show how it can be respected by procedural means, particularly by the preliminary reference procedure according to Article 34 SCA. By describing some national practices with regard to the main elements of that provision, that is, referring to the EFTA Court and, maybe, following its advisory opinions, it has become clear that the jurisprudence of the three EEA EFTA States clearly lacks coherence in more than one way. *Inter alia*, choices seem not always to be made on the basis of legal arguments, but also on that of national politics.

Given the lack of a constitutional framework, unlike in the EU, and hence, the comparatively more important role of the national courts in the three EEA EFTA States, it is all the more important to have information on the different courts' jurisprudence available, put in evidence and exchanged. This was already provided for in the EEA Agreement in Article 106 EEA when it entered into force, although that provision was never applied. In order to enhance homogeneity and to be more transparent on the EFTA side, it should be considered finally after 20 years. This is of utmost importance as a lack of information and transparency with regard to case law might jeopardise the aim of striving towards a homogenous Internal Market, especially now, as the functioning of the EEA Agreement is under scrutiny.[102]

Ultimately, this is about protecting the rights of citizens, especially in the EEA EFTA States.

---

[100] Art 105 para 1 EEA; see also the preamble to Protocol 35: 'aims at achieving a homogeneous European Economic Area (...)'.

[101] See Case E-18/11 *Irish Bank Resolution Corporation Ltd v Kaupthing Bank hf* [2012] EFTA Ct Rep 592, para 57.

[102] See, eg, the Commission Working Paper 'A review of the functioning of the European Economic Area', above n 91 and, with regard to the EEA EFTA States' current transposition deficit, the so-called 'backlog', EEA Joint Parliamentary Committee: Report on Single Market Governance of 26 March 2014, 6.

Part II

Decentred Integration

16

European Integration

XAVIER BETTEL[*]

Dear Judges, dear Carl, Excellencies, Ladies and Gentlemen,

First thing, I would like to directly underline, is that we don't think about 'empire' in Luxembourg—we are happy as a Grand Duchy. And Carl, congratulations to you as the President of the EFTA Court for organising the 20th anniversary of the Court today. But as I know you and your wife—after the dinner the stress won't be over: don't forget that Switzerland is playing football tonight!

Dear guests, I am also proud that the EFTA Court is based in Luxembourg just like the other European judicial institutions and I congratulate you on the 20th anniversary of the EFTA Court.

It was in fact a natural choice that after it was established in 1994, the EFTA Court was moved to Luxembourg in 1996. There is one major characteristic that both the EFTA Court and Luxembourg have in common: they are small, but strong and important.

Luxembourg is a founding member of what is today the European Union, and since then we have always played a constructive role in Europe. As Prime Minister of a country where every second resident does not have Luxembourgish nationality, I am also proud that we have no political party in our Parliament from the extreme right and I am very happy and proud also that in the recent European elections the Luxembourgish people clearly voted pro-European and did not go against European MEPs in Brussels or Strasbourg. Unfortunately, that is not what happened everywhere else in Europe and to be honest, this worries me and it makes me angry at the same time.

It worries me because there is a very clear danger when political forces, who want to destroy a model of peace, become too powerful. It makes me angry because as national politicians, we are at least partly responsible for the rise of anti-European and Eurosceptic parties—and to some extend it is also our own responsibility that an extreme right party, like the *Front National* in France, has become so powerful.

---

[*] Keynote speech given at the EFTA Court's 20th Anniversary Conference on 20 June 2014.

For many years now, there was one main communication strategy for politicians all over Europe. The key element of that strategy was: If something goes well take all the credit for yourself, and if something doesn't go so well, and is publicly criticised, then join the criticism and blame Europe. That is why the European Union has a rather bad public image. That is also why the name of the Belgian capital seems to be a synonym for all the things that make our daily life more complicated and less fun. When it comes to food and European regulation everybody knows the example of the bananas and a directive on the bending of this fruit. Very rarely, however, do people talk about food security, about a policy on the transparency of ingredients, on consumer protection and so on.

When the question of border policy and immigration is discussed, you hear many national politicians talking about illegal immigrants and a possible threat to our labour markets. You are all familiar with the stories about crime and human trafficking.

Of course, problems should be discussed openly but I also expect that we talk about the Erasmus programme, for example. I also expect that we talk about the fact that it has become very easy for people to study, to live and to work in different countries, that it has become totally unbureaucratic to get married when you fell in love with a person who does not come from the same town but rather from across the border.

We need much more positive stories about Europe and much less unfounded criticism of so-called 'Brussels'—as if it were a 'sea monster' with bad influence on our daily life.

There is another thing that we also tend to forget: who is Brussels?

Is it a bureaucratic apparatus that produces lots of paper and very little concrete measures to improve our life?

Yes, sometimes it may appear a bit distant and removed from reality. But then it is the people you voted for who are also responsible for this. And I am not only talking about Members of the European Parliament or the Commission! Europe is also Angela Merkel, François Hollande, David Cameron, as it is Elio di Rupo, Marc Rutte, it is even Viktor Orban and now, it is also Xavier Bettel.

If Europe does something that you think is a very bad idea, then blame your own government first—and of course be aware of the fact that these people were democratically elected to make choices.

As I stand here to address you, there is a place in Eastern Europe where people are shooting each other. Last week a military plane was shot down in the Ukraine and 49 people died. This is a very serious situation and it is a reality we are not used to any more.

Considering the beginning of the conflict in the Ukraine, we probably realise that Europe is something valuable. These were people who put their lives on the line to move closer to Europe.

There were young people who had lost hope in their future and had only one ace up their sleeve, and that was approaching the European Union.

These people risked their lives to have more Brussels. We should keep that in mind when we complain about the European Union and the curvature of bananas.

Ladies and Gentlemen, historically, Luxembourg has always played the role of a mediator in Europe. When we celebrate 175 years of independence, we also celebrate an anniversary of a strong country whose sovereignty was under threat more than once. However, when the darkest period in our history ended in 1945, our ancestors realised very quickly that everything had to be done to prevent the repetition of such a nightmare. It became clear that peace on our continent could only be maintained if Germany and France managed to overcome their mutual distrust. This is where Luxembourg played a major role and since then we were always perceived as a country interested in finding peaceful solutions.

The Luxembourgish DNA has not changed since the end of the Second World War. I still hope, and I also think that there is a way of resolving the conflict in the Ukraine without tanks, helicopters, and rifles. The situation has not become less delicate in the last couple of weeks but European politicians have done a lot to prevent further escalation.

I hope that we will be also able to prove that we have to agree on people and to respect people's choices. Lately, I read some articles about the future president of the European Commission and top positions in the EU. If we agreed on some things before the elections, then we forgot it after the elections. This is also one of the reasons why Eurosceptic parties are becoming so strong.

This is what Europe is in the end: a peacekeeping project and a dream that has become true. We should concentrate all our efforts in keeping that dream alive.

Thank you very much for your attention.

17

Free Movement of People and the European Economic Area

I. INTRODUCTION: THE BENEFITS OF THE EEA AGREEMENT

THE EEA AGREEMENT is the most far-reaching and comprehensive instrument to extend the EU's internal market to third countries. Its two-pillar structure has provided a solid foundation for close EU relations with the EEA EFTA countries for more than 20 years, and benefits all EEA citizens and businesses.

The benefits of the EEA Agreement are best illustrated by concrete examples. Today a Norwegian consumer can easily buy products made in the EU without having to pay any additional taxes and the same applies for a producer in Iceland, who can freely export his products to an EU market of more than 500 million consumers. Twenty years ago, it was almost unthinkable that Icelandic students would have the possibility to choose from a wide range of EU universities at which to study. Today this is a reality, thanks to the Erasmus+ programme, which is part of the EEA Agreement. Nowadays there is no problem for an English chemical engineer to work for Statoil, the Norwegian state oil company, because the EEA Agreement provides for free movement of persons. One should also not forget about the intensive research cooperation through the Horizon 2020 programme. All this is possible thanks to the EEA Agreement.

II. THE FRAMEWORK FOR THE PROTECTION OF THE RIGHT TO FREE MOVEMENT IN EEA COUNTRIES

As one of the core freedoms of the European Internal Market, the free movement of persons is a key element of the EEA Agreement. Free movement of persons is covered by Chapters I and II of Part III of the EEA Agreement, on free movement of workers and self-employed persons and on the right of establishment, including the principle of equal treatment on grounds of nationality (which is also reaffirmed, in general terms, by Article 4 of the Agreement); as well as by Annex V and

Annex VIII to the Agreement, listing the EU acts which are relevant to the application of free movement of workers and the right of establishment in the EEA context.

It is interesting to note that the wording in the EEA Agreement expressly refers to workers and self-employed persons only. This is because free movement of persons was, when the Agreement was signed, synonymous with free movement of workers, since freedom of movement and residence in the EEA EFTA States was granted exclusively to those willing to work or take up an economic activity there, and to their family members.

This restriction of free movement to workers only reflected the legal situation at Community level before the entry into force of the Treaty of Maastricht. It is well known that, notwithstanding the impetus provided by the case law of the Court of Justice of the European Union (hereinafter 'the Court of Justice'),[1] at that time the European Communities' treaties provided guarantees for the free movement of economically active persons, but not, generally, for others.[2]

It was only with the introduction of the status of Union citizenship by the Treaty of Maastricht some 20 years ago[3] that a process of reorientation of the European project from its market-oriented background began. This was largely thanks to a renewed political will to go beyond an area of free trade between nations, where individuals were viewed purely as economic operators, and a shift towards a political Union, putting citizens at its centre.

This evolution was intended to convey a strong political message, foster a genuine European identity and strengthen Union citizens' sense of belonging to the European integration project. The intention of European leaders was to create a European demos and to elicit people's subjective identification with the EU, with a view to preparing the ground for a true area of freedom, security and justice, reflecting the core values on which this Union is founded, such as equality and solidarity.

The dynamic and innovative character of EU citizenship, 'destined to be the fundamental status of nationals of the Member States', as the Court of Justice has

---

[1] See, eg, Case 53/81 *DM Levin v Staatssecretaris van Justitie* [1982] ECR 01035, Case 139/85 *RH Kempf v Staatssecretaris van Justitie* [1986] ECR 01741, Joined Cases 286/82 and 26/83 *Graziana Luisi and Giuseppe Carbone v Ministero del Tesoro* [1984] ECR 00377, Case 186/87 *Ian William Cowan v Trésor public* [1989] ECR 00195. For a commentary see P Craig and G de Búrca, *EU Law: Text, Cases and Materials*, 3rd edn (Oxford, Oxford University Press, 2003) 706–711.

[2] Art 69 of the Treaty of Paris establishing the European Coal and Steel Community of 1951 established a right to free movement for workers in these industries while Title III of the Treaty of Rome of 1957 provided for the free movement of workers and services.

[3] Art 8 of the Treaty establishing the European Community (Consolidated version 1992), as introduced by the Treaty of Maastricht, later Art 17 of the Treaty establishing a European Community (Consolidated version 1997, as amended by the Treaty of Amsterdam), now Art 20 of the Treaty on the Functioning of the European Union (TFEU).

been asserting for the last 15 years,[4] also had a strong spill-over effect on the rights attached to Union citizenship.

As a result, the scope of application of the right to move and reside freely, and consequently also of the EU general principle of non-discrimination on grounds of nationality,[5] was broadened. Non-discrimination now covers all mobile Union citizens, irrespective of the grounds on which they exercise their free movement rights, be it for work, study or simply leisure.

This self-standing right to free movement was thus established in the Treaties to grant every citizen of the Union, as formulated today in Article 21 TFEU, 'the right to move and reside freely within the territory of the Member States, subject to the limitations and conditions laid down in the Treaties and by the measures adopted to give them effect'.[6] The same right was meanwhile also included amongst the fundamental rights guaranteed by the Charter of Fundamental Rights of the European Union (hereinafter 'the EU Charter'),[7] an authentic bill of rights which today has the same legal value as the Treaties.[8]

The EU legislator's determined, forward-looking action, inspired by the Court of Justice's dynamic judicial advances, prompted further developments.

The Free Movement Directive[9] of 2004, which has since become the main legal instrument setting out the conditions and limitations to the exercise of the right to free movement, marked a decisive reinforcement of the legal framework for the protection and promotion of the right to free movement. The Directive codified and reviewed the existing EU instruments, a motley set of nine directives and a regulation that had been adopted between 1964 and 1993. The EU legislators' ambition was to simplify and strengthen the right to free movement and residence for all Union citizens and their family members. Examples of the innovations that were introduced include the introduction of the right of permanent residence, safeguards underpinning the recourse to possible derogations and restrictions to the right to free movement and residence, as well as the extension of the rights granted to family members.

These developments have been mirrored, as adapted for the purposes of the Agreement, in the EEA context. Accordingly, the scope of free movement rules in that context has been gradually broadened to include, besides workers

---

[4] The expression was first used by the Court of Justice in its judgment in Case C-184/99 *Rudy Grzelczyk v Centre public d'aide sociale d'Ottignies-Louvain-la-Neuve* [2001] ECR I-06193, para 31.

[5] See Art 12 of the Treaty establishing a European Community (Consolidated version 1997, as amended by the Treaty of Amsterdam), now Art 18 TFEU.

[6] See Art 8a of the Treaty establishing the European Community (Consolidated version 1992), later Art 18 of the Treaty establishing the European Community (Consolidated version 1997, as amended by the Treaty of Amsterdam).

[7] See Art 45 thereof.

[8] Art 6(1) of the Treaty on European Union (TEU).

[9] Directive 2004/38/EC of the European Parliament and of the Council of 29 April 2004 on the right of citizens of the Union and their family members to move and reside freely within the territory of the Member States, amending Regulation (EEC) No 1612/68 and repealing Directives 64/221/EEC, 68/360/EEC, 72/194/EEC, 73/148/EEC, 75/34/EEC, 75/35/EEC, 90/364/EEC, 90/365/EEC and 93/96/EEC.

and self-employed persons, economically non-active persons, such as students, job-seekers and retired workers.

As a result, all EEA citizens and their family members can enjoy the right to move and reside freely in the territory of the EEA to live, work, set up a business or study, enjoying equal treatment with the nationals of the host country. Such rights shall be exercised in accordance with the conditions set out by relevant EU provisions, and in particular those contained in the Free Movement Directive, which is now among the instruments listed in Annex V to the EEA Agreement. Other EU instruments complement and support the principle of free movement through specific rules in the fields of mutual recognition of professional qualifications and coordination of social security systems.

III. UPHOLDING THE RIGHT TO FREE MOVEMENT: THE IMPORTANT CONTRIBUTION OF THE EFTA COURT

The EFTA Court has been playing a decisive role in ensuring that existing rules on free movement of persons are properly enforced and applied in the EEA context. The aim is to ensure that citizens, when making use of their rights to free movement, are not confronted with disproportionate restrictions, unnecessary administrative hurdles or unequal treatment compared to nationals.

Free movement of persons is one of the areas where the EFTA Court has demonstrated its willingness to interpret EU rules creatively and dynamically which, according to certain scholars, is likely to render the EEA Agreement 'more "supranational" … than originally conceived'.[10]

The EFTA Court has, on the one hand, taken a leading role in the progressive development of EEA law[11] and, on the other hand, avoided legal gaps between the free movement rights that EEA/EU citizens can enjoy, and the restrictions they can be subject to throughout the territory of the Union and of EEA EFTA countries.

The EFTA Court has constantly upheld the principle of homogeneity of substantive law enshrined in the EEA Agreement,[12] as leading to 'a presumption that provisions framed identically in the EEA Agreement and the EC Treaty are to be construed in the same way',[13] also having regard to relevant case law of the Court of Justice. The EFTA Court has, accordingly, rejected all arguments put forward

---

[10] H Haukeland Fredriksen, 'The EFTA Court 15 years on' (2010) 59 *International & Comparative Law Quarterly* 731, 756.

[11] ibid, 757.

[12] See Art 102 of the Agreement, and the implementing measures contained in Section I of Chapter 3 of the Agreement. On the interpretation of this principle by the EFTA Court, see, among others, C Baudenbacher, 'The EFTA Court and Court of Justice of the European Union: coming in parts but winning together' in Court of Justice of the European Union, *The Court of Justice and the construction of Europe: analyses and perspectives on sixty years of case-law* (The Hague, Asser Press, 2013).

[13] Case E-2/06 *EFTA Surveillance Authority v Norway (Waterfalls)* [2007] EFTA Ct Rep 164, para 59.

by some EEA EFTA States to the effect that, 'due to alleged differences of goals and context between EEA and EU law, the substantive rules of the EEA Agreement, such as on the fundamental freedoms, [needed] to be interpreted in a more *State friendly* way than in the EU pillar of the EEA', for example by allowing 'more, and broader, justification grounds for restrictions than EU law' and by refusing the existence of 'a *de minimis* rule in the field of fundamental freedoms'.[14]

On free movement of persons, the EFTA Court has rigorously interpreted the principle, facilitating free movement of workers and self-employed persons, and of possible related restrictions to those principles.

For example, in Case E-1/11 *Dr A*,[15] the EFTA Court interpreted the relevant EU provisions on the mutual recognition of professional qualifications[16] in light of a strict interpretation of the EU general principle of proportionality, as interpreted by the Court of Justice in similar cases. The case concerned the refusal by the Norwegian Registration Authority to grant a medical doctor trained in Bulgaria a licence to practise as a medical doctor in Norway, due to the allegedly poor language and communication skills of the applicant. The EFTA Court applied, by analogy, the solution elaborated by the Court of Justice in similar cases,[17] in order to strike a balance between the objective underlying the restrictive measure adopted by the national authority, in particular the protection of public health, and the principle of automatic recognition on which the EU provisions at stake were based.

Similarly, in Case E-4/07 *Þorkelsson*,[18] relating to the interpretation of EU provisions on the coordination of social security schemes,[19] read in conjunction with EEA provisions on free movement of workers, the EFTA Court referred to relevant case law of the Court of Justice.[20] The Court extended the notion of social security and strictly interpreted possible restrictions, precluding a condition imposed by national law in the case at issue that would have forced the mobile citizen to be a member of several legislation-based social security schemes at the same time, thus contradicting the purpose of the EU provisions concerned. The potential effects of such an approach are not, however, only confined to 'market-related' cases, meaning those concerning the application of rules on free movement of workers or self-employed persons.

---

[14] Baudenbacher, 'The EFTA Court and Court of Justice', 189. See, eg, Case E-3/98 *Rainford Towning* [1998] EFTA Ct Rep 205, para 15; Case E-1/03 *EFTA Surveillance Authority v Iceland* (Air passenger tax) [2003] EFTA Ct Rep 143, para 21; Case E-2/06 *EFTA Surveillance Authority v Norway*, above n 13, para 41.

[15] Case E-1/11 *Dr A* [2011] EFTA Ct Rep 484.

[16] In particular Art 53 of Directive 2005/36/EC of the European Parliament and of the Council of 7 September 2005 on the recognition of professional qualifications.

[17] The EFTA Court referred in particular to Case C-110/01 *Tennah-Durez* [2003] ECR I-6239.

[18] Case E-4/07 *Jón Gunnar Þorkelsson and Gildi-lífeyrissjóður* [2008] EFTA Ct Rep 3.

[19] Regulation (EEC) No 1408/71 of the Council of 14 June 1971 on the application of social security schemes to employed persons and their families moving within the Community.

[20] Case 35/77 *Beerens* [1977] ECR 2249; Case C-168/88 *Dammer* [1989] ECR 4553; Case C-227/89 *Rönfeldt* [1991] ECR 323; Case C-78/91 *Hughes* [1992] ECR I-4839.

In fact, the EFTA Court's meticulous application of the homogeneity principle has also proved useful for strengthening the safeguards for mobile citizens exercising their free movement rights on grounds other than being workers or self-employed.

In this context, I would like to highlight the importance of three recent cases decided by the EFTA Court.

A first case, *Dr Joachim Kottke*,[21] concerns the application of the EU general principle of non-discrimination on grounds of nationality. The case arose from a request to the EFTA for an opinion on the interpretation of the principle reaffirmed by Article 4 of the Agreement, in relation to a provision of the Liechtenstein code of civil procedure. The Liechtenstein code of civil procedure stipulated that a plaintiff resident in another EEA State had the obligation, when filing a case before national courts, to provide a guarantee for the costs of proceedings, on application by the defendant. The same obligation was not imposed on plaintiffs residing in Liechtenstein. Building on relevant case law by the Court of Justice, the EFTA Court's premise was that legislative provisions on national procedure, although falling within the exclusive competence of the EEA States, may not discriminate against persons to whom EEA law gives the right to equal treatment or restrict the fundamental freedoms guaranteed by EEA law. According to the EFTA Court, having in mind the principles established by the Court of Justice,[22] a person in a situation such as Mr Kottke was, although formally resident in his State of origin, exercising a cross-border activity within the meaning of the EEA provisions on free movement of persons, and therefore should enjoy a right to equal treatment. In this case, the EFTA Court found that the national provisions constituted indirect discrimination on grounds of nationality within the meaning of Article 4 of the Agreement, since it made it more difficult for nationals of other EEA States to bring a civil action before the domestic courts than for nationals of the State in question. On this basis, the EFTA Court held that a fair balance had to be struck between the restriction imposed to the right to free movement and the public interest. The national judge subsequently had to assess whether a measure such as that at issue could be considered as necessary and not excessive in attaining the objectives pursued.

The other two cases concern the interpretation of specific provisions of the Free Movement Directive. The 'dialogue' between the EFTA Court and the Court of Justice is particularly lively, and the EFTA Court clearly aims to uphold the rights and safeguards granted by relevant EU provisions. The EFTA Court rejects any restrictive interpretation proposed by EEA EFTA States, to ensure that mobile citizens can fully and effectively enjoy their free movement rights.

---

[21] Case E-5/10 *Dr Joachim Kottke v Präsidial Anstalt and Sweetyle Stiftung* [2009–2010] EFTA Ct Rep, 320.
[22] The EFTA Court referred, among others, to Case C-186/87 *Cowan* [1989] ECR 195.

In Case E-4/11 *Clauder*[23] the EFTA Court was confronted with the claim to a right to family reunification by a German national holding a right of permanent residence in Liechtenstein as an economically inactive person, and recipient of supplementary social welfare benefits there. Mr Clauder's old-age pension revenues were, in fact, relatively modest so that, even combined with the supplementary benefits granted under Liechtenstein law they would not be sufficient to ensure subsistence of himself and his wife without having recourse to additional social welfare benefits. Mr Clauder's wife was a German national for whom he had applied for a residence permit in Liechtenstein. Rejecting all the restrictive interpretations suggested by the intervening governments, the EFTA Court supported the arguments put forward by the European Commission. The Court interpreted the right to permanent residence provided for in the Directive[24] as allowing a person in a situation such as that of Mr Clauder to claim a right to family reunification, irrespective of the fact that the family member may also have to claim social welfare benefits in the host State. According to the EFTA Court, despite the absence of a specific regulation of the right to family reunification of permanent residents under the Directive, a different interpretation would have been in contrast with the purpose of the Directive and would have undermined its full effectiveness, even in situations, such as that at issue, where there is a risk that the family member becomes a burden on the social assistance system of the host State. It is interesting to note that the EFTA Court recalled, in reaching such a conclusion, the importance of ensuring the protection of family life of nationals of EEA States. This principle has been recognised as essential with a view to eliminating obstacles to the exercise of free movement both by the EU legislature[25] and, even before, by the Court of Justice.[26] Moreover, the emphasis on the protection of family life derives from the need to interpret provisions of the EEA Agreement in the light of fundamental rights, and, in particular, Article 8 of the European Convention on Human Rights and Fundamental Freedoms (ECHR) and Article 7 of the EU Charter.

In the *Wahl* case,[27] the EFTA Court followed a similar approach to ensure the effectiveness of rights and safeguards for mobile citizens that the Free Movement Directive guarantees. The Court interpreted the scope of the derogation provided for in the Directive in a strict manner, allowing for restrictions to the right of entry and residence on grounds of public policy and public security.[28] The case concerned a Norwegian national who, while travelling to Iceland on a holiday trip, was denied entry on grounds of his membership of a Norwegian motorcycle club whose activities were considered by Icelandic authorities to constitute a

---

[23] Case E-4/11 *Arnulf Clauder* [2011] EFTA Ct Rep 216.

[24] See Art 16 thereof.

[25] The EFTA Court refers to recital 3 in the preamble of the Free Movement Directive.

[26] The EFTA Court recalls, in particular, the judgment of the Court of Justice in Case C-127/08 *Metock and Others* [2008] ECR I-6241.

[27] Case E-15/12 *Jan Anfinn Wahl v the Icelandic State* [2013] EFTA Ct Rep 534.

[28] See Art 27 of the Free Movement Directive.

threat to public policy and public security. Finding that the situation of Mr Wahl constituted an exercise of the right to free movement granted to nationals of EEA States, which entailed the application of the safeguards provided for in the Directive, the EFTA Court carried out a particularly rigorous assessment of the proportionality of the restriction in question. This approach was based on the premise that requirements for justification for a derogation from the fundamental principle of free movement of persons in the EEA context ought to be interpreted strictly, as affirmed already by the Court of Justice in the EU context,[29] so that the scope of these derogations could not be determined unilaterally by each EEA State without any control by the EEA institutions.

The EFTA Court applied the safeguards provided for in the Directive,[30] interpreted them in the light of relevant case law of the Court of Justice,[31] and indicated to the national court all the elements to be considered to assess whether the restriction at issue had to be considered proportionate to the aim pursued, on the basis of a thorough 'risk assessment'.

The above-mentioned judgments show the EFTA Court's clear willingness to align, as far as possible, the protection granted to all mobile citizens in EEA EFTA States to that granted by the Court of Justice within the EU legal framework.

The contribution of the EFTA Court has been essential not only to ensure a smooth functioning of the system and to avoid legal gaps, but above all to embrace a comprehensive and inclusive concept of the free movement of persons and uphold the effectiveness of the rights granted to all EEA mobile citizens.

IV. LOOKING AHEAD

During the last two decades, the importance and scope of the right to free movement of persons has continuously grown, enabling citizens to draw the full benefits of the EEA-wide Internal Market to travel, study, work, train or live in another European country. The free movement of persons has become a cornerstone of European integration, one of the main achievements of the European Union and the EU Treaty right which citizens cherish the most.[32]

At EU level, the case law of the Court of Justice remains crucial in offering a progressive interpretation of the scope and value of the right to free movement

---

[29] The EFTA Court mentioned, in particular, Case 36/75 *Rutili* [1975] ECR 1219; Case 30/77 *Bouchereau* [1977] ECR 1999; Case C-54/99 *Église de scientologie* [2000] ECR I-1335; and Case C-36/02 *Omega* [2004] ECR I-9609.

[30] See in particular Art 27(2) thereof.

[31] The EFTA Court referred to many relevant judgments of the Court of Justice, among which those in *Rutili* and *Bouchereau*, both cited above n 29, in Case 41/74 *Van Duyn* [1974] ECR 1337, in Joined Cases C-482/01 and C-493/01 *Orfanopoulos and Oliveri* [2004] ECR I-5257, in Joined Cases 115/81 and 116/81 *Adoui and Cornuaille* [1982] ECR 1665, in Case C-348/96 *Calfa* [1999] ECR I-11 and in the recent Cases C-249/11 *Byankov*, judgment of 4 October 2012, nyr, and C-300/11 *ZZ*, judgment of 4 June 2013, nyr.

[32] See the result of the Standard Eurobarometer 79 of Spring 2013.

and the rights related to it. Case law ensures that existing rules are effectively enforced and applied, and interpreting rather strictly applicable conditions and possible limitations.[33] Moreover, the Court of Justice uses the concept of Union citizenship to extend the protection afforded to EU citizens, even in the absence of a cross-border element.[34]

For its part, the European Commission has worked towards supporting and strengthening the legislative framework through comprehensive political action, inspired by the innovative and dynamic potential the status of Union citizenship has and the rights attached to this status. The Commission takes a holistic, multi-disciplinary approach, to overcome the fragmentation which had shaped past EU policies on free movement. The Commission endeavours to tackle the various kinds of concrete obstacles citizens face when seeking to exercise their EU rights, whether as private individuals, as consumers, as students and professionals or as political actors, as reflected in the EU Citizenship Reports.[35] Enhancing the right to free movement and ensuring that existing rules are properly enforced and applied remains essential, and the Commission put forward initiatives to that end, such as the Commission guidelines on the Free Movement Directive issued in 2009[36] and the recent Communication.[37] The aim of the Communication in particular is to clarify EU citizens' rights and obligations and the conditions and limitations of free movement under EU law, as well as helping Member States and their local authorities to effectively apply EU free movement rules.

Thanks to the EFTA Court's progressive approach and the cross-fertilising cooperation between the latter and the Court of Justice, the EEA States were able to adapt to the evolving concept and scope of free movement of persons.

The European Commission is strongly committed to upholding the right to free movement of persons in the broadest sense of the term, as an EEA-wide fundamental principle and a right of all EEA citizens. Mobility is a win-win for all,

---

[33] See, as mere examples, the recent judgment of the Court in Case C-423/12 *Reyes v Migrationsverket* [2014], not yet published, on the notion of dependency of a family member from a Union citizen for the purpose of obtaining residence rights in the host Member State; Joined Cases C-424/10 and C-425/10 *Tomasz Ziolkowski v Land Berlin* [2011] ECR I-14035, on the right of permanent residence; Case C-46/12 *LN v Styrelsen for Videregående Uddannelser og Uddannelsesstøtte* [2013], not yet published, concerning the principle of equal treatment on grounds of nationality; Case C-300/11 *ZZ v Secretary of State for the Home Department* [2013] not yet published, where the Court provided guidance on the interpretation of the procedural safeguards contained in the Free Movement Directive.

[34] See, eg, the well-known Case C-34/09 *Gerardo Ruiz Zambrano v Office national de l'emploi (ONEm)* [2011] ECR I-01177.

[35] EU Citizenship Report 2010 of 27 October 2010—Dismantling the obstacles to EU citizens' rights, COM(2010) 603 final and EU Citizenship Report 2013 of 8 May 2013—EU citizens: your rights, your future, COM(2013) 269 final.

[36] Communication from the Commission to the European Parliament and the Council of 2 July 2009 on guidance for better transposition and application of Directive 2004/38/EC on the right of citizens of the Union and their family members to move and reside freely within the territory of the Member States, COM(2009) 313 final.

[37] Communication from the Commission to the European Parliament, the Council, the European Economic and Social Committee and the Committee of the Regions of 25 November 2013, Free movement of EU citizens and their families: Five actions to make a difference, COM(2013) 837 final.

and the benefits it brings are keenly felt by all citizens, not only those who move but also those who do not.

The continuing and fruitful cooperation between EU and EEA EFTA States, boosted by the forward-looking approach embraced by the EFTA Court, is indeed essential to making mobility easier for EEA citizens, making sure that their rights are respected and that they are treated the same way as nationals, enabling them to fully enjoy the benefits of the Internal Market wherever they are in the EEA.

All these positive developments contribute to a more inclusive and comprehensive strategy for the EEA area, which ultimately aims to make the Internal Market more competitive and beneficial for economic operators, as well as helping citizens to make use of the opportunities that the Internal Market offers.

18

'Shall be Made Part of the Internal Legal Order': The Legislative Approaches

HENRIK BULL[1]

I. THE PROBLEM

D
IRECT EFFECT AND primacy of EU law is a cornerstone of the European integration project that we now know as the European Union. Developed by the Court of Justice of the European Union[2]—the CJEU—and supplementing the Treaty-based direct applicability of regulations and, as the case may be, decisions,[3] these principles have played a major role in ensuring the effectiveness of EU law. In demanding that national authorities apply directly EU norms and decisions that fulfil certain prerequisites, if necessary giving them precedence over conflicting national norms and decisions, they are also the clearest sign that the European Union has ambitions going beyond that of traditional international cooperation.

Obviously, in international law generally, conflicting national law is never a valid excuse for a State's non-fulfilment of its international obligations. However, unlike EU law, international law does not ask of States that internal law, as applied by national authorities, should yield to international obligations so as to prevent a conflict from arising in the first place. Nevertheless, the internal legal systems of some States take this approach to the international legal obligations of the State. Others do not and prefer to live with risk. This is usually referred to as the monist and dualist approach to international law, respectively. As we shall see, there is no clear-cut distinction between the two positions. Some national legal orders that are generally understood to be dualist may contain important monist elements, and vice versa.

---

[1] The author is indebted to Justice Thorgeir Örlygsson of the Supreme Court of Iceland, formerly his colleague on the bench of the EFTA Court, for providing him with information about the situation in Iceland and Icelandic law. Any mistakes in this regard are entirely the author's responsibility.

[2] See especially Case 26/62 *Van Gend en Loos* [1963] ECR 1 and Case 6/64 *Costa v ENEL* [1964] 585.

[3] See Art 288 of the Treaty on the Functioning of the European Union. In this chapter, the concept of 'direct effect' will include direct applicability of regulations and decisions.

Among the current three EFTA States in the EEA, the Norwegian and Icelandic legal systems are dualist, whereas the Liechtenstein legal system is monist. Whereas monism as a voluntary undertaking of the internal legal order itself is fully compatible with the traditional understanding of sovereignty, monism as a requirement imposed from outside is more problematic in this regard, in particular when imposed by an entity from which there is no clear and easy way to secede once you have joined.

Consequently, the EU principles of direct effect and primacy have been seen by many as proof for the EU being, ultimately, a project for the establishment of a 'United States of Europe' not dissimilar to its American counterpart—not least by those who are sceptical of such a development.

There are of course other reasons why one might not like to see one's country join the EU. For Norway, control of marine resources and a Common Agricultural Policy that would mean less generous subsidies to the smallholders that traditionally dominate Norwegian agriculture have been stumbling blocks, as well. Also, decision-making by majority voting rather than unanimity tends to be seen by many as dangerous for smaller States, even when smaller States have more voting power than justified by their relative size. However, the direct effect and primacy of EU law, and earlier of Community law, have always ignited passionate resistance to EU membership in Norway, whose understanding of itself is based to quite some extent on the full national sovereignty regained in 1905 after unions with Denmark (1380–1814) and, much looser, with Sweden (1814–1905).[4] In this perspective, the promise, now found in the preamble to the Treaty on the Functioning of the European Union, the TFEU, of an 'ever closer union' has always seemed more like a threat than a temptation.

During the EEA negotiations, it was therefore of the utmost importance for Norway to avoid as far as possible any form of direct effect and primacy. Article 93 of the Norwegian Constitution does provide for a mechanism, requiring a three-fourths majority in Parliament, for entering into treaties entailing the transfer of sovereign powers to an international organisation, so the problem was not of a strictly legal nature.[5] However, this provision has always been thought of as intended for Norwegian membership of the EU (or EC in earlier days), so a negotiating result that could only be accepted by the use of Article 93 would belie the

---

[4] Leaving the constitutional aspects aside, which basically consisted in the King of Sweden also being King of Norway bound by a separate Norwegian Constitution, the EEA Agreement binds Norway and Sweden much closer together legally and economically than the union between 1814 and 1905 ever did. See generally O Mestad and D Michalsen (eds), *Rett, nasjon, union, den svensk-norske unionens historie 1814–1905* (Oslo, Universitetsforlaget, 2005).

[5] In addition, one may in theory employ the regular procedure for amending the Constitution. However, that is impractical when the question is whether or not to enter into a treaty. For regular amendments to the Constitution, Article 112 prescribes that the proposal must be tabled at least one year before a general election, and the proposal may then only be submitted for a vote in Parliament after the election. To pass, a two-thirds majority is required, and the proposal may not be altered in any way before voting on it. Depending on the circumstances, it could take years after the end of negotiations to get a treaty accepted in this way. There is no mechanism for dissolving Parliament ahead of time—it will always sit its full four-year term.

claim by the Government that the EEA Agreement was something very different from membership. In addition, such a result would also increase the risk that there would not be a three-fourths majority in Parliament in favour of the Agreement.[6]

The same political problems with direct effect and primacy existed in Iceland and for much the same kind of historical reasons as in Norway: full sovereignty only in 1944 after a long union with Denmark.[7] Iceland had the additional legal problem that the Icelandic Constitution, unlike the Norwegian Constitution, had no special clause on ceding sovereign powers.

Liechtenstein did not have the same political or constitutional problems as the two Nordic countries with these aspects of EU law possibly becoming part of EEA law. Both direct effect and primacy of EEA law could have been accommodated within its monist legal order. Liechtenstein's extensive agreements with Switzerland also meant that far-reaching agreements relating to the economy and trade was nothing new to Liechtenstein.

Also Austria, Finland, Sweden and Switzerland took part in the EEA negotiations, Finland and Sweden with dualist legal systems, Austria and Switzerland with monist systems. However, direct effect and primacy seemed to be less controversial for Sweden and Finland than for Norway and Iceland.

In the end, the EFTA States had to accept direct effect of decisions in the field of competition law. For Norway, this meant that Article 93 of the Constitution had to be employed in the parliamentary procedure after all. However, in the public debate, the Government took great care to point out that other aspects of direct effect and primacy were not part of the Agreement.[8]

Iceland decided that the EEA Agreement, including this form of limited direct effect, did not prevent the Agreement from being accepted by the Icelandic Parliament according to existing procedures.[9]

---

[6] The author took part in the EEA negotiations as an official of the Norwegian Ministry of Justice. Statements in this chapter as to the intention behind certain provisions of the EEA Agreement are based on this experience.

[7] Union with Norway from 1262, together with Norway and Denmark from 1380. Iceland got its own Constitution in 1874, an Icelandic Minister for domestic matters in 1904, and in 1918 Iceland gained sovereignty as a separate Kingdom of Iceland in personal union with Denmark. The last constitutional ties with Denmark were severed in 1944 with the declaration of the republic.

[8] See Stortingsproposisjon No 100 (1991–92) pp 317–319 and 335–347. A particular problem with respect to decisions in the field of competition law was the powers of the European Commission, under the EEA Agreement, of subjecting Norwegian undertakings to sanctions. Article 93 only provides for the ceding of sovereign powers to organisations of which Norway is or becomes a member. Clearly, by the EEA Agreement, Norway did not become a member of the EU. This was solved by a unilateral declaration to the Final Act that such sanctions imposed by the European Commission would not be enforced on Norwegian soil. This did not matter much to the EU, as the threat of enforcement anywhere within the rest of the EEA would be effective enough. In response, the EU simply declared that the Commission would keep the situation created by the Norwegian declaration 'under constant review' and 'initiate consultation' should problems arise. To this author's knowledge, no problem has arisen.

[9] See, eg, Alþt 1992, A-deild, pp 50 and 52, and M Elvira Méndez-Pinedo, *EC and EEA Law—A Comparative Study of the Effectiveness of European Law* (Groningen, Europa Law Publishing, 2009) pp 115–118 and 126–129, with further references to Icelandic legal literature.

II. THE SOLUTION IN THE AGREEMENT

The lack of direct effect and primacy may be deduced from, in particular, three provisions of the EEA Agreement.

Article 7 EEA corresponds to Article 288 TFEU, but with some notable differences. Firstly, the lead-in sentence acknowledges the difference between monist and dualist legal orders by stating that the EU legal acts that have been made part of the Agreement either through the Agreement as signed in 1992 or through later decisions by the EEA Joint Committee shall 'be, or be made, part of' the internal legal order of the Contracting Parties. The Article then goes on to provide that regulations 'shall as such be made part of the internal legal order of the Contracting States'. This is quite different from the requirement found in Article 288 TFEU of regulations being 'directly applicable' in the Member States. This shows that there is no obligation for the EEA Contracting Parties to provide for direct applicability of regulations, although it follows from the lead-in sentence of Article 7 EEA ('be, or be made, part of') that those States whose monist system would automatically make a regulation part of the internal legal order, can rely on this.

This being the case for regulations, it would be incoherent to assume that the EEA Contracting Parties would be under an obligation to provide for direct effect of directives,[10] or indeed of the provisions of the main EEA Agreement corresponding to directly effective provisions of the TFEU.

Article 6 EEA, which provides that EEA law should be construed in accordance with the case law of the CJEU up to the date of signature of the Agreement,[11] limits the effect of this undertaking with the words 'in so far as they are identical in substance' and by referring to 'the relevant rulings' of the CJEU. This was intended to exclude case law pertaining to the legal effects of EU law in the Member States' legal orders, as opposed to case law on the substantive content of the provisions.

The absence of any transfer of legislative powers is also spelled out in the preamble to Protocol 35 to the Agreement, laying down an undertaking for the EFTA States to introduce 'if necessary' a 'statutory provision to the effect that EEA rules prevail' in cases of possible conflicts 'between implemented EEA rules and other statutory provision'. The proviso of 'if necessary' makes it clear that EFTA States whose monist systems provide for primacy of international obligations over conflicting rules of national law are not affected by the Protocol. For the other EFTA States, the obligation laid down in Protocol 35 differs from the EU concept of primacy in two ways. First, the primacy required is for the benefit of

---

[10] To the extent directives may have direct effect, see in particular Case C-91/92 *Faccini Dori* [1994] ECR I-3325.

[11] 2 May 1992. The Agreement between the EFTA States on the establishment of a Surveillance Authority and a Court of Justice supplements this by providing, in Art 3, that the Surveillance Authority and the Court 'shall pay due account to' also later case law. Art 6 EEA itself makes reservation for 'future developments of case-law'.

'implemented EEA rules' over 'other' statutory provision. This means that EEA rules that, perhaps in violation of Article 7 EEA, have not been made part of the national legal order through implementing legislation would not benefit from the required primacy—as that would have presupposed direct effect as well.[12] Second, an undertaking to introduce a 'statutory provision', in contrast to a 'constitutional provision', is not a promise of an iron-clad guarantee against the possibility that national legislatures may still choose to enact other statutory provisions violating the EEA Agreement and thus setting aside the primacy provision.[13]

In spite of these arguments, some commentators have interpreted the EEA Agreement as requiring EU-style direct effect and primacy.[14] The EFTA Court, however, has refrained from reading direct effect and primacy into the Agreement. In *Restamark* at paragraph 77,[15] it interpreted Protocol 35 to mean that 'individuals and economic operators in cases of conflict between implemented EEA rules and national statutory provisions must be entitled to invoke and to claim at the national level any rights that could be derived from provisions of the EEA Agreement, as being or having been made part of the respective national legal order, if they are

---

[12] The effect of this is demonstrated by a judgment of the Norwegian Supreme Court reported in *Norsk Retstidend* 2000 p 1811 (*Finanger I*) and a judgment of the Icelandic Supreme Court of 9 December 2010 in Case No 79/2010, the first case concerning insufficient implementation of directives concerning traffic insurance and the second case concerning insufficient implementation of the directive on product liability. Both Supreme Courts found it impossible to reconcile the very clear wording of the national statutes with the requirements of the respective directives. It should be added that both cases concerned directives regulating the relationship between private parties, so there would have been no direct effect and primacy of the directives in EU law, either. (In a judgment reported in *Norsk Retstidend* 2005 p 1365 (*Finanger II*) the victim of the traffic accident was awarded damages from the State instead, based on the doctrine of State liability for violation of EEA law developed by the EFTA Court beginning with Case E-9/97 *Sveinbjörnsdóttir* [1998] EFTA Ct Rep p 95.) In another judgment, of 3 September 2012 in Case No 401/2012, the Icelandic Supreme Court upheld the decision of a lower court not to request an advisory opinion from the EFTA Court on the interpretation of a directive on the grounds that the relevant Icelandic statutory provisions could not in any case be understood in conformity with the directive—something which the parties to the case, both private, agreed on—and therefore the view of the EFTA Court on the interpretation of the directive could not have an impact on the outcome of the case.

[13] Faced with conflicting statutory provisions, national courts may conclude that the newest, or more specific, prevails. However, also in a dualist system, national courts may recoil at the prospect of a judgment violating international obligations and require very clear language in order to accept that the legislature indeed accepted the possibility of such a result with open eyes. This would be the position of Norwegian courts. Thus, the principles of *lex posterior derogate priori* and *lex specialis derogat legi generali* may not necessarily decide the matter.

[14] See, eg, W van Gerven, 'The Genesis of EEA Law and the Principles of Primacy and Direct Effect' (1992–1993) *Fordham International Law Journal* 955–989, L Sevón and M Johansson, 'The protection of the rights of individuals under the EEA Agreement' (1999) *European Law Review* 373–386, T Bruha, 'Is the EEA an Internal Market' in P-C Müller-Graff and E Selvig (eds), *EEA-EU relations, Deutsch-Norwegisches Forum des Rechts* Band 2 (Berlin, Berlin Verlag, 1999) 97–129. Other commentators have taken the opposite view; see, eg, P-C Müller-Graff, 'EEA-Agreement and EC Law: A Comparison in Scope and Content—Overview on the Basic Legal Link between Norway and the European Union' in Müller-Graff and Selvig (eds), *The European Economic Area—Norway's Basic Status in the Legal Construction of Europe* (Berlin, Berlin Verlag, 1997) 17–41, H Haukeland Fredriksen and G Mathisen, *EØS-rett* (2nd edition Bergen, Fagbokforlaget, 2014) 315–317, and H Bull, 'The EEA Agreement and Norwegian Law' (1994) *European Business Law Review* 291–296.

[15] Case E-1/94 *Restamark* [1994–95] EFTA Ct Rep 15.

unconditional and sufficiently precise'. The Court went on to state, in *Karlsson*[16] at paragraph 28, that '[i]t follows from Article 7 EEA and Protocol 35 to the EEA Agreement that EEA law does not entail a transfer of legislative powers. Therefore, EEA law does not require that individuals and economic operators can rely directly on non-implemented EEA rules before national courts'. Finally, in *Criminal Proceedings Against A*[17] at paragraph 40, the Court concluded that Article 7 and Protocol 35 meant that 'EEA law does not require that non-implemented EEA rules take precedence over conflicting national rules, including national rules which fail to transpose the relevant EEA rules correctly into national law'.

The EEA Agreement has no equivalent to the provision contained in Article 288 TFEU on the legal effects of decisions. However, it follows from Article 110 EEA that decisions under the EEA Agreement by the EFTA Surveillance Authority and the EC Commission that impose a pecuniary obligation on persons other than States shall be enforceable. As mentioned above, this element of direct effect, in practice in the field of competition law, led to the EEA Agreement requiring a three-fourths majority in the Norwegian Parliament.

Also Article 103(2) EEA needs to be mentioned in this context. According to this provision, a decision of the EEA Joint Committee to include a new EU legal act into the EEA Agreement 'shall be applied provisionally pending the fulfilment of constitutional requirements unless a Contracting Party notifies that such provisional application cannot take place' if a notification of fulfilment of such requirements has not been given within six months of the Joint Committee making its decision. It has been suggested that this may entail some sort of direct applicability of EU legal acts.[18]

This provision was introduced because of the possibility, under the Swiss Constitution—Switzerland taking part in the EEA negotiations—of an EEA Joint Committee decision being subject to a popular vote, which could take a long time to arrange. The Swiss negotiators pointed to the possibility under Swiss law of provisional application of the decision pending the popular vote.[19] The Nordic EFTA States made it clear that for their part, there was no possibility of provisional application of a decision if its acceptance necessitated a vote in Parliament—which for them would be the only 'constitutional requirements' alluded to in Article 103. However, it would seem that in the cases where constitutional requirements need to be fulfilled before a decision of the EEA Joint Committee can become binding, a notification that provisional application is not possible is not always given. One must assume that one reason may be that

---

[16] Case E-4/01 *Karlsson* [2002] EFTA Ct Rep 240.

[17] Case E-1/07 *Criminal Proceedings Against A* [2007] EFTA Ct Rep 246.

[18] See M Schmauch, 'Reglene om midlertidig anvendelse av EØS-rett i påvente av implementering' (2013) *Lov og Rett* 258, in particular pp 366–370.

[19] See, eg, D Björgvinsson, *EES-réttur og landsréttur* (Reykjavík, Bókaútgáfan Codex, 2006) 58. For Switzerland, with its monist legal system, the question of whether Art 103(2) EEA entailed direct effect in addition to providing for the provisional binding effect of the decision in question, was probably a non-issue.

the State in question foresees that the six months deadline will be kept. That has turned out not always to be the case.[20]

It would seem to be no more possible under Norwegian and Icelandic law to accept 'provisional' direct effect under Article 103 than regular direct effect of EEA law in general.[21] Thus, such an interpretation of Article 103(2) EEA would seem to create more problems than it solved.

The words 'applied provisionally' in Article 103(2) EEA must be read in conjunction with paragraph 1 of that provision, which deals with the procedure of making Joint Committee decisions 'enter into force'.[22] In other words, what follows from Article 103(2) EEA is simply that exceeding the time limit for notifying the fulfilment of constitutional requirements without having notified that provisional application is not possible has the same legal effect for the EFTA State in question as the timely notification according to paragraph 1 would have had: the decision enters into force—becomes binding. It would seem odd indeed if the consequence of exceeding the time limit of six months should be the direct effect, albeit provisionally, of the act in question when the State would be under no obligation to provide for direct effect of the same act had it not exceeded the time limit but, all the same, failed to implement the legal act in question correctly into national law.[23]

---

[20] See Schmauch, above n 18, pp 360–361.

[21] Schmauch, above n 18 suggests that since the main part of the EEA Agreement, containing Art 103, has been incorporated into Norwegian and Icelandic law as statutory Acts of Parliament, this would provide the necessary internal legal basis for provisional application. It is highly doubtful that Art 103, in its capacity as national law, would be capable of being understood as a clause that suspends, albeit in a limited field on each occasion, the constitutional balance of powers between the executive and the legislative branches of government.

[22] In this respect, the provision resembles Art 25 of the Vienna Convention on the Law of Treaties. Art 25 deals with the possibility that a treaty may be 'applied provisionally' pending its entry into force. It must be clear that in this context, provisional application must mean that the full binding effect will apply before the regular entry into force of the treaty for the State in question. If that State, due to its dualist legal system and lack of necessary implementing measures, is unable to fulfil its obligations under the treaty already at a stage prior to the regular entry into force, it will be in violation of the treaty, just as it would be if the necessary implementing measures are not in place after the regular entry into force. Art 25 cannot be understood to mean that dualist States are bound to accept monism on a provisional basis with regard to the treaty in question whenever they accept provisional application of a treaty.

[23] Decision-making in the EEA Joint Committee often lags behind EU decision-making to such an extent that by the time the Joint Committee makes its decisions, the legal acts in question—mostly directives—have not only entered into force in the EU, the time limit for implementation has also lapsed. In most cases, no special time limit for implementation is indicated in the decisions of the EEA Joint Committee. This has the consequence that the time limit for implementation for the EFTA States in fact is identical to the time for entry into force of the Joint Committee decision. It must be assumed that in many cases, full and correct implementation is not in place by then. One should note in this context that the failure to implement correctly a legal act that has been accepted as binding by the EFTA States does not lead to the 'suspension' of the 'affected part' of the relevant annex of the Agreement according to Art 102(5) EEA. Such non-implementation is a matter for the EFTA Surveillance Authority, which may bring the EFTA State in question before the EFTA Court for infringing the EEA Agreement, just as the European Commission can initiate infringement procedures before the CJEU against a Member State for non-implementation of a legal act. Suspension according to Art 102(5) is the reaction reserved for the EFTA States' refusal to accept a new EU legal act as part of the EEA Agreement.

It may of course also be a problem for the EFTA State in question to be bound by a Joint Committee decision before the conclusion of the necessary constitutional procedures. However, under general international law it is possible for a State to become bound by a treaty even if constitutional requirements have not been complied with.[24] This is a risk all States must accept.

III. THE SOLUTION IN NATIONAL LAW

Among the three EFTA States left in the EEA, Liechtenstein with its monist legal system has been faced with the fewest problems in making EEA law corresponding to directly applicable EU law part of the internal legal order. However, a special clause has been added to Article 67 of the Liechtenstein Constitution providing that EEA provisions applicable to Liechtenstein shall be promulgated in a particular EEA compendium. In this way, it is not necessary to promulgate regulations in the ordinary Liechtenstein Legal Gazette in order for them to be applicable.

A second question came to light in the case *Criminal Proceedings Against A* before the EFTA Court.[25] In the EU, direct effect and primacy of EU law are principles to be applied by all courts, regardless of whether, under national law, the power to declare national statutes void or inapplicable is reserved for a Constitutional Court.[26] In Liechtenstein, these powers are indeed vested in the Constitutional Court. Thus, Liechtenstein's form of monism does not fully reflect the EU principles of direct effect and primacy. The EFTA Court accepted this: the lack of an obligation to introduce direct effect and primacy of unimplemented EEA provisions must mean that EFTA States with a monist system must be free to decide which administrative and judicial organs shall have the power to apply the relevant EEA rule directly and thereby avoiding violation of EEA law in a particular case.[27]

As the Court also took the opportunity to point out, monist States remain subject to an obligation to correctly transpose directives into national law.

For Norway and Iceland with their dualist systems, implementing EEA law into their national legal order has been more of a challenge. Both States have given the main part of the EEA Agreement the force of statutory Acts of Parliament.[28] The main part of the Agreement contains the basic principles of free movement whose direct effect have been crucial in making the internal market function within the EU. Even though the EEA Agreement itself—curiously enough—does not establish any obligation to make the main part of the Agreement part of national law, it was clear to both States that this needed to be done.

---

[24] See Art 46 of the Vienna Convention on the Law of Treaties.
[25] Case E-1/07 *Criminal Proceedings Against A* [2007] EFTA Ct Rep 246.
[26] See Case 106/77 *Simmenthal* [1978] ECR 629.
[27] Para 41 of the advisory opinion.
[28] Act No 109/1992 and Act No 2/1993, respectively.

In Norway, the standstill obligation for State Aid until approved by the EFTA Surveillance Authority, and the obligation to pay back illegal State Aid, corresponding to Article 108(2) TFEU but not found in the EEA Agreement but rather in Article 1 of Protocol 3 to the Agreement between the EFTA States on the establishment of a Surveillance Authority and a Court of Justice, follows from a special piece of legislation, the Act on State Aid of 27 November 1992 No 115 on State Aid.

The Icelandic regulatory framework differs in this respect, where the respective Ministry is responsible for State Aid on account of the EEA Agreement, see Act No 2/1993 on the EEA Agreement. Iceland has not enacted a special law on State Aid, as Norway has done.

Enforcement of EEA competition law is ensured through statutory law, in Norway by Act of 5 March 2004 No 11 on implementation and control relating to the competition rules of the EEA Agreement, in Iceland by chapter VII of the Competition Act (Act No 44/2005).

Under a dualist regime, regulations also need to be implemented 'as such', ie word by word.[29] In Norway, this is mostly done by simply enacting provisions stating that regulation so-and-so shall apply as such as a statute, with whatever adaptations that may follow from the relevant annex of the EEA Agreement into which it has been incorporated.[30] This means that incorrect implementation is not really a problem. A regulation is either implemented correctly or not at all. However, it does happen that regulations are not implemented in time.

The same method was originally applied in Iceland. This approach was, however, severely criticised by national courts and the Parliamentary Ombudsman, who argued that this way of implementation did not meet the requirements of the Icelandic Act on publication of laws and regulations. Subsequently, all regulations have been transposed into Icelandic law on a case-by-case basis by the enactment of new legislation or legislative amendments.

With regard to directives, insufficient or incorrect implementation is more of an issue. In Norway and Iceland, however, a strong tradition of treaty-friendly interpretation makes the ambition to avoid violations of international obligation a strong interpretative argument in its own right. The principle of harmonious interpretation found in the case law of the CJEU[31] and adopted by the EFTA

---

[29] See Article 7 EEA. Paragraph 54 of the judgment in case C-431/11UK v European Commission is thus based on a misunderstanding. See also Section II above.

[30] These are typically lists of national institutions etc supplementing similar lists for the EU Member States attached to the regulation, or provisions on cooperation between the EFTA States and the EFTA Surveillance Authority supplanting provisions on the same form of cooperation between the EU Member States and the European Commission.

[31] See especially Case 14/83 *von Colson and Kamann* [1984] ECR 1891 and Case C-282/10 *Dominguez*, nyr.

Court,[32] has therefore met no resistance from national courts. To them, this corresponds to what is already national law.

The traditional principle of treaty-friendly interpretation is also understood to entail competence for courts to set aside administrative decisions, and probably also subordinate legislation enacted by the ministries and sub-ministerial organs, in so far as the decisions or the legislation violates Norway's international obligation, regardless of whether the international norm in question has been made part of Norwegian law.[33]

The Judgments of the CJEU concerning the so-called incidental horizontal effect of Directive 83/189/EEC, now Directive 98/34/EC, as a consequence of a national technical regulation not having been notified before implementation[34]— meaning that the technical regulation may not be invoked even in disputes between private parties—have been dealt with through a special Act, of 15 December 2004 No 101, which enacts this very principle in Norway.

Protocol 35 has led to a provision of the Act incorporating the main part of the EEA Agreement into Norwegian law in which all statutory provisions, whether in Acts of Parliament or in subordinate legislation, that serve to implement obligations under the EEA Agreement shall prevail over other provisions.[35] However, due to the tradition of treaty-friendly interpretation, this provision has not yet played any noticeable part in the application of EEA law in Norway.

With regard to Iceland, in order to fulfil the requirements of Protocol 35, it is stated in Article 3 of Act No 2/1993, incorporating the main part of the EEA Agreement into Icelandic law, that law and regulations shall, as is relevant, be interpreted in conformity with the EEA Agreement and secondary legislation.[36] The provision is thus on the one hand more cautiously worded than its Norwegian equivalent; on the other hand, unlike the Norwegian provision, it does not work in favour of implemented EEA law only.

---

[32]   See Case E-4/01 *Karlsson* [2002] EFTA Ct Rep 240, Case E-1/07 *Criminal Proceedings Against A* [2007] EFTA Ct Rep 246 and Case E-15/12 *Wahl*, nyr.

[33]   See especially the Supreme Court judgment reported in *Norsk Retstidend* 1982 p 241 and, with regard to subordinate legislation, F Arnesen and A Stenvik, *Internasjonalisering og juridisk metode* (Oslo, Universitetsforlaget, 2009) pp 123–124.

[34]   Case C-194/94 *CIA Security* [1996] ECR I-2201 and Case C-443/98 *Unilever Italia* [2000] ECR I-7535.

[35]   Section 2 of Act of 27 November 1992 No 109. The only exception is that a clause in subordinate legislation may not prevail over an earlier Act of Parliament. This would potentially have turned all clauses found in Acts of Parliament enabling the Government or subordinate organs to enact legislation 'about' this or that topic within the scope of application of the Act into clauses enabling the executive branch of government to derogate from the Act in question. This would be constitutionally dubious. However, even in such cases, the traditional principle of treaty-friendly interpretation would apply to the interpretation of the Act in question.

[36]   This has been subject to criticism. See, eg, Ó Jóhannes Einarsson, *Bókun 35 og staða EES-samningsins að íslenskum rétti*, Tímarit lögfræðinga, 4 hefti 57 árg 2007, pp 371–411 and M Einarsdóttir, *Forgangsáhrif réttilega innleiddra EES-reglna*, Tímarit Lögréttu, 1 hefti 7 árg 2010, pp 29–34.

When one takes into account the fact that the main part of the EEA Agreement has the force of an Act of Parliament, and that in the EU, directives do not have direct effect in so far as they impose obligations on individuals,[37] as well as the competence of Norwegian courts to declare an administrative decision void on the basis that it violates (unimplemented) international obligations, Fredriksen and Mathisen are probably right in concluding that the absence of a principle of direct effect in EEA law has little consequence in practice as far as Norwegian application of EEA law is concerned.[38] This seems to be the view also of some Icelandic commentators with regard to Icelandic law.[39]

---

[37] See Case C-91/92 *Faccini Dori* [1994] ECR 3325.
[38] H Haukeland Fredriksen and G Mathisen, *EØS-rett* (2nd edition Bergen, Fagbokforlaget, 2014) p 321.
[39] See Méndez-Pinedo 2009 with references to the debate in Icelandic legal literature on p 129, pp 170–172 and pp 197–201.

19

Climate Change Law and Policy in the EEA—A View from the General Court

MARC JAEGER

IN ITS TWENTY years history, the EFTA Court has only had to deal with a few cases directly concerning environmental and climate change law.[1] However, the importance of those provisions in an EEA context, as well as the specific role played by the EFTA pillar in the sector, is underlined by the fact that one of its landmark cases, the 'Norwegian Waterfalls' case,[2] concerned the compatibility with the Agreement on the European Economic Area (EEA Agreement) of national rules applying to concessions for the acquisition of hydropower resources for the production of green electricity.

In its judgment in that case, the EFTA Court ruled, in particular, that the provisions that govern the management of essential natural energy resources are not exempted from the scope of the EEA Agreement: 'on the contrary, Article 73(1)(c) EEA provides that the Contracting Parties shall, in their actions relating to the environment, pursue the objective of ensuring a prudent and rational utilisation of natural resources'.[3]

---

[1] The cases dealt with by the EFTA Court in this area are those for failure to transpose Directive 2002/49/EC on the assessment and management of environmental noise (Case E-6/06 *EFTA Surveillance Authority v Liechtenstein* [2007] EFTA Ct Rep 239; Case E-8/11 *EFTA Surveillance Authority v Iceland* [2011] EFTA Ct Rep 467) and the case for failure to transpose Directive 2002/91/EC on the energy performance of buildings (Case E-6/08 *EFTA Surveillance Authority v Norway* [2009–2010] EFTA Ct Rep 5). Moreover, in this context, one can also mention the pioneering *Kellogg's* judgment (Case E-3/00 *EFTA Surveillance Authority v Norway* [2000–2001] EFTA Ct Rep 73) concerning the precautionary principle, which was referred to by the General Court in cases T-13/99 *Pfizer Animal Health* [2002] ECR II-3305 and T-70/99 *Alpharma* [2002] ECR II-3495, and then relied upon by the Court of justice in cases C-192/01 *Commission v Denmark* [2003] ECR I-9693, C-41/02 *Commission v Netherlands* [2004] ECR I-11375, C-236/01 *Monsanto Agricoltura Italia and Others* [2003] I-8105 and C-286/02 *Bellio F.lli* [2004] ECR I-3465; on that topic, see especially: C Baudenbacher 'The goal of homogeneous interpretation of the law in the European Economic Area' [2008] *The European Legal Forum (ELF)* 22.

[2] Case E-2/06 *EFTA Surveillance Authority v Norway* [2007] EFTA Ct Rep 167.

[3] Case E-2/06 *EFTA Surveillance Authority v Norway* [2007] EFTA Ct Rep 167, para 60.

Thereby, it confirmed the approach taken by the Contracting Parties to the EEA Agreement, which have deemed EEA relevant and been steadily incorporating into that Agreement almost all the acts adopted by the EU in the area of climate change law, which, in general, directly affect the management of the energy resources in the EEA States.

Indeed, it is a shared objective across both pillars of the EEA to develop legal instruments in order to combat climate change[4] and promote a competitive, climate resilient and sustainable low carbon economy. Despite the current challenges faced by the EU climate change policy, linked, inter alia, to shifting priorities following the financial crisis, they remain committed to the fight against global warming,[5] 'one of the greatest social, economic and environmental threats which the world currently faces'.[6]

Moreover, the EFTA States are fully integrated into the internal market. In view of the impact of climate change policy on the regulatory environment and the conditions of competition in which economic actors operate, the close cooperation in this area between the EFTA States and the EU Member States, as well as between the EEA institutions, is of particular importance. This is even more so as EU policy in the area of climate change has a strong link to the Union's energy policy and the EFTA States play a significant role in the EEA energy internal market, both as regards fossil fuels and renewable energy.

In this context, this chapter aims to provide an overview, from the perspective of the General Court and in an EEA context, of two key instruments in the fight against climate change, for which the case-law of the European Union courts has played a significant role: the European Emissions Trading Scheme and the renewable energy policy.

I. EMISSIONS TRADING SCHEME

Amongst the instruments developed to tackle climate change, the EU's Emissions Trading Scheme (EU ETS) has been the most innovative one.

The EU ETS is a cap and trade system. A limit, or 'cap' is placed on the total quantity of emissions of certain emitters of greenhouse gases, which is reduced over time so that total emissions fall. This limited quantity of emissions is then shared amongst those emitters, through the allocation of allowances, which authorise their holder to emit a certain quantity of CO_2. These allowances are tradable. Every year, each emitter covered by the scheme must surrender to the

---

[4] Climate change is now directly mentioned in the EU treaties, since the Lisbon Treaty: Article 191 TFUE sets as one of the objectives of EU environment policy 'combating climate change', as part of the objective of 'promoting measures at international level to deal with regional or worldwide environmental problems'.

[5] Council of the EEA, 'Conclusions of the 40th meeting of the EEA Council, 19 November 2013' EEE 1611/13, www.consilium.europa.eu/uedocs/cms_data/docs/pressdata/en/er/139648.pdf.

[6] Case T-263/07 *Estonia v Commission* [2009] ECR II-3463, para 49.

competent authority enough allowances to match all his emissions. In order to surrender sufficient allowances, he has the choice between either reducing his emissions or purchasing allowances from another emitter who has reduced his. As each emitter will base his decision on cost-effectiveness, this allows that emissions are cut where it costs least to do so.

The establishment of an emission trading scheme between individual emitters at the scale of 15 Member States, and then, after the successive enlargements, of 28 Member States, and 31 States through incorporation into the EEA Agreement,[7] was, and remains, unprecedented.[8] In view of the novelty and complexity of the scheme, the EU legislator took a step by step approach, progressively widening the scope of the Directive. Moreover, the concrete operation of the scheme led the Commission and then the EU legislator to progressively centralise and harmonise the allocation mechanisms. Those two trends were contested and led the Union courts to clarify the framework within which this gradual approach could be followed.

A. Widening the Scope

Directive 2003/87/EC of the European Parliament and of the Council of 13 October 2003 establishing a scheme for greenhouse gas emission allowance trading within the Community and amending Council Directive 96/61/EC[9] covers the greenhouse gas emissions from activities listed in Annex I to the Directive. Both the initial restricted scope and then the widening of the scope were subject to appeal by affected industries and Member States.

1. When it was adopted, Directive 2003/87/EC covered only carbon dioxide emissions, which account for over 80% of the Union's overall greenhouse gas emissions. It also only covered a limited number of installations, which represented

---

[7] Directive 2003/87/EC was incorporated into the EEA Agreement by Decision of the EEA Joint Committee No 146/2007 of 26 October 2007 amending Annex XX (Environment) to the EEA Agreement ([2008] OJ L100/92), which entered into force on 29 December 2007 and extended the ETS to include the EFTA States.

[8] The main scheme operating at the time of the introduction of the EU ETS was the Acid Rain Program of the United States Environmental Protection Agency, covering emissions of sulphur dioxide (SO2) and nitrogen oxides (NOX). But it started in 1995 with a scope covering only a core set of 110 large electric power plants in 21 US states, and currently covering 1249 electric power plants for SO2 and 368 power plants for NOX (For an overview of the scheme, its history and the current situation: www.epa.gov/airmarkets/progsregs/arp/basic.html). Other emission trading schemes have also been introduced at the national or sub-national level in Australia, New Zealand, Japan, Switzerland, China and United States. The scope of the EU ETS remains the widest, covering many installations (currently approx. 10.000), across many industrial sectors, including the aviation sector, in 31 countries.

[9] Directive 2003/87/EC of the European Parliament and of the Council of 13 October 2003 establishing a scheme for greenhouse gas emission allowance trading within the Community and amending Council Directive 96/61/EC [2003] OJ L275/32.

approximately 41% of estimated EU carbon dioxide emissions in 2005:[10] large combustion installations, oil refineries, coke ovens, installations of the ferrous metals industry, the mineral industry (production of cement clinker, glass and ceramic products), and the pulp and paper industry. The Directive explicitly foresaw the possibility of including other activities (*inter alia* the chemicals, aluminium and transport sectors) and emissions of other greenhouse gases, on the basis of experience of the application of the Directive and of progress achieved in the monitoring of emissions of greenhouse gases and in the light of developments in the international context.[11]

However, this gradual approach was contested by a group of companies from the steel industry, which introduced, in front of the General Court, an application for partial annulment of the Directive and for damages, and, in parallel, an application in front of the French Conseil d'État, which made a reference to the Court of justice for a preliminary ruling on the validity of the Directive. The applicants argued, in particular, that the exclusion of non-ferrous metal and chemical product sectors from the scope of the Directive breached the principle of equal treatment.

The Grand Chamber of the Court of justice,[12] followed by the General Court,[13] rejected that argument and confirmed the validity of the Directive.

Indeed, the EU courts agreed with the applicants that the steel, chemical and non-ferrous metal sectors are, for the purposes of examining the validity of Directive 2003/87/EC from the point of view of the principle of equal treatment, in a comparable position while being treated differently.[14]

However, the courts ruled that the original definition of the scope of Directive 2003/87/EC and the step-by-step approach, taken in order not to disturb the establishment of the system, were within the discretion enjoyed by the Community legislature, in view of the novelty and complexity of the scheme. Moreover, they found that the choice of sectors to be included in the scope of Directive 2003/87/EC had been done on the basis of objective criteria, linked to the quantity of emissions per sector and the administrative burden entailed by the number of installations in that sector; the principle of equality had therefore not been breached.

The courts thus judged that the gradual approach taken by the EU legislator as regards the scope of the Directive, justified by the need to carry out 'legislative experimentation'[15] before generalising such a far-reaching scheme, did

---

[10] Commission, 'Commission staff working document—Accompanying document to the Proposal for a Directive of the European Parliament and of the Council amending Directive 2003/87/EC so as to improve and extend the EU greenhouse gas emission allowance trading system—Impact assessment' SEC(2008)52.

[11] Article 30 of Directive 2003/87/EC.

[12] Case C-127/07 *ArcelorAtlantique et Lorraine and Others* [2008] ECR I-9895, paras 25–73.

[13] Case T-16/04 *Arcelor v Parliament and Council* [2010] ECR II-211, para 168. The General Court declared inadmissible the application for annulment, for lack of direct and individual concern of the applicant, but declared admissible the application for damages.

[14] Case C-127/07 *ArcelorAtlantique et Lorraine and Others* [2008] ECR I-9895, paras 25–38.

[15] See, on that topic: Case C-127/07 *ArcelorAtlantique et Lorraine and Others* [2008] ECR I-9895, Opinion of AG Poiares Maduro, paras 44–48.

not constitute a manifest error of assessment[16] and they upheld the legality of Directive 2003/87/EC.

2. Thereafter, as provided for by Directive 2003/87/EC, the Commission carried out a review of the scope of the Directive, and progressively included other sectors. The first one to be included, as of 2012, was aviation, through the extension of the scope of Directive 2003/87/EC to all flights arriving at or departing from an airport situated in the territory of a Member State by Directive 2008/101/EC of the European Parliament and of the Council of 19 November 2008 amending Directive 2003/87/EC so as to include aviation activities in the scheme for greenhouse gas emission allowance trading within the Community.[17] This was followed by the inclusion of CO_2 emissions from the petrochemical, ammonia and aluminium sectors, of N_2O emissions from certain chemical productions and of perfluorocarbon emissions from the aluminium sector by Directive 2009/29/EC of the European Parliament and of the Council of 23 April 2009 amending Directive 2003/87/EC so as to improve and extend the greenhouse gas emission allowance trading scheme of the Community.[18]

The increase of the scope of the Directive to include new industrial sectors was not subject to new litigation in the Union's courts, but the inclusion of aviation led to proceedings being brought by the American aviation industry, concerning the validity of the measures adopted by the United Kingdom to implement Directive 2008/101/EC, which, in turn, led to a reference to the Court of justice for a preliminary ruling on the validity of the Directive.[19] Whereas the *Arcelor* cases[20] concerned the question whether the EU legislator had not limited too much the scope of the EU ETS, the proceedings introduced by the aviation industry concerned the question whether the EU legislator had not gone too far in including aviation and in particular flights originating from or departing towards third States.

In its judgment, the Court of justice confirmed the competence, for the European Union, to extend the scope of the EU ETS as it did. In particular, it rejected claims founded on the breach of principles of international customary law linked to territoriality, the sovereignty of third States and the freedom to fly

---

[16] See, concerning the nature of the judicial review undertaken by the Court of justice as regards the validity of a Directive in the light of the principle of equal treatment, in particular in economic matters: Case C-127/07 *ArcelorAtlantique et Lorraine and Others* [2008] ECR I-9895, Opinion of AG Poiares Maduro, paras 28–39.

[17] Directive 2008/101/EC of the European Parliament and of the Council of 19 November 2008 amending Directive 2003/87/EC so as to include aviation activities in the scheme for greenhouse gas emission allowance trading within the Community [2008] OJ L8/3. The Directive was incorporated into the EEA Agreement by Joint Committee Decision No 6/2011 of 1 April 2011 amending Annex XX (Environment) to the EEA Agreement [2011] OJ L171/44, which entered into force on 2 April 2011.

[18] Directive 2009/29/EC of the European Parliament and of the Council of 23 April 2009 amending Directive 2003/87/EC so as to improve and extend the greenhouse gas emission allowance trading scheme of the Community [2009] OJ L140/63. It was incorporated into the EEA Agreement by Joint Committee Decision No 152/2012 of 26 July 2012 amending Annex XX (Environment) to the EEA Agreement [2012] OJ L309/38, which entered into force on 27 July 2012.

[19] Case C-366/10 *Air Transport Association of America and Others* [2011] ECR I-13755.

[20] Case T-16/04 *Arcelor v Parliament and Council* [2010] ECR II-211, para 168 and Case C-127/07 *ArcelorAtlantique et Lorraine and Others* [2008] ECR I-9895.

over the high seas, as the Directive is applied to aircrafts physically in the territory of one of the Member States of the European Union and thus subject on that basis to the unlimited jurisdiction of the European Union. It also rejected claims founded on the Open Skies Agreement and the obligation to exempt fuel load from taxes, duties, fees and charges, in the absence of a direct link between the quantity of fuel held or consumed by an aircraft and the financial burden on the aircraft's operator in the context of the operation of the EU ETS. Indeed, the actual cost for the operator, resulting from the number of allowances to be surrendered, a quantity which is calculated inter alia on the basis of fuel consumption, depends, inasmuch as a market-based measure is involved, not directly on the number of allowances that must be surrendered, but on the number of allowances initially allocated to the operator and their market price when the purchase of additional allowances proves necessary in order to cover the operator's emissions.[21]

B. Harmonising and Centralising Allocation Mechanisms

Beyond the issue of the scope of the Directive, the step-by-step approach also concerned the allocation mechanism, something which proved, initially, more problematic. Indeed, the Directive provided for an allocation mechanism driven by the Member States, within a framework giving them significant discretion. In light of the operation of the scheme, the Commission attempted to harmonise the process through administrative measures, but in doing so, went beyond its powers, as ruled by the EU courts. This approach may be interestingly contrasted with the more harmonised approach taken as concerns the EFTA States. In the end, a centralisation of the allocation mechanisms, decided by the EU legislator, addressed the issue.

1. As indicated above, a key element of an emission trading scheme is the allocation of allowances to operators. Directive 2003/87/EC provided that the allocation of allowances to companies would be done by Member States. In doing so, they had to comply with a set of criteria, set out in Annex III to the Directive, which were to ensure that the sectors concerned by the ETS would contribute appropriately to the overall reduction of greenhouse gas emissions and which would guarantee a level playing-field between companies competing within the internal

---

[21] In the meantime, by Regulation (EU) No 421/2014 of the European Parliament and of the Council of 16 April 2014 amending Directive 2003/87/EC establishing a scheme for greenhouse gas emission allowance trading within the Community, in view of the implementation by 2020 of an international agreement applying a single global market-based measure to international aviation emissions [2014] OJ L129/1, the EU temporarily suspended the EU ETS requirements for flights operated from or to non-European countries. This Decision was incorporated into the EEA Agreement by Joint Committee Decision No 62/2014 of 30 April 2014 amending Annex XX (Environment) to the EEA Agreement. For an overview of the issues: Commission, 'Executive summary of the impact assessment accompanying the proposal for a Directive amending Directive 2003/87/EC establishing a scheme for greenhouse gas emission allowance trading within the Community in view of the implementation by 2020 of an international agreement applying a single global market-based measure to international aviation emissions' SWD(2013) 431.

market.[22] Compliance with those criteria was ensured through an examination, by the Commission, of the 'national allocation plans' (NAP) notified by the Member States, which stated the total quantity of allowances that they intended to allocate and how they proposed to allocate them. The Commission could reject a plan incompatible with the criteria of Annex III.

The first phase of the scheme ran between 2005 and 2007, a period preceding the Kyoto Protocol's commitment period, and was conceived as a 'learning by doing' phase to prepare for the second phase, when the EU ETS would need to function effectively.[23] After the first phase, and upon review, it appeared that Member States had over-allocated allowances and that the allocation methods were differing significantly across Member States, causing a lack of a level playing field across the EU.[24] For the second phase, running from 2008 to 2012, the Commission developed an approach for the review of the NAPs which was designed to ensure scarcity in the market and a more harmonised method of allocating allowances, based on guidance documents.

However, the EU courts did not validate the approach taken by the Commission when they were led to examine the decisions of the Commission concerning the Member States' NAPs and, in this context, clarify the respective roles of the Commission and of the Member States.

A first set of challenges to the Commission decisions came from private operators subject to the EU ETS. Their actions were not admissible, as the applicants contesting the decisions of the Commission assessing the NAPs notified by Member States[25] were not directly and individually concerned by the contested acts.[26]

---

[22] Commission, 'Proposal for a Directive establishing a scheme for greenhouse gas emission allowance trading within the Community and amending Council Directive 96/61/EC' COM(2001) 581.

[23] Ibid.

[24] Commission, 'Commission staff working document—Accompanying document to the Proposal for a Directive of the European Parliament and of the Council amending Directive 2003/87/EC so as to improve and extend the EU greenhouse gas emission allowance trading system—Impact assessment' SEC(2008) 52, 14–15.

[25] Case T-130/06 *Drax Power and Others v Commission* [2007] OJ C 211/33 (United Kingdom NAP I), Case T-28/07 *Fels-Werke and Others v Commission* [2007] OJ C283/27 (confirmed in Case C-503/07 P *Saint-Gobain Glass Deutschland v Commission* [2008] ECR I-2217)(German NAP II), T-489/04 *US Steel Košice v Commission* [2007] OJ C297/41 (Slovak NAP I), T-27/07 *US Steel Košice v Commission* [2007] OJ C297/41 (confirmed in Case C-6/08 P *US Steel Košice v Commission* [2008] OJ C285/13) (Slovak NAP II), T-13/07 *Cemex UK Cement v Commission* [2007] ECR II-146 (United Kingdom NAP II), T-195/07 *Lafarge Cement v Commission* [2008] OJ C301/36 (Polish NAP II) and T-208/07 *BOT Elektrownia Bełchatów and Others v Commission* [2008] OJ C327/25 (Polish NAP II). In case Case T-387/04 *EnBW Energie Baden-Württemberg v Commission* [2007] ECR II-1195 (German NAP I), the application was declared inadmissible as the applicant was held to lack *locus standi* to bring an action against the Commission's decision.

[26] More generally, on this topic, see M Jaeger, 'L'accès des personnes physiques ou morales à la justice: les premières interprétations par le Tribunal des nouvelles dispositions de l'article 263, quatrième alinéa, TFUE' in L Weitzel (ed), *Mélanges en hommage à Albert Weitzel: l'Europe des droits fondamentaux* (Pédone, 2013) 91–128 and M Jaeger, 'Private Parties' Access to the Court of Regional (and Sub-Regional) Economic Integration Organisations: a Comparative Analysis' in P Cardonell, A Rosas and N Wahl (eds), *Constitutionalising the EU judicial system: essays in honour of Pernilla Lindh* (Oxford, Hart Publishing, 2012) 25–37.

However, these decisions allowed the General Court to start clarifying the Commission's role in the review of the NAPs. In particular, it insisted on the fact that the Commission's power to consider and reject NAPs is 'severely limited',[27] as its review is restricted to considering whether the NAPs are compatible with the criteria laid down in Annex III to Directive 2003/87/EC and the provisions of Article 10 thereof,[28] and does not constitute an authorisation procedure but an simple ex-ante control. As summarized by the Court of justice thereafter, it is for each Member State, not the Commission, to decide on the total quantity of allowances it will allocate for the period in question, to initiate the process of allocation and to rule on allocation.[29]

This body of case-law, along with the judgments concerning the decisions of the Commission on the first phase NAPs notified by the United Kingdom[30] and Germany,[31] laid the groundwork for when the General Court was led to adjudicate the cases introduced by 8 Member States in 2007, contesting the legality of the Commission decisions on their second phase NAPs.[32]

At the heart of those cases lay the question whether the Commission was exceeding its powers under the Directive when using a harmonised approach to the review of the second phase NAPs. In its judgments, the General Court ruled in the affirmative.

Indeed, the General Court underlined that the drawing up of a NAP required the Member State to make choices, which are neither correct nor incorrect in absolute terms. In reviewing those choices, the Commission had to respect the margin for manoeuvre of the Member States, and, in so far as the latter bases its reasoning on credible and sufficient data and parameters for analysis, having regard to the criteria in Annex III, it could not reject the national allocation

---

[27] Case T-387/04 *EnBW Energie Baden-Württemberg v Commission* [2007] ECR II-1195, para 104. See also: Case T-374/04 *Germany v Commission* [2007] ECR II-4431, para 116, Case T-369/07 Latvia v Commission [2011] ECR II-1039, para 46 and Case C-267/11 P *Commission v Latvia* [2013] OJ C344/6, para 47.

[28] Case T-387/04 *EnBW Energie Baden-Württemberg v Commission* [2007] ECR II-1195, paras 104, 112, 120.

[29] Case C-503/07 P *Saint-Gobain Glass Deutschland v Commission* [2008] ECR I-2217, para 75.

[30] Case T-178/05 *United Kingdom v Commission* [2005] ECR II-4807. The case concerned the refusal, by the Commission, to accept amendments to the UK NAP.

[31] Case T-374/04 *Germany v Commission* [2007] ECR II-4431. The case concerned measures, in the German NAP, for the ex-post adjustment of the amount of allowances allocation to installations.

[32] Case T-183/07 *Poland v Commission* [2009] ECR II-3395 (confirmed in Case C-504/09 P *Poland v Commission* [2012] OJ C151/2), T-263/07 *Estonia v Commission* [2009] ECR II-3463 (confirmed in Case C-505/09 P *Commission v Estonia* [2012] OJ C151/2) and Case T-369/07 *Latvia v Commission* [2011] ECR II-1039 (confirmed in Case C-267/11 P *Commission v Latvia* [2013] OJ C344/6). For an analysis of the General Court's approach: D Mertens de Wilmars, 'Recent Case Law on the European Scheme for Greenhouse Gas Emission Allowance Trading' in *Today's multilayered legal order: liber amicorum in honour of Arjen W.H. Meij* (Paris Legal Publishers, 2011) 211–18. The other cases led to Orders for removal from the Register after the Member States decided to discontinue proceedings: Cases T-499/07 and T-500/07 *Bulgaria v Commission* [2010] OJ C246/39, Case T-368/07 *Lithuania v Commission* [2011] OJ C340/32, Case T-484/07 *Romania v Commission* [2012] OJ C258/27, Case T-221/07 *Hungary v Commission* [2013] OJ C, Case T-194/07 *Czech Republic v Commission* [2013] OJ C171/40.

plan.[33] The Commission's task was to review the choices made by the Member State for the purposes of drawing up its national plan; it was not to make its own choice as to the data to be used, as to the methods to forecast the evolution of emissions or as to the types of parameters to be used to set the quantities of allowances to be allocated, and to express an opinion only on any challenges to that choice by the Member States.[34] It was not for the Commission to select and apply a single method for assessing the NAPs of all the Member States, which would give it a power of uniformisation and a central role in the drawing up of NAPs, which were not conferred on it by the Directive.[35]

As stated by the General Court, in a community governed by the rule of law, administrative measures must be adopted in compliance with the competences attributed to various administrative bodies. Even if the annulment of the contested decisions were to have a negative impact on the proper functioning of the Community's greenhouse gas emissions trading system, that finding would not be enough to justify maintaining the contested decisions in force if those measures were adopted in breach of the competences allocated by the Directive to the Member States and the Commission respectively.[36]

Indeed, the Commission could not attempt to mitigate the perceived shortcomings of the progressive approach taken by the EU legislator through administrative measures.

2. At about the same time that the General Court was issuing its first judgments on that issue, the EFTA States and the EU were adopting the decision to extend the EU ETS to the whole of the EEA. A different approach was taken as regards the review of the NAPs of the EFTA States.

The extension of the EU ETS to the EFTA States posed the challenge of ensuring that homogeneity across the EEA, ie that the same rules apply throughout the European Economic Area, was not jeopardized, while safeguarding the decision-making autonomy of the EU and the EFTA sides[37] through the so-called two pillar structure. The latter means, in short, that the EU side and the EFTA side each take

---

[33] Case T-263/07 *Estonia v Commission* [2009] ECR II-3463, para 69.

[34] Case T-263/07 *Estonia v Commission* [2009] ECR II-3463, para 71–94.

[35] Case T-183/07 *Poland v Commission* [2009] ECR II-3395, para 103–106. See also: Case C-504/09 P *Poland v Commission* [2012] OJ C151/2, para 80 and Case C-505/09 P *Commission v Estonia* [2012] OJ C151/2, para 82 and C-267/11 P *Commission v Latvia* [2013] OJ C344/6, para 54.

[36] Cases T-263/07 *Estonia v Commission* [2009] ECR II-3463, para 39 and T-183/07 *Poland v Commission* [2009] ECR II-3395, para 129. See also: Case C-504/09 P *Poland v Commission* [2012] OJ C151/2, para 78 and Case C-505/09 P *Commission v Estonia* [2012] OJ C151/2, para 80.

[37] On this dialectic of the principles of homogeneity and decision-making autonomy in the EEA Agreement: C Baudenbacher 'Between Homogeneity and Independence: The Legal Position of the EFTA Court in the European Economic Area' (1996/1997) 3 *Columbia Journal of European Law* 169, 175; A Toledano Laredo, 'Principes et objectifs de l'Accord EEE. Eléments de réflexion' in O Jacot-Guillarmod (ed), *Accord EEE: Commentaires et réflexions* (Schulthess, 1992) 565–570; T van Stiphout, 'Homogeneity vs. Decision-Making Autonomy in the EEA Agreement' (2007) *European Journal of Law Reform* 431.

care of their own internal matters, with each side having their own institutions for internal decision-making, surveillance and judicial review.[38]

In the context of Directive 2003/87/EC, and in accordance with the default mechanisms provided for in EEA law, it was for the EFTA Surveillance Authority to undertake the tasks relating to the EFTA States for which the Commission is responsible with respect to the EC Member States under the Directive,[39] and thus to review the EFTA NAPs. To ensure homogeneity, the Joint Committee Decision incorporating the Directive into the EEA Agreement[40] provided that the EFTA Surveillance Authority was to take its decisions in a manner consistent with the criteria of Annex III to the Directive, the relevant provisions of the methodology set out in the Commission's guidance documents and the Commission's decisions on the NAPs of the EU Member States. In effect, the Joint Committee Decision made binding, as concerns the EFTA States, the practice of the Commission, as well as the guidance documents developed by the Commission prior to 2007 for the review of the NAPs of the EU Member States.

In theory, one could thus argue that the EFTA States were made subject to a more harmonised regime than the one which resulted from the Directive, as interpreted by the General Court and the Court of justice. In practice, however, the Joint Committee Decision guaranteed homogeneity. Indeed, it ensured that the EFTA Surveillance Authority would take the same approach towards the EFTA NAPs as the Commission had taken in its decisions on the EU Member States' NAPs, which were all adopted in 2006 and 2007, prior to the rulings issued by the EU courts and which were, except for two annulled by the Court, unaffected in substance by those rulings. Moreover, by the time the decisions on the EFTA NAPs were adopted by the EFTA Surveillance Authority, the latter could draw upon the body of case law issued by the EU courts to assess the EFTA NAPs.[41]

In any event, the problems which led the Commission to attempt a harmonised approach through guidance documents, and, in turn, to the annulment of its decisions by the General Court, were then addressed by the EU legislator.

---

[38] T Blanchet, R Piipponen and M Westman-Clément, *The Agreement on the European Economic Area (EEA): A Guide to the Free Movement of Goods and Competition Rules* (Oxford, 1994) 27; S Norberg, K Hökborg, M Johansson, D Eliasson and L Dedichen, *EEA Law. A Comentary on the EEA Agreement* (Fritzes, 1993) 109.

[39] This follows from the application of point 4(d) of Protocol 1 on horizontal adaptations to the EEA Agreement (OJ L1/37) and Article 1(2) of Protocol 1 on the functions and powers of the EFTA Surveillance Authority, to the Agreement between the EFTA States on the establishment of a surveillance authority and a court of justice (OJ L344/1). It must be noted, however, that this is the default mechanism. Protocol 1 on horizontal adaptations allows a Joint Committee Decision to provide for other mechanisms or an adaptation of the mechanism when incorporating an act into the EEA Agreement.

[40] Directive 2003/87/EC was incorporated into the EEA Agreement by Joint Committee Decision No 146/2007 of 26 October 2007 amending Annex XX (Environment) to the EEA Agreement [2008] OJ L100/92, which entered into force on 29 December 2007, in time for the EFTA States to be able to participate in the second trading period, which started on 1 January 2008.

[41] This is particularly the case for the EFTA Surveillance Authority Decision No 100/09/COL on the Norwegian NAP, which was adopted on 27 February 2009. The EFTA Surveillance Authority Decision No 728/07/COL on the Liechtenstein NAP was adopted on 19 December 2007.

3. As indicated above, the first major change in the EU ETS was an extension of its scope so as to include aviation activities in the scheme for greenhouse gas emission allowance trading within the Community.[42] But instead of relying on NAPs, the Directive specifies a harmonised allocation methodology for determining the total quantity of allowances to be issued and for distributing allowances to aircraft operators, based on the historical aviation emissions. After this first step, the EU legislature, in light of the difficulties encountered with a nationally-driven process based on time-limited allocation plans,[43] made a paradigm shift for the third trading period of the scheme (2013–2020) and introduced a harmonised scheme.

The first major change has been the introduction of an EU-wide cap, which will decrease annually along a linear trend line, instead of national caps. Secondly, instead of distributing most allowances for free to emitters,[44] auctioning becomes the basic principle for allocation of allowances. However, in order to avoid 'carbon leakage', ie the transfer of production from the EU to countries with lower constraints on greenhouse gas emissions, free allocation is maintained for sectors exposed to a risk of such carbon leakage. The free allowances are allocated on the basis of, mainly, product-specific benchmarks set by the Commission, which correspond to the performance of the most efficient installations in the sector. This ensures that only the most efficient installations in each sector receive for free an amount of allowances that may cover all their needs, and thus encourages reduction in emissions.

The benchmarks, once adopted by the Commission, were contested by Poland, in essence on the basis that they discouraged the use of coal and lignite as energy sources, in breach of Article 194(2) TFUE, the principle equal treatment, the principle of proportionality and the rules set out in the revised Directive 2003/87/EC.[45] However, the General Court dismissed the action, noting, in particular, the profound changes made to the allocation methods in favour of a more harmonised scheme.

---

[42] Directive 2008/101/EC of the European Parliament and of the Council of 19 November 2008 amending Directive 2003/87/EC so as to include aviation activities in the scheme for greenhouse gas emission allowance trading within the Community [2008] OJ L8/3. This Directive was subject to a reference for a preliminary ruling on its validity, which confirmed its validity in light of international treaty law and customary international law: Case C-366/10 *Air Transport Association of America and Others* [2011] ECR I-13755.

[43] These difficulties were already identified in the 2006 Commission report on the application of the Directive: Commission, 'Building a global carbon market—Report pursuant to Article 30 of Directive 2003/87/EC' (Communication) COM(2006) 676, 7.

[44] During phases I and II, free allocation had led to windfall profits for certain industries, which had included, in the prices charged to their customers, the value of emission allowances allocated free of charge. The Court of justice has confirmed the legality of the measures adopted by Spain in order to prevent such windfall profits in the electricity sector: Cases C-566/11, C-567/11, C-580/11, C-591/11, C-620/11 and C-640/11 *Iberdrola and Gas Natural* [2013] OJ C367/4. Article 10a(1), §3 of the revised Directive 2003/87/EC now prohibits free allocation in respect of electricity generation, except for transitional free allocation for the modernization of electricity generation, subject to strict constraints.

[45] Case T-370/11 *Poland v Commission* [2013] OJ C114/34. The actions introduced against that same decision by non-privileged applicants were rejected as inadmissible as they lacked direct and individual concern and as the contested decision entails implementing measures within the meaning of the fourth paragraph of Article 263 TFUE: Case T-379/11 *Hüttenwerke Krupp Mannesmann and Others v Commission* [2012] JO C217/23 and Case T-381/11 *Eurofer v Commission* [2012] JO C217/24.

In its judgment, the General Court rejected the plea based on Article 194(2) TFUE and the Member States' right to determine the conditions for exploiting their energy resources, their choice between different energy sources and the general structure of their energy supply. Indeed, the benchmarks are implementing measures of a directive with a legal basis in Article 192(1) TFUE (environmental policy), and thus which is not within the scope of Article 194(2) TFEU. Poland also alleged a breach of the principle of equal treatment linked to the alleged favourable treatment afforded to installations using natural gas compared to those using coal through the equal treatment of all installations despite the fact that they are in different situations due to the use of different fuels. But the General Court judged that this equal treatment was objectively justified, in particular by the fact that a differentiation of product benchmarks according to the fuel used would not encourage industrial installations that use high CO_2 emission fuel to seek solutions to reduce their emissions, but also because such differentiation would not encourage full harmonisation across the European Union of the implementing measures relating to harmonised allocation of free allowances, which the Directive seeks. Finally, after an in-depth examination of the benchmarks, in light of the objectives and provisions of the Directive, the General Court rejected Poland's argument to the effect that those benchmarks would have been set in breach of the principle of proportionality.

C. The Road Ahead

The difficulties faced by the EEA ETS are not resolved. As underlined by the Commission, at the start of the third trading period, the EEA ETS is still confronted with a large imbalance between supply and demand of allowances. This imbalance is primarily caused by a mismatch between the auction supply of emission allowances, which is fixed in a rigid manner, and demand for those allowances, which is flexible and impacted by economic cycles, fossil fuel prices as well as other factors.[46] The imbalance has caused a reduction in the prices of allowances and thereby decreased the incentives for low-carbon investment.[47]

In order to address the problem, the EU legislator has devised a short-term solution through 'back-loading', i.e. postponing the auctioning of 900 million allowances in the early years of the third phase.[48] For the long term, the

---

[46] Commission, 'Proposal for a Decision of the European Parliament and of the Council concerning the establishment and operation of a market stability reserve for the Union greenhouse gas emission trading scheme and amending Directive 2003/87/EU', COM(2014) 20.

[47] Commission, 'The state of the European carbon market in 2012' (Report) COM(2012) 652, 5 and 9.

[48] Decision No 1359/2013/EU of the European Parliament and of the Council of 17 December 2013 amending Directive 2003/87/EC clarifying provisions on the timing of auctions of greenhouse gas allowances [2013] OJ L343/1, incorporated into the EEA Agreement by Joint Committee Decision No 140/2014 of 27 June 2014, which entered into force on 28 June 2014, and Commission Regulation

Commission has proposed, in January 2014, the establishment of a market stability reserve, designed as an objective and rule-based mechanism to adjust auctions in an automatic manner, to be applied as of the fourth phase of the ETS starting in 2021.[49] Only the implementations of these instruments will tell whether they will address the imbalances in the market.

In any event, the difficulties currently faced by the EEA ETS must not hide the achievement represented by the step-by-step establishment, in less than a decade, of a fully functioning market infrastructure and a liquid market producing an EEA-wide carbon price signal, across 31 countries.[50]

II. RENEWABLE ENERGY LEGISLATION

The second instrument developed in order to tackle climate change has been the renewable energy legislation, which aims at fostering the production of energy from renewable sources. The EU's renewable policy started at the time of the negotiation of the Kyoto Protocol and led to the adoption of two successive Directives setting a framework for the development of renewables in the EU and then the EEA. However, one key issue which was not settled is the coexistence of national support schemes in an internal market for energy, thus leaving it up for the EU courts to address.

A. The Legislative Framework

The first community legislative act with respect to the promotion of renewable energy sources has been Directive 2001/77/EC of the European Parliament and of the Council of 27 September 2001 on the promotion of electricity produced from renewable energy sources in the internal electricity market,[51] which was then replaced by Directive 2009/28/EC of the European Parliament and of the Council of 23 April 2009 on the promotion of the use of energy from renewable sources as

---

(EU) No 176/2014 of 25 February 2014 amending Regulation (EU) No 1031/2010 in particular to determine the volumes of greenhouse gas emission allowances to be auctioned in 2013–20 [2014] OJ L56/11.

[49] Commission, 'Proposal for a Decision of the European Parliament and of the Council concerning the establishment and operation of a market stability reserve for the Union greenhouse gas emission trading scheme and amending Directive 2003/87/EC', COM(2014) 20.

[50] Croatia was included as of its accession, on 1 July 2013, and for aviation, as of 1 January 2014: Annexes III and V to the Act concerning the conditions of accession of the Republic of Croatia and the adjustments to the Treaty on European Union, the Treaty on the Functioning of the European Union and the Treaty establishing the European Atomic Energy Community [2012] OJ L112/36.

[51] Directive 2001/77/EC of the European Parliament and of the Council of 27 September 2001 on the promotion of electricity produced from renewable energy sources in the internal electricity market [2001] OJ L 283/33.

and amending and subsequently repealing Directives 2001/77/EC and 2003/30/EC,[52] as part of the 2020 Climate and Energy package adopted on 23 April 2009 ('the RES Directives').

The RES Directives are based on national targets for the share of renewables in energy consumption, which became binding with Directive 2009/28/EC, obliging Member States to introduce measures designed to equal or exceed an indicative trajectory to reach the targets. The RES Directives set an obligation to streamline authorisation procedures and facilitate access to and operation of transmission and distribution grid infrastructure and also provide a framework applicable to guarantees of origin of energy produced from renewable sources as a tool for disclosure to customers.

The RES Directives provides for a clear and binding framework to foster the production of energy from renewable energy. But a key issue which was not settled in either directive has been the support schemes for renewable energy.

B. Support Schemes

Indeed, the production of energy from renewable energy sources requires support, as the market does not provide the optimal level of renewables in the absence of public intervention. This is due to market and regulatory failures: low levels of competition and unfair competition with other fuels (in particular because of the existing subsidies for fossil fuels and nuclear energy), the incomplete internalisation of external costs (air pollution and energy security), and rigid electricity system design.[53]

The Member States use many different support schemes, generally in combination, which often vary depending on the energy source or the technology used to produce energy: feed-in tariffs, feed-in premiums, green certificate systems, tax exemptions, tendering procedures and investment support.[54] Almost all are national in scope.

The Commission, in its proposal for the first renewable Directive,[55] had noted the difficulty of having an internal market in renewable energy, when under all existing support schemes, the support was granted exclusively when production was sold by national producers of green electricity to the national market. But in light of the limited experience with support schemes at the time, it appeared

---

[52] Directive 2009/28/EC of the European Parliament and of the Council of 23 April 2009 on the promotion of the use of energy from renewable sources and amending and subsequently repealing Directives 2001/77/EC and 2003/30/EC [2009] OJ L 140/16.

[53] Commission, 'European Commission guidance for the design of renewables support schemes', SWD(2013) 439.

[54] Commission, 'European Commission guidance for the design of renewables support schemes', SWD(2013) 439, Appendix 1, Table 2; EWEA, *Wind Energy: The Facts* (Routledge, 2009) 231–232.

[55] Commission, 'Proposal for a Directive on the promotion of electricity from renewable energy sources in the internal electricity market' COM(2000) 279, 6.

difficult to decide on the appropriate design of a harmonised mechanism. So Directive 2001/77/EC simply required the Commission to monitor the situation and report on experience gained with the application national schemes.

The two subsequent reports, in 2005[56] and then in 2008,[57] concluded that a harmonised system was not appropriate, in particular as it was not possible to pick a 'winner' between feed-in tariffs and quota based systems. So instead of harmonisation, Directive 2009/28/EC opts for mechanisms to facilitate cross-border support of energy from renewable sources, with effect on target calculation and target compliance: statistical transfers of renewable energy production between Member States, joint projects between Member States or between Member States and third countries and joint support schemes. The objective of those mechanisms is to allow Member States to maintain control on how their renewable energy resources are jointly developed and co-financed and their support schemes joined or harmonised.[58]

But despite the calls from the Commission for greater convergence of national support schemes to facilitate trade and move towards a more pan-European approach to development of renewable energy sources,[59] Member States have continued to focus on national resources and on achieving their 2020 targets on their own,[60] without using the convergence tools provided for in Directive 2009/28/EC.

One major exception has been the cooperation between Sweden and Norway, which led both countries to establish and operate a joint green certificate support scheme under Article 11 of Directive 2009/28/EC. Indeed, Directive 2009/28/EC was incorporated into the EEA Agreement.[61] For the purposes of Directive 2009/28/EC, Iceland and Norway[62] have the same rights and obligation as an EU Member States,[63] including the obligation to reach specific targets for the share of energy from renewable sources, set out in the Joint Committee Decision, but

---

[56] In its report under the Directive in 2005, the Commission analysed the advantages and disadvantages of harmonisation and co-existence of national schemes. It came to the conclusion that a harmonised system, at that stage, was not appropriate, but that a co-ordinated approach, based on cooperation between countries and optimisation of national schemes in light of the existing experience across the EU, would be beneficial. Commission, 'The support of electricity from renewable energy sources' COM(2005) 627.

[57] Commission, 'The support of electricity from renewable energy sources, Accompanying document to the Proposal for a Directive of the European Parliament and of the Council on the promotion of the use of energy from renewable sources' SEC(2008) 57, 13.

[58] Commission, 'Renewable Energy: Progressing towards the 2020 target', COM(2011) 31, 12.

[59] Commission, 'Energy 2020: a strategy for competitive sustainable and secure energy' COM(2010) 639, 10.

[60] Commission, 'Review of European and national financing of renewable energy in accordance with Article 23(7) of Directive 2009/28/EC' SEC(2011) 131, 7.

[61] Its predecessor, Directive 2001/77/EC, had also been incorporated into the EEA Agreement, by Joint Committee Decision No 102/2005 of 8 July 2005 amending Annex IV (Energy) to the EEA Agreement [2005] OJ L 306/34.

[62] As provided for in the Joint Committee Decision 162/2011, the Directive does not apply to Liechtenstein.

[63] Paragraph 8 of Protocol 1 on horizontal adaptations to the EEA Agreement (OJ L1/37).

also the possibility to use the mechanisms of the Directive designed to facilitate cross-border support of energy from renewable sources.

Under the common green certificate scheme, eligible producers established in Sweden or Norway are granted, by the respective competent authority, one certificate per MWh renewable electricity generated. Electricity suppliers and certain consumers, located in both countries, have an obligation to buy a certain number of green certificates. They can purchase them indifferently in either country. As a result, support is independent of whether the power plant is located in Sweden or Norway. This means that investment in renewable power generation is made where profitability is highest and renewable energy resources in both countries are used more effectively than if national green certificate markets had been established.[64]

This remains, to date, the only joint scheme to support renewables.

Private operators have attempted to challenge the national scope of support schemes, which has led to preliminary references being made to the Court of justice on the compatibility of those schemes with EU law. Challenges have also come from the decisional practice of the Commission, which the General Court has currently started to examine.

C. Support Schemes before the Court of Justice

The first judicial challenge to a scheme to support energy from renewable sources to be dealt with by the Court of justice, in case *PreussenElektra*,[65] concerned a German law which obliged electricity supply undertakings to purchase all the green electricity produced within their area of supply and pay for that electricity a fixed minimum purchase price (in essence, a feed-in tariff). In the judgment, given by the Full Court and in the light of an opposite opinion of Advocate General Jacobs, the compatibility of the scheme was examined in light of the rules on State aid as well as those on the free movement of goods.

Concerning the issue of State aid, the Court of justice decided that the obligation imposed on electricity suppliers did not involve any direct or indirect transfer of State resources to undertakings and thus did not qualify as State aid.[66]

Concerning the free movement of goods, the Court noted that the purchase obligation applied only to electricity produced from renewable energy sources

---

[64] Swedish Energy Agency, Norwegian Water Resources and Energy Directorate (NVE) 'The Swedish-Norwegian Electricity Certificate Market, Annual report 2012', 2013, www.nve.no/Global/Elsertifikater/Elcertifikat2013_Eng_TA%20(2).pdf; Agreement between the Government of the Kingdom of Norway and the Government of the Kingdom of Sweden on a common market for electricity certificates, unofficial translation provided on: www.regjeringen.no/upload/OED/pdf%20filer/Elsertifikater/Agreement_on_a_common_market_for_electricity_certificates.pdf.
[65] Case C-379/98 *PreussenElektra* [2001] ECR I-02099.
[66] Case C-379/98 *PreussenElektra* [2001] ECR I-02099, para 58–66. On the application of the State aid rules to feed-in tariffs: Case C-262/12 *Vent De Colère and Others* [2014] OJ C52/11.

within the respective supply area of each undertaking concerned, and was therefore capable, at least potentially, of hindering intra-Community trade.[67] However, the Court noted that the promotion of green electricity is useful for protecting the environment. It also noted that Directive 96/92/EC of 19 December 1996 concerning common rules for the internal market in electricity, applicable at the time, constituted only a further phase in the liberalisation of the electricity market and left some obstacles to trade in electricity between Member States in place. Finally, it noted that mutually-recognisable certificates of origin for green electricity, which were essential in order to make trade in green electricity both reliable and possible in practice, had only just been proposed by the Commission in its proposal for what would become Directive 2001/77/EC. It thus concluded that, in the state of Union law concerning the electricity market as it stood, the German scheme was not in violation of Article 30 of the Treaty.[68] The issue thus appeared settled.

However, it was then reopened through two preliminary reference cases before the Court of justice and which, in light of the opinion of Advocate General Bot in those cases, could have led to a different outcome, not least because of the significant evolution in the legal framework and the European electricity market.

Those cases, *Essent Belgium*[69] and *Ålands Vindkraft*,[70] concerned the compatibility of the green certificate support schemes of, respectively, Belgium and Sweden, with the applicable RES directive, as well as with the provisions on free movement of goods and non-discrimination of the EEA Agreement and the EC/EU treaties. In both those schemes, certificates issued for green electricity produced in another Member State cannot be taken into account to fulfil the national quota obligation.

In his two opinions on these cases, the Advocate General concluded that neither Directive 2001/77/EC, nor Directive 2009/28/EC, require that Member States allow green certificates obtained in another Member State to count towards the fulfilment of the national quota obligation.

However, he concluded that such a prohibition constitutes a discriminatory restriction on the free movement of goods and that this restriction is not justified, suggesting that the Court overturn *PreussenElektra*.[71] The Advocate General agreed that the use of green energies, which the national support schemes seek to promote, contributes to the protection of the environment, in particular by reducing emissions of greenhouse gases. However, he considered that territorial

---

[67] Case C-379/98 *PreussenElektra* [2001] ECR I-02099, para 71.

[68] It is interesting to note that in his opinion in *PreussenElektra*, concerning the justification of the measure under Article 30 EC, Advocate General Jacobs could not see why electricity from renewable sources produced in another Member State would not contribute to the reduction of gas emissions in Germany to the same extent as electricity from renewable sources produced in Germany, and considered that this limitation did not seem proportionate.

[69] Cases C-204/12 to C-208/12, *Essent Belgium*, still pending of July 2014.

[70] Case C-573/12, *Ålands Vindkraft*, EU:C:2014:2037.

[71] However, in his opinion in Case C-66/13 *Green Network* EU:C:2014:156, he states that the justifications of *PreussenElektra* are fully applicable to restrictions to trade with Switzerland (para 95–96).

restrictions such as those at issue were not necessary for securing the attainment of the objective of environmental protection. In that regard, he rejected the justifications based, in particular, on the need to ensure the stability of national schemes, the need to coordinate national schemes before allowing exchanges in green electricity, the need to allow Member State to maintain control over their national energy mix and the need to avoid forcing national consumers to finance green electricity production installations located in other Member States.

He concluded that, as Directive 2009/28/EC can only be interpreted as allowing a restriction to the free movement of green electricity, it must be deemed to be invalid in that regard. In order to avoid negative effects on investments in the renewables sector which could be caused by the confidence crisis due to retroactive amendments to support schemes, he proposed that the Court defer the temporal effects of its judgment for 24 months.

The solution advocated in the opinions raised several concerns. Amongst those, it could have had an effect on the siting of energy production installations, which would not be constrained by national support schemes and become more concentrated in certain areas. Beyond issues of industrial policy and problems linked to the acceptability of such installations by the public, this would have an effect on the flows of electricity across the Union and require significant new additional investment in the electricity grid infrastructure and interconnection between national systems. From an administrative and legal perspective, all Member States would have needed to conclude agreements in order to solve administrative issues linked to the differences between the national support schemes (type of support, eligible technologies, eligibility linked to the date of commissioning of the installations and their size, etc) and linked to the exchange of information between competent authorities, across 31 EEA States, in order to prevent fraud. They would also have had to agree as to how the green energy produced in the different Member States would count towards the national renewable energy targets.[72] It is also noteworthy that it would have led to a situation where consumers and/or taxpayers would be required to finance the development of energy production installations in other Member States, something which might have been politically difficult. Finally, it could not have been excluded that, in light of the ruling of the Court, the Member States would have wanted to amend the RES Directive in a context which has changed since the adoption of the directive in 2009 and where the place of greenhouse gas mitigation, as a driver of energy policy, may have shifted.

---

[72] In that regard, in the recitals to the Environmental and Energy Aid Guidelines 2014–2020, the Commission noted, referring to the opinion of Advocate General Bot, that operating aid schemes should in principle be open to other EEA countries and Contracting Parties of the Energy Community to limit the overall distortive effects. Such an approach would minimise costs for Member States whose sole aim is to achieve the national renewables target laid down in EU legislation. However, the Commission also noted that Member States may want to have a cooperation mechanism in place before allowing cross border support as otherwise, production from installations in other countries will not count towards their national target under the RES Directive (Commission, 'Guidelines on State aid for environmental protection and energy' 2014–2020 COM(2014) 2322, recital 122).

These practical problems will remain hypothetical as the Grand Chamber of the Court of justice, in the judgment in the *ÅlandsVindkraft* case did not follow its Advocate General, as had happened in *PreussenElektra*.

The Court, in its judgment, agreed that the legislation at issue is capable, in various ways, of hindering—at least indirectly and potentially—imports of electricity, especially green electricity, from other Member States. It noted, as the Advocate General, that the objective of promoting the use of renewable energy sources for the production of electricity is, in principle, capable of justifying barriers to the free movement of goods. The Court also agreed that, at first sight, it would seem possible for the environmental protection objective to be pursued regardless of whether that increase originates from installations located in the territory of a specific Member State.

However, after analysis, the Court ruled that the territorial restrictions provided for in the Swedish scheme are indeed appropriate for securing the attainment of the legitimate objective pursued and are necessary for this purpose. In particular, the Court noted that the starting points, the renewable energy potential and the energy mix of each Member State vary, a fact which moved the EU legislature to consider it appropriate, taking into account those differences, to allocate among those States a fair and appropriate share of the effort required to satisfy the EU's international commitments. Furthermore, the Court noted that it is essential, in order to ensure the proper functioning of the national support schemes, that Member States be able to control the effect and costs of their national support schemes according to their different potentials, while maintaining investor confidence. Finally, the Court observed that while preserving the national and, in principle, territorial nature of the existing support schemes, the EU legislature has nonetheless also established various mechanisms to enable Member States to cooperate, insofar as is possible, in order to achieve their mandatory targets under Directive 2009/28/EC.

The Court of Justice thus validated the territorial restrictions provided for in the Swedish green certificates scheme. But the Court went further and examined the proportionality of the other features of the Swedish legislation at issue, considered together with the territorial limitation, thus allowing it to set a framework for support schemes based on green certificates.

In that regard, the Court of justice first confirmed that, as a matter of principle, Member States may introduce a mechanism such as the one at issue, in which the additional cost of producing green electricity is borne directly by the market and, ultimately, by the consumer. Secondly, it confirmed that the incentive effect of a scheme, which constitutes operating aid, as opposed to, for example, investment aid, does not appear to be open to doubt, nor, consequently, does it appear possible to call in question the ability of that scheme to attain the legitimate objective pursued in the circumstances of this case. However, thirdly, the Court stressed that, by its very nature, such a scheme requires, for its proper functioning, market mechanisms that are capable of enabling traders to obtain certificates effectively and under fair terms; it is therefore important that mechanisms be established which ensure the creation of a genuine market for certificates in which supply can match demand, reaching some kind of balance, so that it is actually possible for the relevant suppliers and users to obtain certificates under fair terms; and the fee which suppliers and users which do not meet their quota obligation must pay must not be excessive. Fourthly, the fact that the national legislation at issue in the main proceedings does not prohibit producers of green electricity from selling to traders under the quota obligation both the electricity and the certificates does not render it disproportionate.

In its judgement, the Court thus validated the basic territorial restrictions which are part of most, if not all, national support schemes and also sets out the basic framework within which green certificate schemes must be designed in order to comply with internal market rules.

It may be expected that this framework will be further refined, in particular through the examination of support schemes by the Commission in the context of State aid rules and through the review, by the EU courts, of the decisions adopted by the Commission in this context.

D. Support Schemes and the Commission

Indeed, the issue of cross-border support for green energy may have to be examined in the context of State aid rules, as support schemes may also be subject to those rules if they fulfil the conditions set out by the Court of justice.[73]

As a matter of fact, on the basis of those provisions, the Commission has been examining various national support schemes, including the latest amendments to the German Renewable Energy Act (*Gesetz für den Vorrang Erneuerbarer Energien—* EEG), for which the Commission has decided to initiate the formal investigation procedure. In its letter notifying of its decision to initiate the procedure,[74] the Commission stresses that 'the present decision, like previous decisions on national support schemes for renewable energy, does not put into question the fact that support under the EEG is limited to national production'. But it also recalls that 'when drafting their support schemes, Member States may not introduce discriminatory charges within the meaning of Article 30/110 TFEU'. In its letter, the Commission expresses its doubts concerning the compatibility of certain aspects of the German scheme with Articles 30 and 110 TFEU, and in particular the fact that the German scheme provides for a reduced rate of the surcharge financing the feed-in tariff which seems to be available only when the supplier has purchased 50% of his electricity portfolio from national RES electricity producers.

The Commission's decision to initiate the formal investigation has been appealed by Germany as well as several undertakings in front of the General

---

[73] On this aspect, see: Case C-262/12 *Vent De Colère and Others* OJ C52/11.

[74] Commission, 'Invitation to submit comments pursuant to Article 108(2) TFUE, State aid SA.33995 (2013/C) (ex 2013/NN)—Support for renewable electricity and reduced EEG- surcharge for energy-intensive users' [2014] OJ L37/73.

Court. The latter may, eventually, have to examine the issue of the compatibility of the measure with Articles 30 and 110 TFEU, and thus could be led to rule on restrictions to the free movement of goods linked to national support schemes, further refining the framework for green certificate schemes.

Beyond the internal market issues, the State aid framework will also have an increasing impact on support schemes. In that regard, the latest Environmental and Energy Aid Guidelines 2014–2020 provide a more detailed and prescriptive framework for support schemes for renewables. In particular, they foresee gradual introduction of competitive bidding processes for allocating public support and the gradual replacement of feed-in tariffs by feed-in premiums and green certificates, which expose renewable energy sources to market signals. Indeed, the Commission notes that renewable energy sources have been heavily supported with fixed tariffs, which have 'enormously' supported the growth of renewables and its share in the energy supply. But it also considers that this type of support-scheme has sheltered them from price signals and has led to market distortions. As technologies mature and their production reaches a substantial share of the market, the Commission considers that renewable energy production can and should react to market signals, and aid amounts should respond to falling production costs.[75]

As a result of the evolution in the policy of the Commission as regards support schemes for renewable energy, of the growing maturity of the renewable sector and also, potentially, of the forthcoming case-law of the Court of justice and the General Court, the framework for the development of renewable energy will thus continue to evolve in the near future.

***

It is clear that the development of a robust and effective legal framework to fight climate change and promote a competitive, climate resilient and sustainable low carbon economy, at EEA level, is not a process which was going to be made at once. And the construction will continue, step by step, defined, in part, by the dialogue between the EU legislature and the EU courts, as well as between the EEA institutions. But it must be underlined that the current achievements are immense, particularly in light of the difficulties of setting up such a framework with 28 Member States (or 31 EEA States) with very different economies, natural resources and geographical constraints and taking into account the legacy of energy systems built for national energy markets.

The different parties now have the obligation to find the right solutions, so that the instruments work as well as possible and contribute to the fight against the social, economic and environmental threat of climate change which the world continues to face. We owe it to the next generations.

---

[75] Commission, 'Energy and Environmental State aid Guidelines—Frequently asked questions', MEMO/14/276.

20

Homogeneity or Renationalisation in the European Judicial Area?

Comments on a Recent Judgment of the Norwegian Supreme Court

CHRISTIAN KOHLER

I. THE EFTA COURT AND THE LUGANO CONVENTION

THE LUGANO CONVENTION on Jurisdiction and Judgments is a key element of the European judicial area. It sets out uniform rules on the international jurisdiction of courts and allows for easy recognition and enforcement of judgments in civil and commercial matters. First concluded in 1988[1] between the Member States of the EEC and the EFTA States as a 'parallel convention' to the 1968 Brussels Convention on the same subject, it was replaced in 2007 by a new Convention concluded by the EU, Denmark and three of the four EFTA States, namely Iceland, Norway and Switzerland. Liechtenstein, an EFTA-EEA State like Iceland and Norway, is still not a party to the Convention.[2]

Although the EFTA Court has, so far, no jurisdiction to interpret the Lugano Convention as regards the application by the courts of the EFTA States,[3] it is well aware of the importance of this instrument for the proper functioning of

---

[1] Convention on jurisdiction and enforcement of judgments in civil and commercial matters, of 16.09.1988, OJ L 319/1988.

[2] See G Baur, 'Liechtenstein: eine Lücke von 160 km² im Europäischen Rechtsraum' in Liechtenstein Institut (ed), *Beiträge zum liechtensteinischen Recht aus nationaler und internationaler Perspektive. Festschrift zum 70. Geburtstag von Herbert Wille* (Vaduz, Verlag der Liechtensteinischen Akademischen Gesellschaft, 2014) p 25.

[3] On possible perspectives see C Kohler, 'The Interpretation of the Lugano Convention of 2007 and the Brussels Instruments on Jurisdiction and Judgments in Civil and Commercial Matters' in EFTA Court (ed), *Judicial Protection in the European Economic Area* (Stuttgart, German Law Publishers, 2012) 218, 221f; Kohler, 'Balancing the Judicial Dialogue in Europe: Some Remarks on the Interpretation of the 2007 Lugano Convention on Jurisdiction and Judgments' in J Forner Delaygua, C González Beilfuss and R Viñas Farré (eds), *Entre Bruselas e La Haya. Estudios sobre la unificación internacional e regional del Derecho internacional privado. Liber amicorum Alegría Borrás* (Madrid, Marcial Pons, 2013) 565.

the internal market of the EEA. This became apparent in several cases before the Court when Liechtenstein tried to justify restrictions on market freedoms by the necessity to ensure *domestic* enforcement of civil judgments as these would not be recognised in other EEA States. The argument failed. Considering a residence requirement for a member of the board of a domiciliary company provided for by Liechtenstein law, the Court said in 2002:

> As regards the execution of civil law judgments, the Court acknowledges that certain complications may arise since Liechtenstein is not party to the Lugano Convention ... The Court observes that, if such complications were of vital concern in relation to the public policy objective pursued, accession to this instrument would constitute one remedy. Moreover, the Court recognizes that litigation or execution in foreign jurisdictions often involves costs and complications that will not arise in the domestic jurisdiction. However, the encouragement of cross-border activity is a fundamental objective of the EEA Agreement; and, whenever such activity gives rise to litigation, the enforcement of judgments must often be sought within the jurisdiction of another EEA State ...
>
> For these reasons, the Court finds that considerations relating to the administration of justice in civil matters cannot be held to justify the imposition of a residence requirement in derogation of Article 31 EEA.[4]

The Court thus acknowledged the close link between market freedoms and the legal protection of market operators across borders. That connection is also emphasised in the Preamble to the 2007 Convention where the Contracting Parties declare to be

> aware of the links between them, which have been sanctioned in the economic field by the free trade agreements concluded between the European Community and certain States members of the European Free Trade Association.[5]

The Lugano Convention is not just another instrument for judicial cooperation in civil matters, it is an essential component of the judicial infrastructure of the EEA and serves directly the objectives of the Agreement. The application and interpretation of the Convention is thus a matter of direct concern not only to the States bound by it but also to the EEA institutions. As a matter of fact, any dysfunction in the operation of the Convention may affect the proper functioning of the EEA itself. In that perspective, the recent judgment of Norway's Høyesterett in *Trico Subsea AS v Raffles Shipping Projects Pte Ltd*[6] deserves special attention as neither the outcome of the case nor the reasoning given by the majority of three judges take sufficient account of the EEA link shown above. Moreover, the judgment

---

[4] Case E-2/01 *Dr Franz Martin Pucher* [2002] EFTA Ct Rep 44, para 39. See also Case E-10/04 *Paolo Piazza v Paul Schurte AG* [2005] EFTA Ct Rep 76, para 46 and Case E-13/11 *Granville Establishment v Volker Anhalt and others* [2012] EFTA Ct Rep 400, para 47. *Cf* Baur, above n 2, 45.

[5] An analogous paragraph appeared already in the Preamble of the 1988 Convention. Shortly after, Henrik Bull stressed the link between the Lugano Convention and the forthcoming EEA Agreement in his preface to the Norwegian edition of L Pålsson, *Luganokonvensjonen* (Tano, Norstedts Juridik, 1992).

[6] Judgment of 20.12.2012, HR-2012-2393-A, Norsk Retstidende (Rt) 2012, 1951.

does not seem in line with relevant case law and accepted principles of interpretation of the Lugano Convention. As the case raises seminal issues, a brief recall
of these governing principles seems appropriate before turning to the case itself.

II. THE INTERPRETATION OF THE LUGANO CONVENTION
AND THE QUEST FOR HOMOGENEITY IN
THE EUROPEAN JUDICIAL AREA

A. Protocol 2 on the Interpretation of the Convention

As the 1988 Lugano Convention largely mirrored the 1968 Brussels Convention,
it seemed manifest that its rules should be interpreted in the same way as similar
rules of the mother convention. In 1971, the Court of Justice of the European
Communities (ECJ) had been given jurisdiction to interpret the Brussels
Convention. Although it would have been logical to confer to the ECJ a similar
competence for the Lugano Convention, this appeared not to be feasible for
political and institutional reasons.[7] Instead, a complex mechanism was set up in
Protocol 2 of the Lugano Convention. Its purpose was to come, first, to a uniform
interpretation of its rules by the courts of the Contracting States and, second, to
an interpretation that was 'parallel' to the one given to the rules of the Brussels
Convention. With regard to uniformity, Article 1 of Protocol 2 obliged the courts
of any Contracting State to 'pay due account to the principles laid down by any
relevant decision delivered by courts of the other Contracting States concerning
provisions of this Convention'. In order to maintain the parallelism between the
two conventions, two declarations were annexed to the Protocol, spelling out,
first, that the courts of the EFTA States when interpreting the Lugano Convention
should pay due account to the case law of the ECJ and the national courts on the
Brussels Convention and, second, that the ECJ when interpreting the Brussels
Convention should pay due account to the rulings contained in the case law on
the Lugano Convention. The overall objective was to come to a *homogeneous*
interpretation of both Conventions within the judicial area made up by the territories of the Contracting States.

In 2007, the 1988 instrument was replaced by a new convention.[8] Already
in 2000, after the Amsterdam Treaty had entered into force, the Brussels
Convention had been converted into a community act, namely Regulation
No 44/2001 (the 'Brussels I Regulation'), which incorporated the amendments elaborated in 1998 for a joint revision of the Brussels *and* the Lugano
Conventions. However, it was only in 2007 that the parallelism with the Brussels
rules was restored. As the ECJ had ruled in 2006 that exclusive competence to

---

[7] See the Report on the 1988 Convention by P Jenard and G Möller, OJ C 189/1990, para 110.
[8] OJ L 147/2009.

conclude the new convention was vested in the European Community,[9] the Member States could not become Contracting Parties individually and the new convention had to be concluded by the Community alone. Seen from the perspective of the European Union, the 2007 convention forms part of EU law and the ECJ has jurisdiction to interpret its provisions 'as regards the application by the courts of the EU Member States'.[10] From the EFTA perspective, it remains a multilateral convention, although the EEA States have to take into account the particular elements mentioned above.

As concerns the interpretation of the 2007 convention, the homogeneity objective is confirmed and refined in a twofold way. First, this objective is now integrated in the scope of Article 1 of the revised Protocol 2 which extends the obligation to pay due account to the case law concerning the Brussels instruments.[11] Article 1(1) reads:

> Any court applying and interpreting this Convention shall pay due account to the principles laid down by any relevant decision concerning the provision(s) concerned or any similar provision(s) of the 1988 Lugano Convention and the instruments referred to in Article 64(1) of the Convention rendered by the courts of the States bound by this Convention and by the Court of Justice of the European Communities.

Second, the ECJ's role and function in this process is no longer addressed in mere declarations, separate from the instrument, but in the provisions of the revised Protocol 2 itself. As appears from Article 1, the obligation to pay account to the ECJ's rulings now applies directly also to the courts of the EFTA States. Conversely, the case law of these courts has to be taken into account also by the ECJ, as the term 'any court' in Article 1 is to be interpreted to cover the ECJ.[12]

It should be noted that rulings of the ECJ given *before* the date of signature of the 2007 Convention are of an enhanced effect. It appears from the Preamble of Protocol 2 that the provisions of the Convention are to be applied *in the light of these rulings*.[13] This goes further than the obligation to pay due account. It means that the Contracting Parties agree that the ECJ's rulings on provisions of the Brussels instruments are to be taken as an *authentic interpretation* of similar provisions in the 2007 Convention.

---

[9] See Opinion 1/03 of 7 February 2006.

[10] Para 3 of the Preamble to Protocol 2.

[11] Namely the Brussels I Regulation and other instruments specified in Art 64(1) of the 2007 Convention.

[12] See C Kohler, 'Dialog der Gerichte im europäischen Justizraum' in M Monti et al (eds), *Economic Law and Justice in Times of Globalisation. Festschrift for Carl Baudenbacher* (Baden-Baden/Wien/Bern, Nomos, Verlag Österreich, Stämpfli, 2007) 141, 152.

[13] See the paras 5 and 6 of the Preamble. The same principle applied to the 1988 Convention, see para 3 of the Preamble to Protocol 2 of that Convention, and the Jenard/Möller Report (above, n 7) para 112.

B. Essentials of Homogeneity in the Brussels-Lugano Area

The concept of homogeneity, well known in EEA law,[14] thus precedes the establishment of the common economic area through the EEA Agreement.[15] In the Brussels-Lugano context its main objective is to arrive at a situation where key issues of jurisdiction and enforcement of judgments are dealt with by national courts on the basis of the same principles. Homogeneity is not an end in itself. It serves legal certainty. Its objective is to enhance *predictability* of solutions for market operators and, more generally, individuals engaged in cross-border situations. They should be able to foresee which courts would exercise jurisdiction and under which conditions a judgment would be enforced in other European States. Homogeneity is relevant for both method and substance. Whether a term or a concept used in a rule of the Convention has to be given a 'national' or an 'autonomous' meaning is the point to be decided in the first place. If national law is to govern the interpretation of the term, the subsequent question to be decided is *which* national law is to be applied—the *lex fori* of the court seized or the law applicable according to the conflict rules of the forum. In both alternatives, the interpretation may lead to different solutions depending on the forum before which the case has been brought. If, on the contrary, the concept is to be given an autonomous interpretation, the meaning of the term or the content of the concept will, ideally, be the same in all States of the common area. It is crucial that the preliminary question of the method of interpretation be decided in the same way in all States concerned. This is particularly true as regards the concepts or terms describing the *scope* of the Convention as this will directly impact on the extent to which these States have renounced to apply their national law to the issue concerned. Only an autonomous understanding of the scope of the Convention will ensure that the participating States enjoy the same rights and are subject to the same obligations arising from the Convention. Obviously, it is hardly possible to arrive at an interpretation that is autonomous *and* uniform through a dialogue of national courts alone. As far as the Brussels Convention was concerned, the decision to entrust the ECJ with the interpretation of the Convention was a pragmatic step to solve this difficulty. The same is true for the extension of the ECJ's role to the Lugano Convention through the provisions in Protocol 2 of the Convention first in 1988 and now in the elaborated form of 2007. As access to the ECJ is not open to the EFTA States whereas these States are supposed to follow the ECJ's case law, a further step might be to confer jurisdiction on the EFTA Court to interpret the Convention upon request of the EFTA States. This would enable the two

---

[14] See Art 6 and Arts 105ff of the EEA Agreement; see also Art 3 of the Agreement between the EFTA States on the establishment of a Surveillance Authority and a Court of Justice. *Cf* C Baudenbacher, 'Between Homogeneity and Independence: The Legal Position of the EFTA Court in the European Economic Area' (1997) 3 *Columbia Journal of European Law* 169.

[15] *Cf* Baur (above n 2) 30f, who recalls the Luxembourg Declaration of 9 April 1984 on the rapprochement between the EEC and the EFTA States.

European courts to extend the dialogue experienced in the field of EEA-EU law to the Lugano-Brussels instruments.[16]

III. THE LUGANO CONVENTION IN NORWAY

It has to be acknowledged that throughout the lifetime of the 1988 Lugano Convention, that is mainly until the end of 2009, the objectives of Protocol 2 have been attained. Homogeneity in the European judicial area has been preserved essentially because the national courts of the EU *and* the EFTA States when interpreting the Lugano Convention followed the ECJ's case law on the parallel rules of the Brussels Convention and the Brussels Regulation.[17] Within EFTA, this is true in particular for Switzerland and Norway. Both the Swiss Federal Court and the Norwegian Supreme Court have in a number of leading cases on the interpretation of the Lugano Convention based their decision on the principles laid down in rulings of the ECJ on the similar rules of the Brussels instruments. The Swiss Bundesgericht has repeatedly stated that it was prepared to follow the ECJ rulings for the purposes of the Lugano Convention unless the interpretation of the Brussels rules by the ECJ appeared to be determined by EU law or guided by European integration priorities.[18] Interestingly, there has been so far no case in which this reservation has been applied. Norway's Høyesterett has, in the past, never discussed the question of principle to what extent it should follow, or take 'due account' of, the ECJ's decisions for the purposes of the interpretation of the Lugano Convention.[19] Instead, it has adopted a somewhat pragmatic approach that amounted to the same result as in Switzerland. As shown by numerous rulings, where the Lugano issue before it had already been resolved by the ECJ for the purposes of the Brussels rules, the Høyesterett would base its ruling on the same principles either implicitly or by referring expressly to the relevant ECJ decisions.[20]

---

[16] Above n 3.

[17] See Kohler (above n 12) 145f with further references. More than 600 decisions of the national courts of the contracting States interpreting the Lugano and/or the Brussels conventions are accessible in a database published on the ECJ's website, see *Information pursuant to Protocol 2 annexed to the Lugano Convention*, at http://curia.europa.eu/common/recdoc/convention/en/index.htm.

[18] BGE 124 III 396; see also, for later rulings to the same effect, A Bucher in *Commentaire Romand. Loi sur le droit international privé. Convention de Lugano* (Bâle, Helbig Lichtenhahn, 2011), Art 1-79 CL, para 28.

[19] This contrasts with the Court's approach in the complex situation that exists in relation to the interpretation of EEA law where the courts of the EFTA States, besides being obliged to take due account of the case law of the ECJ, have to abide by the obligations arising from the case law of the EFTA Court; see H Bull, 'European Law and Norwegian Courts' in P-C Müller-Graff and E Selvig (eds), *The Approach to European Law in Germany and Norway* (Berlin, Berliner Wissenschafts-Verlag, 2004) 95; H Haukeland Fredriksen, 'The Two EEA Courts—a Norwegian Perspective' in EFTA Court (ed), *Judicial Protection in the European Economic Area* (above n 3), 187, 189f. See, for the Supreme Court's position to the case law of the two European Courts, the decision Rt 2000, 1811 and, recently, HR-2013–0496-A (Case No 2012/1447) (judgment of 5 March 2013).

[20] See, eg, Høyesterett's decisions included in the ECJ's website on the 1988 Lugano Convention (above, n 17), relating, inter alia, to Art 1(2)(1) (25.04.2000, Rt 2000, 654), Art 5(1) (14.06.2004, Rt

Henrik Bull's statement, related to EEA law, that '[t]he Supreme Court has demonstrated a clear willingness to draw on case law of the ECJ'[21] applies in principle also to the interpretation of the Lugano Convention. It is against this background that the decision in the above-mentioned *Trico Subsea* case has to be assessed.

IV. *TRICO SUBSEA AS v RAFFLES SHIPPING PROJECTS PTE LTD*

A. The Case

Does Article 2 of the Lugano Convention apply in circumstances where a plaintiff domiciled in a non-Convention State sues the defendant in the Norwegian courts in a case that has no connection with Norway except for the defendant's domicile? It was on this issue that the Supreme Court was split in what seemed a rather straightforward case.

Trico Subsea AS, a company with headquarters in Haugesund, Norway, had entered into a contract with Raffles Shipping Projects Pte Ltd, a shipbroking company with headquarters in Singapore. The contract was made there. Two ships were sold under the contract and Raffles claimed the payment of broker fees. In 2011 it brought an action against Trico in Norway. Except for the defendant's domicile the case had no connection with Norway.[22] Both the Haugeland district court and the Court of Appeal, Gulating *lagmansretten*, accepted that the Norwegian courts had jurisdiction over the case. The issue eventually brought before the Supreme Court was whether jurisdiction was governed by Article 2 of the 2007 Lugano Convention or by § 4-3 of *tvisteloven*, the Norwegian Act on Civil Procedure. According to this latter provision, disputes with international elements may only be brought before Norwegian courts if the case has a sufficient connection with Norway.

B. The Supreme Court's Judgment

The judgment of the Høyesterett[23] was given by a divided court. Two judges held in favour of the applicability of the Lugano Convention. The judge speaking for the minority referred to Protocol 2 of the Convention and to previous decisions

---

2004, 981; 09.03.2005, Rt 2005, 221; 29.08.2006, Rt 2006, 1008), Art 5(3) (13.10.2004, Rt 2004, 1539), Art 16(1) (07.09.2006, Rt 2006, 1089; 23.11.2007, Rt 2007, 1646); *adde*, on Art 5(3), HR 07.05.2009, Rt 2009, 572.

[21] H Bull, 'European Law and Norwegian Courts' (above n 18) 108.

[22] Trico was part of a group of companies belonging to Trico Marine Services, Inc., registered in Delaware, USA.

[23] Above n 6. For a critical assessment of the judgment and a comprehensive history of the case see G Cordero-Moss, *Internasjonal privatrett på formuerettens område* (Oslo, Universitetsforlaget, 2012) 33f; see also A Fötschl, 'Keine Anwendung des Lugano-Übereinkommens für Kläger aus

of the Supreme Court[24] according to which the case law of the ECJ shall be an 'important source of law' for the interpretation of the Convention by Norwegian Courts. It followed from the ECJ's judgment in *Group Josi*[25] that plaintiffs from non-Convention States could benefit from the rules of the Convention. Once the domicile of the defendant was in a Convention State, no additional connection with a Convention State was required. That had been decided by the ECJ in *Owusu*[26] and was also the position of the Norwegian legislator who had referred to the ECJ's ruling when discussing the point in the context of the implementation of the 2007 Convention in Norway.[27] Legal literature in Norway and abroad was equally in favour of this position.[28]

The majority of three judges held that jurisdiction was governed by Norwegian law and that the Court of Appeal's order, which was based on the assumption that the Convention applied, had to be set aside. The opinion for the majority relied mainly on two arguments. First, the Lugano Convention did not give a plaintiff from a non-Convention State a right to bring an action in Norway. An international convention did not give rights or duties to other than those States who are parties to the convention. There were no clues that the Lugano Convention was to make a general exception to this 'obvious principle'. As emphasised in its preamble, the Lugano Convention was for the benefit of citizens residing in the territory of the Contracting parties. Giving rights to litigants from third States would result in an imbalance as there were no corresponding obligations of those States for the benefit of litigants from Convention States. It was 'natural' to see the relevant rulings of the ECJ in this light.

The second argument of the majority centred on the 'scope of application' (*anvendelsesområdet*) of the Convention. On the basis of the understanding of the Convention in Norwegian law[29] the judge speaking for the majority concluded that a third State plaintiff had no right to bring an action in Norway *pursuant to the Convention*. The ECJ's case law did not lead to a different conclusion, nor did foreign legal writing. After looking at the judgments in *Group Josi* and *Owusu* the opinion states that neither of those cases governed the issue before the Court. In *Group Josi* there were connections with two EU Member States and in *Owusu* the plaintiff was domiciled in the same Member State as the defendant. The ECJ had

---

Drittstaaten—Zur Entscheidung des norwegischen Høyesterett in *Raffles Shipping v Trico Subsea AS*', *IPRax—Praxis des internationalen Privat- und Verfahrensrechts* 2014, 187.

[24] HR 14.06.2004, Rt 2004, 981.

[25] Case C-412/98 *Group Josi Reinsurance Company SA v Universal General Insurance Company* [2000] ECR I-5925.

[26] Case C-281/02 *Andrew Owusu v NB Jackson and Others* [2005] ECR I-1383.

[27] See para 53 of the judgment.

[28] See paras 49 and 61f of the judgment. See also the engaged debate on the issue in the leading Norwegian law journal between Jens Edvin A Skoghøy and Torstein Frantzen (2012) *Lov og Rett* 193; 379; 438; 573.

[29] The opinion cites statements from the legislative procedure and legal writing on the question whether there has to be a sufficient connection of the case to a Convention State, see paras 74f.

not yet decided whether the sole domicile of the defendant provided a sufficient connection to make the Convention applicable. The question before the Supreme Court was thus an open one according to the international legal sources and there was no reason why the Norwegian courts should go ahead. This was all the more true as Norwegian law provided satisfactory solutions that did not conflict with the Convention. At the new trial the Court of Appeal would have to consider that *pursuant to Norwegian law* it needed a lot to show that a Norwegian company with its domicile in Norway could not be sued in the courts of that State.

C. Subsequent Proceedings[30]

Following the Supreme Court's judgment the Gulating Court of Appeal allowed the case to proceed in the Norwegian courts.[31] The requirement of a sufficient connection in § 4-3, first paragraph, of *tvisteloven* had to be understood in a way that if the defendant was sued in his ordinary venue in Norway, the Norwegian courts had *ipso facto* jurisdiction to hear the case, unless the exceptional nature of the case nevertheless exempted it from Norwegian jurisdiction. No circumstances to that effect were shown in the case before the court. The Court of Appeal's decision was appealed to the Supreme Court, but the appeal was rejected by the Supreme Court's Appeal Selection Committee.[32]

V. THE SUPREME COURT ON THE WRONG TRACK

A. The Disregard for the Obligations Flowing from Protocol 2 of the Convention

The Supreme Court's judgment of 20.12.2012 does not respect the obligations flowing from Protocol 2 and is misconceived about the scope of Article 2 of the Convention. Contrary to the majority's opinion, the question whether Article 2 of the Convention applies in circumstances where a plaintiff domiciled in a non-Convention State sues the defendant in the courts of Convention State in a case that has no connection with that State except for the defendant's domicile is not 'open by international sources of law'. It has been settled by the ECJ under the Brussels Convention. The ECJ held in *Group Josi* that the rules on jurisdiction of the Brussels Convention are in principle applicable 'where the defendant has its domicile or seat in a Contracting State, even if the plaintiff is domiciled in a non-member country'.[33] In *Owusu*, the Court held that 'Article 2 of the Brussels

---

[30] I am grateful to Professor Halvard Fredriksen for kindly informing me on this point.
[31] Judgment of 11.04.2013, LG-2013-3127–RG-2013-502.
[32] HR 14.08.2013, Rt 2013, 1089.
[33] Above n 24.

Convention applies to circumstances … involving relationships of a single Contracting State and those of a non-Contracting State rather than relationships between the courts of a number of Contracting States'.[34] Both judgments have been given *before* the date of signature of the 2007 Lugano Convention. They are therefore to be considered as an authoritative interpretation of the scope and of Article 2 of the Convention. This follows, as has been shown, from Protocol 2 of the Convention.[35] The energy employed in the majority's opinion to distinguish these cases is of no avail. The principles formulated in the ECJ's judgments are independent of the circumstances highlighted in the opinion.[36] Neither is the ruling in *Group Josi* determined by the element that there were connections with two EU Member States nor is the *Owusu* ruling dependent on the fact that the plaintiff had his domicile in the same Member State as the defendant. The argument that the Lugano Convention does not confer rights or duties on third States is equally beside the point.[37] The issue in *Trico* was not whether Singapore was entitled to claim that *Raffles* be given access to the Norwegian courts.[38] The question was whether the domicile of the plaintiff mattered under Article 2 of the Convention, and that question had been answered in the negative by the ECJ already in *Group Josi*.

Moreover, there is case law also from national courts of the Convention States which the majority's opinion does not pay account to. In 2008, the Swiss Federal Court was faced with a case brought in the courts of the domicile of the defendant in Switzerland with no other international connection than the plaintiff's domicile in Pakistan. Relying on *Owusu* and its own previous case law, the Court held that Article 2 of the Lugano Convention applied in these circumstances.[39] According to Protocol 2, the principle laid down in this decision should also have been considered as precedent, but no mention is made of it in the Høyesterett's ruling.[40]

[34] Above n 25.

[35] This instrument is not soft law but creates obligations under international law as it is an integral part of the Convention itself, see Art 75. Protocol 2 is thus *lex specialis* to Art 31(1) of the Vienna Convention on the Law of Treaties.

[36] See also Cordero-Moss (above n 23) 37.

[37] In *Owusu*, where an analogous argument had been advanced, the ECJ has rightly pointed out that the Convention's rules giving jurisdiction to the courts of the Contracting State where the defendant has his domicile in proceedings connected 'because of their subject matter or the claimant's domicile, with a non-Contracting State, [do not] impose an obligation of that State' (para 31).

[38] In the example given below at p 245, Norway would be entitled to claim that German courts refrain from exercising jurisdiction under the Zivilprozessordnung.

[39] Bundesgericht 18.12.2008, BGE 135 III 185, at 189: 'Im Lichte dieser Rechtsprechung ist Art 2 LugÜ auf den vorliegenden Sachverhalt anwendbar, denn die Beklagte hat ihren Sitz in der Schweiz, und aus dem klägerischen Wohnsitz in Pakistan ergibt sich ein Auslandsbezug. Eine solche Konstellation wird vom räumlich-persönlichen Anwendungsbereich des harmonisiert ausgelegten Art 2 LugÜ erfasst.'

[40] The English case of *Lucasfilm Ltd v Ainsworth* [2009] EWCA 1328, cited in argument, gives no support for the majority's position; see T Frantzen, 'Tvisteloven og Luganokonvensjonen—duplikk til Skoghøy' (2012) *Lov og Rett* 573, 574.

B. Misconceptions about Article 2 of the Convention

The ECJ's rulings in *Group Josi* and *Owusu* highlight the pivotal role of the defendant's domicile within the scheme of the Convention. It not only confers jurisdiction on the courts of that State. It blocks the application of national rules of jurisdiction in the other Contracting States: once a person is domiciled in a Contracting State, that person may be sued in another Convention State *only* by virtue of the Convention rules.[41] If Raffles had brought an action in Germany pretending that Trico had assets in Frankfurt am Main, the jurisdiction of the German courts could not have been based on § 23 of the Zivilprozessordnung because of *Trico*'s Norwegian domicile; it would have been impossible for Raffles to argue that § 23 could nevertheless be applied because Trico's domicile was insufficient to trigger the application of the Lugano Convention. This far-reaching effect of the defendant's domicile explains why the exercise of the jurisdiction conferred by Article 2 is mandatory and cannot be left to the discretion of the courts of the State of the domicile.[42]

The result of the Supreme Court's judgment in *Trico* amounts to a unilateral modification of the scope of the Convention. From now on, Norwegian courts will have to determine the effect of a Norwegian domicile in cases like *Trico* according to Norwegian law. It is true that in *Trico* § 4-3 of *tvisteloven* led to the same result as Article 2 of the Convention. But the interpretation of this provision by the Norwegian courts may change,[43] and the provision itself may be modified by the national legislature. The *Trico* judgment leads to an uncertainty that is incompatible with the scheme and the logic of the Convention as interpreted by the ECJ.

VI. RENATIONALISATION v HOMOGENEITY?

A. The National Bias in the Majority's Opinion

The opinion for the majority shows a surprising contrast to earlier case law of the Court on the Lugano Convention. Unlike the minority, the judge speaking for the majority does not refer to the rules and principles governing the interpretation of the Convention. No mention of Protocol 2 is made. The Convention is looked at as an 'international agreement' that has to be interpreted like any treaty under

---

[41] See Art 3(1) of the Convention. This effect of the defendant's domicile has been highlighted by the ECJ in its recent judgment in Case C-9/12 *Corman-Collins*, para 22 (19.12.2013).

[42] See C Kohler, 'Staatsvertragliche Bindungen bei der Ausübung internationaler Zuständigkeit und richterliches Ermessen' in OJ Ballon and JJ Hagen (eds), *Verfahrensgarantien im nationalen und internationalen Prozessrecht. Festschrift Franz Matscher zum 65. Geburtstag* (Wien, Manz, 1993) 251.

[43] Eg by giving the courts enlarged discretionary powers according to the common law doctrine of *forum (non) conveniens;* elements of this doctrine may already be found in § 4-3, see Fötschl (above n 23) 188.

international law. In order to determine the Convention's scope the opinion finds it 'natural' to highlight in the first place how the question is perceived in Norwegian law. The ECJ's case law is then discussed in order to see whether it is in line with the Norwegian understanding of the Convention. This approach is deemed to be self-evident as no reasons are given.[44] The opinion appears to be based on a preconception that the extent to which the Norwegian courts are bound is, primarily, a matter of Norwegian law. After more than 20 years of application of the Lugano Convention and Protocol 2 in the Convention States including Norway this approach is difficult to understand.

B. Access to Justice on the Basis of Reciprocity?

An equally surprising conception underlies the opinion's discussion of whether the Convention allows persons established in non-Convention States to bring actions under the Convention. The majority is of course right in saying that an international convention confers rights and obligations only to the States that are parties to it. However, it does not follow from this principle that individuals and companies that are nationals or residents of non-Contracting States may not be affected by the international convention, be it in a positive or a negative way. In today's world of ever-growing trans-frontier commerce and communication the effects of international conventions on private law and litigation may, directly or indirectly, reach business and people throughout the world. As far as the Lugano Convention is concerned, there is simply no basis for a 'presumption' that individuals and companies from third States are not given the same rights as persons established in the Contracting States unless there is *reciprocity* in the relationship with the respective non-Contracting State.[45] As far as international civil litigation in the twenty-first century is concerned, reciprocity is an outdated concept. In cases sufficiently connected with the forum State, the right to sue is not a privilege granted to foreign nationals that requires an advantage in return. Access to justice on a non-discriminatory basis is an accepted standard recognised by international law.[46] This is particularly true if the State where the defendant has his domicile and his assets would not recognise judgments from alternative forums. In fact, to restrict access to the courts in such circumstances may amount to a denial of justice.[47]

---

[44] Instead, rhetorical formulas ('of course', 'natural', 'obvious') are used, see in particular paras 69, 71, 73 and 86.

[45] See para 70 of the judgment.

[46] See, eg, Arts 6 and 14 of the European Convention of Human Rights and Art 14 of the International Covenant on Civil and Political Rights.

[47] The Gulating Court of Appeal (above n 30) was right in saying that when assessing whether the Norwegian courts should exercise jurisdiction according to § 4-3 of *tvisteloven* it had to be considered where a successful plaintiff could enforce his judgment.

C. The EEA Dimension

The Supreme Court's judgment in *Trico* runs squarely counter to the objectives of Protocol 2 of the Convention. It prefers a national perspective to a uniform and homogeneous interpretation. Moreover, it construes unwritten conditions for the application of the Convention. In the light of what has been said at the outset of this chapter this is a matter of concern not only to the Convention States but also to the EEA as the sound operation of the Lugano Convention is a prerequisite of the proper functioning of the common economic area. The renationalisation of litigation against Norwegian defendants in cases like *Trico* is detrimental to the functioning of the EEA as such. Market operators need predictability as to the forum in potential disputes; they prefer legal certainty to the discretionary application of unwritten rules. Even if the final outcome of the *Trico* case may at first sight seem satisfactory, the effects of the Supreme Court's judgment in practice may be far-reaching and are not limited to third State-connected commercial operations. The underlying approach and the reasoning of the judgment should be reconsidered in an appropriate context. In that respect, the arguments put forward in the minority's opinion are pointing in the right direction.

Part III

General Principles and Fundamental Rights in EEA Law

21

General Principles

CARL LEBECK

I. INTRODUCTION

THE EEA IS a legal order that consists of Norway, Iceland and Liechtenstein on one hand and the Member States of the EU on the other. The EEA is constituted as an international legal order with an independent institutional structure (the EEA Joint Committee, the EFTA Surveillance Authority and the EFTA Court) whose aim is to create a market common to the EFTA States participating in the EEA and the EU. The EFTA Surveillance Authority is charged with overseeing compliance with EEA law in the EEA States. The EEA Member States which are not members of the EU still ratify new secondary legislation through the EEA Joint Committee and their national parliaments before it becomes binding on them. However, the refusal by the EEA States to accept new secondary legislation from the EU within the framework of the EEA Agreement may lead to partial suspension of the EEA Agreement. The EFTA Court is the final arbiter of the meaning of the EEA Agreement with regard to the EEA States. EEA law hence has strong supranational traits in relation to application and interpretation of EEA law but intergovernmental traits concerning legislation. The topic of this chapter is the role of general principles in EEA law in general and in the case law of the EFTA Court in particular. Owing to limited space, I do not attempt to give an exhaustive account of general principles in EEA law but focus on the constitutional and coordinating functions of general principles in the case law of the EFTA Court.

The development of international integration concerning economic and political matters has led to the proliferation of legal orders constituted under public international law, of which EEA is one. Whereas these legal orders create various international regimes for different kinds of problem (international peace and security, environmental protection, human rights, international criminal law, conflicts of law, international trade in goods and services, etc), they lack a defined hierarchy between them. However, they have in common that they make (more or less far-reaching) claims for precedence over other international legal orders as well as in relation to national law. The various supranational legal orders are independent from other legal orders with regard to creation and application of norms, whereas they are dependent on the cooperation of national as well as other supranational legal orders for their substantive effectiveness. The absence of hierarchical relations between international legal orders hence replicates the relations between national legal orders in international law.[1] Since these legal orders have in common that they have overlapping jurisdiction with regard to individuals and territories concerned but different functional areas (such as trade, environment, etc), they also presuppose some kind of coordination to avoid conflicts. Despite tendencies of 'constitutionalisation' of inter- and supranational legal orders, it seems as if international law as a whole and hence the relations *between* supranational legal orders have stubbornly resisted 'constitutionalisation'. The proliferation of inter- and supranational legal orders instead have given rise to different methods to resolve conflicts of norms between legal orders without assuming a hierarchy of norms. They include methods such as 'comity',[2] 'consistent interpretation'[3] and 'judicial dialogue'.[4] These methods have in common that they seek to substitute constitutional hierarchies of norms with methods of legal reasoning in the process of adjudication. They hence share the dilemma that, whereas they may reduce conflicts *between* legal orders and therefore increase their effectiveness, such forms of judicial reasoning may also *lessen* the internal coherence of legal orders by interpretative choices or by taking into account norms that otherwise would be irrelevant.

The relations between EEA and EU law to a great extent fit this picture of relations between international legal orders since they have overlapping functional jurisdictions and a far-reaching normative homogeneity,[5] although they are institutionally independent from each other. However EU law and the EEA Agreement share a commitment to economic integration and the EEA Agreement contains an explicit requirement of homogeneity and consistency between EEA law and EU law, which sets it apart from most other international legal orders. Along with the relations between the EU and EEA law, there are also similar, if not identical, needs for mutual adaptation between EEA law and the European Convention on Human Rights (ECHR) and (to some extent) national law, in order to avoid potentially intractable conflicts of norms. The application of general principles by the EFTA Court has been a way of filling gaps within the EEA Agreement in order to create a more coherent and effective legal order and to align it with EU law. What distinguishes the EEA Agreement from other international legal orders of this kind seems to be the attempt to resolve potential conflicts through a principle of homogeneity and the scope that the EFTA Court has given to that principle.

---

[1] That is not to say that there are no rules of conflicts in public international law. On the contrary, the relations between general international law and *jus cogens*, between the UN Charter and other international treaties, and the rules of conflicts under the 1969 Vienna Convention on the Law of Treaties, provide for rules of conflicts. These rules are in some contexts competing and also have gaps, eg when it comes to secondary norms and the binding character of judgments of international courts.

[2] A-M Slaughter, *A New World Order* (Oxford, Oxford University Press, 2005).

[3] A Nollkaemper, *National Courts and the International Rule of Law* (Oxford, Oxford University Press, 2011) 140ff.

[4] C L'Heureux-Dubé, 'The Importance of Dialogue: Globalization and the International Impact of the Rehnquist Court' (1998) *Tulsa Law Journal* 15.

[5] Art 6 EEA Agreement.

The principle of homogeneity is hence of comparative interest as it gives a constitutional foundation within EEA law for the gradual adaptation of EEA law to EU law. The principle of homogeneity within EEA law however relies on the political will to form a common market, which also provides the ultimate legitimacy for the approach adopted by the EFTA Court.

II. GENERAL PRINCIPLES AS A SOURCE OF LAW

General principles of law are well known in national law, in EU law, EEA law and in public international law as well as in jurisprudence. Dworkin has defined them as norms which 'have a dimension of weight', which means that legal principles unlike rules cannot have their scope of application defined beforehand but their practical effects may vary, depending on which situation they are applied in.[6] It is a definition which is sufficient for the purposes of this essay. General principles may not always be relevant but their application cannot be ruled out in advance. A state may not act, for instance, in a way which is disproportionately burdensome for individuals although it may impose burdens on individuals provided that it does so in the public interest, in compliance with constitutional requirements of legislation and in a way which is proportionate to the importance of the aim pursued. That is a general requirement of public action whose consequences are not clearly determined in advance. General principles with diverging and possibly conflicting content may be simultaneously relevant and in such cases a need to balance them will arise, unlike conflicts between rules where rules of conflict may resolve conflicts.

General principles have played a considerable role as a source of law in the development of the EU legal order.[7] The difficulty associated with the use of legal principles as a source of law which has been illustrated both in the case law of the EU Courts and the EFTA Court is that general principles are not just general, but frequently also vague and open-ended. Hence, the methods for discerning the content of the general principles are as central as the use of the principles themselves. The reconstruction (or creation) of general principles of law in the process of adjudication always implies that courts have a fairly broad discretion in their application. In the context of EU law, general principles have been regarded as unwritten norms that are common to the legal orders of the participating Member States and which hence are to guide the application of EU law too.[8] The EU Courts have, however, declared that, while expressing and interpreting the general principles of EU law, they draw on the legal traditions of the Member States as well as on their international obligations in a selective ('evaluative') manner to establish the content of general principles of law.[9] There is a certain difference between EU and EEA law with regard to general principles, since most

---

[6] R Dworkin, 'The Model of Rules' (1968) 35 *University of Chicago Law Review* 14, 23–24.
[7] T Tridimas, *General Principles of EU Law*, 2nd edn (Oxford, Oxford University Press, 2007) 17–19.
[8] ibid, 23–25.
[9] ibid, 20–23.

general principles in EU law have evolved on very limited basis in the treaties, whereas certain general principles—in particular the principle of homogeneity—have at least a more extensive basis in the treaties within EEA law.[10]

The principle of homogeneity has not just determined the substantive outcomes of cases before the EFTA Court (as discussed below), but it also provides a basis for regarding EU law as a source of law within EEA law. EU law is relied on by the EFTA Court both as a source of substantive rules, as a basis for interpretation of the EEA Agreement as well as a source of general principles of law. The principle of homogeneity has been applied broadly by the EFTA Court when it comes to sources of law, since the EFTA Court has included not just EU law, but also other treaties such as the ECHR.[11] It has also included unwritten principles of law,[12] and by that, to a certain degree, extended the reach of general principles recognised under EU law, into EEA law. Likewise, the EFTA Court has recently referred to the EU Charter of Fundamental Rights.[13] To a great extent, this approach is justified by the fact that the EEA Agreement is supposed to be homogeneous with EU law as well as dynamic. It seems, however, as if the EFTA Court in particular relies on the ECHR to reconstruct the meaning of legal principles.[14] To some extent that approach has been regarded as too open-ended.[15] However, the extension of sources of law through the principle of homogeneity reflects a choice whereby the EFTA Court also enables itself to weigh, for example, protection of human rights against effectiveness of the EEA institutions. The broader set of sources of law introduced by the use of general principles seems to enable the EFTA Court to maintain homogeneity between EEA law and the legal orders relevant to EU law in a way which also preserves its coherence.

III. GENERAL PRINCIPLES OF THE EFTA COURT

In substantive terms, the general principles of the EFTA Court involve several principles, such as loyalty,[16] non-discrimination[17] and the principle

---

[10] S Norberg et al, *The EEA Agreement* (Stockholm, Publica, 1994) 229.

[11] Case E-2/03 *Ásgeirsson* [2003] EFTA Ct Rep 185, para 23.

[12] Eg Case E-1/10 *Periscopus A/S v Oslo Børs ASA and Erik Must A/S* [2009–2010] EFTA Ct Rep 200, paras 47–48.

[13] Case E-15/10 *Posten Norge AS v EFTA Surveillance Authority* [2012] EFTA Ct Rep 246, para 85.

[14] Case E-2/03 *Ákæruvaldið (The Public Prosecutor) v Ásgeir Logi Ásgeirsson, Axel Pétur Ásgeirsson and Helgi Már Reynisson* [2003] EFTA Ct Rep 185, para 23; W Kälin, 'The EEA Agreement and the European Convention for the Protection of Human Rights' (1992) 3 *European Journal of International Law* 341–352.

[15] T Burri and B Pirker, 'Constitutionalisation by Association? The Doubtful Case of the European Economic Area' (2013) 33 *Yearbook of European Law* 207–229.

[16] Art 3 EEA Agreement.

[17] Art 4 EEA Agreement; F Sejersted et al, *EØS-rett*, 2nd edn (Oslo, Universitetsforlaget, 2004) 100–103; F Arnesen and A Borgli, *Institusjoner og Retskildelære i EU og EØS* (Oslo, Universitetsforlaget, 1993) 211–223.

of homogeneity (in relation to EU law),[18] which is also the source of the principles
of effectiveness, proportionality and of the general principles of the protection of
fundamental rights.[19] The principle of homogeneity is also different from most
legal principles within the context of EU law, since it has an express basis within
the text of the EEA Agreement[20] along with the requirements of loyal cooperation
of the EEA States.[21] The need for legal 'homogeneity' between the EU and the
EEA is an effect of the aim of creating a system of uniform rules which have to be
applied uniformly in the absence of a common institutional structure.[22] The principle of homogeneity hence means that the EFTA Court shall, as far as possible,
interpret the EEA Agreement as to create a uniform system of norms with EU
law. However, whereas the principle of homogeneity is expressed in the case law
of the EFTA Court, it is also the case that consistent interpretation in the ordinary
sense seems less common. That is because the EFTA Court, by developing general
principles relying on homogeneity as an overarching constitutional principle,
has been able to avoid the kind of *ad hoc* interpretation typically connected with
consistent interpretation.

In the context of the EFTA Court, the principle of homogeneity (which is
laid down in the EEA Agreement), has served as to make EU law into a central
source of law in EEA law, including also the case law of the EU Courts (including
both the Court of Justice and the General Court of the EU).[23] The principle of
homogeneity has also served as a basis for adopting other general principles such
as proportionality,[24] state liability[25] and substantive protection of fundamental
rights.[26] The homogeneity between EU law and the EEA Agreement means also
that the EFTA Court has included developments of European law in EEA law, in a
broader sense, by increasing reliance on the ECHR[27] as well as on the EU Charter
of Fundamental Rights.[28] It seems as if the strong connection between EEA law

---

[18] Art 6 EEA Agreement; Arnesen and Borgli, above, n 17, 202–203; K Almestad, 'The Essentials', this volume.
[19] DÞ Björgvinsson, 'Fundamental Rights in EEA Law', this volume.
[20] Art 6 EEA Agreement.
[21] Art 3 EEA Agreement.
[22] The proposed EU EFTA Court composed of judges from the Member States of EU and EFTA which was foreseen in the first draft of the EEA Agreement was rejected by the (then) ECJ in Opinion 1/91 as it was held that the autonomy of EU law excluded the option of a common court that would have been superior to the ECJ. See Opinion of the Court of 14 December 1991, delivered pursuant to the second subparagraph of Article 228(1) of the Treaty, Draft agreement between the Community, on the one hand, and the countries of the European Free Trade Association, on the other, relating to the creation of the European Economic Area, Opinion 1/91 [1991] ECR I-6079.
[23] Case E-1/94 *Ravintoloitsijain Liiton Kustannus Oy Restamark* [1994] EFTA Ct Rep 15, para 24.
[24] Case E-1/95 *Ulf Samuelsson v Svenska staten* [1995] EFTA Ct Rep 145, paras 32–33.
[25] Case E-9/97 *Erla María Sveinbjörnsdóttir v Iceland* [1998] EFTA Ct Rep 95.
[26] Case E-2/94 *Scottish Salmon Growers' Association Ltd v EFTA Surveillance Authority* [1995] EFTA Ct Rep 59, para 26.
[27] *Ásgeirsson*, above n. 14.
[28] *Posten Norge AS v EFTA Surveillance Authority*, above, n 13, para 86; H Haukeland Fredriksen, 'Betydningen av EUs Pakt om Grunnlegende Rettigheter for EØS-retten' (2013) *Jussens Venner* 371–399.

and EU law has led to a less discretionary approach of the EFTA Court while defining the content of general principles. The principle of homogeneity has also extended the effects of EEA law within the national legal orders. It has furthermore provided a basis for the application of fundamental rights, of the principle of proportionality as well as of the rules on state liability of EEA States.

A. Effectiveness

Effectiveness is a central principle within EEA law as in EU law.[29] It has also raised the issue of whether there is primacy and direct effect of EEA law. As in EU law, the principle of effectiveness has also been regarded as a basis for a principle of primacy under EEA law.[30] However, the issue of whether the claim to primacy in EEA law also entails direct effect has been problematic. There is no written rule in the EEA Agreement that provides for direct effect of legal rules under it but, certain effects associated with direct effect, in particular state liability, have been upheld by the EFTA Court.[31] Hence there is a reason for ascribing at least some degree of direct effect *ipso facto*, following the dynamic character of EEA law.[32] The relation between the overall concern for effectiveness of EEA law and the role of primacy and direct effect is similar to the development of EU law.[33]

It seems as if the overall principle of effectiveness has led to an approach similar to that of the EU, which indirectly creates legal effects that are akin to the effects created by primacy and direct effect, in particular through the extension of state liability. However, the EEA law is almost exclusively dependent on state liability as a remedy to ensure the effectiveness of EEA law, which is a major difference from the role of state liability in EU law. The link between the principle of effectiveness and state liability was expressed by the EFTA Court in the case of *Sveinbjörnsdóttir*, which concerned liability of an EEA State for failure to implement a directive on time.[34] In this case the EFTA Court, following the reasoning of the EU Court in *Francovich*[35] (however, without any explicit reference to the EU Court), held that the national government was liable for damages that had

---

[29] S Zleptnig and M Accetto, 'The Principle of Effectiveness: Rethinking Its Role in Community Law' (2005) 11 *European Public Law* 375–403.

[30] *Restamark*, above, n 23; Case 57/65 *Lütticke v Hauptzollamt Saarlouis* [1966] ECR-293; Case 27/67 *Fink-Frucht v Hauptzollamt München* [1968] ECR-327.

[31] *Restamark*, above n 23, paras 33 and 34.

[32] On the issue of whether the EEA has direct effect and primacy, see, inter alia, W van Gerven, 'The Genesis of EEA Law and the Principles of Primacy and Direct Effect' (1992)16 *Fordham International Law Journal* 955; M Johansson and S Norberg, 'EES-rätten—dynamisk ipso jure' (2011) 14 *Europarättslig Tidskrift* 627.

[33] *Cf* Case 26/62 *Van Gend en Loos* [1963] ECR-3 and Case 6/64 *Flaminio Costa v ENEL* [1964] ECR-1141.

[34] *Erla María Sveinbjörnsdóttir v Iceland*, above, n 25.

[35] Joined Cases C-6/90 and C-9/90 *Andrea Francovich and others v Italian Republic* [1991] ECR I-5357.

been caused by non-implementation. The overall principle of state liability was subsequently clarified by the EFTA Court in *Karlsson*,[36] where it was stated that in order for an EEA State to be liable for failure to apply EEA law, 'the rule of law infringed must be intended to confer rights on individuals; second, the breach must be sufficiently serious; and third, there must be a direct causal link between the breach of the obligation resting on the State and the damage sustained by the injured party'.[37]

B. Fundamental Rights

I will not go into the details of fundamental rights jurisprudence of the EFTA Court. However, as the EEA Agreement as such does not include any particular rules on protection of fundamental rights, the protection of fundamental rights in EEA law is based on general principles of law. At the creation of the EEA Agreement it was questioned whether the ECHR could be held to be a part of EEA law in the light of the absence of explicit provisions for fundamental rights within the EEA Agreement. The EFTA Court has, however, developed a model of fundamental rights protection similar to that of the EU Courts which relies on the distinction between substantive protection of fundamental rights and procedural rights.[38]

The role of fundamental rights in EEA law is similar to that of fundamental rights in EU law, namely as a shield of interests of citizens, both against the national governments and against supranational authorities. The first case where substantive issues of fundamental rights arose was *TV1000 Sverige*,[39] which concerned national restrictions on broadcasting of pornography, where the EFTA Court held that the EEA Agreement also included protection of freedom of expression. The EFTA Court has also found that equal treatment is a part of EEA law.[40] The EFTA Court has also included legal certainty as a principle in EEA law that includes requirements of predictability and a sufficient legal basis

---

[36] Case E-4/01 *Karl K Karlsson hf v The Icelandic State* [2002] EFTA Ct Rep 240; see also E-8/07 *Celina Nguyen v Staten v/Justis- og politidepartementet* [2008] EFTA Ct Rep 224; C Baudenbacher, 'If not EEA State Liability, Then What? Reflections Ten Years after the Sveinbjörnsdóttir Ruling' (2009) 10 *Chicago Journal of International Law* 333ff.

[37] *Karlsson*, above, n 36, para 32.

[38] Eg on statement of reasons, see Case E-2/94 *Scottish Salmon Growers Association Ltd v EFTA Surveillance Authority* [1995] EFTA Ct Rep 59 and subsequently, Joined Cases E-17/10 and E-6/11 *The Principality of Liechtenstein and VTM Fundmanagement v EFTA Surveillance Authority* [2012] EFTA Ct Rep 114.

[39] Case E-8/97 *TV1000 Sverige AB v Norwegian Government* [1998] EFTA Ct Rep 68.

[40] Case E-1/02 *EFTA Surveillance Authority v Kingdom of Norway* [2003] EFTA Ct Rep 17, paras 37–59.

for a decision and that EEA rules should be sufficiently clear as to provide for guidance to persons affected by legislation,[41] as well as protection of legitimate expectations.[42]

With regard to procedural rights, there has been a gradual expansion of protection of such rights, to include the general principles of access to justice and right to judicial protection[43] as well as good administration.[44]

In both EU and EEA law that has been achieved through the development of protection of fundamental rights through general principles. The protection of fundamental rights serves both to avoid conflicts between EU and EEA law, between the respective supranational legal orders and international obligations of the Member States (for example, under the ECHR) and between supranational law and national constitutional law.

C. Proportionality

Compliance with the principle of proportionality is another general requirement of EEA law, which has been imposed on the EFTA institutions as well as on the national governments by the EFTA Court.[45] In this regard, the EFTA Court has drawn extensively on the case law of the EU Court as well as the case law of the European Court of Human Rights. By invoking the principle of proportionality, the EFTA Court both created a general limitation on exercise of public powers within EEA law and aligned it with the general principles of EU law. The principle of proportionality also means that EEA law imposes a justificatory burden on exercise of public powers whereby public authorities have to justify their actions, not just in relation to specific individual rights, but also in relation to fundamental freedoms under the EEA Agreement and the overall purposes of EEA law.

---

[41] Case E-1/10 *Periscopus A/S v Oslo Børs ASA and Erik Must A/S* [2010] EFTA Ct Rep 198, paras 47–48.

[42] Joined Cases E-5/04, E-6/04 and E-7/04 *Fesil and Finnfjord* [2005] EFTA Ct Rep 117, paras 170–173; and Joined Cases E-17/10 and E-6/11 *Liechtenstein and Others v ESA* [2012] EFTA Ct Rep 114, para 134.

[43] *Posten Norge AS v EFTA Surveillance Authority*, above n 13.

[44] Case E-1/04 *Fokus Bank ASA v The Norwegian State* [2004] EFTA Ct Rep 11, para 41.

[45] Eg *Ulf Samuelsson v Svenska Staten*, above n 24; Case E-1/02 *EFTA Surveillance Authority v Norway* [2003] EFTA Ct Rep 1, para 54 (the postdoc case); E-1/03 *EFTA Surveillance Authority v Iceland* [2003] EFTA Ct Rep 143, para 35 (proportionality and freedom of establishment); Joined Cases E-5/04, E-6/04 and E-7/04 *Fesil ASA and Finnfjord Smelteverk AS, PIL and others and The Kingdom of Norway v EFTA Surveillance Authority* [2005] EFTA Ct Rep 117; Case E-1/05 *EFTA Surveillance Authority v The Kingdom of Norway* [2005] EFTA Ct Rep 234; Case E-2/06 *EFTA Surveillance Authority v The Kingdom of Norway* [2007] EFTA Ct Rep 164 (regulation of hydropower resources).

D. Autonomy as a Central Value?

The general principles of EEA law, as said, include both substantive rights as well as principles that constrain the freedom of action of national and supranational public authorities. The protection of fundamental rights and of proportionality in the context of EEA law implies that the EFTA Court in its construction of general principles regards individual autonomy as a central value. Whereas that has reduced the scope of action of the EEA institutions as well as of national governments, it has created constraints on political decision making which further legal protection of individuals and hence individual autonomy.

IV. THE CONSTITUTIONAL FUNCTIONS OF GENERAL PRINCIPLES: INTERNAL AND EXTERNAL COHERENCE

Legal principles serve a similar purpose in public international law in general, in national law as well as in EU and EEA law, namely to make legal orders coherent in absence of clear rules and hierarchies of norms. In the context of supranational law, general principles also tend to serve the function of reducing conflicts between national, supranational and international (for example, international human rights) law.

General principles in EEA law seem to play a role which is similar but not completely identical to general principles in EU law. In both cases general principles of law establish common principles for the application of law across national legal orders and constitute a major source of fundamental rights protection. Hence it is clear in EEA as well as in EU law that general principles have a constitutional function in that they constrain the exercise of public powers. However, the creation of a constitutional principle of homogeneity is uncommon and, in that regard, EEA law makes a distinctive contribution to legal models of economic and political integration. The absence of such a principle in relations between, for example, EU law and the ECHR or between EU law and WTO law also points to a dilemma of much of international integration, namely the absence of constitutional principles to determine the relations between different inter- and supranational legal orders with competing claims for public authority.

The application of the principle of homogeneity by the EFTA Court is a solution to a problem of normative conflicts which is common in the development of supranational legal orders in general and in relation to the interaction between different supranational legal orders in particular. The principle of homogeneity has—as discussed above—been used by the EFTA Court as a mean to adapt EEA law to EU law in fields such as fundamental rights, state liability and proportionality. The common thread of the case law has been the strengthening of protection of individual rights within the context of the common market. The principle of homogeneity has not reduced the practical importance of the EFTA Court in the development of the EEA law, but it has given a greater degree of coherence to the use of general principles of law. The extensive application of general principles through the principle of homogeneity, and the inclusion of a broad set of sources of law, seems to have led the EFTA Court to a more coherent and principled approach to adjudication, for example concerning the protection of fundamental rights. The inclusion of a broader set of sources of law—in particular the ECHR— also enables the EFTA Court to avoid constitutional conflicts with national legal orders as well as with the EU. The discretionary use of general principles in the development of EEA law in the short term therefore seems to have led to a more coherent approach to the constitutionalisation of EEA law over time.[46]

V. CONCLUSIONS

The development of general principles under the EEA Agreement by the EFTA Court is an example of how an international legal order may be internally constitutionalised as well as aligned with national and supranational legal orders on which it depends for effectiveness, without being a part of a common constitutional structure. The gradual constitutionalisation of the EEA has relied on extensive use of the principles of homogeneity and effectiveness to define the conditions of exercise of public powers under the EEA Agreement. However, despite the principle of homogeneity with EU law, the EFTA Court has interpreted homogeneity as a basis for aligning EEA law with EU law and the ECHR as well as with general legal principles, such as legal certainty. That also means that whereas the principle of homogeneity still requires that EEA law and EU law shall overlap on most issues, the principle of homogeneity as it has been employed does not imply that EEA law is subordinated to EU law. On the contrary, the role of general principles to enhance coherence of EEA law in relation to EU law as well as in relation to national law has created a basis for a jurisprudence that maintains an independent basis for constitutional norms within EEA law. Whereas the combination of homogeneity between EU and EEA law and the internal coherence of EEA law can be maintained over time, however remains to be seen.

---

[46] To compare with the situation in EU law, see A Sweet Stone, *Judges as Constitution-Makers* (Oxford, Oxford University Press, 2001).

22

Fundamental Rights in EEA Law

DAVÍÐ THÓR BJÖRGVINSSON

I. INTRODUCTION

THIS CHAPTER OFFERS some reflections on the protection of fundamental rights under the Agreement on the European Economic Area (EEA
Agreement).[1]

The EEA Agreement, as a treaty under international public law, has several interesting features. This is confirmed by the EFTA Court in the *Sveinbjörnsdóttir* case
where the Court found the EEA Agreement to be an international treaty *sui generis*
containing a distinct legal order of its own. Although the depth of integration of
the EEA Agreement was found to be less far-reaching than under the EU legal system, the Court found that the scope and the objective of the EEA Agreement went
beyond what is usual for an agreement under public international law.[2]

The central feature of the EEA Agreement is that it extends the common
market of the EU to the three non-Member States, namely Iceland, Norway and
Liechtenstein (hereinafter referred to as the EEA states). Accordingly, the EU legislation in the field of the four freedoms and competition (and state aid) is part
or is to be made a part of the legal order of these States despite the fact that they
are not full members of the EU. Moreover, the EEA Agreement and the Agreement
between the EFTA States on the Establishment of a Surveillance Authority and a
Court of Justice, signed on 2 May 1992 (the Surveillance and Court Agreement—
SCA) provide for institutions, separate from the EU institutions, the role of which
is to ensure that EU legislation in these fields is implemented and enforced in the
EFTA States in line with EU standards. In this regard the core concept is 'homogeneity', the content of which will be described below.

---

[1] The Agreement on the European Economic Area of 2 May 1992 (OJ 1994 L 1, p 3) (the EEA
Agreement) was concluded as an association agreement on the basis of Article 238 of the EC Treaty,
now Article 217 TFEU, between the European Communities and their Member States at that time,
on the one hand, and the States then belonging to the European Free Trade Association (EFTA),
namely, the Republic of Austria, the Republic of Finland, the Republic of Iceland, the Principality
of Liechtenstein, the Kingdom of Norway, the Kingdom of Sweden and the Swiss Confederation, on
the other. Presently only Iceland, Norway and Liechtenstein are on the EFTA side of the Agreement.
[2] Case E-9/97 *Erla María Sveinbjörnsdóttir v Iceland* [1997] EFTA Ct Rep 95, § 59.

The EEA Agreement does not contain specific provisions referring to fundamental rights. Moreover, the EU Charter on Fundamental Rights is not a part of the EEA legal system and creates no obligations for the EEA states to adhere to it or adopt it into their national systems. Nevertheless, having in mind the democratic principles upon which the legal systems of these states is based, it goes without saying that such rights must be respected. This chapter aims at offering some reflections on the status on the protection of fundamental rights under EEA law.

II. THE LEGAL NATURE OF THE EEA AGREEMENT

The aim of the EEA Agreement is to extend the common market to the non-Member States, Iceland, Norway and Liechtenstein. Under the agreement these states have an obligation to implement EU legislation in the field of the four freedoms and competition into their national legal order and ensure, in accordance with the principle of homogeneity, that this legislation is applied, interpreted and enforced in compliance with EU standards.

The structure and nature of the EEA Agreement is shaped by two aims. First, the rules should be implemented in the national legal system in order to enable individuals and economic operators to rely on them (direct effect) and, second, this should be achieved without requiring these EFTA States to transfer sovereign powers to common institutions beyond limits set by their constitutions. For the purpose of further comparison with the Community legal order the following is relevant.

First, compared to the EU, the transfer of state powers to common institutions is very limited. In fact it is restricted to certain decisions of the EFTA Surveillance Authority (ESA) and the EFTA Court in competition cases. Second, the EEA Agreement does not provide for direct applicability of secondary EU legislation in the national legal order of the EFTA States concerned.

This approach is reflected in Article 7 EEA providing that acts referred to or contained in the annexes to the Agreement, or in the decisions of the EEA Joint Committee, shall be binding upon the Contracting Parties and be, or be made, part of their internal legal order.[3] Acts corresponding to an EEC regulation

---

[3] It is worth noting that not all secondary EU legislation is relevant for the EEA Agreement. It is mostly limited to legislation directly relevant for the operation of the internal market, ie the four freedoms, competition and state aid. However, the common agricultural and fishery policies are excluded from the scope of the Agreement. It is furthermore the role of the EEA Joint Committee to decide which secondary EU legislation shall be a part of the EEA Agreement. As regards the role of the EEA Joint Committee see also S Norberg, K Höckborg, M Johansson, D Eliasson and L Dedichen, *The European Economic Area. EEA Law. A Commentary on the EEA Agreement* (Stockholm, Fritzes, 1993); L Sevón: 'Primacy and Direct Effect in the EEA. Some Reflections' in *Festskrift til Ole Due. Liber Amicorum* (Copenhagen, Gad, 1994) 339–354; M Cremona: 'The Dynamic and Homogeneous EEA: Byzantine Structures and Variable Geometry' (1994) *European Law Review* 508–526; C Reymond: 'Institutions, Decision-making Procedure and Settlement of Disputes in the European Economic Area' (1993) *Common Market Law Review* 449–480.

shall as such be made part of the internal legal order of the Contracting Parties and acts corresponding to an EEC directive shall leave to the authorities of the Contracting Parties the choice of form and method of implementation. It follows that EU regulations will not become a part of the domestic legal order unless specific measures are taken to implement it. The direct applicability and direct effect of secondary legislation, including EU regulations, is therefore dependent on them having been implemented in the national legal order in accordance with constitutional and other domestic legal standards.[4] Third, as regards the enforcement mechanism under the EEA Agreement there are important similarities to the Community legal order, although there are also important dissimilarities. As regards similarities, the ESA and the EFTA Court are the Union's counterparts of the Commission and the CJEU.[5] As regards dissimilarities, the counterpart to the preliminary rulings procedure under the Union order the EEA counterpart is

---

[4] This conclusion represents the common view. However, it could be argued that this understanding has been challenged by the CJEU in its judgment of 26 September 2013 in Case C-431/11 *United Kingdom v Council of the European Union*. In paras 53–55 the CJEU states the following: '(53) It should also be noted that, pursuant to Article 7 of the EEA Agreement, acts referred to in the annexes to the EEA Agreement or in the decisions of the EEA Joint Committee are to be binding on all the Contracting Parties and made part of their internal legal order. (54) In particular, as regards an EU regulation, Article 7(a) of the EEA Agreement expressly provides that such an act is 'as such' to be made part of the internal legal order of the Contracting Parties, that is to say, without any implementing measures being required for that purpose. (55) Consequently, as the Commission has correctly pointed out, the contested decision does not seek only to regulate the social rights of nationals of the three EFTA States concerned, but also, and in the same manner, to regulate the social rights of EU citizens in those EFTA States. In other words, the amendment to the EEA Agreement contemplated by the contested decision not only enables, in essence, nationals of Iceland, Liechtenstein and Norway to invoke the rights conferred by Regulations Nos 883/2004 and 987/2009 within the European Union, but also enables nationals of the Member States to rely on those rights in Iceland, Liechtenstein and Norway.' It is to be noted that it seems that the CJEU has simply misunderstood the meaning of the words 'as such' in Art 7 EEA when it says 'that is to say, without any implementing measures'. These words, however, have in Iceland and Norway not been understood as meaning 'without implementing measures' but rather such that a given EU regulation shall be implemented in its entirety into the national system, as compared to directives, to which national legislation shall in substance be adapted rather than being implemented 'as such'. This unexpected interpretation of the CJEU of the words 'as such' moreover ignores the fact that the EEA Agreement does not, as is clear from Protocol No 35 EEA, provide for transfer of legislative power. Despite this judgment, at least in the dualist countries Iceland and Norway, no EU regulation will be a part of the national legal order unless measures have been taken, in accordance with domestic legislative procedures, to implement it. This judgment of the CJEU will not change that.

[5] See in particular Arts 108–110 EEA. See also Agreement between the EFTA States on the Establishment of a Surveillance Authority and a Court of Justice, signed on 2 May 1992 (the Surveillance and Court Agreement). Despite certain similarities as regards the role of the Commission on the one hand and the EFTA Surveillance Authority on the other, important differences remain in that the EFTA Surveillance Authority is more limited, especially with regard to policy making and its role in the preparations and adoption of new legislation, where the Authority has no role. See also Norberg et al, above n 3, pp 700–708. Also by Norberg: 'The EEA Surveillance System' (1992) *Svensk Juristtidning* 349–364. As regards the role of the EFTA Court see, eg, *The EFTA Court. Legal Framework, Case Law and Composition 1994–2003* (Luxembourg, EFTA Court, 2004); S Norberg and M Magnussen, 'The EFTA Court' in Plender (ed), *European Court Procedure* (London, Sweet and Maxwell, 2001) 3001–3047. Also by Norberg, 'The EFTA Court and the Homogeneous EEA' (1993–94) 4 *Juridisk Tidskrift* 748–758.

the advisory opinion procedure provided for in Article 34 of the Surveillance and Court Agreement. Under this procedure courts and tribunals in the EFTA States are entitled to request the EFTA Court to interpret the EEA Agreement and secondary EU legislation that has been made part of it, when such questions arise in relation to cases before national courts or tribunals. In comparison to preliminary rulings, two important differences must be mentioned. First, the national courts or tribunals are never obliged to request advisory opinions, and second, they are never binding on the national courts.

III. THE EUROPEAN CONVENTION ON HUMAN RIGHTS AND EEA LAW

Broadly speaking, the issue concerning the relationship between EU law and the ECHR can be approached from two different points of view: first, from the point of view of the ECHR and the Court by analysing case law where states have allegedly violated the ECHR in their enforcement and application of EU legislation; and second, from the point of view of EU law by analysing case law of the CJEU where issues of fundamental rights have been addressed and the significance of the ECHR and the case law of the Court in that respect. These two different viewpoints are also relevant in relation to the EEA Agreement. In the following chapters these two approaches will be examined.

A. The Relevance of EEA Law when the ECHR is Applied

i. Introduction

In the case law of the European Court of Human Rights there is still no reference to the EEA Agreement or the case law of the EFTA Court.[6] Therefore there is little to say on this aspect. Nevertheless, theoretically speaking, it is possible that in the future the Court will have applications from individuals complaining that fundamental rights have been infringed in the implementation and enforcement of the EEA Agreement or secondary legislation in the domestic system. The fact that the substantive EEA rules concerning the internal market are the same as in EU law, and having in mind the fundamental principle of homogeneity, it is a legitimate assumption that the EEA law will on behalf of the European Court of Human Rights be accorded similar status as EU law has.

As regards issues where EU Member States have allegedly violated the ECHR in their enforcement and application of EU legislation, as concerns this aspect of the

---

[6] See, however, the case of *Ališić and Others v Bosnia and Herzegovina, Croatia, Serbia, Slovenia and 'The former Yugoslav Republic of Macedonia'*, application No 60642/08, judgment 16/07/2014. The case was heard by the Grand Chamber of the ECtHR on 10 July 2013. In their submissions the parties made a reference to the *Icesave* judgment of the EFTA Court, [2013] EFTA Ct Rep 3.

interplay between ECHR and the Community legal order the Strasbourg Court has dealt with it on several occasions. The first thing to note is that jurisdiction of the State under Article 1 of the Convention is not excluded in cases concerning implementation of Community legislation or decisions. This is clear from *M & Co v Germany*. In this case the European Commission of Human Rights adopted what has been termed as the 'equivalent-protection test'. Under this test the 'transfer of powers to an international organization is not incompatible with the Convention provided that within this organization fundamental rights will receive an equivalent protection'.[7] There is hardly a doubt that the same approach applies in case of application of EEA legislation in the national order of the respective contracting parties.

In the *Bosphorus Airways* judgment the ECtHR took it one step further.[8] Although no mention of EEA Agreement is to be found in this Grand Chamber judgment it gives an opportunity to ask whether and to what extent the reasoning of the Court in this judgment is also relevant in the context of the EEA Agreement.

ii. The Bosphorus Airways *Judgment*

The *Bosphorus Airways* judgment merits more attention. The case concerned an application brought by an airline charter company registered in Turkey, *Bosphorus Airways*. In May 1993 an aircraft leased by the company from Yugoslav Airlines ('JAT') was seized by the Irish authorities when it was in Ireland for maintenance. From the point of view of Irish domestic law the legal basis for the seizure of the aircraft was EEC Council Regulation No 990/93. This regulation, in turn, implemented the UN sanctions regime against the Federal Republic of Yugoslavia (Serbia and Montenegro). Bosphorus Airways' challenge to the retention of the aircraft was initially successful in the High Court in Ireland, which held in June 1994 that Regulation 990/93 was not applicable to the aircraft. On appeal, the Supreme Court referred a question to the CJEU for a preliminary ruling on whether the aircraft was covered by the Regulation. In its preliminary ruling the CJEU found that it was and, in its judgment of November 1996, the Supreme

---

[7] *M & Co v Germany*, Application No 13258/87. Commission decision of 9 February 1990. See also *Waite and Kennedy v Germany*, application No 26083/94, judgment of 18 February 1999 and *Matthews v United Kingdom*, application No 24833/94, judgment of 18 February 1999. See also L Garlicki: 'The Cooperation of Courts: The role of the supranational jurisdictions in Europe' I. CON, Vol 6, Nos 3 & 4, 2008, pp 509–530 (at 524–525).

[8] See *Bosphorus Hava Yollari Turizm ve Ticraet Anonim şikreti v Ireland*, application No 45036/98, judgment of 30 June 2005. The judgment has been the subject of scholarly writings before by the author of this chapter. See, eg, 'Presumption of Convention Compliance' in A Eide, JT Möller and I Ziemele (eds), *Making Peoples Heard. Essays on Human Rights in Honour of Gudmundur Alfredsson* (Leiden, Martinus Nijhoff, 2011) 293–304; on the interplay between EU law, EEA law and the European Convention on Human Rights see M Johansson, N Wahl and U Bernitz (eds), *Liber Amicorum for Sven Norberg. A European for all Seasons* (Brussels, Bruylant, 2006) 87–99; on the EEA Agreement and Fundamental Rights see L Caflisch et al (eds), *Human rights: Strasbourg views: liber amicorum Luzius Wildhaber = Droits de l'homme : regards de Strasbourg : liber amicorum Luzius Wildhaber* (Kehl, NP Engel Verlag, 2008) 25–40.

Court applied the decision of the CJEU and allowed the State's appeal against the High Court's judgment.

By that time, Bosphorus Airways' lease of the aircraft had already expired. Since the sanctions regime had also been relaxed by that date, the Irish authorities returned the aircraft directly to JAT. Bosphorus Airways consequently lost approximately three years of its four-year lease of the aircraft, which was the only one ever seized under the relevant EU and UN regulations.

Before the Court, Bosphorus Airways complained that the manner in which Ireland implemented the sanctions regime to impound its aircraft was a reviewable exercise of discretion within the meaning of Article 1 of the Convention and a violation of Article 1 of Protocol No 1 of the Convention.

As regards Article 1 of the Convention the Court did not dispute that the impoundment of the aircraft leased by Bosphorus Airways was implemented by the Irish authorities on its territory following a decision by the Irish Minister for Transport. Accordingly it was held that Bosphorus Airways fell within the 'jurisdiction' of the Irish State in the meaning of Article 1 of the Convention.

In relation to Article 1 of Protocol No 1 and the legal basis for the impoundment of the aircraft the Court made several interesting statements, inter alia in paragraph 148 where the Court found that the impugned interference was 'not the result of an exercise of discretion by the Irish authorities, either under EU or Irish law, but rather amounted to compliance by the Irish State with its legal obligations flowing from EU law and, in particular, Article 8 of Regulation 990/93'.

This is an important finding as it forms the basis for the final conclusion of non-violation of Article 1 of Protocol No 1 of the Convention by Ireland. According to the *Bosphorus Airways* judgment it seems that this finding is based on the following special features of the Community legal order. 1) The regulation was 'generally applicable' and 'binding in its entirety' pursuant to Article 249 (ex Article 189) of the EC Treaty. It is moreover emphasised that it was 'directly applicable' and that it became a part of the domestic legal order without the need to implement a special legislation to that effect. The Court therefore held that the Irish authorities rightly considered themselves obliged to impound any departing aircraft that fell under Article 8 of the Regulation. 2) Second, it refers to the rights and duties under Article 234 (ex 177) of the EC Treaty to refer matters of interpretation of EU legislation to the CJEU. In this regard it was pointed out that pursuant to Article 5 (ex Article 10) EU that the duty of loyal co-operation required the State to appeal the High Court judgment to the Supreme Court in order to clarify the interpretation of the EU Regulation. Furthermore, the Court found that the Supreme Court of Ireland had no discretion in the matter as the Supreme Court of Ireland had to make the preliminary reference, the ruling of the CJEU was binding on the Supreme Court and the ruling of the CJEU effectively determined the domestic proceedings by concluding that the regulation applied to the aircraft.

As to the question whether the impoundment of the aircraft was justified, the Court first described the general approach. It stressed that there must be a reasonable relationship of proportionality between the means employed and the aim pursued and that a fair balance has to be struck between the demands of the general interests of society and the interests of the individual company concerned. It emphasised that the State enjoys a wide margin of appreciation in this regard. However, it also stressed that the Convention as such does not prevent Contracting Parties from transferring sovereign powers to international organisations for the purpose of co-operation in certain fields. Furthermore, as stated in paragraph 158 the Court examined whether it could be presumed that Ireland complied with its Convention requirements in fulfilling such obligations and whether any such presumption has been rebutted in the circumstances of the case.

In assessing whether such a presumption of Convention compliance could be made at the relevant time, the Court described the main features for the protection of fundamental rights within the Community legal order. It was found that repeated references by the CJEU to the Convention provisions and the Court's jurisprudence, specific treaty provisions referring to protection of such rights and the Charter of Fundamental rights of the European Union, as well as the as the control and enforcement mechanism offered by the Community, allowed it to conclude the following (paragraph 165):

> In such circumstances, the Court finds that the protection of fundamental rights by EU law can be considered to be, and to have been at the relevant time, 'equivalent' (within the meaning of paragraph 155 above) to that of the Convention system. Consequently, the presumption arises that Ireland did not depart from the requirements of the Convention when it implemented legal obligations flowing from its membership of the EC.

In its reasoning the Court stressed that such a presumption of Convention compliance could be rebutted if, in a particular case, it was considered that the protection of Convention rights was manifestly deficient. In such cases, the interest of international co-operation would be outweighed by the Convention's role as a 'constitutional instrument of European public order' in the field of human rights. To the question of whether the presumption could be rebutted, the Court gave the following answer:

> The Court has had regard to the nature of the interference, to the general interest pursued by the impoundment and by the sanctions regime and to the ruling of the CJEU (in the light of the opinion of the AG), a ruling with which the Supreme Court was obliged to and did comply. It considers it clear that there was no dysfunction of the mechanisms of control of the observance of Convention rights.

> In the Court's view, therefore, it cannot be said that the protection of the applicant's Convention rights was manifestly deficient with the consequence that the relevant presumption of Convention compliance by the respondent State has not been rebutted.

On the basis of these arguments the Court found that the impoundment of the aircraft did not give rise to a violation of Article 1 of Protocol No 1 ECHR.

In earlier case law, the Court has stated as a general position that the text of Article 1 of the Convention requires Member States to answer for any infringement of the rights and freedoms protected by the Convention committed against individuals placed under their 'jurisdiction'.[9]

In the *Bosphorus Airways* case it is not disputed that the act about which the applicant complained was implemented by the authorities of the respondent State on its territory following the Irish Minister for Transport's decision to impound.

Despite this conclusion as regards Article 1 of the Convention, the reasoning and the conclusion of the Court in the *Bosphorus Airways* case seems to imply that the Court is in a sense willing to accept that the fact that the disputed decision on the part of the Irish Authorities is based on Community law may limit the discretional powers of the Court in assessing compliance with the Convention standards. It also seems obvious that this is attributable to some specific features of the Community legal order, although other international obligations also come into play. From the judgment as a whole it would seem to be particularly relevant that the Member States of the European Union have transferred sovereign powers to common institutions and in this way created a legal order of its own, independent to a certain extent of the domestic legal order of the Member States. The following features are of importance in this respect: direct applicability (direct effect) of legislation in the domestic legal order of the Member States (and in case of EU Regulations their general applicability as legislation without specific means of implementation in the national order), an independent enforcement mechanism (in the instant case reflected mainly in the binding nature of preliminary rulings), followed by the lack of discretion on the part of the Member States in interpreting and enforcing the rules deriving from the EU institutions, and, finally, standards for the protection of fundamental rights developed by the EU institutions which are considered equivalent to the standards offered by the Convention.

The judgment in the *Bosphorus Airways* case is followed by a joint concurring opinion of six judges, one of them giving a concurring opinion. Like the majority, these judges found that there had been no violation of Article 1 of Protocol No 1, but they disagree as regards some of the steps in the reasoning of the majority. In particular, they disagree as to the approach used in finding that the protection of fundamental rights under the Community legal order should be presumed to offer a protection equivalent to the one offered by the European Convention on Human Rights and the relevance of such presumption. They argue that the Court should rather simply have examined *in concreto* whether there was a reasonable relationship of proportionality between the means employed and the aim pursued and, consequently, determine whether a fair balance had been struck between the requirement of the general interest and the interest of the applicant company. In

---

[9] See in particular cases *Ilaşcu and Others v Moldova and Russia* [GC], application No 48787/99, judgment of 08/07/2004, § 311; *Gentilhomme, Schaff-Benhadji and Zerouki v France*, application Nos 48205/99, 48207/99 et 48209/99, judgment of 14/05 May 2002, § 20; *Banković and Others v Belgium and 16 other Contracting States* (dec), application No 52207/99, decision of 12/12/200, §§ 59–61, ECHR 2001-XII; and *Assanidze v Georgia*, application Nos 71503/01 and 71503/01, judgment of 08/04/2004, § 137).

view of the minority, not only was the whole approach adopted by the majority questionable, but also the finding that the protection could be considered equivalent, especially in the light of lack of individual petition before the Community institutions. They argue that by adopting this approach the majority has created different obligations for the Contracting Parties to the ECHR, divided into those which have acceded to certain international conventions and those which have not, in this case membership of the EU.

It is to be noted that most of the reasoning in the *Bosphorus Airways* case is based on the specific nature of Community law, both with regard to the limited discretion which the EU Member States have when implementing, applying and enforcing EU legislation and in establishing and justifying the presumption of compatibility with Convention standards. In this regard interesting questions arise as regards decisions taken in the EFTA countries, Iceland, Norway and Liechtenstein, based on legislation deriving from the obligations under the EEA Agreement.

These questions are interesting since, as described earlier, they concern the application and enforcement of the same legislation as would be the case in a Member State of the Community.[10] Therefore it may seem tempting to conclude that the arguments, offered by the majority in the *Bosphorus Airways* judgment, apply equally when assessing the discretion of national authorities when applying and enforcing legislation derived from the EEA Agreement and in establishing the presumption of Convention compatibility. But the problem is that most of the above description of the legal nature of the Community legal order on which the arguments of the majority in the *Bosphorus Airways* case is based, does not apply to the EEA Agreement, as the structure and legal nature of the EEA Agreement is, in important aspects, fundamentally different from the EU. Clearly the system set off by the EEA Agreement in fact lacks most of the characteristics of the Community legal order which were considered to be decisive in the majority's opinion. First, the transfer of sovereign powers is much more limited under the EEA. Second, there is no direct applicability, either of the main text of the EEA Agreement nor the secondary Community legislation deriving from it, unless it has first been implemented in the domestic system. Third, there is no binding preliminary ruling procedure equal to the one within the Community, since it is formally up to the national courts to decide if they want to use the advisory opinion procedure, and even if they do so, whether to follow the opinion given by the EFTA Court. Fourth, the arguments used by the majority to substantiate the presumption of Convention compliance are mostly irrelevant in the context of

---

[10] It is noted that EEC Council Regulation No 990/93 was never made a part of the EEA Agreement. Therefore the EFTA States were not obliged under the EEA Agreement to enforce the UN Security Council Resolution No 1074 (1996) in their domestic legal order, although it was binding for them under public international law. However, the arguments offered by the majority related not only to EEC Council Regulation No 990/93, but to the EC Treaty and the secondary legislation in general, including the rules on the internal market, which are part of the EEA Agreement.

the EEA Agreement. It would require very different arguments from those offered in the *Bosphorus Airways* case, to arrive at the conclusion that the protection of fundamental rights within the EEA legal order is equivalent to the one offered by the Convention.

Obviously, the EEA Agreement sets up a relatively complex system with the aim of securing homogenous interpretation, application and enforcement of secondary EU legislation on behalf of the EEA institutions as well as in the domestic system of the EFTA States. Of particular interest in this regard is Article 6 EEA and Article 3 of the Surveillance and Court Agreement, which make it obligatory for the EEA institutions and the courts in the EFTA States to base their interpretation and application of the EEA Agreement and the secondary legislation on the case law of the CJEU where substantially similar provisions have been interpreted and applied.[11]

iii. Ullens de Schooten and Rezabek v Belgium

On 29 September 2011 the ECtHR gave a judgment in the case of *Ullens de Schooten and Rezabek v Belgium* (Applications Nos 3989/07 and 38353/07). The case concerned the refusal of the Belgian Court of Cassation and the *Conseil d'Etat* to refer questions relating to the interpretation of EU law to the Court of Justice for a preliminary ruling. The applicants complained that the Court of Cassation had refused their request to obtain a preliminary ruling from the Court of Justice. In the second case, Mr Ullens de Schooten complained that the *Conseil d'Etat* had failed to consider the manifestly unlawful nature of Article 3 of the decree and had refused to refer the question to the Court of Justice for a preliminary ruling. The applicants relied on Article 6 ECHR.

The Court reiterated that the ECHR did not guarantee any right to have a case referred by a domestic court to another national or international authority for a preliminary ruling. Nonetheless, it observed that Article 6 § 1 imposed an obligation on the national courts to give reasons for any decision refusing to refer a question, particularly where the applicable law permitted such a refusal only in exceptional circumstances. Accordingly, the Court had to be satisfied that any refusal brought before it was accompanied by such reasons.

In the context of the Treaty establishing the European Community (Article 234), that meant that the highest courts were obliged to give reasons for a refusal to refer, based on the exceptions in the case law of the Court of Justice. The Court observed that, where a question concerning the interpretation of the Treaty establishing the European Community was raised in proceedings before a national court or tribunal against whose decisions there was no judicial remedy (in this case, the Court of Cassation and the *Conseil d'Etat*), the court in

---

[11] Some further remarks on the judgment are warranted, but they will not be offered here. See, by this author, 'Presumption of Convention Compliance' in *Making Peoples Heard. Essays on Human Rights in Honour of Gudmundur Alfredsson*, above n 8, pp 293–304.

question was obliged under Article 234 of the Treaty (Article 267 of the Treaty on the functioning of the EU) to refer the question to the Court of Justice for a preliminary ruling. However, that obligation was not absolute, as was clear from the Court of Justice's *CILFIT* case law. The national courts were not required to refer the question where they had established that it was 'irrelevant' or that the EU provision in question had already been interpreted by the Court of Justice, or where the correct application of EU law was 'so obvious as to leave no scope for any reasonable doubt'.

In the *Ullens de Shooten* case, the *Conseil d'Etat*, like the Court of Cassation, had given reasons for its refusal, citing the exceptions under the *CILFIT* case law.[12] In the light of the reasons given by the two courts and having regard to the proceedings as a whole, the Court held that there had been no violation of the applicants' right to a fair hearing under Article 6 § 1. The reasoning, however, clearly indicates that an unsubstantiated denial to refer a case might have impact for the fairness of the proceedings.

B. The Relevance of the ECHR when EEA Law is Applied

Discussion related to protection of fundamental rights within the Community and on behalf of the Community institutions is well documented and there is no need to repeat this story here.[13] In addition to the increased case law of the CJEU where these issues have been addressed, the most important feature of the present situation is that the approach of the CJEU has been given expression in Article 6 of the Treaty of the European Union providing:

1. The Union recognises the rights, freedoms and principles set out in the Charter of Fundamental Rights of the European Union of 7 December 2000, as adapted at Strasbourg, on 12 December 2007, which shall have the same legal value as the Treaties.

---

[12] The *CILFIT* case states that courts and tribunals are not under the obligation to refer a case to the ECJ if the question is hypothetical, has already been answered or if there exists no reasonable doubt as to the correct interpretation of the EU legislation. See also M Schmauch, 'The Preliminary Ruling Procedure and the Right to a Fair Trial—Strasbourg Demands Reasoned Decisions from National Courts when They Refuse to Refer a Case to the ECJ' (December 2011) *European Law Reporter* 362–367.

[13] Among those from recent years are F Jacobs, 'Interaction of the case-law of the European Court of Human Rights and the European Court of Justice: Recent developments' in *Dialogue between judges* (Strasbourg, European Court of Human Rights, 2005) 65–87 and A Rosas, 'Fundamental Rights in the Luxembourg and Strasbourg Courts' in *The EFTA Court. Ten years on* (Oxford, Hart Publishing, 2005) 161–175. Also by the same author, 'Fundamental Rights in the EU, with Special Emphasis on the Case Law of the European Court of Justice (Luxembourg)' in G Alfredsson, J Grimheden, BG Ramcharan and A Zayas (eds), *International Human Rights Monitoring Mechanisms. Essays in Honour of Jakob Th. Möller*, 2nd revised edn (The Roul Wallenberg Institute Human Rights Library, Martinus Nijhoff, 2009) 579–590. Among recent important judgments, reiterating the earlier case law, is Judgment of the ECJ (Grand Chamber) of 3 September 2008—*Yassin Abdullah Kadi, Al Barakaat International Foundation v Council of the European Union, Commission of the European Communities, United Kingdom of Great Britain and Northern Ireland* (Joined Cases C-402/05 P and C-415/05 P).

The provisions of the Charter shall not extend in any way the competences of the Union as defined in the Treaties.

The rights, freedoms and principles in the Charter shall be interpreted in accordance with the general provisions in Title VII of the Charter governing its interpretation and application and with due regard to the explanations referred to in the Charter, that set out the sources of those provisions.

2. The Union shall accede to the European Convention for the Protection of Human Rights and Fundamental Freedoms. Such accession shall not affect the Union's competences as defined in the Treaties.

3. Fundamental rights, as guaranteed by the European Convention for the Protection of Human Rights and Fundamental Freedoms and as they result from the constitutional traditions common to the Member States, shall constitute general principles of the Union's law.

The Treaty of Lisbon entered into force on 1 December 2009. A special Protocol to the Treaty relates to Article 6(2) of the EU Treaty and contains guidance for further provisions to be adopted in a possible agreement on the accession of the EU to the Human Rights Convention system. These provisions relate, inter alia, to preserving the specific characteristics of the Union and Union law, arrangements for the Union's possible participation in the control bodies of the European Convention, the mechanisms necessary to ensure that proceedings by non-Member States and individual applications are correctly addressed to Member States and/or the Union as appropriate and competences of the Union or the powers of its institutions. The Protocol clearly envisages that some specific arrangements may be needed in order to facilitate the Unions participation in the Convention system. This raises many issues, partly technical and partly political, that will not be discussed here.

Not only does the European Union's accession to the Convention system require legislative measures to be taken on behalf of the Union, but also changes to the Convention itself. These are stipulated in Protocol No 14 to the ECHR mentioned above, which amends Article 59 of the Convention allowing for the European Union to accede to it. After the entering into force the issue of the accession of the Union to the Convention system becomes a very topical one and puts into focus, inter alia, issues relating to the interplay between the ECHR and the Community legal order.[14]

As stated above, the EEA Agreement does not contain any provisions directly concerning the protection of fundamental rights. However, as a starting point it is

---

[14] On 5 April 2013 negotiators for the 47 Council of Europe Member States and the European Union finalised the draft accession agreement of the European Union to the European Convention on Human Rights. A request, as regards its compatibility of the text with EU law, is at the time of writing pending before the CJEU. See Draft Agreement on Accession of the European Union to the European Convention on Human Rights at http://echrblog.blogspot.com/2013/04/accession-of-eu-to-echr-draft-agreement.html.

appropriate to refer to the Preamble to the Agreement, where it is stated that the Contracting parties are convinced 'of the contribution that a European Economic Area will bring to the construction of Europe based on peace, democracy and human rights'. These words obviously contain a general declaration on the basis of which it should be possible to conclude that the whole Agreement rests on the presumption that democracy and fundamental rights should be protected in its implementation and enforcement.

This raises three questions. (1) What are the proper legal criteria to refer to when assessing whether such rights have been respected? (2) Who is responsible for ensuring that fundamental rights are observed when the EEA Agreement and the secondary EU legislation, which forms a part of it, are enforced in the EFTA States? (3) Is it possible, having in mind the answer to these two questions, and the legal scope and nature of the EEA Agreement, to make a similar presumption of Convention compliance as was done in the *Bosphorus* judgment?

As regards standards for the protection of fundamental rights under the EEA Agreement, it should be pointed out that the EFTA Court has in several judgments referred to the ECHR and the jurisprudence of the Court.

First one should mention *TV 1000 Sverige AB v Norway*.[15] In this case the EFTA Court was faced with an interpretation of Council Directive 89/552/EEC of 3 October 1989 on the co-ordination of certain provisions laid down by law, regulation, or administrative action in Member States concerning the pursuit of television broadcasting activities. In its judgment, the EFTA Court referred to the freedom of expression granted by Article 10 ECHR, as well as limitations thereof, and to the *Handyside* judgment of the ECHR (judgment of 7 December 1976, A vol 24).

Another reference is to be found in *Technologien Bau- und Wirstschaftberatung GmbH and Bellona Foundation v EFTA Surveillance Authority*.[16] In this judgment, the EFTA Court found, in a case where action for annulment was brought against a decision of the Authority approving state aid, that access to court is an essential element of the legal system set up by the EEA Agreement. This right was, however, subject to those conditions and limitations provided for by EEA law. It is stated that the EFTA Court is aware of the ongoing debate with regard to the issue of the standing of natural and legal persons in actions against Community institutions. It furthermore added that the significance of the judicial function which was inspired by the idea of human rights appears to be on the increase, both on the national and the international level. Nevertheless the Court found that caution was warranted, not least in view of the uncertainties inherent in the current refashioning of fundamental Community law.

---

[15] Case E-8/97 *TV-1000* [1998] EFTA Ct Rep 68.
[16] Case E-2/02 *Bellona* [2003] EFTA Ct Rep. See also Case E-3/11 *Pálmi Sigmarsson v Seðlabanki Íslands* [2011] EFTA Ct Rep 430 and Case E-5/10 *Dr Kottke* [2009–2010] EFTA Ct Rep 320, § 26.

Another reference is to be found in *Ákæruvaldið* (the Public Prosecutor) against *Ásgeir Logi Ásgeirsson and others*.[17] In this case, one of the defendants in the national proceedings had alleged that the reference of the case to the EFTA Court for advisory opinion prolonged the duration of the proceedings and thereby infringed Article 6 ECHR. The EFTA Court found that provisions of the EEA Agreement, as well as procedural provisions of the Surveillance and Court Agreement, were to be interpreted in the light of fundamental rights and that the provisions of the ECHR were important sources when determining the scope of these rights. With regard to the right to a fair trial within a reasonable time granted by Article 6(1) ECHR, it was observed that the European Court of Human Rights held, in a case concerning a delay of two years and seven months due to reference by a national court to the CJEU for a preliminary ruling, that this period of time could not be taken into consideration in the assessment of the length of proceedings. To do so would adversely affect the system instituted by Article 177 (now 234) EU and work against the aim pursued in substance in that Article. In this regard the EFTA Court referred to *Pafitis and others v Greece*.[18] The EFTA Court furthermore found that the same must apply with regard to the procedure established under Article 34 of the Surveillance and Court Agreement which as a means of inter-court co-operation contributes to the proper functioning of the EEA Agreement to the benefit of individuals and economic operators.

Next to mention is the case of *Arnulf Clauder*[19] where the Court makes the following general statement as concerns the significance of the ECHR for the interpretation and enforcement of EEA law:

> Finally, it should be recalled that all the EEA States are parties to the ECHR, which enshrines in Article 8(1) the right to respect for private and family life. According to established case-law, provisions of the EEA Agreement are to be interpreted in the light of fundamental rights (see, for example, Case E-2/03 *Ásgeirsson* [2003] EFTA Ct Rep 18, paragraph 23, and Case E-12/10 *EFTA Surveillance Authority v Iceland*, judgment of 28 June 2011, not yet reported, paragraph 60 and the case-law cited). The Court notes that in the European Union the same right is protected by Article 7 of the Charter of Fundamental Rights.[20]

This approach is further confirmed in Case E-15/10, *Posten Norge AS v EFTA Surveillance Authority*.[21] In the case, the nature of the competition infringements at issue, and the potential gravity of the fine imposed, were found to fall within the criminal sphere of Article 6 ECHR. The Court therefore found that the guarantees established for criminal proceedings enshrined in Article 6 ECHR should

---

[17] Case E-2/03 *Ásgeir Logi Ásgeirssyni and others* [2003] EFTA Ct Rep 52.
[18] *Pafitis and others v Greece* Application No 163/1996, judgment of 26/02 1998 § 95).
[19] Case E-4/11 of 26 July 2011 [2011] EFTA Ct Rep 216, §49.
[20] A similar general statement is also in § 63 of the judgment in Case E-18/11 *Irish Bank Resolution Corporation Ltd v Kaupþing hf*. See also Case E-14/11 *Schenker North AB and others v EFTA Surveillance Authority* (17.7.2013) paras 166–167, where the court found that certain administrative investigative procedures may constitute an interference with a company's rights pursuant to Art 8 ECHR.
[21] EFTA Ct Rep [2012] 246.

be respected. Moreover, it found that the right to a fair trial requires that the Court must be able to quash in all respects, on questions of fact and of law, the challenged decision by ESA. On the basis of its interpretation of Article 6 ECHR, the Court rejected ESA's submission that the Court's review of complex economic assessments by ESA would be limited to a 'manifest' error standard.

Finally Case E-18/11 *Irish Bank Resolution Corporation Ltd v Kaupþing hf* should be mentioned as it is interesting in the light of Case Nos 3989/07 and 38353/0763 *Ullens de Schooten and Rezabek v Belgium*, mentioned above. In this judgment it would seem that the EFTA Court is flirting with the idea of extending the *Ullens de Schooten* case to the advisory opinion procedure. The Court states at paragraph 64:

> In this regard, it must be kept in mind that when a court or tribunal against whose decisions there is no judicial remedy under national law refuses a motion to refer a case to another court, it cannot be excluded that such a decision may fall foul of the standards of Article 6(1) ECHR, which provides that in 'determination of his civil rights and obligations … everyone is entitled to a fair and public hearing within a reasonable time by an independent and impartial tribunal established by law'. In particular this may be the case if the decision to refuse is not reasoned and must therefore be considered arbitrary (compare *Ullens de Schooten and Rezabek v Belgium*, Case Nos 3989/07 and 38353/07, judgment of the European Court of Human Rights of 20 September 2011, paragraphs 59 and 60, and case law cited). These considerations may also apply when a court or tribunal against whose decisions there is no judicial remedy under national law overrules a decision of a lower court to refer the case, whether in civil or criminal proceedings, to another court, or upholds the decision to refer, but nevertheless decides to amend the questions asked by the lower court.

In this regard it is important to note that in its reasoning the ECtHR gives weight to the fact that national courts are obliged, under certain circumstances, to refer a case for a preliminary ruling, and exceptions should be construed narrowly. These elements are absent in the advisory opinion procedure, under which there is never an obligation to refer a case to the EFTA Court for advisory opinion. Moreover, the opinions are not binding, although they in reality are always followed by the national courts. Although, as manifested in the judgment of the EFTA Court, it cannot be excluded that the judgment of the ECtHR has a bearing on the advisory opinion procedure, it would only be in extreme situations, where a refusal is totally unsubstantiated and arbitrary, that a refusal to defer a case will have an impact on the fairness of the national proceedings in breach of Article 6 ECHR.

From these references in the EFTA Court case law to the Convention, and the case law of the ECtHR, it would seem possible to draw at least two conclusions. First, it is clear that the EFTA Court is aware that in the implementation and enforcement of the EEA Agreement, fundamental rights will have to be respected. Second, the main criterion the EFTA Court uses when assessing whether this is so in the circumstances of the individual case is the ECHR as interpreted by the European Court of Human Rights.

A further question is whether one could go so far as to presume priority of the Convention over the EEA Agreement. This could possibly be supported by reference to the joint declaration of the Contracting Parties from 2 May 1992 concerning the continuing effect of international treaties they adhered to at that time and in the light of the status and nature of the Convention as a 'constitutional instrument of European public order', to use a phrase from the *Bosphorus* judgment. Legal scholars have, however, answered this question in the negative.[22] From a formal point of view, the Convention does not form a part of the EEA Agreement as a binding source of legal norms in the context of the EEA Agreement. Still, the case law of the EFTA Court strongly supports the conclusion that the norms contained in the Convention, which also reflect a common standard and a common denominator for a minimum standard for the protection of fundamental rights on a European level, are a part of the general unwritten principles of EEA law.

When it comes to the question as to who is responsible for ensuring that fundamental rights are observed when the EEA Agreement, and the secondary EU legislation which forms a part of it is, enforced in the EFTA States, the answer depends on the point of departure.

If this issue is viewed from the point of view of the European Convention on Human Rights, it follows from Article 1 of the Convention that the high Contracting Parties are obliged to secure to everyone within their jurisdiction the rights and freedoms defined in the Convention. The fact that an alleged violation follows from application and enforcement of international obligations deriving from the EEA Agreement does not move it from the jurisdiction of the respective Contracting Party.

If, on the other hand, a party to a dispute before the national courts argues that certain EEA legislation, its implementation or enforcement, contradicts fundamental human rights as protected by the constitution, or other domestic legal criteria, it falls upon the national courts to make the assessment. It is hard to see that the fact that legislation, or a decision, has its roots in the EEA Agreement can in any way restrict the discretional powers of the national courts to assess its constitutional validity, although the aims and specific nature of the Agreement may have a bearing in such an assessment. In this respect it is necessary to have in mind that the EEA Agreement does not provide for transfer of state powers to international institutions, except to a very limited degree. Other than a limited transfer of state powers in the field of competition law, there is no transfer of legislative, executive or judicial powers to the EEA institutions. There is therefore no basis from which a right or a duty of these institutions to have a say, not to mention the final say, as regards protection of fundamental rights in the application and enforcement of the EEA Agreement in the national legal systems, can be derived.

In answering the third question concerning the presumption of Convention compliance, in a similar way as was done in the *Bosphorus* case, when alleged violation follows from enforcement of duties under the EEA Agreement, the

---

[22] Kälin: EWR Abkommen und Europäische Menschenrechtskonvention, pp 669–670.

following is relevant. First of all, none of the human rights documents referred to in the *Bosphorus* judgment are directly or formally a part of EEA law, nor are they directly relevant for the application and enforcement of the EEA Agreement and the secondary EU legislation it refers to, in the national legal order of the EFTA States. The EFTA Court has never referred to these instruments and neither have the national courts in the EFTA States when applying EEA law. Any reference on behalf of the European Court of Human Rights to these arguments in an attempt to substantiate a presumption of Convention compliance within the framework of the EEA Agreement, would not only be legally wrong but also, in the wider political context, inappropriate.

The *Bosphorus* judgment also refers to the case law of the CJEU as a basis for the presumption of Convention compliance. This of course immediately raises the question whether such a presumption in the context of the EEA Agreement could be based on Article 6 EEA and Article 3 of the Surveillance and Court Agreement which oblige the EEA institutions and the national courts of the EFTA States to have regard to the case law of the CJEU. This is of course a legitimate question, since many of the judgments of the CJEU concern an interpretation and application of legislation which is a part of the EEA Agreement. It could therefore be argued that judgments of the CJEU containing reference to human rights standards when applying EU legislation, which is also a part of the EEA Agreement, become relevant for the EEA Agreement. The principle of homogeneity supports such a finding. But due to the differences of the legal nature of the EEA Agreement on the one hand and that of the EU on the other, the reasoning of these judgments may not always be suitable in the context of the EEA Agreement, although the outcome could in substance be similar.

IV. CONCLUDING REMARKS

There is limited judicial practice relating to the status of fundamental rights within the framework of the EEA Agreement. The legal literature on the issue is also somewhat limited.

In order to summarise the content of this chapter, and possibly to offer some kind of conclusions, the following should be kept in mind. (1) It is probably safe to assert that fundamental rights, as reflected in the ECHR and the case law of the Court, form a part of the unwritten principles of EEA law. This assertion can partly be supported by reference to the fundamental aims of the EEA Agreement, the case law of the EFTA Court and, with some reservations, by a specific reference to Article 6 EEA and Article 3 of the Surveillance and Court Agreement referring to the relevance of the case law of the CJEU for the application and enforcement of the EEA Agreement. However, and most importantly, this assertion is simply based on the fact that the EFTA States adhering to the EEA Agreement are all Contracting Parties to the ECHR and the general view that any given set of legal rules in states that claim to be based on the rule of law must, in their content, application and enforcement respect fundamental rights. (2) None of the EEA institutions have directly been invested with the powers to uphold fundamental rights. In particular, they do not have any powers to define standards for such a protection that would be different or lower than the standards set up by the EFTA States themselves, as provided for in their constitutions or other binding legal instruments, including the ECHR. At the end of the day it is for the national courts to define these standards, taking into consideration the specific aims and legal nature of the EEA Agreement. The real significance of the ECHR for the interpretation and application of the EEA Agreement will also be defined by them. Although, as stated by the EFTA Court in the *Sveinbjörnsdóttir* case, EEA law is a distinctive legal order of its own, in reality it leaves the EEA institutions with limited possibilities to develop specific EEA standards for the protection of fundamental rights independently of the national courts. (3) This latter point, and the fundamental differences between the Community legal order on the one hand and EEA law on the other, must also lead to the conclusion that the reasoning for the presumption of Convention compliance in the *Bosphorus* case is to a great extent irrelevant in the context of the EEA Agreement. In any case, if such a presumption can be made altogether, it must be based on different arguments relating to the specific nature of the EEA Agreement.

23

Uncharted Waters: Reflections on the Legal Significance of the Charter under EEA Law and Judicial Cross-Fertilisation in the Field of Fundamental Rights

NILS WAHL*

I. INTRODUCTION

MORE THAN 20 years after the EFTA Court started operating under the Surveillance and Court Agreement,[1] the legal landscape has changed profoundly. There have been adjustments *ratione personae*: certain of the States party to the EEA Agreement[2] have migrated from the EFTA wing to the EU wing—including my own country. The main modifications, though, have been *ratione materiae*: in the EU pillar of the European Economic Area (EEA), the Treaties of Amsterdam, Nice and Lisbon caused great change to the way in which the EU operates. In that sense, the cooperation within the EEA is a clear example of the concept of a 'two-speed' or even a 'multi-speed' Europe, the latter especially considering that neither all the EFTA States (Switzerland) nor all EU Member States (Croatia) are party yet to the EEA Agreement.[3]

One clearly noticeable change in the EU pillar of the EEA is the fact that the Treaty of Lisbon made the Charter of Fundamental Rights of the European Union (the Charter)[4] legally binding and placed it on the same level as the Treaties under Article 6(1) TFEU, that is to say, on the level of primary law. The aim here, however, is not to dwell on the lengthy history of how the Charter came about, but

---

* All views expressed are personal. I would like to thank William Lindsay-Poulsen, legal secretary in my chambers, for his most valuable contribution to this chapter.

[1] Agreement between the EFTA States on the establishment of a Surveillance Authority and a Court of Justice (OJ 1994 L 344, p 3).

[2] Agreement on the European Economic Area (OJ 1994 L 1, p 3).

[3] While Croatia is currently acceding to the EEA Agreement on the participation of the Republic of Croatia in the European Economic Area, OJ 2014 L170, P. 18), Switzerland has-as far as I can tell -no intention of doing so.

[4] OJ 2007 C 303, p 1.

rather to focus on the issue of what the Charter means for EEA law, as it stands today.[5]

Admittedly, it is difficult, if not impossible, to provide a starting point from which to determine the legal status of the Charter in EEA law. There are no statutory rules which govern the issue. Indeed, officially, the Charter has *no* legal value in EEA law, as it has not been incorporated into the EEA legal order. Thus, the short (and formally correct) answer to the question of the legal status of the Charter in EEA law is that the Charter has no formal significance for EEA law.

Nevertheless, to simply stop there would risk missing the point (and make this chapter too short for the *Festschrift!*). From the absence of incorporation one cannot just assume that the Charter does not have any effects of a *secondary and/or indirect nature*. Such ancillary effects can be significant and should in any event not be underestimated.

Given the lack of formal legal recognition, it is therefore of interest to ascertain how the relevant players in the EEA legal arena have reacted to the adoption of the Charter and its elevation to the rank of EU primary law. Prior to this, though, I will provide some views of a more theoretical nature.

II. THE THEORETICAL APPROACH: IS THERE ROOM FOR MORE JUDICIAL CROSS-FERTILISATION IN THE FIELD OF FUNDAMENTAL RIGHTS?

The Charter essentially is an instrument whose aim is to safeguard the fundamental rights granted to individuals. For that reason, I will begin this part of my analysis by reiterating certain important features of the EEA/EU *acquis* in respect of fundamental rights.

A. Underlying Foundations

Like the EU Member States, all EFTA States are members of the Council of Europe and have acceded to the European Convention on Human Rights (ECHR)[6] prior to the adoption of the EEA Agreement. The respect for human rights in the EFTA States is therefore also, ultimately, subject to review by the European Court of Human Rights (ECtHR or the Strasbourg Court). Thus, ensuring respect for fundamental rights is a goal which the EU Member States and the EFTA States have

---

[5] However, I will not address the domestic considerations of the EFTA States regarding the Charter's legal status under EEA law. See instead H Haukeland Fredriksen, 'Betydningen av EUs pakt om grunnleggende rettigheter for EØS-retten' (2013) 48 *Jussens Venner* 371–399, who argues that the sovereignty of EFTA States and/or the protection of the rights of individuals limits the application of the principle of homogeneity; see p 378.

[6] Convention for the Protection of Human Rights and Fundamental Freedoms, signed in Rome on 4 November 1950.

in common. As is the case for the EU Treaties, that aim is also mirrored in the EEA Agreement.[7] That has not changed with the advent of the Charter, nor is such a development likely in the future. But what about the aim of ensuring homogeneity and the respect for fundamental rights?

As part of the overarching objective of homogeneity enshrined in the EEA Agreement,[8] Article 6 of the EEA Agreement provides:

> Without prejudice to future developments of case-law, the provisions of this Agreement,[9] in so far as they are identical in substance to corresponding rules of the Treaty establishing the European Economic Community and the Treaty establishing the European Coal and Steel Community and to acts adopted in application of these two Treaties, shall, in their implementation and application, be interpreted in conformity with the relevant rulings of the Court of Justice of the European Communities given prior to the date of signature of this Agreement.[10]

Prior to the entry into force of the Treaty of Lisbon, an official document drawn up by the EFTA Court spelled out the view it took at that time on the relationship between EEA and EU law in the following manner:

> EEA law must be understood against the background of Community law and the case-law of the EFTA Court against the background of the case-law of the Court of Justice of the European Communities and the Court of First Instance of the European Communities.[11]

and

> The judgments of the EFTA Court are ... as a matter of principle, based on case-law of the Court of Justice of the European Communities concerning provisions of Community law that are identical in substance to the provisions of EEA law which the EFTA Court has to apply, as far as such case-law is available.[12]

Following the entry into force of the Treaty of Lisbon, the EFTA Court has stated in its rulings that the objective of establishing a dynamic and homogeneous European Economic Area can only be achieved if EFTA and EU citizens, as well as

---

[7] See, inter alia, recital 1 of the preamble to the EEA Agreement, which states as one of the aims of the Agreement to achieve 'a Europe based on peace, democracy and human rights'.

[8] See, inter alia, recital 15 in the preamble to the EEA Agreement and Arts 1(1), 102(1), 105 and 106 thereof.

[9] Under Art 2(a) of the EEA Agreement, the term 'Agreement' is understood to mean the main Agreement, its Protocols and Annexes as well as the acts referred to therein.

[10] A similar obligation exists as regards Protocols 1 to 4 and the provisions of the acts corresponding to those listed in Annexes I and II to the Surveillance and Court Agreement; see Art 3 of that Agreement. See also Part VII, Chapter 3, Section 1 of the EEA Agreement on homogeneity. Although that obligation does not include the main text of the Surveillance and Court Agreement, the EFTA Court has nevertheless sought to homogenise the rules governing the procedure before it with those applicable to the procedure before the EU Courts. See N Fenger, 'Limits to a dynamic homogeneity between EC law and EEA law' in *Festskrift til Claus Gulmann. Liber Amicorum* (Copenhagen, Thomson, 2006) 134–135.

[11] *Legal Framework and Case-law*, 3rd edn (Luxembourg, EFTA Court, 2008) p 11, available at www.eftacourt.int.

[12] ibid, point 2.1, p 16.

economic operators enjoy, relying on EEA law, the same rights in both the EU and EFTA pillars of the EEA.[13] Furthermore, according to that Court, the application of the principle of homogeneity cannot be restricted to the interpretation of provisions whose wording is identical in substance to parallel provisions of EU law.[14]

At the EU level the Court of Justice of the European Union (the Court of Justice) has, since the late 1960s, ensured respect for fundamental rights within the sphere of EU law.[15] In this respect, the Court of Justice initially referred to international treaties for the protection of human rights on which the Member States have collaborated or of which they are signatories,[16] before referring more specifically to the ECHR itself.[17] The Court has held that the provisions of the ECHR 'must be taken into consideration in [EU] law',[18] and has later pointed out the 'special significance' of the ECHR.[19] Moreover, the duty to observe fundamental rights applies not only to the EU Institutions but also to the EU Member States when implementing[20] or derogating from[21] EU law. As such, the Court of Justice has held that:

> [T]he Community cannot accept measures which are incompatible with observance of the human rights thus recognized and guaranteed ...

> [The Court of Justice] has no power to examine the compatibility with the [ECHR] of national rules which do not fall within the scope of Community law. On the other hand, where such rules do fall within the scope of Community law, and reference is made to the Court for a preliminary ruling, it must provide all the criteria of interpretation needed by the national court to determine whether those rules are compatible with the fundamental rights the observance of which the Court ensures and which derive in particular from the [ECHR].[22]

Thus, the respect for fundamental rights is well rooted in EU law, with the Court of Justice playing an active role in ensuring its respect.

Now, what about the response from the EFTA Court? As stated above, the case law of the Court of Justice on fundamental rights essentially predates the signature of the EEA Agreement.[23] In accordance with the principle of homogeneity and Article 6 of the EEA Agreement, it is therefore logical that the EFTA Court has also, in its case law, confirmed that fundamental rights must be ensured when implementing EEA law. The EFTA Court has stated that the

---

[13] Judgment of 28 September 2012 in Case E-18/11 *Irish Bank Resolution Corporation v Kaupþing*, para 122.

[14] Judgment of 21 December 2012 in Case E-14/11 *DB Schenker v ESA*, para 78.

[15] See *Stauder* (29/69, EU:C:1969:57), para 7; see also *Internationale Handelsgesellschaft* (11/70, EU:C:1970:114), para 4.

[16] See *Nold v Commission* (4/73, EU:C:1974:51), para 13.

[17] See *Rutili* (36/75, EU:C:1975:137), para 32, and *Hauer* (44/79, EU:C:1979:290), paras 15 and 17.

[18] See *Johnston* (222/84, EU:C:1986:206), para 18.

[19] See, inter alia, *ERT* (C-260/89, EU:C:1991:254), para 41.

[20] See *Wachauf* (5/88, EU:C:1989:321), para 19.

[21] See *ERT* (EU:C:1991:254), paras 43 and 44.

[22] ibid, paras 41 and 42.

[23] The Final Act of the EEA Agreement was signed in Oporto on 2 May 1992.

provisions of the EEA Agreement as well as procedural provisions of the Surveillance and Court Agreement are to be interpreted in the light of fundamental rights ... The provisions of the [ECHR] and the judgments of the European Court of Human Rights are important sources for determining the scope of these rights.[24]

This view has been confirmed in later case law.[25] Although the above-mentioned passage only explicitly refers to the ECHR and the case law of the ECtHR as 'important sources', case law prior to the Charter becoming binding also showed that the EFTA Court referred to judgments (or opinions of Advocates General) of the Court of Justice when interpreting the content of a fundamental right.[26]

Therefore, the adherence to and full effectiveness of the principle of homogeneity also ensures, as a corollary, the respect for fundamental rights.[27] This is but one example of the 'cross-fertilisation' in the field of fundamental rights which is ensured through judicial dialogue.

B. Hypothesis

If the conclusion of what has been stated above is that adherence to the principle of homogeneity has entailed, as a positive side-effect, a respect for fundamental rights in EEA law, what is to be done with the Charter now that it has become fully binding? Is it to be actively opposed, ignored quietly or should the judicial organs of the EFTA pillar of the EEA instead take the bull by the horns and acknowledge the Charter for what it is? The way forward is not obvious, given the basic premise that the Charter has not been incorporated into EEA law. Accordingly, I should like to provide some further observations concerning the Charter to stimulate a discussion on which path to follow.

In the EU pillar, it follows from Article 52(3) of the Charter that it may not provide for a lesser degree of protection than that granted under the ECHR.[28] Accordingly, the Court of Justice is obliged to take into account the case law of the ECtHR when interpreting rights and freedoms contained in the ECHR which correspond to provisions of the Charter.[29] However, for the purpose of the present discussion, it is of even greater interest that the Court of Justice quite readily cited

---

[24] See Judgment of 12 December 2003 in Case E-2/03 *Ásgeirsson and Others*, para 23.

[25] See Judgment of 28 June 2011 in Case E-12/10, *EFTA Surveillance Authority (ESA) v Iceland*, para 60.

[26] See, inter alia, Judgments of 12 June 1998 in Case E-8/97 *TV 1000*, para 26 (referring to *Conegate*, 121/85, EU:C:1986:114), and of 19 June 2003 in Case E-2/02 *Bellona* (referring to the Opinion of Advocate General Jacobs in *Unión de Pequeños Agricultores v Council*, C-50/00 P, EU:C:2002:462).

[27] See, in this respect, C Baudenbacher, 'Sven Norberg and the European Economic Area' in *Liber Amicorum in Honour of Sven Norberg. A European for all seasons* (Brussels, Bruylant, 2006), 43.

[28] The explanation to Art 52(3) of the Charter—which must be interpreted 'with due regard to' Art 6(1) TEU—indeed provides that 'the level of protection afforded by the Charter may never be lower than that guaranteed by the ECHR'.

[29] As for provisions of *national* law which provide for a higher level of protection of fundamental rights, see *Melloni* (C-399/11, EU:C:2013:107).

provisions of the ECHR and referred to case law of the Strasbourg Court even at a time where *no* statutory rule such as Article 52(3) of the Charter determined the legal status of the ECHR in EU law. Indeed, the system set up under the ECHR is—at least in formal terms—still an autonomous body of law, entirely distinct from EU law and will remain so, even when the EU accedes to the ECHR as foreseen in Article 6(2) TEU.[30] However, this did not prevent the Court of Justice from placing special emphasis on the ECHR when faced with situations involving potential breaches of fundamental rights. Truly, why should it not have regard for the findings of an international yet equally European court specialising in human rights?[31] Such cross-fertilisation in the field of fundamental rights is in no way an unknown phenomenon, but appears rather to be a positive by-product of the constructive judicial dialogue which takes place amongst the manifold courts and tribunals of Europe, whether at national, supranational or international level.[32]

This, however, begs the question as to which added value the Charter may bring to the equation. Insofar as rights and freedoms corresponding to the ECHR are concerned, why is it necessary to refer to the charter or even to acknowledge it? That issue may, however, have been raised too late. By the same logic, one would also have to question why it was necessary for the EFTA Court to refer, in its case law, to the ECHR which—at least formally speaking—forms part of a legal order which is distinct from EEA law. As noted elsewhere, the EFTA Court has already integrated fundamental rights into the EEA legal order, even where this was not explicitly mandated by provisions of the EEA legal order to preserve the homogeneity imposed by Article 6 EEA and Article 3(2) of the Surveillance and Court Agreement.[33] Actually, President Baudenbacher has acknowledged that the

---

[30] In accordance with Art 6(2) TEU, accession 'shall not affect the Union's competences as defined in the Treaties'. Furthermore, according to Art 1 of the Protocol (No 8) relating to Art 6(2) of the Treaty on European Union on the accession of the Union to the European Convention on the Protection of Human Rights and Fundamental Freedoms (OJ 2012 C 326, p 273), the agreement on accession 'shall make provision for preserving the specific characteristics of the Union and Union law'. Moreover, Declaration No 2 on Art 6(2) of the Treaty on European Union, annexed to the final act of the inter-governmental conference which adopted the Treaty of Lisbon (consolidated version 2012, OJ 2012 C 326, p 339), states that the specific features of EU law must be preserved when arranging for the accession to the ECHR.

[31] As for the EFTA Court, it has been noted that it undertakes the 'process of assessing the status of a fundamental right through looking into various other legal orders', see T Burri and B Pirker, 'Constitutionalization by Association? The Doubtful Case of the European Economic Area' (2013) 32 *Yearbook of European Law* 1, 217.

[32] It is not a new occurrence that, through the medium of EU law, national legal systems have been more readily exposed to the effective enforcement of the ECHR. As a recent example thereof, see Case C-617/10 *Åkerberg Fransson* EU:C:2013:280, and the decision of the Swedish Supreme Court of 16 July 2013 in Case Ö 1526-13 *JS v Riksåklagaren*; and also J Rozenberg, 'Never mind human rights law, EU law is much more powerful', *The Guardian*, 9 October 2013 (available at http://www.theguardian.com/law/2013/oct/09/human-rights-eu-law-powerful), referring to the decision of the UK Employment Appeals Tribunal of 4 October 2013 in the cases of *Janah v Libya* and *Benkharbouche v Sudan*, UKEAT/0401/12/GE & UKEAT/0020/13/GE. See also T Jensen, 'Domstolskontrollen med overholdelse af grundrettigheder' [1995] *Ugeskrift for Retsvæsen* B p 241 at 247.

[33] See Fenger, above n 9, p 138.

EFTA Court was not obliged to express itself on the issue in *Bellona*.[34] However, the acknowledgement by the EFTA Court of the ECHR and the case law of the Strasbourg Court as an important motor of human rights has not appeared to give rise to the same degree of controversy.[35] Rather, it is the *extent* of that protection which has caused some debate.[36]

Against that background, I would simply point to the fact that, owing to their common objectives, EEA law is far more closely intertwined with EU law than with the ECHR system set up under the auspices of the Council of Europe.[37] The EFTA Court has itself held that one of the main objectives of the EEA Agreement is to create a homogeneous EEA, and that that objective has consistently guided the jurisprudence of the Court as well as that of the Court of Justice.[38] In the EU pillar of the EEA this is attested by the fact that, where relevant, the case law of the EFTA Court is cited by the EU Courts.[39] Therefore, in theory at least, one can hardly criticise the EFTA Court for seeking inspiration from the way in which a bill of rights, which includes provisions corresponding to the ECHR, has been interpreted and applied in the context of disputes of an economic law nature involving proceedings strikingly similar to that in which that Court operates.[40] If the EFTA Court were to deny the Charter any value whatsoever for purely formal reasons when interpreting a particular fundamental right that would necessarily entail as a corollary that it could no longer refer to the more recent case law of the Court of Justice either. Readers familiar with the case law of the Court of Justice will have realised that the Charter is now the principal guideline on the basis of which the Court of Justice carries out its task of ensuring that in the interpretation and application of EU law fundamental rights are observed.[41] Such a move would constitute a rather absurd retrogression.

---

[34] C Baudenbacher, 'Fundamental Rights in EEA Law' in S Breitenmoser et al, Human Rights, Domocracy and the Rule of Law. Liber amicorum Luzius Wildhaber (Zürich/St Gallen, DIKE/Nomos, 2007) p 87.

[35] See, eg, Fredriksen, above n 4, p 382.

[36] David Thór Björgvinsson takes the basic view that 'it would require highly sophisticated legal acrobatics … to arrive at the conclusion that the protection of fundamental rights within the EEA legal order is equivalent to the one offered by the ECHR'; see 'EC Law, EEA Law and the ECHR' in *Liber Amicorum in Honour of Sven Norberg. A European for all seasons* (Brussels, Bruylant, 2006) p 98.

[37] Recital 2 in the preamble to the EEA Agreement refers to a 'privileged relationship between the European Community, its Member States and the EFTA States, which is based on proximity, long-standing common values and European identity'.

[38] See Judgment of 23 November 2004 in Case E-1/04 *Fokus Bank*, para 22.

[39] See, for a recent example, *Content Services* (C-49/11, EU:C:2012:419), para 45. As for the application of the principle of homogeneity by the EU Courts, see *Opel Austria v Council* (T-115/94, EU:T:1997:3), para 49.

[40] This should not be taken to mean that the ECtHR does not also occasionally issue rulings within the sphere of economic law. See, eg, *A Menarini Diagnostics SRL v Italy*, No 43509/08, 27 September 2011 (referred to in the Judgment of the EFTA Court of 23 November 2004 in Case E-15/10 *Posten Norge v ESA*, para 88).

[41] See, eg, Discussion document of the Court of Justice of the European Union of 5 May 2010 on certain aspects of the accession of the European Union to the European Convention for the Protection of Human Rights and Fundamental Freedoms, point 2, and Joint Communication from Presidents J-P Costa and V Skouris of 24 January 2011, point 1. Both documents available on the website of the Court of Justice (http://www.curia.europa.eu/).

Furthermore, as has been rightly observed elsewhere,[42] provisions of secondary EU law which have been incorporated into EEA law may, at times, contain a reference to the Charter in their preamble.[43] Absent the specific exclusion of any recitals to that effect during the process of incorporation into EEA law, it is unclear how the EFTA Court could simply ignore such recitals.

Lastly, EEA law itself provides, in certain specific—and admittedly limited—situations, for the possibility of referring a matter to the Court of Justice.[44] In such cases, it is patently clear that the Charter may be *directly* relevant for EEA law.

Paradoxically, the question would therefore rather seem to be: why ought the EFTA Court *not* refer to the Charter?

As for rights of the Charter which *do not* mirror provisions of the ECHR, the situation may admittedly be somewhat different.[45] I will revert to this issue below at point IV.B. Before that, however, I will take a look at the position adopted in respect of the Charter by the relevant players on the EFTA legal scene.

III. THE PRACTICAL APPROACH: HOW HAVE STAKEHOLDERS REACTED?

Even if it would seem natural for the EFTA Court to take the Charter into account, it remains to be seen whether the observations and predictions made above have been confirmed in practice. I will therefore take a closer look at how the EFTA stakeholders have reacted, based on information which is publicly available. It should, however, be borne in mind that the Charter only became binding within the EU pillar at the end of 2009, that is to say, less than five years ago. This may perhaps not be sufficient time for the relevant players to adopt a settled position on this issue.

In the following, I will examine the extent to which the Charter is referred to in proceedings before the EFTA Court by (i) private parties; (ii) the EFTA States; (iii) the EFTA Surveillance Authority (ESA); and (iv) the EFTA Court itself. However, as a point of order, it goes without saying that the statements of private parties, the EFTA States and ESA in no way bind the EFTA Court.

---

[42] See Fredriksen, above n 4, p 378ff.

[43] An important example is to be found in recital 31 in the preamble to Directive 2004/38/EC of the European Parliament and of the Council of 29 April 2004 on the right of citizens of the Union and their family members to move and reside freely within the territory of the Member States (OJ 2004 L 158, p 77), as amended and corrected (the 'Citizenship Directive').

[44] See, eg, Art 111(3) of the EEA Agreement regarding the possibility to refer a dispute which has not been settled by the EEA Joint Committee to the Court of Justice. See also Art 6(2) of Protocol No 24 to that Agreement on challenges brought by EFTA States to the Court of Justice against decisions of the European Commission in the field of concentrations.

[45] On this issue, see also Fredriksen, above n 4, p 383ff.

A. Private Parties Appearing before the EFTA Court

Not surprisingly, perhaps, private parties appearing before the EFTA Court *do* frequently rely on the Charter when putting their case to the judges.[46] A simple explanation for this would be an attempt to bolster one's legal arguments, in particular where the EU Courts have had the opportunity to deal with a similar issue raised in the context of the Charter.

More surprising, however, is the fact that those parties have, at least on one occasion, referred to the Charter even prior to it gaining the force of law in the EU pillar.[47] One reason could be that, at the time, the issue which arose in that case was subject to a lively dialogue in both case law and academic literature.[48]

B. EFTA States

Unlike private parties the EFTA States may not readily be accused of invoking something like the Charter simply to bolster their case, and it is also clear that they have not yet taken a uniform view on the legal impact of the Charter on EEA law in proceedings before the EFTA Court. On the one hand, *Norway* has stated that

> [t]he Kingdom of Norway agrees with ESA that the Court need not address the Charter in the present case. It observes that the Charter has not been incorporated into the EEA Agreement and consequently asserts that it lacks direct relevance for the interpretation of the Agreement.[49]

Whereas the first sentence of that statement is ambivalent in nature, the second sentence is rather more straightforward. In the view of the Norwegian Government, the formal lack of binding effect entails, as a consequence, the lack of 'direct relevance' in EEA law, as it was put to the Court. It is not clear from that statement whether that government would agree that the Charter could have any indirect or secondary relevance. In a memorandum issued by the Norwegian Government on the impact of the Treaty of Lisbon on that EFTA State, that government states that '[t]he fact that the Charter is made legally binding for the

---

[46] See, eg, Order of the President of the EFTA Court of 30 April 2013 in Case E-4/13 *DB Schenker v ESA*, para 8; the report for the hearing in Case E-7/12 *DB Schenker v ESA*, paras 35 and 38; the report for the hearing in Case E-8/12 *DB Schenker v ESA*, paras 110 and 111; the report for the hearing in Case E-5/13 *Schenker North and Others v ESA*, para 69 (all three referring to Art 42 of the Charter on the right of access to documents); and the report for the hearing in Case E-6/09 *Magasin- og Ukepresseforeningen v* ESA, fn 17 (where the applicant referred to Art 41 of the Charter concerning the right to good administration).

[47] See Judgment of 19 June 2003 in Case E-2/02 *Technologien Bau- und Wirtschaftsberatung GmbH and Bellona Foundation v ESA*, para 28, in respect of Art 47 of the Charter concerning the right to effective judicial protection and, more specifically, access to justice.

[48] That discussion concerned whether, in the light of the Opinion of Advocate General Jacobs in *Unión de Pequeños Agricultores v Council* (EU:C:2002:462), the conditions governing access to court for private applicants who were not the addressees of a decision should be loosened.

[49] See the report for the hearing in Case E-12/10 *ESA v Iceland*, para 163.

EU Member States will hardly have any particular effects on Norway'.[50] Although apparently dismissive of any impact that the Charter might have on Norway, the use of the word 'hardly' in that statement nevertheless does not go so far as to exclude *all* thinkable forms of indirect or ancillary effects.

On the other hand, *Iceland* has relied directly on the Charter in infringement proceedings brought against it.[51] More specifically, Iceland has stated that

> it would be unacceptable as a matter of both national policy and EEA law that workers be afforded less protection under EEA law than under EU law. In this respect, [Iceland] refers to Article 9 TFEU and Article 31 of [the Charter].

It would appear from this statement that it was the principle of homogeneity that formed the basis of Iceland's arguments in respect of the Charter. Moreover, it should be pointed out that Iceland relied on Article 31 of the Charter (on the right to fair and just working conditions) and Article 34 thereof (concerning social security and social assistance). Those provisions do not appear to correspond to comparable provisions of the ECHR.

This difference in view between the two governments is paradoxical. The fact that the procedure in question involved infringement proceedings against Iceland may perhaps explain why that State relied directly on the Charter. However, seeing as Norway intervened in that case in support of Iceland, it still remains rather inexplicable how one EFTA State would argue directly on the basis of the Charter, whilst the other would take a diametrically opposite view.

C. ESA

ESA's views on the legal status of the Charter in EEA law seem to be rather opaque. In the infringement proceedings against Iceland referred to above, ESA has argued that

> ESA submits that Article 34 of the Charter, as referred to by Iceland, concerns the right to social security and social assistance in accordance with Community and national law … In any case, ESA is of the opinion that for the purposes of this case it is unnecessary to examine in detail the relationship to provisions of the Charter.[52]

The view put forward by ESA only testifies to the lack of relevance of the Charter *in concreto*, and does not even imply any view on its legal significance in general. A less informed view would perhaps be to argue that it was in ESA's interest if this point were to be left deliberately open to interpretation.

However, subsequent to the Charter becoming legally binding, in a request for intervention in a case before the General Court, ESA has successfully argued that

---

[50] See memorandum of 14 July 2009 issued by the European Policy Section of the Norwegian Ministry of Foreign Affairs, p 32, available at http://www.regjeringen.no/upload/UD/Vedlegg/Europa/090714_Lisboa-traktaten_Virkninger_for_Norge.pdf (unofficial translation).

[51] See the report for the hearing in Case E-12/10 *ESA v Iceland*, para 92.

[52] ibid, para 89.

the case concerns, inter alia, the interpretation of Council Regulation (EC) No 1/2003 of 16 December 2002 on the implementation of the rules on competition laid down in Articles 81 and 82 [EC] (OJ 2003 L 1, p 1), of the [Charter] ... and of the [ECHR] ...

it is clear from the case-law of the EFTA Court that the stipulations of the EEA Agreement must be interpreted in the light of fundamental rights, of which the ECHR and the case-law of the European Court of Human Rights are important sources of interpretation.[53]

Although ESA only explicitly refers to the ECHR and the case law of the ECtHR as an important source of interpretation of fundamental rights in EEA law, that does not as such exclude the idea that the Charter could also serve as such a source. Indeed, the contrary would appear to be true. After all, ESA's request to intervene in the case at hand—which was a domestic EU matter—was essentially based on the proper application of the principle of homogeneity within the field of fundamental rights.

Furthermore, ESA has also relied, in proceedings before the EFTA Court, on the case law of the Court of Justice applying the Charter and specifically mentioned a particular provision thereof.[54] Lastly, ESA has moreover found it unnecessary to distinguish between rights in the Charter and identical or similar rights contained in the ECHR, choosing instead to refer to both.[55]

D. The EFTA Court

From the outset, it is interesting to note that in the above-mentioned infringement proceedings in Case E-12/10 *ESA v Iceland*, the EFTA Court did not mention the Charter at all in its judgment of 28 June 2011. This in spite of the observations submitted on this matter by Norway, Iceland and ESA.

However, that did not last long. Not even a month later, the EFTA Court stated, in its judgment of 26 July 2011 in Case E-4/11 *Arnulf Clauder*, at paragraph 49:

Finally, it should be recalled that all the EEA States are parties to the ECHR, which enshrines in Article 8(1) the right to respect for private and family life. According to

---

[53] See the Order in *Deutsche Bahn and Others v Commission* (T-289/11, EU:T:2012:20) paras 10 and 11.

[54] An example of this can be found in the Order of the President of the EFTA Court of 30 April 2013 in Case E-4/13 *Schenker North and Others v ESA*, para 19, where ESA referred to the order of the President of the Court of Justice of 19 February 2013 in *Commission v EnBW Energie Baden-Württemberg* (C-365/12 P, EU:C:2013:643) regarding Art 47 of the Charter on effective judicial protection.

[55] See the report for the hearing in Case E-5/13 *Schenker North and Others v ESA*, para 154, regarding the right to protection of professional secrets which flows from Art 7 of the Charter and the corresponding provision in Art 8 of the ECHR. At that same paragraph, ESA furthermore refers to case law of the General Court on this issue. Interestingly, one of those cases does not mention Art 8 of the ECHR but only Art 7 of the Charter, see the Order in *InterMune UK and Others v EMA* (T-73/13 R, EU:T:2013:222).

established case-law, provisions of the EEA Agreement are to be interpreted in the light of fundamental rights (see, for example, Case E-2/03 *Ásgeirsson* [2003] EFTA Ct Rep 18, paragraph 23, and Case E-12/10 *EFTA Surveillance Authority v Iceland*, judgment of 28 June 2011, not yet reported, paragraph 60 and the case-law cited). *The Court notes that in the European Union the same right is protected by Article 7 of the Charter of Fundamental Rights* (emphasis added).

Considering that none of the parties seem to have referred to the Charter in their submissions it is not evident why the EFTA Court referred to the Charter at all. One reason could be that the *Clauder* judgment came as the answer to a request for an advisory opinion under Article 34 of the Surveillance and Court Agreement for interpretation of Article 16 of the Citizenship Directive, as adapted into EEA law. As mentioned above, the preamble to that directive refers explicitly to the Charter,[56] which may have prompted the EFTA Court to mention the Charter in its judgment.

Not long after, the EFTA Court referred again to the Charter in its judgment in Case E-15/10 *Posten Norge v ESA*, judgment of 18 April 2012 where the EFTA Court held at paragraph 86:

> The principle of effective judicial protection including the right to a fair trial, which is inter alia enshrined in Article 6 ECHR, is a general principle of EEA law. *It may be noted that expression to the principle of effective judicial protection is now also given by Article 47 of the Charter of Fundamental Rights of the European Union* (see on the latter point Case C-389/10 P *KME v Commission*, judgment of 8 December 2011, not yet reported, paragraph 119; and concerning the right of access to justice, Case E-2/02 *Bellona* [2003] EFTA Ct Rep 52, paragraph 36 and Case E-3/11 *Sigmarsson* [2011] EFTA Ct Rep 430, paragraph 29) (emphasis added).

It may, however, be noted that in this case (concerning an action for annulment of a decision finding an abuse of a dominant position) Posten Norge (according to the report for the hearing) did in fact rely on the Charter—yet on an altogether different provision thereof.[57]

The provisions of the Charter to which the EFTA Court made reference in both *Clauder* and *Posten Norge* concerned rights which were not only protected under the Charter, but also the ECHR (Articles 6 and 8 ECHR). The EFTA Court emphasised in *Clauder* that all EEA States are party to that convention. Both judgments express the idea that the Charter mirrors general principles of EEA law: in *Clauder*, the Court referred to 'the same right', and the *Posten Norge* judgment uses

---

[56] See recital 31 in the preamble to the Citizenship Directive, which states that '[t]his Directive respects the fundamental rights and freedoms and observes the principles recognised in particular by the Charter of Fundamental Rights of the European Union. In accordance with the prohibition of discrimination contained in the Charter, Member States should implement this Directive without discrimination between the beneficiaries of this Directive on grounds such as sex, race, colour, ethnic or social origin, genetic characteristics, language, religion or beliefs, political or other opinion, membership of an ethnic minority, property, birth, disability, age or sexual orientation'.

[57] *Posten Norge* referred to Art 36 on services of general economic interest; see fn 101 of the report for the hearing.

the terms 'now also'. However, it is worth pointing out that in *Posten Norge*, the EFTA Court—like ESA—did not only rely on the Charter, but also on the case law of the EU Courts applying the Charter (as well as the ECHR), and on Opinions issued in such cases by the Advocates General.[58]

E. Confirmation of the Hypothesis?

In the hypothesis stated above, I raised the question why the EFTA Court should decline to refer to the Charter. An empiric analysis of the—admittedly rather limited—data available on the matter has shown that private parties, one EFTA State, ESA and the EFTA Court itself have relied on the Charter in legal proceedings before that Court. Thus, so far, so good—the prognosis of the relevance of the Charter seems to be confirmed.

However, whether the reference to the Charter made by the EFTA Court is more than a purely symbolic gesture of goodwill remains to be seen. On both occasions when the EFTA Court referred to the Charter, the provisions in question mirrored those of the ECHR. Far from being ground-breaking, the reference made to the Charter in those cases seems rather uncontroversial. In fact, it appears as if the references are couched in such a way as to avoid giving the impression that the Charter has any real 'bite'. When the EFTA Court 'notes' that Article x of the Charter exists, it is therefore merely stating the obvious. Unlike with the ECHR, it does not directly state that the Charter is an 'important source' for the protection of fundamental rights, although that might perhaps be inferred from the fact that the level of protection under the Charter is at least the same.

However, one revealing fact is that the EFTA Court does not only refer to the Charter, but also to the case law applying it. First, this testifies to the continuing relevance of the case law of the EU Courts on fundamental rights, irrespective of the Charter becoming binding. However, it also shows that the Charter will undeniably have some practical, albeit indirect, effect on EEA law. Indeed, as mentioned above, the Charter has swiftly become of paramount importance in the recent case law of the Court of Justice. Although it may seem a negligible aspect on the face of it, a reference to a decision of an EU Court applying the Charter in reality also implies some sort of recognition of the way in which the protection which that document confers has evolved since it has become legally binding.

---

[58] See the reference made by the EFTA Court at paras 88 and 91 of its judgment in *Posten Norge* to points 64 and 67 of the Opinion of Advocate General Sharpston in *KME and Others v Commission* (C-272/09 P, EU:C:2011:810). The Advocate General referred specifically, at point of 67 her Opinion, to the Charter. In addition, in *Posten Norge*, the EFTA Court referred to points 81 to 83 and 196 of the Opinion of Advocate General Kokott in *Solvay v Commission* (C-110/10 P, EU:C:2011:257), which in turn contains a reference to the Charter in point 83 thereof.

IV. A 'RIGHT' CONUNDRUM

The discussion so far has broached the issue as to whether a particular right in the Charter corresponds to a right in the Convention. That issue warrants certain further remarks.

From the outset, I would point out that a helpful (albeit non-binding) list has been drawn up in the explanations relating to Article 52(3) of the Charter.[59] That list provides assistance when determining whether a given Charter right corresponds to a right under the ECHR or, as the case may be, offers wider protection than under the latter.

A. Charter Rights which Correspond to Rights in the ECHR

As for *rights in the Charter which correspond in their entirety to rights in the ECHR*, referring to the Charter in an EEA law context appears to be wholly unproblematic. In that instance, the Charter is nothing more, nothing less than the Convention.

Where the protection which flows from the Charter *is greater than under the ECHR*, two remarks should be made.

First, the aim of the EEA Agreement is, according to Article 1 thereof, to provide for equal conditions of competition and the respect of the same rules with a view to creating a homogeneous European Economic Area. It would make for a lop-sided European Economic Area if the level of protection afforded in the EFTA pillar of the EEA Agreement somehow were to remain at the 'lower' level—as provided for under the Convention—in comparison to the EU pillar of the agreement which applies a 'higher' level of protection on the basis of the Charter.[60]

Second, the judicial organs of the EEA legal community need not fear that the possible greater protection provided under EU law should somehow be unjustified or arbitrary. In this connection, I would call to mind that when interpreting the provisions of the ECHR, the Strasbourg Court regularly also takes into consideration the provisions of the Charter.[61] It does so, amongst other things, to ascertain whether the requirements of modern-day society call for a greater level of protection under the convention regime.[62] The Strasbourg Court refers to the Charter even where the Contracting State allegedly responsible for a breach of fun-

---

[59] OJ 2007 C 303, pp 33–34.

[60] The reverse would also be true, I might add. Indeed, nothing prevents the EFTA Court from being a 'first-mover' in how the Charter should be interpreted in a given matter.

[61] See, eg, *GN v Italy*, No 43134/05, § 126, 1 December 2009; *Harkins and Edwards v United Kingdom*, Nos 9146/07 and 32650/07, § 127, 17 January 2012; *Hirsi Jamaa and Others v Italy* [GC], No 27765/09, § 134, 23 February 2012; *Babar Ahmad and Others v United Kingdom*, Nos 24027/07, 11949/08, 36742/08, 66911/09 and 67354/09, § 175, 10 April 2012; and *X v Latvia* [GC], No 27853/09, § 97, 26 November 2013.

[62] Eg concerning the sometimes sensitive issue of legal recognition of same-sex marriage, see *Schalk and Kopf v Austria*, No 30141/04, §§ 60 and 61, 24 June 2010.

damental rights is not an EU Member State—or for that matter an EFTA State.[63] It has furthermore referred to provisions of the Charter prior to it becoming legally binding in EU law[64] and even earlier than the Court of Justice.[65] This is but another example of judicial cross-fertilisation in the area of fundamental rights.

In this case, too, I therefore see no reason why the EFTA Court might not have regard to the Charter and its application—even though it has no formal duty to do so.

B. Charter Rights which do not Correspond to Rights in the ECHR

This leaves us with the rights in the Charter *which do not correspond* to rights contained in the ECHR. How does one deal with them? What status do they have in EEA law? In my view, that very much depends on the particular right.

To begin with, it is necessary to determine *whether the right at issue is at all relevant in an EEA context.* Clearly, that is not the case for some provisions of the Charter. Article 39 thereof, for instance, provides for the right to vote and to stand as a candidate at elections to the European Parliament. Apart from expressing the general idea of democracy, I do not see the relevance of such a provision in an EEA context. The same would apply to Article 43 of the Charter concerning the right to refer to the European Ombudsman cases of maladministration; Article 44 on the Right to petition the European Parliament; and Article 46 on diplomatic and consular protection. If a particular right is *hors sujet* in an EEA context, then it has no legal relevance at all, whether direct or indirect.

Other rights are obviously relevant in an EEA context, such as Article 45 on freedom of movement. That is furthermore the case even though that Charter provision only refers to EU citizens. In this connection, it should be recalled that under Article 52(2) thereof, the right to freedom of movement is to be exercised according to the rules of the FEU Treaty (rules with which the EFTA Court is obviously familiar).

In other cases, the relevance of a Charter provision must be determined on a case-by-case basis. To that end, I will provide the following views.

First, whether those provisions are judicially cognisable on their own as 'free-standing provisions' is in no way certain.[66] By this, I obviously refer to the distinction operated in Article 52(5) of the Charter, read in conjunction with the last sentence of the preamble thereto, between 'rights' (and 'freedoms') on the one hand,

---

[63] See, eg, *Bayatyan v Armenia* [GC], No 23459/03, §§ 106 to 109; 7 July 2011; and *Demir and Baykara v Turkey* [GC], No 34503/97, §§ 80, 105 and 150, 12 November 2008.

[64] See *Demir and Baykara v Turkey* [GC], No 34503/97, §§ 80, 105 and 150, 12 November 2008; and *Scoppola v Italy (No 2)* [GC], No 10249/03, § 105, 17 September 2009.

[65] See *Goodwin v United Kingdom* [GC], No 20957/95, § 100, 11 July 2002.

[66] See, eg, *Association de médiation sociale* (C-176/12, EU:C:2014:2), para 48, where the Court of Justice held that Article 27 of the Charter (on the right of workers to be informed and consulted) could not be relied on directly in the proceedings before the national court.

and 'principles' on the other.[67] That distinction is not straightforward. Many of the provisions of the Charter have yet to be interpreted by the Court of Justice, which remains, it should be emphasised, the final authority in the interpretation thereof.

Second, although not mirrored in the ECHR, certain provisions of the Charter are nevertheless not alien to the EEA Agreement. By way of example, I would refer in this respect to Article 38 of the Charter on consumer protection, which finds an echo in recital 12 of the preamble to the EEA Agreement and Chapter II of Part V thereof. The same can be said of Article 37 of the Charter on protection of the environment, which is reflected in recitals 9 and 10 of the preamble to the EEA Agreement and Chapter III of Part V. It would therefore not be wholly unthinkable for the EFTA Court to pay attention to developments in case law in respect of those Charter provisions (however, whether they can be relied upon directly is, as mentioned above, an altogether different matter).

Personally, I believe that Case E-12/10 *ESA v Iceland* illustrates this second point rather well. In that case, the provisions relied upon by Iceland, namely Article 31 of the Charter (on the right to fair and just working conditions) and Article 34 thereof (concerning social security and social assistance), both concern topics which fall within this grey area. For instance, social security is coordinated, across the entire EEA, by Regulation No 883/2004,[68] and Article 7(2) of Regulation No 492/2011[69] lays down the principle of non-discrimination of workers across that same area in respect of social advantages. Moreover, Annex XVIII contains a list of EU legislation on health and safety at work, labour law, and equal treatment for men and women,[70] and further Community acts on social policy are to be found in Protocol No 31 to the EEA Agreement. In addition, the EFTA Court has, in the past, paid due regard to the (Community) Charter of the Fundamental Social Rights of Workers, annexed to the Final Act to the EEA Agreement.[71] Here it should be recalled that some of the provisions laid down in the Charter of the Fundamental Social Rights of Workers have been reaffirmed in the Charter.[72]

---

[67] According to the explanations relating to Art 52(5) of the Charter, Arts 25, 26 and 37 of the Charter fall under the category of 'principles', and Arts 23, 33 and 34 contain both elements of 'rights' and 'principles'. Having said this, I will limit myself to refer to the extensive analysis undertaken by Advocate General Cruz Villalón in his Opinion in *Association de médiation sociale* (EU:C:2014:2). See also my Opinion in *Pohotovosť* (C-470/12, EU:C:2014:101), point 66 and fn 39.

[68] Regulation (EC) No 883/2004 of the European Parliament and of the Council of 29 April 2004 on the coordination of social security systems (OJ 2004 L 166, p 1), as amended. That regulation is listed in Annex VI to the EEA Agreement.

[69] Regulation (EU) No 492/2011 of the European Parliament and of the Council of 5 April 2011 on freedom of movement for workers within the Union (codification) (OJ 2011 L 141, p 1). That regulation is listed in Annex V to the EEA Agreement.

[70] Such as Council Directive 89/391/EEC of 12 June 1989 on the introduction of measures to encourage improvements in the safety and health of workers at work (OJ 1989 L 183, p 1), as corrected and amended, or Directive 2003/88/EC of the European Parliament and of the Council of 4 November 2003 concerning certain aspects of the organisation of working time (OJ 2003 L 299, p 9).

[71] See, eg, Judgment of 22 March 2002 in Case E-00 *Norwegian Federation of Trade Unions and Others v Norwegian Association of Local and Regional Authorities and Others*, para 43.

[72] See, eg, Art 31(2) of the Charter regarding, among others, the right to an annual period of paid leave. The explanations relating to that provision refer to point 8 in the Community Charter of the

Seen from this perspective—and perhaps contrary to others[73]—I see no reason to take the view that the Charter is of no relevance whatsoever when interpreting an act of secondary EU legislation which has been incorporated into EEA law, even where that right is not comparable to a right under the ECHR. On the contrary, to me it would seem natural to look at the Charter and the case law giving effect thereto in the above-mentioned areas *as an important source for determining the scope of the fundamental rights protected under EEA law.*

V. CONCLUDING REMARKS

To conclude, both a theoretical and an empirical analysis seem to indicate that despite not being incorporated into EEA law, the Charter and, in particular, the case law of the Court of Justice interpreting it cannot be outright excluded as a relevant source when determining the scope of fundamental rights protection under EEA law. This would seem to be a rather more positive outcome of homogeneity than what was predicted some 20 years ago.[74] A reason for this might be the cross-fertilisation of fundamental rights across the various European legal orders. However, the exact extent to which the Charter is relevant, in particular, to the EFTA pillar of the EEA legal order can only be decided by the relevant players in that legal community, notably the EFTA Court.

Time will tell whether the Charter will actually be incorporated into EEA law. Meanwhile, the situation in which the EEA finds itself at present brings to mind the period of time which began with the proclamation of the Charter in Nice on 7 December 2000 and ended with it becoming legally binding following the entry into force on 1 December 2009 of the Treaty of Lisbon. Indeed, during that period, despite its non-binding status, the Charter was referred to by the General Court,[75] by Advocates General,[76] and ultimately also by the Court of Justice.[77]

Fundamental Social Rights of Workers. The Court of Justice has furthermore qualified that provision of the Charter as affirming an important principle of EU social law; see, eg, *Commission v Strack* (C-579/12 RX II, EU:C:2013:570), para 15.

[73] For a different view, see Fredriksen, above n 4, p 385.

[74] See N Wahl, '"Relevanta" avgöranden av EG-domstolen' in J Rosén (ed), *EES-avtalet i svensk rätt. Arbetsstätt, bolagsrätt, immaterialrätt och medierätt—EES-avtalets bakgrund, utformning och tolkning— betydelsen av EG-domstolens praxis* (Stockholm, Juristförlaget, 1993) 181.

[75] See, eg, *max.mobil v Commission* (T-54/99, EU:T:2002:20), at paras 48 and 57, and *Jégo-Quéré v Commission* (T-177/01, EU:T:2002:112), paras 42 and 47.

[76] See, eg, point 97 of the Opinion of Advocate General Mischo in *D and Sweden v Council* (C-122/99 P and C-125/99 P), EU:C:2001:304; point 39 of the Opinion of Advocate General Jacobs in *Unión de Pequeños Agricultores v Council* (EU:C:2002:462); points 59 and 110 and fnn 51 and 58 of the Opinion of Advocate General Geelhoed in *Baumbast and R* (C-413/99, EU:C:2002:493); points 51, 73, 78, 80 to 86 and 89, and fnn 50 to 52 of the Opinion of Advocate General Léger in *Council v Hautala* (C-353/99 P, EU:C:2001:661); and fn 29 of the Opinion of Advocate General Stix-Hackl in *Carpenter* (C-60/00, EU:C:2002:434).

[77] See *Parliament v Council* (C-540/03, EU:C:2006:429), para 38. See also *Salzgitter Mannesmann v Commission* (C-411/04 P, EU:C:2006:548), para 50; *Advocaten voor de Wereld* (C-303/05,

Some of these references to the Charter, perhaps most typically those made by the Court of Justice, can be explained—at least in part—by the fact that the Charter was mentioned in the preamble to the act of secondary legislation at issue in those cases.[78] And so the same explanation might be offered as to why the EFTA Court found it relevant to refer for the first time to the Charter in *Clauder*, despite the fact that none of the parties having submitted observations to the Court had made any mention of it.

EU:C:2007:261), para 46; *Laval un Partneri* (C-341/05, EU:C:2007:809), paras 90 and 91; and *Kadi and Al Barakaat International Foundation v Council and Commission* (C-402/05 P and C-415/05 P, EU:C:2008:461), para 335.

[78] Recitals in the preambles to acts of secondary legislation referring to the Charter were mentioned, inter alia, in the following judgments: *Sweden v Commission* (C-64/05 P, EU:C:2007:802), para 4; *Sweden and Turco v Council* (C-39/05 P and C-52/05 P, EU:C:2008:374), para 5; *Promusicae* (C-275/06, EU:C:2008:54) para 64; and *Metock and Others* (C-127/08, EU:C:2008:449), para 4.

24

The Essentials

KNUT ALMESTAD

T HE EFTA COURT has passed a milestone marking 20 years of conscientious work for the preservation of the two-pillar structure for surveillance and judicial control in the European Economic Area (EEA).

As we will remember, the EFTA Court emerged from the EEA negotiations as a quite different child than the one originally conceived by its negotiators. The idea of establishing a monolithic structure with a mixed crew, safely harboured as a chamber of the European Court of Justice (ECJ), had to be abandoned because of objections from that Court. Instead should appear a separate EFTA Court to operate on top of the two-pillar structure for surveillance in parallel with the ECJ.

On paper, this solution had some symmetric beauty and it removed some fears on the EFTA side with regard to the constitutionality of the original construction. However, it raised deep concerns whether it would be able to maintain the legal homogeneity required for the good functioning of the EEA market. After all, the EFTA Court would be very small in comparison with its big brother and rather far from current events with its planned location in Geneva. Yet, as an independent court it had to acquire excellence and earn respect commensurate with the precarious importance of the tasks it was to be charged with.

I will try to deal with some of the aspects of the Court's task which I consider most essential for the construction which is unique for the European Economic Area, namely to achieve equal rights for individuals and economic operators in a legal environment where the EFTA States[1] have not ceded legislative or judicial powers to the EEA institutions.

I. HOMOGENEITY

The rewritten text of Section 1 of Chapter 3 of the EEA Agreement's Institutional Provisions, which is entitled 'Homogeneity', reveals very clearly the seriousness of

---

[1] The terms 'EFTA' and 'EFTA States' will throughout this chapter refer to the three EFTA States that are Contracting Parties to the EEA Agreement—Iceland, Liechtenstein and Norway—unless otherwise specified.

these concerns. In fact, Article 105 EEA places the EFTA Court under a kind of tutelage of the EEA Joint Committee. In a language which has a note of harshness seldom to be found elsewhere in the Institutional Provisions of the Agreement,[2] the Committee is told to keep the case law of the two Courts under constant review. If a difference in the case law is brought before the Committee and it does not succeed in preserving the homogeneous interpretation of the Agreement within two months, the dispute settlement procedure in Article 111 EEA may be invoked. The Agreement moreover instructs the EEA Joint Committee to set up a system for exchange of information concerning judgments by the Courts of this two-pillar system.

I think that at this particular juncture it is both appropriate and timely to recognise that the part played by the EFTA Court in establishing legal homogeneity in the EEA has turned out to be quite remarkable. A tell-tale indication is the fact that the Article 105 procedure has never been initiated. The only occasion I can remember this possibility being brought up in the EEA Joint Committee was related to *Finanger*.[3] However, once the relevant Commission service could be convinced that the ECJ would not have ruled differently, the matter was dropped altogether.

Even more important has been the informal dialogue between the EFTA Court and the Courts on the EU side which has developed over the years. A good illustration of the significance of this dialogue emerges from the fact that the ECJ, the General Court and the Advocates General by October last year had made references to the case law of the EFTA Court more than 170 times. This means also that the EFTA Court on a number of issues has had to come out first in clarifying EEA law, such as in *Kellogg's*,[4] where the precautionary principle was applied for the first time. Thus, while it is true that the EFTA Court shall follow the case law of the ECJ given prior to the signature of the Agreement and pay due attention to rulings passed by it after that date, the system obviously also works vice versa.

If there still could be any doubt as to the professionalism and independent resolve of the EFTA Court, its ruling in the *Icesave*[5] case certainly must be regarded as its defining moment. Here the Court, in a highly politicised atmosphere and against most expectations, found inter alia that the relevant legal act simply did not provide for the volume of security necessary for dealing with a crisis of such proportions as that which had struck Iceland. The outcome of this ruling was accepted by the Member States having an active interest, whereas the Commission declared that it would respect it, and it will no doubt have an influence in on-going legislative processes.

---

[2] For comparison, see Art 109, which deals with the cooperation between the European Commission and the EFTA Surveillance Authority in a more even-handed way.

[3] Case E-1/99 *Storebrand Skadeforsikring AS v Veronika Finanger* [1999] EFTA Ct Rep 120.

[4] Case E-3/00 *EFTA Surveillance Authority v The Kingdom of Norway* [2000–2001] EFTA Ct Rep 153.

[5] Case E-16/11 *EFTA Surveillance Authority v Iceland* [2013] EFTA Ct Rep 4.

It is on this festive occasion highly relevant to note that this remarkable record has been achieved against rather heavy odds. During the critical moment for the EEA Agreement and its two-pillar model for surveillance and judicial control which followed the accession of Austria, Finland and Sweden to the European Union the EFTA institutions were radically scaled down. The EFTA States seemed at this time not particularly sensitive to the consequences of the EFTA Surveillance Authority and the EFTA Court no longer being able to fulfil their respective task in a credible manner. In particular, it could be expected that the EEA Joint Committee and the dispute settlement procedure in practice would assume active roles as the ultimate guardians of legal homogeneity and the good functioning of the Agreement. In this case, political and even constitutional issues might easily have arisen in the EFTA States alongside concerns in the EU for the balance and reciprocity of the Agreement.

The EFTA Court emerged in 1995 from the scaling-down process with a total manning of only 15 persons, judges included. There were considerable concerns that this was not sufficient to form critical mass for a sustainable operation on the professional level required. Some found consolation in the fact that the number of cases during the first years probably would be limited. On the other hand, the Court would still have to deal with the full scope of the Agreement without the possibility of having recourse to special expertise.

Whereas the EFTA Surveillance Authority, which in 1995 was dealing with many of the same problems, in later years has had a steady increase in its staff, the staff of the EFTA Court remains virtually the same as in 1995. Its modest proposals for staff increases and organisational changes seem in the EFTA States to have been placed on the back burner.

It is perhaps inevitable that an international court with a mandate to assure the rights of individuals and business operators against an opposing State could escape criticisms for 'legal activism' or, as the EFTA catchphrase goes, for being 'more Catholic than the Pope'. Actually, it was the EFTA Surveillance Authority and its leadership which were first honoured this way. These allegations originated in parliamentary circles as reactions of surprise over the broad scope of the EEA Agreement coupled with frustration over the constant demands from the Authority for timely and consistent implementation of secondary legislation which, according to widespread belief, was not taken too seriously in many EU Member States. Ironically, these concerns were raised at a time when literally hundreds of legal acts awaited their incorporation in the EEA Agreement. The critics were obviously also oblivious of the fact that the EU Regulations were directly applicable and that the direct effect of Directives as a last resort would assure the rights of individuals and enterprises in the EU even without implementing measures.

There also existed in EFTA States a persistent belief that since the EEA Agreement did not aim to pursue the very broad objectives of the EU its provisions had to be interpreted more narrowly, that is, more leniently. As these perceptions found little support in the EFTA Court, the Court eventually also became targeted as being 'more Catholic than the Pope'. The criticisms frequently had a rather unfortunate personal direction which was aggravated when certain members of the legal profession in EFTA States also found it opportune to join the chorus. Regrettably, the same quarters have not displayed any great interest in engaging in comparative studies and proper research which could present an objective picture of the practices of the EFTA Court and the EFTA Surveillance Authority as compared to those of their counterparts in the EU.

At any rate, the verdict of the reviews carried out in recent years by the EU is unequivocally in favour of retaining the EEA as a model for future extensions of its Internal Market to neighbouring States. While it is also frequently concluded that 'the Agreement is working well' despite certain misgivings about backlogs and delays in the inclusion of new relevant legal acts, the EFTA Court and the EFTA Surveillance Authority may have every reason to consider that their part of the mission to maintain legal homogeneity in the EEA has been adequately and efficiently carried out.

II. INDIVIDUAL RIGHTS

During the EEA negotiations many attempts were made to find a general description of the Agreement that would be understandable to both politicians and ordinary people. For some time the Agreement was commonly referred to as an enhanced free trade agreement, which of course is quite misleading. The Agreement was to introduce free circulation as defined by EU law and cover economic relations far beyond what commonly is understood as trade.

Even after the objectives of the Agreement had been clearly formulated in the Preamble and the opening Articles of the Agreement a discussion continued which attempted to find a succinct description of this novel institutional construction that could be explained on the basis of known terms and models in international public law. Obviously, the EEA Agreement has all the hallmarks of being an agreement between equal partners typical of a treaty under public international law. And according to the last recital of its Preamble the Agreement does not restrict the decision-making or the treaty-making powers of the Contracting Parties.

At the same time, the objective of the Agreement was to create an economic area which functioned on the basis of common rules taken over from and maintained by a continuous legislative process in one of the Contracting Parties, which happened to be a supranational entity.

The most difficult challenge was undoubtedly to assure that individuals and economic operators would get equal treatment throughout the EEA not only with regard to the four freedoms and conditions of competition,[6] but that they also should be able to exercise individual rights conferred to them by the Agreement and enjoy judicial protection of these rights in national courts.[7]

---

[6] The penultimate Recital of the Preamble of the Agreement.
[7] The eighth Recital of the Preamble of the Agreement.

The underlying problem was that in the EU such individual rights were partly protected by the doctrine of direct effect of Directives and by the direct applicability of Regulations. The general system of the Agreement seemed to indicate that in the EFTA States protection could only result from adequate incorporation of the relevant provision in the national legal systems. Yet, several people close to the negotiations were concerned that in order to provide equal treatment of individuals and market operators the Agreement must be interpreted to have direct effect.

In practice, basic questions related to the protection of individual rights conferred by the Agreement in the EFTA States had to be clarified by the EFTA Court. Only the question of primacy had been settled with full clarity by the negotiators. Protocol 35 of the Agreement provides that implemented EEA rules shall prevail over other statutory rules in the legal systems of the EFTA States, which also undertook to introduce, if necessary, statutory provisions to ensure such primacy. This obligation has been complied with by all EFTA States.

However, some uncertainty remained whether individual rights derived from EEA rules would be identical to those enjoyed by individuals and economic operators in the EU under the doctrine of direct effect. This question was promptly answered by the EFTA Court in its first judgment[8] by stating that it indeed followed from Protocol 35 that individuals and economic operators should be able to invoke and claim before national courts rights derived from implemented EEA rules, provided that these rules were unconditional and sufficiently precise. Furthermore, this Court in 2002 expressly confirmed that according to Protocol 35 such rules should prevail over other national rules.[9]

Whether the EEA Agreement could produce direct effect remained a question that still needed an answer. The Court of First Instance had in *Opel Austria*[10] already concluded that Article 10 of the Agreement in fact did so in Community law. But that did not necessarily mean that non-implemented EEA law would produce such effect in the EFTA States.

In its landmark ruling in *Sveinbjörnsdóttir*[11] the EFTA Court found that EFTA States would be liable to make good financial loss suffered by private parties as a result of faulty implementation of a Directive on condition similar to those laid down by the European Court of Justice in *Francovich*[12] and *Factortame*.[13] Here the Court declared the EEA Agreement a treaty *sui generis*, with objectives going beyond a traditional free trade agreement, and with a distinct legal order of its own. As a legal basis for its ruling the Court relied on the Agreement's objective of homogeneity and equal treatment of individuals and economic operators.

---

[8] Case E-1/94 *Ravintoloitsijain Liiton Oy Restamark* [1994–1995] EFTA Ct Rep 14.
[9] Case E-1/01 *Hörður Einarsson v The Icelandic State* [2002] EFTA Ct Rep 4.
[10] Case T-115/94 *Opel Austria GmbH v Council of the European Union* [1997] ECR II-39.
[11] Case E-9/97 *Erla María Sveinbjörnsdóttir and The Government of Iceland* [1998] EFTA Ct Rep 95.
[12] Joined Cases C-6/90 and C-9/90 *Andrea Francovich and Daniela Bonifaci and others v The Italian Republic* [1991] ECR I-5357.
[13] Joined Cases C-46/93 and C-48/93 *Brasserie du Pêcheur SA v The Federal Republic of Germany and R v Secretary of State for Transport ex parte Factortame Ltd and Others* [1996] ECR I-1029.

Later, in *Karlsson*[14] the Court not only confirmed the principle of State liability but allowed it to be understood that the principle had general application in case of infringements of the EEA Agreement which cause loss or damage to individuals and economic operators. One the one hand, the Court declared that EEA law does not require that individuals and economic operators be able to rely directly on non-implemented rules before national courts. This would in other words mean that the Agreement by itself does not produce direct effect, which seems to be a reasonable reading of its Protocol 35.

On the other hand, the Court went on to remind national courts that it was inherent in the general objective of the EEA Agreement, hereunder the defence of the right of individuals and the principle of effectiveness in international law, that they consider any relevant element of EEA law, whether implemented or not, when interpreting international law.[15]

These statements have in later judgments been honed to even greater sharpness. In HOB-vín III[16] the Court makes it abundantly clear that when it comes to State liability it is irrelevant whether or not a Directive has been made part of the legal order in an EFTA State, as long it has been incorporated in the EEA Agreement. Individuals and economic operators must be able to invoke this principle as soon as a decision of the EEA Joint Committee becomes applicable. That would follow from the obligations of primary law already implemented in the national legal order.

Obviously, this series of rulings adds a new dimension to the word 'binding' in Article 103 EEA. However, the Court's reminder in *Karlsson* takes us beyond the principle of State liability. National courts, even if they cannot according to Protocol 35 rely directly on the material content of non-implemented EEA rules, must nevertheless in the defence of the rights of individuals and economic operators apply general principles of law embodied or inherent in the Main Agreement which, by the way, has been made part of the legal orders of the EFTA States. Likewise, they will in their interpretation of national rules be bound by long-standing principles of public international law.

Consequently, it should not come as a surprise if a national court finds an ample legal basis for setting aside provisions of national law as inconsistent with primary EEA law and its abundant case law, on terms which are quite identical to a non-implemented Directive, particularly when the defence of individual rights is at issue.

III. LOYALTY

Article 3 EEA contains the principle of loyalty, or the principle of good faith. Its prominent position as one of the fundamental objectives and principles of

---

[14] E-4/01 *Karl K Karlsson v The Icelandic State* [2002] EFTA Ct Rep 240.
[15] ibid, para 28.
[16] E-2/12 *HOB-vín ehf v Áfengis- og tóbaksverslun ríkisins* [2012] EFTA Ct Rep 1092.

the Agreement indicates that it was regarded by the negotiators as an essential provision. Yet, the impression is that this provision often has been overlooked by politicians and legal commentators. However, the latter category includes at least one person deserving of our particular praise for keeping us up to date, namely Dr John Temple Lang, author of a long series of articles on the subject.[17]

According to *Norberg et al*[18] the corresponding provision of the EEC Treaty, Article 5, had at the time of the EEA negotiations been cited about 150 times by the ECJ. Article 3 EEA is drafted as closely as possible to that article, except for the institutional differences. This implies that a major part of the substantive elements of the ECJ case law on the subject is part and parcel of the EEA Agreement.

The complicated legal architecture of the EEA Agreement leaves the defence of equal rights for individuals and economic operators to autonomous measures by the EFTA States themselves; acting loyally and in good faith to a greater extent than is the case with EU Member States. In fact, good faith is the keystone which supports the EEA edifice, without which the construction might crumble.

A very important institutional difference between the two pillars for judicial review in the EEA is that the EFTA Court lacks the 'constitutional' competencies of the ECJ. Thus, it cannot set aside secondary legislation, or share an equivalent position to that of its big relative with regard to having the ultimate 'say' in EEA-related legal issues arising in the EFTA States. However, its decisions in direct actions are binding under public international law, and it shares with the ECJ that the implementation and enforcement of their binding rulings will have to be carried out by the national courts and authorities. Yet, they have both no powers to set aside national legislation, enforce fines, award damages, etc.

In the practice of the EFTA Court the principle of loyalty has been cited in a number of cases which now is approaching 50. The majority of these cases, around 30, are legally rather uncontroversial instances of failure to implement legal acts in a timely manner. Here the consistent use of the reference to Article 3 obviously serves to underline this provision's function as a reinforcement of the old principle *pacta sunt servanda*. At the same time, the Court delivers a clear signal with regard to the crucial importance of correct and timely implementation of new legal acts for maintaining the homogeneity and good functioning of the Agreement on the side of the EFTA States.

A second distinct group of cases in which the principle of loyalty play a central role, less important in number but legally extremely significant, deals with individual rights and have been described in part II above. These cases demonstrate that the principle of loyalty goes far beyond a general reinforcement of *pacta sunt servanda* but also serves to clarify and even add essential elements left open in the negotiations.

---

[17] See, eg, 'Article 10 EC—The most important "general principle" of Community law'. The Swedish Network for European Legal Studies, Stockholm Conference, March 2007.
[18] S Norberg, K Hökborg, M Johansson, D Eliasson and L Dedichen: *The European Economic Area EEA Law. A Commentary on the EEA Agreement* (Stockholm, Fritzes, 1993) 99.

However, recent judgments of the EFTA Court[19] remind us that in the cooperation between the EFTA Court and the national courts not everything is running to perfection. One sometimes gets the impression that the reference to the independence of the courts in the penultimate Recital of the Preamble of the Agreement in the context of maintaining a uniform interpretation and application is not fully understood. In democratic states courts shall of course act independently in the exercise of their function but their judicial powers are limited to applying the 'law'. That includes, as stated in the eighth Recital of the Preamble, the judicial defence of individual rights conferred on them by the Agreement.

As organs of the State national courts in the EFTA States have an obligation to give effect to EEA law, including duties following from the principle of loyalty. This was expressly recognised by the Norwegian Supreme Court in *Finanger I*[20] by confirming that the obligation of duty in the EEA Agreement is addressed directly to Norwegian judges.

In *Finanger II*[21] the same Court declared that national judges are in the same position as their colleagues in EU Member States when it comes to interpreting national law in accordance with Community law and with regard to providing sanctions against infringements by the legislative and executive branches of their obligations under the Agreement. This is a good description of duties that follow from the principle of effectiveness embodied in Article 3 EEA. It would seem that this also describes the understanding in the two other EFTA States.

The fact that effective application and enforcement of the EEA Agreement is a shared responsibility makes it incumbent on the institutions both at the national and the EFTA level to act in sincere cooperation, which constitutes another aspect of the principle of loyalty.

Moreover, when it comes to the procedural rights of individuals and economic operators, where the Contracting Parties have procedural autonomy, the principle of equality will to some extent assure them equal treatment in accordance with national rules. However, where that will not suffice to render full effect of EEA rules national courts will sometimes, consistent with the principle of effectiveness, have to resort to inventive methods in order to safeguard their right to fair judicial review as understood by EEA law.

It is a fair assumption that when it comes to procedural rights the principle of homogeneous individual rights also must be achieved in one way or other, regardless of the architectural differences between the two pillars in this regard. This follows from the general scheme of the Agreement and the principle of loyalty. It cannot be that the fundamentals of the right to judicial review in defence of individual rights displays variations in effectiveness in certain parts of the EEA.

---

[19] See Case E-18/11 *Irish Bank Resolution Corporation Ltd v Kaupþing hf* [2012] EFTA Ct Rep 592, paras 58 and 59, and Case E-3/12 *Staten v/Arbeidsdepartementet v Stig Arne Jonsson* [2013] EFTA Ct Rep 136, para 60.

[20] Sak HR-2000-49-B—Rt-2000-1811.

[21] Sak HR-2005-01690-P—Rt-2005-1365.

And obviously, if the courts in the EFTA states should fail in their task in such a way that individuals and economic operators suffer loss or damage these States are under the doctrine of State liability responsible for such failure.[22] This will in the EFTA pillar just as in the EU only depend on the vigilance and resolve of the competent surveillance authority to bring direct actions on its own initiative or following a complaint. However, this is clearly something to be avoided.

It becomes important to keep these factors in mind when trying to understand the contents of Article 34 of the Surveillance and Court Agreement (SCA). Should a court act in open defiance of or misapply a Preliminary Ruling or an Advisory Opinion, as the case may be, there may always be a second round which can set the record straight as far as individual rights are concerned.

Consequently, as regards the first question which the enigmatic Article 34 SCA raises, namely the difference between a binding Preliminary Ruling and a non-binding Advisory Opinion, it may in practice be less acute than the intensity of the legal debates that have enfolded around the subject. At any rate, it seems that the national courts of the EFTA States are in broad agreement that the Advisory Opinions of the EFTA Court shall be accorded considerable weight as a source of law.

The history of the EEA Negotiations will reveal—see in particular *Norberg et al*[23]—that the EFTA States originally wanted a monolithic court system for the EEA Agreement in the form of a chamber with a mixed manning in the ECJ. However, as the European Court of Justice in its much-debated Opinion 1/91[24] found this concept for judicial control in the EEA to be unconstitutional, a new model for assuring legal homogeneity in the EEA had to be elaborated. Neither did the ECJ want to have an EFTA Court at its side which might interfere with its constitutional position in Community law through deviations caused by conflicting but binding interpretations from an EFTA Court.

Article 34 SCA must be read against this backdrop, but it is still a bit difficult to grasp its consistency as long as the EFTA Court could be fully competent to deliver binding judgments in direct actions initiated by the Surveillance Authority.[25] The possibility for EFTA States to ask the ECJ 'to decide' on the interpretation of an EEA rule offered in Article 107 appears to have been offered as a consolation prize. For obvious constitutional and political reasons it has never been used.

Nevertheless, this gives a hint towards understanding why Article 34 uses the word 'may' where the related article in EU law says 'must' when it comes to the

---

[22] See Case C-129/00 *Commission of the European Communities v Italian Republic* [2003] ECR I-14737.

[23] Above n 19, p 194.

[24] Opinion delivered pursuant to the second subparagraph of Art 228(1) of the Treaty [1991] ECR I-06079.

[25] Another reminiscence of the ECJ's sensitivity is the fact that the SCA contains no provision similar to Art 164 EEC which instructs the ECJ to ensure that 'the law' is observed in the interpretation and application of the Treaty in spite of the numerous references to common values in the Preamble of the Agreement.

issue of national courts referring questions to the respective courts in the EEA institutional structure when considered necessary to enable them to give judgment. Article 34 SCA must essentially be read as a provision of an enabling character which bestows on, but also delimits, the competency of the EFTA Court.

It is at the same time important to note that in order to describe the situation in which national courts should seek assistance Article 34 SCA uses the same wording as its EU counterpart, now Article 267 TFEU, namely if it considers it necessary to enable it to give judgment. The slight differences in the wording relate only to the legal format of the answer. Clearly, it does not make much sense to argue that if a national court in an EFTA State feels that this condition is not fulfilled it still has the right to abstain from making a referral to the EFTA Court.

It appears, therefore, that here again one is faced with one of the architectural imperfections of the EEA Agreement which must be held up by the principle of loyalty. In addition, national courts will find most helpful advice in the doctrine of *acte clair*[26] which, *mutatis mutandis*, must be considered to be part of the EEA Agreement, *cf* Article 6 EEA. The *CILFIT* ruling leaves little doubt that when in doubt it is better for national courts to make a reference once too many than to abstain from doing so. While the system of referral does not constitute a means of redress the ECJ found it appropriate to remind national courts of the specific characteristics of Community law, the particular difficulties which its interpretation gives rise to and, not least importantly in the case of national courts in the EFTA States, the risk of divergences in judicial decisions.

It could therefore be concluded that the issue at stake is not related to the independence of the national courts in the EFTA States or the national procedural autonomy but rather, that these courts by their States have been made part of a system of cooperation with the aim of assuring legal homogeneity in the EEA, particularly in the defence of the rights of individuals and economic operators. The principle of loyalty binds them to carry out this duty in good faith.

IV. CONCLUSION

It is not difficult to conclude this chapter with an expression of full appreciation of the ground-breaking work the EFTA Court has accomplished during the last two decades in order to fortify and add credibility to the EFTA pillar for surveillance and judicial review of the EEA Agreement. Taking into account its small staff this has been a capital achievement, not least when it comes to the very high standard of professionalism which it has had to acquire.

In the EFTA States, however, this extraordinary feat has not universally been recognised in the way it deserves. In spite of the fact that recent studies have confirmed a solid political support for the EEA Agreement minimalistic approaches

---

[26] Case C-283/81 *Srl CILFIT and Lanificio di Gavardo SpA v Ministry of Health* [1982] ECR 03415.

and rather one-sided perspectives easily surface when the reciprocal obligations of the Agreement sometimes become politically uncomfortable.

On the festive occasion of having reached an important milestone the EFTA Court can nevertheless fully savour the satisfaction of having contributed decisively to add to the credibility and good functioning of the complicated legal and institutional architecture of the EEA Agreement in a way which makes this model sustainable for many years to come.

Judging by recent developments in the EU's relationship with neighbouring countries the EEA model seems to be the only one on offer which, short of membership, can give individuals and economic operators full access to the Internal Market of the EU on the basis of the four freedoms and equal conditions of competition.

Chapeau!

25

Judicial Protection in the EEA EFTA States—Direct Effect of EEA Law Revisited

MARTIN JOHANSSON

I
N AUGUST 1999, Leif Sevón, then Judge at the EU Court of Justice,[1] and I published an article in the European Law Review, in which we argued that if the homogeneity objective of the EEA Agreement is not to be jeopardised and the balance of the rights and obligations under the Agreement is to be maintained, the EU principles of direct effect (and primacy) have to apply also in the EEA, possibly in a slightly modified form.[2]

Since then, the EFTA Court has delivered judgments recognising the application of the principle of State liability in the EEA,[3] but also noting the absence of recognition of direct effect for non-implemented EEA rules in the EEA EFTA States,[4] thus seemingly closing the debate.

Nevertheless, recent developments, both in the case law of the EFTA Court and in that of the Norwegian Supreme Court, seem to indicate that the question might still be open.

The question of the EEA EFTA States' recognition of direct effect is sensitive and, to the opponents of such a recognition, a question of principle: since the EEA EFTA States have not transferred legislative powers to the EEA, there may be no recognition of direct effect (only in case of membership in the EU would they accept the application of those principles).[5]

In this short chapter I come back to the question of direct effect of EEA law. I first describe the relevant judgments of the EFTA Court concerning the principles

---

[1] Leif Sevón was before that, inter alia, the first President of the EFTA Court and on leaving the EU Court of Justice he became President of the Supreme Court of Finland.

[2] L Sevón and M Johansson, 'The protection of the rights of individuals under the EEA Agreement' (1999) 24 EL Rev 373.

[3] Following the judgment in Case E-9/97 Sveinbjörnsdóttir [1998] EFTA Ct Rep 95.

[4] Case E-4/01 Karlsson [2002] EFTA Ct Rep 240.

[5] See, eg, O Abrahamsson and H Frennered, 'Endast unionsrätten har direct effect-EFTA-domstolen klargör att EES-rätten varken har företräde eller direkt effect ipso jure', ERT 2011 p 627.

of State liability and direct effect and thereafter discuss whether a change of this case law is required and possible.

I. THE DEVELOPMENT OF THE CASE LAW OF THE EFTA
COURT AND THE PRESENT STATE OF PLAY

In *Sveinbjörnsdóttir* the EFTA Court held that the homogeneity objective and the objective of establishing the right of individuals and economic operators to equal treatment and equal opportunities are so strongly expressed in the EEA Agreement that it must be considered a principle of the Agreement that the EFTA States are obliged to provide compensation for loss and damage caused to individuals by breaches of the obligations under the EEA Agreement for which the EFTA States can be held responsible, such as through incorrect implementation of a directive.[6]

This very important judgment, which must be seen as a milestone towards the equal protection of the rights of individuals in the EU and in the EEA EFTA States, was immediately acknowledged by the EU Court of Justice. In its judgment in *Rechberger*, the Court of Justice 'in view of the objective of uniform interpretation and application which informs the EEA Agreement', pointed out that the principles governing the liability of an EFTA State for infringement of a directive referred to in the EEA Agreement were the subject of the EFTA Court's judgment in *Sveinbjörnsdóttir*.[7]

The EFTA Court found:

> that the provisions of the EEA Agreement are, to a great extent, intended for the benefit of individuals and economic operators throughout the European Economic Area. Therefore the proper functioning of the EEA Agreement is dependent on those individuals and economic operators being able to rely on the rights thus intended for their benefit.[8]

> that the EEA Agreement is an international treaty *sui generis* which contains a distinct legal order of its own ... The depth of integration ... is less far-reaching than under the EC Treaty, but the scope and the objective goes beyond what is usual for an agreement under public international law.[9]

> that the homogeneity objective and the objective of establishing the right of individuals and economic operators to equal treatment and equal opportunities are so strongly expressed in the EEA Agreement that the EFTA States must be obliged to provide for compensation for loss and damage caused by an individual by incorrect implementation of a directive.[10]

---

[6]   Case E-9/97 *Sveinbjörnsdóttir* [1998] EFTA Ct Rep 95, paras 60 and 62.
[7]   Case C-140/97 *Rechberger* [1999] ECR I-3499, para 39.
[8]   Case E-9/97 *Sveinbjörnsdóttir* [1998] EFTA Ct Rep 95, para 58.
[9]   ibid, para 59.
[10]   ibid, para 60.

Nevertheless, in *Karlsson*, the EFTA Court accepted the absence of recognition of direct effect for non-implemented EEA rules in the EEA EFTA States. The EFTA Court held:

> It follows from Article 7 EEA and Protocol 35 to the EEA Agreement that EEA law does not entail a transfer of legislative powers. Therefore, EEA law does not require that individuals and economic operators can rely directly on non-implemented EEA rules before national courts.[11]

The case law of the EFTA Court has since developed further. This development is rather well summarised in the 2013 judgment of the EFTA Court 2013 in *Wahl*.[12] Although the EFTA Court limits its statements to directives, it is submitted that there is nothing that indicates that the rules set out do not apply also to regulations.

According to the EFTA Court, there are three main points at which a directive gains effect under the EEA Agreement:[13]

1. The first arises where a decision of the EEA Joint Committee has entered into force and becomes binding pursuant to Article 104 EEA and the directive must be implemented. This must have taken place at the latest on the implementation date in the EU or when the Joint Committee Decision enters into force, whichever is later. Any later date constitutes an infringement of the EEA Agreement.
2. The second is where a directive is implemented pursuant to Article 7 EEA, in which case it shall prevail over national provisions regardless of the form and method of implementation.
3. The third is where a decision of the EEA Joint Committee becomes provisionally applicable pursuant to Article 103 EEA, unless a Contracting Party notifies that such a provisional application cannot take place.

The Court appears to deliberately talk about a directive gaining effect, without indicating which those effects are.

As to the first point, the effect would appear to be that ESA may bring a case before the EFTA Court under Article 31 of the Agreement between the EFTA States on the Establishment of a Surveillance Authority and a Court of Justice, for violation of EEA law.[14] It should also be possible for individuals and economic

---

[11] Case E-4/01 *Karlsson* [2002] EFTA Ct Rep 240, para 28. However, the EFTA Court immediately underlined the importance in this situation of the obligation of EEA conform interpretation, adding, in the same paragraph:

At the same time, it is inherent in the general objective of the EEA Agreement of establishing a dynamic and homogeneous market, in the ensuing emphasis on the judicial defence and enforcement of the rights of individuals, as well as in the public international law principle of effectiveness, that national courts will consider any relevant element of EEA law, whether implemented or not, when interpreting national law.

[12] Case E-15/12 *Wahl* [2013] EFTA Ct Rep 534.

[13] ibid, paras 46–48.

[14] See Case E-1/07 *Criminal proceedings against A* [2007] EFTA Ct Rep 246, para 42.

operators to bring a case against the EFTA State concerned before a national court for compensation for loss and damage caused by the non-implementation.

As to the second point, the EFTA Court noted in *Wahl*[15] that the implementation of a directive does not necessarily require legislative action in each EFTA State, as the existence of statutory provisions and general principles of law may render the implementation by specific legislation superfluous. Nevertheless, provisions of directives must be implemented with unquestionable binding force and the specificity, precision and clarity necessary to satisfy the requirements of legal certainty and the legal situation resulting from national implementing measures must be sufficiently precise and clear and individuals made fully aware of their rights.

The Court then held that 'Article 3 EEA requires the EFTA States to take all measures necessary, regardless of the form and method of implementation, to ensure that a directive which has been implemented and satisfies the conditions set out above prevails over conflicting national law and to guarantee the effectiveness of the directive'.[16] It is interesting to note that it is the directive itself, and not the implemented rules, that shall prevail over conflicting national law.

Finally, as to the third point, it is difficult to say what the effect would be for the provisions of a directive where the decision of the EEA Joint Committee becomes provisionally applicable. It is submitted that the provisional application cannot be more far-reaching than what is required with regard to a non-implemented EEA rule, but that it must go further than what would anyway apply under the public international law principle of good faith, that is, an obligation not to undertake any measures that might compromise the result prescribed by the EEA Joint Committee decision. It is therefore suggested that the EEA EFTA States are obliged to ensure the result sought by the EEA Joint Committee decision concerned through the application of the principle of EEA conform interpretation.[17]

The development of its case law by the EFTA Court in order to compensate for the negative effects of the absence of recognition of direct effect of EEA law has thus come a long way.

Nevertheless, that development now seems to have come as far as it can. It is clear that it does not guarantee equal judicial protection under the EEA Agreement in all the Contracting Parties.

The principle of EEA conform interpretation is limited by the general principles of EEA law, such as the principles of legal certainty and non-retroactivity, and cannot serve as the basis for an interpretation of national law *contra legem* or where there is no national law to interpret.

The application of the principle of State liability is very difficult in practice. Not only does an applicant have to prove that the breach of EEA law on the part of

---

[15] Case E-15/12 *Wahl* [2013] EFTA Ct Rep 534, paras 49–54.
[16] ibid, para 54.
[17] See M Johansson, 'Provisional Application of EEA Law and Obligation on ESA to Take a Position in Infringement Cases' (2012) *European Law Reporter* 298.

the State is sufficiently serious, it must also prove that it has suffered damage and that there is a link between that damage and the breach of the State's obligations. The principle of State liability is a complement to the principle of direct effect and not a substitute.

There has lately been a discussion in the doctrine of whether or not, because of the absence of direct effect of the EEA Agreement in the EEA EFTA States, there exists a strict State liability for breach of EEA law when the provisions concerned correspond to provisions of EU law which would be capable of having direct effect within the EU.

Even though such a strengthened principle of State liability would go some way towards limiting the negative consequences of the non-recognition of direct effect, it would in my view far from take care of the problem: it will still be much more difficult for citizens and economic operators to argue a case of State liability than to have the right to invoke the provisions concerned directly before a national court. Furthermore, the effects are not the same. Through the direct effect of a provision, the citizens and economic operators are able to directly insist on getting their rights. If they manage to win a case of State liability, the whole idea is that they should get economic compensation that corresponds as well as possible to the (economic) damage suffered.

Moreover, if, as suggested by some writers, the applicability of a strict EEA State liability principle is to be limited to cases where the lack of EEA law principle of direct effect constitutes a condition sine qua non for the plaintiff's loss,[18] the advantage of such a strengthened principle will be very small. It will require a plaintiff to first bring a case invoking his EEA rights and the principle of EEA conform interpretation, even if it is rather clear that there is little chance of success. If he does not, he will find it very difficult to prove that he would not have succeeded had he tried to pursue his EEA rights in court.

II. IS A CHANGE REQUIRED AND IS IT POSSIBLE?

The question is therefore whether the time has not come, more than 20 years after the entry into force of the EEA Agreement, for the EFTA Court to recognise the principle of direct effect of EEA law.

Not only does the EEA Agreement expressly state that the objective of the Contracting Parties is to establish a 'dynamic and homogeneous European Economic Area ... providing for the adequate means of enforcement including at the judicial levels' and to arrive at an 'equal treatment of individuals and economic operators'.

In addition, the EFTA Court has in its later case law repeatedly held that '[t]he objective of establishing a dynamic and homogeneous European Economic Area

---

[18] See, eg H Haukeland Fredriksen, 'State Liability and EEA Law: The Same or Different?' [2013] 38 *EL Rev* 884.

can only be achieved if EFTA and EU citizens and economic operators enjoy, relying upon EEA law, the same rights in both the EU and EFTA pillars of the EEA'.[19]

Furthermore, the EFTA Court in *Koch* recalled that access to justice and effective judicial protection are essential elements in the EEA legal framework.[20] This can only partially be achieved through the right to equal access to the courts in both the EU and EFTA pillars of the EEA, recognised by the EFTA Court. As long as the principle of direct effect, allowing citizens and economic operators to rely before national courts on non-implemented EEA rules conferring rights on them, is not recognised, the access to justice and effective judicial protection will not be guaranteed in the EFTA pillar of the EEA.

Moreover, the Supreme Court of Norway, sitting in Full Court, in 2005, in *Finanger v Norway* (the so-called *Finanger II*), accepting the principle of State liability, referred to 'fundamental considerations of homogeneity, equal treatment of individual persons/legal entities and protection of their activities'. Rejecting a plea of the Norwegian Government for a milder State liability regime under the EEA Agreement, the Supreme Court held:

> If a directive is to be in force both in the EC and the EEA, a decisive emphasis should be placed on the principle of homogeneity and the expectation that each and every country and their citizens have that the directives are implemented. The directives in question here are directives which are to give citizens specific rights, and State liability is to ensure that those rights become a reality. It seems then not reasonable that citizens should be in different legal positions when it comes to the protection of these rights.[21]

It is argued that this statement, which was made in relation to State liability, is of general application, and supports the need to recognise the principle of direct effect in the EEA EFTA States.

It should be recalled that in the EU the principle of direct effect was not developed overnight. That principle grew out of a gradually developed case law. A careful analysis of that case law shows that the key elements of direct effect, as identified by the EU Court of Justice, are also present in the EEA Agreement. For example, the Contracting Parties have limited their sovereign rights for the benefit of the EEA legal order, albeit, compared to the EU, within more limited, but nonetheless important, fields. The subjects of this new legal order comprise not only Contracting Parties but also their citizens. The EEA Agreement not only imposes obligations on individuals but also confers rights on them. Those obligations are either expressly granted by the EEA Agreement (or by the acts referred to or contained in the Annexes and Protocols to the Agreement), or result from clearly defined obligations which the Agreement imposes on other individuals,

---

[19] Case E-11/12 *Koch and Others* [2013] EFTA Ct Rep 272, para 116, and case law cited therein.
[20] ibid, para 117, and case law cited therein.
[21] *Finanger v Norway* Rt 2005 p 1365, paras 52 and 58. Unofficial translation, copied from H Haukeland Fredriksen, 'State Liability and EEA Law: The Same or Different?' [2013] 38 *EL Rev* 884.

on the Contracting Parties and on the institutions (EEA, EU as well as EFTA institutions).[22]

In addition, it may be discussed whether or not the Contracting Parties actually have transferred legislative powers to the institutions of the EEA. At the very least, they have limited their right to amend their internal legislation in the areas covered by the EEA Agreement, which include the acts (such as regulations and directives) integrated into the Agreement by decisions of the EEA Joint Committee. It follows from Article 97 in the EEA Agreement that the Contracting Parties are only allowed to amend their internal legislation if either:

(i)   the EEA Join Committee concludes that the legislation as amended does not affect the good functioning of the Agreement, or

(ii)   the EEA Joint Committee, after having completed the EEA decision-making procedure, has decided to amend the Annex or Protocol concerned as required.

The only other way a Contracting Party may regain its freedom to adopt new internal legislation in these areas, without infringing the Agreement, is by withdrawing from the Agreement.

In any case, even if the Contracting Parties are to be considered as not having transferred legislative powers to the institutions of the EEA, one may question whether there is a link between that fact and the question of the direct effect of EEA law. The EEA Joint Committee decisions are adopted with unanimity. They may not enter into force until the necessary internal constitutional requirements have been fulfilled. However, once such requirements have been fulfilled the decisions are binding on the Contracting Parties.

The EFTA States thus do not risk being bound by an act they have not voted for and they have the right to fulfil all necessary internal constitutional requirements before the act becomes binding on them. Under such circumstances, when, after all necessary requirements have been fulfilled, an EEA Joint Committee decision has entered into force, individuals must be able to rely on it before national courts in the EEA EFTA States, in a similar way as they may rely on the corresponding union act before national courts in the EU.

III. CONCLUSION

Not only does the EEA Agreement expressly state that the objective of the Contracting Parties is to establish a 'dynamic and homogeneous European Economic Area ... providing for the adequate means of enforcement including

---

[22] For a more detailed analysis of the elements on which the case law of the EU Court of Justice on direct effect is based, seen in the context of the EEA Agreement, see L Sevón and M Johansson, above n 2.

at the judicial levels' and to arrive at an 'equal treatment of individuals and economic operators'.

Furthermore, the EFTA Court has itself held that '[t]he objective of establishing a dynamic and homogeneous European Economic Area can only be achieved if EFTA and EU citizens and economic operators enjoy, relying upon EEA law, the same rights in both the EU and EFTA pillars of the EEA'.[23]

In addition, the Supreme Court of Norway, sitting in Full Court, in *Finanger II*,[24] underlined that '[i]f a directive is to be in force both in the EC and the EEA, a decisive emphasis should be placed on the principle of homogeneity and the expectation that each and every country and their citizens have that the directives are implemented'. Citizens should not be in different legal positions when it comes to the protection of their rights under the directive.

Nevertheless, it is undeniable that, as long as it is not recognised in the EEA EFTA States that a provision of secondary legislation that has been made part of the EEA Agreement can have direct effect and takes precedence over conflicting national rules, citizens and economic operators do not enjoy the same rights in both the EU and the EFTA pillars of the EEA. Citizens and economic operators will be in different legal positions when it comes to the judicial protection of those rights.

When all is said and done, it is difficult to perceive what constitutional concerns could be so important as to deprive individuals and economic operators of the same right in the EU and the EEA EFTA States to rely before national courts on decisions adopted by the EEA Joint Committee with the agreement of all the Contracting Parties and fulfilling internal constitutional requirements (having been approved, where necessary, by the national parliaments).

A characteristic feature of EU law is its inherent dynamic character, which has allowed it to develop far beyond what the fathers of the Rome Treaty ever could foresee. The EEA legal order, which according to the EEA Agreement shall not only be dynamic but also homogeneous in relation to the corresponding parts of EU law, can evidently not remain static either. This is also clear from the case law of the EFTA Court.

Against the background of the above, it would therefore seem that, after more than 20 years of legal developments, and independently of what the authors of Protocol 35 to the EEA Agreement may originally have contemplated, the time has come for the EFTA Court to reconsider the question of direct effect of EEA law, recognising that the need for judicial protection of the rights of citizens and economic operators outweighs constitutional concerns related to the possible absence of a transfer of legislative powers, under the conditions set out in the EEA Agreement.[25]

---

[23] Case E-11/12 *Koch and Others* [2013] EFTA Ct Rep 272, para 116, and case law cited therein.

[24] *Finanger v Norway* Rt 2005 p 1365, para 58. Unofficial translation, copied from H Haukeland Fredriksen, above n 21, p 884.

[25] See also M Johansson and S Norberg, 'EES-rätten—dynamisk *ipso jure!*' ERT 2011 p 795.

26

The EFTA Court and the Principle of State Liability: Protecting the Jewel in the Crown

HALVARD HAUKELAND FREDRIKSEN

I. INTRODUCTION—THE JEWEL IN THE EFTA COURT'S CROWN

IN THE NOW 20-year-long history of the EFTA Court, 10 December 1998 stands out as a defining moment. On this day, the Court decided one of the most controversial questions of EEA law with the following conclusion in Case E-9/97 *Erla María Sveinbjörnsdóttir v Iceland*:

> It is a principle of the EEA Agreement that the Contracting Parties are obliged to provide for compensation for loss and damage caused to individuals by breaches of the obligations under the EEA Agreement for which the EFTA States can be held responsible.[1]

Given the lack of any express provision establishing a basis for State liability in the Agreement, and the highly sensitive character of the question to the dualist EFTA States, the decision was at the time rightly characterised as 'fairly daring'.[2] This was particularly so because the finding was opposed not only by the governments of Iceland and Norway, but also by the Swedish government and—perhaps somewhat unexpectedly—by the European Commission. Apart from Ms Sveinbjörnsdóttir herself, actually the only participant to the proceedings which argued in favour of an unwritten principle of State liability was the EFTA Surveillance Authority.

For the dualist EFTA States, State liability for loss and damage caused by incorrect implementation of EEA law obligations was a bitter pill. At the 35th Nordic Law Conference in Oslo the following year, several commentators criticised *Sveinbjörnsdóttir*.[3] The Norwegian judge who was the President of the EFTA Court at the time came very close to an extrajudicial dissent by stating that he

---

[1] Case E-9/97 *Erla María Sveinbjörnsdóttir v Iceland* [1998] EFTA Ct Rep 95, para 62.

[2] See the editorial 'European Economic Area and European Community: Homogeneity of legal orders?' (1999) 36 *Common Market Law Review* 697–702.

[3] See several of the contributions referred to in *Forhandlingene ved Det 35 nordiske juristmøtet* [Proceedings of the 35th Nordic Law Conference], Oslo 1999, pp 977–1011.

found it difficult to function as a judge in a court where no dissenting opinions are allowed and by declaring parts of the Court's reasoning in *Sveinbjörnsdóttir* an act *ultra vires*.[4] Only about a month after the EFTA Court had held State liability to be a principle of EEA law, Advocate General Cosmas concluded to the contrary in his Opinion in *Andersson*.[5] At least in Norway, the academic literature was split—whereas some welcomed or at least accepted the decision,[6] others criticised it to the extent that they questioned whether the stand of the EFTA Court could be acknowledged as an authoritative interpretation of EEA law.[7]

When the question of EEA State liability arose anew before the EFTA Court in *Karlsson* in 2002, the Norwegian government seized the opportunity and sought a rematch of *Sveinbjörnsdóttir*.[8] By then, however, the principle of State liability for breach of EEA law had not only been *de facto* accepted by the Icelandic Supreme Court in its final judgment in the case brought by Ms Sveinbjörnsdóttir;[9] it had also been endorsed by the ECJ in an obiter dictum in *Rechberger*.[10] Not only did the ECJ make the referring Austrian court aware of *Sveinbjörnsdóttir*; it did so with an introductory reference to 'the objective of uniform interpretation and application which informs the EEA Agreement' and stated that the EFTA Court had expressed itself upon 'the principles governing the liability of an EFTA State for infringement of a directive referred to in the EEA Agreement'.[11] The ECJ's endorsement of *Sveinbjörnsdóttir* did not go unnoticed by the EFTA Court: When

---

[4]   See the intervention of Bjørn Haug, ibid, pp 1005–1006.

[5]   Opinion of 19 January 1999 in Case C-321/97 *Ulla-Birth Andersson and Susanne Wåkerås-Andersson v Sweden* [1999] ECR I-3551. There is no reference to *Sveinbjörnsdóttir* in the Opinion and it remains uncertain whether AG Cosmas was aware of it. The ECJ did not go into the matter in its judgment of 15 June 1999 as it held that it lacked competence to rule on the consequences of the EEA Agreement in Sweden during the period preceding Swedish accession to the EU.

[6]   See, eg, F Arnesen, 'EFTA-domstolen statuerer erstatningsansvar' (1999) *Europarättslig Tidskrift* 357–362; HP Graver, 'Mission Impossible: Supranationality and National Legal Autonomy in the EEA Agreement' (2002) 7 *European Foreign Affairs Review* 73–90 and F Sejersted et al, *EØS-rett*, 2nd edn (Oslo, Universitetsforlaget, 2004), pp 108–109.

[7]   Among the more outspoken critics were Ingvald Falch, in *Forhandlingene ved Det 35 nordiske juristmøtet*, above n 3, pp 1009–1010 and SL Jervell, *Lovgivningen i EØS* (Oslo, Cappelen, 2002), pp 130–142. See also the criticism from the (then) Director General of the Legislation Department of the Ministry of Justice, Inge Lorange Backer, in his article 'Lovgivere og domstoler ved begynnelsen av det 21 århundre' (2006) 41 *Jussens Venner* 248–266 (at 257 and 261). Note, however, that the reception in academic literature outside Norway was generally of a more friendly nature; see, eg, the overview provided for by Carl Baudenbacher in his article, 'If Not EEA State Liability, Then What? Reflections Ten Years after the EFTA Court's *Sveinbjörnsdóttir* Ruling' (2009) 10 *Chicago Journal of International Law* 333–358, at 344–345.

[8]   See the arguments of the Norwegian Government in Case E-4/01 *Karl K Karlsson hf v Iceland* [2002] EFTA Ct Rep 240 (summarised at length in the Report for the Hearing).

[9]   Judgment of 16 December 1999 in Case 236/1999 *Iceland v Erla María Sveinbjörnsdóttir*. As to the only de facto character of the acceptance of the EFTA Court's stand, see V below.

[10]   Case C-140/97 *Walter Rechberger and Others v Austria* [1999] ECR I-3499, para 39.

[11]   The latter formulation presupposes that the EEA Agreement indeed does entail principles on State liability, something which was the very core of the discussion before the EFTA Court in *Sveinbjörnsdóttir*. (This is even clearer in the authentic German version of the judgment, where the reference is to the 'geltende Grundsätze' of State liability.)

the Court stood its ground and confirmed the existence of the principle of State liability in *Karlsson*, it included a reference to *Rechberger* in the reasoning.[12]

After the defeat in *Karlsson*, the Norwegian government gave up its resistance against *Sveinbjörnsdóttir* when the question of State liability for defective implementation of a directive was raised before Norwegian courts in the *Finanger II* case. In its final judgment in the case in 2005, the Norwegian Supreme Court cited extensively from the reasoning of the EFTA Court in *Sveinbjörnsdóttir* and noted the subsequent confirmation in *Karlsson* as well as the acceptance of the principle by both the government and the Icelandic Supreme Court. Writing on behalf of the full court, Justice Gussgaard added that she found 'the EFTA Court's reasons for State liability to be convincing, with its emphasis on the fundamental considerations of homogeneity, equal treatment of individual persons/legal entities and protection of their activities'.[13]

After *Finanger II*, the only remaining EEA EFTA State whose courts had not acknowledged the principle of State liability was Liechtenstein. When the question of State liability for breach of EEA obligations came before the Supreme Court of Liechtenstein in 2006 in the *Dr Tschannet II* case, the court decided the matter purely on the basis of national tort law and acquitted the government without any reference to *Sveinbjörnsdóttir*.[14] The judgment was quashed by the Constitutional Court of Liechtenstein due to inadequate statement of reasons,[15] but this only led to a new judgment in 2008 in which the Supreme Court explained in greater detail why the government had not committed a fault within the meaning of the Liechtenstein Public Liability Act.[16] However, after this second judgment was also quashed by the Constitutional Court,[17] the Supreme Court finally gave in in 2010 and ruled in favour of the plaintiff in a judgment which at least by implication accepts *Sveinbjörnsdóttir* and *Karlsson*.[18]

If one adds that the Supreme Court of Sweden also acknowledged the principle of State liability for breach of obligations under the EEA Agreement in its final judgment in the *Andersson* case from 2004,[19] and that not only the EEA EFTA States but also the European Commission have accepted the principle in their pleadings in subsequent State liability cases before the EFTA Court,[20] it is clear that one may now speak of a well-established principle of EEA law.[21]

---

[12] *Karlsson*, above n 8, para 25.

[13] Judgment of 28 October 2005 in Case 2005/412 (Rt 2005 p 1365), para 52.

[14] Judgment of 7 December 2006 in Case CO.2004.2-25.

[15] Judgment of 3 July 2007 in Case StGH 2007/15.

[16] Judgment of 5 June 2008 in Case CO.2004.2-38.

[17] Judgment of 24 June 2009 in Case StGH 2008/87.

[18] Judgment of 7 May 2010 in Case CO.2004.2 (final). As to the only de facto character of the acceptance of the case law of the EFTA Court, see V below.

[19] Judgment of 26 November 2004 in Case T-2593-01 (NJA 2004, p 662).

[20] See, eg, the submissions of the Commission in Case E-2/10 *Þór Kolbeinsson v Iceland* [2009–2010] EFTA Ct Rep 234 (as they are summarised in the Report for the Hearing, paras 136ff).

[21] Even though it is true that the ECJ still has not been confronted with a case where it has had to take a definite stand on the matter, the general 'EEA-friendly' approach of the ECJ, the de facto

Looking back at the rather heated discussion in the wake of *Sveinbjörnsdóttir*, it is possible to argue that the opposition in the end proved to be beneficial to the EFTA Court as it only accentuated the court's achievement. There are certainly striking parallels between the criticism of *Sveinbjörnsdóttir* and the criticism which was directed at the ECJ in the wake of *Francovich*.[22] In a sense, the opposition to *Sveinbjörnsdóttir* allowed the EFTA Court to demonstrate its independence of the EFTA States and its commitment to secure judicial protection of EEA-based rights which equals the protection offered in EU law, if need be through a rather dynamic interpretation of the Agreement. Notwithstanding the fact that the EFTA Court has rendered a significant number of other important decisions over the last 20 years, it thus appears justified to describe *Sveinbjörnsdóttir* as the jewel in the Court's crown.

In an attempt to contribute to the EFTA Court's 20th anniversary with something more than just a historical overview of the genesis of the principle of State liability, the attention in the following is directed towards some questions concerning the legal basis of the principle which still may be of practical interest (II); the reach of the principle (III); the conditions for the liability of the States (IV); and the role of the principle in the complex relationship between the EFTA Court, the ECJ and the highest courts of the EEA EFTA States (V and VI).

II. THE LEGAL BASIS FOR THE PRINCIPLE OF STATE LIABILITY—APPRAISAL AND CRITIQUE OF *SVEINBJÖRNSDÓTTIR*

This chapter is not the proper place for an in-depth analysis of the reasons offered by the EFTA Court in *Sveinbjörnsdóttir*.[23] Still, parts of the reasoning are of interest to current discussions concerning the reach of the principle of State liability (as well as other questions of EEA law). Thus, some remarks appear appropriate.

In short, the EFTA Court deduced the principle of State liability from the purposes and legal structure of the Agreement, in particular the Agreement's overarching objective of a homogeneous European Economic Area with 'equal conditions of competition, and the respect of the same rules' (Article 1 EEA).[24]

True enough, the EFTA Court also referred to the need for effective judicial protection of individual rights as well as to the principle of loyalty enshrined in

---

acceptance of the principle of EEA State liability by the Contracting Parties and the pragmatic argument that it is simply not in the EU's best interest to 'liberate' the EFTA States from a principle which is of far greater concern to them than to the EU and the EU Member States, all suggest that the ECJ will not overrule *Sveinbjörnsdóttir* if the occasion should occur.

[22] *Cf*, eg, the submissions from the German government in Joined Cases C-46/93 and C-48/93 *Brasserie du Pêcheur v Germany and Factortame and Others v United Kingdom* [1996] ECR I-1029 at paras 24ff to the arguments of the Norwegian government in *Karlsson*.

[23] For an extensive analysis in the Norwegian language, see HH Fredriksen, *Offentligrettslig erstatningsansvar ved brudd på EØS-avtalen* (Bergen, Fagbokforlaget, 2013), pp 49–79.

[24] *Sveinbjörnsdóttir*, above n 1, paras 47–56.

Article 3 EEA.[25] Still, it is common ground that without the existence of the EU law principle of State liability, there would be no basis for an EEA law principle of State liability either.[26] Thus, the essence of *Sveinbjörnsdóttir* is that the EFTA Court applied the fact that the EEA Agreement as such confers rights on individuals[27] and the fact that Article 3 EEA reproduces textually the loyalty clause of the EU Treaties (now found in Article 4(3) TEU) to support a *functional* (or *effect-related*) conception of the homogeneity objective: the objective of homogeneity does, *as a matter of a legal principle* (not only as a political goal), embrace the question of the *effect of EEA law in the legal orders of the Contracting Parties*. In doing so, the EFTA Court dismissed the understanding of the dualist EFTA States that the reach of the homogeneity principle was limited to the interpretation of the substantive content of the internal market *acquis*, leaving it to the Contracting Parties to secure the effect of the rules through national procedures. Of course, this functional conception of homogeneity has consequences beyond the question of State liability as it establishes *a general presumption for judicial protection of EEA-based rights which, in effect, equals the protection offered in EU law*.[28] One consequence is the EEA-based duty of national courts to do whatever lies within their competence to interpret and apply national law in conformity to obligations under the EEA Agreement;[29] another is the EEA-based duty of administrative authorities to do likewise;[30] a third is the EEA-based obligation to repay charges levied in breach of EEA law[31] and a fourth is what the EFTA Court more recently has described as the procedural branch of homogeneity.[32] Thus, the conception of homogeneity established in *Sveinbjörnsdóttir* continues to influence the judicial development of EEA law.

Less fortunate, at least in this author's view, was the characterisation in *Sveinbjörnsdóttir* of the EEA Agreement as an international treaty *sui generis* which contains a 'distinct legal order of its own'. The striking parallel to the ECJ's

---

[25] *Sveinbjörnsdóttir*, above n 1, paras 57–58 and 61.

[26] See, eg, S Magnússon and ÓÍ Hannesson, 'State Liability in EEA Law: Towards Parallelism or Homogeneity?' (2013) 38 *European Law Review* 167–186, at p 171: 'Without the principle of State liability in EU law, EEA law would not have required this level of protection'. The same view is held by the President of the EFTA Court, Carl Baudenbacher, above n 7 at 356: 'It is clear … that the recognition of this principle [of EEA State liability] has its basis in the jurisprudence of the ECJ.'

[27] See the fourth and eighth recitals of the Preamble.

[28] For a more comprehensive argument for this conception of the homogeneity objective, see HH Fredriksen, 'State Liability in EU and EEA Law: The Same or Different?' (2013) 38 *European Law Review* 884–895, at 885–888.

[29] See *Karlsson*, above n 8, para 28; Case E-1/07 *Criminal proceedings against A* [2007] EFTA Ct Rep 246, para 39; Case E-15/12 *Jan Anfinn Wahl v Iceland ('Hells Angels')* [2013] EFTA Ct Rep 534, para 54; Case E-6/13 *Metacom AG v Rechtsanwälte Zipper & Collegen* [2013] EFTA Ct Rep 856, para 69 and Case E-7/13 *Creditinfo Lánstraust hf v þjóðskrá Íslands and Iceland* [2013] EFTA Ct Rep 970, para 47.

[30] See Case E-1/04 *Fokus Bank ASA v Norway* [2004] EFTA Ct Rep 11, para 41.

[31] See Case E-7/13 *Creditinfo Lánstraust hf v þjóðskrá Íslands and Iceland* [2013] EFTA Ct Rep 970, para 43.

[32] See, eg, Case E-14/11, *DB Schenker v EFTA Surveillance Authority ('Schenker I')* [2012] EFTA Ct Rep 1178, para 77.

characterisation of the EEC Treaty in its seminal judgment in *Van Gend en Loos* met little understanding in Norwegian literature. Critics pointed out that it was evident that the Contracting Parties to the EEA Agreement did not intend to establish a supranational legal order—arguably, this is the very reason for the Agreement's existence.[33] Further, it was objected that the mere characterisation of the EEA as a distinct legal order could not in itself contribute anything to the legal basis for the principle of State liability—the basis had to be found in the purposes and legal structure of the Agreement, not in a philosophical meta-discussion about the legal 'nature' of EEA law.[34]

It is not clear from *Sveinbjörnsdóttir* why the EFTA Court felt it necessary to postulate the *sui generis* character of the EEA Agreement. However, a possible explanation lies in the fact that Iceland, Norway and the European Commission all referred to the alleged common understanding of the Contracting Parties in their arguments against the principle of State liability.[35] Arguably, the notion of a distinct EU legal order has played an important role in the ECJ's 'emancipation' of the interpretation of the treaties from whatever common intentions the original Member States might have had. Still, for the EFTA Court it would have sufficed to note that pleadings from three governments and the Commission hardly proved a common understanding of the 20 parties which signed the Agreement more than six years earlier.[36] It is common ground that the question of the effect of EEA law in the legal orders of the Contracting Parties was a very difficult element of the negotiations and that this is why the Agreement contains no provision which unequivocally settles the matter.[37] Further, a possible common understanding against the existence of an EEA law principle of direct effect is hardly in itself a compelling argument against the principle of State liability.[38] The Icelandic government's view, that the absence of a provision in the EEA Agreement on State liability indicated that the Contracting Parties made a deliberate decision against *Francovich*, could easily have been turned on its head: if there really was such a common understanding, should it not—given the attention which *Francovich* attracted within the EC before the closing of the EEA negotiations—be expected to be put on paper, for example in the preamble or in a joint declaration?

[33] See, eg, T Bekkedal, *Frihet, likhet og fellesskap* (Oslo, Fagbokforlaget, 2008), p 137; HH Fredriksen, 'Bridging the widening gap between the EU treaties and the agreement on the European Economic Area' (2012) 18 *European Law Journal* 868–886, at p 881.

[34] ibid.

[35] See the Report for the Hearing in *Sveinbjörnsdóttir*, paras 60 (Iceland); 71 (Norway) and 96 (European Commission).

[36] See the apt remark by AG Lagrange in his Opinion in Case 8/55 *Fédération Charbonnière de Belgique v The High Authority* [1954–56] ECR (English special edition) 245, at 277: 'the common will … is in most cases difficult to establish with certainty in the case of documents such as international agreements, which are generally the result of compromises reached with more or less difficulty and in which the obscure or imprecise wording often only conceals fundamental disagreements'.

[37] See, eg, H Bull, *Det indre marked for tjenester og kapital* (Oslo, Universitetsforlaget, 2002), p 78 (Bull participated in the negotiations on the Norwegian side).

[38] As the EFTA Court later demonstrated in *Karlsson*, above n 8, para 29.

Interestingly, at the time *Sveinbjörnsdóttir* was pending before the EFTA Court, the French government actually argued *in favour of* EEA State liability before the ECJ in *Andersson*.[39]

Better still, the EFTA Court could have pointed out that as a matter of principle, the interpretation of an Agreement which explicitly confers rights on individuals cannot be guided by an understanding among the Contracting Parties which is not put on paper in a manner which is accessible to the public. However, even though this methodological point was not explicitly made in *Sveinbjörnsdóttir*, it may be inferred from the outcome of the case (as well as subsequent case law).[40] Thus, this too may be seen as a part of the legacy of *Sveinbjörnsdóttir* which continues to inform the interpretation of EEA law.

A final point of interest is the fact that *Sveinbjörnsdóttir* contains no reference to what the EFTA Court more recently has characterised as the fundamental EEA law principle of reciprocity.[41] Arguably, the EFTA Court ought to have pointed out that there already existed a principle of State liability in EU law *which includes breaches of EEA obligations for which the EU Member States can be held responsible* (as the EEA Agreement is recognised as an integral part of EU law) and that reasons of reciprocity thus supported the deduction of a similar principle of EEA law. However, the strength of this argument should not be overestimated. The origins of the reference to reciprocity in the preamble may be traced to Article 310 of the EC Treaty (now Article 217 TFEU) and here the ECJ has clearly stated that it is not to be understood in a strict sense.[42] Thus, at least in the view of this author, a reference to reciprocity is hardly more than an argument in support of the by now already well-established effect-related understanding of the principle of homogeneity.

III. THE REACH OF THE PRINCIPLE

As to the reach of the principle of State liability, the operative part and most of the reasoning in *Sveinbjörnsdóttir* was limited to incorrect implementation of directives.[43] Thus, in *Karlsson*, the Icelandic and the Norwegian government tried to limit the reach of the principle to cases of incorrect implementation of EEA obligations, arguing that in all other cases the effectiveness of EEA law was well taken care of by national law.[44] This reasoning essentially equals the argument by the

---

[39] See the submissions of the French government as they are referred to in the Opinion of AG Cosmas, above n 5, para 46.

[40] See especially Case E-5/06 *EFTA Surveillance Authority v Liechtenstein* [2007] EFTA Ct Rep 296, para 63.

[41] Case E-12/13 *EFTA Surveillance Authority v Iceland*, judgment of 11 February 2014, para 68.

[42] See, eg, Case 104/81 *Hauptzollamt Mainz v CA Kupferberg & Cie KG a.A.* [1982] ECR 3641, para 18.

[43] With the exception of para 62, where the EFTA Court referred to breaches of EEA obligations in general.

[44] See *Karlsson*, above n 8, para 31, read in conjunction with para 69 of the Report for the Hearing.

German, the Irish and the Netherlands governments which failed to convince the ECJ in *Brasserie du Pêcheur/Factortame*.[45] Thus, it was hardly surprising that the EFTA Court followed the ECJ's lead and stated in general that an EEA State may be held responsible for breaches of its obligations under EEA law.[46]

More recently, in *HOB-vín*, the EFTA Court stressed that is irrelevant whether a directive is being made or has been made part of the national legal order: with regard to secondary EEA law, individuals must be able to invoke the principle of State liability from the time when a decision by the EEA Joint Committee to incorporate a legal act in the EEA Agreement becomes applicable.[47] Thus, it is no prerequisite that the competent legislative authorities have actually tried to make the legal act in question part of national law (as in *Sveinbjörnsdóttir*).[48] And further, in cases of provisional applicability of a decision by the EEA Joint Committee, the principle of State liability will apply from the date on which the decision becomes provisionally applicable.[49]

Despite the general wording in *Karlsson*, the question whether the principle of State liability also covers *judicial wrongdoing* remains to be settled by the EFTA Court. It lurked in the background in *Kolbeinsson*, but the EFTA Court limited itself to noting in an obiter dictum that *if* States are to incur liability under EEA law for incorrect application of EEA law by national courts, the infringement would in any case have to be manifest in character.[50] It may hardly be inferred from this statement that the EFTA Court has adopted the ECJ's judgment in *Köbler*.[51] However, the above-mentioned effect-oriented conception of homogeneity suggests that the principle of State liability does encompass breaches of EEA law caused by national courts. Given the very limited role which the ECJ attributed to the duty of national courts of last instance to request preliminary rulings under Article 267 TFEU in its reasoning in *Köbler*,[52] it does not seem convincing to apply the lack of such a duty under Article 34 SCA as an argument against EEA State liability for judicial wrongdoing.[53]

---

[45] *Cf Brasserie du Pêcheur/Factortame*, above n 22, paras 18–22.

[46] *Karlsson*, above n 8, para 32.

[47] Case E-2/12, *HOB-vín v The State Alcohol and Tobacco Company of Iceland (ÁTVR)* [2012] EFTA Ct Rep 1092, para 128.

[48] In Norwegian literature, this question was briefly discussed by Jervell, above n 7 at 141, but the general view has always been that *Sveinbjörnsdóttir* applies also to cases where the State has made no attempt at all to implement the legal act in question.

[49] In cases where one or more of the Contracting Parties has notified the need to fulfil constitutional requirements before a decision of the EEA Joint Committee can be binding, Art 103(2) EEA states that upon the expiry of a period of six months, the decision shall be applied provisionally, unless the Contracting Party in question notifies that such a provisional application cannot take place. As demonstrated by Case E-17/11 *Aresbank SA v Landsbankinn hf, Fjármálaeftirlitið and Iceland* [2012] EFTA Ct Rep 916, there have been cases where Iceland has failed to prevent such provisional applicability.

[50] *Kolbeinsson*, above n 20, para 77.

[51] Case C-224/01 *Köbler v Austria* [2003] ECR I-10239.

[52] See *Köbler*, above n 51, paras 30–50.

[53] As argued by the Norwegian government in *Kolbeinsson*, above n 20, para 70.

Still, at the national level, a claim for compensation for judicial wrongdoing was rejected by Icelandic courts in the case brought by Mr Kolbeinsson. According to the Supreme Court, the City Court of Reykjavik was correct when it held that Icelandic procedural law (the principle of *res judicata*) precludes the possibility to claim damages for a breach of EEA law allegedly caused by a final judgment from the Supreme Court.[54] Neither the City Court nor the Supreme Court discussed the fact that the ECJ in *Köbler* rejected similar objections from several EU Member States, stating that proceedings seeking to render the State liable do not have the same purpose and do not necessarily involve the same parties as the proceedings resulting in the decision which has acquired the status of *res judicata*: the applicant in an action to establish the liability of the State will, if successful, secure an order against it for reparation of the damage incurred but not necessarily a declaration invalidating the status of *res judicata* of the judicial decision which was responsible for the damage.[55] The reasoning of the ECJ may well be criticised on this point, but one still has to acknowledge that the ECJ has recognised that the principle of State liability also applies to decisions of a court adjudicating at last instance.[56] Still, as neither the City Court nor the Supreme Court discussed the matter from the perspective of EEA law, the latter's judgment hardly contributes anything to the discussion; it only makes clear that application of an EEA law principle of State liability for judicial wrongdoing will necessitate changes in the rules on *res judicata* in the Icelandic Code on Civil Procedure.[57]

Another topical question is the reach of the EEA principle of State liability when it comes to its subjects. Throughout its decision in *HOB-vín*, the EFTA Court refers exclusively to the liability of the *EFTA States*.[58] This represents a break with earlier case law, in which the EFTA Court has been careful to refer to the liability of (all of) the Contracting Parties or at least to that of (all of) the *EEA States*.[59] The reason for this change is not clear, but it may perhaps be understood as an attempt to get out of the ECJ's shadow and warn the national courts of the EEA EFTA States that the liability of the EFTA States may not necessarily be coextensive in all respects with that of the EU Member States (see further in VI, below). Be that as it may, the EFTA Court has yet to come up with a convincing argument why the EEA State liability regime may apply to the

---

[54] Judgment of the Supreme Court of 21 February 2013 in Case 532/2012, upholding the City Court's judgment of 9 May 2012.

[55] See *Köbler*, above n 51, para 39.

[56] See, eg, T Tridimas, *The General Principles of EU Law*, 2nd edn (Oxford, OUP, 2006), at 525ff.

[57] It remains to be seen whether the EFTA Surveillance Authority will pursue the apparent conflict between an EEA law principle of State liability for judicial wrongdoing (which ESA argued in favour of before the EFTA Court in *Kolbeinsson*) and the Icelandic rules on *res judicata*.

[58] *HOB-vín*, above n 47, paras 119, 121 and 129–131.

[59] See *Sveinbjörnsdóttir*, above n 1, paras 61–62 and 68; *Karlsson*, above n 8, paras 32–34; Case E-8/07 *Nguyen v Norway* [2008] EFTA Ct Rep 224, paras 31–34 and *Kolbeinsson*, above n 20, paras 78–85. Note, for the sake of completeness, that the EFTA Court in para 60 of *Sveinbjörnsdóttir* referred to the liability of the EFTA States only, but in the rest of the grounds, as well as in the conclusions, the references are to the liability of (all) the Contracting Parties.

EFTA States only. The only possible explanation appears to be the assumption that the liability of the EU Member States for breaches of their EEA obligations is taken care of by the existing EU law principle of State liability and that this is to be seen as the *fulfilment of an EEA law obligation* (and not only as a generous concession on the part of the EU and its Member States for the benefit of private parties and economic operators from the EFTA States). Admittedly, Protocol 35 to the Agreement does lend some support for such a conclusion. According to this Protocol, the *EFTA States only* are obliged to introduce, if necessary, a statutory provision to the effect that EEA rules prevail in cases of possible conflict between implemented EEA rules and other statutory provisions. It may be inferred from this that the direct effect and supremacy that EU law grants to EEA rules in the EU Member States are to be seen as *part of the Agreement on the EEA*. Still, it appears questionable if this is sufficient to rebut the natural presumption that the EEA law principle of State liability, as it follows from the EEA Agreement as such, has to apply to all of the Contracting Parties—the EFTA States, the EU Member States and the European Union itself.[60] It will be interesting to see how the EFTA Court will handle this question in future State liability cases.

IV. THE CONDITIONS FOR THE LIABILITY OF THE STATES

As to the conditions for the liability of the Contracting Parties, the EFTA Court simply adopted verbatim the conditions which the ECJ set out in *Brasserie du Pêcheur/Factortame*. First, the EEA rule infringed must be intended to confer rights on individuals; second, the breach must be sufficiently serious; and third, there must be a direct causal link between the breach and the damage sustained by the injured parties.[61]

True enough, the only reference to ECJ case law in *Sveinbjörnsdóttir* was a reference to *Francovich* with regard to the first of the three conditions. Still, there was little doubt as to their origin.[62] Even though the EFTA Court did not refer to the principle of homogeneity, it did not attempt to give any other explanation for the formulation of the conditions.[63] And subsequent cases such as *Karlsson*, *Kolbeinsson* and *HOB-vín* all include at least some references to ECJ case law in relation to the conditions for the liability.[64]

---

[60] For a more detailed analysis, see Fredriksen, above n 28, at 888–890.

[61] See *Sveinbjörnsdóttir*, above n 1, para 66; *Karlsson*, above n 8, para 32 and *Kolbeinsson*, above n 20, para 121. Note, for the sake of completeness, that the requirement of a *direct* causal link was overlooked in *Sveinbjörnsdóttir*, but that this was corrected in *Karlsson*.

[62] See, eg, Baudenbacher, above n 7, at 344.

[63] Compare *Sveinbjörnsdóttir*, above n 1, para 66 to paras 39ff of *Brasserie du Pêcheur/Factortame*, where the ECJ explains why the liability of the EU Member States depends upon the existence of a sufficiently serious breach of their EU law obligations.

[64] See *Karlsson*, above n 8, paras 37, 40 and 47; *Kolbeinsson*, above n 20, para 77 and *HOB-vín*, above n 47, para 124.

Still, in *Karlsson* the EFTA Court followed up with an important reservation:

> The finding that the principle of State liability is an integral part of the EEA Agreement differs, as it must, from the development in the case law of the Court of Justice of the European Communities of the principle of State liability under EC law. Therefore, the application of the principles may not necessarily be in all respects coextensive.[65]

In *Karlsson*, this reservation was seen by the EFTA Court as necessary in order to repudiate the Norwegian government's assertion that the differences between EU and EEA law concerning the question of direct effect precluded the very existence of an EEA law principle of State liability.[66] As such, the statement said nothing about how the application of the principles may differ. Given the context in *Karlsson*, however, it was hardly surprising that the Norwegian government interpreted it as support for a narrower interpretation under EEA law than under EU law of the condition that there must be a sufficiently serious breach in order to establish State liability. In *Karlsson*, the Norwegian government argued for this proposition in the alternative,[67] whereas no one appearing before the EFTA Court in that case suggested that the EEA State liability regime might actually be stricter than its EU law model.

However, in the above-mentioned *Finanger II* case, the Norwegian Supreme Court forcefully rejected the government's interpretation, stating that a decisive emphasis should be placed on the principle of homogeneity and that it would not be reasonable if citizens should be in different legal positions under EU and EEA law when it comes to the protection of their EU/EEA rights.[68] Interestingly, this has not stopped the Norwegian government from reiterating before the EFTA Court that there may be situations in which EU State liability could come so close to direct effect that such a form of liability would be incompatible with the characteristics of the EEA Agreement.[69] However, in light of the above-mentioned functional conception of the homogeneity objective, and supported by the Norwegian Supreme Court's clear rejection of the case for a milder EEA State liability regime, it is very hard indeed to see the circumstances under which the EFTA Court might be persuaded by this line of argument.

Rather to the contrary, the effect-related conception of the homogeneity objective established in *Sveinbjörnsdóttir* (and endorsed by the Norwegian Supreme Court through the above-mentioned statements in *Finanger II*) suggests that the EEA State liability regime may be *stricter* than its EU model in cases where this is necessary in order to compensate for the lack of EEA law principles of direct

---

[65] Karlsson, above n 8, Para 30.
[66] See *Karlsson*, above n 8, paras 26–30.
[67] See the Report for the Hearing in *Karlsson*, paras 74–76.
[68] *Finanger II*, above n 13, para 58 (unofficial translation).
[69] See *Kolbeinsson*, above n 20, Report for the Hearing, para 94 and Case E-19/11 *Vín Tríó ehf v Iceland* [2012] EFTA Ct Rep 974, Report for the Hearing, paras 95–96.

effect and supremacy.[70] The EFTA Court has not yet had the opportunity to express itself on the matter, but the recent renaissance of the *Karlsson* reservation in *HOB-vín* and *Schenker II* may perhaps be interpreted as support for an answer in the affirmative.[71]

With this possible exception, the homogeneity principle strongly suggests that the application of the EU and EEA law principles of State liability indeed is coextensive. This is reflected in the case law of the EFTA Court, where the conditions for the liability of the Contracting Parties are explained and applied in accordance with ECJ case law.[72] Even though much remains to be said about the common conditions for the liability of the States, this is not the proper occasion on which to do so. Thus, with the exception of some brief comments in the next section on the role of discretion for the assessment of the seriousness of a breach, the conditions for the obligation of the EEA Contracting Parties to provide for compensation for damage caused to individuals by breaches of EEA law will not be discussed further in this chapter.

V. THE PRACTICE OF THE HIGHEST COURTS OF THE EEA EFTA STATES: ATTEMPTING TO SIDELINE THE EFTA COURT?

Even though the Norwegian Supreme Court's above-mentioned stand in *Finanger II* is to be welcomed from the perspective of homogeneity, it does at the same time pose a potential problem to the EFTA Court. Writing on behalf of the full court, justice Gussgaard concluded as follows:

> In my opinion, the considerations behind State liability within the EEA lead to the conclusion that it has the same scope and is at the same level as State liability in the EC. The ECJ's decisions on this matter thus hold significant interest.[73]

The Supreme Court has reiterated this in subsequent State liability cases and so have other Norwegian courts.[74] As a result, the attention of Norwegian courts in State liability cases is firmly directed towards ECJ case law concerning the principle of State liability under EU law. Both in *Finanger II* and the *Edquist* case from 2010, pleas from the plaintiffs for a request to be made to the EFTA Court under Article 34 SCA were rejected by the Supreme Court. Both cases raised unresolved

---

[70] As suggested by Baudenbacher, above n 7, at 357–358 and later discussed by, eg, Magnússon and Hannesson, above n 26, and Fredriksen, above n 28.

[71] The reference to the *Karlsson* reservation in *HOB-vín* and *Schenker II* is briefly discussed in VI below.

[72] See *Karlsson*, above n 8, paras 36ff; *Nguyen*, above n 59, paras 32ff; *Kolbeinsson*, above n 20, paras 77ff; *HOB-vín*, above n 47, paras 121ff.

[73] *Finanger II*, above n 13, para 58 (unofficial translation).

[74] See, in particular, the Supreme Court's judgments of 7 December 2010 in Case 2010/821 *Edquist and Others v Norway* (Rt 2010, p 1500), paras 91–92 and of 22 November 2012 in Case 2012/963 *Personskadeforbundet v Norway* (Rt 2012, p 1793), para 40. A recent example from Oslo City Court is the judgment of 8 January 2014 in Case 10-045497TVI-OTIR/06 *Norfrakalk v Norway*.

questions concerning the principle of State liability, but the Supreme Court chose to resolve them alone by relying upon existing ECJ case law.

This approach was continued in the *Personskadeforbundet* case from 2012. Here, the Supreme Court was confronted with the very same question which it refused to refer to the EFTA Court in *Finanger II*—how important is the measure of discretion which the infringed rule of EEA law leaves to the national authorities in the assessment of whether there has been a sufficiently serious breach of EEA law? In short, the majority in *Finanger II* stated that a general distinction has to be drawn between situations in which the EEA rule in question leaves the EEA States a wide discretion and situations where they have only limited or even no discretion. The minority, on the other hand, held that the breach in any case has to be manifest and grave and that the existence or non-existence of discretion is thus only a criterion in the assessment of whether this threshold is exceeded.[75] In the opinion of the government, the approach of the minority raises the threshold for liability in cases where the EEA States have only limited or even no discretion.[76] In *Personskadeforbundet*, the government argued that subsequent judgments from the ECJ had proved the minority right.[77] The Supreme Court addressed the question and hinted that the government might be correct. However, the matter was ultimately left open, as the court chose to concentrate on the degree of clarity of the directives infringed.[78] By implication, the judgment suggests that the structural disagreement in *Finanger II* need not have any practical consequences for the assessment of whether there has been a sufficiently serious breach of EEA law. This may very well be correct, but the same may not, at least in this author's view, be said about the underlying assumption that the 'manifest and grave' threshold applies also to situations where the EEA States have only limited or even no discretion.[79]

In the present context, the concern of the EFTA Court lies in the fact that a preliminary reference under Article 34 SCA was not requested by either the plaintiff or by the government, and that the possibility of a referral *ex officio* appears not even to have been contemplated by the Supreme Court. As a result, the EFTA Court has been denied a say in any of the three EEA State liability cases which so far have

---

[75] See *Finanger II*, above n 13, paras 59ff (the majority) and paras 111ff (the minority).

[76] As illustrated by the fact that the majority of nine justices in *Finanger II* upheld the judgment of the City Court awarding Ms Finanger damages, whereas the minority of four voted for the government.

[77] The government referred to Case C-446/04 *Test Claimants in the FII Group Litigation v Commissioners of Inland Revenue* [2006] ECR I-11753; Case C-278/05 *Robins and Others v Secretary of State for Work and Pensions* [2007] ECR I-1053 and Case C-452/06 *The Queen, on the application of Synthon BV v Licensing Authority of the Department of Health* [2008] ECR I-7681.

[78] *Personskadeforbundet*, above n 74, para 48.

[79] Admittedly, the ECJ's approach to the national authorities' measure of discretion in the assessment of whether there has been a sufficiently serious breach is complex and confusing. Still, as far as the application of the 'manifest and grave' threshold is concerned, cases such as C-424/97 *Haim v Kassenzahnärztliche Vereinigung Nordrhein* [2000] ECR I-5213; C-118/00 *Gervais Larsy v INASTI* [2001] ECR I-5063 and, in particular, C-278/05 *Robins and others v Secretary of State for Work and Pensions* [2007] ECR I-1053 suggest that the majority in *Finanger II* was correct. Support for this view may now arguably also be found in the EFTA Court's decision in *HOB-vín*, above n 47, para 130.

been heard by the Norwegian Supreme Court. Actually, the only Norwegian case concerning EEA State liability which was referred to the EFTA Court is *Nguyen*, where the referral came from Oslo City Court. Importantly, the lack of referrals to the EFTA Court may not be interpreted as Norwegian courts protecting the government from presumed unwelcome answers from Luxembourg: out of the three State liability cases decided by the Supreme Court, the government has lost two (*Finanger II* and *Personskadeforbundet*). Evidence from State liability cases from other EEA States suggests that this is a rather good record from the perspective of judicial protection of individuals. Still, as in other parts of EEA law, the Supreme Court's 'ECJ-centred' approach to the principle of State liability poses a threat to the authority and functioning of the EFTA Court.[80]

The same approach is evident in the Liechtenstein Supreme Court's decisions in the above-mentioned *Dr Tschannet II* case. Pleas for a reference to the EFTA Court under Article 34 SCA were twice rejected and even as the Supreme Court ruled in favour of Dr Tschannet in the final judgment from 2010, it did so without any references to *Sveinbjörnsdóttir*.[81] Instead, the Supreme Court referred at length to *Brasserie du Pêcheur/Factortame* and construed the national rules on the tort liability of public authorities in conformity with the standards developed by the ECJ.[82] As demonstrated by the outcome of the case, this was unproblematic from the perspective of judicial protection. To the EFTA Court, however, this *de facto* 'hand-over' of the control of the principle of State liability to the ECJ warrants some concern.

As to Icelandic courts, the picture is more nuanced. *Sveinbjörnsdóttir*, *Karlsson*, *Kolbeinsson* and *HOB-vín* are all Icelandic cases, brought before the EFTA Court by the City Court of Reykjavik. As to the Icelandic Supreme Court's final judgment in the case brought by Ms Sveinbjörnsdóttir, however, it is striking how the liability of the State is based upon interpretation of the national rules on the tort liability of public authorities and not upon open acknowledgement of the reasoning of the EFTA Court.[83] Still, the outcome of the case may only be characterised as very 'EEA friendly' indeed: the Supreme Court ruled in favour of Ms Sveinbjörnsdóttir even though the breach hardly could be described as

---

[80] For a critical analysis of the Supreme Court's attitude towards the EFTA Court, see HH Fredriksen, 'The Troubled Relationship between the Supreme Court of Norway and the EFTA Court—Recent Developments' in P-C Müller-Graff and O Mestad (eds), *The Rising Complexity of European Law* (Berlin, Berliner Wissenschafts-Verlag, 2014), pp 11–37.

[81] Judgment of 7 May 2010 in Case CO.2004.2 (final).

[82] *Cf* para 29 of the judgment.

[83] Judgment of 16 December 1999 in Case 236/1999 *Iceland v Erla María Sveinbjörnsdóttir*. Apparently, the Supreme Court was of the opinion that the act incorporating the main part of the EEA Agreement into Icelandic law gives individuals a legally protected expectation of correct implementation of EEA obligations. To a Norwegian lawyer, this reasoning is difficult to harmonise with dualism. The same line of argument was made before the Norwegian Supreme Court in *Finanger II*, above n 13, but it was unanimously rejected by the full court.

sufficiently serious from an EEA law perspective.[84] The outcome of later Icelandic State liability cases, however, has been less fortunate for the plaintiffs. In the case brought by Mr Kolbeinsson, the Supreme Court first prevented the question of State liability for judicial wrongdoing from being put to the EFTA Court and then, in its final judgment in the case in 2013, answered it in the negative it with an interpretation of the principle of *res judicata* which is in conflict the ECJ's judgment in *Köbler*.[85] However, as the judicial wrongdoing in question hardly was manifest in character, the outcome of the case still appears to be in line with the minimum requirements of EEA law. The same applies to the acquittal of the Icelandic State in the case brought by Karl K Karlsson hf and the partial acquittal in the case brought by HOB-vín ehf.[86]

The cases referred are perhaps not enough to conclude that the highest national courts of the EEA EFTA States deliberately attempt to sideline the EFTA Court. Still, to the EFTA Court, there is no denial that this is the practical consequence of the approach of the national courts.

VI. THE REACTION OF THE EFTA COURT: PROTECTING THE JEWEL IN THE CROWN

Regardless of the motivation of the national courts, it is certainly tempting to read the most recent State liability decisions of the EFTA Court as an attempt to reclaim its position on the playing field.

To start with, the above-mentioned *Karlsson* reservation concerning possible differences between the EU and EEA law principles of State liability somewhat unexpectedly re-emerged in *HOB-vín*.[87] The case did not raise any EEA-specific questions concerning State liability which called for an elaboration of this reservation (nor did the EFTA Court offer any). As the reservation was not mentioned in either *Nguyen* or *Kolbeinsson*, its re-emergence in *HOB-vín* inevitably attracts attention. And shortly thereafter, the reservation was highlighted again in *Schenker II*.[88]

Second, it is hard to overlook the EFTA Court's consistent references in *HOB-vín* to the liability of the *EFTA States* only. As noted above in III, this is a striking change from earlier State liability cases, where the EFTA Court has been careful

---

[84] Suffice to note the EFTA Court's own reference to the discrepancies between the various language versions of the provision in question in *Sveinbjörnsdóttir*, above n 1, paras 25–32 and the Commission's express view of the breach as not sufficiently serious (as it is referred in the Report for the Hearing, para 99).

[85] Reference is made to the discussion in III above.

[86] The case brought by Karl K Karlsson hf failed because the company was unable to prove the alleged loss of profit, see the judgment of the Supreme Court of 15 February 2007 in Case 120/2006. The case brought by HOB-vín ehf was only partially successful before the City Court of Reykjavik, see the judgment of 21 February 2014 in case E-2381/2011 (this judgment is not final).

[87] Cf *HOB-vín*, above n 47, para 120.

[88] Case E-7/12 *DB Schenker v EFTA Surveillance Authority ('Schenker II')*, [2013] EFTA Ct Rep 356, para 120.

to refer to the liability of (all of) the *Contracting Parties* or to that of (all of) the *EEA States*. It is carried through in such a systematic manner that it cannot be a mere coincidence and it leaves one with the impression that the EFTA Court strengthens the message to the national courts of the EFTA States that the liability of the EFTA States may not necessarily be coextensive in all respects with that of the EU Member States.

Third, *HOB-vín* is characterised by extensive paraphrasing of passages taken from the State liability jurisprudence of the ECJ, but without any references to the sources.[89] True enough, the EFTA Court has not been too eager to refer to ECJ case law concerning the principle of State liability under EU law in other cases either, but the reluctance in *HOB-vín* seems particularly apparent. If compared to the many references to relevant ECJ case law in cases dealing with other aspects of EEA law, the lack of any such references in *HOB-vín* is even more striking. Again, one is left with the impression that the EFTA Court is eager to avoid a complete 'hand-over' of the principle of State liability to the ECJ.

Further, a final opportunity for the EFTA Court to increase its appeal in the eyes of national judges lies in a wide interpretation of the allocation of competences between the EFTA Court and the referring national court under Article 34 SCA. Just as for the ECJ under Article 267 TFEU, the competence of the EFTA under Article 34 SCA is limited to 'interpretation' of the law, whereas the application of the law to the facts of the case is left to the national courts.[90] Disregarding objections from the Norwegian government in particular,[91] the EFTA Court has in recent years demonstrated a firm will to assert itself as primary adjudicator of whether a breach of EEA law is sufficiently serious to entail State liability.[92] According to the Court's President, this may be justified by the need to ensure effective protection of individual rights.[93] The implicit distrust of the national courts is unlikely to improve relations to the highest courts of the EFTA States, but the EFTA Court may perhaps hope that the approach will encourage references from lower courts more interested in opportunities to ease their own caseload than in general questions concerning the allocation of competences between the EFTA Court and the national judiciary.

---

[89] The passage in para 125 *in fine* is clearly taken from Case C-445/06 *Danske Slagterier v Germany* [2009] ECR I-2119, para 23; para 130 is a paraphrase of Case C-5/94 *The Queen v Ministry of Agriculture, Fisheries and Food, ex parte Hedley Lomas* [1996] ECR I-2553, para 28 (and subsequent ECJ case law) and para 131 is a paraphrase of Case C-278/05 *Robins v Secretary of State for Work and Pensions* [2007] ECR I-1053, para 73.

[90] See generally M Broberg and N Fenger, *Preliminary References to the European Court of Justice* (2nd edn, Oxford, OUP, 2014), at 154f and 428ff.

[91] *Cf*, eg, *Kolbeinsson*, above n 20, Report for the Hearing, para 75.

[92] *Cf Karlsson*, above, n 8, paras 42–46; *Nguyen*, above n 59, paras 32–35; *Kolbeinsson*, above n 20, paras 81–84; *HOB-vín*, above n 47, paras 132–136.

[93] See C Baudenbacher, 'The Implementation of Decisions of the ECJ and the EFTA Court in Member States' Domestic Legal Orders' (2005) 40 *Texas International Law Journal* 383–416, at 410 (concerning the similar approach of the ECJ).

VII. OUTLOOK—WILL THE PRINCIPLE OF STATE
LIABILITY 'SQUARE THE CIRCLE'?

More than 15 years after *Sveinbjörnsdóttir*, important questions concerning the reach of the principle of State liability still remain to be settled. At the level of principle, the question of strict liability in cases where the plaintiff's loss is caused by the lack of EEA law principles of direct effect and supremacy is of considerable interest. Strict liability for breach of EEA law in these circumstances will 'square the circle': the EEA Agreement does not entail transfer of legislative powers, but it nonetheless secures judicial protection of EEA-based rights, which, in effect, equals the protection offered in EU law. By accepting such an understanding of the EEA State liability regime, the EFTA States will put to rest possible allegations from the EU side of 'cherry picking'.

However, the principle of State liability as such, and the effect-related conception of homogeneity upon which it is based, is by now well established. No one can tell for sure how the EEA Agreement would have fared if the EFTA Court had not recognised the principle of State liability. Still, it is certainly tempting to tie the ECJ's clear change of opinion of the Agreement to the endorsement of *Sveinbjörnsdóttir* in *Rechberger*. From the deep scepticism voiced in Opinion 1/91 and, albeit to a lesser extent, in Opinion 1/92, the ECJ has come to recognise that it may indeed be possible to realise the EEA Agreement's objective to extend the internal market to the EEA EFTA States.[94] Given the weight which the ECJ seems to put on reciprocity when interpreting international agreements, it may be assumed that the EFTA Court's protection of EEA-based rights in the EFTA pillar has contributed to the ECJ's willingness to offer individuals and economic operators from the EEA EFTA States the same judicial protection in the EU as enjoyed by individuals and economic operators from the EU Member States. As the fate of the EEA Agreement relies on its continued acceptance by the ECJ, this may well be the most important legacy of *Sveinbjörnsdóttir*.

---

[94] See HH Fredriksen, 'The EFTA Court 15 Years On' (2010) 59 *International and Comparative Law Quarterly* 731–760, at 750–756.

27

Fine-tuning Transparency

FERGAL O'REGAN[*]

I. INTRODUCTION

FOR 35 YEARS, from 1957 until 1992, the Treaties provided for no right of public access to information or documents in the possession of the then Community institutions.[1] This legal framework did not, for decades, lead to any significant public disquiet.[2] With deepening integration, however, came growing concerns about the so-called 'democratic deficit' within the European project. This democratic deficit had numerous aspects, not least the need for greater electoral accountability. Confronting this 'democratic deficit' therefore involved, primarily, enhancing the role of Parliament through the greater use of co-decision. Dealing with the 'democratic deficit' also encompassed, however, the idea that institutions should act more openly towards the public.[3] The perception that greater openness was needed was fed by the relative complexity of the institutional structures and mechanisms, a complexity which many citizens may have (mis)understood as a deliberate means of excluding them from the levers of power.

---

[*] All views expressed herein are personal. They should not be understood to reflect the views of the European Ombudsman.

[1] In contrast, Member States have always ensured that they are provided with extensive rights of access to information and documents held by the EU institutions, bodies, offices and agencies (for an early example, see Art 10 of Regulation 17/62, which stated that the competent authorities of the Member States, through an Advisory Committee on Restrictive Practices and Monopolies, must be provided with in-depth information concerning competition law matters. Art 10 of Regulation 17/62 goes on to state that the Commission must closely and constantly liaise with the competent authorities of the Member States, who shall have the right to express their views upon the Commission's completion law procedures).

[2] This observation should be understood in context. The absence of openness toward individuals (until the Treaty of Maastricht), and the connected absence of rules on access to documents held by the EU institutions, was, for much of this period, also the dominant paradigm at national level. Until the late 1970s, none of the founding Member States had public access to document rules. Even today, not all Member States have public access to document rules.

[3] See, eg, G Majone, 'The Credibility Crisis of Community Regulation' (2002) 38 *Journal of Common Market Studies* 273; K Lenaerts, 'In the Union We Trust: Trust—Enhancing Principles of Community Law' (2004) 41 *CML Rev* 317, 318–319; K Lenaerts, 'The principle of democracy in the case law of the European Court of Justice (2013) 62(2) *ICLQ* 271–315; and J Lodge, 'Transparency and Democratic Legitimacy' (1994) 32 *Journal of Common Market Studies* 343.

The Treaty of Maastricht thus placed the openness of the institutions, towards those who had now become EU citizens, at the core of the nascent EU.[4] Article 1 TEU states that the Treaty 'marks a new stage in the process of creating an ever closer union among the peoples of Europe, in which decisions are taken as openly as possible and as closely as possible to the citizen'. Alongside this recognition that openness is a value underpinning the EU came Declaration 17, which declared that transparency of the decision-making process strengthens the democratic nature of the institutions and the public's confidence in the administration.[5]

Subsequently, when Article 255 EC of the Treaty of Amsterdam gave a specific legal basis for legislation on public access to documents, Regulation 1049/2001[6] was adopted. Regulation 1049/2001 provides for a right of public access to documents held by the Commission, the Council and Parliament,[7] subject to certain defined exceptions.

Regulation 1049/2001 gives any citizen of the Union, and any natural or legal person residing or having its registered office in a Member State, a right to have access to all documents[8] held by the Commission, Parliament or Council, that is to say, documents drawn up or received by the institution concerned and in its possession, in all areas of activity of the European Union.[9]

---

[4] Art F of the Treaty on European Union also introduced, for the first time, the term democracy to the Treaties (it referred to democracy as a principle on which the Union is founded and which is common to the Member States).

[5] While Declaration 17 had, strictly speaking, no legal effects—it was not until the Treaty of Amsterdam (Art 255 EC) that a specific legal basis for a right of public access to documents was introduced into the Treaties—its adoption marked a sea change. It recognised, for the first time, the need to strengthen the democratic nature of the EU institutions and the public's trust in these institutions through transparency. It also explicitly stated that transparency requires the adoption of measures allowing the public access to the information available to the institutions. Subsequently, the Council and the Commission adopted decisions on dealing with requests for public access to documents in their possession (respectively, Decision 93/731/EC on public access to Council documents and Decision 94/90/ECSC, EC, Euratom on public access to Commission documents).

[6] Regulation 1049/2001 of the European Parliament and of the Council of 30 May 2001 regarding public access to European Parliament, Council and Commission documents, [2001] OJ L 145/43.

[7] While Regulation 1049/2001 only applies to the Commission, Council and Parliament, most EU agencies operate under a legal renvoi to Regulation 1049/2001 (see, eg, Art 73 of Regulation 726/2004 laying down procedures for the authorisation and supervision of medicinal products for human and veterinary use and establishing a European Medicines Agency, which states that the Agency shall apply Regulation 1049/2001). Other institutions, bodies, offices and agencies have adopted specific rules on public access, which reflect the principles underpinning Regulation 1049/2001 (see, respectively, the EIB Transparency Policy, approved by a Decision of the EIB Board of Directors of 2 February 2010, and the Europol Decision of 8 July 2009 laying down the rules concerning access to Europol documents).

[8] The concept of 'document' covers 'any content whatever its medium (written on paper or stored in electronic form or as a sound, visual or audiovisual recording) concerning a matter relating to the policies, activities and decisions falling within the institution's sphere of responsibility' (see Art 3(a) of Regulation No 1049/2001).

[9] See Arts 2(1) and 2(3) of Regulation 1049/2001. An interesting aspect of Art 2(3) is the precise meaning of the term 'documents drawn up ... by it', 'it' being the institution holding the requested documents. The use of this terminology would seem, to this author, to imply that documents drawn up by individual members of staff, but not yet finalised, do not fall within the scope of Regulation 1049/2001 (they would only fall within the scope of Regulation 1049/2001 when they have been finalised and either archived or transmitted to other actors within or outside the institution). The EU Courts have not yet had reason to rule on the meaning of Art 2(3) of Regulation 1049/2001.

This right of public access is made subject to certain defined exceptions set out in Article 4 of the Regulation. Article 4(1) of the Regulation sets out a series of exceptions[10] which are absolute, that is, they are not subject to any requirement that they be balanced with any public interest in disclosure. In contrast, Article 4(2)[11] and 4(3)[12] of the Regulation sets out a series of exceptions that must be balanced with the public interest in disclosure. In principle, that balancing exercise can give rise to a finding that a document can be disclosed (when there is an overriding public interest in disclosure) even though its disclosure would undermine a protected interest disclosure.[13] The exception set out in Article 4(3) of the Regulation, relating to the protection of an institution's decision-making process, only applies where the decision-making process is *seriously* undermined. This is a higher threshold than that applied to the exceptions set out in Article 4(2) of the Regulation, where it is only necessary to demonstrate that the interests concerned are undermined.

All the above outlined exceptions must be interpreted and applied strictly.[14] If an institution refuses a request for access to a document, it must justify why access could specifically and effectively undermine the interest protected by an exception laid down in Article 4 of the Regulation. Moreover, the risk of the interest being undermined must be reasonably foreseeable and must not be purely hypothetical.[15]

The EU courts have recognised, however, that an institution may, in certain circumstances, rely on a general presumption that an exception applies to a category

---

[10] Art 4(1) allows for access to be denied where access would undermine the protection of the public interest as regards public security, defence and military matters, international relations, the financial, monetary or economic policy of the EU or a Member State. It also allows for access to be denied where access would undermine the protection 'privacy and the integrity of the individual', in particular in accordance with EU legislation on data protection.

[11] Art 4(2) states that access can be denied where access would undermine the protection of commercial interests of a natural or legal person, including intellectual property, court proceedings and legal advice, the purpose of inspections, investigations and audits, unless there is an there is an overriding public interest in disclosure.

[12] Art 4(3) states that access can be denied where access would *seriously* undermine the decision-making process of the institution concerned, provided that there is no 'overriding public interest' in disclosure. As such, a higher benchmark is set for the application of Art 4(3) when compared to Art 4(2) of Regulation 1049/2001. Art 4(3) distinguishes between requests for access to documents the release of which will affect an on-going decision-making process and requests for access to documents the release of which will affect a decision-making process that has already ended. Whereas there is no formal limitation on the type of document that can fall within the exception while the decision-making process is on-going, when the decision-making process has ended the exception only applies to documents that contain 'opinions for internal use as part of deliberations and preliminary consultations within the institution concerned'.

[13] While it is open to an applicant to put forward reasons why an institution should consider that there is an overriding public interest in disclosure, it would also appear correct that an institution must carry out an analysis, *ex officio*, as to whether or not there is an overriding public interest in disclosure, at least, as we shall see, as regards legislative documents (see below, n 49).

[14] See Case C-266/05 P *Sison v Council* [2007] ECR I-1233, para 63; Joined Cases C-39/05 P and C-52/05 P *Sweden and Turco v Council* [2008] ECR I-4723, para 36; Cases C-514/07 P, C-528/07 P and C-532/07 P *Sweden and Others v API and Commission* [2010] ECR I-8533, para 73.

[15] Case C-506/08 P *Sweden v MyTravel and Commission* [2011] ECR I-6237, para 76 and the case law cited.

of documents to justify a decision refusing access.[16] General presumptions thus effectively reverse the burden of proof that normally applies in relation to requests for public access to documents. If a general presumption is deemed to apply, the burden of proof, rather than lying with the institution holding the requested document, lies with the person requesting access, who must rebut the application of the general presumption in order to obtain access to the requested document.

This chapter will examine in detail the origin, extent and limits of such general presumptions. In order to provide a complete understanding of this issue, we will examine its application in relation to public access to 'legislative documents' and public access to administrative documents relating to investigatory procedures, with special emphasis on documents relating to competition law proceedings. The chapter will, in this context, define and connect two trends. One trend, that concerning access to 'legislative documents', reflects the understanding that access to documents can be one means of deepening the democratic nature of the EU, by ensuring that legislative procedures are carried out with maximum transparency. This trend towards maximum transparency as regards 'legislative documents' is characterised by the view that transparency does not normally produce any signif-icant negative impact on the legislative process, rather the opposite is understood to be true, and an implicit recognition that the public interest in disclosure of documents relating to that process will normally outweigh any possible negative impact resulting from transparency. As regards this trend, we shall see that the application of general presumptions that access can be denied is strictly limited. The other trend, relating to access to documents generated in the context of inves-tigatory procedures, in particular competition law proceedings, is characterised by a recognition of a need to protect the investigatory capacity of the Commission, in a context where the Commission relies, to a great extent, on the willingness of parties to provide, voluntarily, sensitive information to the Commission. As regards this trend, the general presumptions that access can be denied are given an extensive application.

II. ACCESS TO 'LEGISLATIVE DOCUMENTS'

Recital 2 of Regulation 1049/2001 states that 'openness contributes to strengthen-ing the principles of democracy and respect for fundamental rights as laid down in Article 6 of the EU Treaty and in the Charter of Fundamental Rights of the European Union'. While the principle set out in Recital 2 can be applied to requests for public access to any document in the possession of the institutions, and not only documents received or produced in the context of the adoption of legisla-tion, it is evident that the connection between transparency and the democratic

---

[16] See Joined Cases C-39/05 P and C-52/05 P *Sweden and Turco v Council*, para 50; and Case C-139/07 P *Commission v Technische Glaswerke Ilmenau* [2010] ECR I-5885, paras 55–61).

nature of the institutions is of particular importance when the institutions participate in the adoption of legislation.

The close connection between transparency of the decision-making process relating to the adoption of legislation, and the democratic nature of the institutions, has found an echo in the case law of the European Courts. The Court of Justice has held, in *Sweden and Turco v Council*,[17] that:

> [o]penness in that respect contributes to strengthening democracy by enabling citizens to scrutinize all the information which has formed the basis for a legislative act. The possibility for citizens to find out the considerations underpinning legislative action is a precondition for the effective exercise of their democratic rights.

The views of Advocate-General Cruz Villalón in *Council v Access Info Europe*[18] provide a clear and convincing perspective on the importance of this case law. He states that:

> Legislating is, by definition, a law-making activity that in a democratic society can only occur through the use of a procedure that is public in nature and, in that sense, 'transparent'. Otherwise, it would not be possible to ascribe to 'law' the virtue of being the expression of the will of those that must obey it, which is the very foundation of its legitimacy as an indisputable edict. In a representative democracy, and this term must apply to the EU, it must be possible for citizens to find out about the legislative procedure, since if this were not so, citizens would be unable to hold their representatives politically accountable, as they must be by virtue of their electoral mandate.

In sum, openness allows citizens to scrutinise all the relevant information which is used in the formulation of future legislative acts, acts which will impact directly on them.[19] Citizens are thereby provided with the knowledge and insights they require to take part in the public debate on the various considerations underpinning new legislation,[20] and to hold their political representatives accountable for the positions they take in relation to that new legislation. This may not only lead to better legislative outcomes, it also enhances the democratic legitimacy of the EU legislation,[21] the EU institutions that participate in the adoption of such legislation and of the EU.[22]

The special position of access to documents relating to the adoption of legislation is reflected in Recital 6 of Regulation 1049/2001, which states that wider access should be granted to documents in cases where the institutions are acting

---

[17] See *Sweden and Turco v Council*, para 46.

[18] See the Opinion of Advocate General Cruz Villalón of 16 May 2013 in Case C-280/11 P *Council v Access Info Europe*, nyr, para 63.

[19] In contrast, the impact of administrative decisions may only be felt (directly) by those to whom those decisions are addressed.

[20] See *Sweden and Turco v Council*, para 46.

[21] See the Opinion of Advocate General Cruz Villalón of 16 May 2013 in Case C-280/11 P *Council v Access Info Europe*, para 64.

[22] For an insightful and comprehensive account of the impact of greater transparency and greater public participation, see A Alemanno, 'Unpacking the principle of openness in EU law: transparency, participation and democracy' (2014) *European Law Review* 72.

in their 'legislative capacity', including under delegated powers, while at the same time preserving the effectiveness of the institutions' decision-making process. It adds that such documents should be made directly accessible to the greatest possible extent. Recital 6 is given effect through Article 12(2) of Regulation 1049/2001, which states that 'in particular, legislative documents, that is to say, documents drawn up or received in the course of procedures for the adoption of acts which are legally binding in or for the Member States, should, subject to Articles 4 and 9, be made directly accessible'.

Clearly, documents drawn up or received by the co-legislators themselves, the Council and the Parliament, in the context of the adoption of legislation, are 'legislative documents'. Many such documents are made available proactively on the websites of the Council[23] and the Parliament.[24]

Article 12(2) of Regulation 1049/2001, however, understands the term 'legislative documents' broadly, as covering documents drawn up or received 'in the course of procedures' for the adoption of 'acts which are legally binding in or for the Member States'.

Documents produced by working groups within the legislative body thus fall within the category of 'legislative documents' since they are clearly drawn up 'in the course of procedures' for the adoption of acts which are legally binding in or for the Member States. This was well illustrated by *Council v Access Info Europe*,[25] a case where the Council refused public access to working party documents containing the proposals for amendments put forward by a number of Member States concerning a proposal by the Commission (the proposal, coincidentally, sought to amend Regulation 1049/2001 itself).

'Legislative documents' would also include documents prepared by the services of the institutions *to assist* the legislator.[26]

A key area, for the future,[27] as regards transparency of 'legislative documents' is the issue of public access to documents produced in the context of the so-called informal 'trilogues'. Trilogues are informal tripartite meetings, attended

---

[23] See www.consilium.europa.eu/documents/legislative-transparency?lang=en (site checked April 2014). The available documents include:
— timetables and agendas of meetings of the Council and other preparatory bodies;
— summaries of legislative and non-legislative acts adopted by the Council, including the results of votes, explanations of voting and statements for the minutes when the Council is acting in its capacity as legislator;
— minutes of Council meetings, including the results of votes and explanations of votes by Council members.

[24] See www.europarl.europa.eu/RegistreWeb/search/typedoc.htm?codeTypeDocu=LTPED (site checked April 2014). Parliament's site contains extensive information. As regards 'legislative documents' the site includes Plenary documents, Committee documents and Conciliation documents.

[25] Judgment of the Court of Justice of 17 October 2013, *Council v Access Info Europe* (nyr).

[26] Indeed, in *Sweden and Turco v Council*, the document at issue was not a document *of* the legislator as such, but rather an opinion of the Council's legal service advising the Council on aspects of proposed legislation.

[27] Neither the Courts nor the Ombudsman have had the opportunity, to date, to examine this issue.

by representatives of Parliament, the Council and the Commission,[28] which aim to reach agreements on amendments to proposed legislation before the Council adopts its Common Position or the Parliament adopts its formal opinion. Trilogues can thus increase the likelihood that legislation is adopted at first reading. Documents relating to trilogues, such as the minutes of the negotiations drawn up by each institution, are not, however, made available proactively on the websites of the three institutions taking part in the trilogues. It would be difficult, however, to envisage how any requests for public access to such minutes could be systematically denied. The agreements reached in trilogues can be, and often are, decisive in terms of the eventual content of legislation. As such, the public's knowledge of the negotiations in trilogues can be key to ensuring that the public's political representatives can be held accountable to the public for the compromises they agree to. Without such knowledge, and the resultant accountability that it brings, the democratic nature, and therefore the legitimacy of the legislation subsequently adopted, would be questionable.[29]

The term 'legislative documents', and the consequent enhanced right of public access that should apply thereto, should also cover documents produced by the Commission when *preparing* proposals for legislation, such as documents produced for the purposes of inter-service consultations relating to up-coming proposals for legislation. Such documents may also be key to understanding the considerations underpinning legislative action. Public access to such documents is thus also a precondition for the effective exercise of citizens' democratic rights.

It follows that the term 'legislative documents', and the enhanced right of public access that should apply thereto, could also be understood to apply to technical assessments which feed into the legislative process, whether produced by the Commission or by the specialised agencies for the Commission. For example, documents produced by the European Aviation Safety Agency in the context of the process which would lead to the adoption of an EASA Opinion on the modification of flight and duty time limitations and rest requirements for commercial air transport could be

---

[28] As a general rule, trilogues involve the MEP rapporteur (accompanied at times by shadow rapporteurs), the chairperson of COREPER I (or the relevant Council working party) and representatives of the Commission (usually the expert in charge of the dossier and his or her direct superior, assisted by the Commission's Secretariat-General and Legal Service). Exceptionally, the political representatives of the Council and the Commission, namely Ministers and Commissioners, may take part in trilogues. The growing relative importance of trilogues can be gauged by the fact that between 1999 and 2004, less than 30% of (co-decision) legislation was adopted at first reading, whilst between 2004 and 2009, this was nearly 70%. Since 2009 this trend has continued upwards (see M Shackleton, 'The European Parliament' in J Peterson and M Shackleton (eds), *The Institutions of the European Union*, 3rd edn (Oxford, OUP, 2012), 136–137.

[29] See H Farrell and A Heritier, *The invisible transformation of co-decision: problems for democratic legitimacy* (Swedish Institute for European Policy Studies, 2003). Access to documents will, however, only shed light on trilogues if trilogues are properly documented. This may not, however, be the case to date, according to a Transparency International Report (see *The European Union Integrity System*, available at http://www.transparencyinternational.eu/wp-content/uploads/2014/04/EU_Integrity_System_Report.pdf, p 29), where it is suggested that no comprehensive minutes are produced. For an example of how effective trilogues can be in adopting legislation quickly, yet opaquely, see below, n 118.

understood to be 'documents drawn up or received in the course of procedures for the adoption of acts which are legally binding in or for the Member States'[30]. While EASA has no formal role in the legislative process, it nonetheless plays an important role in that process when it prepares the ground for the Commission on technical issues relating to air transport safety. The Commission, which has the exclusive right to propose legislation, and also plays a role in conciliating the possibly divergent positions of Parliament and Council, can be significantly influenced by such opinion of EASA. The Commission, and indirectly the co-legislators, thus rely heavily on the scientific work of EASA. EASA's work therefore impacts significantly on the interests of all EU citizens since it can be decisive in terms of the eventual content of legislation.[31]

Likewise, technical assessments from outside experts, requested by the Commission, or by an Agency assisting the Commission, for the purposes of evaluating legislative options, would also fall within the broad definition of a 'legislative document' for the purposes of applying Regulation 1049/2001.

It would also follow that any documents submitted by lobbyists to the Commission with a view to influencing a proposal for legislation, or to the Council or Parliament for the purposes of seeking to influence the legislative process in those institutions,[32] could also be understood as falling within the category of a document drawn up or received 'in the course of procedures for the adoption of acts which are legally binding in or for the Member States'.

The above examples relate to documents used in procedures which give rise to 'legislative acts'. The enhanced public access that applies to 'legislative documents' should not be limited, however, *ratione materiae*, to documents relating to the adoption of 'legislative acts'. For example, while 'delegated acts' are 'non-legislative acts',[33] they are nonetheless acts that will be 'legally binding in or for the Member States' within the meaning of Article 12(2) of Regulation 1049/2001. As a result, documents generated in the context of the adoption of such acts are, for the purposes of applying Regulation 1049/2001, 'legislative documents'.[34] This is

---

[30] See the Draft recommendation of the European Ombudsman in her inquiry into complaint 726/2012/(RA)FOR against the European Aviation Safety Agency, available at: www.ombudsman.europa.eu/en/cases/draftrecommendation.faces/en/52883/html.bookmark.

[31] The purpose of the EASA Opinion was to propose to the European Commission an update of the current rules on flight and duty time limitations and rest requirements for commercial aeroplane transport. See also Case T-121/05 *Borax Europe Ltd v Commission* [2009] ECR II-27, para 105, which states that scientific opinions obtained by an institution for the purpose of the preparation of legislation must, as a rule, be disclosed, even if they might give rise to controversy or deter those who expressed them from making their contribution to the decision-making process of that institution.

[32] A significant weakness in the access to documents rules is, in this respect, the fact that documents communicated in the context of the lobbying of individual Member States for the purposes of influencing their position in the Council, and in the context of the lobbying of individual MEPs or of political groups in the Parliament, do not fall under EU access to documents rules, since these rules only documents in the possession of the EU institutions, bodies, offices and agencies.

[33] Art 290 TFEU refers to 'delegated acts' as 'non-legislative acts of general application to supplement or amend certain non-essential elements of a legislative act'.

[34] Eg, any documents relating to consultations in the preparation and drawing up of delegated acts, such as consultations with experts from the national authorities of Member States responsible

a particularly important observation since the traditional system of 'comitology' was not characterised by a great degree of transparency toward citizens.[35,36]

The enhanced public access that applies to 'legislative documents' may also cover documents drawn up or received in the course of negotiations of international treaties by the EU since these international treaties may give rise to rules which are 'legally binding in or for the Member States'. There is, however, a temporal limitation on such access. Access can certainly be denied while the international negotiations are on-going. However, it would, this author argues, run counter to the principles set out in the *Turco* and *Access Info Europe* case law, to impose an absolute limit[37] on public access to the documents produced and used during the negotiation of an international treaty once that international treaty is submitted to the EU legislator for ratification.[38]

III. REFUSING ACCESS TO LEGISLATIVE DOCUMENTS

Regulation 1049/2001 does not exclude, however, the possibility that an exception to public access might justly not release any document held by the institutions, including legislative documents.[39] However, a particularly high barrier must be surpassed before an exception to public access could be deemed to apply to legislative documents.

As noted above, the Court of Justice has acknowledged that a refusal to grant public access to a document can be based on general presumptions which apply to certain '*categories*' of documents, as considerations of a generally similar kind are likely to apply to requests for disclosure relating to documents 'of the same nature'. That principle was first set out in *Sweden and Turco v Council*,[40] which concerned a request for public access to a 'legislative document', namely a legal opinion of the Council's legal service on a proposal for a Council Directive laying down minimum standards for the reception of applicants for asylum in Member States.

---

for implementing the delegated acts once they have been adopted, should fall within the scope of the enhanced public access applying to legislative documents.

[35] In contrast, Member States have always ensured that they have had detailed access to information and a control function relating to 'comitology' (see, eg, Regulation 182/2011 of the European Parliament and of the Council of 16 February 2011 laying down the rules and general principles concerning mechanisms for control by Member States of the Commission's exercise of implementing powers, OJ L 55, 28/02/2011, pp 13–18). The European Parliament also retains a general right of information as regards the activities of the Committees working on 'delegated acts'.

[36] See G Brandsma, D Curtin and A Meijer, 'How Transparent are EU Comitology Committees?' (2008) 14 *ELJ* 827.

[37] The General Court has not excluded that the end of international negotiations can have some impact upon whether a document relating to those negotiation can be disclosed (see Judgment of the General Court of 19 March 2013, *Sophie in 't Veld v European Commission*, nyr, paras 126–127).

[38] See Decision of the European Ombudsman in his inquiry into complaint 2393/2011/RA against the European Parliament, para 62 (at www.ombudsman.europa.eu/en/cases/decision.faces/en/50947/html.book-mark).

[39] See Art 12(2) of Regulation 1049/2001.

[40] See *Sweden and Turco v Council*, para 50.

As we will see in the section relating to investigatory documents, the use of a general presumption that an exception to public access applies can be used to justify the non-disclosure of broad categories of documents. However, its application as regards legislative documents is strictly limited.

In *Turco*, the Court of Justice first rejected the Council's argument that access could be denied to each and every legal advice relating to legislative matters.[41] It added, however, that public access to legal advice given in the context of a legislative process could be denied if that legal advice was of a 'particularly sensitive nature' or of a 'particularly wide scope', going beyond the context of the legislative process in question.[42] In such a case, it would be incumbent on the institution concerned to give a detailed statement of reasons for such a refusal.[43]

The Court of Justice, in sum, implies that very exceptional circumstances indeed must prevail before any document, or any category of document, relating to the legislative process can be withheld from the public. Documents relating to a legislative process that contains advice which is not sensitive, or which is merely sensitive but not particularly sensitive, will not surpass this threshold. Advice which may seek to highlight weaknesses in the proposed legislation would not, for example, meet this threshold. In this regard, it is of interest to note that, in *Turco*, the Court referred to the fear expressed by the Council that disclosure of an opinion of its legal service relating to a legislative proposal could lead to doubts as to the lawfulness of the legislative act concerned. The Court then observed that it is precisely openness in this regard that contributes to conferring greater legitimacy on the institutions in the eyes of European citizens and increasing their confidence in them by allowing divergences between various points of view to be openly debated. It added that it is in fact rather a lack of information and debate which is capable of giving rise to doubts in the minds of citizens, not only as regards the lawfulness of an isolated act, but also as regards the legitimacy of the decision-making process as a whole.[44] It should be noted that the Court is effectively, in the context of a balancing exercise between the interests of disclosure and the interests of non-disclosure, transferring to the other side of the balance, the

---

[41] See *Sweden and Turco v Council*, paras 57–68.

[42] See *Sweden and Turco v Council*, para 69. If a document were to contain advice of a particularly wide scope going beyond the context of the legislative process in question it would presumably still be possible to release the document by redacting the legal advice contained therein which goes beyond the scope of the legislative process in question (assuming that the redacted text could be shown to fall within an exception set out in Art 4 of Regulation 1049/2001). By way of example, if the advice included reflections on how future legislation might impact on specific operational or strategic decisions, it might be deemed advice of a 'particularly wide scope going beyond the context of the legislative process in question'.

[43] See *Sweden and Turco v Council*, para 69. If 'legal' advice can only be withheld if it is of a 'particularly sensitive nature', it would follow that other types of advice feeding into the legislative process could only be withheld if it too was of a particularly sensitive nature. Indeed, given that such advice could only be withheld under Art 4(3) of Regulation 1049/2001, which can only apply where the decision-making process is 'seriously' undermined by disclosure of a document, it should be even more exceptional that such other advice could be withheld.

[44] See *Sweden and Turco v Council*, paras 59–60.

side favouring disclosure, what the Council considered to be a general argument against disclosure. This approach by the Court demonstrates its willingness to delimit strictly any limitation on the right of access to 'legislative documents', in particular any limitations based on general presumptions.

The Courts have not yet had the opportunity to provide guidance as regards what might constitute advice of a 'particularly sensitive nature'. It is arguable, however, that advice to an institution relating to proposed legislation would be more likely to be considered 'particularly sensitive' advice if that legislation (or aspects of it), and therefore the advice relating to it, falls within the scope of the matters referred to in Article 4(1)(a) of Regulation 1049/2001. Article 4(1)(a) of Regulation 1049/2001, it will be recalled, allows for public access to be denied to a document where such access would undermine the protection of the public interest as regards public security, defence and military matters, international relations, the financial, monetary or economic policy of the EU or a Member State.[45] It should be recalled, in this context, that while an overriding public interest in disclosure can apply in relation to interests protected under Articles 4(2) and 4(3) of Regulation 1049/2001, no overriding public interest can apply in relation to documents which would undermine the 'particularly sensitive' interests set in Article 4(1)(a) of Regulation 1049/2001.[46]

Outside the scope of legislation relating to the matters referred to in Article 4(1) (a) of Regulation 1049/2001, it should be more exceptional for access to 'legislative documents' to be denied on the basis of the particularly sensitive nature of the requested documents, primarily because of the likely application of an overriding public interest in disclosure of the requested documents. The *Access Info Europe* case illustrates this point well. In *Access Info Europe*, the Council argued that the redaction of the names of those Member States putting forward amendments to a Commission proposal to modify Regulation 1049/2001 itself, by arguing that disclosure of the names of the Member States that put forward the amendments contained in the document would adversely affect the efficiency of the Council's decision-making process. The Court of Justice ruled that if the institution applies one of the exceptions provided for in Article 4 of Regulation 1049/2001, it should

> weigh the particular interest to be protected through non-disclosure of the document concerned against, inter alia, the public interest in the document being made accessible, having regard to the advantages of increased openness ... in that it enables citizens to participate more closely in the decision-making process and guarantees that the administration enjoys greater legitimacy and is more effective and more accountable to the citizen in a democratic system.[47]

---

[45] A hypothetical example could be the following. After the attacks of 11 September 2001, the European Parliament and the Council adopted Regulation 2320/2002 (now replaced by Regulation 300/2008) establishing common rules in the field of civil aviation security. It is arguable that advice provided in the context of the adoption of those Regulations would, given the very subject matter of the legislation, be deemed 'particularly sensitive'.

[46] See *Sophie in 't Veld v European Commission*, paras 108–110, and the case law cited therein.

[47] See *Council v Access Info Europe*, para 32.

The Court added that openness in that respect contributes to strengthening democracy by enabling citizens to scrutinise all the information that has formed the basis for a legislative act, which is a precondition for the effective exercise of their democratic rights.[48,49]

The above may lead to the conclusion that even though it was in relation to a request for access to a 'legislative document' that the Court first recognised that public access to a document can be denied based on general presumptions which apply to certain 'categories' of documents, such general presumptions should be of very limited relevance and application as regards 'legislative documents'.

IV. ACCESS TO DOCUMENTS USED IN INVESTIGATORY PROCEDURES

The European Commission has extensive powers to gather the information necessary to permit it to determine whether there exists an infringement of the EU competition law rules.[50] Article 28 of Regulation 1/2003 states that the information collected by the Commission pursuant to the powers granted to it under Regulation 1/2003 shall be used only for the purpose for which it was acquired. The Commission can thus, pursuant to Regulation 1/2003, only grant parties deemed to be 'interested parties' access to such information, with the exception of documents containing 'business secrets', 'other confidential information' and 'internal documents'.[51] All documents held by the Commission, however, fall within the scope of Regulation 1049/2001, which would imply that *any* member of the public can be granted access to documents containing information gathered pursuant to Regulation 1/2003, unless an exception set out in Article 4 of Regulation 1049/2001 applies. How can these rules be reconciled?

---

[48] ibid, para 33.

[49] As the Council had failed to weigh those competing interests properly—its arguments were too general and abstract to establish a sufficiently serious and reasonably foreseeable risk justifying the application of the exception—its decision refusing access was annulled. It would appear that the Court suggests that the institution holding the requested document must carry out the analysis as regards whether the public interest in disclosure outweighs the interest in non-disclosure *ex-officio* (see also *Sweden and Turco v Council*, para 44, where it is stated that 'if the Council takes the view that disclosure of a document would undermine the protection of legal advice as defined above, it is incumbent on the Council to ascertain whether there is any overriding public interest justifying disclosure'). A failure to carry out the balancing exercise *ex-officio* as regards requests for access to 'legislative documents' could, this author argues, be grounds for an annulment given that it should be obvious that such a public interest in disclosure of such documents always exists, therefore implying that, at least, the balancing exercise would always need to be carried out.

[50] As regards the enforcement of Arts 101 and 102 TFEU, see Council Regulation 1/2003 (OJ L1, 4.1.2003, pp 1–25) and Commission Regulation 773/2004 (OJ L 123, 27.4.2004, pp 18–24). The Commission also has extensive powers to gather information in the context of merger control and State aid investigations.

[51] See Art 28 of Regulation 1/2003 and Arts 6, 8, 15 and 16 of Regulation 773/2004. Documents obtained through access to the file can only be used by interested parties for the purposes of judicial or administrative proceedings relating to the application of Arts 101 and 102 TFEU.

First, it should be noted that neither Regulation has primacy over the other. It is therefore necessary to ensure that each of the regulations is applied in a manner which is compatible with the other and enables them to be applied consistently.[52]

As noted above, the Court of Justice has acknowledged that a refusal to grant public access to a document can be based on general presumptions which apply to certain categories of documents, as considerations of a generally similar kind are likely to apply to requests for disclosure relating to documents of the same nature. Whereas this principle has been applied strictly in relation to access to 'legislative documents', we shall see that it has been given an extensive application in relation to documents used in a procedure for reviewing State aid,[53] documents exchanged between the Commission and notifying parties or third parties in the course of merger control proceedings,[54] the pleading lodged by institutions in court proceedings,[55] documents concerning an infringement procedure during its pre-litigation stage[56] and documents relating to the enforcement of Article 101 TFEU.[57,58]

V. GENERAL PRESUMPTIONS BASED ON THE NEED NOT TO MODIFY THE NATURE OF A PROCEDURE

The first case in which the Court of Justice recognised the application of general presumptions in relation to documents in an investigatory file was *Commission v Technische Glaswerke Ilmenau*,[59] which related to a request for access to a file used in a State aid procedure. The Court of Justice recognised that since the State Aid Regulation[60] established special accessibility arrangements for such documents (only the Member State responsible for granting the aid is given the right to consult the documents in the administrative file), there was a general presumption that public access to the requested documents could adversely affect the purpose served by the State Aid procedure.[61] The Court found that if interested parties (such as the

---

[52] See Judgment of the Court of Justice of 28 June 2012 *Commission v Éditions Odile Jacob* (nyr), para 110; and Judgment of the Court of Justice of 28 June 2012 *Commission v Agrofert Holding* (nyr), para 52. See also, as regards compatibility of Regulation 1049/2001 with Regulation 45/2001, Case C-28/08 P *Commission v Bavarian Lager* [2010] ECR I-6055, para 56.

[53] See *Commission v Technische Glaswerke Ilmenau*, para 61.

[54] see *Commission v Éditions Odile Jacob*, para 123, and *Commission v Agrofert Holding*, para 64.

[55] See *Sweden and Others v API and Commission* [2010] ECR I-8533, para 94.

[56] See Judgment of the Court of Justice of 14 November 2013 in Joined Cases C-514/11 P and C-605/11 P, *LPN and Finland v Commission* (nyr), para 65.

[57] See Judgment of the Court of 27 February 2014, C-365/12 P, *Commission v EnBW Energie Baden-Württemberg AG* (nyr).

[58] The Ombudsman has also applied these concepts in relation to a request for public access to documents contained in a trade law investigation file (see Decision of the Ombudsman closing his inquiry into complaint 1039/2008/FOR against the Commission at http://www.ombudsman.europa.eu/en/cases/decision.faces/en/5404/html.bookmark).

[59] See above, n 16.

[60] See Council Regulation 659/1999, OJ 1999 L 83, p 1.

[61] See *Commission v Technische Glaswerke Ilmenau*, paras 55–61. However, the institution concerned must at least establish, in each case, whether the general presumption, adjudged to be normally

recipients of State aid or their competitors) were able to obtain access, on the basis of Regulation 1049/2001, to the documents in the Commission's administrative file, the system for the review of State aid would be called into question.

What does the Court mean by 'calling into question' the system for the review of State aid? The Court stated that public access to documents would enable interested parties (in the case at hand the requesting party was the recipient of the State aid) to obtain all the observations and documents submitted to the Commission. It could thereby adopt a position on those matters in their own observations to the Commission. It then stated that this 'is likely to modify the nature of such a procedure'.[62] This statement must be understood, according to this author, in the context of much older case law relating to access to documents concerning the application of Article 258 TFEU.[63] The purpose of the pre-litigation stage under Article 258 TFEU is to enable a Member State, which the Commission considers is not in compliance with its obligations under EU law, to conform voluntarily with EU law. State aid procedures have a similar purpose, since they have as their purpose, in the pre-litigation stage, convincing the Member State concerned that it should bring itself into compliance with EU State aid rules.[64] In infringement proceedings under Article 258 TFEU, the Member State may, after a letter of formal notice from the Commission, or even after receiving a reasoned opinion, decide to address the Commission's concerns by voluntarily bringing itself into compliance with its obligations under EU law. A Member State can do likewise in State aid procedures. In this context, we can see that the *nature* of the pre-litigation administrative proceedings can be characterised as a process of negotiation centred on a sincere dialogue, with genuine cooperation and an atmosphere of mutual trust[65] between the Commission and the Member State concerned. The preservation of that objective, namely an amicable resolution of the dispute between the Commission and the Member State concerned justified, the Court of First Instance found in those old cases, a refusal of access to the letters of formal notice and reasoned opinions drawn up in connection with the Article 258 TFEU proceedings. The same reasoning would underpin the analysis of a request for access to documents in a State aid file.

Since the specific type of damage to a State aid investigation which the *Technische Glaswerke Ilmenau* suggests will occur to the State aid procedure as a result of public access can only occur while the State aid procedure is on-going, the general presumption, at least to the extent that it is based on that specific type

---

applicable to a particular type of document, is in fact applicable to the specific document which it has been asked to disclose.

[62] See *Commission v Technische Glaswerke Ilmenau*, para 59.

[63] See Case T-309/97 *Bavarian Lager v Commission* [1999] ECR II-3217 and Case T-191/99 *Petrie v Commission* [2001] ECR II-3677.

[64] The Commission can close a state aid investigation procedure if the Member State under investigation takes steps, during the investigation, to ensure that the measure communicated to the Commission by the Member State does not constitute 'aid' or (if it is 'aid') that the aid is compatible with the common market (see Council Regulation 659/1999, Arts 7(2) and 7(3)).

[65] See *Petrie v Commission*, paras 67 and 68.

of damage, would not necessarily apply once the State aid investigation has ended. The same observation can be made as regards merger proceedings or proceedings relating to the enforcement of Articles 101 or 102 TFEU.[66]

But when have such procedures ended? The Court of Justice has ruled, in relation to access to documents concerning proceedings under Article 101 TFEU,[67] that a procedure cannot be regarded as completed when the Commission's decision has been adopted. Investigations relating to such proceedings may be regarded as completed only when the decision adopted by the Commission is no longer subject to judicial review.[68] Up to that point in time, the Commission may be prompted, if the decision to which the documents relate is annulled, to resume its investigations with a view to the possible adoption of a new decision.[69]

The Court of Justice has also held that, separate from the issue of protecting the Commission's (on-going) investigatory process, limitations on access to the investigation file may be necessary to ensure the protection of the court proceedings in which the annulment of the Commission decision is sought. In the Court's view, the protection of those proceedings implies that compliance with the principles of equality of arms and the sound administration of justice must be ensured. The Court added that access to documents by one party in those court proceedings could well upset the vital balance between the parties to a dispute—the state of balance which is at the basis of the principle of equality of arms—since only the institution concerned by an application for access to its documents, and not all the parties to the court proceedings, would be bound by the obligation of disclosure.[70]

VI. ACCESS TO INTERNAL DOCUMENTS AFTER A PROCEDURE HAS BEEN COMPLETED

Once an investigation has definitively ended, the first general presumption referred to above, which relates to the need to ensure that public access would not *modify the nature of a procedure*, by giving parties the opportunity to use information in that procedure which they would otherwise not have access to, can no longer

---

[66] See also the Decision of the Ombudsman closing his inquiry into complaint 2953/2008/FOR against the Commission (at http://www.ombudsman.europa.eu/cases/decision.faces/en/5168/html. bookmark), where the Ombudsman noted that in order for this dialogue to be properly carried out in state aid procedures there must be genuine cooperation and an atmosphere of mutual trust between the Commission and the Member State concerned. In the Ombudsman's view, exactly the same point could be made as regards an on-going commitments procedure under Art 9 of Regulation 1/2003, where the Commission seeks to enter into a dialogue with a party under investigation with a view to obtaining commitments which would put an end to an infringement of EU competition law.

[67] See *Commission v EnBW Energie Baden-Württemberg AG*, para 99. Similar conclusions could not be drawn as regards state aid proceedings and merger proceedings (see *Commission v Edition Odile Jacob*, paras 128–131).

[68] This will occur if the decision is not appealed or when the judicial remedies have been exhausted.

[69] See *Commission v EnBW Energie Baden-Württemberg AG*, para 114.

[70] See *Commission v Éditions Odile Jacob*, para 132; and *Sweden and Others v API and Commission*, paras 84, 85 and 87.

apply. As we shall see below, a second general presumption can apply after the investigation has definitively ended. However, since that general presumption is based on the likelihood that documents in an investigatory file will contain commercially sensitive information, and the connected harm that disclosure of such information will have on the capacity of the Commission to gather information, it can only apply to requests for public access to documents received from third parties or documents of the Commission incorporating commercially sensitive information obtained from third parties. That first general presumption should not apply to internal documents provided they do not contain any of the information gathered in the context of the investigation or references to that information. Even if the general presumption is given a broad application, to cover all documents in the investigation file, including purely internal documents that do not contain any of the information gathered in the context of the investigation or references to that information, it should be possible, as regards such internal documents, to rebut the general presumption.

Thus, at that stage, unless another general presumption, based on alternative reasoning, can be deemed to apply, the Commission would be required, if it wishes to refuse access to an internal document in the regulatory file, to explain how access to the requested document is likely, actually and specifically, and not on the basis of general and abstract considerations, to undermine the interest protected by an exception under Regulation 1049/2001.[71] The most obvious exception under Regulation 1049/2001 that would be invoked is Article 4(3), second subparagraph. However, that provision covers only documents containing '*opinions*' for internal use as part of '*deliberations and preliminary consultations*'.[72] Thus, not all internal documents can benefit from this exception. Further, it should be demonstrated, specifically, how disclosure of those documents containing opinions for internal use would seriously undermine the decision-making process of the Commission.[73] A high standard of proof is required in this respect.

In *MyTravel*, the Court of Justice[74] rejected the position taken by the General Court,[75] which was that disclosure of internal notes of DG Competition would risk communicating to the public information on the state of internal discussions between DG Competition and the Commission's legal service on the lawfulness of the assessment of the compatibility of a merger with EU law, which would risk affecting decisions which might fall to be made as regards the same parties or in the same sector. The Court of Justice stated that, as regards the fear that disclosure could lead to doubts as to the lawfulness of the final decision, it is precisely openness in this regard that contributes to conferring greater legitimacy on the institutions in the eyes of European citizens and increasing their confidence in them by allowing divergences between various points of view to be openly debated. It is, it added, in

---

[71] See *Sweden and MyTravel v Commission*, paras 110, 115 and 117.
[72] See above, n 12.
[73] See *Sweden and MyTravel v Commission*, para 82.
[74] See *Sweden and MyTravel v Commission*, paras 113–114.
[75] See Case T-403/05 *MyTravel v Commission* [2008] ECR II-2027, para 124.

fact rather a lack of information and debate which is capable of giving rise to doubts in the minds of citizens, not only as regards the lawfulness of an isolated act, but also as regards the legitimacy of the decision-making process as a whole.

The General Court had also taken the view in *MyTravel*[76] that disclosure of internal documents would be liable to lead the legal service to display reticence and caution in the future in the drafting of such notes. This argument was also rejected by the Court of Justice,[77] who stated that such an argument would need to be supported by concrete and detailed evidence, and not based solely on general and abstract considerations.[78]

In sum, given that there is no general presumption that access can be denied to purely internal documents after an investigation has been definitively completed, the Commission must make a concrete examination of the content of the internal document at issue in order to evaluate if the nature and intensity of the risk which arises as a result of the public disclosure of the document is sufficient to undermine seriously its decision-making processes.

VII. GENERAL PRESUMPTIONS BASED ON THE NEED TO PROTECT INFORMATION-GATHERING POWERS

State aid procedures, merger procedures and procedures under Articles 101 and 102 TFEU are characterised by the need for the Commission to gather possibly sensitive commercial information about the undertaking under investigation and about the sector in which they operate.[79]

The protection afforded to this information under Regulations 1/2003 and 773/2004, under the Merger Regulation and under the State Aid Regulation, serves to reassure parties that submit such information to the Commission that disclosure of such information will be strictly controlled. Such reassurances are important in terms of the effectiveness of the Commission's investigations. If the Commission cannot successfully gather such information, because those that hold it become unwilling to provide it to the Commission, the Commission will have difficulties carrying out its investigatory role properly and completely. The Court

---

[76] ibid, para 125.

[77] *Sweden and MyTravel v Commission*, paras 115–117.

[78] See Case T-121/05 *Borax Europe Ltd v Commission* [2009] ECR II-27, paras 70–71.

[79] As regards cartel procedures, the Court of Justice has stated that, having regard to the objective of a proceeding under Art 101 EC, which is to ascertain whether or not an agreement between undertakings is compatible with the common market, the Commission is likely to gather, in the context of such a proceeding, commercially sensitive information concerning, inter alia, the commercial strategies of the undertakings concerned, their sales figures, their market shares or their business relations, so that disclosure of documents relating to such a proceeding may undermine the protection of the commercial interests of those undertakings. Accordingly, the exceptions relating to the protection of commercial interests and the protection of the purpose of investigations are, in such a procedure, closely connected (see *Commission v EnBW Energie Baden-Württemberg AG*, para 79). See also, as regards merger procedures, *Commission v Editions Odile Jacob*, para 115, and *Commission v Agrofert Holding*, para 56.

of Justice has thus recognised that the need to protect commercial interests and the need to protect the purpose of investigations are closely connected.[80]

In this context, the Court of Justice also acknowledged the existence of a separate general presumption, whereby it is presumed, first, that such investigatory files contain documents which may, if disclosed to the public, undermine the protection of the commercial interests of the undertakings involved in the investigatory proceedings,[81] and second, that such disclosure will, as a consequence of the undermining of the confidence of investigated parties and interested parties that their commercial interests will be protected, also undermine the protection of the purpose of investigations.[82,83]

This additional general presumption would continue to apply *even after* the proceedings in question have definitively ended. If parties that are requested to provide information to the Commission in the context of an investigation fear that their commercially sensitive information will be released, even after the investigatory procedure has ended, they may be less willing to cooperate during that procedure. Are there any time limits to this general presumption? As we will see, the case law considers that there are not. However, it is useful to explore this issue in some detail before looking at the position taken by the Courts.

The information gathered by the Commission in merger proceedings will relate to the commercial strategies of the undertakings concerned, their sales figures, their market shares or their business relations. This information is likely to be, by its very nature, commercially sensitive. It is also, at least at the time the merger is notified, up-to-date. Information supplied in a merger notification concerning commercial strategies may also be projected into the future. Similar conclusions could be drawn as regards documents submitted in the context of State aid procedures, since the nature of State aid procedures seeks to evaluate the financial and commercial situation of the State aid recipient at the time the State aid is notified to the Commission and also its future financial and commercial prospects.

Notwithstanding these observations, a request for public access to documents in such files may be made many years after such procedures have ended, when such information may have become commercially obsolete.

The potential for information in a requested document to be commercially obsolete when a request for access is made is even more likely as regards documents obtained from undertakings during proceedings under Articles 101 and 102 TFEU, since the information gathered (which may also include commercial strategies of the undertakings concerned, their sales figures, their market shares or their business relations) can only relate to commercial activities that have ended (possibly many) years prior to the adoption of the decision finding an infringement of Article 101 or 102 TFEU.

---

[80] See *Commission v EnBW Energie Baden-Württemberg AG*, para 90, *Commission v Éditions Odile Jacob*, para 121, and *Commission v Agrofert Holding*, para 62.

[81] See the first indent of Art 4(2) of Regulation 1049/2001.

[82] See the third indent of Art 4(2) of Regulation 1049/2001.

[83] See *Commission v Éditions Odile Jacob*, para 123; and *Commission v Agrofert Holding*, para 64; *Commission v EnBW Energie Baden-Württemberg AG*, para 80.

In sum, time alone cannot shield such documents from public disclosure.

It is also interesting to examine closely the precise manner in which the Commission gathers information.

As noted above, the close connection between the need to protect commercial interests and the need to protect the purpose of investigations, which forms the basis of this separate general presumption, is based on the understanding that the Commission's capacity to gather sensitive information could be undermined if undertakings become unwilling to provide the Commission with that information for fear that this information might be released to the public subsequent to the closure of the proceedings. The general presumption would thus appear to be based on a need to ensure cooperation from interested parties. However, the Commission's powers to gather information under Regulations 1/2003 and 773/2004 do not all require the active cooperation of the undertakings holding the required information. Articles 20 and 21 of Regulation 1/2003 empower the Commission to conduct, with or without the active cooperation of the undertakings concerned, all necessary inspections of undertakings and associations of undertakings, which encompasses the right (a) to enter any premises, land and means of transport; (b) to examine the books and other records related to the business, irrespective of the medium on which they are stored; (c) to take or obtain in any form copies of or extracts from such books or records; and (d) to seal any business premises and books or records for the period and to the extent necessary for the inspection. Any failure to submit to an inspection can give rise, under Article 23 and 24 of Regulation, to a financial penalty. Many documents obtained in inspections are obtained notwithstanding the unwillingness of the party concerned to provide such documents to the Commission. In this context, it might be questioned whether there is, as regards information gathered using these powers, a close connection between the need to protect commercial interests and the need to protect the purpose of investigations.

In contrast, when documents are obtained under Article 18 of Regulation 1/2003, where parties are required to provide the Commission with all necessary information requested by the Commission, it is evident, despite the power of the Commission to impose fines on undertakings that refuse to comply with a request, that the willingness of the parties concerned to cooperate with the Commission may have at least some impact on the amount of information the Commission obtains.[84] Such willingness could, arguably, be undermined if the undertakings fear that the information provided may be disclosed to the public at some future time. The argument is even stronger in relation to statements gathered under Article 19 of Regulation 1/2003, since Article 19 only empowers the Commission to interview any natural or legal person *who consents to be interviewed*. Likewise, and importantly, such considerations also apply as regards information obtained

---

[84] A similar observation could be made as regards information obtained under Art 20(1)(e) of Regulation 1/2003.

by the Commission subject to its leniency programme.[85] Referring to national leniency programmes, the Court of Justice has noted that such programmes

> are useful tools if efforts to uncover and bring an end to infringements of competition rules are to be effective and thus serve the objective of effective application of Articles 101 TFEU and 102 TFEU. The effectiveness of those programmes could be compromised if documents relating to leniency proceedings were disclosed to persons wishing to bring an action for damages. The view can reasonably be taken that a person involved in an infringement of competition law, faced with the possibility of such disclosure, would be deterred from taking the opportunity offered by such leniency programmes.[86]

It should be recalled, at this stage, that the system of general presumptions, first set out in *Turco*, implies that a general presumption can be deemed to apply to certain 'categories' of documents, as considerations of a generally similar kind are likely to apply to requests for disclosure relating to documents 'of the same nature'. The extent of the general presumption is thus dependent on the extent of the 'category of documents of the same nature'. It is clear that the category of documents can be defined broadly if the nature of the documents concerned is defined vaguely. Conversely, a more precise definition of the 'nature of the documents' concerned will lead to a narrower 'category' of documents, and therefore a more narrowly construed general presumption.

For example, if, for the purposes of establishing a general presumption that access can be denied, the nature of documents were defined broadly as 'all documents obtained by the Commission from third parties and documents containing information obtained from third parties, irrespective of the manner in which these documents and information were obtained', the resulting general presumption would cover all documents and information obtained under Articles 18–21 of Regulation 1/2003 and through a leniency application. The distinctions set out above would thus have no relevance as regards the extent of the general presumption. If, however, the nature of documents were defined taking account of the specific manner in which these documents (or the information used to create them) were obtained (that is, taking into account whether they were obtained, on the one hand, under Articles 18 and 19 of Regulation 1/2003 or through leniency, and, on the other hand, under Articles 20 and 21 of Regulation 1/2003), arguably, a general presumption might not be deemed to apply to the category of documents obtained pursuant to Articles 20–21 of Regulation 1/2003.

As we shall see, the case law of the EU Courts ignores the arguments in favour of narrower categories when establishing the general presumption that exceptions to public access apply to investigatory documents (the case law includes all documents in the investigatory file that are obtained from third parties in a single broad category). Before examining this case law, it is useful to examine the approach of the EFTA Court.

---

[85] See Commission notice on immunity from fines and reduction of fines in cartel cases (OJ C 298, 8 December 2006, p 17).

[86] Case C-360/09 *Pfleiderer* [2011] ECR I-5161, paras 25–27.

VIII. THE APPROACH OF THE EFTA COURT: *SCHENKER*

The EFTA Surveillance Authority applies rules on public access to documents[87] which are essentially identical to Regulation 1049/2001. In *Schenker*,[88] the EFTA Court examined a decision of the EFTA Surveillance Authority denying the applicant, Schenker, access to 350 documents seized during the inspection of Norway Post's premises (Schenker had sought access in order to prepare a claim for damages against Norway Post, who had been found to have abused its dominant position in the business-to-consumer parcel market in Norway).

The Surveillance Authority argued that these documents contained both commercially sensitive information and information concerning private individuals.

The EFTA Court ruled that the limitations to public access had to be applied strictly. It added that the Surveillance Authority had not broken down the requested documents into groups of the same category or nature, or listed them individually, in such a way as to allow either the applicant or the EFTA Court to determine their nature or the Surveillance Authority's grounds for determining that they contained information which was liable to undermine the commercial interests of Norway Post.[89] The EFTA Court went on to suggest that the categorisation that should take place should distinguish leniency documents from other documents in the file.[90] In sum, the EFTA Court, applying a rigorous and logical reasoning, sought to apply the general presumption theory through a strict understanding of the nature of the documents at issue.

In addition, the EFTA Court ruled that the Surveillance Authority had erred by failing to consider whether the private enforcement of competition law and institutional transparency might constitute an overriding public interest in disclosure.[91]

IX. THE APPROACH OF THE EU COURTS

The EU Courts have taken an alternative approach.[92]

In *Commission v EnBW Energie Baden-Württemberg AG*,[93] the Court of Justice overturned the ruling of the General Court in *EnBW Energie Baden-Württemberg*

---

[87] Decision No 407/2008/COL of 27 June 2008 on Rules on Access to Documents.

[88] See Judgment of the EFTA Court of 21 December 2012, in Case E-14/11, *Schenker North AB v EFTA Surveillance Authority* [2013] 4 *Common Market Law Reports* 17.

[89] See *Schenker*, para 191.

[90] See *Schenker*, paras 222–224.

[91] See *Schenker*, paras 132 and 241. It should be noted that the EFTA Court was not required, in *Schenker*, to examine the scope of general presumptions since the decision of the Surveillance Authority refusing access in the case before the Court had not relied on a general presumption.

[92] It is worth noting that the EFTA Court is required to ensure a homogenous interpretation of EFTA access rules and Regulation 1049/2001, so as to ensure at least the same degree of openness as provided for by Regulation 1049/2001 (see Recital 7 of Decision No 407/2008/COL and *Schenker*, para 121). The EFTA Court would not appear to be constrained, however, from giving an interpretation which provides for a broader level of public access.

[93] See above n 57.

AG v Commission.[94] The Court of Justice noted that the documents at issue relate to an 'investigation' within the meaning of the third indent of Article 4(2) of Regulation 1049/2001, and that they *may* contain commercially sensitive information for the purpose of the first indent of Article 4(2) of Regulation 1049/2001.[95] In this respect, it noted that, given the objective of a proceeding under Article 101 TFEU, which is to ascertain whether or not an agreement between undertakings is compatible with the common market, the Commission *is likely* to gather, in the context of such a proceeding, commercially sensitive information concerning, inter alia, the commercial strategies of the undertakings concerned, their sales figures, their market shares or their business relations, so that disclosure of documents relating to such a proceeding may undermine the protection of the commercial interests of those undertakings.[96]

The Court of Justice then held that the *close connection* between the need to protect commercial interests and the need to protect the purpose of investigations creates a general presumption that disclosure of documents would both undermine the protection of the commercial interests of the undertakings involved in proceedings, as well as the protection of the purpose of investigations relating to proceedings.

It should be understood that the Court's position as to the existence of this general presumption (which is, as will see, rebuttable) is not based on the view that all documents in a defined category *will*, necessarily, if disclosed to the public, undermine an interest protected under Article 4 of Regulation 1049/2001. Rather, the general presumption is based on the view that disclosure of such documents *is likely* to undermine an interest protected under Article 4 of Regulation 1049/2001, that likelihood being based on the fact that competition law enforcement requires the gathering of commercially sensitive information concerning, inter alia, the commercial strategies of the undertakings concerned, their sales figures, their market shares or their business relations. In sum, the general presumption does not require certainty, but rather requires likelihood (that the documents requested will contain commercially sensitive information).

In this respect, in order to support the view that the documents are likely to contain commercially sensitive information, the Court noted that it is relevant (if not determinative) that the parties to a proceeding under Article 101 TFEU (and 102 TFEU) do not, under Regulations 1/2003 and 773/2004, enjoy an unlimited right of access to the documents in the Commission's file (their rights are subject to the protection of the business secrets and other confidential information

---

[94] See Case T-344/08, *EnBW Energie Baden-Württemberg AG v Commission*, paras 113–150 and 174. The General Court took the view that a general presumption concerning the protection of commercial interests did not apply to requested documents since most of the information in the file dated from long before the decision refusing public access was taken. The General Court thus found that the Commission should have carried out a specific, individual examination of the documents concerned to demonstrate how their disclosure would undermine the protection of the commercial interests of the persons concerned.
[95] See *Commission v EnBW Energie Baden-Württemberg AG*, para 78.
[96] ibid, para 79.

of undertakings) and that third parties, with the exception of complainants, do not, under such a proceeding, have *any* right of access to the documents in the Commission's file. The Court added that if persons other than those with a right of access under Regulations 1/2003 and 773/2004, or those who enjoy such a right in principle but have not used it or have been refused access, were able to obtain access to documents on the basis of Regulation 1049/2001, the (limited and con-trolled) access system introduced by Regulations 1/2003 and 773/2004 would be undermined.[97] This would, the Court underlined, jeopardise the balance which the EU legislature sought to ensure, in Regulations 1/2003 and 773/2004, between the obligation on the undertakings concerned to submit to the Commission possi-bly sensitive commercial information to enable it to ascertain whether a concerted practice was in existence and to determine whether that practice was compatible with Article 101 TFEU, on the one hand, and the guarantee of increased protec-tion, by virtue of the requirement of professional secrecy and business secrecy, for the information so provided to the Commission, on the other.[98]

No distinction is made by the Court of Justice, in terms of establishing this general presumption, as regards the manner in which the information contained in the requested documents is gathered, namely whether it was obtained, on the one hand, under Articles 18 and 19 of Regulation 1/2003 or through leniency, or, on the other hand, under Articles 20 and 21 of Regulation 1/2003.[99]

X. REBUTTALS OF THE GENERAL PRESUMPTION

The existence of the general presumptions referred to above does not rule out the possibility of demonstrating that a specific document is not covered by such general presumptions, or that there is an overriding public interest in disclosure of the document.[100] This section will only examine the issue of overriding public interests in disclosure.

It was suggested above (see notes 13 and 49) that while it is open to a person seek-ing access to put forward reasons why an institution should consider that there is an overriding public interest in disclosure, an institution must carry out an analysis,

---

[97] ibid, para 88. See also *Commission v Technische Glaswerke Ilmenau*, para 58; *Sweden and Others v API and Commission*, para 100; *Commission v Éditions Odile Jacob*, para 122; *Commission v Agrofert Holding*, para 63; and *LPN and Finland v Commission*, para 58.

[98] *Commission v EnBW Energie Baden-Württemberg AG*, para 90. See also, by analogy, *Commission v Éditions Odile Jacob*, para 121, and *Commission v Agrofert Holding*, para 62.

[99] See *Commission v EnBW Energie Baden-Württemberg AG*, para 97, where the Court stated that it is irrelevant that certain documents were provided to the Commission voluntarily by the parties con-cerned with a view to obtaining immunity or a reduction in the amount of the fines imposed, since it is common ground that disclosure of such documents, regardless of whether they were provided to that institution on a voluntary basis or under compulsion, is in any event strictly governed by Regulations 1/2003 and 773/2004.

[100] See *Commission v Technische Glaswerke Ilmenau*, para 62; *Commission v Éditions Odile Jacob*, para 126; *Commission v Agrofert Holding*, para 68; and *LPN and Finland v Commission*, para 66; *Commission v EnBW Energie Baden-Württemberg AG*, para 100.

ex officio, as to whether or not there is an overriding public interest in disclosure, at least as regards 'legislative documents'. The Court has implied, however, as regards the general presumptions relating to investigatory documents, that there is no obligation on the Commission to examine any specific document to determine if the general presumption applies to that document *or* to determine if there is an overriding public interest in disclosure of the document. Such a requirement would deprive that general presumption of its proper effect, which is to permit the Commission to reply to a global request for access in a manner equally global.[101] It would thus appear for the person seeking access to such documents to argue why there is, for a specific document or specific documents, an overriding public interest in disclosure.

Whereas, as noted above, the specific content and the specific nature of a document is irrelevant as regards whether a general presumption is established that one or more of the interests set out under Article 4(2) and 4(3) of Regulation 1049/2001 applies, this author argues that the specific content and the specific nature of a document should be of relevance as regards establishing whether there is an overriding public interest in disclosure.

In a case dating from 2010,[102] the Ombudsman took the view that amongst the factors which should be taken into consideration, when assessing whether there is an overriding public interest in disclosure, is whether the documents at issue contain information which may be useful in an action for damages before national courts. The Ombudsman noted that the Court of Justice had stated, in *Courage v Crehan*,[103] that the full effectiveness of Article 101 TFEU and, in particular, the practical effect of the prohibition laid down in that Article would be put at risk if it were not open to any individual to claim damages for loss caused by a contract or by conduct liable to restrict or distort competition. The Court added that the existence of such a right strengthens the working of the EU competition rules and discourages agreements or practices which are liable to restrict or distort competition. From that point of view, the Court concluded that actions for damages before the national courts can make a significant contribution to the maintenance of effective competition in the EU. The Ombudsman thus understood that actions for damages have a close link with the public enforcement of competition rules and that they serve to further a 'public interest' (in addition to furthering a 'private interest').

The view that there may be public interest in disclosure of information in a cartel file is also supported by the *Bank Austria Creditanstalt* ruling, where the General Court found that:

> [T]he interest of an undertaking which the Commission has fined for breach of competition law in the details of the offending conduct of which it is accused not being

---

[101] See *LPN and Finland v Commission*, para 68; and *Commission v EnBW Energie Baden-Württemberg AG*, para 101.

[102] See Decision of the European Ombudsman closing his inquiry into complaint 3699/2006/ELB against the European Commission (at http://www.ombudsman.europa.eu/cases/decision.faces/en/4752/html.bookmark).

[103] Case C-453/99 *Courage v Crehan* [2001] ECR I-629, paras 26–27.

disclosed to the public does not warrant any particular protection, given the public interest in knowing as fully as possible the reasons behind any Commission action, the interest of the economic operators in knowing the sort of behaviour for which they are liable to be penalised and the interest of persons harmed by the infringement in being informed of the details thereof so that they may, where appropriate, assert their rights against the undertakings punished.[104]

In *Donau Chemie*, the Court of Justice stated that the right to take private action

strengthens the working of the Community competition rules by deterring anticompetitive conduct as well as fully compensating those who have suffered harm as a result of the conduct.[105]

The EFTA Court in *Schenker* was even more explicit. It stated that private actions provide

a significant contribution to the maintenance of effective competition in the EEA ... While pursuing his private interest, a plaintiff in such proceedings contributes at the same time to the protection of the public interest.[106]

If it is accepted that a public interest may be served by actions for damages, and a request for public access is made for the purposes of pursuing such an action, it should be necessary to carry out a balancing exercise to determine if that public interest outweighs the interests protected by non-disclosure.

In order to carry out the balancing exercise properly, with a view to establishing whether there is an overriding public interest in disclosure of certain documents, the specific 'weight' of specific documents to be placed on that 'balance' must be established. This requires, on the one hand, knowledge of the *precise* damage disclosure of a given document may cause to protected interest (such as the precise damage to a (legitimate) commercial interest or the precise damage to an investigatory process), and knowledge of the *precise* benefit to the public interest identified above.

This view is reflected in the Ombudsman's decision referred to above relating to a request for access to documents in a competition enforcement file.[107] In that decision the Ombudsman noted that when the protection of commercial interests is weighed against the public interest in disclosure, in order to verify whether the public interest in disclosure does, in fact, override the interest in the protection of commercial interests, the specific content of each document must be taken into account. The Ombudsman added that the categorisation of a series of documents as containing commercially sensitive information does not imply that all the documents are equally sensitive. The sensitive nature of documents can vary insofar as certain information may be highly sensitive, whereas other information may be less sensitive. When carrying out the analysis, account must be taken

---

[104] See Case T-198/03, *Bank Austria Creditanstalt AG v Commission* [2006] ECR II-1429, para 78.
[105] See *Donau Chemie* [2013] 5 *Common Market Law Reports* 19, paras 23–24.
[106] See *Schenker*, paras 132 and 241.
[107] See above n 102.

of the specific content of each document, and the nature and importance of the commercial interests to be protected, in order to balance private and public interests accurately. If the applicant can show that the requested documents contain commercial information which is 'old', and the applicant proves, in a reasoned manner, that the markets concerned were not characterised by great stability, the conclusion should be that the information has ceased to be commercially sensitive.[108]

The Ombudsman also considered that it is necessary, when weighing interests against each other, to distinguish between documents on the basis of how they were gathered by the Commission, namely documents voluntarily submitted to the Commission in the framework of a leniency programme;[109] documents obtained following a request from the Commission in accordance with Article 18 of Regulation 1/2003; documents obtained following an inspection carried out by the Commission in accordance with Article 20 of Regulation 1/2003.

The Ombudsman also considered that, amongst the factors which should be taken into consideration when assessing whether there is an overriding public interest in disclosure, the Commission should evaluate whether the documents which form the object of the request for access do actually contain information which will be useful in any action for damages before national courts. It could well be that many documents in a requested file have no bearing on the successful outcome of an action for damages. Such information could, for example, relate to damage caused to third parties or to a causal link between the infringement of EU competition law and the damage caused to those third parties. If the documents do actually contain information which may be useful to enable the national court to evaluate an action for damages before it, it should be more likely that there will be an overriding public interest in disclosure of those documents. We can call this a necessity test.

Finally, the Ombudsman also considered that amongst the factors which should be taken into consideration, when assessing whether there is an overriding public interest in disclosure, is whether the national court can effectively request access to the documents in question, pursuant to Article 15 of Regulation 1/2003.[110] The Ombudsman stated[111] that, as regards whether there are other alternatives, other than giving public access to the documents, which would achieve the same end result of increasing the deterrent effect of EU competition law through a

---

[108] This idea is supported by recent case law (see Case T-380/08, *The Netherlands v Commission*, nyr, para 100 (*a sensu contrario*)).

[109] The Ombudsman did not exclude the possibility that it may be necessary, in order to protect the public interest, to ensure the protection of the information voluntarily submitted to the Commission in the framework of a leniency programme. In effect, the effectiveness of the leniency programme should not be compromised.

[110] Art 15.1 of Regulation 1/2003 states the following: 'In proceedings for the application of [Art 101 or Art 102] of the Treaty, courts of the Member States may ask the Commission to transmit to them information in its possession or its opinion on questions concerning the application of the [EU] competition rules ...'.

[111] See paras 112–114 of the Ombudsman's Decision.

more effective system of private enforcement, Article 15 of Regulation 1/2003 empowers national courts to request documents from the Commission for the purposes of applying Article 101 TFEU and 102 TFEU. National courts may thus have access to documents containing commercially sensitive information, without revealing their content to the public. The public interest of increasing the deterrent effect of EU competition law through a more effective system of private enforcement can thus be achieved without giving public access to the documents. This fact is directly, the Ombudsman stated, relevant to the balancing exercise which the Commission is required to carry out pursuant to Regulation 1049/2001. The fact that the same public benefit of having a more effective system of private enforcement of EU competition law can be achieved through an alternative channel, namely, through Article 15 of Regulation 1/2003, and that this channel offers guarantees to protect the legitimate interests of third parties, diminishes significantly the weight of the need to grant public access, in the context of the balancing exercise, to these documents. This observation does not imply that Regulation 1/2003 applies to the documents in question to the exclusion of Regulation 1049/2001, but rather that a full analysis under Regulation 1049/2001 takes into account, as a relevant factor, the diverse effects of Regulation 1/2003.

In sum, the Ombudsman also recognised an indispensability test as part of the balancing exercise under Regulation 1049/2001. If the same public interest could not be achieved through an alternative mechanism, such as through Article 15 of Regulation 1/2003, it would be more likely that there would exist an overriding public interest in the public disclosure of the documents concerned.

Recent case law could support certain of the views expressed above. In *Commission v EnBW Energie Baden-Württemberg AG*, the Court of Justice recognised that in order to ensure effective protection of the right to compensation enjoyed by a claimant, there is no need for every document relating to a proceeding under Article 101 TFEU to be disclosed to that claimant on the ground that that party is intending to bring an action for damages, as it is highly unlikely that the action for damages will need to be based on all the evidence in the file relating to that proceeding.[112] The Court added that any person seeking compensation for the loss caused by a breach of Article 101 TFEU must establish that it is *necessary* for that person to be granted access to documents in the Commission's file, in order to enable the latter to weigh up, on a case-by-case basis, the respective interests in favour of disclosure of such documents and in favour of the protection of those documents, taking into account all the relevant factors in the case.[113] *In the absence of any such necessity*, the Court ruled, the interest in obtaining compensation for the loss suffered as a result of a breach of Article 101 TFEU cannot constitute an overriding public interest within the meaning of Article 4(2) of Regulation

---

[112] See *Commission v EnBW Energie Baden-Württemberg AG*, para 106; see also *Donau Chemie*, para 33.
[113] See *Commission v EnBW Energie Baden-Württemberg AG*, para 107 (see also, by analogy, *Donau Chemie*, paras 30 and 34.

1049/2001.[114] It would seem to follow, from the above, that if such necessity were shown to exist, and balancing all the other relevant factors, an overriding public interest in disclosure might apply as regards the disclosure certain documents in files relating to the enforcement of Articles 101 and 102 TFEU.

XI. FURTHER FINE-TUNING THE BALANCING EXERCISE

The issues of necessity and of indispensability have been touched on above, and will be commented upon again below in relation to recent legislative developments.[115] A number of other relevant factors which impact on the balancing exercise, relating to precisely how information is gathered and whether that information remains commercially sensitive, have also been mentioned above. There may be other factors, however.

It is questionable whether the Commission should release documents that relate to an undertaking that has been the subject of an investigation, but which has not been found to have infringed EU competition rules. This issue arose in *Pergan*,[116] which, while it did not relate to the application of Regulation 1049/2001, is a case which sets out principles that may be of relevance to the balancing exercise set out above. While the Commission addressed a statement of objections to Pergan in the organic peroxides cartel investigation, no decision finding an infringement of Article 101 TFEU was directed to Pergan. Pergan then opposed the release of any information that might demonstrate to third parties its involvement in the cartel. The General Court, hearing an appeal from Pergan, considered that the scope of the right to confidentiality under Regulation 1/2003 needed to be interpreted in the light of general principles and fundamental rights, including the presumption of innocence. It then found that the presumption of innocence excludes even any allusion to the liability of an accused person in a final decision unless that person has enjoyed all the usual guarantees in terms of the exercise of the rights of defence. In sum, the Court found that non-addressees of a Commission decision cannot defend themselves against the findings contained therein and, therefore, deserve special protection under the rules on confidentiality. Such a finding would also appear to be of relevance if a request were made for *public* access to documents containing information about the party to whom the Commission had not addressed its decision finding an infringement.

---

[114] See *Commission v EnBW Energie Baden-Württemberg AG*, para 108.

[115] On 17 April 2014, the European Parliament adopted a text of the Directive on antitrust damages actions (after agreement between the European Parliament and the Council in a trilogue). The agreed text of the Directive has been sent to the EU Council of Ministers for final approval.

[116] See Case T-474/04 *Pergan Hilfsstoffe für industrielle Prozesse GmbH v Commission* [2007] II-04225.

XII. LEGISLATIVE DEVELOPMENTS

As noted above, on 17 April 2014, Parliament adopted a text of the Directive on antitrust damages actions.[117] The agreed text of the Directive has now been sent to the EU Council of Ministers for final approval.[118] The Directive puts forward a number of measures which will facilitate antitrust damages claims in Member States. Notably, parties will have easier access to the evidence they need to pursue an action for damages. In particular, if a party needs specific pieces or categories of evidence to prove a claim or a defence, it will have the possibility to ask the national court hearing the action for damages to order other parties or third parties to produce this evidence.[119] It may also request such information from a competition authority, be that the Commission or a national competition authority.[120]

The national judge will, when dealing with such requests, ensure that disclosure orders are proportionate and that confidential information is duly protected. First the party requesting disclosure must provide a reasoned justification, containing reasonably available facts and evidence, to support the plausibility of its claim for damages.[121] Member States shall also ensure that national courts limit disclosure of evidence to that which is proportionate. In determining whether any disclosure requested by a party is proportionate, national courts shall consider the legitimate interests of all parties and third parties concerned. They shall, in particular, consider: (a) the extent to which the claim or defence is supported by available facts and evidence justifying the request to disclose evidence; (b) the scope and cost of disclosure, especially for any third parties concerned, also to prevent non-specific search of information which is unlikely to be of relevance for the parties in the procedure; (c) whether the evidence to be disclosed contains confidential information, especially concerning any third parties, and the arrangements for protecting such confidential information.[122] Reflecting the General

---

[117] The text approved by Parliament is available at http://www.europarl.europa.eu/sides/getDoc.do?pubRef=-//EP//NONSGML+AMD+A7-2014-0089+002-002+DOC+PDF+V0//EN (checked 29 April 2014).

[118] The manner in which this important legislation progressed through the legislator provides, coincidentally, an interesting insight into the power and importance of trilogues (see above, n 29). The Commission submitted its Proposal for a Directive on 11 June 2013. On 2 December 2013, the Council adopted its general approach on the Commission's proposal. On 27 January 2014, the ECON Committee of Parliament provided the Parliament Rapporteur with a mandate to start trilogue negotiations. In February and March 2014, three political trilogues and several technical meetings took place. Agreement was reached on 20 March 2014. On 26 March 2014, COREPER endorsed the agreed result. On 17 April 2014, the European Parliament adopted a text of the Directive based on the agreed result. At the time of writing (April 2014), it only remained for the Council to adopt formally the agreed text. The entire legislative process will take, as a result of trilogues, less than one year, which is impressive, especially given the complexity and importance of the subject. However, this efficiency comes at a cost; the precise content of the discussions at the trilogues and compromises reached at the trilogues, in relation to this important legislation, are not (as yet) publicly available.

[119] See Art 5 of the (draft) Directive.

[120] See Art 6 of the (draft) Directive.

[121] See Art 5(1) of the (draft) Directive.

[122] See Art 5(3) of the (draft) Directive.

Court's view in the *Bank Austria Creditanstalt* ruling, the Directive states that the interest of undertakings to avoid actions for damages following an infringement of competition law shall not constitute an interest that warrants protection.[123] Importantly for the purposes of determining whether there will remain a possibility of an overriding public interest in the public disclosure of such documents, the Directive states that Member States shall ensure that national courts have the power to order disclosure of evidence containing confidential information where they consider it relevant to the action for damages.[124] The Directive states that Member States shall ensure that those from whom disclosure is sought are provided with an opportunity to be heard before a national court orders disclosure.

However, and reflecting the detailed discussions above, the Directive states that leniency statements[125] and settlement submissions[126] can never be disclosed.[127] The purpose of this exception is to preserve the incentive for companies to provide information to competition authorities, which the Directive considers to be a key instrument without which many cartels would never be discovered in the first place. In this respect, Recital 24 of the Directive states that leniency programmes and settlement procedures are important tools for the public enforcement of Union competition law as they contribute to the detection, the efficient prosecution and the imposition of penalties for the most serious competition law infringements. It adds that undertakings may be deterred from cooperating in this context if self-incriminating statements such as leniency statements and settlement submissions, which are solely produced for the purpose of such cooperation, were disclosed. Such disclosure poses a risk of exposing cooperating undertakings or their managing staff to civil or criminal liability under worse conditions than the co-infringers that do not cooperate with competition authorities. Thus, to ensure the undertakings' continued willingness to voluntarily approach competition authorities with leniency statements or settlement submissions, such documents should be excluded from disclosure.[128]

If promulgated, the Directive will, when implemented at national level, imply that the indispensability test set out above will no longer be met. It will be recalled that such a test is arguably included in the assessment of whether the public interest in *public* access to antitrust documents outweighs the interests in non-disclosure. This will mean that it will be exceedingly difficult to rebut the general presumption that public access can be denied to such documents. Thus, while Article 6(3)

---

[123] See Art 5(4) of the (draft) Directive.

[124] Art 5(5) of the (draft) Directive.

[125] See, in this respect, para 72 of the 2010 Decision of the European Ombudsman closing his inquiry into complaint 3699/2006/ELB against the European Commission (at http://www.ombudsman.europa.eu/cases/decision.faces/en/4752/html.bookmark).

[126] See, in this respect, the 2010 Decision of the Ombudsman closing his inquiry into complaint 2953/2008/FOR against the Commission (at: http://www.ombudsman.europa.eu/cases/decision.faces/en/5168/html.-bookmark), which dealt with such procedures.

[127] See Art 6(6) of the (draft) Directive.

[128] For an early commentary on the Proposal of the Commission, see R Gamble, 'Whether neap or spring, the tide turns for private enforcement: the EU proposal for a Directive on damages examined' *European Competition Law Review* 611.

of the Directive states that the Chapter on disclosure of evidence in the Directive is without prejudice to the rules and practices on public access to documents under Regulation 1049/2001, the Directive will have, this author argues, a significant impact on the manner in which those rules and practices are applied.

XIII. CONCLUSIONS

The purpose of this chapter was to trace the origin, extent and limits of general presumptions that public access can be denied to documents held by EU institutions. The precise delimitation of these general presumptions reflects a simple underlying concept. As the Court has consistently stressed, the administrative activity of an institution does not require such extensive access to documents as that required by the legislative activity of an EU institution.[129] Thus, in situations where the institutions act in the capacity of a legislature (or where they provide input to the legislative process), even wider access to documents should be authorised[130] than is the case for other documents.

In relation to legislative documents, the use of a general presumption that access can be denied has been limited to such an extent that its existence, in practical terms, is negligible, if not completely absent in most circumstances. In an EU which seeks to bolster its democratic credentials through openness, it could only be so. It should not be forgotten that critics of the European project, and they are increasingly numerous, will not lose any opportunity to highlight absences of openness in relation to legislating. Thus, every opportunity must be taken to give effect to the wording, and moreover the spirit, of Article 1 TEU, which seeks to mark 'a new stage in the process of creating an ever closer union among the peoples of Europe, in which decisions are taken as openly as possible and as closely as possible to the citizen'.

In contrast, as regards administrative documents, and specifically in relation to documents in an investigatory file, where an important public interest, the effective enforcement of competition law, is at stake, general presumptions can be broadly construed and applied. Such general presumptions can only be rebutted where public access would prove indispensable to achieve a related and important public interest, namely the private enforcement of competition law. This view has now been copper-fastened by the legislator, which has both recognised the importance of protecting the enforcement capacity of competition authorities, whilst introducing alternative disclosure mechanisms, made effective through national courts, to ensure that actions for damages are reinforced and made effective. This legislative development will all but obviate the public interest in the public disclosure of documents of third parties held by competition authorities.

---

[129] See, eg, *Commission v Technische Glaswerke Ilmenau*, para 60; *Sweden and Others v API and Commission*, para 77; and *Sweden v My Travel and Commission*, para 87.
[130] See *Commission v Technische Glaswerke Ilmenau*, para 60.

Part IV

EEA Business and Economic Law

28

The Free Movement of Goods in EEA Law: The Philip Morris Norway, Commission v Italy and Mickelsson and Roos Cases

KOEN LENAERTS*

I. INTRODUCTION

A BAN ON all forms of advertising of tobacco products is nothing new in Norway. As a matter of fact, such a prohibition has been in force since 1973 when the Norwegian Parliament passed the Act relating to the Prevention of the Harmful Effects of Tobacco (the 1973 Act). However, in 2009, in order to increase the level of protection of public health, the Norwegian Parliament decided to amend the 1973 Act by extending the ban laid down therein to the visual display of tobacco products and smoking devices (the 2009 legislation).

Needless to say, that was not good news for Philip Morris Norway, the Norwegian subsidiary of one of the world's largest tobacco producers which imported tobacco products from other EEA States to Norway. With a view to having the visual display ban, provided for in the 2009 legislation, set aside Philip Morris Norway brought proceedings before the Oslo District Court against the Norwegian State, on the ground that that ban constituted a measure having equivalent effect to quantitative restrictions on imports (MEE) within the meaning of Article 11 EEA, which could not be justified under Article 13 EEA. For its part, the Norwegian State argued that the visual display ban was compatible with EEA law, since it did not fall within the scope of application of the free movement of goods. In the alternative, it argued that the ban could, in any event, be justified by public health considerations.

Accordingly, in the *Philip Morris Norway* case,[1] the Oslo District Court made a reference to the EFTA Court under Article 34 SCA. It asked, in essence, whether the visual display ban set out in the 2009 legislation was compatible with EEA law.

---

* All opinions expressed herein are strictly personal to the author.
[1] Case E-16/10 *Philip Morris Norway AS v Norwegian Sate* [2011] EFTA Ct Rep 330.

Philip Morris Norway is an important case because it gave the EFTA Court the opportunity to express its views on the extent to which it would 'pay due account'[2] to the framework of analysis applied by the European Court of Justice (ECJ) in the *Commission v Italy* and *Mickelsson and Roos* cases.[3]

The purpose of this chapter is to celebrate the 20th anniversary of the EFTA Court, by exploring those three cases which highlight the fact that, when interpreting Articles 11 and 13 EEA, the EFTA Court follows closely the developments in the case law of the ECJ relating to Articles 34 and 36 TFEU. This is a reason for celebration given that legal convergence between EU law and EEA law is of vital importance for the proper functioning of both the EU internal market and the EEA. The remainder of this chapter is divided into four sections. Section II provides a historical background of the ECJ's case law on the free movement of goods. Section III examines the rulings of the ECJ in *Commission v Italy* and in *Mickelsson and Roos*. Section IV is devoted to an examination of the EFTA Court's ruling in the *Philip Morris Norway* case. Finally, a brief conclusion (Section V) takes the view that the ruling of the EFTA Court in *Philip Morris Norway* is fully consistent with the rationale underpinning the rulings of the ECJ in *Commission v Italy* and in *Mickelsson and Roos*.

II. HISTORICAL BACKGROUND

Before the rulings of the ECJ in *Commission v Italy* and *Mickelsson and Roos* were delivered, the law on the free movement of goods was governed by three seminal judgments, namely *Dassonville*,[4] *Cassis de Dijon*[5] and *Keck*,[6] which have contributed to defining the types of national measures considered to be MEEs.

As is well known, in *Dassonville* the ECJ held that 'all trading rules enacted by Member States which are capable of hindering, directly or indirectly, actually or potentially, intra-Community trade are to be considered as [MEEs] and are, on that basis, prohibited by [Article 34 TFEU]'.[7] Known as the '*Dassonville* formula', that definition of a MEE is drafted in very broad terms. For example, in order for a measure to be regarded as a MEE, it suffices that it produces a potential and indirect effect on intra-EU trade.[8] That formula is neither formalistic, nor purpose-driven, but rather focuses on the effects of the measure in question. As a result, a broad range of measures have fallen within its scope of application. To

---

[2] See Art 3 II SCA.

[3] Case C-110/05 *Commission v Italy* [2009] ECR I-519 and Case C-142/05 *Mickelsson and Roos* [2009] ECR I-4273.

[4] Case 8/74 *Dassonville* [1974] ECR 837.

[5] Case 120/78 *Rewe-Zentral* ('*Cassis de Dijon*') [1979] ECR 649.

[6] Joined Cases C-267/91 and C-268/91 *Keck and Mithouard* ('*Keck*') [1993] ECR I-6097.

[7] *Dassonville*, above n 4, para 5.

[8] See, generally, C Barnard, *The Substantive Law of the European Union*, 3rd edn (Oxford, Oxford University Press, 2010).

name just a few, import licences,[9] labelling requirements,[10] price controls,[11] rules relating to the composition of a product,[12] rules limiting channels of distribution[13] and rules favouring national products[14] are all to be considered as MEEs. As Oliver suggests, 'the list is almost endless'.[15] That formula also covers both types of discriminatory measure, that is those that are overtly discriminatory (for example, imposing additional requirements on imports) as well as those that formally apply to imports and domestic products alike but, in fact, give rise to a particular burden on the former (that is, 'same burden in law, but different burden in fact').[16] In addition, the ECJ has held that the *Dassonville* formula applies regardless of whether the impact of the national measure in question upon intra-EU trade is slight. Unlike the Treaty provisions on competition law, there is no *de minimis* rule under Article 34 TFEU.[17] However, the application of the *Dassonville* formula does not automatically entail the incompatibility of the measure in question with EU law. As Article 36 TFEU makes clear, a MEE can be justified on the grounds laid down therein, provided that it does not constitute a means of arbitrary discrimination and that it complies with the principle of proportionality.

Moreover, whilst drafted in broad terms, the *Dassonville* formula has its limits. In particular, in light of cases such as *Krantz* and *Peralta*,[18] a national measure whose effects upon intra-EU trade are 'too uncertain and too indirect' is not considered to be a MEE.

In *Cassis de Dijon*, the ECJ endorsed the principle of mutual recognition, according to which 'in the absence of harmonisation of national legislation, obstacles to the free movement of goods which are the consequence of applying, to goods coming from other Member States where they are lawfully manufactured and marketed, rules that lay down requirements to be met by such goods constitute [MEEs] even if those rules apply to all products alike'.[19] That principle entailed a 'revolution' for the law of the internal market, as it shifts the burden of proof from the economic operator to the host Member State which has to justify its legislation. Indeed, the principle of mutual recognition does not preclude Member States from justifying obstacles to free movement of goods on the basis not only of the grounds listed in Article 36 TFEU, but also of a non-exhaustive list of mandatory requirements of public interest.

---

[9] Case 41/76 *Donckerwolcke and Schou* [1976] ECR 1921.
[10] Case C-470/93 *Mars* [1995] ECR I-1923.
[11] Case 13/77 *GB-Inno-BM* [1977] ECR 2115.
[12] Case 261/81 *Rau* [1982] ECR 3961.
[13] Case 104/75 *De Peijper* [1976] ECR 613.
[14] Case 113/80 *Commission v Ireland* [1981] ECR 1625.
[15] P Oliver, 'Of Trailers and Jet Skis: Is the Case Law on Article 34 TFEU Hurtling in a New Direction?' (2011) 33 *Fordham International Law Journal* 1423, at 1429.
[16] See, generally, Barnard, above n 8, at 90.
[17] Case C-67/97 *Ditlev Bluhme* [1998] ECR I-8033.
[18] Case C-69/88 *Krantz v Ontvanger der Directe Belastingen* [1990] ECR I-583; Case C-379/92 *Peralta* [1994] ECR I-3453.
[19] *Cassis de Dijon*, above n 5, paras 6, 14 and 15.

The principle of mutual recognition follows a 'market-access' rationale. This meant, in the aftermath of *Cassis de Dijon*, that the question whether a national measure discriminated against imports was no longer the primary focus of the analysis. The combined effect of the broad definition of a MEE laid down in *Dassonville* and the principle of mutual recognition encouraged transnational litigation. Economic operators began to challenge all types of rules which, whilst 'quite far removed from imports and manifestly not targeted at them',[20] restricted the exercise of commercial activity. Notably, they began to challenge 'market circumstances rules', that is, rules that regulate 'when', 'where', 'how' and 'by whom' a product may be marketed.[21] The problem was that those rules do not generally apply to producers or importers, but to retailers. Arguably, the primary purpose of litigation was not therefore to remove obstacles to intra-EU trade, but rather to allow operators to exercise their commercial activities under more liberalised market conditions.[22]

The question whether market circumstances rules fell within the notion of a MEE raised important constitutional questions. Drawing parallels with the US experience, notably the infamous *Lochner* case,[23] one could argue that Article 34 TFEU ran the risk of enshrining some sort of 'European economic due process clause'.[24] At first, the ECJ did not provide a clear answer to that question, as the 'Sunday trading cases' showed.[25] This lack of clarity led AG Tesauro in *Hünermund* to argue that Article 34 TFEU should not apply to national measures that neither insulate national markets nor target imports directly nor discriminate against them.[26] This paved the way for the ECJ to revisit its case law. In *Keck*, the ECJ took the view that the time was right to address that difficult question. In paragraphs 16 and 17, it held that:

---

[20] Oliver, above n 15, at 1435.

[21] See Barnard, above n 8, at 117 et seq.

[22] In his seminal article, E White, 'In Search of the Limits to Article 30 of the EEC Treaty' (1989) 26 *Common Market Law Review* 235, invited the ECJ to reform its case law so as to deter litigants from challenging market circumstances rules which, in his view, fell outside the scope of application of Art 34 TFEU. In the same vein, K Mortelmans, 'Article 30 of the EEC Treaty and Legislation Relating to Market Circumstances: Time to Consider a New Definition?' (1991) 28 *Common Market Law Review* 115 (who opposed the application of Article 34 TFEU to rules with a 'territorial element', such as Sunday trading rules).

[23] *Lochner v New York*, 198 US 45 (1905).

[24] For a comparison between the US and EU experience, see M Poaires Maduro, *We the Court: The European Court of Justice and the European Economic Constitution* (Oxford, Hart Publishing, 1998).

[25] See Case C-145/88 *Torfaen Borough Council v B&Q* [1989] ECR 3851; Case C-312/89 *Conforama and Others* [1991] ECR I-997; Case C-169/91 *Stoke-on-Trent Council v B&Q* [1992] ECR I-6635. See also C Barnard, 'Sunday Trading: A Drama in Five Acts' (1994) 57 *Modern Law Review* 449.

[26] See Opinion of AG Tesauro in Case C-292/92 *Hünermund* [1993] ECR I-6787, para 28 ('I am persuaded that the *Dassonville* test neither can nor should be so construed as to include in the definition of [MEEs] even those national laws which, because they affect supply and/or demand and therefore, but on that account alone, the volume of sales, may bring about a reduction in the volume of imports, that is to say, where there exists no obstacle whatsoever to the movement within the Community of the products concerned and no connection whatsoever with the disparity between the laws in question').

By contrast, contrary to what has previously been decided, the application to products from other Member States of national provisions restricting or prohibiting certain selling arrangements is not such as to hinder directly or indirectly, actually or potentially, trade between Member States within the meaning of the *Dassonville* judgment (Case 8/74 [1974] ECR 837), so long as those provisions apply to all relevant traders operating within the national territory and so long as they affect in the same manner, in law and in fact, the marketing of domestic products and of those from other Member States.

Provided that those conditions are fulfilled, the application of such rules to the sale of products from another Member State meeting the requirements laid down by that State is not by nature such as to prevent their access to the market or to impede access any more than it impedes the access of domestic products. Such rules therefore fall outside the scope of Article [34] of the Treaty.

The primary purpose of *Keck* was to clarify the law on the free movement of goods. By putting forward a 'clear-cut' rule, the ECJ sought to provide guidance to the national courts as to the type of measures falling outside the scope of application of Article 34 TFEU. *Keck* only excluded 'certain selling arrangements' from the scope of application of that Treaty provision. That meant that product requirements continued to be governed by *Dassonville* and *Cassis de Dijon*.

The *Keck* ruling has been (and still is) subject to criticism by Advocates General and scholars.[27] First, its detractors argue that the ECJ failed to define what is to be understood by 'selling arrangements', to specify what it meant by '*certain* selling arrangements', and to identify the particular judgments that were overruled. However, subsequent case law has clarified that the expression 'selling arrangements' relates to market circumstances.[28] Second, scholars note that it might be difficult to determine whether a national measure concerns a product requirement or a selling arrangement. In that regard, the ECJ has ruled that those two categories are mutually exclusive[29] and that, in case of doubt, it will tend to lean towards the application of Article 34 TFEU.[30] Third, some scholars question whether *Keck*

---

[27] See, eg, A Mattera, 'De l'arrêt Dassonville à l'arrêt Keck: l'obscure clarté d'une jurisprudence riche en principes novateurs et en contradictions' (1994) *Revue du Marché unique européen* 117; S Weatherill, 'After *Keck*: some thoughts on how to clarify the clarification' (1996) 33 *Common Market Law Review* 887; F Picod, 'La nouvelle approche de la Cour de justice en matière d'entraves aux échanges' (1998) 34 *Revue Trimestrielle de Droit européen* 169, and J Stuyck, 'L'arrêt Keck et Mithouard (vente à perte) et ses conséquences sur la libre circulation des marchandises' (1994) *Cahiers de droit européen* 435. More recently, see A Tryfonidou, 'Was Keck a Half-baked Solution After All?' (2007) 34 *Legal Issues of Economic Integration* 167; D Wilsher, 'Does Keck discrimination make any sense? An assessment of the non-discrimination principle within the European Single Market' (2008) 33 *European Law Review* 3.

[28] Restrictions on when (see, eg, Joined Cases C-69/93 and C-258/93 *Punto Casa and PPV* [1994] ECR I-02355), where and by whom (Case C-322/01 *Deutscher Apothekerverband* [2003] ECR I-14887; Case C-391/92 *Commission v Greece* [1995] ECR I-1621) goods can be sold. They also include price controls (*Keck*, above n 6) and restrictions on advertising (Case C-405/98 *Gourmet International Products* [2001] ECR I-1795).

[29] Oliver, above n 15, p 1439.

[30] ibid, p 1441 (referring to Case C-470/93 *Mars* [1995] ECR I-1923 and Case C-368/95 *Familiapress* [1997] ECR I-3689).

has actually brought legal certainty to the law on the free movement of goods. By looking at subsequent developments, they argue that the ECJ has favoured a broad interpretation of indirect discrimination so as to include selling arrangements within the scope of application of Article 34 TFEU.[31] As Spaventa points out, since *De Agostini*,[32] in only two cases has the ECJ found that a selling arrangement was non-discriminatory.[33] Thus, they observe that the flexibility with which the ECJ has applied the principle of non-discrimination has made it more difficult for national courts to identify the outer limits of that Treaty provision.[34] Fourth, the *Keck* ruling is said to be at odds with the other freedoms which have moved beyond the discrimination paradigm.[35] Notwithstanding the distinctive features of the free movement of goods, a common and single criterion should govern all fundamental freedoms, namely market access. Last but not least, *Keck* might be too broad in some cases, whilst too narrow in others. *Keck* is overinclusive when it allows national measures hindering market access to fall outside the scope of application of Article 34 TFEU. Thus, in *Leclerc-Siplec*, AG Jacobs opined that a discrimination-based test, such as that endorsed by the ECJ in *Keck*, was not sufficient to counter the risks of market fragmentation, 'since traders would have to accept whatever restrictions on selling arrangements happened to exist in each Member State, and would have to adapt their own arrangements accordingly in each State'.[36] 'Restrictions on trade should not', he wrote, 'be tested against local conditions which happen to prevail in each Member State, but against the aim of access to the entire [EU] market'.[37] *Keck* is also underinclusive because it left open the question whether a residual category of measures, namely those that neither impose product requirements nor prohibit certain selling arrangements, are to be governed by the new test or by the *Dassonville–Cassis de Dijon* approach. However,

---

[31]   P Wennerås and K Boe Moen, 'Selling arrangements, keeping Keck' (2010) 34 *European Law Review* 387, at 396ff (who argue that, regarding selling arrangements, 'it seems possible to discern three categories which are subject to distinct assessments as concerns discriminatory effects'. First, 'restrictions on those sales methods which constitute "more significant ways of gaining direct access to the … market" for imported goods than domestic ones [eg internet or mail-order sales] will be considered discriminatory in fact'. Second, regarding sales methods and sales promotions (eg advertising), the ECJ will look at the intensity of the restriction: an outright ban will often be qualified as discriminatory, whilst a more limited restriction will not. Finally, 'restrictions on sales methods which by nature are completely neutral in terms of gaining access to the market for imported and domestic products' (eg restrictions of retail distribution) are not caught by Art 34 TFEU).

[32]   Joined Cases C-34/95 to C-36/95 *De Agostini and TV-Shop* [1997] ECR I-3843.

[33]   Case C-20/03 *Burmanjer and Others* [2005] ECR I-4133 and Case C-441/04 *A-Punkt Schmuckhandel* [2006] ECR I-2093.

[34]   E Spaventa, 'Leaving *Keck* behind? The free movement of goods after the rulings in *Commission v Italy* and *Mickelsson and Roos*' (2009) 34 *European Law Review* 914, at 919.

[35]   See Opinion of AG Poiares Maduro in Joined Cases C-158 and 159/04 *Alfa Vita* [2006] ECR I-8135, para 33.

[36]   See Opinion of AG Jacobs in Case C-412/93 *Leclerc-Siplec* [1995] ECR I-179, para 40.

[37]   ibid.

by looking at cases such as *Canal Satélite Digital*,[38] *Toolex Alpha*[39] and *Monsees*,[40] scholars point out that Article 34 TFEU applies to that residual category of measures.[41] Notably, in *Commission v Portugal*,[42] decided shortly before *Commission v Italy*, the ECJ ruled that a measure prohibiting the affixing of tinted film to the windscreen and windows alongside passenger seats in motor vehicles fell within the scope of Article 34 TFEU. Applying the *Dassonville* formula, the ECJ reasoned that such a measure constituted an obstacle to the free movement of tinted films as 'potential customers, traders or individuals [had] practically no interest in buying them in the knowledge that affixing such [films was] prohibited'.[43]

III. *COMMISSION V ITALY* AND *MICKELSSON AND ROOS*

In *Commission v Italy*,[44] the Commission brought infringement proceedings under ex Article 226 EC (now Article 258 TFEU) against Italy on the ground that Italian law prohibited mopeds, motorcycles, tricycles and quadricycles from towing trailers. According to the Commission, that prohibition prevented the use of trailers lawfully produced and marketed in the Member States where there was no such prohibition and to hinder their importation into, and sale in, Italy. Accordingly, the Commission argued that Italy had failed to fulfil its obligations under ex Article 28 EC (now Article 34 TFEU).

The *Mickelsson and Roos* case involved a reference for a preliminary ruling to the ECJ which was made in the context of criminal proceedings brought by the Swedish Public Prosecutor's Office against P Mickelsson and J Roos for having, on 8 August 2004, in infringement of the national regulations, operated personal watercraft on waters other than general navigable waterways or waters in respect of which the local authority had issued rules permitting their use (designated waterways). In this regard, the referring court asked whether Articles 34 TFEU and 36 TFEU opposed national provisions which prohibited the use of personal watercraft on waters other than designated waterways.

---

[38] Case C-390/99 *Canal Satélite Digital* [2002] ECR I-607 (concerning a market authorisation).

[39] See Case C-473/98 *Toolex* [2000] ECR I-5681 (concerning a prohibition against the industrial use of trichloroethylene).

[40] Case C-350/97 *Monsees* [1999] ECR I-2921 (concerning restrictions on transport).

[41] P Oliver and S Enchelmaier, 'Free movement of goods: Recent developments in the case law' (2007) 44 *Common Market Law Review* 649, at 681 (who argued that '[a] new tendency can be discerned in these cases. Until recently, a distinction was made between (i) product-bound measures and (ii) selling arrangements. As mentioned earlier, that left a third group of restrictions falling outside both categories. Now, the Court would seem to have acknowledged the need to accommodate the third group, since it appears to recognize two categories of measure, namely (i) selling arrangements and (ii) other measures; and with respect to all the measures in the second category, there appears to be no need to prove discrimination'). In the same vein, see Spaventa, above n 34, at 920.

[42] Case C-265/06 *Commission v Portugal* [2008] ECR I-2245.

[43] ibid, para 33.

[44] Case C-110/05 *Commission v Italy* [2009] ECR I-519.

In essence, the parties submitting observations to the ECJ were divided into two camps. On the one hand, the Commission argued that rules concerning the use of a product fell within the scope of the free movement of goods. On the other hand, some Member States supported the contention that *Keck*[45] should apply by analogy to a national provision which restricts or prohibits certain forms of use of a product. Stated simply, the question was whether non-discriminatory 'arrangements for use' fell within the scope of Article 34 TFEU. In those two cases, the ECJ held that arrangements for use fell within the scope of the free movement of goods.

In so doing, the ECJ also sought to consolidate and systematise the existing case law, whilst shedding light on the scope of Article 34 TFEU.[46] In accordance with *Commission v Italy* and *Mickelsson and Roos*, three categories of measures, namely product requirements, selling arrangements and 'any other measures' are to be distinguished.[47]

First, product requirements continue to be governed by *Dassonville* and *Cassis de Dijon*. In order for that type of measure to be compatible with Article 34 TFEU, they must be based on a legitimate interest recognised by the EU legal order and must comply with the principle of proportionality.

Second, *Commission v Italy* and *Mickelsson and Roos* confirm that *Keck* remains good law. Selling arrangements which do not discriminate, either in law or in fact, against imports do not prevent market access and thus do not fall within the scope of application of Article 34 TFEU. This is demonstrated by the ruling of the ECJ in *Ker-Optika*, decided after those two judgments.[48] In that case, the ECJ ruled that a national measure prohibiting the sale of contact lenses via the Internet concerned a selling arrangement.[49] Accordingly, the ECJ proceeded to examine 'whether [that prohibition applied] to all relevant traders operating within the national territory and whether it affect[ed] in the same manner, in law and in fact, the selling of domestic products and the selling of those from other Member States'.[50] Referring to its previous ruling in *Deutscher Apothekerverband*,[51] it found that it did not, since that prohibition deprived 'traders from other Member States of a particularly effective means of selling those products and thus significantly impedes access of those traders to the market of the Member State concerned'.[52] The prohibition at issue in *Ker-Optika* therefore fell within the scope of Article 34 TFEU as it had a discriminatory effect.

Third, it follows from *Commission v Italy* and *Mickelsson and Roos* that *Keck* is confined to selling arrangements. Any other type of measure—such as

---

[45] Joined Cases C-267/91 and C-268/91 *Keck and Mithouard* ('*Keck*') [1993] ECR I-6097.
[46] Wennerås and Boe Moen, above n 31, at 387.
[47] Oliver, above n 15, at 1462. See also P Pecho, 'Good-Bye Keck?: A Comment on the Remarkable Judgment in Commission v Italy, C-110/05' (2009) 36 *Legal Issues of Economic Integration* 257, at 262.
[48] Case C-108/09 *Ker-Optika* [2010] ECR I-12213. See also Case C-531/07 *LIBRO* [2009] ECR I-3717.
[49] ibid, para 45.
[50] ibid, para 53.
[51] Case C-322/01 *Deutscher Apothekerverband* [2003] ECR I-14887, para 74.
[52] *Ker-Optika*, above n 48, para 54.

arrangements for use—is governed by a market-access test. Those two judgments thus stress the fact that, just as happens with the other fundamental freedoms, the market-access rationale pervades the law on the free movement of goods, which covers both obstacles that hinder the entry of imports into the market of the host Member State and obstacles that prevent exports from exiting the market of the home Member State. Indeed, in relation to the latter, the first indications of a market-access-based approach can be found in *Gysbrechts*.[53] It is worth recalling that, prior to that case, Article 35 TFEU only applied to overtly discriminatory measures.[54] However, in *Gysbrechts*, the ECJ ruled that Article 35 TFEU applies to measures which, whilst formally applying to exports and domestic products alike, have an 'effect [that] is none the less greater on goods leaving the market of the exporting Member State than on the marketing of goods in the domestic market of that Member State'.[55] It follows from the foregoing that *Keck* must be read in light of the market-access rationale, that is, as containing an irrebuttable presumption that non-discriminatory selling arrangements do not by their nature hinder market access.[56]

Logically, the question is then how the ECJ will apply the market-access test to measures that are neither product requirements nor selling arrangements and that do not discriminate, either in law or in fact, against imports.[57] It follows from *Commission v Italy* and *Mickelsson and Roos* that the irrebuttable presumption laid down in *Keck* does not apply. Rather, (i) measures which impose a total ban on use, (ii) measures which 'have the effect of preventing users of [a product] from using [it] for the specific and inherent purposes for which [it was] intended' and (iii) measures which have the effect 'of greatly restricting [its] use',[58] fall within the scope of Article 34 TFEU. But what does the adverb 'greatly' mean?[59] Does it cover measures which render more difficult or discourage access to the market for a product?[60] If so, to what extent? It follows from his Opinion in *Commission v Italy* that AG Bot would, as a matter of principle, favour including measures that

---

[53] Case C-205/07 *Gysbrechts* [2008] ECR I-9947.

[54] Case 15/79 *Groenveld* [1979] ECR 3409.

[55] *Gysbrechts*, above n 53, para 43.

[56] However, see Barnard, above n 8, at 141, who considers that a possible reading of *Commission v Italy* may suggest that non-discriminatory selling arrangements (such as a total ban on the sale of a particular product) may fall within the scope of Art 34 TFEU if they prevent access to the market. Accordingly, she posits that *Keck* has been modified (corrected) so as to include a market access test. However, such a reading of *Commission v Italy* does not modify or correct *Keck* but simply overrules it, something which clearly the ECJ did not do.

[57] See J Snell, 'The Notion of Market Access: A Concept or a Slogan?'(2010) 47 *Common Market Law Review* 437, at 470–471 (who argues that 'the notion of market access obscures rather than illuminates'. In his view, there is no middle ground between the two different ways in which the fundamental freedoms can be understood (anti-protectionism v economic freedom). Accordingly, he invites the ECJ to abandon the notion of 'market access' altogether).

[58] See *Mickelsson and Roos*, above n 3, para 28.

[59] See, in this regard, S Weatherill, 'The Road to Ruin: "Restrictions on Use" and the Circular Lifecycle of Article 34 TFEU' (2012) *European Journal of Consumer Law* 343, at 364ff.

[60] See Spaventa, above n 34, at 923–924, who criticises the fact that the ECJ did not provide further guidance in this respect.

are less restrictive than those that render the use of a product futile. Former AG Jacobs agrees. Provided that the measure at issue constitutes a 'substantial restriction' to the free movement of goods, Article 34 TFEU should apply.[61] However, for Wennerås and Boe Moen, applying a market-access test to non-discriminatory measures which merely render a product's access to the market more difficult would run the risk of broadening the scope of Article 34 TFEU excessively. They also observe, as had AG Jacobs,[62] that such a reading of the word 'greatly' would require a *de minimis* test that the ECJ has time and again rejected.[63] Accordingly, in their view, the market-access test should apply restrictively.[64] This would allow national courts to apply the market-access test in a clear and systematic manner.[65]

Commission v Italy and *Mickelsson and Roos* also show that, when determining the compatibility of a measure with Article 34 TFEU, the ECJ will not only look at the effects of such a measure on economic operators, but also on consumers. In both cases, the ECJ considered that the measure in question prevented market access because the prohibition had 'considerable influence on the behaviour of consumers'.[66] If a product cannot be used by consumers, it will certainly not be bought by them and thus economic operators will not import such a product. Consumer behaviour is therefore an important factor that national courts must take into account when determining whether a measure hinders market access.[67]

Moreover, it is worth noting that neither *Commission v Italy* nor *Mickelsson and Roos* affects the line of case law according to which measures whose effect on intra-EU trade is 'too uncertain and too indirect' fall outside the scope of application of Article 34 TFEU. As Stuyck suggests, the *Krantz* test may provide the ECJ with useful tools to clarify the outer limits of the market-access test embraced by the ECJ in those two judgments. Unfortunately, he notes that the *Krantz* test has been 'rarely applied'.[68]

As to justification, the ECJ did not follow the Opinions of the Advocates General. Instead, it decided to uphold the compatibility of the measure in question with EU law. In so doing, the ECJ applied a 'soft' version of the principle of proportionality set out in *Commission v Italy*. Whilst acknowledging that it was possible to envisage less restrictive alternatives to the free movement of trailers,

---

[61] AG Jacobs in *Leclerc-Siplec*, above n 36, para 42.
[62] ibid.
[63] In the same way, Snell, above n 57, at 458–459.
[64] Wennerås and Boe Moen, above n 31, at 395.
[65] ibid, at 399.
[66] *Commission v Italy*, above n 44, para 57.
[67] The same applies when determining whether a measure produces a discriminatory effect. In this regard, see *Gourmet*, above n 28, para 21, where the ECJ held that 'in the case of products like alcoholic beverages, the consumption of which is linked to traditional social practices and to local habits and customs, a prohibition of all advertising directed at consumers in the form of advertisements in the press, on the radio and on television, the direct mailing of unsolicited material or the placing of posters on the public highway is liable to impede access to the market by products from other Member States more than it impedes access by domestic products, with which consumers are instantly more familiar'.
[68] J Stuyck, 'Is *Keck* still alive and kicking?' (2012) *European Journal of Consumer Law* 343, at 355. See also Pecho, above n 47, at 264.

the ECJ ruled that Member States were entitled to enforce a simple and general rule to guarantee road safety. In *Mickelsson and Roos*, the ECJ opted to look at the proportionality of the restriction more closely. However, in so doing, the ECJ did not seek to second-guess the policy decisions taken by the Swedish authorities but to apply the principle of proportionality in a procedural fashion. The ECJ thus examined whether the national measure in question was free from internal contradictions. In that regard, since Swedish regulations provided that local authorities were to designate waters open to navigation by personal watercraft, it found that limiting the operation of personal watercraft to general navigable waterways went beyond what was necessary to protect the environment. Thus, the proportionality of the measure depended on the action to be taken by local authorities. That is why the ECJ decided to focus on making sure that the designation by those authorities of waters open to navigation by personal watercraft takes place within a reasonable time and is not arbitrary.

The application of a process-oriented proportionality test can also be seen in *Sandström*.[69] In that case, criminal charges were brought against Mr Sandström on the ground that he had driven his jet-ski on waters other than those designated by Stockholm County. Thus, unlike the situation at issue in *Mickelsson and Roos*, local authorities had actually designated the waters open to navigation by personal watercraft. The ECJ decided to provide some guidance to the national court regarding the concrete application of the three conditions listed in paragraph 44 of that judgment. In particular, it held that it was for the national court to ascertain whether the decision adopted by Stockholm County had left out waters which were not liable to give rise to risks or pollution deemed unacceptable for the environment. If so, then the national measure at issue would not comply with the principle of proportionality.[70] It was also for the national court to determine whether the period of 11 months for designating the waters open to navigation by personal watercraft was reasonable. In carrying out such determination, the national court had to bear in mind that Stockholm County had adopted its decision at the end of a consultation procedure with municipalities and other stakeholders.[71]

IV. *PHILIP MORRIS NORWAY*

In *Philip Morris Norway*, the EFTA Court followed the framework of analysis applied by the ECJ in *Commission v Italy* and *Mickelsson and Roos*. After referring to the key passages of those judgments, it held that the visual display ban on tobacco

---

[69] Case C-433/05 *Sandström* [2010] ECR I-02885. For a study on process-oriented review, see K Lenaerts, 'The European Court of Justice and Process-Oriented Review' (2012) 31 *Yearbook of European Law* 1, at 3.

[70] ibid, para 38.

[71] ibid, para 39.

products laid down in the 2009 legislation constituted a selling arrangement. This meant that that ban fell within the scope of application of Article 11 EEA, unless it applied to all relevant traders operating within the national territory and affected the marketing of domestic products and of those from other EEA States in the same manner, both in law and in fact.[72] Whilst it was not contested that the visual display ban applied to all traders operating in Norway and affected all products alike, as a matter of law, the question arose whether that ban was discriminatory in fact. In the view of the Norwegian government, that was not the case, given that since 2008 there had been no tobacco production in Norway.[73]

The EFTA Court was, in light of the information before it, unable to determine whether the visual display ban 'affect[ed] the marketing of products from other EEA States to a greater degree than that of imported products that were, until recently, manufactured in Norway'.[74] Consequently, it was for the referring court to undertake that determination, whilst taking account of the following factors. First, referring to the ruling of the ECJ in the *Commission v Greece* case and to its previous ruling in the *Pedicel* case,[75] the EFTA Court pointed out that 'the question whether there [was] domestic production [was] not decisive when it [came] to determining the effects of a restrictive measure', as '[it could not] be excluded that production in Norway [would] resume at a later time'.[76] Second, the national court had to examine whether the effects of the visual display ban on products which were new on the Norwegian market were greater than the effects it produced on products bearing an established trademark in that EEA State. Third, it had to determine whether the effects of the visual display ban were too uncertain and indirect for that ban to constitute a MEE.[77]

On the assumption that a restriction contrary to Article 11 EEA had been found by the national court, the Norwegian State argued that such a restriction could be justified on grounds of public health as provided for in Article 13 EEA. Again, the EFTA Court pointed out that it was for the referring court to identify the aims which the visual display ban was actually intended to pursue. It noted, however, that all parties to the proceedings agreed that the visual display ban aimed to protect public health.[78] It was also for the referring court to determine whether the visual display ban complied with the principle of proportionality, that is, whether it was appropriate for securing public health and did not go beyond what was necessary in order to attain that objective. That being said, it decided to provide the referring court with detailed guidance. First, the EFTA Court recalled—as had the ECJ in *Commission v Italy* in respect of road safety—that it was for each

---

[72] *Philip Morris Norway AS*, above n 1, para 44.
[73] ibid, para 25.
[74] ibid, para 49.
[75] Case C-391/92 *Commission v Greece* [1995] ECR I-1621 and Case E-4/04 *Pedicel* [2005] EFTA Ct Rep 1.
[76] *Philip Morris Norway AS*, above n 1, para 48.
[77] ibid, para 50.
[78] ibid, para 78.

EEA State 'to determine the degree of protection that it wishes to afford to public health and the way in which that protection is to be achieved'. Accordingly, 'the fact that one EEA State imposes less strict rules than another does not mean that the latter's rules are disproportionate'.[79] Second, 'where there is uncertainty as to the existence or extent of risks to human health, an EEA State should be able to take protective measures without having to wait until the reality of those risks becomes fully apparent'.[80] Third, in spite of the fact that there may be some scientific uncertainty as regards the suitability of the visual display ban, the EFTA Court pointed out that the national court should apply a 'rational basis' scrutiny: the visual display ban would be an appropriate means of protecting public health, if it was reasonable to assume that it would be able to contribute to the protection of human health.[81] Fourth and last, the EFTA Court observed that the question whether there was an alternative to the visual display ban relied on findings of fact which the referring court was in a better position to make than the EFTA Court.[82]

V. CONCLUDING REMARKS

In summary, *Commission v Italy* and *Mickelsson and Roos* are two judgments of paramount constitutional importance. Vertically, the ECJ took the opportunity to clarify the contours of Article 34 TFEU. Those two judgments did not revolutionise the law on the free movement of goods, as *Keck* remains good law. The same applies for the free movement of goods in EEA law. *Philip Morris Norway* shows that the EFTA Court is willing to apply the framework of analysis put forward by the ECJ in those two judgments. This means that, under EEA law, *Keck* can be regarded as good law.

However, both courts did stress the fact that the market-access rationale pervades that freedom. As the EFTA Court held in *Philip Morris Norway*, three principles underpin Article 11 EEA, namely the principle of non-discrimination (for selling arrangements), the principle of mutual recognition (for product-related requirements) and the principle of free market access (for other types of measures).[83] This suggests *Keck* must be read narrowly, that is, it is confined to selling arrangements.

Commission v Italy and *Mickelsson and Roos* also reassure the Member States that Article 34 TFEU does not seek to deprive them of their regulatory autonomy. In light of *Philip Morris Norway*, the same applies to Article 11 EEA. Both courts agree that measures whose effect on intra-EU trade is 'too uncertain and too indirect' as well as non-discriminatory selling arrangements fall outside the scope of

---

[79] ibid, para 80 (referring to Case C-141/07 *Commission v Germany* [2008] ECR I-6935, para 51).
[80] ibid, para 82.
[81] ibid, para 83.
[82] ibid, para 86.
[83] ibid, para 40.

the law on the free movement of goods. Arguably, the same applies to measures which do not 'greatly' restrict the use of a product. However, *Commission v Italy* and *Mickelsson and Roos* did not define what the precise meaning of the adverb 'greatly' conveys. Nor did the ECJ determine the degree to which consumer behaviour has to be influenced in order for Article 34 TFEU to be applicable. In the same way, since the visual display ban at issue in *Philip Morris Norway* constituted a selling arrangement, the EFTA Court did not need to resolve the issue whether only measures which 'greatly' restrict the use of a product fall within the scope of Article 11 EEA. It follows that those questions were left open to be resolved at a future date.

Horizontally, when examining the justifications put forward by the Member States, the ECJ strives not to second-guess the policy choices made by the national legislator. Instead, it prefers to focus on examining whether the justifications put forward by the Member State concerned are free from internal contradictions. In other words, the ECJ favours a process-oriented review. In the same way, the EFTA Court is respectful of the choices made by the national legislator as to the level of protection that it wishes to afford to public health.

Finally, as mentioned above, *Commission v Italy*, *Mickelsson and Roos* and *Philip Morris Norway* left open some important questions. However, I do not think that this should be seen as a shortcoming. On the contrary, the fact that the ECJ did not immediately answer all the questions to which *Commission v Italy* and *Mickelsson and Roos* gave rise should be seen as evidence of judicial prudence. Likewise, in *Philip Morris Norway*, the EFTA Court limited its answer to the questions referred by the Oslo District Court. This shows that breakthrough judgments must be accompanied by a progressive development of the case law, following a 'stone-by-stone' approach. As I have argued elsewhere,[84] the inter-judicial dialogue that takes place under Article 267 TFEU is deeply intertwined with the way in which the ECJ builds up its argumentative discourse. The same applies to the relationship between the EFTA Court and national courts, in relation to which the EFTA Court has observed that 'Article 34 SCA establishes a special means of judicial cooperation between the [EFTA] Court and national courts with the aim of providing the national courts with the necessary interpretations of elements of EEA law in order to decide the cases before them'.[85] As such, 'Article 34 SCA is based on a clear separation of functions between the [EFTA] Court and the national courts'.[86]

Accordingly, if the ECJ or the EFTA Court were to follow a model based on 'expository justice' (under which they would each provide exhaustive, albeit abstract, answers based on logic to the points of law raised by the questions referred), they

---

[84] In this regard, see K Lenaerts, 'The Court's outer and inner selves: Exploring the external and internal legitimacy of the European Court of Justice' in M Adams, J Meeusen, G Straetmans and H de Waele (eds), *Judging Europe's Judges* (Oxford, Hart Publishing, 2013) 13.

[85] E-18/11 *Irish Bank Resolution Corporation Ltd v Kaupþing hf* [2012] EFTA Ct Rep 592, para 53.

[86] *Philip Morris Norway AS*, above n 1, para 87.

would actually prevent national courts from engaging in a constructive dialogue. When presenting their legal discourse, the ECJ and the EFTA Court must strike the appropriate balance between different levels of specificity and generality in their reasoning. It must not be laconic and cryptic, nor too abstract, since this would deter national courts from making a reference. In essence, the preliminary reference procedure laid down in Article 267 TFEU and the proceedings under Article 34 SCA being a mechanism of dialogue between courts, the quality of the order for reference will substantially influence the drafting style of the answer given by the ECJ or the EFTA Court respectively. The judgment rendered by the latter must indeed constitute, first and foremost, a practical contribution to the solution of the case pending before the referring court. For this reason also, it is best for the ECJ and for the EFTA Court, in hard cases of constitutional importance, to follow an incremental approach.

29

The EFTA Court—A Court of Business Law?

ERIC MORGAN DE RIVERY AND ALEXANDRE FALL*

T HE EFTA COURT, a court of business law? Is this a legitimate question for a court which by virtue of its founding statute is deemed to be a general court designed to review EFTA Surveillance Authority (ESA) decisions imposing fines, settle disputes between EFTA states, give advisory opinions on the interpretation of the EEA Agreement, handle actions brought by an EFTA State, or a legal person against a decision or a failure to act of the ESA, or in view of obtaining compensation for a damage caused by ESA or its civil servants?[1]

At first glance, EFTA at large appears as a regional union essentially driven by economic and business-related principles. The EEA for its part, which is based on two pillars (that is, the EFTA pillar and the EU pillar), is an enhanced free trade zone that has been designed to extend the EU's internal market to the EEA EFTA Countries.[2] The EEA Agreement with its Annexes and Protocols forms its legal basis. This Agreement implements, in particular, economic freedoms and competition law rules which are similar in substance to those of the EU legal order. However, unlike the EU, the EEA EFTA States have not opted for deeper integration through a common foreign and security policy or a single currency, not even a common foreign trade policy. Thus, on the one hand, it is tempting to assert that the case law of the EFTA Court deals with economic issues and therefore is mostly business-oriented. On the other hand, however, the EFTA Court has never been meant to handle disputes like a commercial court but rather to ensure the implementation of EEA primary and secondary law[3] to the benefit of the EEA EFTA States, economic operators, and individuals. Moreover, the EFTA Court is

---

* The authors would like to thank Eileen Lagathu for her insightful comments.
[1] Agreement between the EFTA States on the establishment of a Surveillance Authority and a Court of Justice (OJ L 344, 31.1.1994, p 3; and EFTA States' official gazettes), Arts 31–37 and 39.
[2] Case E-1/03 *EFTA Surveillance Authority v The Republic of Iceland* [2003] EFTA Ct Rep 143, para 27.
[3] EU secondary legislation is incorporated into the EEA Agreement (Annexes or Protocols) upon decision of the EEA Joint Committee (this committee is composed of the EFTA Standing Committee and the European External Action Service). See Arts 7 and 92 EEA Agreement and Council Regulation (EC) No 2894/94 of 28 November 1994 concerning arrangements for implementing the Agreement in the European Economic Area.

a Supreme Court and a court in charge of giving interpretation to any questions that may be raised on any provision of the EEA Agreement.

Against this background, the rationale behind the question that the authors modestly attempt to address may rather be the objective observation that over its lifespan of 20 years, the EFTA Court has issued numerous decisions which have had, de jure or de facto, directly or indirectly, an effective impact on the development of business transactions within the territory of the EFTA pillar of the EEA (I).

Moreover and beyond the vast array of business-related issues reviewed by the EFTA Court, the judicial protection offered to economic operators, as well as the specific style and methodology adopted, all reveal a willingness of the EFTA Court to deliver judgments that are easy to understand and implement and likely to ensure a level playing field between the administration and private operators. These characteristics, together with a scrupulous effort to issue a case law that is perfectly compatible with that of its EU sister courts, have broadened the impact of the EFTA Court case law and made it a reliable reference for economic operators within the European Economic Area as a whole (II). In that context, business operators from both the EFTA and the EU pillar are, at least indirectly and potentially, all affected by the judgments of the EFTA Court. We will thus examine whether the topics before the EFTA Court and the principles relied upon by this Court justify a conclusion that the EFTA Court is truly a Court of business law.

I. THE EFTA COURT ISSUES JUDGMENTS WITH A DIRECT IMPACT ON BUSINESS OPERATIONS

The correct implementation of the four freedoms to the benefit of individuals and economic operators has been a constant preoccupation of the EFTA Court (hereafter the Court) since its creation. The imagination of the States (be it the EEA EFTA or EU States) to set up barriers aimed at 'protecting' their own industries by recreating artificial partitioning of the EEA, has never weakened. In the EU we all have in mind the *Cassis de Dijon*,[4] *Italian Pasta*[5] or the *Rioja Wine*[6] judgments. As the years go by, the pretexts used by the Member States have become increasingly sophisticated. The limited number of cases (in comparison with the ECJ) has not precluded the EFTA Court from relentlessly and without ambiguity condemning any artificial barrier in various decisions involving economic operators (A). However, the Court remains a Supreme Court and as such is meant to handle issues going beyond the mere implementation of the economic freedoms enshrined in the EEA Agreement. Thus, the Court also deals, as will be demonstrated by focusing on selected cases, with other types of issues (concerning inter alia the interpretation of EU directives that have been incorporated into the EEA

---

[4] Case C-120/78 *REWE*, 'Cassis de Dijon' [1979] ECR-649.
[5] Case C-90/86 *Giorgi Zoni*, 'Italian pasta' [1988] ECR-4285.
[6] Case C-388/95 *Kingdom of Belgium v Kingdom of Spain*, 'Rioja Wine' [2000] ECR I-3123.

Agreement). Nevertheless, one must admit that even in this context, the Court's judgments have had an indirect but nevertheless clear impact on economic operators (B).

A. The Court Deals with a Wide Array of Issues Having a Direct Impact on Business

i. Lifting Barriers to the Free Movement of Goods

The *Grund* case, based on a referral from the Reykjavík District Court, is a topical example of the implementation of the freedom of circulation of goods.[7] The plaintiff, an Icelandic nursing home, purchased four medicinal products from a wholesaler in Norway which it intended to give to its own patients under medical supervision. The defendant, the Icelandic Medicines Agency, refused to allow these imports, allegedly on the basis of Directive 2001/83 laying down common rules on the control of medicinal products, if a control report was not issued confirming that each batch of medicinal products met the requirements on which the Icelandic marketing authorisation was based. The referring Court essentially asked: (i) whether medical institutions could freely import medicinal products distributed to end users (and not intended for further resale) from another EEA State on the sole basis of the marketing authorisation given in the state of export or whether the importing medical institution had to present a control report to the competent agency in the country of import, and (ii) whether the labelling and package leaflet should be in Icelandic. Interestingly enough, both the EU Commission and the ESA in their submissions were in favour of a strict interpretation of the relevant texts, requesting in particular that a marketing authorisation be issued by the state of import.

On the first issue, the EFTA Court began by putting the problem into perspective by recalling first that the goal of market authorisations is to safeguard public health and second, that it is almost a given fact that parallel importers in the pharmaceutical sector will generally offer goods at a lower price than an official distributor.

Second, on a more technical basis, the Court noted that the products have marketing authorisations in Norway (country of export) and that products with the same names have marketing authorisations in Iceland (country of import).[8] Thus it considered that these products were imported not like products being placed on the market for the first time, but rather as a parallel import of a product similar or identical to a product already covered by a marketing authorisation in Iceland (that is, the EEA country of import).

---

[7] Case E-7/11 *Grund, elli- og hjúkrunarheimili v Lyfjastofnun* [2012] EFTA Ct Rep 188.
[8] ibid, para 56.

Third, the Court noted that in such conditions, there was no need to require the parallel importer to provide the import authorities with traceability information in the form of control reports. Such reports requiring the parallel importer to obtain from the manufacturer all the pharmaceutical specifications to which it has no access[9] would therefore constitute a disproportionate request. The Court concluded that such requirement would be tantamount to a measure having an equivalent effect to a quantitative restriction on imports contrary to Article 11 EEA.[10]

Finally, the Court reached a practical solution, inspired by the principle of proportionality, that is, that the parallel importer be subjected to the production of a mere parallel import licence which would be limited to establishing that the imported product is identical or essentially similar to products having the marketing authorisation in the EEA State of import.

On the second issue, again, after having recalled the primary objective of the Directive that is, the protection of health, the Court opined that at least in the circumstances of the case (that is, the distribution of the relevant medicines directly to the patients under appropriate professional supervision), the exemption from the language requirements for holders of parallel licences did not entail a higher risk for public health than when granted to holders or applicants for a marketing authorisation. In this context, the Court acknowledged the discretion of the authorities regarding the possibility to grant a language exemption so that the nursing home could dispense with the notice and labelling in Icelandic which are normally provided with the relevant medicines. However the Court clearly indicated that such discretion was limited by the general principles of EEA law and that consequently, it must not be exercised in a disproportionate, arbitrary or abusive, and in particular protectionist manner.

This practical line of reasoning, previously developed in two other cases (*Paranova*[11] and *Astra Norge*[12]) demonstrates both the Court's commitment to such fundamental principles as free trade and its consequence of unfettered parallel imports, but also the Court's ability to provide practical solutions (that is, the parallel licence such as proposed) based on fundamental as well as commonsense principles which can be used beyond the circumstances of the case as a precious tool to resolve disputes regarding the interpretation of the law. Such line of reasoning and conclusion is in fact akin to the use of *'effet utile'*, which has sometimes been used as a guiding principle in cases adjudicated by the EU Courts.[13]

---

[9]   ibid, para 66.

[10] ibid, para 62.

[11] Case E-3/02 *Paranova AS v Merck & Co, Inc and Others* [2003] EFTA Ct Rep 101.

[12] Case E-1/98 *The Norwegian Government v Astra Norge AS* [1998] EFTA Ct Rep 140. In the *Paranova* and *Astra Norge* cases the court condemned artificial arguments (eg derived from copyrights or trademark legislation), the effect of which was to partition the market in pharmaceuticals by prohibiting de facto parallel imports.

[13] See, eg, Case C-453/99 *Courage Ltd v Crehan* [2001] ECR I-6297; Joined Cases C-6/90 and C-9/90 and C-9/90, *Andrea Francovich and Others v Italian Republic* [1991] ECR I-5357.

Adopting the same pragmatic approach in the *Kellogg's* case,[14] the EFTA Court accepted the precautionary principle but within certain practical limits, that is, it should not be used as another barrier to free trade. The Norwegian government had argued in essence that the nutritional fortification (in particular with iron) of the complainant's cornflakes were likely to have negative consequences on health. The Court accepted the precautionary principle as a justification for restricting trade:

> In the absence of harmonization of rules, when there is uncertainty as to the current state of scientific research, it is for the Contracting Parties to decide what degree of protection of human health they intend to assure, having regard to the fundamental requirements of EEA law, notably, the free movement of goods within the European Economic Area.[15]

However, it made it clear that measures taken by a State pursuant to the precautionary principle must comply with EEA law and are subject to judicial review indicating that 'the need to safeguard public health must be balanced against the principle of the free movement of goods'.[16] *In casu*, the Court concluded that the justifications given by the Norwegian Health Authority remained purely hypothetical or academic and noted that Norway accepted without any difficulty the fortification with iron of its own brown whey cheese. This cheese was given to all the schoolchildren on a daily basis. It is no surprise that such realistic reasoning of the Court has inspired the ECJ in various cases.[17]

ii. Lifting Barriers to the Free Movement of Services

Regarding the protection against restrictions to the freedom to provide services, the EFTA Court delivered another interesting judgment in the *Ladbrokes* case[18] relating to the gaming industry,[19] a sector which has also given rise to numerous cases before the ECJ.[20] In this case, the Court had to determine upon request of the Oslo District Court to what extent State monopolies, which denied access

---

[14] Case E-3/00 *EFTA Surveillance Authority v The Kingdom of Norway* [2000–2001] EFTA Ct Rep 73 (*Kellogg's*).
[15] ibid, para 25.
[16] ibid, para 28.
[17] Case C-192/01 *Commission v Denmark* [2003] ECR I-9693, paras 46–53 and Advocate General Mischo's opinion, para 79; Case C-236/01 *Monsanto Agricoltura Italia* [2003] ECR I-8105, para 106; Case T-13/99 *Pfizer Animal Health* [2002] ECR II-3305, paras 115 and 143.
[18] Case E-3/06 *Ladbrokes Ltd and the Government of Norway, Ministry of Culture and Church affairs/ Ministry of Agriculture and Food* [2007] EFTA Ct Rep 86 (*Ladbrokes*).
[19] See also Case E-1/06 *EFTA Surveillance Authority v The Kingdom of Norway* [2007] EFTA Ct Rep 8.
[20] Joined Cases C-338/04, C-359/04 and C-360/04 *Placanica and Others* [2007] ECR I-1891; Case C-42/02 *Lindman* [2003] ECR I-13519; Case C-243/01 *Gambelli and Others* [2003] ECR I-13031; Case C-6/01 *Anomar and Others* ECR [2003] I-8621; Case C-67/98 *Questore di Verona v Diego Zenatti* [1999] ECR I-7289; Case C-124/97 *Läärä and Others* [1999] ECR I-6067; Case C-275/92 *HM Customs and Excise v Schindler* [1994] ECR I-1039.

to the market to private operators, restricted the free movement of services (Article 36 EEA). More specifically the referring court asked:

— whether the fundamental freedoms preclude a national legislation from establishing that certain forms of gaming may only be offered by a State-owned gaming company, while horse-race betting and other forms of gaming could only be entrusted to non-profit organisations or operators with a special purpose; and
— whether national statutory rules can prohibit the provision and marketing of gaming by an undertaking that does not have permission to operate.

In reaching its decision, the Court considered carefully the justifications given by Norway to impose such restrictions, namely fighting gambling addiction, crime and malpractice. First and in line with ECJ case law,[21] the Court recalled that the restriction of fundamental freedoms must not only be justified, but also necessary and proportionate. The Court set stringent conditions to justify such restrictions: (i) 'the restrictive measures [must] reflect a concern to bring about a genuine diminution in gambling opportunities'[22] (ii), and gaming policy must provide for a lower level of gambling addiction in society than in a liberalised system.

Regarding the proportionality test, the Court considered that the system must limit gaming activities in a consistent and systematic manner. Hence, the restrictive policy applied to EEA-based new entrants shall not be inconsistent with marketing activities or the development of new games authorised by public authorities in favour of their national operators.

Regarding the necessity test, the Court indicated that where other less restrictive measures would have achieved the objective level of protection sought, an exclusive rights system could not be considered necessary simply because it might offer an even higher level of protection. Thus, the Court indicated that the national court should determine in practice whether and to what extent a given game can lead to a gambling addiction.[23]

Second, the Court, having noted that the licensing of gaming has not been harmonised between Member States, acknowledged with a remarkable pragmatism and sense of reality that 'different levels of protection may exist throughout the EEA'[24] as regards gaming policy. However, the Court tried to reconcile the need for a level of consumer protection that suits the characteristics of each society with the freedom to provide services. The Court considered that Member States 'must take into account the requirements already fulfilled by the provider of the services

---

[21] Case C-243/01 *Gambelli* [2003] ECR I-13031, para 62.
[22] *Ladbrokes*, above n 18, para 45.
[23] ibid, para 57.
[24] ibid, para 85.

for the pursuit of activities in the home state'.[25] The ECJ followed this line in the *Liga Portuguesa* case.[26]

Third, the Court set aside in a series of very clear paragraphs, justifications for existing or new games linked to the financing of benevolent or public interest activities. Such arguments were considered by the Court as beneficial but *incidental* to the only acceptable grounds mentioned above.

The case carried out an in-depth review of gambling services and applied fully the principle of freedom of circulation of services broadly, where previously that industry was considered as a political issue to be dealt with by the (generally biased) national governments.

iii. Lifting Barriers to the Free Movement of Capital

Regarding the principle of free movement of capital the Court decided in the *Fokus Bank* case[27] that the EEA law provisions on free movement of capital should prevail over bilateral tax agreements. A Norwegian court essentially questioned the Court to know whether (i) Article 40 EEA (on free movement of capital) opposes a legislation providing that the benefit of a tax credit on dividends paid by a Norwegian company will only be granted to shareholders residing in Norway, and whether (ii) the Norwegian administration could engage in tax administrative proceedings exclusively with the distributing company when assessing the withholding tax.

Before addressing these issues, the Court insisted on the wide scope of EEA law by stating: 'As a general rule, the tax system of an EFTA State party to the EEA Agreement is not covered by the EEA Agreement. The EEA/EFTA States must, however, exercise their taxation power consistent with EEA Law'.[28]

First, the Court reasserted the prevalence of fundamental freedoms over any bilateral tax agreement and more specifically held that the legislation at stake was restricting the 'free movement of capital, [as it] may adversely affect the profit of non-resident shareholders and ... thereby have the effect of deterring them from investing capital in companies having their seat in Norway'.[29] Second, the Court adopted the same posture regarding the principle of non-discrimination.

Based on the above, the Court concluded that the favourable tax credit paid to resident shareholders (as opposed to the tax credit paid to non-resident shareholders) was incompatible with Article 40 EEA.

Finally, the Court addressed the question of whether procedural rights had been denied to shareholders residing outside Norway, inasmuch as they had not been notified of the changes in their tax positions and were not party to the

---

[25] ibid, para 86.
[26] Case C-42/07 *Liga Portuguesa de Futebol Profesional and Bwin International* [2009] ECR I-7633, para 69.
[27] Case E-1/04 *Fokus Bank ASA and The Norwegian State, represented by Skattedirektoratet* [2004] EFTA Ct Rep 11 (*Fokus Bank*).
[28] ibid, para 20.
[29] ibid, para 26.

administrative proceedings.[30] In this respect, the Court clearly considered that in the light of the principle of free movement of capital, it is of prime importance to facilitate access to information in order to guarantee substantive rights.[31] Therefore, non-resident shareholders cannot be excluded from the administrative procedure. The Court indicated that the fact for non-residents to see their procedural rights denied ('to the extent they are not notified of and cannot be a party to tax administrative proceedings') entails differential treatment amounting to an unjustified discrimination under Article 40 EEA. The Court added that this is a matter of principle and that the exact extent of this advantage is irrelevant. Thus, the Court not only asserted the prevalence of free movement of capital but also ensured that the corporate entities have the appropriate tools to exercise their rights.

B. The EFTA Court Provides Advice to Other Courts or Decides Last Resort Cases on Subjects which Have an Indirect but Clear Impact on Business Operators

The Court mainly rules on disputes relating to the interpretation of the EEA Agreement (four economic freedoms, competition law, state aid, harmonised law). We have made the demonstration above that its contribution is of prime interest to economic operators. However, as a Supreme Court, the EFTA Court has also been called upon to decide cases or provide advice to other courts on subjects which, although on the face of it are not directly related to business, in fact frequently affect the interests of business operators.

Thus, the Court has been asked to give its interpretation of the equal treatment directive in a case involving public servants. In this case,[32] the EFTA Court considered that Norway, by keeping in force a rule which allows for a number of academic posts to be reserved for members of the underrepresented gender, had failed to fulfil its obligations under Articles 7 and 70 of the EEA Agreement and Directive 76/207/EEC on the implementation of the principle of equal treatment for men and women. The Court pointed out that any derogation from the right of equal treatment of men and women must be appropriate, necessary and proportionate (that is, in the case at hand, there must be a possibility for the best-qualified candidate to obtain the post). In this case, the Norwegian legislation allowed positions to be attributed *automatically* to the underrepresented gender. Therefore, the Court concluded that the directive had not been implemented properly.

Of course, the interpretation of this directive relating to 'equal treatment for men and women as regards access to employment, vocational training and

---

[30] ibid, para 40.
[31] ibid, para 43, 'procedural rights are prerequisite to the protection of substantive rights under the EEA Agreement'.
[32] Case E-1/02 *EFTA Surveillance Authority v The Kingdom of Norway* [2003] EFTA Ct Rep 1.

promotion, and working conditions' is not confined to the academic world and is equally applicable to corporate entities.

In another case, the Labour Court of Norway made a reference relating to the conditions under which Norwegian municipalities could switch to a different pension insurance scheme provider from the one referred to in the collective agreements. The Court had to establish essentially whether (i) and to what extent Article 53 EEA (equivalent to Article 101 TFEU) applies to a collective agreement concluded by an employer organisation and whether (ii) the concerned agreement that imposed, inter alia, an obligation for the employer to discuss beforehand the possible change of pension company and to submit occupational pension schemes offers to union representatives for approval, was compatible with Articles 53 and 54 EEA (equivalent to Articles 101 and 102 TFEU).

The Court engaged on the key question of the relationship between collective agreement and EEA competition law. Building on ECJ case law, the Court pointed out that the pursuit of social policy objectives foreseen in particular in the EEA Agreement[33] must be balanced against the need to guarantee the effective functioning of the market.

The Court essentially held that collective bargaining agreements between employers and employees are, inasmuch as they pursue the objective of improving working conditions and employment, sheltered from EEA competition law, and in particular from the application of the provisions relating to the prohibition of cartels. However, provisions pursuing objectives extraneous to that objective may come within the scope of competition law. In order to determine whether provisions of a collective agreement pursue the said objective of improving conditions of work and employment, the Court took a pragmatic stance: 'where it is clear that the intended, immediate and practical effect of any such clause is to improve conditions of work and employment, inherent restrictions on competition must be accepted'.[34] The Court also urged national courts to take into account in their assessment the good faith of the parties in concluding and implementing the agreement and the aggregate effect of the provisions.

Once again, this ruling, which *in casu* applied to public entities (Norwegian municipalities), is equally applicable to corporate entities and sets a clear framework for business operators operating within the EFTA pillar.

Regarding the financing of municipal kindergartens, the Court provided insightful remarks in the field of state aid. In this case, an association of private kindergartens initiated an action for annulment against an ESA decision not to open a formal investigation procedure under State aid rules regarding the public financing of municipal kindergartens in Norway. As a matter of fact, public and private Norwegian municipal kindergartens received equal state subsidies capped at 20% of the cost of services. However, the applicant claimed that the financing

---

[33] Art 66 EEA provides that 'the contracting parties agree upon the need to promote improved working conditions and an improved standard of living for workers'.

[34] *EFTA Surveillance Authority v The Kingdom of Norway*, above n 32, para 55.

system discriminated against private kindergartens, as the costs incurred by public kindergartens were systematically higher than those incurred by their private counterpart.

The Court dismissed the applicant's claims on the substance for reasons which need not be developed here. Nevertheless, the Court used this case to give indications on the concept of economic activity.

Before engaging with the notion of economic activity, the Court restated that 'the concept of an undertaking encompasses every entity engaged in an economic activity, regardless of the legal status of the entity and the way in which it is financed'.[35]

The Court then pointed out that an undertaking provides services as an economic activity only if it receives remuneration. However, in the absence of remuneration or if the remuneration does not constitute consideration for the service rendered (for example, the remuneration only constitutes a fraction of the real cost of the service), it is a public service founded by the State.[36]

In the case at hand, the Court noted, inter alia, that 80 per cent of the costs of municipal kindergartens are state funded and that there is no connection between the actual costs of the service provided and the fee paid by the parents. It therefore deducted that municipalities have a statutory duty to ensure that sufficient places for young children (below the age of compulsory school) exist. In such circumstances, the Court concluded that the ESA 'did not need to entertain doubts as to whether the municipal kindergartens might constitute undertakings'.[37]

As highlighted by the foregoing, even when the EFTA Court's judgments do not directly deal with business issues, the interpretation which it provides of the EEA Agreement or of secondary legislation or economic concepts appears to be intentionally geared at providing extremely valuable pointers to business operators.

II. THE EFTA COURT THROUGH ITS ORIGINAL METHODOLOGY AND DISPENSATION OF A HIGH DEGREE OF JUDICIAL PROTECTION POSITIVELY AFFECTS ECONOMIC OPERATORS OUTSIDE THE EFTA PILLAR

The Court, in the best tradition of Nordic countries, has been quite demanding in terms of transparency vis-à-vis national administrations or vis-à-vis the EFTA administration and it has also made clear that judicial protection would correct any asymmetry or imbalance in favour of said administrations (A). Meanwhile, the Court has adopted from the date of its creation a style and an approach privileging unambiguous as well as practical solutions or recommendations, so that the referring courts or the parties might infer clear conclusions from the relatively

---

[35] ibid, para 78.
[36] ibid, paras 80–84.
[37] ibid, para 84.

short judgments issued (B). All these characteristics have benefited business operators in and outside the EFTA pillar.

A. An Approach Introducing a Higher Standard of Judicial Review in Order to Correct any Imbalance or Disadvantage which Would Play against Private Operators

The Court, far from merely implementing the procedural guarantees as interpreted by the ECJ, has in a number of occasions provided further guidance to economic operators in order to correct unfair imbalances or even possible abuses by administrations. In this respect, the Court unambiguously places the judge as the ultimate protector of the corporate citizen.

i. Better Control of Administrative Decisions Imposing Fines

It cannot be denied that the welcome conjunction of the incorporation of the Charter of Fundamental Rights of the European Union as of the entry into force of the treaty of Lisbon on 1 January 2009, along with the adoption of the landmark *Menarini* judgment of the European Court of Human Rights on 27 September 2011,[38] have caused a great leap forward towards qualifying competition procedures and fines to criminal charges.[39] As a result thereof, an appropriate adjustment of the judicial review of the EFTA and EU administrative authorities had to be made in order to ensure the compatibility with fundamental rights of the EU/EFTA antitrust enforcement system.[40] Indeed, in the famous twin cases *KME*[41] *and Chalkor*,[42] both delivered on 8 December 2011, the Court of Justice made a clear statement on the role of the judiciary as regards the review of legality.[43] Yet even today, a good faith examination of the EU case law conveys the impression that the EU Courts are still undecided as to how in practice such judicial control of legality is effectively understood and/or exercised. Thus,

---

[38] *Menarini (A) Diagnostics SRL v Italy* No 43509/08, 27 September 2011.

[39] ibid, para 42; see also Advocate General Sharpston's Opinion of 10 February 2011, Case C-272/09 P *KME Germany AG et al v Commission* [2011] ECR I-12789, para 67 (competition law fines fall under the scope of Art 6 ECHR).

[40] See on the scope of review *Menarini*, above n 38, paras 63–75; see contra W Wils, 'The compatibility with fundamental rights of the EU antitrust enforcement system in which the European Commission acts both as investigator and as first-instance decision maker' (2014) 37(1) *World Competition* 5.

[41] Case C-272/09 P *KME Germany AG et al v Commission*, above n 39, para 121.

[42] Case C-386/10 *Chalkor AE Epexergasias Metallon v Commission* [2011] ECR I-13085, para 54.

[43] It is true that when doing so, the Court of justice pretended to merely endorse a position which had been adopted by the Court of First Instance on the occasion of the *Tetra Laval* case as early as 2005. However, it must be acknowledged that the enlarged judicial control described in this judgment had somewhat remained a rather isolated viewpoint often justified by the allegedly specific nature of merger and not followed by a general as well as effective change in the exercise of judicial control over the Commission by the EU judicature.

some judges of the Tribunal (i) continue to refer to the manifest error concept,[44] (ii) while others seem to be happy with a very minimal degree of justifications[45] or even substitute largely, while exercising their review of legality, their own appreciation to that of the administration to the extent that the latter's appraisal does not take into account all the circumstances of the case,[46] and finally others (iii) prefer to implicitly conclude by way of a global or en bloc approach (which aggregates in its comments the review of legality and the unlimited jurisdiction enjoyed by the EU judicature when reviewing fines) that the reasoning of the Commission is compatible with the Charter of fundamental rights, the *Menarini* judgment and Article 6 of the Convention of the Human Rights.[47] Even the Court of Justice seems at times to slightly stray from the *Chalkor/KME* interpretation of the review of legality in connection with the Commission's duty to reason its decisions.[48]

Finally, the presumption of innocence is often sacrificed on the ground that the EU judicature considers that a presumption of guilt (at least in theory rebuttable) can prevail with a view to ensuring an effective implementation of competition law.

Against that background, the content of the *Posten Norge* judgment of 18 April 2012 is clear and reassuring.[49] It should be noted at the outset that the EU Charter of Fundamental Rights is not part of EEA law. But the EFTA Court has long recognised that EEA law must be interpreted in the light of fundamental rights and that the provisions of the European Convention of Human Rights and the judgments of the European Court of Human Rights are important sources for determining the scope of these rights.[50]

First, the Court held, regarding the limited perimeter of the control of legality:

— 'This case law must be seen against the background of the limitation of the Court's powers of review which is inherent in the concept of review of legality ... This is the reason for which the Court, when conducting its review of ESA's decision, must not substitute its own assessment of complex economic circumstances for that of ESA';[51] or 'the fact that the Court is restricted to a review of legality precludes it from annulling the contested decision if there can be no legal objection to the assessment of ESA, even if it is not the one which the Court would consider to be preferable'.[52]

---

[44] See, eg, Case T-439/07 *Coats Holdings v Commission*, nyr, para 185.

[45] See, eg, Case T-154/10 *Commission v France*, nyr, para 120 and C-559/12 P *Commission v France*, nyr, para 66.

[46] See, eg, Case T-360/09 *E.ON Ruhrgas v Commission*, para 301; Case T-370/09 *GDF Suez v Commission*, para 462.

[47] See, eg, T-379/10 *Keramag Keramische Werke and Others v Commission*, nyr, para 34.

[48] *Cf* Case C-247/11 P *Areva and Others v Commission*, nyr, paras 56 and 57 with Case C-272/09 P *KME Germany AG et al v Commission*, above n 39 ECR I-12789, paras 128 and 132.

[49] Case E-15/10 *Posten Norge AS v EFTA Surveillance Authority* [2012] EFTA Ct Rep 246.

[50] Case E-2/03 *Ákæruvaldið (The Public Prosecutor) v Ásgeir Logi Ásgeirsson, Axel Pétur Ásgeirsson and Helgi Már Reynisson* [2003] EFTA Ct Rep 185, para 23.

[51] ibid, para 96.

[52] ibid, para 98.

Second, regarding the intensity of judicial review in that context, it found:

— 'Not only must the Court establish, among other things, whether the evidence relied on is factually accurate, reliable and consistent, but also whether that evidence contains all the information which must be taken into account in order to assess a complex situation and whether it is capable of substantiating the conclusions drawn from it';[53] with the consequence that since the control is akin to the control of a criminal sanction imposed by an administrative body, 'the Court must be able to quash in all respects, on questions of fact and of law, the challenged decision'.[54]
— Besides, the presumption of innocence must be kept in mind by the judge.[55]
— Finally and against this background, 'the submission that the Court may intervene only if it considers a complex economic assessment of ESA to be manifestly wrong must be rejected'.[56]

Hence, the Court allows for an effective control of legality but within the clearly defined boundaries of the specific concept of legality review. On the contrary, the European Court of Justice often seems to define the control of legality in a much broader way[57] than its traditional sense. In practice, however, the EU Courts do not seem to draw the effective consequences of this broad definition.

As a result, the EFTA Court supplies businesses with clearer and more accurate guidance on what constitute the key elements of judicial control. This approach has been taken over by several Advocates General.[58]

ii. Facilitate Access to Documents, in Particular for the
Purpose of Private Enforcement Actions

The Court also managed to develop a concrete approach as regards the thorny issue of access to documents for the purpose of private enforcement actions. In this respect, the *DB Schenker* case[59] provides felicitous clarifications regarding, inter alia, the standard for the assessment of requests, the possible justifications for the administration's resistance and the need to facilitate private enforcement actions.

Building on the above-mentioned *Posten Norge* case, the Court issued a judgment on 21 December 2012, *DB Schenker*, whereby it interpreted the EFTA

---

[53] ibid, para 99.
[54] ibid, para 100.
[55] ibid, para 101.
[56] ibid, para 102.
[57] See, especially, *KME Germany*, above n 39, para 121 and *Chalkor*, above n 42, para 54.
[58] AG Kokott, Opinion of 18 April 2013 in Case C-501/11 P *Schindler Holding Ltd v Commission*, fn 18; AG Wathelet, Opinion of 26 September 2013 in Case C-295/12 P *Telefónica v Commission*, fn 63; AG Mengozzi, Opinion of 30 January 2014 in Case C-382/12 P *Mastercard v Commission*, fnn 102 and 105.
[59] Case E-14/11 *DB Schenker North AB v EFTA Surveillance Authority*, not yet published (*DB Schenker*).

legislation governing the right of access to ESA's documents. The issue arose within the framework of a claim for follow-on damages, initiated by DB Schenker against Posten Norge for losses allegedly caused by the abuse of dominance which had formed the subject of the above-mentioned *Posten Norge* judgment of 18 April 2012. ESA had taken a decision which denied access to 350 documents in the case file which had been seized during the inspection of the premises of Posten Norge in June 2005. ESA argued that giving access to such documents would undermine the privacy and integrity of private individuals and that there was no overriding public interest in the disclosure of such documents. In addition, it underlined the huge burden that would result for ESA and on Posten Norge if non-confidential versions of the inspection documents were to be prepared. Finally, Posten Norge raised the sensitive nature of many of these documents which contain business secrets.

On the occasion of this case, the Court once again revealed both its attachment to transparency and the rights of victims of competition law infringements to be able to obtain damages thanks to the evidence gathered by way of access to documents. Beyond that, the Court once again was able to express its attachment to fundamental principles[60] and to give another example of its pragmatism and commonsense approach.

First, the Court clearly stated that in conformity with the relevant law, access to documents is the rule and refusal to access the exception.[61] In this respect, and more specifically, the Court added that there cannot be any general presumption regarding the purpose of inspections and investigations where the infringement decision is final (that is, there is no appeal pending) and the documents do not relate to voluntary submissions by leniency applicants.[62] The EFTA Court seems to be more generous towards corporate entities than the European Commission in its draft directive on private enforcement. The latter only protects corporate leniency statements and does not encompass leniency documents that have not been drafted for the purpose of the investigation.[63] The Court also provided further guidance on the exception for allegedly excessive burden on the administration put forward by ESA. On that latter aspect, the Court made it clear that the application of such exception requires a concrete and individual assessment whereby ESA must prove the unreasonableness of the administrative burden that would be caused by granting access to documents. In this case, the pragmatic approach of the Court was particularly relevant since the situation merely concerned three ring binders.[64] Moreover, the Court considered that all the information concerning a company and its business contacts cannot be protected as business secrets. Instead, a case-by-case assessment ought to be carried out. In this respect,

---

[60] ibid, para 78: referring, in particular, to legal certainty or the principle of equal access to justice for individuals and economic operators.

[61] ibid, paras 118–125.

[62] ibid, paras 133 and 224.

[63] Directive proposal 2013/34/UE of the European Parliament and Council as amended by the Council on 24 March 2014 [2013/0185 (COD)], Article 6(2a).

[64] *DB Schenker*, above n 56, para 270.

the Court highlighted that the age of information is a significant consideration in assessing whether access to that document could violate business secrets.[65]

Further, the Court, in its typical reasonable and balanced approach, held that applicants must provide indications allowing to identify the documents targeted and justifications concerning their relevance.[66]

Last but not least, departing specifically from the EU case law, the Court found that private enforcement may be regarded as constituting an overriding public interest.[67] As specified in the EFTA Rules on Access to Documents (RAD),[68] the exceptions foreseen (for example, commercial interest) under Article 4 RAD may be set aside if there is an 'overriding public interest' in disclosure. The Court did not hesitate to state that the objectives of transparency and private enforcement may override confidentiality concerns.

Thus, the *Schenker* judgment provides greater access to files, while reinforcing procedural guarantees concerning the judicial review of the administration's decisions to the benefit of corporate entities.

B. An Approach Providing Clear and Practical Decisions Thanks to an Original Methodology

One of the strengths of the Court pertains to the fact that it has developed an interpretation of the EEA Agreement over the last 20 years, which is consistent with that of the EU case law. This is perfectly in line with the homogeneity principle which is enshrined in the EEA Agreement and provides for a 'homogeneous and dynamic European Economic Area', along with a coherent interpretation of case law within the EEA area.[69] Such principle is also foreseen by the EFTA Surveillance Agency and the EFTA Court agreement.[70] Therefore, the articles which are identical to the corresponding EU rules in the TFEU and secondary EU legislation ought to be interpreted in conformity with the ECJ case law for the period prior to the signing of the EEA Agreement (2 May 1992) and 'as uniform

---

[65] This exception is foreseen by Art 4 of the Transparency regulation 1049/2001, see *DB Schenker*, paras 125 and 278.

[66] *DB Schenker*, above n 56, para 92.

[67] ibid, para 132. See *contra* Case T-109/05 *Navigazione Libera des Golfo v Commission* [2011] ECR II-2479, para 148.

[68] This is the mirror legislation of the EU Transparency regulation 1049/2001.

[69] Paras 4 and 15 of the Preamble and Art 1, 6, 105, 106, 107, 111 of the EEA Agreement. The Preamble states that the 'objective is to establish a dynamic and homogeneous European Economic Area, based on common rules and equal conditions of competition'.

[70] Agreement between the EFTA States on the establishment of a Surveillance Authority and a Court of Justice (OJ L 344, 31.1.1994, p 3; and EFTA States' official gazettes), Art 3 'in so far as they are identical in substance to corresponding rules of the Treaty establishing the European Economic Community and the Treaty establishing the European Coal and Steel Community and to acts adopted in application of these two Treaties, shall in their implementation and application be interpreted in conformity with the relevant rulings of the Court of Justice of the European Communities given prior to the date of signature of the EEA Agreement'.

as possible'[71] after that date. In practice, the EFTA Court has always followed closely the ECJ case law, and the EFTA jurisprudence regularly refers to this principle considered to be a quasi-fundamental principle.[72] The Court even considers that homogeneity 'cannot be restricted to the interpretation of provisions whose wording is identical in substance to parallel provisions of European Union Law'.[73] As a result thereof, EEA law is akin to a *mirror legislation*. Various EFTA cases relate to the interpretation of EU law, such as Directives[74] or Regulations.[75]

The Court has also developed an advanced integration system, in particular with respect to fundamental freedoms.[76] As acknowledged by the case law, 'the aim of the EEA Agreement … is the realisation of the four freedoms within the whole of the European Economic Area, so that the internal market is extended to the EFTA states'.[77]

Securing a homogeneous development of EEA law in cooperation with the ECJ brings innovative solutions to business operators in the EEA and the EU. Fully aware of this fact, the Court has been keen to embrace this principle and constantly refers to the decisions of the EU judges and that of their Strasbourg counterparts inasmuch as they are relevant to the case at hand.[78] For instance, in the above-mentioned *Posten Norge* case, the EFTA court referred to no fewer than five cases of the ECHR and 21 cases of the European Court of Justice (General Court and Court of Justice of the European Union). This practice is welcomed as it enhances legal certainty and gives full credibility as such to the Court's contribution and, as it is recognised by EU Courts,[79] benefits to all EEA economic operators.

---

[71] Agreement between the EFTA States on the establishment of a Surveillance Authority and a Court of Justice (OJ L 344, 31.1.1994, p 3; and EFTA States' official gazettes), Art 105. See also Case C-452/01 *Ospelt and Schlössle Weissenberg* [2003] ECR I-9743, para 28: 'one of the principal aims of the EEA Agreement … so that the internal market established within the European Union is extended to the EFTA States'. This requirement applies to procedural matters in order to ensure equal access to justice or protection of fundamental principles for all individuals and all economic operators throughout the EEA as this region is meant to be a seamless and borderless economic zone: see *Posten Norge*, above n 48, para 110.

[72] *Fokus Bank*, above n 27, paras 22 and 30; Case E-1/03 *EFTA Surveillance Authority v The Republic of Iceland* [2003] EFTA Ct Rep 143, para 27.

[73] *DB Schenker*, above n 56, paras 77 and 78.

[74] See, eg, Case E-2/04 *Reidar Rasmussen, Jan Rossavik, and Johan Käldman v Total E&P Norge AS, v/ styrets formann* [2004] EFTA Ct Rep 57; Case E-1/02 *EFTA Surveillance Authority v Kingdom of Norway* [2003] EFTA Ct Rep 1; Case E-7/11 *Grund, elli- og hjúkrunarheimili v Lyfjastofnun* [2012] EFTA Ct Rep 188 and Case E-16/11 *EFTA Surveillance Authority v Iceland*, not yet published.

[75] See, eg, Case E-3/04 *Tsomakas Athanasios and Others with Odfjell ASA as an accessory intervener v The Norwegian State* [2004] EFTA Ct Rep 95.

[76] See C Baudenbacher, 'The EFTA Court Ten years on' in C Baudenbacher, P Tresselt and T Örlygsson (eds), *The EFTA Court: Ten Years On* (Oxford, Hart Publishing, 2005) 20: '[t]he Court has rejected attempts to construe fundamental freedoms in a less integration-friendly way than the ECJ does in Community law'.

[77] Case E-1/03 *EFTA Surveillance Authority v The Republic of Iceland* [2003] EFTA Ct Rep 143, para 27.

[78] See, eg, *DB Schenker*, above n 56, para 125 and *Fokus Bank*, above n 27, paras 22, 29, 33 and 37.

[79] See, eg, Case C-286/02 *Bellio F.lli Srl v Prefettura di Treviso* [2004] ECR I-3465, para 34; see also the *Kellogg's* case, referring to Case 174/82 *Sandoz BV* [1983] ECR-2443 and Case C-355/98 *Commission v Belgium* [2000] ECR I-1221.

i. The Court Judgments are Easily Acceptable throughout the EEA because the Court Provides Useful Information or Suggests Reforms, in Particular through Commonsense Solutions and Subtle Obiter Dicta

More regularly and without overtly departing from the case law of its big sister courts, the EFTA Court has made a soft but significant contribution to the EU legal order by proposing pragmatic and commonsense solutions.[80] Moreover, the Court often makes use of a suggestive obiter dictum methodology.[81] Thus, in the above-mentioned *Kellogg's* case, the Court provided a *vademecum* on judicial review of decisions based on the precautionary principle,[82] and indicated the type of documents required along with an appropriate analysis in order to justify quantitative restrictions on imports on grounds of health protection. Subsequent ECJ rulings refer to this case, and make an extensive use of the reasoning of the EFTA Court.[83]

In the *Municipal Kindergarten* case,[84] the Court did not hesitate to provide a definition of the notion of 'doubts' on which the ESA relied to initiate a formal investigation[85] and to state that the ESA may only refuse to open a formal investigation where a measure cannot be classified as state aid pursuant to the initial investigation. Further, the Court indicated the scope of the legal review that ought to be exercised in that context: 'It follows that judicial review by the Court of the existence of 'doubts' … will, by nature, go beyond simple consideration of whether or not there has been a manifest error of assessment by ESA in not initiating a formal investigation procedure.'[86] Such methodology certainly proves useful to economic operators.

ii. A Court Achieving a Realpolitik

Another important feature of the EFTA Court pertains to its ability to tackle hard economic facts within the limits imposed by EEA/EU law. The economic crisis has given the Court the opportunity to make full use of its *marge de manoeuvre* and to provide solutions based primarily on practical and material considerations, rather than ideological positions.

---

[80] See, eg, E Morgan de Rivery, E Lagathu, E Chassaing and Z Genova, 'DB Schenker: The EFTA Court sets a high threshold for transparency and reasoning (2013) 3 *European Law Reporter* 91.

[81] See, eg, *Fokus Bank*, above n 27, para 47.

[82] *Kellogg's*, paras 29–33.

[83] Case C-192/01 *Commission v Denmark* [2003] ECR I-9693, paras 46–53 and Advocate General Opinion para 79; Case C-236/01 *Monsanto Agricoltura Italia* [2003] ECR I-8105, para 106; Case T-13/99 *Pfizer Animal Health* [2002] ECR II-3305, paras 115 and 143.

[84] Case E-5/07 *Private Barnehagers Landsforbund v EFTA Surveillance Authority* [2008] EFTA Ct Rep 62.

[85] Art 4(4) in Part II of Protocol 3 of the Surveillance and Court Agreement provides that the ESA may initiate a formal investigation procedure when 'doubts are raised on the compatibility with the functioning of the EEA Agreement'.

[86] Case E-5/07 *Private Barnehagers Landsforbund v EFTA Surveillance Authority* [2008] EFTA Ct Rep 62, para 76.

In this respect, the most iconic case is the *Icesave* judgment.[87] An Icelandic bank, Landsbanki, had opened internet branches in the United Kingdom and in the Netherlands in 2006 and 2008, which accepted online deposits under the brand name Icesave. The crisis caused a run on Icesave accounts in the UK between February and April 2008. In late 2008, compensation to depositors was paid under the Netherlands and British deposit-guarantee schemes. However, Iceland did not pay to depositors in the Netherlands and in the UK the minimum amount of compensation provided by the relevant provisions of Directive 94/19/EC of 30 May 1994 on deposit-guarantee schemes. ESA therefore initiated an infringement action against Iceland.

ESA claimed that (i) Iceland was responsible for the compensation of depositors once all the credit institutions meant to finance the deposit-guarantee fund under the Directive had failed, and that (ii) Iceland had breached the principle of non-discrimination by providing full protection to domestic depositors moving their assets to a new bank while failing to compensate overseas depositors.

The EFTA Court dismissed these arguments on two grounds. First, it insisted that the ruling must be based on the Directive as it stood at the time the fact occurred. It did not include amendments meant to improve the protection of depositors, that is, the States were under no obligation to ensure payment under all circumstances at the time. The EFTA Court then rejected an extensive interpretation of the text on economic grounds (in particular with regard to the adverse effect on competition and moral hazard of state liability).[88] Thus, Iceland was under no obligation to ensure payment of compensation to overseas depositors. Second, the EFTA Court considered that domestic and overseas depositors were not in a similar situation since the transfer of accounts to a new bank was part of the bank restructuring plan and was not conducted under the deposit-guarantee scheme provided for in the Directive. Hence, neither domestic nor overseas depositors were actually compensated. Against this background and the limited scope of the form of order sought by ESA in respect to discrimination, the Court dismissed the action.

Again, the EFTA Court used a pragmatic approach and provided numerous details through its reasoning in order to support its findings. More importantly, the Court not only pointed out the exceptional circumstances of the case but in addition underlined the unprecedented scale of the crisis ('in a systemic crisis of the magnitude experienced by Iceland'). Indeed, the claims following the collapse of Icesave (equivalent to 44 per cent of Iceland's GDP) exceeded by far the resources of the deposit scheme established under the Directive.

The Court conducted a meticulous analysis of the Directive (which included reviewing the Commission's conclusions in its Impact Assessment of the Directive)[89]

---

[87] Case E-16/11 *EFTA Surveillance Authority v Iceland*, not yet published (*Icesave*).
[88] ibid, para 167.
[89] ibid, para 153. See also Commission Staff Working document, 'Impact Assessment of 12 July 2010', SEC (2010) 834/2.

in order to determine what had been foreseen in terms of who should be called upon in case of default payment. Based on this thorough study, the Court concluded that, as drafted at the relevant time, the Directive expressly aimed to preclude an excessive shifting to the States of the costs arising from a major banking failure.[90] However, the Directive did not provide for systemic failure of deposit-guarantee schemes (hence the rewording of Article 7 in the subsequent 2009 Directive).

The Court proposed to check what the underlying economic consequences of an extensive interpretation of the Directive would be. On this basis, the Court indicated that it considered that 'increasing consumer protection may reach a point where the costs outweigh the benefits'.[91] Such judgment is reassuring for business, as the Court demonstrated its ability to deal with complex economic and political issues while adopting a reasonable (albeit carefully reasoned) approach.

III. CONCLUSIONS

After 20 years of existence, it is clear that the EFTA Court remains a general court and a Supreme Court in full compliance with its statutes. However, its impact on business is undoubtedly more important than what could have been anticipated when it was created, considering its powers, its relatively low number of cases and its limited geographic sphere of influence. Several developments have contributed to enhancing the role of the Court as well as its impact on business. Thus, beyond cases directly addressing business issues, other cases concerning procedural issues or interpretation of the legislation in fact have impact on business organisation or business policies or priorities. The EFTA Court seems perfectly aware of this situation and of its role as a useful and unique complement to the EU Courts. The EFTA judges have lived up to that role and responsibility in particular vis-à-vis business operators through an original mix of prudence and boldness, modesty and self-assurance when dealing with principles relating to free trade or other principles recognised as important in the Nordic mentality. Of course, this situation may be partly attributed to the homogeneous profile of the judges, not to mention their strong personalities.

No doubt other judges will step in in the future with their own views and personalities. Things may therefore evolve, but the EFTA Court has found its place not only on the *plateau du Kirchberg* but also and more generally in the judicial landscape of the EEA, in particular as a welcome source of reference and inspiration for the business community of the EU.

---

[90] ibid, para 176.
[91] ibid, para 170.

30

Icesave—Limited Homogeneity and Unlimited Judicial Interpretation

DAMIAN CHALMERS

I. INTRODUCTION

THE CENTRAL ISSUES in the infringement proceedings brought by the EFTA Surveillance Authority against the Icelandic State following the collapse of the Icelandic Landsbanki bank in 2008 were two relatively simple ones. The first went to whether the Icelandic government could lawfully refuse to cover deposits held with branches of Landsbanki's Icesave subsidiary in the Netherlands and the United Kingdom in the event that these could not be covered by the deposit-guarantee schemes which had been put in place in Iceland. The second went to whether it made any legal difference that the Icelandic government had largely protected its own nationals by securing the deposits held in Landsbanki branches based in Iceland. The surrounding context was, however, incendiary. In Iceland, two referenda had voted, by a large majority, against public money being used to indemnify these losses.[1] The views of some in the international financial community were equally strident that the Icelandic government should be liable.[2] Independently of this, the redistributive effects of any decision, one way or the other, were considerable. The amounts involved were about €4 billion without interest. As the British and Dutch governments had rushed in to protect their savers, the dispute was largely about which government should bear the loss, something which would have to be absorbed to the detriment of other fields of public expenditure.

These circumstances may make it dangerous to extrapolate from the following *Icesave* judgment of the EFTA Court.[3] However, the judgment, nevertheless, represents a potential watershed. Prior to *Icesave*, the EFTA Court had emphasised similarities between EEA law and EU law. *Icesave* opens this up to question, for

---

[1] There were two referenda held in Iceland on structured settlements agreed between the Icelandic, Dutch and British governments. The first was rejected by 98% of Icelandic citizens and the second by 59%.

[2] 'In the cooler: the Court ruling is a blow to global banking,' *The Economist* 2 February 2013.

[3] Case E-16/11 *EFTA Surveillance Authority v Iceland*, Judgment of 28 January 2013.

whilst the EFTA Court did not question EU law the reasoning was nevertheless quite restrictive. If a difference can be justified because the EU and EEA are different organisations, there remains the question of how this is to be incorporated into the EFTA Court's style of reasoning. In *Icesave*, this was reflected in a less assertive form of teleological reasoning than might have been deployed by the Court of Justice. This chapter will suggest that there might be a steadier foundation for distinguishing its reasoning. This is to structure judgments such as *Icesave* around three principles. The first, the homogeneity principle, requires the EFTA Court to give presumptive effect to EU law and to the methods of reasoning of the Court of Justice. The second, the less integration principle, acts as a countervailing principle which recognises that the EEA places fewer demands on its Member States than the European Union. This states that EEA law should cede to national law wherever it transgresses on national principles of democratic or constitutional identity or social justice, or generates social polarisation. The third is the principle of mutual accommodation. This states even where a State is not bound by EU legal instruments that will within the scope of the EEA Agreement, it still owes duties to other EEA States to accommodate their interests. These require it to enter into negotiations to see if mutual accommodation can be reached.

II. THE LIMITS OF HOMOGENEITY AFTER *ICESAVE*

A. The Homogeneity Tradition in EEA Law

Arguably, the central organising principle of the European Economic Area Agreement is the homogeneity principle. The principle has two dimensions. The first, set out in the fourth recital of the Preamble, is to create a homogenous market place across the EEA based on common rules and equal conditions of competition. As the EEA comprises not only the EEA EFTA States of Iceland, Liechtenstein and Norway but also the European Union, the second follows from this, and is that of alignment. Article 6 EEA, in particular, requires EEA provisions where they are identical in substance to EU legal provisions to be interpreted in conformity with interpretations provided by the Court of Justice.[4] These do not have to be interpreted *identically* with EU law but in such a way that there is no breach of EU law. Different interpretations can be given, for example the EFTA Court may find a breach of gender discrimination or competition law where the Court of Justice does not, and this has occasionally taken place.[5]

---

[4] The Article, in fact, only requires that these be interpreted in line with judgments given prior to the signing of the Agreement. This time restriction has, by and large, been ignored, however. See also Art 102(1) EEA, which requires the EEA Joint Committee to update the Annexes to the EEA Agreement to be as close to possible to newly concluded Union legislation.

[5] The EFTA Court has therefore ruled that public monopolies on gambling breach the freedom to provide services: Case E-1/06 *EFTA Surveillance Authority v Kingdom of Norway* [2007] EFTA Ct Rep 8; Case E-3/06 *Ladbrokes v The Government of Norway, Ministry of Culture and Church Affairs and*

Notwithstanding this, over the years, the EFTA Court has deployed the homogeneity principle along five axes. First, it has been used, by and large, to give the material provisions of EEA law the same meaning as those given by the Court of Justice. Court of Justice interpretations are thus regularly cited as authority in its judgments.[6] Second, it has been deployed to develop the autonomy of EEA law. The EFTA Court stated famously that:

> [T]he EEA Agreement is an international treaty sui generis which contains a distinct legal order of its own. The EEA Agreement does not establish a customs union but an enhanced free trade area ... The depth of integration of the EEA Agreement is less far-reaching than under the EC Treaty, but the scope and the objective of the EEA Agreement goes beyond what is usual for an agreement under public international law.[7]

From this, it has been argued that the EEA Treaty does not have primacy over national law in the same way as the EU Treaties,[8] and is not capable of direct effect. It can generate indirect effect and State liability, however.[9] The third consequence has been that the EFTA Court has been ready to follow much of the Court of Justice's constitutionalising jurisprudence, be it on the development of fundamental rights or EU citizenship.[10] The fourth has been that, quite self-consciously, the EFTA Court has tried to create a position for itself within the EEA that parallels that of the Court of Justice within the European Union.[11] Fifth, and finally, a consequence of this alignment was that the EFTA Court largely bought in to the style of the reasoning of the Court of Justice.[12] In particular, it had to be prepared to engage in teleological reasoning in which provisions were interpreted in the light of objectives of EU legislation. Otherwise, it would not be able to align its case law with that of the Court of Justice.

Ministry of Agriculture and Food [2007] EFTA Ct Rep 86. This is not the case in EU law: Case C-42/07 *Liga Portuguesa de Futebol Profissional and Bwin International Ltd v Departamento de Jogos da Santa Casa da Misericórdia de Lisboa* [2009] ECR I-7633.

[6] With regard to the case law on Art 34 TFEU see Case E-5/96 *Ullensaker commune etal v Nile* [1997] EFTA Ct Rep 30.

[7] Case E-9/97 *Sveinbjörnsdóttir v Government of Iceland* [1998] EFTA Ct Rep 95, para 59.

[8] See, however, Protocol 35 to the EEA, which requires the parties to put in place national mechanisms which grant primacy to EEA law over national law.

[9] Case E-9/97 *Sveinbjörnsdóttir v Government of Iceland* [1998] EFTA Ct Rep 95; Case E-1/07 *A* [2007] EFTA Ct Rep 246.

[10] On this see T Burri and B Pirker, 'Constitutionalization by Association? The Doubtful Case of the European Economic Area' (2013) 32 *Yearbook of European Law* 207, 215–220.

[11] On this see the views of the President of the EFTA Court, Carl Baudenbacher: C Baudenbacher, 'The EFTA Court Ten Years On' in C Baudenbacher et al (eds), *The EFTA Court Ten Years On* (Oxford, Hart Publishing, 2005); C Baudenbacher, 'The EFTA Court: An Actor in the European Judicial Dialogue' (2005) 28 *Fordham International Law Journal* 353.

[12] Although, arguably, there is no specific duty on the EFTA Court, Art 105(1) EEA requires parties to ensure as uniform an interpretation as possible between EEA law and EU law.

B. Homogeneity and the CJEU Counterfactual in *Icesave*

The homogeneity principle therefore invited not only comparison, in *Icesave*, between any judgment given by the EFTA Court and the case law of the Court of Justice, but also generated anticipations about how it would reason based on expectations associated with the latter. This was particularly constraining in relation to both the central issues in the case.

The first legal issue centred on government obligations under Directive 94/19/ EC on deposit-guarantee schemes.[13] The Directive required States to ensure that deposit-guarantee schemes were established to protect depositors both for branches within its territory but also for EEA subsidiaries of its domestic banks.[14] These guarantee schemes were required, at the time of Landsbanki's collapse, to protect nearly all depositors up to the value of €20,000.[15] Such schemes were set up around the EEA using funds from the domestic banking sector rather than public money. Nobody contested that Iceland had set up a scheme. The challenge was that between 2008 and 2009, the banking crisis wiped out 93 per cent of the Icelandic banking industry. There were, thus, insufficient funds for the guarantee scheme to cover the deposits. At issue, however, was the question whether the Directive required the Icelandic government itself to step in to cover depositors up to the €20,000.

The teleological and contextual style of reasoning favoured by the Court left the Icelandic government exposed in this regard. The latter could, on the one hand, point to the 24th recital of the Directive, which stated:

> Whereas this Directive may not result in the Member States' or their competent authorities' being made liable in respect of depositors *if* [author's italics] they have ensured that one or more schemes guaranteeing deposits or credit institutions themselves and ensuring the compensation or protection of depositors under the conditions prescribed in this Directive have been introduced and officially recognized.

However, this only seemed to absolve governments from liability if they had observed an additional duty of care to secure the effective protection of depositors. It was not enough under this recital for a government to ensure that a deposit-guarantee scheme had been established. The government had also to ensure that the scheme protected and compensated depositors.

This sense of a prior duty of care was also present in the case law of the Court of Justice. In *Paul*, a number of German depositors took action against the German government when they lost their deposits following the bankruptcy of a German bank.[16] These were compensated €20,000 each for the failure of the German authorities to transpose Directive 94/19/EC. They also claimed that they had

---

[13] OJ 1994, L 135/5.
[14] ibid, Art 3(1).
[15] ibid, Art 7(1).
[16] Case C-222/02 *Paul et al v Bundesrepublik Deutschland* [2004] ECR I-9425.

only lost their deposits because of negligent oversight by the German supervisory authorities, and they sought further compensation for this. The Court rejected their action. It stated that if the compensation of depositors was ensured in the event that their deposits were unavailable, the Directive did not confer any right to have the competent authorities take supervisory measures. The lack of rights was, therefore, predicated on the payment of the prior compensation. The judgment implied a fairly strong duty on the State, therefore, to secure protection which extended beyond simply ensuring the formalities for a deposit-guarantee scheme were in place.

Other elements of the Directive confirmed this line of reasoning. Article 3(2) required that if a credit institution did not comply with its deposit-guarantee scheme obligations, competent authorities were required to take all appropriate measures including the imposition of sanctions to ensure that it did. 'All appropriate measures' could no doubt include recapitalising the bank so that it had sufficient funds to enable the operation of the scheme. In line with this, the eighth recital of the Preamble stated that harmonisation was 'confined to the main elements of deposit-guarantee schemes and … [to] ensure payments under a guarantee calculated on the basis of a harmonized minimum level'. This suggested that the two obligations were separate and the duty to guarantee deposits was not met by establishing such a scheme.

If a strong case could be made that adoption of the style of reasoning of the Court of Justice might well lead to a duty to secure the depositors on the part of the Icelandic State, this was also true of the second main bone of contention, possible discrimination against non-Icelandic depositors by virtue of the exclusive protection of deposits held at domestic branches of Landsbanki. Article 4 EEA prohibits within the scope of application of the EEA Agreement any discrimination, be it direct or indirect, on grounds of nationality. There was little doubt that the actions of the Icelandic government had been done to protect the deposits of Icelandic citizens with awareness that this was at the expense of citizens from other EEA States. The only question was whether it fell within the scope of application of the EEA Agreement. No discrimination was carried out by the Icelandic deposit-guarantee scheme. It was, after all, largely defunct. The discriminatory measure was a piece of emergency legislation adopted by the Icelandic parliament which, the day after the collapse of Landsbanki, transferred the assets and liabilities of domestic branches into a new bank whilst leaving the deposits in foreign branches to the mercy of the markets. It arguably fell outside the scope of Directive 94/14/EC insofar as this did not directly regulate such conduct, but there was still the question of whether it fell within the scope of the EEA Agreement.

The Court of Justice judgment most on point on this is *Fransson*, which stated that EU fundamental rights laws and general principles of law (in this instance the non-discrimination principle) bind national institutions when they act within the scope of EU law. This will not be the case where it is something on which the Union has competence but rather where EU law imposes an obligation on national authorities with regard to some aspect of the dispute or requires national authorities to carry out some task for the Union.[17] In *Fransson*, therefore, EU law duties on States to ensure that VAT was collected and to counter fraud imposed a sufficient obligation on the Swedish State that the imposition of both regulatory and criminal penalties for non-payment of tax could be challenged on the grounds that this might violate the principle not to be tried twice for the same office. In this regard, if Directive 94/19/EC did place any obligation on the Icelandic State with regard to the new bank then other EEA legislation clearly did. Directive 2006/48/EC on the taking-up and pursuit of the business of credit institutions indicates that this cannot take place without the authorisation of national authorities. These are to lay down requirements for the authorisation and notify these to the Commission.[18] It might be argued that the judgment in *Icesave* was given just under a month before that in *Fransson*, and therefore cannot be governed by the latter. If this argument has some sway in the field of EU fundamental rights law, generally, it is less compelling in respect of the non-discrimination principle, in particular, which has bound Member States acting within the scope of EU law since the *Mangold* judgment in 2005.[19]

C. *Icesave* and the Limits of Homogeneity

The EFTA Court adopted an alternative approach, and it is instructive to see how its reasoning differed.

With regard to the interpretation of Directive 94/19/EC, the EFTA Court adopted a form of teleological reasoning but one which differed from that of the Court of Justice. With regard to the Preambles of Directives, which set out the objectives of the latter, the EFTA Court noted that these are not included in the Annexes of legislation to be adopted by the EEA EFTA States but regard can be had to these to the extent necessary for a proper interpretation of the relevant legal provisions.[20] They are accorded a role but a less central role than in EU law. They are something which may be used where it is deemed proper for the interpretation of EEA law and to be balanced against other considerations rather than being, as in EU law, the central tool for interpretation.

The EFTA Court, thus, sees Directive 94/19 as setting out two objectives: freedom to provide services on the one hand, and the security and stability of the banking sector and protection of savers on the other. However, it does not go on to refer back to these objectives to interpret the substantive provisions governing possible national duties (Articles 3 and 7). It relies, instead, on four

---

[17] Case C-617/10 *Fransson*, Judgment of 26 February 2013. For similar reasoning see Case C-418/11 *Texdata Software*, Judgment of 26 September 2013; Case C-206/13 *Siragusa v Regione Sicilia— Soprintendenza Beni Culturali e Ambientali di Palermo*, Judgment of 6 March 2014.

[18] OJ 2006, L 177/1, Art 6. On specific EU law requirements in addition to any national requirements that may be imposed see Arts 7–12.

[19] Case C-144/04 *Mangold v Helm* [2005] ECR I-9981, para 75.

[20] See Case E-16/11 *EFTA Surveillance Authority v Iceland*, Judgment of 28 January 2013, para 122.

different arguments. First, it noted that the Directive is amended in 2009 to increase the threshold of cover to €50,000.[21] The new Directive also talks of Member States rather than deposit-guarantee schemes being responsible for this protection. It deduced from this change that if Directive 94/19 had been intended to impose duties of protection on national governments, this would have been done explicitly. Second, it noted that Article 7(6) requires States to make provision for depositors to sue for compensation where they suffer loss as a result of deposit-guarantee schemes breaching their obligations under the Directive. The presence of this duty detailed, in the Court's view, the obligations of the State in the event of failure, thereby precluding more open-ended duties. From these two lines of reasoning, the EFTA Court ruled that Directive 94/19 was not intended to regulate deposit guarantees exhaustively, and therefore, any duty on the part of the State to compensate depositors lay outside EEA law. It then went on to reason further why this should be so. The third reason was that the Directive, in the view of the Court, only anticipated failure of individual credit institutions, and talked in those terms. It did not address the question of systemic risk where the whole sector collapsed. The final reason was moral hazard. If States were under a duty to guarantee deposits, this ultimately resulted in the public purse bearing the risk of bankruptcy, and reduced the incentives for disciplined behaviour by the banking sector.

With regard to the argument on discrimination, the EFTA Court did not look at *Mangold*. Instead it quoted its own case law which stated that Article 4 EEA, the provision prohibiting discrimination, only applied to situations which were already governed by EEA law.[22] In this instance, in the light of its earlier reasoning, the only relevant activity governed by EEA law in its view was the operation of the Icelandic deposit-guarantee scheme. This, it noted, had acted in a non-discriminatory manner. As an aside, it noted that there was a possibility, in any case, that differential treatment between deposits in Icelandic and non-Icelandic branches could be justified by the wide margin of discretion enjoyed by EEA States in fundamental choices of economic policy in the event of a systemic crisis.

III. HOMOGENEITY, LIMITED INTEGRATION AND MUTUAL ACCOMMODATION

The adoption of a different style of reasoning from the Court of Justice is, to be sure, fully justified. If the EEA is conceived as a less integrated area than the European Union then the style of legal reasoning of the Court of Justice which requires EU law to be interpreted in the light of the objectives of the Union integration process cannot be readily transferred to the EEA. A level of reasoning

---

[21] Directive 2009/14/EC amending Directive 94/19/EC on deposit-guarantee schemes as regards the coverage level and the pay-out delay, OJ 2009 L 68/3, Art 7(1).

[22] Case E-1/00 *Íslandsbanki-FBA* [2000-2001] EFTA Ct Rep 8.

seeking to secure a less integrated area than the Union whilst not disrupting legal relations between the EFTA EEA States and the Union contains both a tension between these demands and is extremely underspecified.

It can lead, therefore, to reasoning which is very de-anchored. This played itself out in the judgment which involves a mixture of formal, *ex post*, and policy-based reasoning. Furthermore, for every reason adduced as to why Iceland had not broken the law, a counter-argument could be found that it did. The 2009 legislative amendment is, thus, seen as evidence of intent of the legislature in 1994, but judicial interpretation is meant to be independent of that provided by other arms of government, so how could a subsequent legislative re-interpretation in 2009 be deployed to explain a 1994 instrument? The requirement that States allow depositors to sue for compensation could be seen as exhaustive of their duties, but could also be seen as illustrative of a more general principle on States to secure compensation. The 1994 Directive does not exclude or mention issues of systemic risk, so could equally be deemed to incorporate these dangers within its purview as to exclude them. The moral hazard argument also applies to deposit-guarantee schemes. Set up by the sector, they de-incentivise individual banks to be prudential as the costs can be picked up by their competitors if they go bust.

If this sounds critical, it is because trying to argue that an ambiguous, internally contradictory legal instrument clearly resolves matters in black and white terms is inevitably fraught. It is like trying to argue whether orange is really a form of red or a form of yellow. The difficulties would also have been as great in any judgment declaring Iceland to be in breach of EEA law. For this reason, it is suggested that it is important that the reasoning be unpackaged to identify in a more structured manner the central constitutional issues at stake. It will be suggested that these issues find expression in the EEA law in the homogeneity principle, the limited integration doctrine and the duty of mutual accommodation. A word will be said about each.

The homogeneity principle is a commitment, in principle, by EEA EFTA States to give effect to EU law where this falls within the scope of the EEA Agreement. This commitment is evidenced in the EEA articles described earlier, but it is also present in the practices of EEA and national institutions, be it the work of the EEA Joint Committee aligning EEA law with EU law, the EFTA Surveillance Authority policing EEA law, the EFTA Court providing authoritative interpretations, or national administrations and courts giving effect to it. Membership of a system of regional cooperation requires, as the German Constitutional Court has noted, an openness to its norms which, in turn, implies a commitment to obey them the overwhelming majority of the time.[23] Such openness also implies a commitment, as has been the usual practice of the EFTA Court, to observe them in the manner observed by other parties: in this case, the European Union. It implies, therefore,

---

[23] 2 BvE 2/08 *Lisbon Treaty*, Judgment of 30 June 2009 (German Constitutional Court), paras 225 and 240.

as mentioned earlier, a disposition to accept the interpretive style of the Court of Justice, as without a commonality of interpretation, it would increasingly be difficult to talk of common obligations across the EEA.

The second principle, the limited integration principle, qualifies the homogeneity principle by noting that it is no more than a presumption. Even within the Union there will be circumstances where States will not give effect to the primacy of EU law, even if the Union is acting *intra vires*. This has been held to be the case where it adopts measures which transgress on the constitutional or democratic identity of a State. Fields identified as where this is likely to be the case include budgetary policy, foreign and defence policy, central elements of social policy, policing and criminal justice, education, religious law and family law.[24] If the EEA is a less demanding model of integration than the European Union, it follows that the scope for leeway granted to EEA EFTA States should be greater.

Moreover, two EEA provisions recognise this. The first, the 'constitutional requirements' provision in Article 103(1) EEA allows EEA EFTA States extra time to implement an EEA measure if it raises difficulties in respect of some part of their constitution. Indeed, they may even derogate from the measure if it clashes with their constitution, albeit that this raises the rights granted to them under that part of the EEA being suspended.[25] Second, by virtue of Article 113(1) EEA, EEA States can take safeguard measures, albeit subject to consultation and proportionate counter-measures, where serious economic, societal or environmental difficulties of a sectorial or regional nature arise and are liable to persist.[26]

These procedures suggest that EEA law should not transgress on questions which go to significant matters of democratic political community or would cause significant social conflict within an EEA EFTA State. Examples would include the fields identified by the German Constitutional Court with regard to the Union; anything likely to touch on issues of national citizenship or social justice;[27] or, finally, any measure which generates widespread opposition in the form of demonstrations or petitions. The opposition of many Icelanders to indemnification was, indeed, based mainly on these terms. They felt that a key element of citizenship was the entitlement to a secure bank account, and that the Icelandic State had a pre-eminent duty to secure that before anything else. This idea of a secure place to leave one's money in a territory is completely in keeping with modern ideas of citizenship which emphasise a State's responsibility to offer their citizens security within a precarious world.[28] There is, however, no EEA citizenship so it could not be said that Iceland offered this duty to non-Icelanders.

---

[24] ibid, paras 252/260. For a list of other national constitutional courts who do likewise see 2 BvR 2728/13 *ECB/ESM*, Judgment of 14 January 2014, para 30.

[25] Art 103(2) EEA.

[26] The procedures are set out in Arts 112–114 EEA.

[27] On this as something which limits the application of EU law see K 32/09 *Lisbon Treaty*, Judgment of 24 November 2010, section 2.1 (Polish Constitutional Court).

[28] B Turner, 'The Erosion of Citizenship' (2001) 52 *British Journal of Sociology* 189.

There is a third principle which goes to the mediation of the homogeneity and limited integration principles: that of mutual accommodation. The EEA Agreement requires parties to cooperate to realise its objectives[29] and to find mutually acceptable solutions.[30] Common agreement might not always be possible, and there had been attempts by both sides to reach agreement, which ultimately collapsed in *Icesave*. However, a problematic feature of any judicial dispute is its all-or-nothing quality. Only the most hawkish protagonists on either side of the dispute in *Icesave* advocated this, with the central issue being the amount to be identified to British and Dutch savers and the priority to be given to it. In this regard, courts are good at identifying structures for mediation of such differences and for ascertaining whether parties have made *bona fide* attempts to recognise the perspective of the other in the reasons that they provide for their positions. Ultimately, such an approach would be more likely to generate reconciliation than a winner-takes-all approach.

IV. CONCLUSION

As Iceland made significant attempts to negotiate with the British and Dutch governments over the interests of depositors of non-domestic subsidiaries of Icesave, it might be asked why it should be necessary to suggest a different form of reasoning when the result would, in all likelihood, have been the same. There are two reasons. The first goes to the legal identity of the EEA after *Icesave*. It is undoubtedly different from that of the European Union but the contours of this are left not simply ambiguous but highly unspecified. This generates misunderstandings on the part of operators, contracting parties, but above all, citizens within the EEA as to what it can ask of and give them and how it relates to cherished national institutions or values. Setting this out more clearly would be worthwhile. The second goes to the place of the judgment within the EEA legal order. The high stakes in the case may allow it to be seen as something exceptional with little predictive value for the future. It would be a pity if this were so. The stakes were high not simply because of the sums involved but because there was conflict about the values institutionalised by the EEA. As it generated interest across the EEA, *Icesave*, therefore, marked a possibility for these to be communicated in an iconographic way to citizens. This possibility could still be taken up but it was not seized in the judgment.

---

[29] Art 3(3) EEA.
[30] Art 102(5) EEA.

31

Standard of Review in Competition Law Cases: Posten Norge and Beyond

ERIC BARBIER DE LA SERRE

THE RULE ACCORDING to which the EU Courts limit their control of complex economic assessments to 'manifest errors of appreciation' has been applied in an impressive number of EU law judgments. Yet, nearly 60 years after its beginnings in *Consten and Grundig*,[1] the scope and meaning of this rule remain unclear. With the exception of a handful of judgments, it is as if the EU Courts had deliberately sought to remain vague, and therefore confirm the principle according to which '[b]reath spent repeating dicta does not infuse it with life'.[2]

But vagueness is not a deadly sin. The main problem with this rule is not that it is obscure, but rather that it raises very serious questions as to its compatibility with the requirement of full effective judicial review under Art 6 ECHR and Art 47 of the Charter. An impressive series of articles have been published on this topic over the last 20 years,[3] and the debate has not remained purely academic, as during the last three years the European Court of Human Rights (ECtHR) and

---

[1] Joined Cases 56/64 and 58/64 *Consten and Grundig* [1965] ECR 382. ·

[2] *Metro Stevedore Co v Rambo*, 515 US 291, 300 (1995) (Kennedy J).

[3] See, eg, D Waelbroeck and D Fosselard, 'Should the Decision-Making Power in EC Antitrust Procedures be left to an Independent Judge?—The Impact of the European Convention of Human Rights on EC Antitrust Procedures' in A Barav and DA Wyatt (eds), *1994 Yearbook of European Law* (Oxford, Clarendon Press, 1995); W Wils, 'La compatibilité des procedures communautaires en matière de concurrence avec la Convention européenne des droits de l'homme' (1996) *Cahiers de droit européen* 329, and more recently D Slater, S Thomas and D Waelbroeck, 'Competition Law Proceedings before the European Commission and the Right to a Fair Trial: No Need for Reform?' (2009) *European Competition Journal*, April, 97; I Forrester, 'Due process in EC competition cases: A distinguished institution with flawed procedures' (2009) *EL Rev* 817; H Schweitzer, 'The European Competition Law Enforcement System and the Evolution of Judicial Review' in C-D Ehlermann and M Marquis (eds), *European Competition Law Annual 2009: Evaluation of Evidence and Its Judicial Control in Competition Cases* (Oxford, Hart Publishing, 2011) 79; M Bronckers and A Vallery, 'Fair and effective competition policy in the EU: Which role for authorities and which role for the courts after Menarini?' (2012) *European Competition Journal* 283; R Nazzini, 'Administrative enforcement, judicial review and fundamental rights in EU competition law: A comparative contextual-functionalist perspective' (2012) *CML Rev* 971; H Schweitzer, 'Judicial Review in EU Competition Law' in D Geradin and I Lianos (eds), *Handbook on EU Antitrust Law* (Cheltenham, Edward Elgar Publishing, 2013) 491; W Wils, 'The Compatibility with Fundamental Rights of the EU Antitrust Enforcement System in Which the European Commission Acts Both as Investigator and as First-Instance Decision Maker' (2014) 37(1) *World Competition* 5.

the Court of Justice have delivered several landmark judgments in relation to this issue.[4] Yet, it is a judgment from the youngest European Court—the EFTA Court—that contains the clearest and most elaborate developments on this issue.

Contrary to the proverb, youth is not wasted on the young: in *Posten Norge*, the EFTA Court opted for a courageous outcome, since it assertively refused to limit the review of complex economic assessments made by the EFTA Surveillance Authority to a 'manifest error' standard.[5] For this sole reason, *Posten Norge* is a milestone judgment. At this stage, it is the clearest sign that the 'manifest error' standard has started waning. In fact, as will be shown below, while the EU Courts still abundantly—and sometimes unjustifiably—refer to this standard, there are signs that the armour is cracking. If the current trend continues, the 'manifest error' standard may well be living its last years, at least for the review of decisions finding a breach of Art 101 and/or 102 TFEU. This is, in our view, not only the most desirable outcome, but also the most likely.

Yet, even if this happened, this would not imply that judicial review would increase. In fact there are indications that the 'manifest error' standard is declining not because the EU Courts are increasingly eager to control complex economic decisions, but because it is the very notion of a standard of judicial review that loses of its importance. This means that even if the 'manifest error' standard did disappear, this would not necessarily be the sign of more stringent judicial review: this may well be evidence that litigants' rights are genuinely protected better, but this may also be a mere methodological clarification. The real test is, and will be, how the European Courts will perform their duty beyond the applicable standard.

I. *POSTEN NORGE*: A MILESTONE

A. 'The Long and Winding Road' (A Short History of Limited Review)

As is well known, unlike the ECSC Treaty,[6] the EEC Treaty did not contain any provision directing the Court of Justice to restrict the judicial review that it performs on decisions involving economic appreciations. In 1966 the Court of Justice nonetheless decided in *Consten and Grundig* that the review of 'complex economic evaluations concerning [Article 101(3)] exemptions' should be limited.[7] While in theory this may have been explained by (and therefore restricted to) the

---

[4] Case C-272/09 P *KME Germany and Others v Commission*; Case C-389/10 P *KME Germany and Others v Commission*; Case C-386/10 P *Chalkor v Commission*; judgment of the European Court of Human Rights in *A Menarini Diagnostics SRL v Italy*, No 43509/08, 27 September 2011.

[5] Case E-15/10 *Posten Norge v EFTA Surveillance Authority* [2012] EFTA Ct Rep 248. See comment by A-L Sibony, *Concurrences* No 4-2012, p 74.

[6] See Art 33 ECSC: 'the Court may not review the conclusions of the High Authority, drawn from economic facts and circumstances, which formed the basis of such decisions or recommendations, except where the High Authority is alleged to have abused its powers or to have clearly misinterpreted the provisions of the Treaty or of a rule of law relating to its application'.

[7] Joined Cases 56/64 and 58/64 *Consten and Grundig* [1965] ECR 382.

Commission's then monopoly for applying Article 85(3) EEC (now Article 101(3) TFEU),[8] in 1985 the *Remia* judgment extended this standard to the review of the conditions for the application of Article 101(1) TFEU (then Article 85 EEC).[9] The standard now applies to all types of complex economic assessments, and in fact, more generally, to all 'complex technical appraisals'.[10]

The justifications for this limitation have never been clearly articulated by the EU Courts. The reasons generally advanced are the Commission's prerogatives to shape the Union's competition policy,[11] as well as its expertise in complex economic matters.[12] While there is some truth in these justifications, and in particular the first one, their practical added value remains limited, as they do not allow a clear delineation of the Courts' limited review.[13]

To make things even worse, the inherent obscurity of the 'manifest error' standard was increased by the fact that, to many observers, it has been applied with varying rigour. For instance, in 2002 the famous *Airtours/Schneider/Tetra Laval* trilogy gave the impression that the General Court was reinforcing its control on economic appreciations.[14] Three years later, the ruling of the Court of Justice in *Tetra Laval* prolonged this trend by confirming that the review resulting from the 'manifest error' standard may be meaningful.[15] Yet to many the *Microsoft* judgment came as a disappointment, as it gave the impression that the EU Courts

---

[8] See in particular M Siragusa, 'Celebration of 20 years of the Court of First Instance of the European Communities' (available at http://curia.europa.eu/jcms/upload/docs/application/pdf/2009-10/siragusa. pdf); I Forrester, 'A Bush in Need of Pruning: the Luxuriant Growth of "Light Judicial Review"' in C-D Ehlermann and M Marquis (eds), *European Competition Law Annual 2009: Evaluation of Evidence and Its Judicial Control in Competition Cases* (Oxford, Hart Publishing, 2011) 407, and Opinion of Advocate General Mengozzi in Case C-382/12 P *MasterCard and Others v Commission*, fn 97.

[9] Case 42/84 *Remia* [1985] ECR 2545, para 34.

[10] Case T-201/04 *Microsoft v Commission* [2005] ECR II-1491, para 88. On the history of the 'manifest error' standard, see, eg, I Forrester, 'A Bush in Need of Pruning: the Luxuriant Growth of "Light Judicial Review"', above n 8.

[11] Opinion of Advocate General Léger in Case C-40/03 P *Rica Foods v Commission* [2005] ECR I-6811, paras 45 and 46 (who draws a distinction between discretion of a 'political' nature and discretion of a 'technical' nature). For a more detailed classification, see A Fritzsche, 'Discretion, Scope of Judicial Review and Institutional Balance in European Law' (2010) *CML Rev* 361. On the political justification, see also Opinion of Advocate General Tizzano in Case C-12/03 P *Commission v Tetra Laval* [2005] ECR I-987, para 89, and Opinion of Advocate General Mengozzi in Case C-382/12 P *MasterCard and Others v Commission*, para 118.

[12] A Fritzsche, above n 11.

[13] A-L Sibony, *Le juge et le raisonnement économique en droit de la concurrence* (Paris, LGDJ, 2008) 719ff; A-L Sibony and É Barbier de La Serre, 'Charge de la preuve et théorie du contrôle en droit communautaire de la concurrence: pour un changement de perspective' (2007) *RTD eur* 205ff.

[14] Case T-342/99 *Airtours v Commission* [2002] ECR II-2585; Case T-310/01 *Schneider Electric v Commission* [2002] ECR II-4071; Case T-5/02 *Tetra Laval v Commission* [2002] ECR II-4381.

[15] Case C-12/03 P *Commission v Tetra Laval* [2005] ECR I-987, para 39 (while the Commission 'has a margin of discretion with regard to economic matters, that does not mean that the [EU] Courts must refrain from reviewing the Commission's interpretation of information of an economic nature. Not only must the [EU] Courts, inter alia, establish whether the evidence relied on is factually accurate, reliable and consistent but also whether that evidence contains all the information which must be taken into account in order to assess a complex situation and whether it is capable of substantiating the conclusions drawn from it').

were still inclined to perform a very light review, including in those cases where the Commission imposes a fine.[16]

The obscurity of the 'manifest error' standard has been troubling from its very beginnings. Yet, for decades, this seems to have given rise to a relatively well contained level of frustration. At the turn of the millennium this situation changed radically, under the influence of two factors. First, in the late 1990s there was growing discontent among practitioners due to the perception that the Commission's merger control decisions were not reviewed with sufficient rigour. These concerns have been partly allayed by the *Airtours/Schneider/ Tetra Laval* trilogy. By contrast, the frustration created by the second factor—the increase of the level of fines imposed for breaches of Articles 101 and 102 TFEU—has not abated. On the contrary, there have been growing concerns that the 'manifest error' standard was not compatible with the right to a fair trial enshrined in Article 6 ECHR, in particular in criminal, or quasi-criminal, cases.

The question derives from the ECtHR's traditional requirement that, if at first instance in a criminal case the sanction is not imposed by an impartial tribunal, the decision must be reviewed by judicial bodies that have 'full jurisdiction'.[17] As regards the application of this test to competition law, there is a consensus on at least one point: nearly everybody now agrees that competition law qualifies as criminal law within the meaning of Article 6 ECHR.[18] This was confirmed by the ECtHR itself in its *Menarini* judgment of September 2011.[19] By contrast, the meaning of the 'full jurisdiction' requirement remains unclear.[20] This is in part a consequence of the *Jussila* judgment, in which the ECtHR found that the guarantees of criminal law does not apply with their full stringency in non-hardcore criminal cases.[21] The crux of the issue has therefore become whether competition law qualifies as hardcore criminal law, which triggers the full application of the guarantees of Article 6 ECHR, or whether it is soft criminal law, in which case those guarantees may be adapted. If competition law is not hardcore, where does it lie on the spectrum, and what type of judicial review does this imply?

---

[16] In particular due to the extension of the 'manifest error' standard to 'complex technical assessments' (I Forrester, 'A Bush in Need of Pruning: the Luxuriant Growth of "Light Judicial Review"', above n 8. See *contra* W Wils, 'The Compatibility with Fundamental Rights of the EU Antitrust Enforcement System in Which the European Commission Acts Both as Investigator and as First-Instance Decision Maker', above n 3).

[17] See, eg, ECtHR, 23 October 1995, *Schautzer v Austria*, No 15523/89, para 36.

[18] See W Wils, 'The Compatibility with Fundamental Rights of the EU Antitrust Enforcement System in Which the European Commission Acts Both as Investigator and as First-Instance Decision Maker', above n 3.

[19] *Menarini Diagnostics v Italy*, above n 4, para 38–42.

[20] According to case law concerning hardcore matters and predating *Menarini*, the tribunal must have 'full jurisdiction, including the power to quash in all respects, on questions of fact and law, the challenged decision' (ECtHR, Judgment of 31 May 2007, *Bistrović v Croatia*, No 25774/05, para 51), and must be able to perform a *de novo* analysis of the case (ECtHR, Judgment of 27 January 2004, *Kyprianou v Cyprus*, No 73797/01, para 44).

[21] ECtHR, 23 November 2006, *Jussila v Finland*, No 73053/01, para 43.

B. 'Dear Prudence' (*Menarini, KME* and *Chalkor*)

In *Menarini* the ECtHR gave a puzzling response to this fundamental question and, in particular, on the notion of 'full jurisdiction'. On the one hand, the ECtHR found it important that the Italian court reviewing the matter was entitled to assess whether the administrative authority had 'made an appropriate use of its powers', which literally implies the existence of powers going beyond a mere control of legality.[22] However, the ECtHR also held that some limitations to the review of competition law decisions were acceptable, and, in practice, it applied a very loose notion of 'full jurisdiction'.[23]

The Court of Justice's judgments of December 2011 in *KME* and *Chalkor* also came as a relative disappointment: on the one hand, the Court found it sufficient that the EU Courts review both the law and the facts, and have the power to assess evidence, to annul the contested decision and to alter the amount of a fine.[24] Yet, on the other hand, the Court held that the EU Courts cannot use the Commission's margin of discretion as a basis for dispensing with the conduct of an in-depth review of the law and of the facts, as long as (with the exception of matters of public policy) the applicant requests it.[25] *KME* was a significant step forward, as it may be interpreted as meaning that the General Court is required to go as far as the applicants ask it to go. However, as recently noted by Advocate General Mengozzi, while this 'dictum ... has in itself the potential to neutralise de facto the very principle of the recognition of a margin of economic assessment to the Commission', its scope 'is not yet clear'.[26]

While *Menarini, KME* and *Chalkor* immediately appeared as landmark rulings, in these judgments the ECtHR and the Court of Justice seemed hesitant, if not clearly beating around the bush. This is one of the reasons that makes *Posten Norge* so remarkable, as in this judgment the EFTA Court had the audacity of directly confronting the issue avoided by its sister courts.

---

[22] *Menarini Diagnostics v Italy*, above n 4, paras 63 and 64. See also para 59 (in which the ECtHR holds that one of the characteristics of a tribunal with 'full jurisdiction' is that it must have the 'power to quash in all respects, on questions of fact and law, the decision', and 'must have jurisdiction to examine all questions of fact and law relevant to the dispute before it' (free translation)).

[23] ibid, para 62.

[24] Case C-389/10 P *KME Germany and Others v Commission*, para 133.

[25] ibid, paras 63–64, 129 and 131–132. See also Case C-272/09 P *KME Germany and Others v Commission*, paras 55–56, 102 and 104–105, and Case C-386/10 P *Chalkor v Commission*, paras 62 and 64–66.

[26] Opinion of Advocate General Mengozzi in Case C-382/12 P *MasterCard and Others v Commission*, para 119. See also A-L Sibony, Note on Case C-272/09 P, *KME Germany and Others v Commission* (2012) *CML Rev*, 1977 (who notes in particular that the ambiguous formulas of *KME* fall short of a coherent framework), and R Nazzini, above n 3.

C. 'We Can Work it Out' (*Posten Norge*)

Posten Norge concerns a decision of the EFTA Surveillance Authority sanctioning Posten Norge for an abuse of a dominant position and imposing a fine of €12.89 million. In line with *Jussila*, the EFTA Court accepted that Article 6 ECHR does not in all cases apply with its full stringency and that the scope of the guarantees applied in a given case must be determined with regard to the weight of the criminal charge at issue.[27] Yet, in the case at hand, having regard to the nature and the severity of the charge at hand, the matter could 'not be considered to concern a criminal charge of minor weight'. In the Court's view, the amount of the charge in this case is 'substantial' and, moreover, 'the stigma attached to being held accountable for an abuse of a dominant position is not negligible'. Thus, while the form of administrative review may influence, with regard to several aspects, the way in which the guarantees provided by the criminal head of Article 6 ECHR are applied, 'this cannot detract from the necessity to respect these guarantees in substance'.[28] Criminal penalties of the kind at issue may be imposed by an administrative body which does not itself comply with the requirements of Article 6 ECHR, provided that the decision of that body is subject to subsequent control by a judicial body that has full jurisdiction and does in fact comply with those requirements.[29]

As far as complex economic appreciations are concerned, the Court held that it is precluded from annulling the contested decision 'if there can be no legal objection to the assessment … even if it is not the one which the Court would consider to be preferable'.[30] The Court must nonetheless establish whether the evidence relied on is factually accurate, reliable and consistent, but also whether that evidence contains all the information which must be taken into account in order to assess a complex situation and whether it is capable of substantiating the conclusions drawn from it.[31] This is in substance the standard already applied by the EU Courts.[32]

More importantly, the EFTA Court ruled that 'when imposing fines for infringement of the competition rules, [the EFTA Surveillance Authority] cannot be regarded to have any margin of discretion in the assessment of complex economic matters which goes beyond the leeway that necessarily flows from the limitations inherent in the system of legality review'.[33] Moreover, the Court recalled that in a criminal case, 'the question whether the evidence is capable of substantiating the conclusions drawn from it by the competition authority must be answered having regard to the presumption of innocence'. As a consequence,

---

[27] *Posten Norge*, para 89.
[28] ibid, para 90, referring to *Menarini Diagnostics v Italy*, para 62.
[29] ibid, para 91.
[30] ibid, para 98.
[31] ibid, para 99.
[32] Case C-12/03 P *Commission v Tetra Laval* [2005] ECR I-987, para 39.
[33] *Posten Norge*, para 100.

although the Court may not replace the authority's assessment with its own and, accordingly, the legality of the assessment is not affected if the Court merely disagrees with the weighing of individual factors in a complex assessment of economic evidence, 'the Court must nonetheless be convinced that the conclusions drawn by [the authority] are supported by the facts'.[34]

In other words, the Court itself must be convinced of the merits of the case, a requirement that sounds perfectly normal since, as noted by the Court of Justice in *Tetra Laval*, 'the essential function of evidence … is to establish convincingly the merits of an argument or … of a decision'.[35] The EFTA Court nonetheless comes to the blunt conclusion, which the Court of Justice never expressed so clearly, that 'the submission that the Court may intervene only if it considers a complex economic assessment to be manifestly wrong must be rejected'.[36] As noted by several observers, the EFTA Court did not pay lip service to the new standard: in the rest of its judgment, it did not refer to the EFTA Surveillance Authority's discretion and exercised an in-depth review of the challenged decision.[37]

In spite of its audacity, the *Posten Norge* ruling has two limits of very different significance.

The first limit is the restriction of the ruling to the judicial review of decisions imposing a fine.[38] Yet, the EFTA Court has not excluded extending the principle to non-criminal decisions. In this connection, it has been argued that the standard of judicial review in civil law matters should not be lower than in criminal law matters.[39] However an extension to civil cases remains uncertain in light of the Court's insistence on the stigma and seriousness of criminal charges.

The second limit derives from the fact that, according to the EFTA Court, there are 'limitations inherent in the system of legality review'.[40] According to the EFTA Court, one of these limits is that it cannot annul a decision without finding an illegality, in other words cannot annul a decision simply because in its view another outcome would be more appropriate.[41] This reflects the view—expressed in *Posten Norge* and later approved by the Court of Justice—according to which the analysis performed by an administrative court 'has neither the object nor the effect of replacing a full investigation of the case in the context of an administrative

---

[34] ibid, para 101.
[35] Case C-12/03 P *Commission v Tetra Laval* [2005] ECR I-987, para 41.
[36] *Posten Norge*, para 102.
[37] See A-L Sibony, above n 26; M Bronckers and A Vallery, above n 3.
[38] *Posten Norge*, para 101.
[39] H Schweitzer, 'Judicial Review in EU Competition Law', above n 3.
[40] *Posten Norge*, para 100.
[41] ibid, para 98. However, as noted by W Wils, in light of the principle of *nullum crimen sine lege*, 'the existence of the infringement cannot depend on something that is beyond legal assessment' ('The Compatibility with Fundamental Rights of the EU Antitrust Enforcement System in Which the European Commission Acts Both as Investigator and as First-Instance Decision Maker', above n 3). See also M Bronckers and A Vallery, above n 3 ('The exercise of discretion by definition is not predictable. If certain key aspects of a fining decision become too complex for judicial review, one is inclined to think that they must also be too complex for a company to have anticipated in defining its conduct').

procedure'.[42] However, this limitation is expressed in rather vague terms, and it is uncertain whether the distinction between the legality and the appropriateness of a given outcome will have a real impact in competition law cases. Provided that the court seized of the matter applies the *Tetra Laval* test vigorously, there is not much scope left to discretion.[43]

Under a narrower view, two limits that are inherent to the system of legality review come to mind. First, as explained by the Court of Justice in *KME* and *Chalkor*, a court performing its control cannot do so of its own motion, with the exception of pleas involving matters of public policy.[44] Second, the Court can only annul a decision, without replacing it by its own decision, except for those matters for which it has full jurisdiction.[45]

Nevertheless, within these boundaries, a court has ample room to perform a strong judicial review. In particular, the fact that (except for matters of public policy) it is incumbent on the applicant to raise arguments does not prevent the Court from controlling a decision in full, provided that the parties' arguments are sufficiently sophisticated. Similarly, the fact that the Court can only annul a decision—and not replace it—does not prevent it from performing very intense judicial review: it merely limits the scope of the remedies that it may order.[46] As a result, a direct consequence of *Posten Norge* is that, at least in the criminal sphere, judicial review does not appear to be significantly limited.

II. BEYOND *POSTEN NORGE*—AND BEYOND STANDARDS

Posten Norge already appears as a milestone in the complex history of judicial review, and as demonstrated by recent Court judgments[47] and Advocate General Opinions referring to it,[48] sometimes implicitly,[49] it has not gone unnoticed on

---

[42] *Posten Norge*, para 96. Case C-510/11 P *Kone v Commission*, para 26: 'It should also be recalled that the analysis by the European Union judicature of the pleas in law raised in an action for annulment has neither the object nor the effect of replacing a full investigation of the case in the context of an administrative procedure. As such a limitation of judicial review is, however, inherent in the notion of the review of legality, it cannot be understood as unduly limiting the review of legality which the European Union judicature is authorised to carry out.'

[43] While the authority may, in particular, choose its preferred theory of harm, it must still prove that it is plausible and supported by the evidence (A-L Sibony, *Le juge et le raisonnement économique*, above n 13, 755, and A-L Sibony and É Barbier de La Serre, above n 13). Judicial review may be intense if the discretion left to the Commission only covers its basic methodological choices (H Schweitzer, 'Judicial Review in EU Competition Law', above n 3).

[44] Case C-272/09 P *KME Germany and Others v Commission*, para 104.

[45] Art 261 and 263 TFEU.

[46] A-L Sibony and É Barbier de La Serre, above n 13.

[47] See, eg, Case T-442/08 *CISAC v Commission*, nyr, para 95.

[48] Opinion of Advocate General Mengozzi in Case C-382/12 P *MasterCard and Others v Commission*, fn 102; Opinion of Advocate General Kokott in C-501/11 P *Schindler Holding and Others v Commission*, fnn 18 and 20.

[49] See Case C-510/11 P *Kone v Commission*, para 26, referring implicitly to para 96 of *Posten Norge* for the proposition that judicial review 'has neither the object nor the effect of replacing a full investigation of the case in the context of an administrative procedure.'

the other side of the Kirchberg. It cannot be excluded that—following the *Posten Norge* example—the EU Courts will soon abandon the 'manifest error' standard. In fact, while the *KME* judgment is unclear, it may already be interpreted as a first step in this direction.[50] Yet, it is probably underestimated that, even if the EU Courts stop applying the 'manifest error' standard, this will not necessarily result in an increased judicial review.

A. Standards Will Always be Standards

Standards are vague by essence.[51] A standard of review may give an indication of the Courts' general eagerness to review a decision. However, it cannot achieve more than that: the review that can be expected from a court is influenced by too many factors to translate into a single test.

As the EFTA Court rightfully noted in *Posten Norge*, a decision finding an infringement and imposing a fine should be controlled very proactively, and in fact probably with more stringency than other types of decision.[52] However, beyond this basic distinction, a judicial review standard is bound to remain vague for the simple reason that the intensity of the review that a court must exercise depends, among other things, on the nature of the facts that need to be proved and the applicable standard of proof.[53] In particular the intensity of the review exercised on a complex economic fact may depend on the degree of consensus existing among economists on this issue.[54]

In addition, beyond the nature of the facts that need to be proved and the applicable standard of proof, a too-often forgotten factor is the sophistication of the arguments and evidence presented to the Court.[55] In *KME* and *Chalkor* the Court of Justice highlighted the significance of this factor, as it held that, with the exception of pleas involving matters of public policy, 'it is for the applicant

---

[50] Opinion of Advocate General Mengozzi in Case C-382/12 P *MasterCard and Others v Commission*, para 119.

[51] See A-L Sibony, *Le juge et le raisonnement économique en droit de la concurrence*, above n 13, 706.

[52] *Posten Norge*, para 100. On the possible existence of different standards for those decisions that involve the exercise of prosecutorial discretion, see W Wils, 'The Compatibility with Fundamental Rights of the EU Antitrust Enforcement System in Which the European Commission Acts Both as Investigator and as First-Instance Decision Maker', above n 3.

[53] See A-L Sibony, *Le juge et le raisonnement économique en droit de la concurrence*, above n 13, 715–718, and 746ff; A-L Sibony and É Barbier de La Serre, above n 13. On the inseparable nature of standards of proof and standards of review, see, eg, B Vesterdorf, 'Standard of Proof in Merger Cases: Reflections in the Light of Recent Case Law of the Community Courts' (2005) *European Competition Journal* 3; B Vesterdorf, 'Certain Reflections on Recent Judgments Reviewing Commission Merger Control Decisions' in M Hoskins and W Robinson (eds), *A True European: Essays for judge David Edward* (Oxford, Hart Publishing, 2004) 117.

[54] See, eg, B Vesterdorf, articles cited above, n 53.

[55] A-L Sibony and É Barbier de La Serre, above n 13. In a two-tier system, the required level of judicial review also depends on the procedural guarantees offered to parties during the administrative proceedings (R Nazzini, above n 3). This leads Nazzini to conclude that the path to reform is not a switch to full review, but rather a reform of the administrative proceedings (ibid).

to raise pleas in law against that decision and to adduce evidence in support of those pleas'.[56] As noted above, these rulings may be read as meaning that (with the exception of matters of public policy) the General Court is required to go as far as the applicant's arguments lead it. Nothing less. In our view this confirms that the sophistication of the courts' review is primarily determined by the sophistication of the applicant's arguments.[57] This also explains why a court may look more demanding in a merger matter than in a quasi-criminal case. This may happen for instance if the parties' arguments in the merger matter were incisive, whereas the applicant's arguments in the quasi-criminal case were superficial.

To sum up, considering the number of parameters that may have an impact on the courts' review, standards of judicial review will likely never be able to address in detail what the courts must do in any given situation.[58] This may be precisely one of the reasons for the success of the 'manifest error' mantra in the courts' case law: as one author noted, 'the complexity formula has become a rhetorical façade substituting a real discourse about the courts' powers under the Treaty'.[59]

This does not mean that standards of review are useless. As noted above, they reflect the Courts' general level of proactivity and therefore give an indication of how they interpret their duty. This explains why judges should not rely on a standard that does not reflect how they actually perform their review.[60] However standards of review have poor explanatory value. They have, in fact, so little intrinsic value that, according to several recent judgments of the Court of Justice, it does not matter that the General Court refers to the wrong standard as long as it carries out the review that is, in law and in fact, 'required of it.'[61] This reflects the now well-established rule according to which 'account is not to be taken of the abstract and declaratory descriptions of judicial review': what matters is the criterion that the Court 'in fact applied'.[62]

---

[56] Case C-272/09 P *KME Germany and Others v Commission*, para 104. See also para 102 ('the Courts must carry out the review of legality incumbent upon them on the basis of the evidence adduced by the applicant in support of the pleas in law put forward').

[57] A-L Sibony, above n 26, 1977.

[58] See, in this connection, D Simon, 'Une théorie de l'intensité du contrôle juridictionnel est-elle possible?' (2000) *Europe*, chron 4.

[59] A Fritzsche, above n 11. Fritzsche also notes that, according to certain authors, the intensity of the review performed by the Courts is part of the Courts' discretion (see in particular the references at fnn 89 and 134) (a position with which he—rightfully—disagrees).

[60] R Nazzini, above n 3; W Wils, 'The Compatibility with Fundamental Rights of the EU Antitrust Enforcement System in Which the European Commission Acts Both as Investigator and as First-Instance Decision Maker', above n 3.

[61] Case C-389/10 P *KME Germany and Others v Commission*, para 136. See also Case C-501/11 P *Schindler v Commission*, paras 156–158; Case C-510/11 P *Kone v Commission*, paras 44–45, 48–57 and 92–93, and Case C-382/12 P *Master Card and Others v Commision*, paras 157–160.

[62] Case C-510/11 P *Kone v Commission*, para 43. See also Case C-386/10 P *Chalkor v Commission*, paras 47 and 82. In *Menarini* Judge Sajò had proposed the same approach, which seems to have been followed by the ECtHR (Opinion of Advocate General Mengozzi in Case C-382/12 P *MasterCard and Others v Commission*, para 122; H Schweitzer, 'Judicial Review in EU Competition Law', above n 3).

B. Why Varying a Standard May not be Enough

The poor added value of standards has an important consequence. Since all the factors that influence judicial review cannot be captured in a standard and are specific to each case, it is extremely difficult to compare the review exercised by the same court—or even the same judges—in different matters. One may even doubt that there are two comparable cases. For instance, is it possible to compare two judgments ruling on a finding of predatory pricing under Article 102 TFEU? While the practices at stake may be similar, the details of the theory of harm and the quality of the evidence supporting the Commission's decision may vary significantly. Above all, the arguments and the evidence submitted to the courts will vary in scope and sophistication. Since these elements have a decisive influence on the review that can be expected from a court, it is complicated, if not impossible, to compare the intensity of the review exercised on the two decisions.

For the same reason, an outside observer may find it difficult to determine whether the Court has met the applicable standard of review even when focusing solely on a given case. Since a decisive factor of judicial review is the sophistication of the applicant's arguments, making a truly informed assessment of how the Court has performed its duty in a specific matter would require having access to all the arguments made by the applicant. While the EFTA Court and the EU Courts summarise the parties' arguments in their judgments, the summary is not sufficient to reflect the full sophistication of the pleas, let alone the evidence adduced in their support. One has to be realistic: only the applicant and the Courts themselves are in a position to make an informed assessment in this regard.

To summarise, precise comparisons cannot be made by outside observers. This has an important consequence: it is possible for a court to vary the standard of review that it applies without changing its review. For instance, even if the EU Courts referred to a 'full review' standard when they deal with complex economic appreciations, they may well continue to perform the review applied under the previous 'manifest error' standard. For the reasons mentioned above, it is likely that nobody—except maybe the Court itself—could notice it. Should this happen, those who criticise the 'manifest error' standard may well triumph, but the change would be cosmetic. As Giuseppe Tomasi di Lampedusa famously professed, sometimes 'things will have to change so that things can stay the same'.[63]

In fact it cannot be ruled out that this may be what is happening under our eyes. On the one hand, *KME* and *Chalkor* can be interpreted as a first step towards a more exacting standard. Yet, on the other hand, in *KME Germany* the Court of Justice held that the General Court had performed the 'full and unrestricted review, in law and in fact, required of it' when in fact the General Court itself

---

[63] T di Lampedusa, *Il gattopardo* (Milano, Mondadori, I Meridani, 1958) 39.

thought that it had applied the 'manifest error' standard.[64] Similarly, in two recent judgments the Court of Justice felt compelled to disapprove of the references made by the General Court in its judgments to the question whether the Commission had 'manifestly' exceeded its margin of discretion.[65] However, it did not quash these judgments, as in its view the General Court had actually performed an in-depth review.[66] A possible explanation for these rulings is that, in the judgments challenged, the General Court was genuinely proactive. However, there is also room for another interpretation according to which the review performed by the General Court was limited but nonetheless sufficient to meet the 'full review' standard expected by the Court of Justice.

C. Why, Beyond a Change of Standard, Strong Judicial Review Is Needed More Than Ever

It has been shown above that if judicial review is to be increased, abandoning a standard is not sufficient: judicial review must also be increased in practice. This takes us back to the most fundamental question: irrespective of the standard on which the Courts rely, should they strengthen their judicial review?

As noted above, without having access to the detail of the applicant's arguments and the evidence on which it relied in its pleadings, it is impossible to make a detailed assessment of the level of control that a court exercises. It is therefore extremely complex to analyse whether the court has performed its duties, and how judicial review has evolved compared to other cases.

One may nonetheless try to identify broad trends. In particular, it is accepted that, as a whole, the creation of the Court of First Instance (now the General Court) has led to more intense judicial review,[67] which was one of its purposes.[68] In addition, several authors consider that the EU Courts' review is intense and that the use of the margin of appraisal standard has now become rhetorical.[69] It is also accepted that the EU Courts have performed a meaningful review of the

[64] Case C-389/10 P *KME Germany and Others v Commission*, para 136. Bronckers and Vallery rightly note that this is regrettable in view of the well-established principle according to which justice must not only be done, but also be seen to be done (M Bronckers and A Vallery, above n 3).

[65] Case C-501/11 P *Schindler v Commission*, para 156; Case C-510/11 P *Kone v Commission*, para 44.

[66] Case C-501/11 P *Schindler v Commission*, paras 156–158; Case C-510/11 P *Kone v Commission*, paras 44–45, 48–57 and 92–93.

[67] See, eg, A Fritzsche, above n 11, in particular fn 78, and M Siragusa, cited above.

[68] Council Decision 88/591/ECSC, EEC, Euratom of 24 October 1988 establishing a Court of First Instance of the European Communities (OJ L 319, p 1), fourth Recital.

[69] H Schweitzer, 'Judicial Review in EU Competition Law', above n 3; F Castillo de la Torre, 'Evidence, Proof and Judicial Review in Cartel Cases' (2009) *World Competition* 505; Editorial Comments (2011) *CML Rev* 1405; W Wils, 'The Compatibility with Fundamental Rights of the EU Antitrust Enforcement System in Which the European Commission Acts Both as Investigator and as First-Instance Decision Maker', above n 3.

Commission's decisions in a number of cases.[70] This is consistent with the main-tenance of a 'manifest error' test, as the review exercised under this standard—as specified in *Tetra Laval*,[71] or even earlier tests[72]—may be very comprehensive. Even under the 'manifest error' standard, as long as the applicant does (and can) present sufficiently sophisticated arguments, it may oblige the courts to carry out an in-depth analysis of the challenged decision.

Yet, there are also reasons to believe that there is no uniform trend towards an increase—or even a lack of decrease—of judicial review. At best the EU Courts have sent mixed signals.

First, the General Court regularly uses expressions that convey the view that certain economic appraisals—such as the definition of the relevant market—are always 'complex',[73] which is blatantly incorrect.[74] Second, in certain cases the EU Courts' limited review has spilled over into factual issues that did not involve complex appreciations. For instance, in 2011 the General Court applied twice the standard of the manifest error of appreciation to the question of whether an undertaking had contested the facts on which the Commission based its allega-tions.[75] Why did this factual finding require the kind of complex appreciation that normally justifies limited review? Third, in several recent cases the Courts have applied the 'manifest error' standard even in those areas where it has full

---

[70] See, eg, J Ratliff, 'Judicial Review in EC Competition Cases Before the European Courts: Avoiding double renvoi' in C-D Ehlermann and M Marquis (eds), *European Competition Law Annual 2009: Evaluation of Evidence and its Judicial Review in Competition Cases* (Oxford, Hart Publishing, 2011) 453; *Woodpulp* (Joined Cases C-89/85, C-104/85, C-114/85, C-116/85, C-117/85 and C-125/85 to C-129/85 A). *Ahlström Osakeyhtiö and Others v Commission* [1993] ECR I-1307) is often cited as a judgment in which the Court of Justice exercised strong review (see, eg, F Castillo de la Torre, above n 69; D Bailey, 'Scope of Judicial Review Under Article 81 EC' (2004) *CML Rev* 1327; N Forwood, 'The Commission's "More Economic Approach"—Implications for the Role of the EU Courts, the Treatment of Economic Evidence and the Scope of Judicial Review' in C-D Ehlermann and M Marquis (eds), *European Competition Law Annual 2009: Evaluation of Evidence and Its Judicial Control in Competition Cases* (Oxford, Hart Publishing, 2011) 255; I Forrester, 'A Bush in Need of Pruning: the Luxuriant Growth of "Light Judicial Review"', above n 8.

[71] Case C-12/03 P *Commission v Tetra Laval* [2005] ECR I-987, para 39 ('[n]ot only must the [EU] Courts, inter alia, establish whether the evidence relied on is factually accurate, reliable and consistent but also whether that evidence contains all the information which must be taken into account in order to assess a complex situation and whether it is capable of substantiating the conclusions drawn from it'). On this issue, See A-L Sibony, above n 26, 1977.

[72] Case T-380/94 *AIUFASS and AKT v Commission* [1996] ECR II-2169, para 59 ('In order to establish that the Commission committed a manifest error in assessing the facts such as to justify the annulment of the contested decision, the evidence adduced by the applicants must be sufficient to make the factual assessments used in the decision implausible').

[73] Case T-446/05 *Amann & Söhne and Others v Commission* [2010] ECR II-1255, para 54 ('[I]nas-much as it involves complex economic appraisals on the part of the Commission, the definition of the relevant market is amenable to only limited review by the Community judicature') (the French version of the judgment is even clearer in this respect). See also paras 106, 110 and 186.

[74] N Forwood, above n 70; I Forrester, 'A Bush in Need of Pruning: the Luxuriant Growth of "Light Judicial Review"', above n 8; M Jaeger, 'The Standard of Review in Competition Cases Involving Complex Economic Assessments: Towards the Marginalisation of the Marginal Review?' (2011) *JECLAP* 295.

[75] Case T-33/05 *Cetarsa v Commission*, para 271; Case T-37/05 *World Wide Tobacco España v Commission*, para 197.

jurisdiction, such as for the assessment of fines.[76] This will likely not last, as in *Kone* and *Schindler* the Court of Justice has indicated that making a reference to this standard was 'not consonant with' its case law.[77] Furthermore, several judgments of 2013 show that—in the course of its control of legality—the General Court is now willing to carry out its own assessment of the fine, in particular of the reduction granted for leniency.[78] Yet there is at least one judgment post-*Schindler* in which the General Court still applied the 'manifest error' standard to the assessment of the applicant's cooperation.[79]

Here again it must be kept in mind that, as such, referring to the 'manifest error' standard does not mean that the court did not control the decision proactively. However, using this standard in cases where this is clearly unjustified even under the most traditional line of case law (that is, when there are no genuine complex appreciations at stake or when the Court is required to exercise its full jurisdiction) reveals the Court's lack of eagerness to exercise a close review of the Commission's decisions.

The situation was worsened by a recent procedural evolution. Classically, the EU Courts consider that where the EU institutions have a broad margin of appreciation, procedural guarantees are particularly important.[80] Yet, in several recent judgments the EU Courts seem to have considered the opposite, that is, that procedural guarantees may be limited precisely because of the existence of a broad margin of appreciation.[81] This is a troubling development.

Abandoning the 'manifest error' standard would therefore be a welcome move,[82] but it is important that the EU Courts also send clearer signals of their

---

[76] See, eg, Case T-439/07 *Coats Holdings v Commission*, para 185.

[77] Case C-501/11 P *Schindler v Commission*, para 44; Case C-510/11 P *Kone v Commission*, para 44.

[78] See, eg, Case T-154/09 *MRI v Commission*, paras 352–359, and Case T-146/09 *Parker v Commission*, paras 251–257.

[79] Case T-375/10 *Hansa Metallwerke and Others v Commission*, paras 136–138.

[80] Case C-269/90 *Technische Universität München* [1991] ECR I-5469, para 14 ('[W]here the Community institutions have such a power of appraisal, respect for the rights guaranteed by the Community legal order in administrative procedures is of even more fundamental importance.' 'Those guarantees include, in particular, the duty of the competent institution to examine carefully and impartially all the relevant aspects of the individual case, the right of the person concerned to make his views known and to have an adequately reasoned decision. Only in this way can the Court verify whether the factual and legal elements upon which the exercise of the power of appraisal depends were present').

[81] See in particular Case C-441/07 P *Commission v Alrosa* [2010] ECR I-5949, para 96 (in which the Court seems to consider that because of the Commission's broad margin of appreciation to accept commitments it is not required to allow interested third parties to know the reasons why a set of commitments is rejected, nor to consider their position in this respect). In the same vein, see Case C-290/07 P *Commission v Scott* [2010] ECR I-7763, paras 79–84 (in which the complex economic assessment required to determine the existence of a State aid seems to justify a decrease of the need to comply with the duty to exercise due diligence).

[82] On this question, see W Wils, 'The Compatibility with Fundamental Rights of the EU Antitrust Enforcement System in Which the European Commission Acts Both as Investigator and as First-Instance Decision Maker', above n 3, and H Schweitzer, 'Judicial Review in EU Competition Law', above n 3.

appetite to control the Commission's decisions in competition law matters. Meaningful judicial review in competition law cases is more needed than ever.

The main reason for this is the success of the commitment procedure under Article 9 of Regulation No 1/2003. For certain types of case, in particular proceedings concerning the application of Article 102 TFEU, the commitment procedure has now become the standard procedure. Since the entry into force of Regulation No 1/2003 on 1 May 2004, there have been only seven Commission decisions finding an infringement of Article 102 TFEU,[83] a very low number that results from the now quasi-systematic use of the commitment procedure in abuse of dominance cases.[84] Similarly, the settlement procedure in cartel cases seems to have recently gained traction. In April 2014, the Commission adopted its thirteenth settlement decision since the introduction of the settlement procedure for cartels in June 2008.[85]

It cannot be repeated enough that, for these commitments and settlements to remain voluntary, the EU Courts must exercise an in-depth review of the Commission's decisions finding an infringement. If the Courts leave too much discretion to the Commission to find infringements and impose fines, filing a commitment or a settlement submission will be the result of a false choice.[86]

III. CONCLUSION—WHY, WITHOUT PROPER REGARD FOR THE APPLICANTS' PROCEDURAL RIGHTS, INCREASED JUDICIAL REVIEW MAY LEAD TO LESS EFFECTIVE JUDICIAL REVIEW

As Advocate General Jacobs mentioned in his opinion concerning the Union de Pequeños Agricultores case, 'the Court should, for reasons of legal certainty, depart from settled case law only where there are compelling arguments in favour

---

[83] Case COMP/38.096 *Clearstream* (Clearing and Settlement), Commission Decision of 2 June 2004; Case COMP/A.37.507/F3 *AstraZeneca*, Commission Decision of 15 June 2005. Case COMP/E.-1/38-113 *Prokent-Tomra*, Commission Decision of 29 March 2006; Case COMP/38.784 *Wanadoo España v Telefónica*, Commission Decision of 4 July 2007; Case COMP/C3/37.990 *Intel*, Commission Decision of 13 May 2009; Case COMP/39.525 *Telekomunikacja Polska*, Commission Decision of 22 June 2011; Case COMP/39.984 *OPCOM/Romanian Power Exchange*, Commission decision of 5 March 2014.

[84] For a recent analysis, see D Gérard, 'Negotiated Remedies in the Modernization Era: The Limits of Effectiveness', in P Lowe and M Marquis (eds), *European Competition Law Annual 2013: Effective and Legitimate Enforcement* (Oxford and Portland, Hart Publishing, forthcoming). See also É Barbier de La Serre, 'Competition Law Cases before the EU Courts: is the Well Running Dry?', in M Merola and J Derenne (eds), *The Role of the Court of Justice of the European Union in Competition Law Cases* (Brussels, Bruylant, 2012) 87.

[85] Antitrust: Commission fines producers of steel abrasive €30.7 million, IP/14/359, 2 April 2014.

[86] Another reason why meaningful review is needed is the Commission's willingness to resort to the more economic approach of Arts 101 and 102 TFEU. This may be a poisonous gift to undertakings if this resulted in less judicial review by the EU Courts. See in particular Communication from the Commission—Guidance on the Commission's enforcement priorities in applying Article 82 of the EC Treaty to abusive exclusionary conduct by dominant undertakings (OJ 2009, C 45, 7).

of, and the time is ripe for, such a step'.[87] The 'manifest error' standard meets both limbs of this test. First, it is excessively vague and may be reconciled with Article 6 ECHR and Article 47 of the Charter only if the EU Courts apply the *Tetra Laval* test in full, which they often refrain from doing. There are therefore compelling reasons to abandon this test, at the very least in criminal cases. Second, the time is ripe for such a step, not only because this rule has given rise to intense frustration (which was unnecessarily imposed if indeed the Courts, although they referred to the 'manifest error' standard, performed intense judicial review), but also in view of the future accession of the EU to the ECHR.

By abandoning the 'margin of appreciation' standard in *Posten Norge*, the EFTA Court has therefore made a very significant contribution to the improvement of the right to a fair trial in the EU. Hopefully this will encourage the EU Courts to clarify their doctrine on this issue. As noted above, it cannot be excluded that they have already started the process that will lead them to abandoning the 'margin of appreciation' standard. Our own prognosis is that, in the coming years, the EU Courts will stop referring to this test in Articles 101 and 102 TFEU matters. However, as noted above, this does not imply that the EU courts will strengthen their review. In practice, standards are nothing more than a general signal that the EU Courts send to express their eagerness to review a decision. Obviously symbols matter. However, as explained above, it must not be forgotten that the EU Courts have ample room to stop using the 'margin of appreciation' standard without increasing their review. The real test will be what the courts do in practice, not what they say about what they do.

This is not the only paradox of judicial review that the EU Courts will need to address in the coming years. Another puzzling issue lies in the fact that, if judicial review is reinforced without sufficient regard for the applicants' procedural rights, this may lead to less effective judicial review. This results from the fact that, following the *Airtours/Schneider/Tetra Laval* trauma of 2002, the Commission has increased the length and detail of its decisions. Competition law decisions are increasingly well reasoned, which is of course a welcome development, but which also means that to successfully challenge a competition law decision an applicant must often present more detailed arguments than in the past. Yet, in the past few years the EU Courts have progressively limited the acceptable length of the applicants' briefs.[88] In many cases these limits are not unreasonable, and it is not submitted here that lawyers should never make an effort to streamline their appeals. That being said, it is illusory to believe that a 400-page decision including hundreds of references to the Commission's file may always be contested in 50 pages. As noted above, the sophistication of the Courts' review is primarily determined

---

[87] Opinion of Advocate General Jacobs in Case C-50/00 P *Unión de Pequeños Agricultores v Council* [2002] ECR I-6677, para 82.

[88] Practice directions to parties before the General Court (OJ 2012, L 68, 23), para 15. See also the line of case-limiting references to annexes (Case T-201/04 *Microsoft v Commission* [2007] ECR II-1491, paras 94–99).

by the sophistication of the applicant's arguments. The courts may well abandon the 'margin of appreciation' standard, but if they restrict the applicants' procedural rights to the level where they cannot challenge all the problematic aspects of the decision, in particular if they need to contest thousands of factual references on which the Commission relies, this is bound to remain a cosmetic change.

32

Third Party Access to File in Competition Cases

ROMINA POLLEY*

I. INTRODUCTION

A CCESS OF THIRD parties, that is, of natural or legal persons that are not parties to competition law proceedings, to documents from the case file is an issue almost as old as the EFTA Court, whose 20th anniversary is celebrated by this Festschrift. It first emerged at EU level with the *Postbank* case, where the Court of First Instance dealt with the possibility for a national court to use the confidential version of a statement of objections transmitted to it by the Commission in national follow-on damages proceedings.[1]

Third party requests for access to documents became more frequent after the adoption of Regulation 1049/2001 (the 'Transparency Regulation')[2] in 2001, which fleshed out the principle of transparency set out in Article 42 of the Charter of Fundamental Rights of the EU (CFREU) and in Article 15 of the Treaty on the Functioning of the European Union (TFEU). The Transparency Regulation was soon discovered by private plaintiffs as a possible route to get access to information from cartel proceedings. For example, it served a consumer organisation intending to file a damages action against Austrian banks that had participated in a price-fixing cartel as a legal basis for its request for access to the Commission's cartel case file.[3]

The number of third party requests for access to documents in competition law cases and the frequency of litigation following decisions partly or fully rejecting such requests has increased steadily in the last 20 years. This has led to a particularly interesting line of case law, at the core of which lies the key question to what extent third parties should get access to the competition case file so as to ensure

---

* The author would like to thank her colleague Ioannis Thanos for his valuable contribution to this chapter.
[1] Case T-353/94 *Postbank v Commission* [1996] ECR II-926.
[2] Regulation (EC) No 1049/2001 of the European Parliament and of the Council of 30 May 2001 regarding public access to European Parliament, Council and Commission documents [2001] OJ L145/43.
[3] Case T-2/03 *Verein für Konsumenteninformation v Commission* (*VKI*) [2005] ECR II-1121.

both an efficient public enforcement of competition law and to avoid rendering private enforcement excessively difficult.

After the Court of Justice of the European Union (ECJ) issued its *Pfleiderer* preliminary ruling in June 2011,[4] where it dealt for the first time with a request for access to the file in cartel proceedings of a national competition authority (NCA), in that case the German Federal Cartel Office, the EFTA Court dealt in December 2012 in *Schenker*[5] with third party access to the file of the EFTA Surveillance Authority (ESA) in which the EFTA Court stressed that the private enforcement of competition law may constitute an overriding public interest and should be encouraged, since it can make a significant contribution to the maintenance of effective competition in the EEA.[6] The ECJ's later *EnBW* judgment[7] lays down when the private enforcement of competition law may prove to be an overriding interest referring to a test of 'necessity'.[8]

As the President of the EFTA Court, Carl Baudenbacher, rightly observed,[9] questions regarding competition law enforcement are subject to the principle of homogeneity and require a uniform response by the judiciary. Divergences in interpretation are not favourable to legal certainty in EU and EEA law. Further, access to evidence is a corollary of the right of access to justice, a right enshrined in Article 6 of the European Convention on Human Rights (ECHR).[10] In the light of the importance of legal certainty in the area of third party access to documents in cartel proceedings across the EEA the ECJ's *EnBW* judgment and the Commission's Directive on Antitrust Damages Actions[11] (Antitrust Damages Directive) are to be welcomed.

This chapter portrays the more recent development of case law on third party access to the file of a competition authority (Commission and NCAs) including the partially diverging recent rulings of the EFTA Court and the ECJ and presents the solution adopted in the Antitrust Damages Directive with regard to third party access to documents at national level and concludes with some comments on the practical implications of the interplay between the case law of the EFTA Court, the EU Courts and the Antitrust Damages Directive.

---

[4] Case C-360/09 *Pfleiderer AG v Bundeskartellamt* [2011] ECR I-5186.

[5] Case E-14/11 *Schenker North AB and Schenker Privpak AB and Schenker Privpak AS v ESA* [2012] EFTA Ct Rep 1181.

[6] Case E-14/11 *Schenker*, para 241.

[7] Case C-365/12 *Commission v EnBW* (ECJ, 27 February 2014).

[8] Case C-365/12P *Commission v EnBW*, paras 107–108.

[9] C Baudenbacher, *The EFTA Court in action* (Stuttgart, German Law Publishers, 2010) 71.

[10] JT Lang, 'The Duty of National Courts to Provide Access to Justice in the EEA' in EFTA Court (ed), *Judicial Protection in the European Economic Area* (Stuttgart, German Law Publishers, 2012) 100, 104ff.

[11] Proposal for a Directive of the European Parliament and of the Council on certain rules governing actions for damages under national law for infringements of the competition law provisions of the Member States and of the European Union, COM(2013) 404, 11.6.2013; see also fn 107.

II. LEGAL FRAMEWORK FOR THIRD PARTY ACCESS
TO DOCUMENTS IN THE EEA

The right of access to documents and the right of access to file, although similar from a functional point of view, as they allow disclosure of documents held by a public body, are legally distinct.[12] The right of access to documents serves primarily the democratic legitimacy of the EU and ensures transparency in the work of its institutions.[13] On the other hand, the right of access to the file forms part of the rights of defence of any person against which an authority has opened proceedings and serves to ensure compliance with the principle of professional secrecy.[14] In competition law proceedings, it allows a natural or legal person faced with the objections of a competition authority to exercise its right to be heard, which is also a fundamental right protected by Article 47(2) CFREU, and ensures equality of arms, as the parties get knowledge of the evidence collected by the authority. As becomes apparent from the objective of the right of access to file, its material, personal and temporal scope is much narrower than that of the right of access to documents.[15] However, none of these rights and the respective regulations is specific or superior to the other.[16]

A. Third Party Requests for Access to the Commission's or ESA's file

It follows from the legal distinction between access to file and access to documents that there are two main options for third parties seeking access to documents from the Commission's or ESA's file or to documents from the file of an NCA. A third party may rely either on the Transparency Regulation or use the indirect way provided for in Article 15(1) Reg 1/2003, which entitles a national court to request from the Commission transmission of documents from its case file.

i. *Request for Access to Documents under EU/EEA Competition Law Rules*

EU and EEA competition rules do not provide for a general right to obtain access to documents being part of the Commission's or ESA's cartel investigation file. Access to the Commission's case file is part of the rights of defence and as such reserved to the addressees of a statement of objections.[17] Parties are entitled to access the whole

---

[12] Case T-380/08 *Netherlands v Commission (Dutch Bitumen)* (GC, 13 September 2013), para 32.
[13] Case C-365/12 *Commission v EnBW* (ECJ, 27 February 2014), para 83.
[14] Case C-365/12 *Commission v EnBW*, para 83 referring to Case C-404/10P *Commission v Éditions Odile Jacob* (ECJ, 28 June 2012), para 109.
[15] G Goddin, 'Recent Judgments Regarding Transparency and Access to Documents in the Field of Competition Law: Where Does the Court of Justice of the EU Strike the Balance?' (2011) *Journal of European Competition Law and Practice* 10, 15.
[16] Case C-365/12, *Commission v EnBW* (ECJ, 27 February 2014), para 84.
[17] Art 23(2) Reg 1/2003 and Art 15(1) Reg 773/2004. The precise modalities of access to the Commission's file are described in the Commission's Notice for Access to File (Commission Notice on

file except for business secrets, otherwise confidential information and internal documents of the Commission or NCAs. With regard to leniency statements, the Commission Leniency Notice provides for a limited access of the parties to the proceedings.[18] The same ground rule applies also with respect to settlement submissions. Parties that opted against settlement can be granted access to the submissions, provided they do not copy them and that they use the information they get only in judicial or administrative proceedings for the enforcement of EU competition rules.[19]

Third parties have no right of access to file at all under the relevant competition rules.[20] However, third parties preparing an action for damages against cartelists can obtain the information necessary for the substantiation of their claim either from the non-confidential version of the fine decision published pursuant to Article 30 Reg 1/2003 or by relying on Article 15(1) Reg 1/2003.[21] Pursuant to that provision, 'courts of the Member States may ask the Commission to transmit to them information in its possession'. The latter approach has some drawbacks. First, it presupposes that a cartel victim has already filed an action with a national court. Damages claimants need, however, very often access to the information provided in the competition authority's file in order to assess the success chances of a potential damages claim. Second, a damages claimant cannot request access to documents itself but has to use the court as an intermediary. The outcome of such a plan is uncertain and depends largely on whether national procedural rules grant the plaintiff a right to obtain such a request by the court or merely provide for the plaintiff's possibility to encourage the court to make such a request, leaving the final decision to the court's discretion.[22]

Where a national court submits to the Commission a request for transmission of documents for which confidentiality is claimed, it is for the Commission to decide whether or not a particular document contains business secrets. The Commission is, however, obliged to give the documents' producer the chance to state its views and to issue a duly reasoned decision on the request for transmission.

---

the rules for access to the Commission file in cases pursuant to Articles 81 and 82 of the EC Treaty, Articles 53, 54 and 57 of the EEA Agreement and Council Regulation (EC) No 139/2004 [2005] OJ C325/7. A similar notice has been issued by ESA with regard to the modalities of access to the ESA file: Notice on the rules for access to the EFTA Surveillance Authority file in cases pursuant to Articles 53, 54 and 57 of the EEA Agreement [2007] OJ C250/16 (ESA Notice on rules for access to the file)).

[18] Commission Notice on immunity from fines and reduction of fines in cartel cases [2006] OJ C298/17, paras 33–34.

[19] Commission Notice on the conduct of settlement procedures in view of the adoption of Decisions pursuant to Articles 7 and 23 of Council Regulation (EC) 1/2003 in cartel cases [2008] OJ C167/01, paras 35–36.

[20] Complainants have, however, a limited right of access to file based on Art 8 Reg 773/2004 where the Commission intends to reject their complaint. Access is limited to the documents on which the Commission bases its rejection and does not extend to business secrets or confidential information of the parties or of third parties.

[21] See, generally, M Kellerbauer, 'The Recent Case Law on the Disclosure of Information Regarding EU Competition Law Infringements to Private Damages Claimants' (2014) *European Competition Law Review* 56.

[22] See M Kellerbauer, 'The Recent Case Law on the Disclosure of Information Regarding EU Competition Law Infringements to Private Damages Claimants' (2014) *European Competition Law Review* 56, 62.

Further, in view of the serious damage that disclosure of confidential information may cause, the company concerned must be given the opportunity to appeal the Commission's decision in order to prevent transmission.[23]

ii. Request for Access to Documents on the Basis of Regulation 1049/2001 or the RAD

The Transparency Regulation lays down the details of the exercise of third party right of access to documents.

a. The Principle of Widest Possible Access

The principle underlying the Transparency Regulation is to confer to the public widest possible access to documents of the EU institutions.[24] Beneficiaries of the right of access to documents are EU citizens and any natural or legal person with its place of residence or seat in an EU Member State.[25] As a result of its purpose of ensuring legitimacy and accountability of the administration in a democratic regime, the right of access to documents has a smaller weight in administrative proceedings for the enforcement of competition law than in the context of a legislative procedure.[26] Even though it is not the purpose of the Transparency Regulation to facilitate follow-on damages actions and to support injured parties that suffered damages from a cartel in obtaining the necessary information to substantiate their claim, it has increasingly been used by private plaintiffs as a route to obtain information as will be further explained below at III.B.

A legal instrument almost identical in substance to the Transparency Regulation has been introduced in EEA law by virtue of the decision on Rules on Access to Documents (RAD)[27] in 2008. The RAD, as revised in 2012,[28] stipulate a right of access to documents produced or held by the ESA for every EEA citizen and for every natural or legal person with its residence or seat in an EEA State. It is necessary to make clear that the EEA Joint Committee did not bring over Regulation 1049/2001 into the EEA legal order.

b. The Exceptions

Article 4 Transparency Regulation sets out the limits of the right of access to documents. Article 4 RAD provides for the same exceptions to the general right of access

---

[23] Case C-36/92P *Samenwerkende Elektriciteits-productiebedrijven NV v Commission* [1994] ECR I-1911, para 38; Case 53/85 *Akzo Chemie v Commission* [1986] ECR 1965, para 29.

[24] Case T-181/10 *Reagens v Commission* (GC, 20 March 2014), para 85.

[25] Art 2(1) Transparency Regulation.

[26] Case T-181/10 *Reagens v Commission* (GC, 20 March 2014), para 140.

[27] Rules on Access to Documents, Decision 407/08/COL of 27 June 2008.

[28] ESA Decision 300/12/COL of 5 September 2012 to adopt revised Rules on public access to documents, and repealing Decision 407/08/COL.

to documents as Article 4 Transparency Regulation.[29] Article 4(1) Transparency Regulation provides for a set of absolute exceptions, where disclosure of documents would compromise the protection of a) public interest with regard to public security, defence and military matters, international relations and the financial or economic policy of the EU or of a Member State, or of b) the privacy and integrity of the individual. Paragraphs 2 and 3 of Article 4 stipulate relative exceptions to the general rule of access. Access shall be refused unless there is an overriding public interest in disclosure, if disclosure would undermine the protection of (i) the commercial interests of a natural or legal person, (ii) court proceedings or legal advice, (iii) the purpose of inspections, investigations or audits, or, in case of requests regarding internal or preparatory documents, (iv) the institution's decision-making process. These exceptions have in general to be construed as strictly as possible.[30]

The mere fact that a document concerns one of the interests protected by an Article 4 exception does not justify a rejection of the request for access.[31] The authority has to assess whether access to the document would specifically and actually undermine the protected interest. A purely hypothetical risk does not suffice; the risk has to be rather reasonably foreseeable. In order to comply with these requirements, an institution dealing with an access request normally has to conduct a concrete and individual assessment of the contents of each document requested and to make such assessment visible in its decision on the request.[32]

An institution dealing with a request for access to documents can only under exceptional circumstances invoke a high administrative burden as a justification for a refusal to undertake a concrete, individual assessment, after having balanced the interest in public access against the workload required.[33] The institution has to clearly demonstrate that a concrete, individual examination of the documents requested exceeds the limits of what may be reasonably required and to consult with the applicant in order to try to find a less onerous solution.[34]

A concrete and individual examination is, however, not required, when it is obvious that access must be refused or granted. This is, inter alia, the case when certain documents are either manifestly covered in their entirety by an exception to the right of access or have already been the subject of a concrete, individual assessment in similar circumstances.[35]

In the past, the ECJ had already acknowledged the existence of such presumptions in four particular cases, namely in State Aid, merger control cases, pleadings lodged by one of the institutions in court proceedings and documents concerning an infringement procedure during its pre-litigation phase. For such situations, the

---

[29] See also G Goddin, 'Access to Documents in Competition Files: Where Do we Stand, Two Years after TGI?' (2013) *Journal of European Law and Practice* 112, 116.
[30] Case T-2/03 *VKI* [2005] ECR II-1121, para 106.
[31] ibid, para 69.
[32] ibid, paras 73–74.
[33] ibid, paras 102–103.
[34] Case T-2/03 *VKI* [2005] ECR II-1121, paras 112, 114.
[35] Case T-2/03 *VKI* [2005] ECR II-1121, para 75.

ECJ acknowledged that it is open to the Commission to base its decision for or against disclosure of documents on general presumptions which apply to certain categories of documents, as similar general considerations are likely to apply to requests for disclosure relating to documents of the same nature.[36]

Recently the applicability of a presumption against disclosure of documents has also been confirmed by the ECJ in *EnBW* for competition law proceedings which ended legal uncertainty created by diverging decisions of the GC in *EnBW* and *Bitumen Netherlands*.[37]

B. Third Party Requests for Access to the Case File of an NCA

Where third parties seek access to documents from the case file of an NCA, they may take recourse to national civil procedure rules and national legal instruments ensuring transparency. In that context the national judge deciding on the request for access to documents has to take into account the ECJ preliminary rulings in *Pfleiderer* and *Donau Chemie* (see below under III.C). The entry into force of the Antitrust Damages Directive (described in more detail below under IV) in 2016 will, if correctly implemented by the Member States, harmonise the rules on access to an NCA's case file across Member States and reduce the legal uncertainty created by the *Pfleiderer* and *Donau Chemie* rulings.

III. CASE LAW OF THE EU COURTS AND THE EFTA COURT ON THIRD PARTY ACCESS TO DOCUMENTS IN COMPETITION CASES

A. Indirect Third Party Access to File through Article 15 Reg 1/2003

Instead of directly requesting access to documents from the competition authority, private plaintiffs also have the option to request the national court seized with the follow-on damage claim to ask the Commission for transmission of the documents.

i. The Alstom *Order of the GC*

A case where a damages claimant tried to obtain documents from the Commission's file through a national court's request on the basis of Article 15(1) Reg

---

[36] Case C-139/07P *Commission v Technische Glaswerke Ilmenau* [2010] ECR I-5885, para 54, Case C-404/10 P *Commission v Éditions Odile Jacob* (ECJ, 28 June 2012), para 116; Case C-477/10 P *Commission v Agrofert Holding* (ECJ, 28 June 2012), para 57, Joined Cases C-514/07 P, C-528/07 P and C-532/07 P *Sweden and Others v API and Commission* [2010] ECR I-8533, para 94; Case C-514/11 *LPN and Finland v Commission* (ECJ, 14 November 2013), para 65.

[37] See Case C-365/12 *Commission v EnBW* (ECJ, 27 February 2014), Case T-344/08 *EnBW v Commission* (GC, 22 May 2012) and Case T-380/08 *Dutch Bitumen* (GC, 13 September 2013). See also below under III.B.

1/2003 is *National Grid*. National Grid Electricity Transmission plc brought a claim for damages before the High Court of England and Wales (the High Court) against several gas insulated switchgear producers which were fined by the Commission in 2007 for their participation in bid-rigging and being in a price-fixing cartel.[38] In those proceedings the plaintiff filed an application for disclosure of the replies of some cartel participants to the Commission's statement of objections. The High Court decided that, in order to protect the confidentiality of the documents requested, they should be disclosed to a so-called confidentiality ring, and requested their transmission from the Commission.

By virtue of a decision of 26 January 2012, the Commission communicated to the companies concerned its intention to accede to the High Court's request and a list of the documents that it intended to transmit. On 10 April 2012, Alstom, one of the defendants in the High Court proceedings, filed an action for annulment of the Commission's decision and an application for interim measures with the GC.

On 29 November 2012, the President of the GC ordered the suspension of the transmission of the documents that related to the interim relief applicant.[39] The President of the GC acknowledged that the applicant had a *prima facie* case and that disclosure of the documents may cause serious and irreparable harm to it. According to the GC, the Commission failed to properly assess the implications of the confidentiality ring established by the High Court for the guarantee of protection of professional secrecy. In its conclusion the GC took into account the inclusion of in-house counsels in the confidentiality ring and the respective ECJ case law on in-house counsels and their professional obligations.[40]

ii. *The* Pilkington *Order of the ECJ*

The *Alstom* order reinforced the position of companies trying to protect confidentiality of their submissions to a competition authority. It has, however, to be qualified in view of the ECJ's statement in *Pilkington*, an order of the ECJ issued in September 2013 in a case concerning the appeal of a cartelist against the Commission's decision to reject its request for confidential treatment of some parts of the car glass cartel decision.[41] The information whose confidentiality was at issue allowed to identify individual customers harmed by the cartel and details about the functioning of the cartel. The Vice-President of the ECJ held that claiming, in general, an irreparable breach of fundamental rights does not suffice to establish urgency of the request for interim relief.[42] The party seeking relief has to establish the likelihood of such harm in each particular case.[43]

---

[38] Case 38.899 Gas Insulated Switchgear, summary decision [2008] OJ C5/7.
[39] Case T-164/12R *Alstom v Commission* (GC, Order of the President, 29 November 2012).
[40] Case T-164/12R *Alstom v Commission* (GC, Order of the President, 29 November 2012), para 57.
[41] Case C-278/13P(R) *Commission v Pilkington* (ECJ, Order of the Vice-President, 10 September 2013).
[42] Case C-278/13P(R) *Commission v Pilkington*, para 40.
[43] ibid, para 41.

Harm in case of disclosure of information that may be used by damages claimants in bringing actions for damages is normally of a pecuniary nature. Pecuniary damage can, however, only in exceptional circumstances be considered as serious and irreparable harm, since it can normally be made good by an action for damages. This is not the case when the harm, even after having occurred, is unquantifiable.[44] The Vice-President of the ECJ concluded that the harm from disclosure of confidential information by publishing a Commission decision is indeed unquantifiable, and therefore serious and irreparable, since it is impossible to identify the number and status of all the persons who in fact got knowledge of the information published.[45]

In a reverse conclusion, the ECJ's Vice-President's statement in *Pilkington* means that, where disclosure is confined to a limited number of identifiable persons, the harm will usually be identifiable and, hence, not irreparable.[46] Disclosure to a confidentiality ring, such as that ordered by the High Court in *National Grid*, can be considered as disclosure to an identifiable number of persons, allowing the conclusion that applications for interim measures by companies harmed by such disclosure to third parties will in future cases have a low chance of success.

B. Third Party Access to Documents on the Basis of Regulation 1049/2001

The Transparency Regulation has until now been the most favoured legal basis for third parties seeking access to the Commission's file in cartel, merger control and State Aid cases. In all cases brought before the GC and, upon appeal, the ECJ, the interpretation of the relative exceptions to the public access principle laid down in Article 4(2) and (3) Regulation 1049/2001 was of particular importance. While the GC, at least initially, construed these exceptions narrowly, the ECJ interpreted them in a broader sense by taking into consideration the particularities of the procedure for the enforcement of EU competition law.[47] The prime example of this broad interpretation is the acknowledgement by the ECJ of the Commission's possibility to rely on general presumptions applying to certain categories of documents in order to reject third party requests for access to documents not only in State Aid and merger control cases[48] but more recently also in cartel cases.[49] This clarification by the ECJ is not only of tremendous practical importance in light of the size of cartel files at the Commission, but also put an end to legal uncertainty created by divergent case law of the GC (see below under i).

---

[44] ibid, paras 46–52.
[45] ibid, para 55.
[46] ibid, para 57.
[47] G Goddin, 'Recent Judgments Regarding Transparency and Access to Documents in the Field of Competition Law: Where Does the Court of Justice of the EU Strike the Balance?' (2011) *Journal of European Competition Law and Practice* 10, 17.
[48] See, eg, Case C-139/07P *Commission v Technische Glaswerke Ilmenau* [2010] ECR I-5885, paras 54–55.
[49] Case C-365/12P *Commission v EnBW*, para 93.

i. The GC's Case Law from CDC *and* EnBW *to* Dutch Bitumen

a. The *CDC* Judgment

Initially, the GC took a more access-claimant-friendly approach. In *CDC*, the GC annulled a Commission decision that had rejected the application of a damages claimant in the hydrogen peroxide cartel for disclosure of the table of contents of the Commission's case file.[50] The GC held that the Commission's broad interpretation of the concept of the purpose of the investigation as including all of the Commission's policy for punishment and prevention of cartels would allow the Commission to exclude without any time limit any document in competition cases from the application scope of the Transparency Regulation and, thus, frustrate the principle of widest possible access to documents.[51]

b. The *EnBW* Judgment

The GC's *EnBW* judgment,[52] where a German power supplier seeking to file an action for damages against members of the gas insulated switchgear cartel appealed a decision of the Commission rejecting its request for access to documents of the relevant cartel case file, seemed to herald a new era of easier access to the Commission's file. The Commission refused access by relying primarily on the Article 4(2) Regulation 1049/2001 exception for protection of commercially sensitive information. The GC annulled the Commission's decision as the Commission failed to perform a concrete and individual examination of the documents requested to establish whether they actually fell within the exception invoked.[53]

More importantly for damages claimants the GC held that there is no presumption that third party access to the Commission's file in cartel cases would undermine the Commission's ability to detect and sanction cartels. Neither could such an assumption be inferred from the existence of specific rules regarding access of third parties to the file in antitrust cases.[54] The shift away from the ECJ's case law was more than obvious, since the ECJ had earlier based the adoption of such a presumption in the fields of State Aid and merger control on the existence of specific rules on access to the file in these procedures.[55] It is likely that the rejection of a general presumption against disclosure in cartel cases was perceived as a way

---

[50] Case T-437/08 *CDC Hydrogen Peroxide Cartel Damage Claims v Commission (CDC)* [2011] ECR II-8251.

[51] Case T-437/08 *CDC* [2011] ECR II-8251, paras 70–71.

[52] Case T-344/08 *EnBW v Commission* (GC, 22 May 2012).

[53] Case T-344/08 *EnBW v Commission*, paras 79, 85, 110–112 and 176.

[54] ibid, para 61.

[55] See with regard to request for access to file of state aid proceedings Case C-139/07P *Commission v Technische Glaswerke Ilmenau (TGI)* [2010] ECR I-5885, paras 54–55, and with respect to access to a merger control case file Case C-477/10P *Commission v Agrofert* (ECJ, 28 June 2012), para 64; Case C-404/10P *Commission v Éditions Odile Jacob* (ECJ, 28 June 2012), para 123.

to foster private enforcement of competition law, or at least to treat it on equal terms with public enforcement of competition rules after the ECJ had refused to give primacy to either of the two in *Pfleiderer*.

The GC also stated that the interest of a company that violated competition law in avoiding damages actions by victims of such infringement does not constitute a commercial interest, despite the fact that actions may cause high costs to be incurred, and does not deserve protection when weighed against the right of every person to claim damages for loss suffered by a breach of competition rules.[56]

c. The *Dutch Bitumen* Judgment

The damages-claimant-friendly approach endorsed by the GC in *EnBW* and *CDC* was, however, recently revised and aligned to the ECJ's approach in merger control and State Aid cases. In the *Dutch Bitumen* judgment,[57] the GC dismissed an appeal of the Netherlands against a Commission decision that had refused the Dutch Government's request for access to confidential parts of the Commission's decision in the *Dutch Bitumen* cartel decision.[58] The GC explicitly recognised that for the purposes of interpretation of the exceptions of the first and third indent of Article 4(2) Regulation 1049/2001 a general presumption applies according to which disclosure of documents drawn up by the Commission during Article 101 TFEU proceedings undermines in principle both the protection of the purpose of investigations and the protection of commercial interests.[59] This judgment contrasted sharply with the GC's earlier *EnBW* precedent.

Regarding the temporal scope of such presumption, the GC clarified that it applies irrespective of whether the proceedings to which the request refers are finally closed or not, as disclosure of commercially sensitive information may harm a company at any time. Further, the prospect of disclosure of such data after closure of proceedings may reduce a company's willingness to cooperate during the proceedings.[60]

ii. *The ECJ's Case Law:* EnBW *and the General Presumption against Disclosure*

The ECJ's ruling in the appeal proceedings concerning the GC's *EnBW* judgment affirmed the GC's approach in the *Dutch Bitumen* judgment and ended the uncertainty on the applicability of the presumption against the disclosure of documents to third parties in cartel cases.[61] In the judgment rendered in February 2014, the ECJ annulled the GC's judgment, which had rejected the existence of a

---

[56] Case T-344/08 *EnBW v Commission*, para 148.
[57] Case T-380/08 *Dutch Bitumen* (GC, 13 September 2013).
[58] Case COMP/38.456—Bitumen Nederland, summary decision [2007] OJ L196/40.
[59] Case T-380/08 *Dutch Bitumen*, para 42.
[60] ibid, para 43.
[61] Case C-365/12P *Commission v EnBW* (ECJ, 27 February 2014).

general presumption with regard to documents from the cartel case file. The ECJ reiterated its settled case law that an EU institution rejecting a request for access to documents can fulfil its obligation to explain how access would specifically and actually undermine one of the interests protected by the exceptions of Article 4(2) and 4(3) Regulation 1049/2001 by relying on general presumptions applying to certain categories of documents.[62] Such presumptions facilitate the handling of global applications for disclosure of documents by the EU institutions.[63]

Contrary to the GC's findings, the ECJ found in *EnBW* that for the purposes of application of the exceptions laid down in the first and third indents of Article 4(2) Regulation 1049/2001 the Commission is entitled to rely on a general presumption that disclosure of documents from the competition file will, in principle, undermine the protection of the commercial interests of the parties to the competition proceedings and of the Commission's investigation purpose as the access system introduced by Regulations 1/2003 and 773/2004 would otherwise be undermined. Generalised access on the basis of the Transparency Regulation would jeopardise the balance sought in these regulations between the obligation of the undertakings to submit commercially sensitive information to the Commission in order to enable it to ascertain whether there was an infringement on the one hand and the guarantee of increased protection of information so provided to the Commission through professional secrecy and business secrecy on the other hand.[64]

This presumption against disclosure allows the Commission to lawfully dispense with a specific and individual examination of each of the documents requested.[65] With respect to the protection of the purpose of investigation exception, the presumption applies at least until the Commission decision becomes final, as an annulment of its decision may force the Commission to resume its investigations.[66] The ECJ discarded the GC's approach, which had found that the Commission's proceedings were closed with its decision notwithstanding pending appeals and that the Commission could therefore no longer invoke that disclosure would undermine its investigation.

The ECJ decided that for the applicability of the presumption it was not relevant whether documents were provided voluntarily by leniency applicants or under compulsion, since it is common ground that disclosure is governed by Regulations 1/2003 and 773/2004.[67]

The ECJ emphasised that the general presumption against disclosure of documents is a rebuttable one. The access applicant has to establish either that a specific document, whose disclosure it seeks, does not fall under the presumption, or

---

[62]   Case C-365/12P *Commission v EnBW*, paras 64–65.
[63]   ibid, para 68.
[64]   ibid, para 90.
[65]   Case C-365/12P *Commission v EnBW*, para 93.
[66]   Case C-365/12P *Commission v EnBW*, para 99.
[67]   Case C-365/12P *Commission v EnBW*, para 97.

that there is an overriding public interest in disclosure by virtue of Article 4(2) Regulation 1049/2001.[68] This does not mean, however, that the Commission has to individually examine each document requested, as such a requirement would render the general presumption devoid of purpose.[69] Further, general considerations such as the fostering of private enforcement of competition rules through a damages action do not constitute an interest overriding the need to protect confidentiality because it is unlikely that the damages action will need to be based on all evidence in the file relating to that proceeding.[70] A damages claimant seeking access to documents from the competition authority's file rather has to establish that access is essential for its case, so that the Commission can weigh on a case-by-case basis the interests for and against disclosure. According to the ECJ, it is only when such information would have enabled it to obtain the evidence needed to establish its claim for damages as it has no other way of obtaining the information that it can constitute an overriding public interest.[71]

This is the point where the ECJ's case law on the Transparency Regulation is linked to the *Donau Chemie* and *Pfleiderer* case law that concerns third party requests for access to documents in the file of an NCA (see below under C).

Such a link is twofold: first, the ECJ refers to the Commission's obligation to weigh the interests for and against disclosure on a case-by-case basis, as it did in *Donau Chemie* and *Pfleiderer* with respect to the national courts' obligation to weigh the interests in the case of requests for access to the NCA's case file.[72] Second, the ECJ emphasises in *EnBW*, exactly as it did in *Donau Chemie*,[73] that access to the authority's case file may in some cases be the only way for a damages claimant to obtain the evidence necessary for the substantiation of its claim. The ECJ implies that in such circumstances the interest of a third party seeking access to the file for the substantiation of a damages claim could prevail over the protection of confidentiality.

While the ECJ made the existence of an overriding public interest in disclosure of documents contingent upon the lack of any other possibility for the damages claimant to get the evidence necessary for bringing an action for damages, the EFTA Court at least at first sight seems to have reached a more far-reaching conclusion in *Schenker*.

iii. The EFTA Court's Case Law: Schenker *and Private Enforcement as Overriding Public Interest*

In *Schenker*, the EFTA Court had to review an ESA decision that had rejected Schenker Privpak AB, Schenker Privpak AS and Schenker North AB's (together

---

[68] Case C-365/12P *Commission v EnBW*, para 100.
[69] ibid, para 101.
[70] ibid, paras 104–105.
[71] ibid, para 107, 132.
[72] Case C-536/11 *Bundeswettbewerbsbehörde v Donau Chemie* (ECJ, 6 June 2013), para 30; Case C-360/09 *Pfleiderer v Bundeskartellamt* [2011] ECR I-5161.
[73] Case C-536/11 *Donau Chemie*, paras 32, 39 and 44.

'Schenker') request on the basis of the RAD for access to certain documents of the ESA file in Case No 34250 *Norway Post/Privpak*. The case goes back to a fine imposed in July 2010 by ESA against Norway Post, the state-owned postal company of Norway, for abuse of its dominant position in the business-to-consumer parcel market with over-the-counter delivery, where Schenker was also active. Schenker pursued a follow-on damages claim against Norway Post for loss allegedly suffered by Norway Post's breach of Article 54 EEA. For that purpose it formally requested access to the case file. ESA, however, only granted partial access. It refused to disclose 350 documents that were seized during an inspection at Norway Post's premises in June 2004 by relying on the need for protection of the privacy and integrity of private individuals involved in the practices of Norway Post and on the need for protection of Norway Post's commercial interests. Further, ESA found that there was no overriding public interest in disclosure of these documents.[74] In October 2011, Schenker filed an appeal with the EFTA Court seeking annulment of the ESA decision.

The EFTA Court stressed the importance of RAD as part of the principles of transparency and good administration common to the democratic traditions of the EEA/EFTA States.[75] It then placed emphasis on the indispensability of a homogeneous interpretation of the RAD and Regulation 1049/2001.[76] After clarifying that access to documents is the rule and refusal to disclose the exception,[77] the EFTA Court held that ESA is in general entitled to base its decisions refusing access to documents on general presumptions that apply to certain categories of documents.[78]

It found that certain limits apply to the use of such general presumptions. The general presumption regarding the purpose of inspections and investigations does not apply when ESA's decision has become final, where the decision has not been appealed or where the Court has dismissed an appeal in a situation where the relevant information has not been obtained by way of voluntary submission from a leniency applicant.[79] The Court reasoned that access to documents after closure of proceedings cannot undermine the purpose of investigations and inspections, as the authority can always ensure compliance with the inspection by imposing fines in a situation.[80] The EFTA Court was not required to consider whether the presumption should apply after closure of the proceedings because the effectiveness of public enforcement would be undermined by discouraging leniency applications. It is thus clear that documents obtained from leniency applicants will retain protection so as to maintain the efficacy of the public enforcement of competition law.

The EFTA Court added that, as a general presumption shifts the burden of proof to the applicant, ESA has to provide the applicant with sufficient and

---

[74]   Case E-14/11 *Schenker*, para 44.
[75]   ibid, para 118.
[76]   ibid, para 121.
[77]   ibid, para 125.
[78]   ibid, para 130.
[79]   Case E-14/11 *Schenker*, paras 133, 224.
[80]   Case E-14/11 *Schenker*, para 222.

adequate information, such as a detailed index of the documents in the file, to allow him a rebuttal of the presumption.[81] It found that certain limitations to the use of general presumptions are justified by the specific policy consider-ations arising in requests for access to documents in follow-on antitrust damages actions before national courts. Private damages actions can contribute to main-taining effective competition in the EEA. Contrary to the views of ESA and the Commission, a damages claimant not only pursues its private interest in recoup-ing its loss but also contributes to a more effective competition and, hence, to the public interest.[82] The EFTA Court relied in this context on the ECJ's findings in *Courage*: 'actions for damages before the national courts can make a significant contribution to the maintenance of effective competition in the Community.'[83]

Even in the situation that a general presumption against disclosure of docu-ments from the antitrust case file applies, a competition authority dealing with a request for access to documents has to examine on its own motion and appropri-ately explain whether there is any overriding public interest justifying disclosure.[84] The EFTA Court found that transparency may insofar be considered an overrid-ing public interest in that it allows the public to ensure that ESA acts in accor-dance with the principle of good administration.[85] Moreover, private enforcement of competition law may also constitute an overriding public interest as it can significantly contribute to the maintenance of effective competition in the EEA.[86] The EFTA Court found that ESA erred by failing to consider whether private enforcement and transparency could constitute overriding public interests.

iv. Differences between the EnBW and the Schenker Judgments

While the EFTA Court confirmed before the ECJ that a presumption against dis-closure exists in cartel cases, it concluded at the same time that it cannot apply after final closure of the proceedings at least in the absence of leniency documents in the file. In contrast the ECJ left this question open and did not comment on whether the presumption might under certain circumstances apply also after the Commission's decision has become finally binding, but only confirmed that in the light of the possible resumption of the investigation by the Commission and reuse of evidence in the file the presumption continues to apply after the Commission has adopted its decision.

The EFTA Court also took a more private-plaintiff-friendly approach than the ECJ by finding that third parties at least need to get an index of the docu-ments in the file in order to be able to rebut the presumption. By recognising that

---

[81] Case E-14/11 *Schenker*, para 134.
[82] ibid, para 132; see also W Frenz, 'Dokumentenzugang vs Kronzeugenregelung' (2013) *Europäische Zeitschrift für Wirtschaftsrecht* 778, 780.
[83] Case C-453/99 *Courage v Crehan* [2001] ECR I-6297, para 27.
[84] Case E-14/11 *Schenker*, para 239.
[85] Case E-14/11 *Schenker*, para 240.
[86] Case E-14/11 *Schenker*, para 241.

private enforcement may constitute an overriding public interest that can limit the application of the general presumption it sounds at least at first sight as if the EFTA Court puts greater emphasis on private enforcement than the ECJ. In contrast the ECJ explicitly stated that general considerations such as boosting private enforcement of competition law do not constitute as such a public interest overriding the need to protect confidentiality and made the existence of such interest contingent upon the lack of any other possibility for the damages claimant to get the evidence necessary for bringing an action for damages.[87] While the EFTA Court did not explicitly make the assumption of an overriding public interest in disclosure conditional upon the non-existence of another opportunity to get the necessary evidence it should be noted that the EFTA Court only criticised ESA for not having considered private enforcement as possible overriding public interest in its decision that rejected access to documents. This does not mean that third parties will automatically be able to claim access to documents, but their legal interest in obtaining the information and possible alternative ways to get access to it should form part of the reasoned decision of the authority whether an overriding public interest in disclosure exists or not. The discrepancy between the EFTA Court's and the ECJ's judgment may therefore in practice be less significant than it seems at first sight.

The ECJ also found in *EnBW* that for the applicability of the presumption it does not matter whether documents have been provided voluntarily by leniency applicants, since the disclosure of such documents regardless of whether they were provided voluntarily or under compulsion is in any event strictly governed by the specific regime of Regulations 1/2003 and 773/2004. It therefore did not engage in any discussion whether the potential disclosure of leniency documents even after the final closure of proceedings risks undermining public enforcement. In contrast the EFTA Court put great emphasis in its reasoning in *Schenker* on the fact that ESA had not relied on leniency documents in the proceedings and could therefore not argue a risk of undermining its investigation after ESA's final decision. Nevertheless, it made clear that leniency documents will be shielded from disclosure after the cartel proceedings are closed in order to secure the effectiveness of public enforcement.[88]

C. Third Party Access to Documents on the Basis of National Law

While the *EnBW* case dealt with third party access to the Commission's file in competition cases, a parallel stream of ECJ case law deals with the parallel situation at national level.

---

[87] Case C-365/12P *Commission v EnBW*, paras 104–105.
[88] Case E-14/11 *Schenker*, paras 131–133 and 224.

i. The ECJ Judgment in Pfleiderer

The *Pfleiderer* case was the first time the ECJ dealt with a third party's claim for disclosure of leniency documents from a NCA's case file. Pfleiderer was a customer of decorative paper manufacturers that were fined in January 2008 by the German Federal Cartel Office (FCO) for operating a price-fixing cartel. In order to prepare a follow-on action for damages, Pfleiderer requested on the basis of German criminal procedure rules access to the whole content of the FCO's decorative paper cartel case file. The FCO granted access to non-confidential versions of documents other than internal documents and documents voluntarily submitted by the cartel participants under the leniency cooperation programme. Pfleiderer appealed the FCO's partial rejection decision to the Bonn District Court, which stayed the proceedings and requested a preliminary ruling from the ECJ on whether exclusion of third parties from access to leniency documents was compatible with EU law.

The ECJ held that in the absence of EU rules it was for the Member States to establish and apply rules on the right of access to leniency documents.[89] Such rules should, however, not jeopardise the effective application of EU law and, in particular, of Articles 101 and 102 TFEU, or render it impossible or excessively difficult.[90] Effective application of EU competition rules encompasses the leniency programme, which is a very useful investigative tool, and the right to claim damages from a cartelist. Therefore, any national rule on disclosure of leniency documents should take into account and balance two conflicting interests: the interest of a competition authority in preserving the attractiveness of leniency programmes (public enforcement) and the interest of any person seeking damages for loss suffered as a result of a competition law infringement in getting access to evidence necessary for bringing a claim (private enforcement). This weighing exercise has to be performed by national courts on a case-by-case basis while considering all the relevant circumstances of a case.[91]

ii. The ECJ Judgment in Donau Chemie

The ECJ's judgment in *Donau Chemie*[92] confirmed and elaborated on the *Pfleiderer* ruling. The case goes back to a fine imposed in 2010 by the Vienna Court of Appeals—sitting as a Cartel Court—on wholesale distributors of printing chemicals for participation in a cartel. Verband Druck & Medientechnik, a customer of the cartelists intending to assess its loss and prepare an action for damages, requested access to the case file on the basis of a provision of the Austrian Law on Cartels then in force stating that third parties may get access to

---

[89] Case C-360/09 *Pfleiderer*, para 23.
[90] Case C-360/09 *Pfleiderer*, para 24.
[91] Case C-360/09 *Pfleiderer*, paras 30–31.
[92] Case C-536/11 *Donau Chemie*.

the Cartel Court's file only with the consent of the parties. The Austrian Cartel Court referred to the ECJ the question whether the Austrian statutory provision making disclosure dependent on the parties' consent was compatible with EU law and, in particular, with the ECJ's findings in *Pfleiderer*.

The ECJ reiterated that private enforcement increases the effectiveness of EU competition law.[93] Member States have to establish rules that safeguard rights of victims of competition law infringements and that do not affect effective application of Articles 101 and 102 TFEU.[94] Regarding third party access to documents of the authority's file, the ECJ clarified by reference to *Pfleiderer* that the judge applying the relevant national disclosure rules has to weigh the interest of the applicant in obtaining access to the documents in order to prepare a damages action, in particular in light of other possibilities the applicant may have to get to the evidence required, against the actual harmful consequences that granting of access may have on public interests or legitimate interests of the parties.[95]

Any rigid rule may undermine the effectiveness of Article 101 TFEU.[96] A rule precluding third party access to documents from the antitrust case file may render the right to compensation devoid of any meaning, especially in cases where a victim has no other way to obtain the evidence necessary to bring a damages claim. On the other side, a rule providing for generalised access may adversely affect public enforcement of competition law, as it may deter cartel participants from voluntarily coming forward with information on infringements, and violate other EU rights, such as the right to protection of business secrets and the right to protection of personal data.[97]

The ECJ held further that national rules on third party access to the NCA's file should not be drafted in a way barring the courts from the case-by-case balancing exercise.[98] Public policy considerations, such as the need to maintain effectiveness of the leniency tool, may justify refusal to disclose certain documents contained in the file. Any blanket refusal, however, violates the principle of effectiveness of EU law.[99] According to the ECJ, simply stating that access to the documents contained in a competition authority's file may undermine the effectiveness of a leniency programme does not justify, in view of the private enforcement's importance for maintenance of effective competition in the EU, a refusal to grant access to the file content. A competition authority rather has to demonstrate that there is a risk that a particular document may specifically and actually undermine the effectiveness of the leniency programme.[100] On the basis of these considerations, the ECJ concluded that the Austrian rule on access violated EU law, since, by making

---

[93] Case C-536/11 *Donau Chemie*, para 23.
[94] ibid, paras 24–27.
[95] ibid, paras 44, 45, 30 and 34.
[96] ibid, paras 30–31.
[97] Case C-536/11 *Donau Chemie*, paras 32–33.
[98] Case C-536/11 *Donau Chemie*, para 35.
[99] Case C-536/11 *Donau Chemie*, paras 42–43.
[100] Case C-536/11 *Donau Chemie*, paras 46–48.

disclosure contingent upon the parties' consent, it did not leave national courts any possibility of balancing the clashing interests.[101]

Although the *Donau Chemie* ruling further developed and clarified the ECJ's findings in *Pfleiderer*, both decisions have contributed to an increased legal uncertainty regarding the conditions of third party access to the case file of a competition authority, because they advocate a case-by-case assessment in order to strike the right balance between the different interests at stake speaking for and against disclosure. However, at the same time both rulings have to be regarded as the result of the ECJ's judicial self-restraint in a field where the EU legislator had not established any rules until the adoption of the Antitrust Damages Directive (see IV, below).[102]

IV. THE DIRECTIVE ON ANTITRUST DAMAGES AND THE CASE LAW ON THIRD PARTY ACCESS TO DOCUMENTS

A. The Commission's Proposal

On 11 June 2013, only a few days after the delivery of the preliminary ruling in *Donau Chemie*, the Commission presented its Draft Antitrust Damages Directive.[103] The Antitrust Damages Directive codifies the ECJ's premise that victims of competition law infringements not only have a right to full compensation but also that they must have the possibility to effectively claim compensation.[104] "Effectively" means in particular that potential claimants have the possibility to obtain disclosure of evidence, usually held either by the cartelists or by third parties, such as competition authorities. Disclosability is a very important element in ensuring effectiveness of private enforcement, as antitrust litigation is characterised by information asymmetry.[105]

The Antitrust Damages Directive aims to deal with this information asymmetry by stipulating in Article 5(1) that 'Member States shall ensure that in proceedings relating to an action for damages in the Union upon request of a claimant who has presented a reasoned justification containing reasonably available facts and evidence sufficient to support the plausibility of its claim for damages, national courts are able to order the defendant or a third party to disclose relevant evidence

---

[101] Case C-536/11 *Donau Chemie*, para 49.

[102] See in particular the wording of para 25 in *Donau Chemie*: 'In the absence of EU rules governing the matter, it is for the domestic legal system of each Member State to lay down the detailed procedural rules governing actions for safeguarding rights which individuals derive from EU law.'

[103] COM(2013) 404.

[104] Joined Cases C-295/04 to C-298/04 *Vincenzo Manfredi v Lloyd Adriatico Assicurazioni SpA* [2006] ECR I-6641, paras 100 and 60; Case C-453/99 *Courage v Crehan* [2001] ECR I-6314, para 27. See with respect to the 'codification' A Howard, 'The Draft Directive on Competition Law Damages— What Does it Mean for Infringers and Victims?' (2014) *European Competition Law Review* 51, 52.

[105] See Recitals 13 and 14 of the Antitrust Damages Directive in the version adopted by the EP on 17 April 2014.

which lies in their control … Member States shall ensure that courts are also able to order the claimant or a third party to disclose evidence upon the request of the defendant.'[106]

The Antitrust Damages Directive also tries to balance out the inherent tension between public and private enforcement of EU competition law.[107] It incorporates, with slight amendments, the differentiated disclosure model suggested by Advocate General Mazak in *Pfleiderer*. Advocate General Mazak suggested that third party access to voluntary self-incriminating statements made by a leniency applicant should be in principle precluded.[108] Access should, however, be granted to pre-existing documents that were not drafted for a competition authority but were merely submitted by a leniency applicant.[109]

Regarding disclosure of evidence from the file of a competition authority, Article 6(1) of the Antitrust Damages Directive in the version proposed by the Commission provided for a per se exclusion of leniency corporate statements and settlement submissions from disclosure ('black-listed documents'); Article 6(2) stipulated that information prepared by a natural or legal person specifically for the proceedings of a competition authority or information drawn up by a competition authority during the proceedings shall be disclosable only after closure of the authority's proceedings ('grey-listed documents'). All other evidence included in the authority's file, such as pre-existing documents, shall be disclosable at any time without restrictions (Article 6(3)) ('white-listed documents').

B. The Final Text Adopted by the European Parliament

The final text of the Antitrust Damages Directive adopted by the EP on 17 April 2014,[110] which basically reflects the compromise text adopted after relatively short negotiations between the Commission, the European Parliament and the Council on 18 March 2014, did not materially change this differentiated disclosure approach on the basis of black-, grey- and white-listed documents. Disclosure of leniency corporate statements and settlement submissions is still excluded (Article 6(6)). The exception applies also to literal quotations from a leniency statement or a settlement submission.[111]

---

[106] Art 5(1) of the Antitrust Damages Directive in the Compromise Text Version published by the Council of the EU on 24 March 2014: Note 8088/14.

[107] See also C Kersting, 'Removing the tension between public and private enforcement: disclosure and privileges for successful leniency applicants' (2014) *Journal of European Competition Law and Practice* 2, 3.

[108] Case C-360/09 *Pfleiderer v Bundeskartellamt* [2011] ECR I-5163, Opinion of AG Mazak, para 46.

[109] Case C-360/09 *Pfleiderer v Bundeskartellamt* [2011] ECR I-5163, Opinion of AG Mazak, para 47.

[110] See EP, Texts adopted at the sitting of Thursday 17 April 2014, P7_TA-PROV(2014)04-17—PE 531.387, 96ff. The text adopted will now be ratified by the Council of Ministers of the EU, according to latest news in September 2014. Following ratification, Member States will have two years and 20 days to transpose the directive into their national law.

[111] Recital 24 of the Antitrust Damages Directive in the version adopted by the EP on 17 April 2014.

However, an access applicant can request that a national court verifies that the documents excluded from disclosure are indeed leniency statements and/or settlement submissions. Notwithstanding this review possibility, a national judge is not entitled to disclose the transmitted documents to the parties of the national proceedings or to third parties. Should the judge find that only parts of the requested documents are leniency statements or settlement submissions, he can order disclosure of the parts not covered by the exception (Article 6(7) and (8)).

The grey-listed documents were also extended to cover—apart from documents drafted from a company especially for the proceedings, such as answers to requests for information, and evidence gathered by an authority during the investigation—withdrawn settlement submissions.[112] The latter amendment is unfortunate because it risks to discourage companies from engaging in settlement discussions.

C. Compatibility of the Antitrust Damages Directive with EU Primary Law

The question arises whether the disclosure approach adopted by the Commission in the Antitrust Damages Directive and endorsed by the EP in April 2014, in particular the per se rule excluding leniency statements and settlement submissions from disclosure at any time, is in line with the principle of effectiveness of EU law and the right of everyone to claim damages for loss suffered from a cartel. It has been argued that, in view of the ECJ's finding in *Donau Chemie* that 'any rule that is rigid, either by providing for absolute refusal to grant access to the documents in question or for granting access to those documents as matter of course, is liable to undermine the effective application of, inter alia, Article 101 TFEU and the rights that provision confers on individuals',[113] the solution adopted in Article 6 of the Antitrust Damages Directive with respect to leniency statements and settlement submissions violates the primary EU law principle of effectiveness, as it introduces a blanket ban on disclosure of leniency statements and settlement submissions.[114]

However, Article 6(6) of the Antitrust Damages Directive clashes only at first sight with EU primary law.[115] The ECJ refers both in *Donau Chemie* and *Pfleiderer* to the absence of EU rules on third party access to leniency documents.[116]

---

[112] Art 6(5) of the Antitrust Damages Directive in the version adopted by the EP on 17 April 2014.

[113] Case C-536/11 *Donau Chemie*, para 31.

[114] See, eg, C Kersting, 'Removing the tension between public and private enforcement: disclosure and privileges for successful leniency applicants' (2014) *Journal of European Competition Law and Practice* 2, 3; T Kapp, 'Grundsatz der Einzelabwägung sticht Gesetzgebungskompetenz aus' (2013) *Betriebsberater* 1556.

[115] See also L Fiedler and A Huttenlauch, 'Der Schutz von Kronzeugen- und Settlementerklärungen vor der Einsichtnahme durch Dritte nach dem Richtlinien-Vorschlag der Kommission' (2013) *Neue Zeitschrift für Kartellrecht* 350, 354.

[116] Case C-536/11 *Donau Chemie*, para 25; Case C-360/09 *Pfleiderer*, para 23.

Therefore it may be reasonably assumed that it is for the EU legislature to perform the balancing exercise between the interest in disclosure and the interest in confidentiality protection by means of a general abstract provision. Legislative freedom finds its limits where the solution adopted violates EU primary law. In the case of the Antitrust Damages Directive, this limit is everyone's right to claim damages for loss suffered from a competition law infringement, which derives directly from the need to ensure the *effet utile* of Article 101 TFEU. It follows that any legislative solution with regard to third party access to leniency and settlement documents adopted on the basis of the legislator's assessment prerogative should not render claiming damages excessively difficult or even impossible.[117] Article 6(6) of the Antitrust Damages Directive fully respects that premise.

Contrary to the Austrian statutory provision examined in *Donau Chemie*, which did not stipulate any balancing of interests by the legislator, but shifted the decision-making authority to the authors of the documents, and was found to contravene EU primary law, the Antitrust Damages Directive provides for a general abstract weighing of interests by the EU legislator. The fact that the balancing is in favour of non-disclosure of leniency statements and settlement submissions is a clear expression of the legislator's assessment prerogative. The Antitrust Damages Directive does not render bringing an antitrust damages action more cumbersome but rather facilitates conditions for private antitrust damages litigation—not least through the harmonisation of national procedural rules and the provision for disclosability of substantial evidence after the closure of an authority's proceedings and for access to pre-existing evidence at any time.

Further, the general abstract balancing in favour of protection of confidentiality of leniency statements and settlement submissions and the harmonisation achieved throughout the EU enhance the effectiveness of the right to full compensation for harm suffered from a cartel, as they reduce the uncertainty inherent in the case-by-case assessment of the national judge required by the ECJ. Moreover, the existence of uniform rules on disclosure relieves national courts from the need to engage in a detailed and cumbersome assessment of every document requested, and enhances procedural economy, which in turn benefits damages claimants.

Finally, the importance of third party access to leniency and settlement documents seems to be slightly overrated. Leniency statements and settlement submission are usually fact-intensive and do not contain the kind of information that damages claimants need in order to establish crucial factors for the success of their claims, such as the existence and quantification of damage[118] or the causal link between infringement and damage suffered.[119] It is more probable that damages claimants

---

[117] See C Palzer, 'Unvereinbarkeit der österreichischen Regelung zur Akteneinsicht Kartellgeschädigter mit EU-Recht' (2013) *Neue Zeitschrift für Kartellrecht* 324, 326.

[118] See with respect to the difficulties in quantification of damages A Howard, 'The Draft Directive on Competition Law Damages—What Does it Mean for Infringers and Victims?' (2014) *European Competition Law Review* 51, 53.

[119] See L Idot and F Zivy, 'L'Accès au Dossier des Autorités de Concurrence dans le Cadre des Actions Privées: État des Lieux Deux Ans après l'arrêt Pfleiderer' (2013) *Concurrences* 34, 53; L Fiedler and

find the evidence required in documents other than leniency statements and settlement submissions that are disclosable. Moreover, Article 9 of the Antitrust Damages Directive further alleviates the evidentiary burden of damages claimants by declaring final decisions of a competition authority or a court finding an antitrust infringement as *prima facie* evidence for the establishment of that infringement.

V. CONCLUSIONS

The EU Courts, the EFTA Court in their case law and the Commission in its Antitrust Damages Directive have performed a highly delicate balancing act between public and private enforcement of competition law in the field of third party access to documents from a competition authority's file. Public and private enforcement are at the same time complementary and inversely correlated. They both contribute to effective competition within the EEA, but promoting one of them may have adverse effects on the other.[120] However, despite the fact that there is no *de iure* hierarchy between the two enforcement tools, there is a factual primacy of public enforcement owed to the following reasons: i) public enforcement seems to be better placed to serve the policy goals of competition law, as it can rely on state power and has a lower potential of abuse,[121] and ii) in light of the procedural systems in most Member States, private enforcement is under-developed in Europe and depends highly on public enforcement (almost no stand-alone actions, relatively few follow-on actions).[122] Even though the ECJ does not explicitly acknowledge the supremacy of public enforcement it has strengthened the Commission's position in its recent *EnBW* precedent. Its finding of a general presumption against disclosure in antitrust cases alleviates the burden for the Commission to deal with third party access to document requests that put a strain on its resources and raises the bar for damages claimants seeking access to documents on the basis of the Transparency Regulation because they have to refute the presumption by invoking a specific need for certain documents to substantiate their damage claim.[123]

A Huttenlauch, 'Der Schutz von Kronzeugen- und Settlementerklärungen vor der Einsichtnahme durch Dritte nach dem Richtlinien-Vorschlag der Kommission' (2013) *Neue Zeitschrift für Kartellrecht* 350, 353.

[120] C Nowak, 'Richtlinienvorschlag der Europäischen Kommission zur Stärkung der privaten Kartellrechtsdurchsetzung sowie zur Optimierung der Interaktion zwischen behördlicher und privater Durchsetzung des EU-Kartellrechts' (2013) *Zeitschrift für Vertriebsrecht* 376, 377.

[121] See in this regard W Möschel, 'Should private enforcement of competition law be strengthened' (2013) *Global Competition Litigation Review* 1, 3f; E Camilleri, 'A decade of EU antitrust private enforcement: chronicle of a failure foretold?' (2013) *European Competition Law Review* 531, 536f.

[122] Case C-360/09 *Pfleiderer v Bundeskartellamt* [2011] ECR I-5163, Opinion of AG Mazak, para 40; W Möschel, 'Should private enforcement of competition law be strengthened?' (2013) *Global Competition Litigation Review* 1.

[123] See also M Lavedan, 'Netherlands v Commission: General Court Confirms Refusal to Access to the Full Version of the Bitumen Cartel Decision' (2014) *Journal of European Competition Law and Practice* 80, 81.

Whether the EFTA Court's approach is more plaintiff-friendly[124] than the ECJ's remains to be seen. What can be said today is that both the ECJ's and EFTA Court's approaches are compatible with one another. The differences for the reader are merely superficial. The ECJ has left the door open to take a plaintiff-friendly approach in future regarding what it considers 'necessary'. So far it is a matter of whether one looks at the solutions as either half full or half empty.

Risking a forecast, one may assume that the Antitrust Damages Directive, if correctly implemented, increases legal certainty for leniency applicants and damages claimants, and will therefore hopefully contribute to a reduction of access to documents-related litigation in the EU and EEA. It is less clear at this stage how significantly it will contribute to a more effective, and hence increased, private enforcement of competition law.[125]

---

[124] G Goddin, 'Access to Documents in Competition Files: Where do we Stand, Two Years after TGI?' (2013) *Journal of European Competition Law and Practice* 112, 116.

[125] See also S Wisking, K Dietzel and M Herron, 'European Commission Finally Publishes Measures to Facilitate Competition Law Private Actions in the European Union' (2014) *European Competition Law Review* 185, 193.

33

To Tax or Not to Tax: Reflections on the Case Law of the EFTA Court

ALEXANDER RUST

IN ITS 20 years of existence, the EFTA Court has only had to opine in four cases on the conformity of national tax rules with the fundamental freedoms of the EEA Agreement.[1] However, these four tax cases, *Fokus Bank*,[2] *Seabrokers*,[3] *Arcade Drilling*[4] and *EFTA Surveillance Authority v Iceland*[5] stand out. They have influenced the jurisprudence of the Court of Justice and national courts alike. The Advocates General of the Court of Justice have referred to these decisions on numerous occasions.[6] In this chapter, I will analyse the four tax

---

[1] In the meantime, a fifth seminal decision in the area of taxation, Joined Cases E-3/13 and E-20/13 *Olsen and Others* was published on 9 July 2014, http://www.eftacourt.int/uploads/tx_nvcases/3_13_20_13_Judgment_EN.pdf (last visited 26 August 2014).

[2] EFTA Court of 23 November 2004, Case E-1/04 *Fokus Bank ASA* [2004] EFTA Ct Rep 11; see the comments by A Cordewener, 'Körperschaftsteueranrechnung für Gebietsfremde versus Kapitalverkehrsfreiheit—Zum Gutachten des EFTA-Gerichtshofs in Sachen Fokus Bank ASA' (2005) *Finanzrundschau* 345; A Bullen, 'Norwegian Withholding Tax Contrary to Rules on Free Movement of Capital in EEA Agreement' (2005) 45 *European Taxation* 75; A Bullen, 'The Norwegian Response to the EFTA Court Judgment in the Fokus Bank Case' (2007) 47 *European Taxation* 273.

[3] EFTA Court of 7 May 2008, Case E-7/07 *Seabrokers AS* [2008] EFTA Ct Rep 172; see the comments by B Arnold, 'Tax Treaty News' (2008) 62 *Bulletin for International Taxation* 454; P Gruner, 'EFTA Court rules on Norwegian Tax Credit' (2008) 36 *Intertax* 412.

[4] EFTA Court of 3 October 2012, Case E-15/11 *Arcade Drilling AS* [2012] EFTA Ct Rep 676; see the comments by D Dürrschmidt and F Wobst, 'Anmerkung' (2013) *Internationales Steuerrecht* 202.

[5] EFTA Court of 2 December 2013, Case E-14/13 *EFTA Surveillance Authority v Iceland* nyp.

[6] Regarding the function of the opinions of Advocates General as an important gateway for EFTA Court case law into the ECJ's jurisprudence see C Baudenbacher, 'The EFTA Court, the ECJ, and the Latter's Advocates General—a Tale of Judicial Dialogue' in A Arnull et al (eds), *Continuity and Change in EU Law—Essays in Honour of Sir Francis Jacobs* (2008) 90, 98; C Baudenbacher, 'The EFTA Court's Relationship with the Advocates General of the European Court of Justice' in *Mélanges en l'honneur de Paolo Mengozzi* (2013) 341; Opinion of Advocate General Trstenjak of 5 July 2012, Case C-300/10 *Vítor Hugo Marques Almeida* fn 25. For the *Fokus Bank* judgment see Opinion of Advocate General Geelhoed of 23 February 2006, Case C-374/04 *ACT Group Litigation* fn 83; Opinion of Advocate General Geelhoed of 27 April 2006, Case C-170/05 *Denkavit International* fn 28; Opinion of Advocate General Mengozzi of 7 June 2007, Case C-379/05 *Amurta* fn 23; CJEU of 11 June 2009, Case C-521/07 *Commission v Netherlands* [2009] ECR I-4873 para 15; CJEU of 3 June 2010, Case C-487/08 *Commission v Spain* [2010] ECR I-4843 paras 17, 29, 32; Opinion of Advocate General Jääskinen of 29 April 2010, Case C-72/09 *Établissement Rimbaud* fn 39; Opinion of Advocate General Trstenjak

judgments, illustrate their innovative approaches and compare their results and their reasoning with those of similar judgments of the Court of Justice.

I. FOKUS BANK

A. Facts of the Case (Simplified)

Fokus Bank, a joint stock company resident in Norway, made a dividend distribution to its shareholders. Among those shareholders were a company resident in Germany and a company resident in the United Kingdom. While shareholders resident in Norway did not have to pay any taxes on the dividend distribution—as they benefited from an indirect credit equal to their tax liability on the dividends—non-resident taxpayers were subject to a withholding tax on the dividends at a rate of 15 per cent. The indirect credit was denied to non-resident shareholders. The tax treaties concluded between Norway and Germany, as well as between Norway and the United Kingdom, preserved the taxation in Norway and obliged the respective residence state to grant a credit for the taxes levied in Norway. The EFTA Court was asked whether the denial of the indirect credit to the non-resident shareholders violated the EEA Agreement.

B. Reasoning of the EFTA Court

The EFTA Court held that the distribution of dividends from a Norwegian company to a German or a UK company was protected by the free movement of capital enshrined in Article 40 EEA Agreement.[7] As denying an indirect credit to non-resident shareholders deterred investors from buying shares in Norwegian companies and impeded these companies from raising capital outside Norway, the denial constituted a restriction of Article 40 EEA. The Court also decided that, with regard to the receipt of dividends, non-resident and resident shareholders were in a comparable situation. The Norwegian tax law had the purpose of avoiding economic double taxation. Both resident and non-resident shareholders suffered from economic double taxation. Therefore, the purpose of the legislation to avoid economic double taxation would not in any way be affected by extending the indirect credit to non-resident taxpayers. The Court then turned to the interesting question of whether the existence of a double tax treaty could justify the denial of the indirect credit. In the tax treaties the Contracting State had agreed

---

of 2 June 2010, Case C-81/09 *Idryma Tipou* fn 100. For the *Seabrokers* judgment see Opinion of Advocate General Trstenjak of 2 June 2010, Case C-81/09 *Idryma Tipou* fn 53. For the *Arcade Drilling* judgment see Opinion of Advocate General Paolo Mengozzi of 1 April 2014, Case C-83/13 *Svenska Transportarbetareförbundet, Facket för Service och Kommunikation* fn 53.

[7] EFTA Court of 23 November 2004, Case E-1/04 *Fokus Bank ASA* [2004] EFTA Ct Rep 11 para 22ff.

that the source state Norway could levy a tax of 15 per cent on the dividends while the residence states Germany and the United Kingdom obliged themselves to grant a credit for the taxes paid in Norway. The Norwegian tax administration had argued that forcing Norway to effectively exempt the dividends in the hands of the German and UK shareholders would relieve Germany and the United Kingdom from deducting Norwegian taxes from their own tax liability and, therefore, shift the taxation right from the source state to the residence state. This would run counter to the agreed solution in the tax treaties and negate a principle of international taxation according to which it is the task of the residence state to avoid economic double taxation. The Court rejected this argument stating that the free movement of capital prevailed over tax treaties. Countries were not allowed to derogate from the rights conferred by the EEA Agreement by concluding a tax treaty.[8] Finally, the tax administration advanced the argument that the shareholders were not adversely affected by the denial of the indirect credit. As the Norwegian taxes were credited in the residence state of the shareholders, their overall tax burden remained constant. The tax liability in both countries contemplated together was not higher if Norway levied a dividend tax as this dividend tax reduced the tax liability in the residence state accordingly. At the end of the day, the dividend tax was neutralised by the credit in the residence state. For the taxpayer, it should not matter whether he paid the tax to the treasury of the source state or to the treasury of the residence state. The EFTA Court rejected this neutralisation argument as well. It held that a more disadvantageous tax treatment in one state could not be offset by a more favourable tax treatment in the other state. Each country was obliged to comply with the EEA Agreement. It was not possible to transfer this obligation in a tax treaty to the residence state even if the residence state obligated itself in the treaty to make good for the disadvantages caused by the taxation in the source state. The Court further elaborated that the principle of legal certainty would be infringed if in each case the obligation by the source state to grant an indirect credit would depend on whether or not the residence state taxed the dividends and granted a credit for the taxes levied in the source state.[9] As a result, the Court concluded that it was irrelevant whether the residence state effectively granted a credit. Norway violated the free movement of capital by not granting an indirect tax credit to the shareholders resident in Germany and in the United Kingdom.

C. Comparison with the Jurisprudence of the Court of Justice

With regard to two aspects, the EFTA Court had to play a pioneer role. Neither the question whether resident and non-resident shareholders are in a comparable

---

[8] EFTA Court of 23 November 2004, Case E-1/04 *Fokus Bank ASA* [2004] EFTA Ct Rep 11 para 31.
[9] EFTA Court of 23 November 2004, Case E-1/04 *Fokus Bank ASA* [2004] EFTA Ct Rep 11 para 37.

situation, nor the question whether a credit in the residence state of the share-holder can neutralise discrimination, had been decided by the CJEU before the *Fokus Bank* judgment. The findings of the EFTA Court that non-resident and resident shareholders are in a comparable situation (once they are both subject to taxation on the dividends) and that the residence state of the distributing com-pany has to extend an indirect tax credit to non-resident shareholders, were then picked up by the CJEU and can now be regarded as settled case law.[10]

Concerning the possibility of a neutralisation of discriminatory taxation, the jurisprudence of both Courts resemble each other. In the *Denkavit* judgment, the Court of Justice did not have to decide the issue whether a discriminatory source tax can be healed by a credit in the residence state, as in this particular case, the residence state Netherlands did not alleviate double taxation through a credit but through exemption.[11] In *Amurta*, the Court of Justice finally had to settle the issue and decided in a slightly different way from the EFTA Court. In line with the rea-soning of the EFTA Court the Court of Justice held that a tax advantage granted unilaterally by another Member State cannot neutralise discriminatory source taxation.[12] However, a Member State may comply with its obligations under the TFEU by ensuring in a tax treaty with the residence state of the shareholders that the discrimination is neutralised through a tax credit.[13] In this respect the judg-ments of the two courts differ; the EFTA Court had excluded the possibility of a neutralisation even through a tax treaty. Due to the judgment in *Commission v Italy*[14] the Court of Justice attenuated the effects of its judgment in *Amurta*. In *Commission v Italy* the Court of Justice held that a neutralisation—even through a treaty—is generally not possible unless 'the tax withheld at source ... can be set off against the tax due in the other Member State in the full amount'.[15] As the source state cannot guarantee that the residence state will in effect sufficiently tax the dividends so that a credit is possible there is a risk that the discrimination in the source state persists.[16] A mere conclusion of a tax treaty with the other

---

[10] ECJ of 12 December 2006, Case C-374/04 *ACT Group Litigation* [2006] ECR I-11673 para 68 and 70; of 14 December 2006, Case C-170/05 *Denkavit Internationaal, Denkavit France* [2006] ECR I-11949 para 35; of 8 November 2007, Case C-379/05 *Amurta* [2007] ECR I-9569 para 38; of 19 November 2009, Case C-540/07 *Commission v Italian Republic* [2009] ECR I-10983 para 52.

[11] ECJ of 14 December 2006, Case C-170/05 *Denkavit Internationaal, Denkavit France* [2006] ECR I-11949 para 47: 'It must therefore be held that the combined application of the Franco-Netherlands Convention and the relevant Netherlands legislation does not serve to overcome the effects of the restriction on freedom of establishment that was held to exist'.

[12] ECJ of 8 November 2007, Case C-379/05 *Amurta* [2007] ECR I-9569 para 78; see also ECJ of 11 September 2008, Case C-43/07 *Arens-Sikken* [2008] ECR I-6887 para 65 stating that the credit in the residence state would be beyond the control of the source state.

[13] ECJ of 8 November 2007, Case C-379/05 *Amurta* [2007] ECR I-9569 para 79ff; see in detail G Kofler, 'Tax Treaty "Neutralization" of Source State Discrimination under the EU Fundamental Freedoms?' (2011) 65 *Bulletin for International Taxation* 684.

[14] ECJ of 19 November 2009, Case C-540/08 *Commission v Italian Republic* [2009] ECR I-10983.

[15] ECJ of 19 November 2009, Case C-540/08 *Commission v Italian Republic* [2009] ECR I-10983 para 37.

[16] ECJ of 19 November 2009, Case C-540/08 *Commission v Italian Republic* [2009] ECR I-10983 para 38.

Member States which contains a credit obligation is, therefore, not enough to neutralise the discrimination. This conclusion has a similar effect to the findings of the EFTA Court. However, differences between the two decisions continue to exist if the source state unilaterally assures that all withholding taxes on dividends which are not creditable in the residence state will be reimbursed by the source state.[17] In this situation, the EFTA Court would still assume a violation of the free movement of capital while the Court of Justice would regard the discrimination as neutralised.

D. Conclusion

The EFTA Court is often confronted with new legal problems which have not yet been decided by the Court of Justice. In this situation it tries to prudently develop the existing jurisprudence. As can be seen in the follow-up of the *Fokus Bank* judgment, the Court of Justice concurs for the most part with the result of this jurisprudence even if at first glance the reasoning seems to be different.

II. *SEABROKERS*

A. Facts of the Case (Simplified)

Seabrokers AS is a private limited company resident in Norway. It carried out part of its business through a branch located in the United Kingdom. The majority of its profits were attributable to the UK branch. Norway taxed the worldwide income of Seabrokers but allowed a credit for the taxes paid to the United Kingdom. However, the credit was subject to a limitation, the so-called maximum creditable amount. Norway only credited the UK taxes against its own taxes on the Norwegian income. The maximum creditable amount prevented the UK taxes from reducing the Norwegian tax liability on income earned in Norway. In the relevant tax years, Seabrokers made significant interest payments and deductible group contributions. The Norwegian tax authorities apportioned the interest expenses and the group contributions between the Norwegian head office and the UK branch in accordance with the net income (before interest and group deductions) earned in each part of the enterprise. As the UK branch was very profitable and earned nearly two thirds of the net profits of the enterprise, two thirds of the interest expenses and group deductions were allocated to the UK branch. However, the United Kingdom attributed the expenses to the head office in Norway and taxed the branch without allowing a deduction for the expenses. As a source state, the United Kingdom was not obliged to deduct expenses which were

---

[17] For this argument see G Kofler, 'Tax Treaty "Neutralization" of Source State Discrimination under the EU Fundamental Freedoms?' (2011) 65 *Bulletin for International Taxation* 684, 689.

not linked to the business of the branch in the United Kingdom. Consequently, the Norwegian rules governing the maximum creditable amount made it impossible for Seabrokers to credit all of its UK taxes in Norway as the UK tax liability on the branch profit was much higher than the Norwegian tax liability on the branch profit. Seabrokers argued that for calculating the maximum creditable amount, the interest expenses and the group deductions should have been attributed to the head office in Norway as the expenses arose in Norway. Seabrokers wanted to attribute the expenses in accordance with the direct method.

B. Reasoning of the EFTA Court

The EFTA Court held that the establishment of a branch in another EEA State was protected by the freedom of establishment contained in Article 31 EEA Agreement. Seabrokers as a company could rely on the freedom by virtue of Article 34 EEA Agreement. The Court went on to state that it constituted a restriction of the freedom of establishment if expenses which were linked to the business in Norway were attributed to the branch in the United Kingdom for the calculation of the maximum creditable amount. A company which conducts all its business in its residence state, and has expenses linked to its business in that state and a company which carries on its business through a head office in the residence state and a branch in another EEA State, but having all its expenses linked to the residence state, are in a comparable situation with regard to the expenses.[18] The fact that Norway attributed the interest expenses to the income of the UK branch worked to the detriment of the taxpayer as it reduced the maximum creditable amount. The attribution of expenses to the foreign income had the same effect as if Norway only allowed a portion of the expenses when calculating the global net income on which Norwegian tax is assessed.[19] This rendered a cross-border investment less attractive than a domestic investment. However, if the expenses are linked to the branch in the United Kingdom, Norway may attribute them to the foreign branch; if the expenses cannot be linked to a particular business activity, a proportionate attribution to the foreign branch is admissible.[20]

The Court ruled that the EEA Agreement did not oblige Norway to grant relief for double taxation within the Economic Area. The Agreement does not contain any criteria for the allocation of taxing rights between Norway and the United Kingdom either. However, once Norway has decided to grant a tax credit, the tax credit mechanism must not be implemented in a discriminatory way. As a result, the EFTA Court came to the conclusion that attributing expenses to the foreign branch for the calculation of the maximum creditable amount, although they

---

[18] EFTA Court of 7 May 2008, Case E-7/07 *Seabrokers AS* [2008] EFTA Ct Rep 172 para 56.
[19] EFTA Court of 7 May 2008, Case E-7/07 *Seabrokers AS* [2008] EFTA Ct Rep 172 para 47.
[20] EFTA Court of 7 May 2008, Case E-7/07 *Seabrokers AS* [2008] EFTA Ct Rep 172 para 54ff.

were linked with the activity of the head office in Norway, constituted a violation of the freedom of establishment enshrined in Article 31 EEA Agreement.

C. Comparison with the Jurisprudence of the Court of Justice

In December 2002, the Court of Justice had already rendered its judgment in the *de Groot* case.[21] The case dealt with the comparable tax problem whether the residence state may apportion certain personal allowances to the foreign income when exempting this foreign income. The Court of Justice came to the conclusion that it was the task of the residence state to take personal allowances into account. The residence state may not defect from this obligation just because it exempts foreign income. The EFTA Court followed this line of reasoning: irrespective of whether the residence state avoids double taxation through the credit or the exemption method, the taxpayer may not lose personal allowances in the residence state just because of the fact that he earns income in another EEA state. The judgment in *Seabrokers* is then followed by the judgment of the Court of Justice in *Beker*.[22] In this case, the Court of Justice evolved its jurisprudence in *de Groot* applying the same principles to the credit method. It followed the reasoning of the EFTA Court in *Seabrokers* and confirmed that the residence state may not disallow certain personal expenses as a result of the taxpayer's activity in another Member State when calculating of the amount of the credit.[23]

D. Conclusion

When deciding its *Seabrokers* judgment, the EFTA Court paid due account to the jurisprudence of the Court of Justice. Correspondingly, *Seabrokers* laid the ground for the later judgment of the Court of Justice in *Beker*. It remains interesting to see whether the Court of Justice will follow the EFTA Court also with respect to business expenses. *De Groot* and *Beker* state that personal expenses, which by definition cannot be attributed between the residence and the source state, have to be taken into account by the residence state. This speaks in favour of obliging the residence state to fully take business expenses into account when these expenses are not attributable to a branch in the other state.

---

[21] ECJ of 12 December 2002, Case C-385/00 *de Groot* [2002] ECR I-11819.
[22] ECJ of 28 February 2013, Case C-168/11 *Beker* ECLI:EU:C:2013:117.
[23] ECJ of 28 February 2013, Case C-168/11 *Beker* ECLI:EU:C:2013:117 paras 41 and 56.

III. *ARCADE DRILLING*

A. Facts of the Case (Simplified)

Arcade Drilling AS is a limited liability company incorporated in Norway. It operated oil rigs on the UK continental shelf but did not exercise any activity in Norway. While, during the first years, its board meetings took place in Norway, Arcade Drilling later held its board meetings in the United Kingdom. With the shift of its place of effective management to the United Kingdom, Arcade Drilling became a resident of the United Kingdom under the double tax convention between Norway and the United Kingdom and was no longer taxable with its profits in Norway.[24] It was disputed between the Norwegian tax authorities and Arcade Drilling whether the transfer of the real seat to the United Kingdom led to an obligation to liquidate. Irrespective of this dispute, the Norwegian tax authorities subjected Arcade Drilling to a liquidation tax as a result of its transfer to the United Kingdom. The taxation was based on the Norwegian general anti-avoidance rules as—according to the Norwegian tax authorities—Arcade Drilling did not meet its obligation to liquidate. Arcade Drilling appealed against the assessment of the liquidation tax, arguing that the tax constituted a violation of the EEA Agreement. The district court of Oslo asked the EFTA Court for an advisory opinion.

B. Reasoning of the EFTA Court

The EFTA Court first had to decide whether Arcade Drilling could rely on the freedom of establishment under Articles 31 and 34 EEA when it transferred its real seat to the United Kingdom. As the Court of Justice had ruled that a Member State of incorporation can prevent a company from transferring its seat to another Member State, and from retaining its status as company governed by the law of the Member State of incorporation, it was necessary to see whether Norwegian companies have the right to emigrate.[25] In the absence of a clear rule in Norwegian law stating that a company transferring its real seat outside Norway must liquidate, the EFTA Court held that Arcade Drilling could rely on the freedom of establishment. This conclusion was also supported by the fact that Arcade Drilling still existed despite the relocation to the United Kingdom. The Court went on to state that the levy of a tax at the occasion of the transfer of the real seat to another EEA

---

[24] See Arts 4(1) and (3) DTC Norway/United Kingdom 2000. Norway generally applies the credit method for the avoidance of double taxation in accordance with Art 28(2) DTC Norway/United Kingdom 2000.

[25] ECJ of 16 December 2008, Case C-210/06 *Cartesio* [2008] ECR I-9641 para 110; for the argument that the exit tax jurisprudence of the CJEU and the EFTA Court might incite countries to switch to the internal market-hostile real seat system see B Terra and P Wattel, *European Tax Law*, 6th edn (2012) 972.

State restricted the freedom of establishment as the Norwegian tax authorities applied the anti-avoidance legislation only in a cross-border setting. However, this restriction could be justified by the need to achieve a balanced allocation of the power to impose taxes between the EEA States[26] if the measure did not go beyond what was necessary to attain this result. The Court then analysed the proportionality of the liquidation tax. It distinguished between the establishment of the tax and the recovery of the tax. The establishment of the tax at the time of the transfer of the real seat could lead to more legal certainty and, therefore, did not violate the freedom of establishment. However, the immediate recovery of the tax resulted in a cash flow disadvantage which may in some cases even force the company into liquidation. In order to be proportionate, the company should be given the choice between a deferral of the tax until the assets are actually sold and an immediate payment of the tax upon emigration. If the company chose the deferred payment, the tax administration may take measures to secure the eventual payment of the amount of tax, such as asking for a bank guarantee. However, such safeguarding measures were only proportionate if there was a genuine and proven risk of non-recovery.[27] As a result, a bank guarantee might be unnecessary if the risk of non-recovery was already covered by the personal liability of the shareholders for the outstanding tax debts of the company. If the company chose the deferred payment, the tax administration was also allowed to ask for interest payments for the deferral in accordance with the applicable national legislation.[28] An immediate payment of the tax upon emigration might be more advantageous for the company if the administrative burden for the company in connection with tracing the relocated assets was high.

C. Comparison with the Jurisprudence of the Court of Justice

The judgment in *Arcade Drilling* neatly fits in a row of judgments rendered by the Court of Justice in *Lasteyrie du Saillant*,[29] *N*,[30] *National Grid Indus*[31] and *Commission v Portugal*,[32] dealing with exit taxes. *Arcade Drilling* is followed by the judgment in *DMC Beteiligungsgesellschaft*.[33] In the two first decisions, *Lasteyrie du Saillant* and *N*, concerning the emigration of individual taxpayers, the Court of Justice came to the conclusion that an immediate taxation at the moment of emigration was not in

[26] EFTA Court of 3 October 2012, Case E-15/11 *Arcade Drilling AS* [2012] EFTA Ct Rep 676 para 91.
[27] EFTA Court of 3 October 2012, Case E-15/11 *Arcade Drilling AS* [2012] EFTA Ct Rep 676 para 102.
[28] EFTA Court of 3 October 2012, Case E-15/11 *Arcade Drilling AS* [2012] EFTA Ct Rep 676 para 103; against the duty to pay interest see, however, D Dürrschmidt and F Wobst, 'Anmerkung' (2013) *Internationales Steuerrecht* 202, 203.
[29] ECJ of 11 March 2004, Case C-9/02 *Hughes de Lasteyrie du Saillant* [2004] ECR I-2409.
[30] ECJ of 7 September 2006, Case C-470/04 *N* [2006] ECR I-7409.
[31] ECJ of 29 November 2011, Case C-371/10 *National Grid Indus* [2011] ECR I-12273.
[32] ECJ of 6 September 2012, Case C-38/10 *European Commission v Portuguese Republic* ECLI:EU:C:2012:521.
[33] ECJ of 23 January 2014, Case C-164/12 *DMC Beteiligungsgesellschaft* ECLI:EU:C:2014:20.

line with the fundamental freedoms and that bank guarantees may not be sought in order to safeguard the eventual payment of the tax at the moment of the sale of the assets.[34] The decisions in *National Grid Indus* and in *Commission v Portugal* concerned the emigration of companies. Here the Court of Justice held that companies should be given the choice between an immediate taxation upon emigration and a deferral of the payment of the taxes until actual realisation, together with interest, in accordance with the applicable national legislation and the provision of a bank guarantee, if there was a risk of non-recovery of the tax.[35] The EFTA Court judgment continued this jurisprudence. It confirmed that the company Arcade Drilling must be given the choice between immediate taxation and deferral of the payment and that the deferral of the payment might involve interest in accordance with the national legislation. Concerning the provision of a bank guarantee, it further developed the jurisprudence of the Court of Justice. Applying the principle of proportionality, the EFTA Court held that the tax administration was not automatically entitled to ask for a bank guarantee. In certain situations, if the risk of non-recovery was only remote, a bank guarantee may not be necessary. The Court of Justice followed this reasoning in the *DMC* judgment, stating that the requirement to provide a bank guarantee must respect the principle of proportionality. It cannot be imposed without prior assessment of the risk of non-recovery.[36]

D. Conclusion

This line of judgments shows very well how the EFTA Court pays due account to the principles laid down in the jurisprudence of the CJEU with regard to exit taxes and how it prudently evolves the jurisprudence. In its latest judgment, the CJEU then picked up the ideas developed by the EFTA Court.

IV. *EFTA SURVEILLANCE AUTHORITY V ICELAND*

A. Facts of the Case (Simplified)

In this case, the EFTA Surveillance Authority had launched an infringement proceeding against Iceland. Iceland treated domestic and cross-border mergers in a different way. It granted a deferral to shareholders if an Icelandic company merged into another Icelandic company and the shareholders of the absorbed

---

[34] ECJ of 11 March 2004, Case C-9/02 *Hughes de Lasteyrie du Saillant* [2004] ECR I-2409 para 69 and for bank guarantees see paras 47 and 57; ECJ of 7 September 2006, Case C-470/04 *N* [2006] ECR I-7409 para 55 and for bank guarantees see para 51.

[35] ECJ of 29 November 2011, Case C-371/10 *National Grid Indus* [2011] ECR I-12273 para 73 and for bank guarantees see para 74; ECJ of 6 September 2012, Case C-38/10 *European Commission v Portuguese Republic* ECLI:EU:C:2012:521 para 32.

[36] ECJ of 23 January 2014, Case C-164/12 *DMC Beteiligungsgesellschaft* ECLI:EU:C:2014:20 para 65ff.

company received shares of the absorbing company in exchange for their shares in the absorbed company. However, Iceland taxed the difference between the fair market value and the cost basis of the shares if an Icelandic company merged into a foreign company. Concerning upstream mergers, the absorbed company was subject to taxation if it merged into a foreign company. However, a deferral was granted if the upstream merger took place between two Icelandic companies.[37] For the EFTA Surveillance Authority, this different treatment constituted a violation of the freedom of establishment under Article 31 EEA and of the free movement of capital under Article 40 EEA. During the court proceeding, the Icelandic government did not try to justify the different treatment.

B. Reasoning of the EFTA Court

The EFTA Court started by referring to its prior case law and stated that while Article 31 EEA is aimed at ensuring that foreign nationals are treated in the same way as nationals of the host state, it also prohibits the state of origin from hindering a company incorporated under its legislation to establish itself in another EEA State.[38] In a cross-border merger, the shareholders of the absorbed company are protected by the free movement of capital if they hold shares below the threshold of definite influence and they are protected by the freedom of establishment if their holding is above the threshold of definite influence.[39] As the different tax treatment of domestic mergers and cross-border mergers could not be justified, the Court concluded that the Icelandic tax provision violated the EEA Agreement.[40]

C. Comparison with the Jurisprudence of the Court of Justice

The Court of Justice already decided, in the *Sevic* judgment, that cross-border mergers constitute particular methods of the exercise of the freedom of establishment.[41] The *Sevic* case dealt with an inbound merger while this decision concerned outbound mergers. It can now be regarded as *acte clair* that both inbound and

---

[37] See EFTA Court of 2 December 2013, Case E-14/13 *EFTA Surveillance Authority v Iceland* nyp, para 6. According to JE Gudmundsson, 'The Icelandic Case' in Lang et al (eds), *ECJ—Recent Developments in Direct Taxation 2013* (2014) 104, Art 51 of the Icelandic ITA granted deferral at the level of the absorbed company and at the level of the shareholder while in case of a cross-border merger both the absorbed company and the shareholder were subject to immediate taxation.

[38] EFTA Court of 2 December 2013, Case E-14/13 *EFTA Surveillance Authority v Iceland* nyp, para 24.

[39] EFTA Court of 2 December 2013, Case E-14/13 *EFTA Surveillance Authority v Iceland* nyp, para 28.

[40] EFTA Court of 2 December 2013, Case E-14/13 *EFTA Surveillance Authority v Iceland* nyp, para 29 and 32.

[41] ECJ of 13 December 2005, Case C-411/03 *Sevic Systems AG* [2005] ECR I-10805 para 19.

outbound mergers are protected by the freedom of establishment.[42] With regard to the shareholders, the EFTA Court entered uncharted territory. Before *EFTA Surveillance Authority v Iceland*, it was not clear whether the shareholders may also benefit from the fundamental freedoms in a merger situation as the shareholders do not actively make use of their freedoms. It can be assumed that the Court of Justice will follow the reasoning of the EFTA Court. It is, however, deplorable that Iceland did not try to justify its discriminatory taxation.[43] In *Italy v Commission* the Court of Justice held that the case law concerning restrictions on the exercise of the fundamental freedoms within the European Union cannot be transposed in its entirety to situations where the EEA Agreement applies as the legal context is different.[44] The Mutual Assistance Directive for the exchange of information does not apply outside the European Union. Iceland has not concluded tax treaties with every other EU Member State which contain a provision providing for an effective exchange of information. One could therefore argue that an immediate taxation of the shareholders, in the case of a cross-border merger, is justified by the overriding reason in the public interest regarding the fight against tax evasion. However, exchange of information is clearly not necessary for resident shareholders as Iceland will be able to find out on its own when the shareholders sell their shares. Non-resident shareholders should not even be liable to tax, when selling their shares, as they are protected by a provision similar to Article 13(5) OECD MC in the tax treaties concluded by Iceland. So exchange of information does not seem to be necessary for the tax collection.

D. Conclusion

The judgment in *EFTA Surveillance Authority v Iceland* is of utmost importance for all reorganisations. It confirms that not only the merging companies but also the shareholders are protected by the fundamental freedoms.[45] This is especially relevant if the absorbed company merges into an absorbing company resident in a third state. Here, the freedom of establishment does not apply with respect to the merging companies but the shareholders can nevertheless rely on the free movement of capital. Another interesting aspect of the judgment is that the fundamental freedoms render Article 8 of the merger directive,[46] in most cases, meaningless.

---

[42] The EFTA Court did not explicitly deal with the situation of the merging company but focused on the entitlement of the shareholders to invoke the fundamental freedoms. However, it can be inferred from para 24 of the judgment that the merging company is also protected by Arts 31 and 34 EEA.

[43] See also JE Gudmundsson, 'The Icelandic Case' in Lang et al (eds), *ECJ—Recent Developments in Direct Taxation 2013* (2014) 104, 112.

[44] ECJ of 19 November 2009, Case C-540/07 *Commission v Italy* [2009] ECR I-10983 para 69.

[45] See already D Hohenwarter, 'Internationale Verschmelzungen nach dem BudBG 2007' (2007) *RDW* 568, 570.

[46] Council Directive 2009/133/EC of 19 October 2009, OJ L310/34.

If a country grants a deferral to the shareholders, in case of a domestic merger, it has to extend this beneficial treatment to the shareholders, also in the case of a cross-border merger. Article 8 of the merger directive is still relevant, though, if the shareholders do not benefit from a deferral in a domestic setting. In contrast to Article 6 of the directive, Article 8 goes beyond a mere non-discrimination provision. It grants deferral in a cross-border merger, even if the shareholders do not benefit from deferral in a domestic reorganisation. The decision in *EFTA Surveillance Authority v Iceland* is especially significant in all situations where the merger directive does not apply.[47]

V. FINAL THOUGHTS

With respect to these four tax cases, the EFTA Court had to decide, in *Fokus Bank* and in *EFTA Surveillance Authority v Iceland*, on uncharted territory. The relevant issues had not yet been dealt with before by the Court of Justice. In *Seabrokers* and in *Arcade Drilling* the EFTA Court could partly rely on the jurisprudence of the Court of Justice. The EFTA Court prudently evolved this jurisprudence. The reasoning of the EFTA Court then manifestly found its way into the judgments of the Court of Justice via the opinions of the Advocates General.

For the academic and practitioner alike, a judicial dialogue between Courts facilitates the understanding of the TFEU and the EEA Agreement. A different reasoning may also shed additional light on the meaning of a particular provision. It also allows the Courts to pause for a moment and to rethink whether the former line of reasoning should be continued.

The author wishes to congratulate the EFTA Court on the occasion of its twentieth anniversary and hopes that the Court will have many opportunities in the future to further evolve its jurisprudence in the area of tax law.

---

[47] The merger directive does not apply in Iceland, Liechtenstein and Norway nor does it apply within the EU if the respective company is not listed in the annex of the directive.

Part V

Actors in the EEA

34

The EEA Joint Committee—A Political Assessment

NIKOLAUS VON LIECHTENSTEIN

I. INTRODUCTION

T HE AGREEMENT ON the European Economic Area (EEA) remains, even after 20 years of existence and great advancements in the field of economic integration in Europe and throughout the world, one of the most comprehensive and institutionally complex association agreements. It has a dualistic governance system: the European Union (EU) on the one side and the European Free Trade Association (EFTA) with the three Member States, Iceland, Liechtenstein and Norway, on the other, each have their own institutions to monitor the obligations of the Contracting Parties of the Agreement and act judicially in surveillance procedures and decide on competition cases. On the EFTA side, these are the EFTA Surveillance Authority and the EFTA Court. Both bodies have proved throughout the years that they fulfil their responsibilities admirably, in spite of their smaller size and capacities compared to the corresponding EU institutions. The EFTA Court, for most of its existence ably presided over by Professor Carl Baudenbacher, has already significantly contributed to the jurisprudence in the field of internal market legislation.

Because of this two-pillar system, the EEA has few common bodies responsible for all Contracting Parties together. The central institution in this respect is the EEA Joint Committee. The Agreement gives it the legislative and executive powers to implement and operate it. Unlike other multilateral treaties, decisions are taken not by all the Contracting Parties but by agreement between the EU on the one hand and the EEA EFTA States, 'speaking with one voice', on the other. This can be explained by the history of the origin of the Agreement.

II. HISTORICAL BACKGROUND

When the internal market of the EU took shape in the second half of the 1980s, the then seven EFTA States absolutely wanted to be associated with it in one way or another. They had understood that the EU—or European Communities, as the EU was then called—would definitely be the crystal nucleus for further European integration and that it was vital for their economies to participate in the so-called 'four freedoms'. For the Community also there was a strong interest to get the EFTA States on board, as they were by far their biggest trading partners at the time.

After some years of preliminary talks and analysis of different options to bring the two sides together, the speech of the then President of the Commission of the European Communities, Jacques Delors, before the European Parliament on 17 January 1989 was the starting signal for concrete exploratory talks and negotiations towards a comprehensive association agreement.

He had already given a rough sketch of what would become the EEA, with an institutional vision of two pillars—the European Communities and EFTA—forming together common decisional and administrative organs. This presupposed major changes for EFTA, which had been a pure intergovernmental free-trade organisation since its beginnings in 1960. It would have to accept a certain 'supranational spirit' and build impartial institutions 'policing' the internal market.

Two issues then dominated the negotiations from 1989 up to the signature in 1992. The first was the extent to which the EFTA States would take over the internal market *acquis* of the Community (plus other policies) and how far specific exceptions on the *acquis* for individual EFTA States could be possible. The second was the decision-making process in the EEA and what influence the EFTA States would have on decisions about new legal acts governing the four freedoms.

The political circumstances underwent important changes during the negotiations, influencing its outcome, not least on the institutional set-up: most EFTA members, and not just the smallest ones, had applied for EC membership at this time. It was soon clear that the European Community wanted to remain the 'sole architect' in its house, as President Delors expressed in his speech of 17 January 1989, and that the EFTA States would not be part of the decision making for new internal market law. Agreement was found for them to be included in what was called decision shaping: they could participate, in the same way as the EC States, in expert and other groups of the Commission preparing legal acts.

This negotiating compromise had the consequence that the main task of a common decision-making body of the Contracting Parties would be to decide what acts of secondary internal market legislation would be covered by the primary law of the EEA, incorporate them into EEA law and determine what adaptations were therefore necessary (transitional periods, technical adaptations, specific national circumstances etc).

This common body of the Agreement became the EEA Joint Committee. At first sight, it resembles the joint decision bodies of other international public law treaties. Due to the composition of the Contracting Parties, the supranational characteristics and the vast code of law it has to administer, however, its legislative and executive importance, and its working methods, cannot be compared with others.

One can say that it was prefigured by the main EC-EFTA negotiating group for the EEA, the High Level Negotiating Group (HLNG), composed of leading diplomats of the EFTA States and the Director-General of the Commission, responsible at that time for external affairs and trade, or a higher ranking functionary. Quite a few of the EFTA chief negotiators later became the first representatives of their authorities in the EEA Joint Committee. It then became the practice that the EFTA Ambassadors to the EU were chief representatives of their country in the EEA Joint Committee, accompanied by members of their staff and, depending on the agendas, experts and other representatives from the capitals. On the EU side, the Director at the Commission, and later on at the External Action Service responsible for EEA, EFTA and Western countries or, more frequently in recent years, the Head of the EEA desk, led the delegation. Besides other functionaries, sometimes a representative of the EU Presidency or, more seldom and depending on the agenda, other Permanent Representations, might be present at meetings.

Also, the sub-structure of the High Level Negotiating Group basically was mirrored in the structures of the EEA Joint Committee, though simplified in the course of recent years (see below).

It is interesting to note that, when a few years after the EEA Agreement's entry into force, the EFTA States concluded association agreements on the so-called Schengen and Dublin *acquis*, another governance system was chosen. There is no two-pillar system, no speaking with one voice and de facto no separate institutional structure for these agreements; the EFTA States participate as observers in the different bodies of the EU, from expert groups up to Council of Ministers level, when Schengen and Dublin issues are on the agenda. They can voice their interests and concerns directly in decision-making organs, though not being represented in all relevant institutions (the European Parliament and Court). At first sight this seems to be a simpler governance system for an association agreement extending legislation to outside partners and a more effective representation for them, not least because of a more direct flow of information for both sides. However, one has to take into account the different scope of the two associations and the much more limited code of law in the case of Schengen and Dublin. There is, for instance, much less need for their own surveillance and judicial authority, which is a central element for the EFTA side in the EEA.

III. TREATY BASE

The EEA Joint Committee is the only organ that has a wide array of competences given to it directly by the Agreement. More than 20 articles refer to such specific competences. Additional competences derive from Protocols and legal acts in the Annexes. In many cases these are only notification duties by the Contracting Parties and respective consultations in the EEA Joint Committee. But more decisive competences, like vetting national legislations, amending Annexes and Protocols, settling interpretative disputes, participation in EU programmes and financial contributions by the EFTA States, rule setting in specific fields, review of case law and decisions on safeguard measures, are also foreseen in the Agreement, besides the decisions on the incorporation of new internal market *acquis*. Article 92 EEA states a general competence: 'It shall ensure the effective implementation and operation' of the Agreement.

IV. FUNCTIONING OF THE EEA JOINT COMMITTEE

A. Relationship to Other Bodies in the EEA

i. The EEA Council

The EEA Council, consisting of representatives of the Contracting Parties on a ministerial level, is the superior authority to the EEA Joint Committee. It is responsible for 'laying down the general guidelines for the EEA Joint Committee'. The agenda and the conclusions for the twice-yearly meetings are mainly prepared in the EEA Joint Committee and by direct diplomatic contacts between the Contracting Parties. It mostly adopts the conclusions as prepared and tends to evaluate the functioning of the EEA in a general way, besides discussing political topics of actuality. So, its impact on the daily running of the EEA is limited, which gives the EEA Joint Committee an even more central role.

ii. The EEA Joint Parliamentary Committee

The Joint Parliamentary Committee, composed of members of the European Parliament and members of Parliaments of the EEA EFTA States, is a forum of dialogue and has no decision-making power. Nevertheless, it has an impact on the work of the EEA Joint Committee and its demands for information and positioning are sometimes difficult to fulfil, as they may lay open existing divergences between the Parties.

iii. The EEA Consultative Committee

The Consultative Committee, composed of representatives of the social partners, has exchanges of views with the Presidency of the EEA Joint Committee. In its field of action, it helps the EEA Joint Committee to assess the role of the social partners in the Agreement.

iv. The EFTA Bodies of the EEA

The EFTA Standing Committee

The EFTA Standing Committee is an important body in the governance of the EEA: it fulfils, in the EFTA pillar, some of the duties the Commission and the External Action Service would take care of in the EU for the daily running of the internal market. Together with the External Action Service, and with the help of the EFTA Secretariat, it would also prepare the agenda for the EEA Joint Committee. In practice, perhaps its primary role, besides EFTA internal management, would be the harmonisation of the EFTA States' positions, so that they can speak with one voice in the EEA Joint Committee as the Agreement demands. Therefore, the EFTA Standing Committee meetings normally take place just before those of the EEA Joint Committee and its agenda primarily consists of the same agenda points. Its substructures are the same with few exceptions.

The EFTA Surveillance Authority

Though the competences and work of the Surveillance Authority are clearly delimited from those of the Standing and Joint Committees, members of the Authority would participate in the meetings and make their positions known, where required, which by the structure of the Agreement is mostly in the EFTA Standing Committee.

The EFTA Court

The EFTA Court is normally not represented in the EEA Joint Committee, and in the Standing Committee only for administrative matters of its direct concern. Article 105 foresees that the Joint Committee 'shall keep under constant review the development of the case law of the Court of Justice of the European Union and the EFTA Court' in view of a homogenous interpretation of the Agreement. In practice this task has not led to major discussions.

The EFTA Secretariat

A fairly large number of staff of the EFTA Secretariat in Brussels, compared to the small EEA desk of the External Action Service, works on EEA matters. Together, they provide the secretariat services for the EEA Joint Committee, in accordance with the rotating presidencies.

v. EU Bodies Concerned with the EEA

As the EEA is basically just an extension of the internal market to three smaller states, the awareness of the Agreement within the EU is limited. Mainly, the External Action Service would take care of the EEA Joint Committee and EEA matters in general. In the Commission, the Directorate General for the internal market would be quite regularly concerned with them, as well as the Legal Service, and other services depending on the issues at stake. The so-called EFTA Group of the Council would monitor the work in the Joint Committee. In recent years it also tends to have more direct links to representatives of the EFTA States. Political bodies of the EU would rarely have EEA matters on their agenda, depending on treaty and internal rule requirements. The concerned services would try to avoid this as much as possible, in view of cumbersome procedures.

B. Daily Running of the EEA Joint Committee

The EEA Joint Committee has about eight meetings a year. Very rarely, extraordinary meetings take place. In the first few years, meeting frequencies were higher until the necessary procedures were run in and the reduction of six to three EFTA members had been adapted to.

The meetings are normally a short and rather formal affair, mostly following prepared speaking notes, read by the Presidents on both sides. All points on the agenda would have been thoroughly prepared. Most substantive issues for negotiation would be taken up by the EEA EFTA States in direct informal talks with the relevant services or at least be tackled in the preparation of the agenda.

Also, the four subcommittees, installed by the EEA Joint Committee, prepare the decisions to incorporate legal acts and would try to clear, as far as possible, problems arising when taking over new legislation into the EEA. There are four permanent subcommittees: Subcommittee I for the free movement of goods, Subcommittee II for the free movement of services and capital, Subcommittee III for persons, and Subcommittee IV for horizontal and flanking policies. The EFTA Standing Committee has a fifth subcommittee dealing with institutional affairs, only meeting occasionally at a Joint Committee level.

The points on its agenda would change little from one meeting to another: decisions to incorporate legal acts, approval or taking note of minutes and reports, monitoring of outstanding legal acts, notifications of measures taken by individual Contracting Parties, and EEA EFTA comments to be forwarded to the EU institutions would form its main programme. Sometimes the Joint Committee deals with problems that are politically more delicate. Negotiations on bigger financial contributions for the participation in EU programmes or in the context of the EFTA Financial Mechanism in favour of disadvantaged regions, for instance, are followed closely by the political masters in the capitals and in the EU institutions.

V. CHALLENGES

There is a general agreement that the EEA has functioned well since its entry into force 20 years ago and that the EEA Joint Committee has performed its tasks well. Nevertheless, some challenges have to be tackled so as to avoid a slow grinding down of the EEA machinery. Among them are the following.

A. Changes in the Political Environment

The EU has changed dramatically in the last two decades and continues to do so. Not least, its treaty relationships with third countries are expanding and deepening. These changes will have increasing effects on the EEA and its EFTA States. A more structured and comprehensive political dialogue evaluating together possible consequences of these changes in the political environment for the EEA might help to avoid sudden shocks that are in nobody's interest.

B. Updating the Agreement

The EEA Joint Committee has until now always succeeded in finding pragmatic solutions to a widening gap between the primary law of the EU and the EEA when incorporating new internal market *acquis*. This might become more and more difficult, as can be seen for instance with the new institutions for the Banking Union. Some, perhaps very limited, adaptations to the Agreement might have to be examined.

C. Reducing the Backlog of New *Acquis*

It takes too much time to incorporate new *acquis* into the EEA. This is mainly a problem on the EFTA side and it needs to be solved.

D. Speaking with One Voice

The EFTA States have to march perfectly in step when it comes to the incorporation of new legal acts or the adoption of programmes. A further strict application of this one voice rule seems to be outdated as the EU has concluded rather far-reaching association agreements with other third countries without this condition. The more the EFTA States are integrated in new EU policies, the more difficult it becomes to find fit-for-all solutions, as divergences of interests naturally increase among them.

E. Streamlining the Working Methods of the EEA Joint Committee

The Joint Committee has improved its working methods throughout the years. More could still be done to cut down the rubber stamping, notably by a wider use of electronic communication means. Changes in the working methods might help to concentrate on new challenges as sketched above.

35

The EEA Surveillance Mechanism

SVEN NORBERG

> Laws and institutions must go hand in hand
> with the development of human mind.
>
> Thomas Jefferson

I. INTRODUCTION

WHEN SEVEN EFTA States together with the European Community and its 12 Member States signed the Agreement on the European Economic Area (EEA) on 2 May 1992 in Oporto, a new legal order, EEA law, was formally created. This new legal order should, in parallel to EC law, for the areas covered by the EEA Agreement be able to deliver the same results as EC law as far as the four freedoms of the Internal Market was concerned. The quite ambitious objective of the EEA Agreement, set from the outset, was in practice to extend the EC Internal Market to encompass the EFTA States and thus to create a dynamic and homogeneous EEA. By the entry into force of the Agreement on 1 January 1994 the EEA covered 12 EC and five EFTA States. Today, 20 years later, the EEA comprises 28 EU Member States and three EFTA States,[1] with a total population of some 500 million inhabitants.

The principle of homogeneity is the single most important legal principle of the EEA Agreement. It explains the genesis of the EEA Agreement and guarantees its continued existence. It is of fundamental importance for the application and interpretation of the EEA Agreement to understand correctly this principle and the relevance thereof for the sustainability of the EEA Agreement. At the same time as the EEA has to be 'homogeneous' it should also be 'dynamic', which primarily means that it in areas common with the EU also should develop in parallel with the EU.

In celebrating the first 20 years of the EEA with the publication of a Festschrift for the EFTA Court it may be quite appropriate to pay some attention to another

---

[1] Iceland, Liechtenstein and Norway. On 1 January 1995 Austria, Finland and Sweden left EFTA and acceded to the EU. Switzerland, however, also an original signatory to the EEA Agreement, failed to ratify following a negative referendum in December 1992.

essential EEA institutional mechanism, the good functioning of which is also vital for the EFTA Court and the exercise of the serious tasks entrusted to it. Initially a summary background[2] will be given from the perspective of what has turned out to be essential for the operation of the EEA and more specifically the particular EEA 'two-pillar' surveillance mechanism created for the monitoring of the good functioning of the Agreement.

Next will follow an explanation of how this surveillance mechanism was worked out and set up. After some reflections on the political and practical challenges for this system and how they have been met in practice, some concluding thoughts on future perspectives are given.

II. BACKGROUND

When Denmark and the United Kingdom left EFTA for the European Communities (EC) on 1 January 1973, the remaining EFTA countries concluded the EC bilateral Free Trade Agreements (FTAs) for industrial goods. To celebrate the abolition of the last duties and quotas under these FTAs a first Ministerial meeting was held 30 years ago between the two groupings on 9 April 1984 in Luxembourg. In the declaration adopted at the end of that meeting, EC and EFTA Ministers and the EC Commission[3] expressed their conviction of the importance of further actions to consolidate and strengthen cooperation, with the aim of creating of a dynamic European economic space (EES) of benefit to their countries.

Particularly important for the development of the so-called Luxembourg follow-up was the 1985 EC Commission White Paper on 'Completing the Internal Market'. The subsequent adoption of the Single European Act, implying a radically simplified and improved decision-making procedure for the EC internal market, suddenly made the White Paper, with its close to 300 specific measures, quite a realistic possibility. Numerous EFTA analyses showed that the White Paper project represented a major threat with considerable risks for discrimination of the EFTA States, their economies and their citizens, if this development could not be met by guarantees for their equal treatment in the EC Internal Market. The work on the follow-up of the Luxembourg declaration on the EES thus took quite new dimensions. A first expression of this was the decision in June 1986 in Reykjavík by the EFTA Ministers and the EC Commissioner in charge of external relations to characterise the EES not only as dynamic but also as homogeneous.

Both sides worked intensively during the following two and a half years on the setting up of this EES. Although there were several areas in which substantial progress was made, it became clear towards the end of 1988 that the creation of

---

[2] For a more comprehensive presentation of the historical background, see Norberg, 'Justice in the European Economic Area—The role of the EFTA Court' in EFTA Court (ed), *Judicial Protection in the European Economic Area* (German Law Publishers, Stuttgart, 2012).

[3] Twenty-fourth Annual report of the European Free Trade Association, Geneva, 1985.

the dynamic and homogenous EES required a completely new approach regarding the legal issues and the institutional framework.

Almost five years after the Luxembourg meeting, the President of the EC Commission, Jacques Delors, in an address to the European Parliament on 17 January 1989, raised the question on how the relationship between the EC and the EFTA countries should be developed. He thereby put the question whether the EFTA States really were prepared to go as far in their cooperation with the Community as they sometimes seemed to indicate. Were they prepared to harmonise their legislation to ensure free circulation of goods, to accept judicial control by the ECJ and to accept the same discipline on State aid and rules of competition as the Community Member States? If they were ready for this and to strengthen the EFTA structures, Delors saw possibilities on the basis of one EC pillar and an EFTA pillar to develop a far-reaching joint cooperation.

On 12 March 1989 the EFTA Heads of Government delivered an unequivocally positive reply in Oslo,[4] stating that negotiations should lead to the fullest possible realisation of free movement of goods, services, capital and persons, with the aim of creating a dynamic and homogeneous EES. They would explore ways and means to strengthen the institutional links between the EFTA states and the EC and would not exclude any option. It may here be of interest to note that, after referring to the need 'for equally strong and reliable surveillance and enforcement procedures', they also, inter alia, declared: 'We will also strengthen our mechanism for surveillance and enforcement of treaty obligations in order to ensure their harmonious and uniform application and interpretation.'

The EC and its Member States and the Member States of EFTA then met in Brussels on 20 March 1989. Their Declaration clearly reflects the important progress made by the EC in completing its Internal market, and in noting that important results also had been achieved in the process of creating the single EES, Ministers discussed the scope for broadening and deepening their cooperation in the areas linked to the internal market—free movement of goods, services, capital and persons—and in other areas such as research, technology, education, environment, social policy aspects, transport. An EC-EFTA Ministerial meeting on 19 December 1989 welcomed a report on the exploratory talks and decided to commence and conclude formal negotiations as soon as possible. Just six months later, the formal EC-EFTA negotiations commenced on 20 June 1990.[5]

As mentioned, the main objective of the EEA Agreement is to establish a dynamic and homogeneous EEA with equal conditions of competition and respect of the same rules.[6] To achieve that aim the rules must be implemented, interpreted and applied in a uniform way throughout the EEA. Since the beginning of the exploratory talks in

---

[4] Declaration of EFTA Heads of Government, Oslo, 14 and 15 March 1989, Twenty-ninth Annual Report of EFTA, Geneva, 1990.
[5] At the opening of the negotiations the EC side suggested that the term so far used in English, 'the European Economic Space', should be changed for linguistic reasons to 'European Economic Area'. No substantive change was intended but the UK Prime Minister, Mrs Thatcher, had expressed a preference for a more down-to-earth expression. The EFTA side accepted the proposal.
[6] Fifteenth recital of the Preamble of the EEA Agreement.

April 1989 the EFTA side gradually tried out and developed various scenarios of how to organise an appropriate surveillance system for the future EEA. The final solution of how the EEA judicial mechanism would look played an important role here. In March 1991 the EFTA side—with Switzerland still reserving its position—envisaged a stipulation in the EEA Agreement that the fulfilment of the obligations under the EEA Agreement should be ensured, as regards the Communities and their Member States and natural and legal persons operating within the EC by the EC Commission and the ECJ, and as regards the EFTA Member States and natural or legal persons operating within those States by an independent EFTA Surveillance Authority, to be set up by the EFTA Member States, and an EEA Court.[7]

After 10 months of negotiations, only two major issues remained to be settled, the judicial mechanism and trade in fish, the latter being an issue that by experience never can be settled in a trade negotiation until all other issues are solved. The EFTA side had concluded from what Delors had stated in his 1989 speech that they would be more directly involved in a real joint decision making with the EC Member States. At this stage, however, they understood that they would only be able to give input during the decision-shaping phase, while the EC took a decision that they would later also have to approve for the EEA. In view of the considerable disappointment this caused in many EFTA capitals, it became even more important for the EFTA side to get a judicial mechanism, where all parties to the agreement would be on an equal footing.

A Joint Ministerial Meeting in Brussels on 13 May 1991 reached a political agreement on the creation of a Joint EEA Court,[8] functionally integrated with the ECJ, which would function in a composition of five judges from the ECJ and three judges from the EFTA States. The EEA Court was to give rulings concerning dispute settlement (including interpretation of EEA rules) on request of the Joint Body or the Contracting Parties; disputes between the EFTA Surveillance Body and an EFTA country; cases brought by enterprises or states against decisions of the EFTA Surveillance Body in the field of competition (including state aid). This agreement was generally welcomed as a major breakthrough in the EEA negotiations and in October 1991 the negotiators also came to an agreement regarding trade in fish. In parallel, the EC Commission submitted the draft agreement to the ECJ for an opinion under Article 228 EC (now Article 264(11) TFEU).

However, on 14 December 1991 the ECJ in Opinion 1/91[9,10] firmly rejected the idea of a Joint EEA Court by concluding that '[T]he system of judicial

---

[7] EFTA document LA 33/91.

[8] Declaration from the Ministerial meeting between the European Community, its Member States and the EFTA Countries of the European Free Trade Association, Thirty-first Annual Report of the European Free Trade Association, Geneva June 1992.

[9] Opinion 1/91 ECR [1991] I-6079. For comments upon this opinion and some erroneous factual findings of the Court regarding the text of the Agreement and in particular its Preamble relating to its dismissal of the feasibility to achieve 'the objective of homogeneity in the interpretation and application of the law in the EEA' (para 29), reference is made to this author's article mentioned above n 2, pp 44–47.

[10] It would seem that the ECJ does not want its erroneous findings to be known. Anyone who tries via the Court's website to find the full text of Opinion 1/91 will only find the final parts of the Opinion

supervision which the agreement proposes to set up is incompatible with the Treaty establishing the European Economic Community.'

The considerable political ambitions behind the project encouraged the negotiators to find solutions to overcome the criticism of the Court, and on 14 February 1992 the negotiations on the necessary modifications to the EEA Agreement were concluded.

The new solution implied that the idea of a joint judicial mechanism through an EEA Court had been abolished and also that the EEA judicial mechanism would follow the general two-pillar structure of the EEA with the ECJ for the Community pillar and a new EFTA Court for the EFTA pillar. Disputes between the two pillars would have to be settled by the EEA Joint Committee. The EFTA Court would be created with corresponding competences for the EFTA countries to those of the ECJ with regard to the EC and its Member States. In addition, considerable efforts were spent on reinforcing the provisions on homogeneity, surveillance and dispute settlement in the Agreement. Modifications were also made regarding Article 56 in the Agreement, dealing with the sharing of competences between the Commission and the EFTA Surveillance Authority in the field of competition.[11] The Commission submitted the new text to the ECJ for a new opinion on the compatibility with the EEC Treaty of the renegotiated version of the Agreement and more specifically of the new Articles regarding the distribution of competences in the field of competition between the EC Commission and the EFTA Surveillance Authority and the dispute settlement mechanism of the Agreement.

The ECJ in Opinion 1/92[12] had no objections and declared compatible with the EEC Treaty:

"(1) the provisions of the Agreement which deal with the settlement of disputes, as long as the principle that decisions taken by the Joint Committee are not to affect the case law of the Court of Justice is laid down in a form binding on the Contracting Parties;[13]

(2) Article 56 of the Agreement, dealing with the sharing of competences in the field of competition."

The EFTA States in Oporto on 2 May 1992 also signed several agreements between themselves called for by their participation in the EEA. Particularly important is the Agreement on the Establishment of a Surveillance Authority and a Court of

---

(pp 6099 to 6112). The introductory sections: I Description of the request, II Procedure, III Appraisal of the agreement and IV Summary of written observations submitted by the Institutions and the Governments (pp 6084 to 6098) are neither there, nor are they to be found on Eurolex. Today the full text is only available for those who have access to the printed edition of the ECR.

[11] A persistent rumour was that the ECJ, if asked a second time, would focus upon the question whether the EC Commission through the EEA could cede competence to the EFTA pillar. It was thus agreed to limit the duties for the EFTA Surveillance Authority in comparison to what first had been agreed.

[12] Opinion 1/92 [1992] ECR I-2821 was delivered on 10 April 1992.

[13] Such a provision was now transferred from an Agreed Minute to become Protocol 48. In order to avoid any conclusion *a contrario*, the Final Act states that the Agreed Minutes have a binding character.

Justice (Surveillance and Court Agreement), by which the new and independent EFTA Surveillance Authority and the EFTA Court were set up.

III. THE SURVEILLANCE SYSTEM

A. Treaty Provisions

The institutional provisions of the EEA Agreement are laid down in Part VII of the Agreement, where Chapter 1 (Articles 89–96) is called 'The structure of the association', Chapter 2 (Articles 97–104) 'The decision-making procedure', Chapter 3 (Articles 105–111) 'Homogeneity, surveillance procedure and settlement of disputes', and Chapter 4 (Articles 112–114) 'Safeguard measures'.

The general rules on the surveillance system are contained in Articles 108–110. While Article 108 first lays down the obligations for the EFTA States to establish an independent surveillance authority (EFTA Surveillance Authority) and a court of justice (EFTA Court), it also provides that the EFTA States are to establish procedures similar to those existing in the Community, including procedures for ensuring the fulfilment of obligations under the Agreement. This means infringement procedures similar to those under Articles 169 and 171 EEC (now Articles 258 and 260 TFEU), and procedures for control of the legality of acts of the surveillance authority regarding competition, which means procedures similar to those under Article 173 EEC (now Article 263 TFEU). From this, it follows that the EFTA Surveillance Authority (ESA), with regard to its surveillance activities, is to have competences corresponding to those of the EU Commission. Further details regarding this are laid down in various other parts of the EEA Agreement, such as in Protocols 21 and 26, which, inter alia, deal with the powers and functions of ESA in the fields of competition and State aid. These Protocols contain far-reaching provisions regarding the daily cooperation between the two surveillance authorities.

Article 109(1) spells out the obligation for each of ESA and the EU Commission to monitor the fulfilment of the obligations under the agreement by their respective side. This fundamental provision thus reads:

> 1. The fulfilment of the obligations of this Agreement shall be monitored by, on the one hand, the EFTA Surveillance Authority and, on the other, the EC Commission acting in conformity with the treaty establishing the European Economic Community, the Treaty establishing the European Coal and Steel Community and this Agreement.

It goes without saying that for this two-pillar mechanism to function well a close cooperation and in-depth understanding between the two surveillance authorities is of fundamental importance. Article 109(2) obliges the two bodies to cooperate, exchange information and consult each other on surveillance policy issues and individual cases in order thereby to ensure a uniform surveillance throughout the EEA. Under Article 109(3) both authorities shall receive any complaints concerning the application of the Agreement as well as inform each other of complaints received. It follows from Article 109(4) that each body shall examine all complaints falling within its competence and pass to the other body complaints falling within the competence of that body. Article 109(5) provides that in case of disagreement between the two bodies with regard to the action to be taken in relation to a complaint or with regard to the result of the examination either body may refer the matter to the EEA Joint Committee which shall deal with it in accordance with the dispute settlement provisions laid down in Article 111.

Article 110, which reproduces the wording of Article 192 EEC (now Article 299 TFEU), concerns the possibility of enforcing not only decisions of ESA and the EU Commission but also the ECJ, the CFI and the EFTA Court.

The further provisions regarding ESA and its organisation and functioning are laid down in the Surveillance and Court Agreement, which contains 53 Articles, seven Protocols and two Annexes. The main part of the Agreement contains mainly provisions regarding the competences, setting up and organisation of ESA and the EFTA Court. Four of the Protocols concern specifically the functioning of ESA in specific fields of surveillance or surveillance-related activities. While Protocols 2 and 3 deal with the functions and powers in the fields of procurement and State aid, respectively, Protocol 4 contains all rules regarding the functions and powers of ESA in the field of competition reproducing the corresponding EU rules in the field of competition.

The provisions regarding the members of the surveillance authority are similar to those for the appointment of members of the Commission, although there is no public scrutiny by any parliamentary body. Under Article 6 of the Surveillance and Court Agreement, the Surveillance Authority consists of three members[14] who, under Article 9, shall be appointed by common accord of the Governments of the EFTA. Their term of office is four years. Under Article 12 the President of ESA shall be appointed from among its members by common accord of the Governments of the EFTA States for a period of two years.

B. Political Challenges

The new responsibilities for the EU Commission under Chapter 3 EEA may not have implied major changes for the Commission's daily activities, but there are nevertheless two aspects worth mentioning. First, the Commission is now for the first time treaty- bound to discuss its surveillance policy as well as individual cases with a party outside the EU, the ESA, with whom it will in principle have to come to an agreement. Second, the Commission is further obliged to see to it that the rights under the EEA Agreement of the EFTA Member States and their economic

---

[14] Originally the 'ESA College' was expected to be composed of seven members. At the entry into force of the EEA there were five, and the present number follows the withdrawal of Austria, Finland and Sweden.

operators and individual citizens are respected. Although this has certainly in practice been a natural part of its obligations as 'guardian of the treaty', it now also follows from Article 109 EEA laying down the obligations of the two surveillance authorities in charge of monitoring the EEA Agreement.

With regard to the ESA, the political challenges were from the outset of two kinds. On the one hand, it would have to acquire the necessary substantial knowledge and know-how to be able to be at par with the Commission and its more than 40 years of experience. Very much linked to this was of course the need to equip it with sufficiently competent and experienced staff to carry out all the different duties which would have to be undertaken by it in its capacity of surveillance authority. At the same time it was obvious that with an EU that at the entry into force of the EEA counted 12 Member States with a population of some 300 million inhabitants, the five EFTA States had a population of less than a tenth thereof, that is, 26.5 million inhabitants. The challenge for the ESA, which would never be able to match the huge resources of the Commission, was nevertheless to be sufficiently strong quality-wise and politically.

During the EEA negotiations the EFTA side had carefully analysed all the different tasks of the Commission, both those following more directly from the texts of the treaties but not least all those sometimes quite important tasks laid down in various provisions in acts of secondary legislation. While some of these tasks may be of a legislative character and include mandates to issue implementing provisions, others may be more of a monitoring or information collecting and reporting type. This analytical work had been carried out with a view precisely to identify which of those tasks would be absolutely necessary to give to ESA in its capacity as surveillance authority. The fact that it here concerned the establishment of an independent authority with supra-national competences made this work a very sensitive exercise. The result is reflected in the Surveillance and Court Agreement and in particular in Protocols 1–4 thereof.

Thus while ESA, with regard to the surveillance activities, has been equipped with competences corresponding to those of the EU Commission, it lacks some of the more fundamental Commission competences, which play an important role for the latter, when it monitors the compliance by Member States, economic operators and individual citizens with relevant treaty provisions. Thus unlike the Commission, ESA has been given no legislative competence, nor has it any right to take legislative initiatives.

With the decision to create the EFTA pillar in the surveillance mechanism as a pure monitoring, policing and prosecuting institution without legislative competences and with no right to take initiatives, the EFTA governments from the outset created a political disequilibrium between the EU Commission on the one hand, and ESA on the other. Clearly, the EFTA States would prefer an ESA that would interfere as little as possible with their own prerogatives and the Commission could hardly object, as long as it could count on ESA being able to carry out its functions as surveillance authority. In the short term perspective, this might not be of major importance. Over a longer term, however, it might risk weakening or undermining the authority of ESA and thereby diminishing the level of respect that ESA ought to deserve both among the EFTA States and in relation to the EU Commission.

The fact that the EU Commission has not only a legislative competence that in certain fields, such as competition, is rather far-reaching, but also has the monopoly on initiating new legislation, is of utmost importance also for its exercise of the function as 'guardian of the treaty'. When taking new legislative initiatives, the Commission regularly builds upon experiences gained from the surveillance activities.

Nor is ESA involved in the joint EU-EFTA discussions, where proposals for new or amended legislation are discussed between the Commission and the EFTA States. In internal EFTA meetings within the five EFTA sub-committees the role of ESA is limited to that of an observer with no right to comment or participate in the discussion.

C. Practical Challenges

i. Recruitment, Training of Staff, etc

For ESA, which formally started to operate with the entry into force of the EEA Agreement 20 years ago, as well as for the EFTA States, the surveillance obligations represented entirely new and untested ground. Most urgent was as quickly as possible to bring on board key staff to fill the most sensitive posts where it would be vital for ESA to be fully operational from day one of the entry into force of the EEA Agreement, for example experts on competition and the veterinary and phytosanitary fields. Thus the recruitment procedure for ESA staff was initiated immediately after the signing of the EEA Agreement in May 1992. This resulted in a considerable part of the new staff being recruited and in place at the new ESA headquarters in Geneva in the early autumn of 1992. The EC Commission had also been extremely open to assist in their training, and the first ESA staff members were immediately welcomed by various Commission services. This meant that for longer or shorter training periods they were serving with those Commission services that handled corresponding activities to those for which they were recruited by ESA.

One of the most important tasks at this stage was also for the new ESA staff to lay down the different procedures and work on manuals which ESA and its different clients, be they government administrations or private companies and their legal advisers, would have to follow. Obviously the Commission procedures would play a leading role, since the overriding homogeneity objective must not be jeopardised. However, as with the EFTA Court, nothing would prevent new ideas or simpler procedures, as long as this would not risk the EEA's homogeneity. These preparations were well advanced, not least in the most sensitive areas of competition and veterinary and phytosanitary issues respectively, when it became clear that the negative outcome of the Swiss referendum on the EEA on 6 December

1992 would prevent the Agreement from entering into force as expected on 1 January 1993.

Originally, it had been decided by the EFTA EEA Member States to maintain the EFTA headquarters in Geneva but expand the EFTA Secretariat offices in Brussels and to locate the Court and the Surveillance Authority, each in separate premises, in Geneva. As a consequence of Switzerland's non-accession to EEA, the five remaining Governments immediately decided to move the ESA headquarters from Geneva to Brussels. This was obviously done with a view to facilitate a close cooperation with the EU Commission. To mark independence from the EFTA States it was, however, decided to maintain the location of ESA in a separate building from that of the EFTA Secretariat. Another measure to that effect was the setting up of a separate Staff Insurance Scheme for the EFTA Court and ESA, which contained identical rules to that of the EFTA Secretariat, but nevertheless was entirely independent. The same went for the Budget and the Staff rules, which were separate for each of the Secretariat, the EFTA Court and ESA.

ii. Differences in Employment Conditions

An important difference between the two surveillance authorities that is of a fundamental nature appeared from 1995, when in relation to the accession on 1 January 1995 of Austria, Finland and Sweden to the EU, profound changes were introduced in EFTA regarding staff policy.

The EU Commission is a permanent EU institution with permanently employed staff that can make their whole career therein and stay until retirement. It is not necessary to stress what that means for the building up of competence, the maintaining of continuity of the institution and not the least its integrity and independence in relation to the Governments.

The situation for ESA has since 1995 differed fundamentally. When it was clear that Austria, Finland and Sweden would leave EFTA, the remaining EEA EFTA States, Iceland and Norway,[15] with the support of Switzerland and Liechtenstein, decided to change the staff rules to the effect that there would no longer be any permanent contracts in EFTA, neither in the Secretariat nor in ESA or the EFTA Court. All staff would be on fixed-term contracts, normally of three years but allowing for a maximum service period of six years. This was an expression of the firm view that the EFTA States would no longer take on any pension obligations regarding its staff.[16] At the same time it was decided to terminate the contracts for all old staff. With this new staff policy also focusing on nationals of the remaining EFTA States, the number of total staff was reduced.

---

[15] Liechtenstein only became a Member of the EEA on 1 May 1995.

[16] Instead, the staff member would participate in a savings fund to which both he or she and the employer would contribute with one third and two thirds respectively. Upon leaving, the amount thus accrued would be reimbursed with interest to the employee.

This fundamental difference in employment conditions between the two surveillance authorities has obviously had an impact on the recruitment of staff, although ESA, unlike the Secretariat, engages quite a number of EU nationals among its staff.[17] Nevertheless, the short-term contracts and the absence of career possibilities have no doubt an impact not only on the continuity in the maintaining of a well-functioning surveillance policy but also on the possibility to recruit the best candidates.

IV. SOME OBSERVATIONS ON THE FUNCTIONING OF EEA SURVEILLANCE

While it in no way would be within the limited scope of this chapter to make a comprehensive review of the activities during the first 20 years of the EEA Surveillance Mechanism, a few more scattered observations will be made.

A. The EU Commission

To start with, very soon after the entry into force of the EEA Agreement, actually in the first case which came up before an EU Court on the interpretation thereof, the EU Commission behaved as if it had entirely forgotten everything regarding the nature of the EEA—as, in practice, an extension of the EU Internal Market—that it had worked with the EFTA side to achieve during years of negotiations and preparatory work.

Opel Austria[18] was the first case before one of the EU Courts, in which outright interpretations of provisions of the EEA Agreement had to be given. The dispute before the Court of First Instance (CFI) concerned an EU Council Regulation adopted on 20 December 1993 but coming in force only in January 1994 after the entry into force of the EEA Agreement. Thereby a customs duty for certain gearboxes produced by Opel Austria and exported to the Community was reintroduced to counter distortive effects of Austrian state aid to the company. Opel Austria as applicant claimed that the measure violated Article 10 EEA prohibiting customs duties and measures of equivalent effect. The Council referring to *Opinion 1/91* claimed that there were major differences between the EC Treaty and the EEA Agreement, which required Article 10 EEA to be interpreted differently. Also the Commission, in supporting the Council position, argued that Article 10 EEA and the corresponding provisions of the EC Treaty were not identical in substance and that therefore Article 6 EEA was not applicable.

---

[17] At present, it has a staff of 15 nationalities. The one post at senior level that since its second incumbent has been held by an EU national is the post of Director of Legal and Executive Affairs.
[18] Case T-115/94 *Opel Austria GmbH v Council of the European Union* [1997] ECR II-39, judgment of 22 January 1997.

The CFI first concluded that, since Article 10 EEA was unconditional and precise, it had had direct effect ever since the entry into force of the EEA Agreement. It then stated that it could not accept the Council's contention that major differences between the EEA Agreement and the EC Treaty meant that, notwithstanding the wording of Article 6 EEA, Article 10 should not be interpreted in the same way as corresponding provisions of the EC Treaty. The Court then, at some length (paragraphs 106 to 108), elaborated on the main characteristics of the EEA Agreement, which 'involves a high degree of integration, with objectives which exceed those of a mere free-trade agreement' (paragraph 107). The Court also referred to the case law of the EFTA Court, inter alia *Restamark*[19] (paragraph 108). As to the Council's arguments, based upon ECJ Opinion 1/91, the Court stated:

> Contrary to the Council's contention, the significance in regard to the interpretation and application of the Agreement of the Contracting Parties' objective of establishing a dynamic and homogeneous EEA has not been diminished by the Court of Justice in Opinion 1/91, cited above. When the Court held that the divergences existing between the aims and context of the Agreement, on the one hand, and the aims and context of Community law on the other, stood in the way of the achievement of the objective of homogeneity in the interpretation and application of the law in the EEA, it was considering the judicial system contemplated by the EEA Agreement for the purposes of ascertaining whether that system might jeopardize the autonomy of the Community legal order in pursuing its own objectives; and not a specific case in which it is necessary to determine whether a provision of the EEA Agreement identical in substance to a provision of Community law must be interpreted in conformity with the rulings of the Court of Justice and the Court of First Instance. (paragraph 109)

The CFI concluded that Article 10 EEA is identical in substance to Articles 12, 13, 16 and 17 of the EC Treaty and must be interpreted in conformity with the relevant rulings of the ECJ and the CFI (paragraph 112). The Court, which also addressed a number of other issues regarding the obligations of the Council when it adopted the Regulation and had it published, for the rest rejected the Council's and the Commission's arguments and annulled the Council Regulation.[20] The judgment was never challenged before the ECJ.

The CFI in *Opel Austria* thoroughly elaborated on the special characteristics of the dynamic and homogeneous EEA and the considerable efforts of the Contracting Parties to ensure that both the Agreement itself, and the institutions in charge of its implementation and interpretation, would be able to live up to the explicitly expressed objectives of the EEA. By so clearly dismissing both the Council's and the Commission's efforts to play down the qualities and the credibility of the EEA Agreement, the Court in this, the very first judgment where one of the EU Courts interpreted the EEA Agreement, also did the whole EEA venture an immense service. The EFTA Court had until then been the only Court within

---

[19] E-1/94 *Ravintoloitsijain Liiton Kustanus Oy Restamark* [1994–1995] EFTA Ct Rep 15.
[20] Rapporteur in the case was Judge Pernilla Lindh, previously one of the most senior Swedish EEA negotiators.

the EEA judicial mechanism which had pronounced itself on the interpretation of the EEA Agreement. By this judgment of the CFI, the EFTA Court was no longer alone in strongly defending the EEA. Although the case had been launched early in 1994, three years had passed during which sceptics of the EEA had criticised the line taken by the EFTA Court.

It was nothing less than a scandal that these two EU institutions, right after the entry into force of the EEA Agreement, in order to save their own skin after the late adoption of a very minor customs regulation, did not hesitate to use arguments that, if accepted by the Court, would have seriously threatened to undermine the credibility of the whole EEA.

Fortunately, *Opel Austria* would seem to be a unique example of the Commission's handling of the EEA Agreement during the 20 years since it came into force. Thus, the Commission stood fully behind the conclusions of the ECJ in its judgment on 26 September 2013, where the EUCJ dismissed an action by the United Kingdom[21] to annul a Council decision concerning an amendment to Annex VI (Social Security) and Protocol 37 to the EEA Agreement. The United Kingdom claimed that Article 48 TFEU was the wrong legal basis for that decision and that instead Article 79 (2)(b) TFEU, which allows for the adoption of measures as part of the EU's immigration policy, should have been used. If accepted, this would have excluded Denmark and allowed the United Kingdom and Ireland to exercise their opt-out. This would not have been in line with the EU commitments in relation to the EFTA States under the EEA Agreement. The Court dismissed the action as unfounded.[22]

Furthermore, the Commission has, ever since the entry into force of the EEA Agreement, been applying the competition provisions of the EEA Agreement in all decisions in antitrust cases, where it regularly applies Articles 101 and 102 TFEU as well as Articles 53 and 54 EEA. Other important examples of Commission actions regarding the EEA Agreement are all the actions before the EFTA Court undertaken through its legal service supported by the service competent in the matter. The Commission thus regularly intervenes both through written submissions and with oral pleadings in the cases before the EFTA Court. This had been foreseen by the EEA negotiators as an important means for the maintenance of a consistent surveillance policy as well as serving the overall objective of homogeneity throughout the EEA. Evidently, this input from the Commission with its long experience should be most helpful, especially in the situation where the EFTA Court, due to the overall more rapid procedures on that side, becomes the first European court to give an interpretation of a new legal issue without any

---

[21] Case C-431/11 *United Kingdom v Council* EU: C:2013:589.

[22] The Court stated, inter alia: 'As the Court already had occasion to state, one of the principal aims of the EEA Agreement to which the United Kingdom and Ireland are also parties, is to provide for the fullest possible realisation of the free movement of goods, persons, services and capital within the whole of the EEA, so that the internal market established within the European Union is extended to the EFTA States (Case C-452/01 *Ospelt and Schlössle Weissenberg* [2003] ECR I-9743, para 29)' (para 50).

precedent from an EU Court being available. This had from the outset been foreseen and has actually happened in quite a number of cases. The Court was faced with this situation in one of its very first judgments in the cases *Mattel* and *Lego*,[23] which concerned the interpretation to be given to the EC Directive 'Television without frontiers' (Directive 89/552) in relation to a Norwegian ban on television advertising directed towards children. Another of the most famous such cases has been *Kellogg's*,[24] the fortified corn flakes case.[25]

B. The EFTA Surveillance Authority

With regard to ESA, the delayed entry into force of the EEA Agreement, following the negative outcome of the Swiss referendum in December 1992, meant that it could use the year 1993 for the removal to Brussels and for training and preparing the new tasks. However, even before its first year of full operations was over, in the late autumn of 1994, ESA—following the successful referenda on the EU Accession Treaty in Austria, Finland and Sweden—had to down-scale its activities and adjust to a very different situation from five Member States with a total of around 26.5 million inhabitants to that of only two or three Member States[26] with a population of just below 5 million. This meant that very early in the life of ESA, and well before everyone could have become familiar with the new responsibilities, a great number of the staff, as well as three experienced Members of the ESA College, had to leave. In spite of this, and benefiting from the experiences of one of the most seasoned EEA negotiators on the EFTA side, the first ESA President, the Norwegian Knut Almestad, the reduced ESA demonstrated very quickly that it nevertheless was fully operational.

Although a major part of the surveillance activities of ESA, as well as of the Commission, will consist in monitoring the implementation of acts of secondary legislation and receive complaints claiming lacking or erroneous implementation or application, the fact that the provisions of EEA law are or have been made directly applicable in Member States implies that a number of issues on their interpretation are raised in disputes before national courts. As in the EU, the instrument of preliminary rulings—in EFTA called Advisory Opinions but otherwise in no way different—is here of key importance.

In the very first case before the EFTA Court, *Restamark*,[27] ESA demonstrated its independence in relation to the EFTA Governments. This case concerned the politically very sensitive issue of the compatibility of the Nordic alcohol monopolies with the fundamental rules of competition and free movement in the

---

[23] Cases E-8/94 *Forbrukerombudet v Mattel Scandinavia A/S* and E-9/94 *Forbrukerombudet v Lego Norge A/S* [1994-1991] EFTA Ct Rep 143.

[24] Case E-3/00 *EFTA Surveillance Authority v Norway (Kellogg's)* [2000–2001] EFTA Ct Rep 73.

[25] In both these cases the line taken by the EFTA Court was later followed by the EU. See more about this in the article mentioned above n 2, p 50.

[26] As mentioned above, Liechtenstein joined the EEA on 1 May 1995.

[27] See above n 15.

internal market. The focus was the Finnish import monopoly for wine and spirits, regarding which the Finnish Customs Appeals Board (the Tullilautakunta) had made a reference for an advisory opinion from the Court. While the Governments of Finland and Norway on various grounds submitted that the monopoly in question, as well as its operation, was compatible with the EEA rules, as well as corresponding EU rules and the interpretation thereof by the ECJ, ESA was of a different opinion, as was the Commission. The conclusion of the EFTA Court was inter alia that the operation of the Finnish monopoly violated Articles 11 and 16 EEA.

Over the years there have certainly been many other cases, where ESA—either by taking a direct action against one or more of the three Member Governments or when Advisory Opinions have been sought by national courts—has clearly distinguished its positions from those of the Member States. Although this is not more than what one would have the right to expect from an independent authority with such a mandate as the one that has been given to ESA, it must be admitted that ESA has been and is in a particular situation due to the limited number and size of the three EFTA States. In the following, only two of the most important cases will be very briefly mentioned.

To start with the so-called *Hjemfallsaken*,[28] a direct action case, where ESA in an action brought before the EFTA Court in 2006 successfully questioned the legality of the almost century-old Norwegian regime for acquisition of hydropower resources and the rules on transfer of property rights from private undertakings to the State at a certain time without compensation. This system was established by a national law of 1917. The EFTA Court found unlawful the concession regime that granted private undertakings a time-limited concession with the obligation to surrender all installations to the Norwegian state without compensation, while Norwegian public undertakings benefited from concessions for an unlimited period of time. The Court found that this regime violated both Article 31 EEA on freedom of establishment and Article 40 EEA on freedom of capital. By successfully bringing this action against a concession system for hydroelectric power resources that had been practised for such a long period, which provoked quite strong reactions in Norway and from the side of the Norwegian government, ESA gave very clear proof of its independence which no doubt contributed to the overall strengthening of its credibility.

Another very important case, in which ESA acted fully independently under circumstances where it no doubt was exposed to a very heavy political pressure, is the *Icesave* case.[29] This was also a direct action case, which in short concerned the situation following the collapse on 7 October 2008 of the Icelandic bank *Landsbanki Íslands hf (Landsbanki)* and the question of compensation to depositors in Icesave. The bank had undertaken previous operations in the United Kingdom and the Netherlands of online savings accounts under the name Icesave that had drawn in

---

[28] Case E-2/06 *EFTA Surveillance Authority v The Kingdom of Norway* [2007] EFTA Ct Rep 167.
[29] Case E-16/11 *EFTA Surveillance Authority v Iceland*, judgment of 28 January 2013.

substantial deposits from both private and public investors in these countries. In connection with the worldwide financial crisis in 2008 there was a run on Icesave accounts in the UK, and now the question had been raised under quite dramatic circumstances—the UK government taking action under its 2001 Anti-Terrorism, Crime and Security Act to formally freeze Landsbanki's assets—of the responsibility of Iceland's Depositors' and Investors' Guarantee Fund to step in in favour of British and Dutch depositors who had lost their deposits.

Although all three pleas of ESA were dismissed by the EFTA Court, and the surveillance authority's action was thus unsuccessful, this is another example of ESA acting independently and with integrity against one of its Member governments in a highly political and very sensitive situation. By doing this ESA demonstrated once more that, in spite of its small size, limited resources and quite exposed situation, it did not hesitate in an extremely heated political situation to provoke a Member State by bringing a serious action, with potentially very considerable economic consequences, against its Government. Thereby it also rightly allowed the EFTA Court to address these very controversial and far from obvious issues and in the end to adjudicate them.

V. CONCLUDING REMARKS

During the 20 years that have passed since it came into force, the application and interpretation of the EEA Agreement have become well established within the EEA institutional set-up and its constituent two pillars. The EU now has a well-consolidated case law in relation to the EEA Agreement and in particular the defence of the rights for individuals and operators created thereby. There are no reasons to believe that this situation will change, although—as illustrated by the recent action by the United Kingdom[30]—it will always be important for the Council and the Commission to defend this *acquis* vigilantly.

Nevertheless, the continued success of the EEA cannot depend on the EU only. If the EFTA side were unable to carry out its tasks in a credible way, the whole project might be jeopardised rather quickly. Fortunately, the same situation as in the EU also reigns on the EFTA side, with a solid amount of case law established by the EFTA Court actively supported by ESA, which through its direct actions, submissions in the procedures for advisory opinions and decisions against which appeals are brought, has made a vital contribution to the EFTA Court's ongoing development of the EEA case law.

There is no doubt that the whole situation looked completely different when the EEA was in a preparatory stage some 25 years ago. In those days it was still a question, on the one hand, of a European Community recently enlarged to 12 with Portugal and Spain that was trying to overcome all the failures during its

---

[30] See above n 22.

first 35 years, and finally realise the four freedoms of the Treaty of Rome and thus complete its Internal Market and, on the other, a group of seven EFTA States, which under the fear that they would become excluded from or discriminated on that Single Market, were trying to get full access to it without being ready to seek full membership. It was in this perspective that the EEA was born and that its institutional set-up was devised.

It has, over the years, not been unusual for questions to be raised regarding the continued ambition and ability of ESA to act fully independently and objectively towards the Governments of the EFTA States, as it is claimed that the Commission always does in relation to the Governments of its Member States. Although it is quite obvious that ESA, with its much smaller size and considerably more exposed situation, with no permanent staff and with College members who do not have the political background or public standing of their colleagues, the EU Commissioners, may have difficulties to compare themselves with the latter. With their background mostly as senior public officials in a national foreign service it would be more appropriate to compare them with senior Commission officials. It should also be clear that with all the political and practical challenges described above, it would not be fair to expect of ESA, with its staff of around 70 officials and its three Member States of 5 million inhabitants, that it always should be able to act as fast, strongly and intensively as the EU Commission with its more than 30,000 officials and 28 Member States with 500 million inhabitants. Nevertheless, and in spite of all these challenges, it must be said that ESA, in an impressive way overall, has managed surprisingly well both to keep up with the Commission and to defend its integrity and independence in relation to the EFTA Governments and thereby to contribute to the credibility of the EFTA pillar in the EEA.

From this, it must also be concluded that in spite of the political disequilibrium between the Commission and ESA, which the original EFTA Governments devised on purpose when they created ESA, ESA has succeeded well in maintaining a good and trustful relationship with the Commission. This has no doubt been an essential explanation as to why the EEA Surveillance Mechanism and its two pillars have succeeded extremely well during these first 20 years of the EEA.

Since it furthermore seems more and more likely that the EEA will have a much longer future than anyone had ever expected, and that the likelihood for new members on the EFTA side does not seem very high, the question remains of how to maintain the present situation in the long run. The main challenges for the future lie obviously on the EFTA side, which in no way can allow itself to relax and be satisfied with a successful past. On the contrary, the EFTA governments and the EFTA institutions will constantly have to demonstrate, both to themselves and to their EU partners, that the EEA still continues to be a valid and credible way in practice to extend the scope of the EU internal market to the EFTA States.

36

The EFTA Surveillance Authority and the Surveillance of the EEA Agreement

ODA HELEN SLETNES

B OTH THE TREATY on the Functioning of the European Union (TFEU) and the Agreement on the European Economic Area (EEA) establish a unique and remarkable system for ensuring compliance by the States that are party to them: they both establish independent institutions to monitor and enforce compliance. Those institutions are, in the case of the European Union, the European Commission and the Court of Justice, and the EFTA Surveillance Authority and the EFTA Court in the case of the EEA.

I. A ROLE SIMILAR TO THAT OF THE EUROPEAN COMMISSION

The EFTA Surveillance Authority is entrusted by the EEA with a role similar to that of the European Commission which is commonly referred to as the guardian of the Treaties (Judgment of the Court of Justice in Case C-76/08 *Commission v Malta*, EC:C:2009:535 paragraph 23). Indeed, Article 108(1) EEA provides that 'the EFTA States shall establish an independent surveillance authority (EFTA Surveillance Authority) as well as procedures similar to those existing in the Community including procedures for ensuring the fulfilment of obligations under this Agreement and for the control of the legality of the acts of the EFTA Surveillance Authority regarding competition.'

It is not only the role attributed to the EFTA Surveillance Authority that is similar to that of the European Commission. The procedures applicable to infringement actions brought by the Authority against the Contracting States are similar to those which the Commission applies. Like Article 258 TFEU, Article 31 of the Agreement between the EFTA States on the establishment of a Surveillance Authority and a Court of Justice (SCA) lays down a three-step process by which the Authority first sends a letter of formal notice to the State concerned, then may deliver a reasoned opinion to the State and finally may apply to the EFTA Court for a declaration that the State has breached EEA law.

The effects of those three procedural steps are the same. The letter of formal notice gives the addressee State the opportunity to submit its observations. The reasoned opinion invites the State concerned to comply with EEA law within a deadline fixed in that document, which is usually two months. Finally, if compliance is not achieved, the Authority may decide to bring the infringement case before the EFTA Court.

The purpose of the infringement procedure is likewise the same. That purpose is best described by the Court of Justice itself in its recent judgment in Case C-514/11 *LPN and Finland v Commission*,[1] in which it held that:

> [The purpose of the infringement procedure is] to begin a process of negotiation and to reach an agreement between the Commission and the Member State concerned putting an end to the infringement alleged, in order to enable European Union law to be respected and to avoid legal proceedings.

Thus, the purpose of infringement proceedings is to bring the States into compliance with EEA law. The procedural steps prescribed in Article 31 SCA provide the framework in which compliance can be achieved through a process of discussions and negotiations with the State authorities concerned.

Although it is not legally obliged to do so, the Authority may begin the process of engaging with the authorities of the Contracting States by first sending an informal inquiry to them, also known as a 'pre-Article 31 letter'. That informal step puts the national authorities on notice that something may be amiss in the legal order, or in their administrative practice, and gives them an opportunity to provide information and explanations to the Authority. If the reaction of the national authorities is such that any doubts as to the existence of a possible infringement are not dissipated, the Surveillance Authority may decide to begin formal proceedings by sending a letter of formal notice.

That process of engagement and negotiation enables the Authority to obtain compliance from the national authorities in the vast majority of cases without recourse to litigation.

Thus the Authority shares the view of the infringement process clearly set out by the Court of Justice that recourse to litigation is not an end in itself. Indeed, litigation and recourse to the EFTA Court is a tool to be used in the process of obtaining compliance with EEA law.

II. ESA AT THE HEART OF THE SURVEILLANCE SYSTEM

While the role and procedures of the Surveillance Authority and the Commission are, for all intents and purposes, the same in infringement procedures, the EFTA Surveillance Authority has fewer governance tools at its disposal than the European Commission to ensure a well-functioning internal market. Over the last few years

---

[1] Judgment 14 November 2013, EU:C:2013:738, para 63.

the Commission has developed a broad set of mechanisms, rules and practices to help Member States implement, apply and enforce the common rules in a uniform manner. The increased use of new instruments and procedures like SOLVIT, EU-Pilot, IMI and Points of Single Contact might also contribute to solve problems at an early stage bearing in mind that formal infringement procedures might take years to complete. The number of infringement cases initiated by the Commission has thus decreased over the last few years while the Authority has launched a record number of such cases lately, but that is mainly due to an unprecedented high number of non-implementation and non-incorporation cases.

One useful instrument which the EFTA Surveillance Authority does not have at its disposal, unlike the Commission, is the administration of the EU Funds, such as the Cohesion, Social, Structural or Regional Funds. To ensure good governance of funds from EU budgets the Commission cannot accept that expenditure is incurred by the Member States in breach of EU law. If a breach is suspected by the Commission, it will suspend or even definitively reduce payment to the Member State. That has proved a useful tool for ensuring compliance with EU law.

Lastly, but not unimportantly, the Commission always has the option to propose legislative change if experience shows that the practical application of common rules does not deliver as expected or wished for. Such an avenue would of course never be open to the EFTA Surveillance Authority.

To sum up, for the Authority the infringement procedure is the key and indeed the only formal instrument at its disposal to ensure compliance by the EFTA States. This makes it even more important to ensure good quality and substance discussions in contacts with national authorities in the EFTA States both before and during the formal procedure.

III. ENFORCEMENT BY STATES AND ECONOMIC OPERATORS

The Authority is, however, not the only body that can bring cases to the EFTA Court when there is disagreement on the interpretation and application of the EEA Agreement. As is the case in the EU (Article 259 TFEU), an EFTA State may according to Article 32 SCA bring an action before the Court against two or more EFTA States for breaching EEA law. Such a procedure is rarely used in the EU because Member States prefer to complain to the Commission and intervene in its support before the Court of Justice rather than assuming the role of the plaintiff (see, for example, Case C-195/90 *Commission v Germany*[2] in which Belgium, Denmark, France, Luxembourg and the Netherlands intervened in support of the Commission). Nevertheless, Member States have commenced proceedings against other Member States five times. On two occasions the cases were settled and withdrawn before a judgment was delivered (once in a case brought by Ireland against

---

[2] EU:C:1992:219.

France in Case 58/77 *Ireland v France* and once in a case brought by Spain against the United Kingdom in Case 349/92 *Spain v United Kingdom*[3]). On four occasions the Court of Justice gave judgment (Case 141/78 *France v United Kingdom*[4] and Case C-388/95 *Belgium v Spain*,[5] Case C-145/04 *Spain v United Kingdom*[6] and Case C-364/10 *Hungary v Slovakia*[7]). In the EEA the procedure has not been used and one would assume for the same reasons. It would be easier to complain to the EFTA Surveillance Authority than to put at risk the relationship between two EFTA States in seeking a solution before the Court of an issue of disagreement related to the interpretation or application of the EEA Agreement.

EEA law does not require direct effect.[8] To what extent economic operators can rely on non-implemented EEA law is thus up to each EFTA State and depends on national law and legal tradition. Direct effect is one of the essential characteristics of EU law, which makes it possible for economic operators in some cases and independent of national law to act as 'private attorneys general' by bringing actions against Member States in national courts. The lack of direct effect of a non-implemented measure in an EFTA State leaves economic operators alleging a breach of EEA law with fewer means of enforcement in domestic courts of the Contracting States. And in some cases, the only recourse available to such operators may be either to complain to the Authority or to attempt to seek damages in national courts for any loss and damage that they may have incurred as a consequence of the breach of EEA law.

IV. SIMILAR ROLE BUT DIFFERENT POWERS

The roles of the Commission and of the EFTA Surveillance Authority are similar but their powers are not.

The Authority has no power similar to Article 260(3) TFEU. That provision of the TFEU, introduced by the Lisbon Treaty, allows the Commission to request the Court of Justice to impose a lump sum or penalty payment on a Member State which has failed to notify to it measures transposing a directive adopted under a legislative procedure.

Likewise, there is no equivalent in the EEA to Article 260(2) TFEU, which allows the Commission to request the Court of Justice to impose a lump sum or penalty payment on a Member State which has failed to comply properly with a judgment of the Court of Justice.

---

[3] OJ 1992 C 256, p 14.
[4] EU:C:1979:225.
[5] EU:C:2000:244.
[6] EU:C:2006:543.
[7] EU:C:2012:630.
[8] Case E-4/01 *Karl K Karlsson hf v Icelandic State* [2002] EFTA Ct Rep 240 and Case E-1/07 *Criminal Proceedings v A* [2007] EFTA Ct Rep 248.

V. SIMILAR BUT NOT IDENTICAL PROCEDURES

As is apparent from the description of the procedure above, both the Authority and the Commission use the same three-stage process in the formal administrative procedure. The Authority has even aligned itself with the Commission's practice in the handling of complaints as laid down in the Commission communication to the European Parliament and the European Ombudsman of 20 March 2002 on relations with the complainant in respect of infringements of Community law.[9] Accordingly, before it intends to close a complaint procedure, it gives the complainant the opportunity to make his or her views known on the Authority's intentions.

Despite the similarity in the infringement procedures at the Authority and the Commission, the EFTA Court has recently signalled that it could depart from the case law of the Court of Justice on how such procedures are handled. In its judgment of 16 July 2012 in Case E-9/11 *ESA v Norway*,[10] the EFTA Court held in paragraph 68:

> When ESA, whether upon a complaint or on its own motion, considers that an EFTA State has failed to fulfil an obligation under the EEA Agreement, it is in the interest of the proper functioning of the EEA Agreement that ESA proceeds within an appropriate time when assessing whether to bring a Contracting Party before the Court. The Court recalls that the aim of the Agreement is, *in particular*, to promote a continuous and balanced strengthening of trade and economic relations between the Contracting Parties with equal conditions of competition for citizens and economic operators, and the respect of the same rules. In the matter brought before the Court in the present case, i.e. the proceedings that result from the letter of formal notice issued on 16 December 2009, ESA has *acted without undue delay*.

The judgment is the first in which the EFTA Court has considered the time taken by the Authority in the exercise of the powers conferred upon it by Article 31 SCA. Paragraph 68 of the judgment is also a departure from the well-established case law of the Court of Justice. That Court has considered the question of the speed with which the Commission brings infringement proceedings on a number of occasions. Its case law on the issue is constant. The Court of Justice recently repeated this in its judgment of 21 January 2010 in Case C-546/07 *Commission v Germany*,[11] in which it held:

> In accordance with settled case-law, it is for the Commission to judge at what time it will bring an action for failure to fulfil obligations; the considerations which determine its choice of time cannot affect the admissibility of the action (see, inter alia, Case C-317/92 *Commission v Germany* [1994] ECR I-2039, paragraph 4).

---

[9] COM/2002/0141 final; OJ 2002 C 244, p 5, paras 7, 9 and 10.
[10] [2012] EFTA Ct Rep 444 (emphasis added).
[11] EU:C:2010:25.

The rules of Article 226 EC must be applied and the Commission is not obliged to act within a specific period, save where the excessive duration of the pre-litigation procedure in that provision is capable of making it more difficult for the Member State concerned to refute the Commission's arguments and of thus infringing the rights of the defence. It is for the Member State concerned to provide evidence that it has been so affected (see, inter alia, Case C-490/04 *Commission v Germany* [2007] ECR I-6095, paragraph 26).

It follows from that passage that:

— the Court of Justice allows the Commission almost unlimited discretion to decide when it should bring an infringement action;
— the admissibility of an application to the Court will not be affected by the duration of the administrative phase of the proceedings;
— the Court will not raise the issue of the duration of the procedure of its own motion and requires that the defendant State demonstrates that the delay in the procedure affected its ability to defend itself.

To date, no Member State has succeeded in demonstrating that mere delay by the Commission in bringing infringement proceedings has affected its rights of defence and convinced the Court of Justice to dismiss the application on that ground alone.

Given the clear position expressed many times by the Court of Justice on the timeliness of infringement proceedings, paragraph 68 of the judgment of 16 July 2012 in Case E-9/11 is a departure from the case law of the Court of Justice in two respects:

— first, the EFTA Court seems willing to examine *of its own motion* the speed with which the Authority brings infringement cases whereas the Court of Justice requires that the defendant State claims and proves that any delay impaired its ability to defend itself; and
— second, the EFTA Court may seem intent *to reduce the margin of discretion* of the Authority to start infringement proceedings when it considers it appropriate to do so.

It is unclear what consequences the EFTA Court might draw for the outcome of infringement proceedings should it ever conclude that the Authority had acted with undue delay. That could in the Authority's view have the paradoxical effect of reducing the Authority's possibility to achieve compliance in the case of long-lasting infringements by the Contracting States. Nevertheless, paragraph 68 of the judgment in Case E-9/11 *ESA v Norway* is a reminder that both the Authority and the Contracting States should pay special attention to the timeline of an infringement procedure. The Authority will continue to act without undue delay and use the instruments it has at its disposal to ensure compliance with EEA law.

37

The EFTA Secretariat: Steward of the EEA

KRISTINN F ÁRNASON

I. INTRODUCTION

THE EUROPEAN FREE Trade Association (EFTA) and the European Union (EU) are the oldest free trade areas in modern times and arguably the most successful. The histories of EFTA and the EU are intertwined and it is hard, if not impossible, to understand the origins and development of one without reference to the other. Both were born in the post-war era and their roots are to be found in the idea and conviction that further and closer cooperation through trade was vital not only for European reconstruction and economic growth but also for long-term stability and prosperity—although they have chosen different routes to achieve these goals.

After the Second World War, a great deal of discussion took place on the nature, scope, organisation and coverage of closer cooperation between European States. In 1957, six European States signed the Treaty of Rome, creating the European Economic Community (EEC). Three years later, seven other European States signed the EFTA Convention in Stockholm, forming their own free trade area. The authors of the EFTA Convention were pragmatic in their approach. While they made firm commitments in tariff reduction and the elimination of quantitative restrictions among the EFTA States, they otherwise satisfied themselves with a statement of guiding principles rather than laying down binding rules and procedures. Today, the liberalisation of intra-EFTA trade relations has been achieved in most areas through the development of the EFTA Convention.

Interaction between the EU and EFTA through the decades has been substantial and tremendously important to both organisations. As early as 1972 and 1973, the EFTA States and the EU signed wide-ranging free trade agreements (FTAs). In 1992, three of the EFTA States, together with the EU Member States, created the European Economic Area (EEA), which is possibly the most comprehensive and dynamic trade agreement in history, effectively including Iceland, Liechtenstein and Norway, the 'EEA EFTA States', in the Internal Market.

The EFTA Secretariat is only incidentally mentioned in the EFTA Convention.[1] It has, however, in its history of more than 50 years, proved to be a highly flexible and effective instrument for the EFTA States as they have pushed for further trade liberalisation and adapted to evolving political and economic realities.

Aside from maintaining the EFTA Convention, the EFTA Secretariat has two substantive tasks today: to assist the EFTA States in negotiating and maintaining FTAs with non-EU countries; and to assist Iceland, Liechtenstein and Norway in the operation and development of the EEA. Work on FTAs is carried out in EFTA's headquarters in Geneva, while day-to-day EEA matters are managed in Brussels. In this chapter, I will shed some light on the *practical* role of the Secretariat in the management of the Agreement on the European Economic Area (EEA Agreement), as this publication focuses on its 20th anniversary.

Participation in the Internal Market through the EEA Agreement involves the incorporation of EU legislation by the EEA EFTA States. The EFTA Secretariat in Brussels plays a key role in the day-to-day management of this process. Importantly, the Secretariat's role is not limited to overseeing the incorporation of EU *acquis* into the EEA Agreement. Officers at the Secretariat have diverse tasks ranging from ensuring EEA EFTA participation in EU programmes to organising consultations between the two sides, for example discussions between parliamentarians and social partners. In sum it can be said that the EFTA Secretariat assisted in the negotiation of the EEA Agreement and that its contribution has been important for EEA cooperation since the Agreement entered into force 20 years ago.

In order to set the scene, I will begin by outlining some of the key elements of our history and structure. I will then go on to set out in some detail the key tasks the Secretariat performs in support of the EEA EFTA States. Finally, I will offer a few thoughts on the potential future of the EEA and the role of the Secretariat in securing the continued participation of the EEA EFTA States in the EEA.

II. FROM A SMALL LISTENING POST TO THE CENTRE OF EEA ACTIVITIES

The office of the EFTA Secretariat in Brussels initially began as a two-man show in 1988 for a trial period of three years. The original aim of having an office in Brussels in addition to the one in Geneva was to create an 'antenna' for the EFTA Member States, which at the time were Austria, Finland, Iceland, Norway, Sweden and Switzerland. The purpose of the Brussels office was to 'provide technical

---

[1] According to Art 44(b) of the Convention establishing the European Free Trade Association of 1960, '[t]he Council shall … make arrangements for the secretariat services required by the Association'.

services for EFTA activities in Brussels' by assisting staff from the Geneva Secretariat and experts and Missions from the EFTA countries.[2]

The EEC[3] was busy preparing for the launch of its Single Market when the initiative of what eventually became the EEA was conceived. It was clear from the outset—the Delors initiative in January 1989 and the positive response at the EFTA summit two months later—that this would be a joint endeavour between EFTA and the European Communities (EC), involving all Member States of both organisations.[4] Another key point was that the EFTA States soon agreed that they would speak 'with one voice' in the negotiations on the EEA.[5] It was then natural that not only would EFTA as such be involved, but also that the Secretariat would play a role. The bulk of the work of the Secretariat relating to the negotiations was executed in Geneva. However, as the work intensified, the office in Brussels was enlarged to five staff members who mainly assisted the Member States with the negotiations.

Once the EEA Agreement was signed in 1992, the role of the EFTA office in Brussels changed considerably. As stated in the Annual Report of 1992, 'the Secretariat, which had previously served as a listening post and facility for Brussels-based meetings, became the centre for EEA-related activities'. By the end of the year, all departments of the EFTA Secretariat were represented in Brussels and some 60 staff members out of a total of 160 were based there. Since 1993, the EFTA office in Brussels has been fully operational and deals with all matters concerning the EEA Agreement. The headquarters and governing structure of EFTA remain in Geneva.

It should be noted that it was soon predicted that the EEA Agreement might serve as a mere stepping stone towards EU membership, at least for some of the EFTA States. Indeed, Austria, Finland and Sweden all joined the EU only a year after the EEA Agreement had entered into force. With the adoption of the Bergen Declaration[6] in June 1995, it was clear that the EEA would have a future for the remaining EFTA States which had ratified the EEA Agreement: Iceland, Liechtenstein[7] and Norway. Switzerland signed the EEA Agreement, but when membership of the EEA was put to the vote in a referendum in December 1992, it was rejected by a slim majority. No further developments have taken place

---

[2] Decision of the EFTA Council No 11 of 1987.

[3] The EEC was created by the Treaty of Rome in 1957. As of 1965 it formed one of the pillars of the European Communities, along with the European Coal and Steel Community and the European Atomic Energy Community.

[4] The anomaly of involving EFTA (which was not a party itself and with some of its Member States not being involved) only resulted from the Swiss 'no' vote in December 1992.

[5] This was later confirmed in the Joint Declaration issued after the EFTA-EC ministerial meeting in Brussels on 19 December 1989, at which point it was decided to launch formal negotiations, which stated that the EFTA countries would be 'acting as a single interlocutor' in the talks.

[6] EFTA ministerial meeting in Bergen, 13 and 14 June 1995. The Bergen Declaration states that after the accession of several former EFTA States to the EU, there has been a smooth transition and EFTA Ministers are satisfied with the good functioning of the EEA.

[7] Following the positive result in the second referendum on the EEA in Liechtenstein in April 1995.

510 Kristinn F Árnason

in EFTA's membership and so the EFTA office in Brussels has served the three EEA EFTA States for more than two decades. The structure and nature of the Secretariat's work have remained remarkably stable since the mid 1990s.

There is one major exception to this, which relates to the development of the so-called 'financial mechanism', a system included in the EEA Agreement with the aim of reducing economic and social disparities between the contracting parties to the EEA Agreement.[8] The two five-year mechanisms (1994–1998 and 1999–2003) were managed by a dedicated unit in the Secretariat office in Brussels—initially consisting of a single staff member. Then, in connection with the EU and EEA enlargement to Central and Eastern Europe in 2004, there was a ten-fold increase in the amounts provided under the financial mechanisms.[9] As a result of this increase, it was decided to set up a distinct Financial Mechanism Office (FMO) administratively linked to the Secretariat, with a considerable boost in staff and resources to manage the grants. Today, the FMO in Brussels has some 65 staff members.

The EFTA office in Brussels currently has a staff of 63. Most of these work on EEA-related issues in one of the three main divisions: i) EEA Coordination, ii) Goods, and iii) Services, Capital, Persons and Programmes. Fluctuations in terms of staffing have been minor over the years, with small peaks in connection with specific projects, such as during the enlargement of the EEA in 2004, 2007 and 2014.

III. THE EFTA PILLAR OF THE EEA

The EEA Agreement provides that the EEA EFTA States are required to speak with one voice in the decision-making bodies of the EEA. This is sometimes referred to as 'one for all and all for one'. In order to facilitate decision making, administration and management between the EEA EFTA States, it was agreed that a Standing Committee would be established on the EFTA side, and that '[t]he Secretariat services for the Standing Committee shall be provided by the EFTA Secretariat'.[10] The Rules of Procedure of the EEA Joint Committee and the Standing Committee of the EFTA States further specified that the Standing Committee would be assisted by five subcommittees to mirror the joint subcommittees established under the EEA Agreement, as well as the possibility of establishing working groups, which in turn may decide to set up expert groups. The Secretariat services these subcommittees and working and expert groups. Considering that there are currently 31 EFTA working groups and 26 expert groups, these decisions had significant consequences for the Secretariat, as its workload increased considerably.

---

[8] Arts 115–117 and Protocol 38 to the EEA Agreement.
[9] Since 2004, there have been two mechanisms: the EEA Financial Mechanism and the Norwegian Financial Mechanism.
[10] Art 8 of the Agreement on a Standing Committee of the EFTA States, signed in Porto on 2 May 1992.

EFTA officers serve as secretaries to these various committees and working groups. Their tasks range from organising and preparing meetings, drafting documents and providing technical and legal advice, monitoring EU developments and managing contacts with EU counterparts, to providing information on EFTA and the EEA to the outside world.[11]

The EEA Agreement provides for a rotating presidency of the EEA Council and the EEA Joint Committee. As a corollary of its support to the Standing Committee, the EFTA Secretariat also assists the EEA EFTA Presidency in the various EEA joint bodies—the EEA Council, the EEA Joint Committee and the Joint Subcommittees—even though this is not explicitly provided for in any formal texts. Furthermore, the Secretariat provides secretariat services to the EEA EFTA delegations, that is, members of the EFTA Parliamentary and Consultative Committees, and to the joint EEA advisory bodies: the EEA Joint Parliamentary Committee (JPC) and the EEA Consultative Committee.[12]

A. Coordinator and Intermediary

The Standing Committee and its subcommittees, working groups and expert groups usually hold their meetings at the EFTA premises in Brussels. All in all, there are more than 100 of these meetings per year, as the Standing Committee and the subcommittees normally meet seven to eight times per year, with each working or expert group meeting a few times each year.

It is the task of the Secretariat to issue the invitations to these meetings and prepare and forward all relevant documents to participants. These include traditional meeting documents such as agendas, conclusions and minutes, as well as key documents such as decisions to be made by the Joint Committee for the incorporation of new EU legislation into the EEA Agreement.

One of the issues discussed at the working group and subcommittee meetings is input to be provided to new EU initiatives and legislative proposals through the submission of so-called 'EEA EFTA Comments'. In 2013, for example, the EEA EFTA States submitted a total of 12 EEA EFTA Comments. The Secretariat supports the EEA EFTA States in this process by coordinating their positions in the relevant EFTA working groups and sometimes by assisting in the drafting of the text of the EEA EFTA Comment.

Another way in which the EEA EFTA States can provide input into the EU legislative process is through their right to participate in the hundreds of EU

---

[11] In addition, a number of formal tasks are assigned to the Secretary-General of EFTA, such as the co-signing of Standing Committee minutes and decisions, and the transmission of information on decisions made and positions taken in case of absence of EFTA States from meetings of the Standing Committee.

[12] According to Rule 21 of the JPC Rules of Procedure, its Secretariat 'shall be provided jointly by the Secretariat of the E[uropean]P[arliament] and the EFTA Secretariat'.

committees and expert groups involved in EEA-related matters. The Secretariat also plays an important role in assisting the Member States in this process. The Secretariat maintains contact with the relevant EU institutions and often acts as an intermediary between the EEA EFTA States and the EU institutions to ensure that the EEA EFTA States are able to participate in the various committees and expert groups, as stipulated in the EEA Agreement.

The Secretariat also uses its contacts with the EU institutions and the Permanent Representations of the EU Member States to ensure that the EEA EFTA States are kept informed about developments within the EU, and that expert knowledge is passed on when needed. For example, the Secretariat regularly invites EU officials or seconded national experts to the relevant EFTA working group to give an overview of a potential new EU initiative.

B. Advice and Analysis

The EFTA Secretariat, upon request of the EEA EFTA States, provides a range of both legal advice and political analysis.

First, the Secretariat has an advisory role when it comes to the incorporation of EEA-relevant EU *acquis* into the EEA Agreement. It analyses EU developments and identifies which aspects are potentially relevant to the EEA EFTA States. When the EU then amends or adopts an EEA-relevant legal act, the Secretariat provides a general assessment of whether this act could pose any challenges in relation to its incorporation into the EEA Agreement. The Secretariat also assists the delegations in drafting any necessary adaptations. While this is not provided for in the Rules of Procedure, it has become usual practice that the Secretariat drafts the so-called 'Joint Committee Decision' (JCD) incorporating the legal act into the EEA Agreement. The number of JCDs drafted by the Secretariat and subsequently adopted by the EEA Joint Committee has steadily increased from 50 per year in the mid 1990s to around 200 annually in recent years.

Further in its role of serving the Standing Committee and advisory bodies, the Secretariat regularly drafts background documents and resolutions and assists in the writing of speaking notes for the chair. Most of the first drafts of the main documents for the EEA Joint Committee and the EEA Council—such as the Annual Report and Progress Report of the Joint Committee, and the EEA Council Conclusions—are drawn up by the Secretariat, in close coordination with the European External Action Service (EEAS) and/or the EU Council Secretariat. When the Chair of the Standing Committee briefs the trade unions and employers' organisations or the EFTA Parliamentary Committee on recent developments in the EEA, it is likely that the Secretariat has assisted in drafting the speaking notes. Similarly, when EFTA parliamentarians make their annual visits to third countries, the Secretariat prepares a detailed background note about these countries. The Secretariat also drafts the opinions and resolutions for the Consultative Committee, which are then presented to the EFTA authorities and EEA bodies.

The Secretariat also serves 'Subcommittee V on Legal and Institutional Matters', a forum for discussing both formal procedures and legal questions affecting overall EEA cooperation. In particular, the Secretariat provides advice on how to upgrade and optimise legal practices and procedures in the institutional setup of the EEA Agreement. Upon request of the EEA EFTA States, it also provides in-depth legal analyses and opinions on questions of both specific and general application. Finally, it supports the work of the EEA EFTA States in other EEA-related matters, such as enlargement of the EEA and, upon request of the EEA EFTA States, the monitoring and analysis of EU developments that may be of relevance to the EEA.

IV. THE SECRETARIAT'S ROLE IN SECURING A SUCCESSFUL FUTURE FOR THE EEA AGREEMENT

An EFTA Bulletin from 1989 states that 'EFTA never intended to build a large bureaucracy, let alone one with executive powers comparable to the Commission or the European Communities'. The EFTA Secretariat was expected to give legal advice, observe, inform and coordinate—in other words, to serve the Member States in a flexible and effective manner.

Seen from today's perspective, the EEA Agreement is far from being a mere stepping stone to EU membership. Both the EU and the EEA EFTA States have in recent years acknowledged that the Agreement is both a durable and a well-functioning instrument. It has succeeded in extending the EU's Internal Market to the EEA EFTA States while at the same time ensuring its integrity. I am proud to say that the Secretariat has certainly been a central player in ensuring that it functions well.

While its tasks have expanded and diversified, the Secretariat has also stayed true to its principle of serving the Member States. So whichever direction the EEA Agreement takes, the EEA EFTA States are in the pilot seat, while the Secretariat is the steward of the craft doing its best to ensure a smooth and comfortable journey—for many years to come.

Part VI

A Look from the Outside

38

EEA Law, Unexpected Success:
A Japanese Perspective

YOICHI ITO

I. INTRODUCTION

THE EFTA COURT celebrates its twentieth anniversary this year. In 1992, however, Community lawyers were not at all enthusiastic about the EEA. On the contrary, they feared the risk of contamination by 'the EEA virus'[1] and had a deep scepticism about the future functioning of the new-born EEA. The famous ECJ Opinion 1/91 expressed a profound distrust of the EEA Agreement as an ordinary international treaty ([1991] ECR I-6079). Such distrust was understandable if we consider the difficulties of its institutional design which have been often described as 'squaring the circle'. The EEA Agreement was indeed an attempt to attain contradictory objectives. On the one hand, the EFTA countries sought to obtain the benefits of a future internal market without fully sharing its burdens—more precisely, without transferring their legislative power to the EEA institutions. On the other hand, the EC was no longer so generous as to give unilateral benefits of 'cherry-picking' to the EFTA States where neither direct effect nor primacy of the EFTA Treaty had been recognised. True, the principle of homogeneity between Community law and EEA law was provided in Article 6 EEA, but Community lawyers, and most of all the ECJ in Opinion 1/91, remained profoundly sceptical of its prospects of success. It was absolutely normal to ask oneself: Does the EEA Agreement really work?

In the eyes of Community lawyers, there was another fatal defect: the EEA advisory opinion procedure. After the first EEA opinion, a new EFTA Court and an advisory opinion procedure between the EFTA Court and national courts were created in order to ensure homogeneity in the EFTA pillar of the EEA. However, national courts in an EFTA State are never obliged to refer questions to the EFTA Court and *advisory* opinion is, by definition, not binding on the national court which made reference to the EFTA Court. It is not surprising that Professor

---

[1] R Barents, 'The Court of Justice and the EEA-Agreements' (1993) *Rivista di diritto europeo* 751, 763.

Boulouis found a sort of 'caricature' of EC preliminary ruling procedure in the EEA advisory opinion procedure.[2]

Worse still, the viability of the EEA itself seemed to be threatened because of successive accession of some EFTA States to the EU. The EEA was regarded by some commentators to be like an 'interim' scheme before formal accession to the EU. So Professor Schermers predicted: 'It is unlikely that the compromises found will lead to a system which remains workable in the long term. They are too much of an effort to combine the uncombinable. Most probably the Agreement will only apply during an interim period.'[3]

In view of such a discouraging prediction, who could ever foresee in 1992 that the EFTA Court would celebrate its twentieth anniversary? Even Sven Norberg, at the time Head of the EFTA Legal Service and influential negotiator of the EEA Agreement, acknowledges that '[t]he EEA judicial mechanism has become much more long-lived than most could ever have expected'.[4] The history of the EEA Agreement is indeed 'one of unexpected success'.[5]

A natural question would be how and why such an expected success could be possible. These questions are all the more natural since the EEA is often said to have successfully established a legal system which is, in practice, no less effective than the Community law.[6]

This chapter is intended to shed some light on these questions taking examples of the EEA principle of State liability and the EEA advisory opinion. In Section II, we will focus on major logic used in the EFTA case law. In Section III, we will discuss the secret of its success. Finally, we will attempt to draw some lessons from EEA law.

II. EEA, UNEXPECTED SUCCESS

From the outset, there has been an intense debate about the 'relevance' of the Community principle of State liability to EEA law. The 'Red Book', the first authoritative commentary on the EEA Agreement written by mainly Swedish negotiators, has already pointed out this issue with respect to the famous

---

[2] J Boulouis, 'Les avis de la Cour de justice des Communautés sur la compatibilité avec le Traité CEE du projet d'accord créant l'Espace économique européen (EEE)' (1992) *Revue trimestrielle de droit européen* 457, 461.

[3] HG Schermers, 'Case note on Opinion 1/91 of 14 December 1991; Opinion 1/92 of 10 April 1992' (1992) 29 *CML Rev* 991, 1005; see also J Dutheil de la Rochère, 'L'Espace économique européen sous le regard des juges de la Cour de justice des Communautés européennes' (1992) *Revue du Marché Commun* 603, 612.

[4] S Norberg, '20 Years On: Some Reflections on the European Economic Area Judicial Mechanism' in P Cardonnel, A Rosas and N Wahl (eds), *Constitutionalising the EU Judicial System: Essays in Honour of Pernilla Lindh* (Oxford, Hart Publishing, 2012) 57, 74.

[5] H Haukeland Fredriksen, 'Bridging the Widening Gap between the EU Treaties and the Agreement on the European Economic Area' (2012) 18 *ELJ* 868, 868.

[6] Eg H Haukeland Fredriksen, 'State Liability in EU and EEA Law: The Same or Different?' (2013) 38 *EL Rev* 884, 895.

Francovich case law of the ECJ[7] and concluded that 'that principle would also have to be considered in relation to the EEA Agreement'.[8] Even if the question remained open, it was perfectly arguable that *Francovich* should be regarded as 'relevant' in the sense of Article 6 EEA, since *Francovich* was delivered in 1991, well before the signature of the EEA Agreement (2 May 1992).[9]

However, the EFTA Court held, in *Sveinbjörnsdóttir*, that 'the principle of State liability must be seen as *an integral part of the EEA Agreement as such*'[10] (emphasis added). In other words, *Francovich* principle was *not* considered as 'relevant' in the technical meaning of Article 6 EEA. This Article provides an obligation to interpret the provisions of the EEA Agreement in conformity with the relevant rulings of the ECJ, only 'in so far as they are identical in substance to corresponding rules' of the EEC Treaty. Contrary to the substantive provisions in the EEA Agreement, it was difficult to affirm the 'relevance', in the sense of Article 6, of 'constitutional' principles of EC law. The Court examined rather the question as to 'whether such a State obligation is to be derived from the stated purposes and the legal structure of the EEA Agreement' (para 47).

The EFTA Court has nevertheless emphasised the importance of the homogeneity objective in EEA law and took the homogeneity objective very seriously. It should be noted that, in this context, the principle of homogeneity has a broader meaning than that in the technical meaning of Article 6. It is important to note that the Court emphasised that 'the homogeneity objective and the objective of establishing the right of individuals and economic operators to *equal* treatment and *equal* opportunities are so strongly expressed in the EEA Agreement that the EFTA States must be obliged to provide for compensation for loss and damage caused to an individual by incorrect implementation of a directive' (para 60, emphasis added). Later, President Baudenbacher wrote extra-judicially, but more clearly, that denying the EEA principle of State liability 'would have been incompatible ... with the legitimate *reciprocity* expectations of the Community and of its citizens'[11] (emphasis added). The point is that, without the EEA principle of State liability, a homogeneous economic area would not be able to be achieved because of imbalance in judicial protection between the EFTA pillar and the EU pillar.

The background of this reciprocity argument is of course the fact that neither principles of EC-styled direct effect nor primacy are recognised in EEA law. The EFTA Court held in *Restamark* that only *implemented* provisions of EEA law may have direct effect and primacy (Case E-1/94, para 77). The result is that 'the same

---

[7] Joined Cases C-6/90 and C-9/90, *Francovich and Bonifaci v Italy* [1991] ECR I-5357.

[8] S Norberg, K Hökborg, M Johansson, D Eliasson and L Dedichen, *EEA Law. A Commentary on the EEA Agreement* (Deventer/Stockholm, Kluwer/Fritzes, 1993) 208.

[9] See also a very interesting testimony by S Norberg reported by S Magnússon and, OI Hannesson, 'State Liability in EEA Law: Towards Parallelism or Homogeneity?' (2013) 38 *EL Rev* 167, 168, fn 6.

[10] Case E-9/97 *Sveinbjörnsdóttir v Iceland*, para 63.

[11] C Baudenbacher, 'If not EEA State Liability, then What? Reflections Ten Years After the EFTA Court's *Sveinbjörnsdóttir* Ruling' (2009) 10 *Chicago Journal of International Law* 333, 358.

rules of EEA law will have absolute primacy in the EU, and only partial primacy in the EFTA States'.[12]

This is why an EEA principle of State liability is regarded as, contrary to the situation in EC law, the *sole* means to compensate for the lack of direct effect and primacy in cases of *non-implemented*—in particular secondary—EEA law and to protect individual rights in the EFTA pillar. As President Baudenbacher clearly put it, 'the homogeneity goal includes an *obligation de résultat* on the part of EEA/EFTA side with regard to the level of protection of individual rights'.[13] Consequently, a principle of State liability is even more important in the EFTA pillar of the EEA than in the EC pillar.[14] This reciprocity argument is thus an extremely powerful one in favour of the EFTA Court's case law on the level of judicial protection of individual rights in EEA law.

Recently, the EFTA Court further held in *HOB-vín (No 3)* that '[w]ith regard to secondary EEA law, individuals and economic operators must be able to invoke the principle of State liability *when a decision by the EEA Joint Committee becomes applicable*'[15] (emphasis added). EEA State liability can therefore be engaged *before* national implementation measures of those secondary EEA provisions even though the aforementioned EEA provisions cannot have direct effect before national courts. It is henceforth sufficient for the purpose of State liability that the EEA Joint Committee has incorporated the secondary EEA law in the Annex to the EEA Agreement.[16]Such construction clearly contributes to compensate for the lack of direct effect of non-implemented EEA secondary law.

Most interestingly, the reciprocity argument is now invoked by some authors in order to propose a lower threshold for EEA State liability in the EEA/EFTA States than in the EU States. Magnússon and Hannesson have recently submitted in the name of 'effect-based homogeneity' that '[i]f a rule has a direct effect according to EU law, a breach of this rule should, in the case of non-implementation, automatically be considered sufficiently serious under EEA law'.[17]

The starting point is the well-known *Karlsson* judgment (Case E-4/01), which confirmed the *Sveinbjörnsdóttir* case law and rejected the Norwegian government's submission against that case law. In its paragraph 30, the EFTA Court held that '[t]he finding that the principle of State liability is an integral part of the EEA Agreement differs, as it must, from the development in the case law of the Court of Justice of the European Communities of the principle of State liability under

---

[12]   F Sejersted, 'Between Sovereignty and Supranationalism in the EEA Context' in P-C Müller-Graff and S Erling (eds), *The European Economic Area: Norway's basic status in the legal construction of Europe* (Berlin, Berlin Verlag, 1997) 43, 59.

[13]   C Baudenbacher, 'The EFTA Court Ten Years On' in C Baudenbacher, P Tresselt and T Örlygsson (eds), *The EFTA Court: Ten Years On* (Oxford, Hart Publishing, 2005) 29.

[14]   Baudenbacher, above n 11, 333, 358.

[15]   Case E-2/12 *HOB-vín ehf v The State Alcohol and Tobacco Company of Iceland (ÁTVR)*, para 128.

[16]   A Alemanno, 'The HOB-vín III Judgment: Stories on Sex (labels), Alcohol (pops) and … EEA State liability' (2012) *European Law Reporter* 330, 337.

[17]   Magnússon and Hannesson, above n 9 (2013) 38 *EL Rev* 167, 179.

EC law. Therefore, the application of the principles *may not necessarily be in all respects coextensive*' (emphasis added). Interestingly, the EFTA Court has never made any direct reference to the ECJ case law in determining the conditions for State liability under EEA law.[18] It is not surprising that the Norwegian government was to interpret, in *Finanger-II* before the Norwegian Supreme Court, the aforementioned paragraph 30 in *Karlsson* as setting a *higher* threshold for State liability in EEA law than in EC law. The Supreme Court, however, rejected the government's interpretation and held that 'EEA State liability has the same scope and is at the same level as State liability in the EC'.[19] So it has been settled in academic literature that the threshold of EEA State liability is *at least* the same level as that in the EC pillar.[20]

The proposition by Magnússon and Hannesson goes further and seems a very bold one. No wonder it has provoked immediately heavy criticism by Fredriksen. However, what is interesting here is that Fredriksen conceded nevertheless that their proposition applies to 'situations where the plaintiff's loss is caused by the lack of an EEA law principle of direct effect'.[21] It remains to be seen whether the EFTA Court will introduce stricter State liability at least in such situations. In any case, it should be noted that it is surprising indeed for Community lawyers to observe such development in EEA law where a principle of State liability itself was questioned initially.

As to the EEA advisory opinion procedure, it is worthwhile to consider briefly a recent development of the reciprocity argument in EFTA case law. Until recently, authors have agreed to conclude that, according to the wording of Article 34 SCA, there is no obligation on national courts, including those of the last instance, to make a reference to the EFTA Court. However, a newer doctrine has been growing to contend that national courts are not always totally free to refuse to refer questions to the EFTA Court.[22] And recently, the EFTA Court finally held in *Irish Bank* that there can be situations where refusal to make a reference to the EFTA Court might be incompatible with Article 6 of the European Convention on Human Rights.[23] According to this 'new approach', national courts might be obliged to make a reference to the EFTA Court, which is without doubt new to EEA law. A reference to the EFTA Court is no longer regarded as a simple faculty of national courts, but as a means for the protection of *a right to access to justice* (Article 6 ECHR).

---

[18] Baudenbacher, above n 11, 350; Magnússon and Hannesson, above n 9, 176.

[19] Judgment of 28 October 2005, Case No 2005/412, *Finanger II* (unofficial translation by the EFTA Court for which the author is grateful to the registry office of the Court). See Baudenbacher, above n 11, 356–357.

[20] See, eg, G Gorton, 'Bestätigung der Staatshaftungsrechtsprechung des EFTA-Gerichtshofs' (2002) *European Law Reporter* 260, 262.

[21] Fredriksen, above n 6, 884, 893.

[22] C Baudenbacher, *The EFTA Court in Action* (Munich, GLP, 2010) 22; J Temple Lang, 'The Duty of National Courts to Provide Access to Justice in the EEA' in EFTA Court (ed), *Judicial Protection in the European Economic Area* (Munich, GLP, 2012) 100, 114; C Baudenbacher, 'Das Vorabentscheidungsverfahren im EFTA-Pfeiler des EWR' (2013) *EuR* 504, 516.

[23] Case E-18/11, paras 63–64. See also Case E-3/12, *Jonsson*, para 60.

This is why the Court again put forward the reciprocity argument in this context.[24] It held that 'EFTA citizens and economic operators benefit from the obligation of courts of the EU Member States against whose decision there is no judicial remedy under national law to make a reference to the ECJ' (para 58) and emphasised that the homogeneity objective 'can only be achieved if EFTA and EU citizens and economic operators enjoy, relying upon EEA law, the same rights in both the EU and EFTA pillars of the EEA' (para 122).

Finally it should be added that there is little difference in practice between reference practice in the EFTA pillar and that in the EU pillar.[25]

All things considered, it seems that, notwithstanding some institutional differences, there is, in practice, not so great a difference in effectivity between EEA law and EC law as expected in 1992.

III. THE SECRET OF SUCCESS

Surprisingly for many Community lawyers, the EEA has thus successfully overcome institutional 'flaws' by dynamic judicial evolution and pragmatism and achieved essentially the same results. But why was it possible? Two marked factors should be borne in mind in the EEA: structural specificity of the EEA (A) and the role of judicial dialogue in Europe (B).

A. Structural Specificity of the EEA

Its first specificity is that the EEA has had what we would like to call 'late development advantages'. If the success of the EEA owes much to the EFTA Court's determination to take the homogeneous objective seriously, it is nevertheless true that the EFTA Court could benefit considerably from the ECJ's experience. To take our example of State liability, without *Francovich* case law, the *Sveinbjörnsdóttir* ruling would have never been delivered. It might be useful to recall a brief chronology in this context. After the *Van Gend en Loos* ruling,[26] the ECJ took nearly 30 years to establish a principle of State liability in *Francovich* whereas the EFTA Court took only four years to establish, in *Sveinbjörnsdóttir*, an EEA principle of State liability after it took office. Moreover, the ECJ took no less than three years to clarify, in *Brasserie du Pêcheur and Factortame*,[27] the conditions of State liability whereas the EFTA Court could, from the very start

---

[24] See also Baudenbacher, 'Das Vorabentscheidungsverfahren im EFTA-Pfeiler des EWR' (2013) *EuR* 504, 519.

[25] Baudenbacher, above n 13, 34–35; H-P Graver, 'The Effects of EFTA Court Jurisprudence on the Legal Orders of the EFTA States' in Baudenbacher et al (eds), above n 13, 79, 86.

[26] Case 26/62 [1963] ECR 1.

[27] Joined Cases C-46/93 and 48/93, *Brasserie du Pêcheur and Factortame [III]* [1996] ECR I-1029, para 51.

in *Sveinbjörnsdóttir*, rely on the conditions already elaborated carefully by the ECJ. It is true that the EFTA Court did not make a direct reference to the ECJ case law on the precise conditions and could deduce the principle directly from the EEA Agreement and the implementation legislation of the Member States, which enabled the Court to reserve for itself the possibility to elaborate conditions which are 'not necessarily be in all respects coextensive' (*Karlsson*, para 30).[28] However, the fact remains that the EFTA Court applied in these cases the famous three conditions laid down in *Brasserie du Pêcheur and Factortame*. It is clear that the EFTA Court could, in any case, benefit from the ECJ's invaluable experience.

The second specificity of the EEA is a growing imbalance of bargaining power between the EFTA side and the EC side. This is of great importance when the EFTA Court has to win general acceptance of its case law in EEA/EFTA States.

In 1992, there were seven states on the EFTA side while there were 12 states on the EC side. After the exit of Sweden, Finland and Austria from the EFTA, only three states remain on the EFTA side while the EC/EU has been enlarged to 15, 27, and now 28. It is undeniable that the imbalance of negotiation power between the two sides has grown considerably. Besides, all the remaining EEA/EFTA States are small states. In view of such a double imbalance, it is hardly conceivable that a future renegotiation of the EEA Agreement would be more favourable for the EEA/EFTA States than that concluded in 1991. As President Baudenbacher observed, 'it can probably not be renegotiated, it cannot be amended anymore'.[29] The EEA/EFTA States would have little chance to ameliorate greatly their bargaining position vis-à-vis the enlarged EU in the foreseeable future. This means first that the EEA/EFTA States can no longer ignore their *obligation de résultat* with impunity, since the EC side has become less tolerant of the lack of reciprocity in judicial protection of individuals in EEA law, and second that they would have virtually no chance to reverse, by way of treaty revisions, the EFTA Court's established case law favourable to such protection. Moreover, the EFTA Court can reasonably expect to receive support from the EU.

True, the EFTA States have, in theory, a right of veto in the EEA Joint Committee (Article 102 EEA) and may decide to withdraw from the EEA if they are willing to pay the price. However, this right of veto has never been used,[30] so that Pascal Lamy, former European Commissioner for trade, is reported to have said that the EEA represented 'fax democracy'.[31] And in view of such practice, Professor Hamamoto, one of my colleagues in our research project, goes so far as to begin his article with this somewhat provocative remark: 'The EEA Agreement

---

[28] SM Stefánsson, 'State Liability in Community Law and EEA Law' in Baudenbacher et al (eds), above n 13, 145, 153.

[29] Baudenbacher (2010), above n 22, 67.

[30] Fredriksen, above n 5, 868, 869.

[31] J Forman, 'Parallel Legislation in the EEA: Automatic or Manual?' in T Bruha et al (Hrsg), *Liechtenstein—10 Jahre im EWR* (Schaan, Verlag der Liechtensteinischen Akademischen Gesellschaft, 2005) 52, 53.

is a curious treaty, it is something like a modern version of an unequal treaty'.[32] Understandably, the economic as well as the political price might be, in practice, too exorbitant for the EFTA States to exercise the right of veto, not to mention the right of withdrawal. Exercising such a drastic right might be all the more difficult that the overall benefits of EU market access surely far outweigh such relatively minor legal problems.

However, it is not completely excluded that the EEA/EFTA States might be tempted to resist the EFTA Court's case law because, on the one hand, non-implemented EEA law enjoys neither direct effect nor primacy over national provisions and because, on the other hand, an advisory ruling of the EFTA Court is not binding on the national court. That is why it is essential to pay particular attention to multi-level judicial dialogue in EEA law.

B. Multi-level Judicial Dialogue

The role of the EFTA Court is particularly important in the EFTA pillar for two reasons. First, there is, as mentioned above, practically no prospect of renegotiation of the EEA Agreement for the near future. Consequently, the EEA/EFTA States would have little chance to attack EFTA Court's case law by way of treaty revisions. Second, in spite of successive revisions of the EEC Treaty after 1992, the main part of the EEA Agreement has not been revised, which means that it is up to the EFTA Court to bridge a growing gap between EEA law and EC law as well as to ensure homogeneity in EEA law. However, the EFTA Court could not have, by itself, imposed its case law on a recalcitrant EFTA State. This is why the EFTA Court has tried to make maximum use of judicial dialogue with European and national courts.

EEA/EFTA States actually expressed a considerable reluctance to a new EEA principle of State liability. The Norwegian government notably manifested its resolute opposition to the *Sveinbjörnsdóttir* case law invoking the famous ECJ Opinion 1/91 in order to deny applicability of State liability in EEA law. Fortunately for the EFTA Court, precious support came from that very ECJ in *Rechberger* (Case C-140/97 [1999] ECR I-3499). The ECJ held in this case that 'in view of the objective of uniform interpretation and application which informs the EEA Agreement, it should be pointed out that the principles governing the liability of an EFTA State for infringement of a directive referred to in the EEA Agreement were the subject of the EFTA Court's judgment of 10 December 1998 in *Sveinbjörnsdóttir*' (para 39). For some commentators, such reference by the ECJ to the *Sveinbjörnsdóttir* ruling did not mean to support the EFTA Court's case

---

[32] S Hamamoto, 'Law-making process in the EEA and the status of EEA law in the domestic legal orders of the member States' (2013) 85 *Horitsu Jiho*, No 8, 56 (this author's translation from Japanese).

law.[33] Although another ruling on a similar case which was rendered by the ECJ on the same day (Case C-321/97 *Andersson* [1999] ECR I-3551) made no such reference, such reference in *Rechberger* should have been regarded as an indirect support by the ECJ to the EFTA case law. As Fredriksen convincingly submitted, '[i]t would, however, be rather odd if the ECJ were to have made the Austrian court explicitly aware of the EFTA Court's position on the issue if it disagreed with it'.[34] In any case, for the majority of commentators, the ECJ had indeed endorsed, though implicitly, the EFTA Court's case law.[35] And such an interpretation was shared by a judge of the EFTA Court.[36]

In *Karlsson*, the EFTA Court was to refer, for its part, explicitly to *Rechberger* in order to reaffirm its *Sveinbjörnsdóttir* case law: 'the principle of State liability must be seen as an integral part of the EEA Agreement as such ... This was noted by the Court of Justice of the European Communities in Case C-140/97 *Rechberger and Others* [1999] ECR I-3499, at paragraph 39' (para 25). It goes without saying that such reference by the EFTA Court to the ECJ case cannot be fortuitous, since, in the *Karlsson* case, the Norwegian government contested the *Sveinbjörnsdóttir* case law bitterly and sought a 'replay'. President Baudenbacher recalled this episode extra-judicially, stating 'how important judicial dialogue can be in such a power game'.[37]

Moreover, it should be emphasised that dialogue between the EFTA Court and national supreme courts is no less important, since it was national supreme courts' support for the EEA case law that enabled the EFTA Court to overcome recalcitrant governments' resistance. In the context of EEA State liability, the first support for the EFTA Court came from the Icelandic Supreme Court in the *Sveinbjörnsdóttir* case (Judgment of 16 December 1999),[38] the second from the Swedish Supreme Court in *Andersson* (Judgment of 26 November 2004),[39] and finally the third from the Norwegian Supreme Court in *Finanger-II* (Judgment of 28 October 2005). It was after this *Finanger-II* judgment that the Norwegian government gave up contesting the EEA principle of State liability laid down in the *Sveinbjörnsdóttir* case.[40] It should be also pointed out that the Swedish and Norwegian Supreme Courts have both made reference to the Icelandic Supreme

[33] A Ott, 'Die anerkannte Rechtsfortbildung des EuGH als Teil des gemeinschaftlichen Bestizstandes (acquis communautaire)' (2000) *EuZW* 293, 297; Stefánsson, above n 28, 145, 154.
[34] H Haukeland Fredriksen, 'The EFTA Court 15 Years On' (2010) 59 *ICLQ* 731, 752–753.
[35] See, eg, Editorial comments, 'European Economic Area and European Community: Homogeneity of legal orders?' (1999) *CML Rev* 697, 700; T Bruha, 'Is the EEA an Internal Market?' in P-C Müller-Graff and E Selvig (eds), *EEA-EU Relations* (Berlin, Berlin Verlag, 1999) 97, 119, fn 79.
[36] C Baudenbacher, 'Staatshaftung im gesamten Europäischen Wirtschaftsraum: EuGH und EFTA-Gerichtshof im Doppelpass'(2000) *EWS* 425, 431.
[37] Baudenbacher (2010), above n 22, 43.
[38] T Örlygsson, 'Iceland and the EFTA Court. Twelve Years of Experience' in M Monti et al (eds), *Economic Law and Justice in Times of Globalisation: Festschrift für Carl Baudenbacher* (Baden-Baden, Nomos, 2007) 225, 238–240.
[39] M Johansson, 'State Liability within the EEA from a Swedish perspective: *Sveinbjörnsdóttir* confirmed' (2005) *European Law Reporter* 50.
[40] Baudenbacher (2010), above n 22, 46; Fredriksen, above n 34, 731, 759.

Court's judgment. A *horizontal* judicial dialogue has thus played an important role for the establishment of EEA State liability principle.

As to the EEA advisory opinion procedure, we find another example of judicial dialogue, this time between the EFTA Court and the European Court of Human Rights. In *Irish Bank* (para 64), the EFTA Court cited *Ullens de Schooten and Rezabek v Belgium* (ECtHR judgment of 20 September 2011) in order to affirm the possibility of arbitrary refusal to refer questions to the EFTA Court.

Without doubt such subtle and ingenious cross-references in the course of multi-level judicial dialogue—inconceivable in Asia—have contributed considerably to the development of EEA law.

IV. CONCLUSION

What lessons can we draw from the experience of EEA law?

From the Community lawyers' point of view, EEA law has been no more than an imperfect Community law. Without the principles of direct effect and of primacy on its own, EEA law seemed to be deprived of its 'heart' of Community law.[41] There is no denying that, in theory, EC law differs radically from EEA law. However, EEA law now seems to offer, in practice, essentially the same level of judicial protection in the EFTA/EEA countries. In other words, the experience of EEA law shows that, notwithstanding their fundamental importance, the EC-styled principles are not always decisive if there are other conditions capable to ensure the *obligation de résultat*.

In this respect, the role of the legal community of judges and lawyers seems to be of crucial importance, since jurists tend to think of effectiveness of legal norms in terms of effective judicial protection of individuals. Even before the *Sveinbjörnsdóttir* ruling, Sejersted rightly concluded: 'As long as matters are left to the lawyers, my prediction is that EEA law will evolve in a supranational direction.'[42]

Thanks to the judicial dynamism of the EFTA Court, EEA law has become more than an imperfect Community law. To cite a beautiful metaphor by President Baudenbacher, 'in EEA law we do not have the giant gothic cathedral with the three naves—direct effect, primacy, and State liability—which is characteristic for EC law. Instead, our construction resembles a simple Nordic stave church. But worshipping is possible in both places, with essentially the same results.'[43]

---

[41] W Van Gerven, 'The Genesis of EEA Law and the Principles of Primacy and Direct Effect' (1992–1993) 16 *Fordham International Law Journal* 955, 972–973.
[42] Sejersted, above n 12, 43, 70.
[43] Baudenbacher, above n 11, 333, 358.

In conclusion, the EEA model seems not only to be more accessible, as a model of economic integration, to Asian countries than the EC model. But EEA law also offers a possible mechanism to ensure homogeneity between two legal orders. If one day two distinct regional organisations happen to be established in Asia because of the rivalry between Japan and China, EEA model might be useful to bridging the two. This is why some EU law and international law scholars in Japan have, perhaps not 'huge', but certainly intense interest in EEA law.[44]

---

[44] Baudenbacher (2010), above n 22, 97: 'There is huge interest in the EEA in Japan ... One could say that the EEA is more popular in the Far East than in some of our capitals.'

39

EU Law, EEA Law and International Law—The Myth of Supranational Law and Its Implications for International Law

TAKAO SUAMI

I. INTRODUCTION[*]

THE EFTA COURT has made enormous contributions to the development of the European legal orders in the past 20 years. Not only has the EFTA Court clarified the interpretation of EEA law provisions, it has also pushed the progress of EU law, because in quite a few instances the EFTA Court's judgments were cited by the EU Courts despite no legal obligation to do so.[1] As the recent *Icesave* judgment indicates, as regards issues which the EU Courts have not dealt with, the EFTA Court's adjudication would constitute a valuable reference point for them.[2] European legal orders are multi-layered, namely international, regional and national. These separate orders are intertwined and interacting with each other. The structure of legal orders in East Asia is much simpler. Only two-layered orders, international and national, exist in the region. In addition, there is a lack of interaction among different courts. These differences make the European experience crucial for the future of East Asia.

Against such a backdrop, this chapter will try to pertinently recognise the relevance of European experience for international law as a whole. For that purpose, its analysis will focus on the legal nature of EU law, EEA law and international

---

[*] The author would like to express his gratitude to Philipp Speitler for giving comments on an early draft of this chapter.
[1] A Rosas, 'The European Court of Justice and Public International Law' in J Wouters, A Nollkaemper and E de Wet (eds), *The Europeanisation of International Law* (The Hague, TMC Asser Press, 2008) 71, 82; C Baudenbacher, *EFTA Court, Legal framework and case law*, 3rd edn (Luxembourg, EFTA Court, 2008) 18.
[2] Case E-16/11 *EFTA Surveillance Authority v Iceland (Icesave)*, 28 January 2013; M Hanten and M Plaschke, 'EU law impact on deposit protection in the financial sector: *Icesave*' (2014) 51 *CML Rev* 295–310.

law. First, it will analyse the differences between EU law and international law; second, it will examine how the European Court of Justice (ECJ) and the EFTA Court distinguish between EEA law, EU law, and international law. After that, it will show how that distinction has become blurred because of recent legal phenomena. Finally, the chapter suggests that the time will come when it is necessary to discuss all three legal orders within the common framework.

II. EU LAW VERSUS PUBLIC INTERNATIONAL LAW

A. The Birth of a Supranational Legal Order

The early days of the ECJ were a period when EC law (nowadays EU law) tried to establish its own identity as a *sui generis* and 'supranational' legal order. Many judgments of the ECJ, beginning with *Van Gend en Loos* and *Costa v ENEL*, emphasised a stark difference in terms of legal nature between EC law and international law, and regarded EC law as being supranational.[3] The ECJ established primacy and direct effect, which altered the nature of EC law in a manner that it was no longer to be considered traditional international law. That understanding of EC law has been further developed. First, the Founding Treaties have been characterised as being of a constitutional nature,[4] and second, the autonomy of the EC's legal order has been repeatedly accepted and confirmed.[5]

B. National Responses to the Supranational Understanding

Today, the supranational nature of EU law is widely accepted.[6] As regards primacy, national courts have gradually come to accept EU law's primacy over ordinary national legislation, although tension between EU law and national constitutions still continues to exist.[7] In this process, most constitutional courts have more or less recognised the *sui generis* character of EU law.[8] However, one constitutional court still takes the view that EU law is to be considered as international law. From

---

[3] In the early 1960s, the European Community law was established as a *sui generis* legal order by a series of judgments by the ECJ (Case 26/62 *Van Gend en Loos v Nederlandse Administratie der Belastingen* [1963] ECR 1; Case 6/64 *Costa v ENEL* [1964] ECR 585; Case 106/77 *Amministrazione delle Finanze dello Stato v Simmenthal* [1978] ECR 629).

[4] Case 294/83 *Les Verts v European Parliament* [1986] ECR 1365, para 23; Opinion 1/91, *Draft Treaty on the establishment of a European Economic Area* [1991] ECR I-6102, para 21.

[5] Joined Cases C-402/05 P and C-415/05 P *Kadi and Al Barakaat International Foundation v Council*, 3 September 2008, para 282; Case C-459/03 *Commission v Ireland* [2006] ECR I-4635, para 123.

[6] J Wouters, A Nollkaemper and E de Wet, 'Introduction: The "Europeanisation" of International Law' in Wouters et al (eds), above n 1, p 5.

[7] D Chalmers, G Davies and G Monti, *European Union Law*, 2nd edn (Cambridge, Cambridge University Press, 2010) 188–190.

[8] ibid, 190–191 and 194–197.

the Polish Constitutional Court's point of view, the Founding Treaties of the EU must be considered as an ordinary international agreement and therefore, in case of conflict, the Polish Constitution will always prevail over EU law.[9]

In general, EU law is recognised as an independent legal order which enjoys immunity from interference of international law.

III. EU LAW VERSUS EEA LAW, INTERNATIONAL LAW VERSUS EEA LAW

Based on the above, one can say that EU law is fundamentally different from international law. The next issue is where EEA law is to be positioned. In order to specify this, its relationship with EU law and international law will be assessed.

A. EU Law versus EEA Law

i. Identical Provisions, Same Interpretation and Homogeneity

Substantive provisions of EEA law are similar or identical in substance to those of EU law. Under the EEA Agreement, new EU legislation with EEA relevance is incorporated into the EEA Agreement by Joint Committee Decision and implemented into the national legal orders of the EEA EFTA States (Article 7 EEA). Given the EEA's purpose of expanding the Internal Market to the EEA EFTA countries (Article 1, paragraph 1 EEA), it is a natural consequence that both the EU and the EEA are sharing the same or similar legal provisions. In addition, in order to achieve 'homogeneity' in the EEA (Article 1, paragraph 1 EEA), EEA law provisions, in so far as they are identical in substance to the EU Treaties' provisions, must be interpreted in conformity with the ECJ's rulings from the time before the signature of the EEA Agreement and due account shall be taken of relevant case law which has been rendered after the signing of the EEA Agreement.

ii. The ECJ's Historical Understanding of EEA Law

Despite their affinity in substance and interpretation, the ECJ historically found dissimilarity between two legal orders. In its opinion on the original EEA Agreement, the ECJ observed in 1991 that unlike the EEC Treaty, which is a constitutional charter, the EEA Agreement is an international treaty, without the transfer of sovereign rights to an international organisation, which merely creates rights and obligations between the Contracting Parties.[10] It held that as the EEA essentially differs from the EC, the EEA Agreement has to provide for other means

---

[9] Polish Constitutional Court, Judgment K18/04 of 11 May 2005, paras 6 and 13.
[10] See Opinion 1/91, above n 4, paras 20–21; Opinion 1/91 also points out that the EEA Treaty 'provides for no transfer of sovereign rights to the inter-governmental institutions' (para 20).

of guaranteeing the homogeneity on the EFTA side of the EEA.[11] The necessity of other means was further supported by the ECJ's critical attitude towards fundamental EU principles in an EEA context. It goes without saying that both primacy and direct effect of EU law are indispensable elements of the Internal Market. However, despite conformity requirements with case law, Opinion 1/91 stated that the EEA Agreement did not recognise the principles of direct effect and primacy,[12] and further explained that compliance with the ECJ's case law did not extend to 'essential elements of that case-law which are reconcilable with the characteristics of the (EEA) Agreement'.[13] In sum, the ECJ's initial and historical view presupposed that EEA law will be enforced in accordance with international law.[14]

iii. The EFTA Court's Understanding on EEA Law

Under the EEA framework, the EFTA Court is placed as a counterpart of the ECJ on the EFTA side of the EEA, and is responsible for ensuring homogeneity within the EFTA states (Article 108, paragraph 2 EEA). The EFTA Court did not accept the principles of primacy and direct effect of EEA law in the EEA.

The starting point of the EFTA Court's analysis was a distinction between implemented and non-implemented EEA law. In case of the former, as far as EEA law has already been incorporated into a national legal order, the EFTA Court has acknowledged quasi primacy and quasi direct effect.[15] However, the former is not a quintessential case where these fundamental principles are required to function. In the EU, they are important in cases where EU law has not yet been domestically implemented. Accordingly, the EFTA Court's attitude to the latter is more important than the former, and the EFTA Court has expressed its cautious approach to the latter in its advisory opinions. In conclusion, as to non-implemented EEA law, the EFTA Court has been cautious to apply primacy and direct effect.

According to the EFTA Court, individuals cannot directly rely on non-implemented EEA law before national courts,[16] and EEA law does not require non-implemented EEA rules to take precedence over conflicting national rules.[17] As a result, there is a gap in terms of the protection of individual rights between

---

[11] See Opinion 1/91, above n 4, paras 22–23; M Elvira Méndez-Pinedo, *EC and EEA Law, A Comparative Study of Effectiveness of European Law* (Europa Law Publishing, 2009) 99–104; S Norberg, K Hökborg, M Johansson, D Eliasson and L Dedichen, *EEA Law, A Commentary on the EEA Agreement* (Stockholm, Fritzes, 1993) 191.

[12] See Opinion 1/91, above n 4, para 27.

[13] See Opinion 1/91, above n 4, para 28.

[14] In fact, the EFTA states, namely Iceland and Norway, with a strong dualist tradition take the view that EEA law will not become part of their national laws without a proper implementation into the national legal orders (see Elvira Méndez-Pinedo, above n 11, at 113–141 and 164.

[15] Case E-1/94 *Restamark*, 16 December 1994, paras 77 and 80; Case E-1/01 *Einarsson v Iceland*, 22 February 2002, paras 50–51; see also Case E-6/12 *ESA v Norway*, 11 September 2013, paras 65 to 67, and case law cited.

[16] Case E-4/01 *Karlsson v Iceland*, 30 May 2002, para 28.

[17] Case E-1/07 *Criminal Proceedings against A*, 3 October 2007, paras 40–41.

EU law and EEA law in that respect. This indicates that the EFTA Court treats EEA law differently from EU law.

It follows from the above consideration that one can see almost a consensus between the ECJ and the EFTA Court about the considerable differences between EU law and EEA law.

B. International Law versus EEA Law

i. More Subtle Issue than Other Distinctions

The previous examinations confirmed the differences between EU law and international law on one hand, and between EU law and EEA law on the other. The final issue still remains whether or not EEA law is part of international law. As compared with the previous distinctions, the differences between international law and EEA law constitute a more subtle and nuanced issue. Originally, the EEA was considered as a legal framework on the basis of international law, because it did not intend to transfer legislative and judicial powers to supranational institutions.[18] In its Opinion 1/91 the ECJ was not aware of any difference between EEA law and international law,[19] but such understanding has to be seen as a chapter in a history book. As of today, it is widely recognised that EEA law cannot be considered traditional international law.

ii. The ECJ's Perspective

The ECJ has not officially overruled its understanding of EEA law in Opinion 1/91. However, we can perceive a change in the case law. In *Opel Austria v Council*, for example, the European Court of First Instance (ECFI) expressed its view that 'the EEA Agreement involves a high degree of integration, with objectives which exceed those of a mere free-trade agreement', and then listed up a number of similarities between the EEA and the EU in terms of their aims, scopes, institutions and substantive provisions.[20] Most likely, the ECFI did not share the view that was taken in Opinion 1/91 by the ECJ. Moreover, in *UK v Council* the ECJ held recently that the EEA Agreement is to provide for the fullest possible realisation of the free movement of goods, persons, services and capital within the whole EEA, so that the internal market established within the European Union is extended to the EFTA States.[21] As regards an EU regulation, Article 7(a) of the EEA Agreement expressly provides that such an act must 'as such' be made part of the internal legal order of the Contracting Parties, that is to say, without any implementing measures

---

[18] Preamble of Protocol 35 on the Implementation of EEA Rules.
[19] See Opinion 1/91, above n 4, para 20.
[20] Case T-115/94 *Opel Austria v Council* [1997] ECR II-39, paras 107–108.
[21] Case C-431/11 *UK v Council*, judgment of 26 September 2013, para 50.

being required for that purpose.[22] With reference to *UK v Council*, Advocate General Mengozzi repeated in a recent opinion that the scope of the fundamental freedoms should be the same within the two pillars. Moreover, he highlighted the *sui generis* nature of the EEA Agreement by reference to EFTA Court's case law.[23] Giving much stress on the similarities between EU law and EEA law makes on us an impression that EEA law is closer to EU law than international law.

iii. The EFTA Court's Perspective

From early on, the EFTA Court demonstrated a clearer view on EEA law than the ECJ. The opinion in *Erla María Sveinbjörnsdóttir v Iceland* concludes that 'the EEA Agreement is an international treaty *sui generis* which contains a distinct legal order of its own'.[24] According to the opinion, '[t]he depth of integration of the EEA Agreement is less far-reaching than under the EC Treaty, but the scope and the objective of the EEA Agreement goes beyond what is usual for an agreement under public international law'.[25] Today, it is settled case law that EEA law is neither to be considered supranational EU law nor international law in a classical sense.[26]

C. EEA Law as a Hybrid of International Law and EU Law

As a consequence of the development of both the ECJ's and the EFTA Court's case law, it is generally explained in academic literature that EEA law is situated in the middle between traditional international law and EU law. For example, the EFTA Court's President, Professor Baudenbacher, explains that EEA law is no longer 'classical public international law, but a *sui generis* being closer to supranational EU law than to traditional public international law.[27] It is not certain that everybody agrees to his exact localisation, but most scholars seem to agree to the intermediate character of EEA law. They say that EEA law is a complex hybrid between classic international law and EC law,[28] or that EEA law is to be considered 'quasi-supranational law'.[29]

---

[22] ibid, para 54.

[23] See AG Mengozzi's Opinion in Case C-83/13 *Fonnship A/S*, fn 54.

[24] Case E-9/97 *Erla María Sveinbjörnsdóttir v Iceland*, 10 December 1998, paras 57–59.

[25] ibid, para 59.

[26] See Case E-4/01, above n 16, para 25; Case E-2/03 *The Public Prosecutor v Ásgeir Logi Ásgeirsson and Others*, 12 December 2003, para 28; Case E-1/07, above n 17, para 37.

[27] C Baudenbacher, *The EFTA Court in Action, Five Lectures* (Stuttgart, German Law Publishers, 2010) 67.

[28] See Elvira Méndez-Pinedo, above n 11, at 31, 34, 46 and 97.

[29] A Epiney and B Hofstötter in collaboration with M Wyssling, 'The Status of "Europeanised" International Law in Austria, Switzerland and Liechtenstein' in *The Europeanisation of International Law*, above n 1, 137, 157–159.

These explanations have a high level of persuasion. Nobody can deny that in many senses, EEA law contains not only elements of international law, but also of EU law. For example, the denial of primacy and direct effect of EEA law in a narrow sense does not mean that individuals are not able to claim their rights deriving from EEA law. The EFTA Court takes due account of the rights of individuals, and understands that the institutional framework providing for the protection of individuals' rights as well as the effective supervision and judicial review is an essential feature of the EEA legal order.[30] Therefore, the EFTA Court's case law ensures that individuals can claim their rights through the principles of consistent interpretation and state liability.[31] Finally, one can reasonably reach the conclusion from the above examinations that the overall picture in Europe is the coexistence of the three distinct and autonomous legal orders.

IV. UNCERTAINTY WITHIN THREE DISTINCT LEGAL ORDERS

A. Continuous Discussion on the Position of EU Law

Nevertheless, the essence of science always lies in having doubts about truism. The main point of this chapter is a hypothesis that the distinction among three legal orders, namely EU law, EEA law and international law, is becoming blurred, and will be even more so in the future.

First of all, the foregoing distinctions among the three legal orders are fundamentally based upon a clear-cut differentiation between EU law and international law. Should this distinction become uncertain, the whole picture would inevitably change. To begin with, one must remember that academic opinions are still divided over the legal nature of EU law, although most of them find something special in EU law. For example, Professor Hartley raised serious doubts about the separation of EU law from international law at the end of 1990s.[32] Even in East Asia, a leading international lawyer from Japan recently expressed his critical view of distinction between EU law and international law. After careful examination of several issues, he concluded that EU law, including legal acts adopted by the EU institutions, is still part of international law.[33] It is undisputed that the majority

---

[30] See Case E-2/03, above n 26, para 28.

[31] See Case E-4/01, above n 16, para 28; Case E-9/97, above n 24, paras 44–63; see for a broader State liability regime Case E-2/12 *HOB-vín ehf v ATVR*, paras 120–138.

[32] TC Hartley, *Constitutional Problems of the European Union* (Oxford, Hart Publishing, 1999) 138–139.

[33] He examined (1) legislative procedures on the basis of a qualified majority voting in the Council, (2) non-application of Vienna Convention on the Laws of Treaties, (3) compulsory jurisdiction of the ECJ, (4) the position of individuals and (5) direct application of EU law (S Hamamoto, '*EU-Ho to Kokusai-Ho—Kokusai-Hogaku no kanten kara*—'[EU Law and International Law—From the perspective of International Law]' in H Hirano, Y Kamemoto and N Kawahama (eds), *Gendai-Ho no Henyo* [*Transformation of Modern law*] (Tokyo, Yuhikaku, 2013) 209–240.

seems to accept that EU law is to be considered supranational and this seems to be convincing. But it does not mean that there is an overall consensus.

In addition, the development of international law over the decades has made the discussion on this issue complicated. As far as international law governs the mutual relationship between sovereign states, its impact does not extend to that of EU law. This is mainly because the fundamental principle of EU law directly affects individuals in their national legal orders.[34] However, international law itself has not yet stopped developing.[35] In the 1960s, international law paid much less attention to non-state actors than today. However, based on the extended scope of human rights treaties, the emergence of investment treaties and of international criminal courts, and the activiation of non-state actors such as NGOs, international law already applies to individuals and multi-national corporations. In brief, international law has changed tremendously over the last decades. The specific nature of EU law was developed by using international law as a yardstick. Nevertheless, that yardstick itself has come closer to EU law. This transition may have narrowed the gap between two legal orders.

B. Recent Phenomena in the EU Legal Order

i. Constitutional Tension between EU law and National Constitutions

Another incident affecting the distance between EU law and international law are unresolved tensions between EU law and national constitutions in the Member States. As aforesaid, the ECJ has firmly established the principle of primacy of EU law over all domestic laws including constitutions. Although accepting the EU law's primacy in principle, however, national courts, particularly many constitutional courts, have not accepted the primacy of EU law over national constitutions in full.[36] In fact, until the beginning of the 1990s, the conflict between the ECJ and constitutional courts had been ameliorating step by step,[37] but such relatively peaceful relationship between the ECJ and national courts had not lasted forever. The Maastricht judgment by the German Constitutional Court (the GCC) in 1993 was a turning point.[38] In this judgment, the GCC not only reconfirmed the theoretical possibility of reviewing EU law in the light of human rights standards under the German constitution, but also added a new possibility of reviewing EU

---

[34] K Lenaerts and P Van Nuffel (R Bray and N Cambien, eds), *European Union Law*, 3rd edn (London, Sweet & Maxwell, 2011) 16–21.

[35] MN Shaw, *International Law*, 6th edn (Cambridge, Cambridge University Press, 2008) 43–49.

[36] P Craig and G de Búrca, *EU Law, Text, Cases and Materials*, 4th edn (Oxford, Oxford University Press, 2008) 353–374; see Lenaerts and Van Nuffel, above n 34, at 772–809.

[37] Case 29/69 *Stauder* [1969] ECR 419; *Solange I*, BVerfGE 37, 271 (1974); *Solange II*, BVerfGE, 73, 339 (1986).

[38] *Maastricht*, BVerfGE 89, 155 (1993); *Brunner v European Union Treaty* (German Constitutional Court) [1994] 1 *CMLR* 57.

law in terms of whether or not the EU institutions' actions did not exceed its competences conferred by the EU Treaties (the *ultra vires* review). The GCC developed its approach further in the Lisbon judgment of 2009. This judgment clarified that the GCC was able to carry out the third type of review, namely whether or not the inviolable core of the constitutional identity in the German constitution was duly observed (the identity review).[39]

More importantly, constitutional or supreme courts in many Member States have followed the GCC's view by and large.[40] To conclude, these national courts do not resist day-to-day application of EU law, but seek confirmation that 'they could set aside EU law on constitutional grounds under certain circumstances'.[41] Since the early 1990s, the distance between the ECJ and the constitutional courts has not narrowed and is not likely to disappear in the foreseeable future. Every legal order necessarily includes some exceptional situations to which law does not properly apply, but these constitutional courts' judgments go beyond such permissible exceptions. The ECJ is given an exclusive authority to interpret EU law (Article 19 TEU). On that basis, EU law has partly lost a ground why it is considered to be of a *sui generis* nature.

ii. Combination of EU Law Measures and International Law Measures

EU measures to escape from the sovereign debt crisis in the eurozone have also added a new element to the relation between EU law and international law. After the crisis that threatened the sustainability of the euro erupted, the EU made a great deal of effort to control the crisis, and has adopted a number of legal measures to that end. One of the conspicuous features of such post-crisis measures is the combination of EU law instruments with extra-EU law, namely international law, instruments.[42]

The typical example is the Treaty on Stability, Coordination and Governance (TSCG) in the Economic and Monetary Union among 25 Member States. The conclusion of the TSCG as a complement of the EU Treaties raises reasonable doubt about the difference in nature between EU law and international law. In order to strengthen the financial stability of the whole euro area, the TSCG intends to foster budgetary discipline and to improve the governance of the euro area (Article 1, paragraph 1 TSCG). At the beginning, the EU Member States

---

[39] *Lisbon*, 2 BvE 2/08, 2 BvE 5/08, 2 BvR 1010/08, 2 BvR 1022/08, 2 BvR 1259/08 and 2 BvR 182/09, 30 June 2009; D Thym, 'In the Name of Sovereign Statehood: A Critical Introduction to the Lisbon Judgment of the German Constitutional Court' (2009) 46 *CML Rev* 1795–1822.

[40] Danish Supreme Court, Case No 1361/1997, 6 April 1998; Corte costituzionale, Judgment of No 103 of 2008, 12 February 2008; French Constitutional Council, Decision no 2007-560 DC, 27 December 2007; Czech Constitutional Court, Pl US 5/12, 31 January 2012.

[41] M Kumm, 'The Jurisprudence of Constitutional Conflict: Constitutional Supremacy in Europe before and after the Constitutional Treaty' (2005) 11 *ELJ* 262, 263.

[42] E Chiti and P Gustavo Teixeira, 'The Constitutional Implication of the European Responses to the Financial and Public Debt Crisis' (2013) 50 *CML Rev* 683–708.

negotiated an amendment to the TFEU provisions, but when they faced the veto of two Member States, they changed their mind and decided to rely upon an inter-governmental agreement to deal with issues within the scope of the EU Treaties.[43] Such substitutive relationship is also shown by the expected incorporation of the TSCG's substance into the legal framework of the EU within five years (Article 16 TSCG).[44] More remarkably, the TSCG is complicatedly intertwined with EU law. The EU Treaties are complemented by the TSCG, and it is surprising that the TSCG is complemented by EU law, too. While the Member States must put in place a budgetary and economic partnership programme, it is clearly stipulated in the TSCG that the content and format must be defined by EU law (Article 5, paragraph 1 TSCG). As a consequence of such inter-complementarity, the TSCG has become inseparable from EU law. In fact, the TSCG and EU law constitute one united body of law, so that the jurisdiction of the Court of Justice of the EU totally covers the TSCG (Article 8 TSCG).[45] It is not uncommon for EU law to be complemented by an international treaty,[46] but such a high level of interdependence has never taken place before. Therefore, the TSCG arrangement can be considered as evidence which demonstrates the closing gap between EU law and international law.

C. High Level of Effectiveness of EEA law

If the distance between EU law and international law has narrowed, the position of EEA law will inevitably become delicate. The practical application of EEA law as well as the development of EFTA Court advisory opinions has also cast some doubts about three types of grouping, namely supranational, quasi-supranational and international.

At first glance, the EFTA Court's opinions are of an advisory nature, unlike legally binding preliminary rulings by the ECJ. Based on that assumption, the former is totally different from the latter. However, according to EEA law experience, this does not necessarily mean that the former's impact in national legal orders is much less than the latter's.

In the first place, Professor Baudenbacher points out a possibility that disregard of such an advisory opinion would cause a breach of the EEA Agreement, and

---

[43] K Tuori and K Tuori, *The Eurozone Crisis, A Constitutional Analysis* (Cambridge, Cambridge University Press, 2014) 109–110 and 171–180.

[44] Art 16 means that the TSCG's provisions are first expected to be incorporated into the EU Treaties through revision procedures, and if their revision is not possible, secondly, to be integrated into EU law through the use of 'enhanced cooperation' between Member States (Art 10).

[45] The jurisdiction is given to the ECJ on the basis of Art 273 TFEU (Art 8, para 3 TSCG). Other EU institutions including the European Commission and the Council of the EU are also given certain tasks under the TSCG (Arts 6, 7 and 8).

[46] The Schengen Agreement and Convention implementing the Schengen Agreement are often mentioned as such an example (see K Tuori and K Tuori, above n 43, at 173).

then be assessed as a failure to fulfil an obligation under the EEA Agreement.[47] Dealing with a slightly different question, an EFTA Court judgment of 2012 confirmed that national courts of last instance may be obliged to make a reference to the EFTA Court because they are bound to fulfil their duty of loyalty (Article 3 EEA).[48] This decision can be interpreted as implying a possibility that non-referral of national courts might constitute a breach of the EEA Agreement. In sum, it is not likely that the EFTA Court's advisory opinions do not produce any legal effect under the EEA framework. In the second place, it is often reported that actual effectiveness of these advisory opinions is comparable to the ECJ rulings, although it is not the same.[49] Despite the lack of binding effect, it is likely that most advisory opinions are properly followed by national courts.[50] After all, if advisory opinions were always less effective than binding rulings, it would be almost impossible to achieve homogeneity in the EEA. In other words, the EEA presupposes that the EFTA States can achieve the similar level of integration by following advisory opinions. It is noteworthy that EU law cannot be legally enforced without voluntary assistance from national courts of the Member States. Although most European lawyers do not explicitly stress this point, the lack of compelling power is a common feature which is shared by both EU law and EEA law. There is no European police either in the EU or in the EEA. As long as we focus on this aspect, the difference between these two legal frameworks is a matter of degree. In conclusion, international courts with compulsory jurisdiction are essential for the autonomous progress of an international organisation,[51] but the binding nature of their decisions is not a decisive element for their success under the lack of compelling power. It seems to be more important how persuasive their reasoning is for national courts as well as other international courts.

V. CONCLUSIONS

EU law, EEA law and international law are not static, but dynamic. All three may develop as regards their legal nature and characteristics. Both EU law and EEA law are enjoying their autonomy and are exempted from the application of international

---

[47] C Baudenbacher, 'Some Thoughts on the EFTA Court's Phases of Life' in EFTA Court (ed), *Judicial Protection in the European Economic Area* (Stuttgart, German Law Publishers, 2012) 2, 15.

[48] Case E-18/11 *Irish Bank v Kaupthing Bank*, 28 September 2012, para 58.

[49] See Elvira Méndez-Pinedo, above n 11, at 150 and 171.

[50] Eg the Supreme Court of Iceland stated that advisory opinions should in principle be followed (see Elvira Méndez-Pinedo, above n 11, at 181). It is reported that following the EFTA Court's opinion in *Sigmarsson* (Case E-3/11 *Sigmarsson v the Central Bank of Iceland*, 14 December 2011), the plaintiff withdrew the case before the judgment of the national court (D Guðmundsdóttir, 'Case note on Sigmarsson' (2012) 49 *CML Rev* 2019, 2037).

[51] A Cassese, 'Gathering Up the Main Threads' in A Cassese (ed), *Realizing Utopia, The Future of International Law* (Oxford, Oxford University Press, 2012) 645, 667.

law principles.[52] Accordingly, both the EU Courts and the EFTA Court can develop their way of interpreting their own legal orders. As far as their daily practice is concerned, each court does not need to pay much attention to the legal nature of EU law or EEA law. Once they face a constitutional conflict, the issue of their legal nature arises. However, the consideration about their legal nature can also have inspiring or indicating effects on the development of international law. This is especially important for countries and regions outside of Europe.

Certainly, the internal law of an international organisation has to be regarded as a specialised and particularised part of international law.[53] However, this does not always hold true, because as the case of a protectorate by a treaty of protection suggests,[54] it is possible for two or more independent states to establish a single sovereign entity by concluding a treaty and to replace domestic law with other domestic law. In sum, international law does not exclude the possibility that, based upon an international treaty, a legal order is established among states which differs from international law. The author has an impression that after a series of Kadi judgments, 'constitutional pluralism' in EU law gives more influence to arguments for 'global constitutionalism'.[55] If this holds true, the time might have already come when the three legal orders can be examined in a common overall framework. This might lead to a redefinition of international law. If this is the case, East Asia will not be immune from its impact. The tripartite relationship among EU law, EEA law and international law provides for much food for legal thought and discussion, even for East Asia. The author further believes that the EFTA Court will play a key role in that context because of EEA law's intermediary character.

---

[52] R Barents, *The Autonomy of Community Law* (The Hague, Kluwer Law International, 2004) 213–215 and 239–274.

[53] See Shaw, above n 35, at 1310.

[54] J Crawford, *The Creation of States in International Law*, 2nd edn (Oxford, Oxford University Press, 2006) 282–294.

[55] J Klabbers, 'Setting the Scene' in J Klabbers, A Peters and G Ulfstein (eds), *The Constitutionalization of International Law* (Oxford, Oxford University Press, 2009) 1–3; D Halberstam, 'Local, global and plural constitutionalism: Europe meets the world' in G de Búrca and JHH Weiler (eds), *The Worlds of European Constitutionalism* (Cambridge, Cambridge University Press, 2012) 150, 185–187.

40

A Look at the EEA from Switzerland

CHRISTA TOBLER

I. INTRODUCTION: SWITZERLAND AND THE EEA

AS THE EFTA Court celebrates its twentieth birthday, Switzerland is a
bystander. This may appear astonishing given that, at the time when
the EEA Agreement was negotiated, Switzerland was one of the driving
forces—so much so that the system eventually set up was tailored towards it, in
particular on the institutional level.[1] However, whilst the (then) Swiss Federal
Government was in favour of EEA membership, citizens critical towards the project launched a referendum that led to the rejection of the EEA Agreement in a
popular vote held on 6 December 1992.

Thereafter, Switzerland in its relationship with the EEA EFTA countries continued to rely on the EFTA Convention of 1960 which, after a fundamental revision
in 2001, now covers the free movement not only of goods but also of persons,
services and capital.[2] In order to maintain a workable legal framework in the
relationship between Switzerland and the EU and its Member States, the parties
agreed to continue on what in the former is commonly termed the 'bilateral path',
that is the conclusion of agreements in selected sectors.[3] Since then, the 'bilateral
law' has grown into a complex and unwieldy system comprising more than 130
Agreements, of which some 20 regulate market access.[4] Further, in order not to
be a legal island in fields not covered by these agreements, Switzerland is comple-
menting the bilateral approach with so-called autonomous adaptation in selected

---

[1] See, eg, P du Bois, 'La négotiation EEE vue par un historien' in O Jacot-Guillarmod (ed), Accord
EEE. Commentaires et reflexions/EWR-Abkommen. Erste Analysen/EEA Agreement. Comments and
reflexions (Zürich/Bern, Schulthess/Stämpfli, 1992) 13–22 and, more recently, PG Nell, Suisse—
Communauté européenne. Au coeur des negotiations sur l'espace économique européen (Paris, Economica,
2012); D Freiburghaus, Königsweg oder Sackgasse? Sechzig Jahre schweizerische Europapolitik (Zürich,
NZZ Libro, 2009) 197ff.
[2] Convention establishing the European Free Trade Association of 4 January 1960 (Stockholm
Convention), as revised by the Vaduz Convention of 2001.
[3] See generally C Tobler and J Beglinger, Grundzüge des bilateralen (Wirtschafts-)Rechts.
Systematische Darstellung in Text und Tafeln, 2 vols (Zurich/St Gallen, Dike, 2013). T Cottier et al, Die
Rechtsbeziehungen der Schweiz und der Europäischen Union (Bern, Stämpfli, 2014).
[4] See II.A.

fields, that is, approaching or even aligning of Swiss law to the relevant EU law in spite of the absence of any legal obligation to do so.

With respect to the EEA, the above means that since 6 December 1992 Switzerland has been in the role of an onlooker. As a consequence, EEA law does not play any meaningful role in Switzerland, and it is often neglected, even from a comparative point of view (though it should be added that the Swiss Federal Tribunal, in the context of Swiss competition law, has referred to the EFTA Court's case law).[5] However, more recently the EEA has moved into the Swiss focus again from a rather different angle, namely that of the EU's wishes for a renewal of the institutional system of the bilateral agreements.[6] In 2006, on the occasion of a visit of the President of the Swiss Federal Government to Brussels, Commission President Barroso referred to the administrative burden caused by the bilateral law and suggested that the best way to improve the situation would be Swiss EEA membership or an association agreement between the EU and Switzerland covering such matters.[7] Subsequently, various EU institutions stated that the Union desires a renewed institutional system for those bilateral agreements that concern market access (that is, the selective access of Switzerland to the EU internal market and, vice versa, the access of the EU Member States to the Swiss market), and that the EU is not willing to conclude any new such agreements before a solution can be found for this matter.[8] In fact, the various statements on this issue make clear that the new system envisaged by the Union is modelled on the EEA Agreement.

Since then, the Swiss Government has agreed on a mandate for negotiations on these institutional issues[9] (at the time of writing of this chapter, the EU was yet to do so and has since done it). This, then, is the focus of the present chapter, which will contrast the EU's wishes with the mandate adopted by the Swiss Government and compare them to the model existing in the EEA, where the EFTA Court plays a particularly interesting and important role (II). To some extent, the chapter

---

[5] BGE 139 I 72 of 29 June 2012, para 4.4.

[6] See also, eg, A Epiney, 'Der EWR und die institutionellen Probleme des "Bilateralismus"' in D Freiburghaus and G Kreis (eds), *Der EWR—verpasste und noch immer bestehende Chance* (Zürich, NZZ Libro, 2012) 139–151.

[7] 'Die Harmonie in Brüssel im Vordergrund. Besuch Bundespräsident Leuenbergers bei der EU-Kommission', *Neue Zürcher Zeitung*, 11 July 2006.

[8] See in particular the Council of Ministers Conclusions on EU relations with EFTA countries of 2010 (http://eeas.europa.eu/norway/docs/2012_final_conclusions_en.pdf) and 2012 (http://eeas.europa.eu/norway/docs/2012_final_conclusions_en.pdf). For further references, see Tobler and Beglinger, above n 3, 40ff.

[9] Mandate of 17 December 2013, content as communicated by the Swiss Federal Council in particular through its Press Release of 21 August 2013 ('Europa: Bundesrat schickt Entwurf für ein Verhandlungsmandat über institutionelle Fragen in die Konsultation', http://www.news.admin.ch/message/index.html?lang=de&msg-id=49947). It should be noted that in the summer of 2012 the Swiss Government had sent suggestions of a somewhat different nature to the European Commission, suggestions, however, that were rejected as insufficient in December 2012; both documents are available at the following website of the Swiss Federal Government: www.europa.admin.ch/themen/00499/00503/01777/index.html?lang=de.

relies on work previously published by the present writer in German.[10] However, following the acceptance in Switzerland of the initiative on mass immigration on 9 February 2014, the issue has now to be seen in a new political and legal framework (III).

II. THE INSTITUTIONAL ISSUES OF THE BILATERAL
LAW IN COMPARISON TO EEA LAW

A. The Wishes of the EU

The EU's main concern is that of homogeneity between its own internal market law and the bilateral law, through which selected aspects of this market regime are extended to Switzerland. Homogeneity in this context relates to the *acquis* of the bilateral market access law as well as to its interpretation and application.[11] Accordingly, the EU has listed four focus points for the renewal of the institutional aspects of the bilateral market access agreements, namely:[12]

1) a system of continued updating of the bilateral market access law in view of changes in the relevant EU law;
2) an interpretation of this law in line with the case law of the European Court of Justice (CJEU) on the same EU law matters;
3) an effective mechanism to supervise the application of this law;
4) a supranational mechanism for the resolution of disputes between the parties.

The above raises the question of what is a market access agreement. From an EU law perspective, it is clear that this term refers to those agreements within the larger framework of the bilateral law that cover the access to the market in goods, persons and services (there is to date no bilateral agreement on the free movement of capital, but here the EU's own rules under Article 63 TFEU *et seq* apply to a certain extent).[13]

---

[10] In particular C Tobler, 'Die Erneuerung des bilateralen Wegs: Eine wachsende Annäherung an den EWR in den zur Diskussion gestellten Modellen', *Jusletter*, 3 June 2012, and 'Die flankierenden Massnahmen der Schweiz in einem erneuerten System des bilateralen Rechts', *Jusletter*, 30 September 2013.

[11] Very early on, Van Gerven spoke in this context of legislative and judicial homogeneity: W Van Gerven, 'The Genesis of EEA Law and the Principles of Primacy and Direct Effect' (1992–1993) *Fordham International Law Journal* 956–989.

[12] In addition to the documents referred to in n 8, see also M Reiterer, 'Die Beziehungen zwischen der EU und der Schweiz "dynamisieren" oder die "Grenzen des Bilateralismus"', *Basler Schriften zur Europäischen Integration* Nr 95 (Doppelschrift Ambühl/Reiterer) (Basel, Europainstitut der Universität Basel, 2011) 26–39.

[13] See, eg, Case C-157/05 *Winfried L Holböck v Finanzamt Salzburg-Land* [2007] ECR I-4051.

In the field of goods and in the opinion of the present writer, this includes the agreements on cheese[14] and watches[15] of 1967; also the Free Trade Agreement of 1972[16] (including in particular the amendment through the Agreement on Processed Agricultural Goods of 2004);[17] the Agreement on Agricultural Products of 1999[18] (including in particular the amendment through the Agreement on Designations of Origin of 2011);[19] the Agreement on the Mutual Recognition of Conformity Assessments of 1999;[20] and the Customs Agreement of 2009.[21]

In the field of persons, the following agreements deal with market access: the Insurance Agreement of 1989 (establishment of insurance companies);[22] the Air Transport Agreement of 1999;[23] the Agreement on the Free Movement of Persons of 1999;[24] (workers and establishment for natural persons and their family members) and, possibly, the Agreement on the Taxation of Pensions of Retired EU Officials in Switzerland, which was concluded by the Swiss Federal Government and the European Commission in 2004.[25]

---

[14] Tariff agreement with Switzerland, negotiated under Art XXVIII of GATT, concerning certain cheeses falling within heading ex 04.04 of the Common Customs Tariff, signed at Geneva on 29 June 1967, OJ 1969 L 257/5.

[15] Council Decision of 6 October 1969 concluding tariff agreements with Switzerland, Finland and Austria concerning certain cheeses listed in position ex 4.04 of the common customs tariff, OJ 1969 L 257/3; see also the Additional Agreement to the Agreement concerning products of the clock and watch industry between the European Economic Community and its Member States and the Swiss Confederation, OJ 1974 L 118/12.

[16] Agreement between the European Economic Community and the Swiss Confederation, OJ 1972 L 300/189.

[17] Agreement between the European Community and the Swiss Confederation amending the Agreement between the European Economic Community and the Swiss Confederation of 22 July 1972 as regards the provisions applicable to processed agricultural products, OJ 2005 L 23/19.

[18] Agreement between the European Community and the Swiss Confederation on trade in agricultural products, OJ 2002 L 114/132.

[19] Agreement between the European Union and the Swiss Confederation on the protection of designations of origin and geographical indications for agricultural products and foodstuffs, amending the Agreement between the European Community and the Swiss Confederation on trade in agricultural products, OJ 2011 L 297/3.

[20] Agreement between the European Community and the Swiss Confederation on mutual recognition in relation to conformity assessment, OJ 2002 L 114/369 (as amended).

[21] Agreement between the European Community and the Swiss Confederation on the simplification of inspections and formalities in respect of the carriage of goods and on customs security measures, OJ 2009 L 199/24.

[22] Agreement between the European Economic Community and the Swiss Confederation on direct insurance other than life assurance, OJ 1991 L 205/3.

[23] Agreement between the European Community and the Swiss Confederation on Air Transport, OJ 2002 L 114/73.

[24] Agreement between the European Community and its Member States, of the one part, and the Swiss Confederation, of the other, on the free movement of persons, OJ 2002 L 114/6.

[25] Not published in the Official Journal of the European Union. For Switzerland (German version): Abkommen vom 26. Oktober 2004 zwischen den Schweizerischen Bundesrat und der Kommission der Europäischen Gemeinschaften zur Vermeidung der Doppelbesteuerung von in der Schweiz ansässigen ehemaligen Beamten der Organe und Agenturen der Europäischen Gemeinschaften, SR 0.672.926.81.

Market access in the field of services is covered by the Agreement on Road Transport[26] and by the above-mentioned Agreement on Air Transport of 1999; also—despite its name—by the above-mentioned Agreement on Free Movement of Persons of 1999 (provision of services within a limited framework by natural persons as well as by companies and firms);[27] and finally by the Agreement on Public Procurement of 1999.[28]

In Switzerland, it has been suggested that also the Agreement on the Cooperation of Competition Authorities of 2013 (not yet in force)[29] falls within the category of market access agreements.[30] However, this is clearly not in line with the EU legal system, as was pointed out in response by, among others, the EU Ambassador to Switzerland.[31] Whilst competition law is functionally linked with internal market law, it is distinct from it (Protocol No 27 attached to the TFEU).

Returning to the four focus points indicated by the EU in view of a renewal of the institutional system of the bilateral market access law, with these the EU has in fact invited Switzerland to revisit, and have a fresh look at, the mechanisms that apply under EEA law, and to agree to transpose them to the bilateral market access law between the EU and Switzerland. What this means is further explained below, by comparing the EU's suggestions with the mechanisms provided for under EEA law, and by sketching the present system under the bilateral law as well as the attitude of the Swiss Federal Government as reflected in its mandate for the negotiations on the institutional matters.

B. Updating the Law

With respect to the updating of the legal *acquis*, EEA law provides for a dynamic system of adapting EEA law to new EU law in the fields covered by the Agreement (Articles 102 and 103 EEA). Whilst the system of updating is dynamic, it is not automatic but is based on formal decisions to be made by the Joint EEA Committee. Should the Joint EEA Committee not be able to agree on an update, the consequence is that, in principle, the relevant part of the EEA Agreement is provisionally suspended. With respect to the adoption of the EU law in question,

---

[26] Agreement between the European Community and the Swiss Confederation on the Carriage of Goods and Passengers by Rail and Road, OJ 2002 L 114/91.

[27] In addition to persons and services, this Agreement also contains rules on persons who are not economically active.

[28] Agreement between the European Community and the Swiss Confederation on certain aspects of government procurement, OJ 2002 L 114/430.

[29] The Agreement was concluded on 17 May 2013, and the ratification process is ongoing. Accordingly, the Agreement has not yet been published in the EU's Official Journal.

[30] S Breitenmoser and R Weyeneth, 'Warum der bilaterale Weg nicht am Ende ist', *Neue Zürcher Zeitung*, 25 January 2013, and 'Die Bilateralen sind nicht am Ende', *Neue Zürcher Zeitung*, 15 February 2013.

[31] R Jones, 'Äpfel und Birnen', *Neue Zürcher Zeitung*, 5 February 2013, and K Armingeon, 'Die Rechnung mit dem Wirt machen', *Neue Zürcher Zeitung*, 5 February 2013.

there is a right of the EEA EFTA states to participation in the so-called decision shaping, though not the decision making on this legislation (Article 99 EEA *et seq*).

It would appear that what the EU has in mind for the renewal of the institutional framework for the bilateral market access law with Switzerland is a system of the type just described. Indeed, even though such a dynamic system may imply a certain delay in updating as compared to the entry into force of the original EU law, it provides the best guarantee of homogeneity with that law.

However, for the bilateral law such a new system would differ markedly from that applicable at present. Among the agreements in force, only three provide for a dynamic updating mechanism, and only one of these is a market access agreement, namely the above-mentioned Customs Agreement (the other two being the Schengen[32] and Dublin Agreements).[33] As for other market access agreements, there is no uniform approach. In most cases, the Joint Committee in charge of a particular agreement is competent to update (certain) annexes, and exceptionally also the body of the agreement itself. In addition, there is always the possibility of a formal revision of the agreement. However, not only the rules are different, but also the practice. Whilst the Insurance Agreement has never been changed fundamentally since its conclusion in 1989,[34] other market access agreements are updated quite regularly, among them in particular the Air Transport Agreement but also the Agreement on the Free Movement of Persons. In practice, the fact that the updating mechanism is not dynamic within the meaning of the EEA law and in particular the lack of legal consequences if an update is not made, has meant that not everything deemed necessary by the EU is updated. The most famous example concerns the Union Citizenship Directive 2004/38,[35] in so far as it is an updated version of previous secondary law on the free movement of persons and services and on non-economically active persons (the Directive also contains aspects related to EU citizenship). Whilst the EU wished this instrument to be incorporated into the bilateral law, the Swiss Federal Government refused. Accordingly, the bilateral Agreement on the Free Movement of Persons remains

---

[32] Agreement between the European Union, the European Community and the Swiss Confederation on the Swiss Confederation's association with the implementation, application and development of the Schengen *acquis*, OJ 2008 L 53/52.

[33] Agreement between the European Community and the Swiss Confederation concerning the criteria and mechanisms for establishing the State responsible for examining a request for asylum lodged in a Member State or in Switzerland, OJ 2008 L 23/5.

[34] The Joint Committee decided only once on certain changes: Decision No 1/2001 of the EC–Switzerland Joint Committee of 18 July 2001 amending the Annexes and Protocols to the Agreement between the European Economic Community and the Swiss Confederation on direct insurance other than life assurance and finding that the domestic legislation of the Contracting Parties is compatible with that Agreement, OJ 2001 L 291/52.

[35] Directive 2004/38/EC of the European Parliament and of the Council of 29 April 2004 on the right of citizens of the Union and their family members to move and reside freely within the territory of the Member States amending Regulation (EEC) No 1612/68 and repealing Directives 64/221/EEC, 68/360/EEC, 72/194/EEC, 73/148/EEC, 75/34/EEC, 75/35/EEC, 90/364/EEC, 90/365/EEC and 93/96/EEC, OJ 2004 L 158/77.

based on old secondary law of the then EC or even the EEC in this field.[36] By way of comparison: in the EEA, the inclusion of the Union Citizenship Directive at first also caused certain resistance on the EEA EFTA side, but was then effected with a reservation with regard to EU citizenship. It is submitted that this could also be a model for the bilateral law between the EU and Switzerland.[37]

When formulating the mandate for negotiations on a future institutional system of the bilateral market access agreements, the Swiss Government stated that it is in principle prepared to accept a dynamic system along the lines of EEA law, with the decisions on updating to be taken by the Joint Committee in charge of the relevant agreement. However, this is meant only for *future* EU legislation that falls within the fields covered by the bilateral agreements. It is very explicitly not meant for previous legislation not already incorporated before adopting the new system, including in particular the Union Citizenship Directive, as mentioned above. In fact, leaving this Directive out is part of the Swiss Federal Government's 'red lines'. It remains to be seen whether the EU is willing to discuss such an approach, of which it is quite clear that it cannot result in the degree of homogeneity desired by the EU and guaranteed by the EEA Agreement, which is the EU's model for a new system with Switzerland.

C. Homogeneity in the Interpretation of the Law

Homogeneity in the interpretation of the law is safeguarded under EEA law by a combination of sophisticated elements. In particular, this includes a system of preliminary rulings, which, if a matter arises in an EEA EU State, is the same as under EU law (Article 267 TFEU) and if a matter arises in an EEA EFTA State, leads to the EFTA Court (Article 109 EEA). Both under EU and EEA law, the system of preliminary rulings has proved to be a powerful instrument of private enforcement and a means for the Courts to make the law uniform and effective.

On the EEA/EFTA side, the EFTA Court (as well as any other court faced with an issue of interpretation of EEA law) must observe the homogeneity principle under Article 6 EEA, according to which the provisions of the EEA Agreement, in so far as they are identical in substance to corresponding rules of EU law,[38] shall be interpreted in conformity with the relevant rulings of the CJEU given prior to the date of signature of the EEA Agreement. In the interest of the effectiveness of

---

[36] Whilst some of the relevant instruments are referred to in the Agreement, the content of others has been incorporated into the provisions of the Agreement. This is the case with Regulation 1612/68/EEC on freedom of movement for workers within the Community, OJ 1968 L 257/2.

[37] See C Tobler, 'Bikers Are(n't) Welcome (*Jan Anfinn Wahl v The Icelandic State*, EFTA Court, Judgment of 22 July 2013, E-15/12)' (2013) *European Law Reporter* 246–255.

[38] The wording of Art 6 EEA refers to the Treaty establishing the European Economic Community and the Treaty establishing the European Coal and Steel Community. As the latter has since expired and the former has been incorporated in the EU Treaty through the Lisbon Treaty Revision, the Article should now be read as referring to EU law.

EEA law, the EFTA Court goes beyond this date and also takes into account subsequent case law.[39] Ultimately, the homogeneity principle is an expression of the fact that the EEA Agreement provides for an extension of the EU internal market to the EEA EFTA states.[40] At the same time, it should be noted that homogeneity does not have to be slavish but can be creative.[41]

Again, the situation is different under the bilateral law between the EU and Switzerland. Here, the preliminary ruling system exists only on the side of the EU and its Member States, where the bilateral law is conceived of as part of EU law. There is no such mechanism on the Swiss side. With respect to the homogeneity principle, a similar approach as under EEA law is provided for only under two bilateral agreements, namely in Article 16(2) of the Agreement on the Free Movement of Persons, and in Article 1(2) of the Air Transport Agreement. The Schengen and Dublin Agreements in their preambles mention the objective of ensuring the most uniform possible application and interpretation. In the case of the Free Trade Agreement, the (then) EEC added a Declaration to the effect that it would interpret the competition law provisions of that Agreement in line with EEC (now EU) competition law. This is the background to diverging interpretations of the state aid rules under the Agreement with respect to certain aspects of the corporate taxation systems of some Swiss Cantons.[42] Most of the bilateral agreements, however, do not mention homogeneous interpretation at all, meaning that here, there are only the interpretation rules of the Vienna Convention on the Law of Treaties to fall back on (Article 31 of the Vienna Convention). In such cases, the Swiss Federal Tribunal likes to emphasise its approach of autonomous interpretation. This has led to instances where the Tribunal interprets bilateral rules different from the CJEU interpretation of the parallel rules under EU law. A famous example is the Swiss Federal Tribunal's express refusal to interpret the prohibition of measures having equivalent effect to a quantitative restriction to imports under Article 13 of the Free Trade Agreement in line with the EU *Cassis de Dijon* case law[43] (Federal Tribunal Decision *Physiogel*, BGE 2A.593/2005). In 2009, this led the Swiss Federal legislator to introduce into Swiss law an approach

---

[39] On homogeneity, see further also Arts 105 EEA et seq. In order to further the aim of homogeneity, Art 106 EEA provides for a system of exchange of information to be set up by the EEA Joint Committee concerning judgments by the EFTA Court, the CJEU and the Courts of last instance of the EFTA States.

[40] H Haukeland Fredriksen, 'One Market, Two Courts: Legal Pluralism vs. Homogeneity in the European Economic Area' (2010) *Nordic Journal of International Law* 481–499.

[41] See, eg, C Timmermans, 'Creative Homogeneity' in M Johansson, N Wahl and U Bernitz (eds), *Liber amicorum in Honour of Sven Norberg: A European for all Seasons* (Brussels, Bruylant, 2006) 471–484.

[42] In the English language, see, eg, C Tobler, 'State aid under Swiss–EU bilateral law: The example of company taxation' in M Bultermann, L Hancher, A McDonnell and H Sevenster (eds), *Views of European Law from the Mountain. Liber Amicorum Piet Jan Slot* (Austin/Boston/Chicago/New York/The Netherlands, Wolters Kluwer, Law & Business, 2009) 195–205, and M Maresceau, 'EU–Switzerland—Quo vadis?' Tribute to Gabriel M Wilmer (2011) *Georgia Journal of International & Comparative Law* 39, 728–755.

[43] Case 120/78 *Rewe-Zentral AG v Bundesmonopolverwaltung für Branntwein* [1979] ECR 649.

based on the *Cassis de Dijon* principle unilaterally for the import of goods from the EEA into Switzerland.[44]

When communicating the key elements of its mandate for negotiations on a future institutional system for the bilateral market access agreements, the Swiss Government mentioned neither a homogeneity principle nor a preliminary ruling system. Unofficial sources indicate that the Government is not keen on the latter but if it should prove inevitable, the Government would envisage the competence of the CJEU. It is submitted that such a solution would have the—within Switzerland politically important—disadvantage that representation of Switzerland in the CJEU is not realistically conceivable. Conversely, it may be assumed that the EFTA Court would be more open in this respect. It is therefore submitted that entrusting this Court with bilateral preliminary rulings coming from the Swiss side presents a valuable alternative.

D. Supervision

With respect to supervision, the EEA Agreement provides for a system that is modelled on that of EU law, though transposed to a two-pillar system. Again, for the EU Member States the usual mechanisms apply. Thus, the Commission monitors the observation of EU law by the Member States and may initiate infringement proceedings that may lead to proceedings before the CJEU (Articles 258 and 260 TFEU).[45] With respect to the EEA EFTA States, the monitoring role is fulfilled by the EFTA Surveillance Authority (ESA) and the Court to which it can turn is the EFTA Court (Article 108 EEA). The system is generally very effective.[46]

It is against this background that the EU also wishes for a supranational supervision mechanism for the bilateral market access agreements with Switzerland. At present, it exists only partially. Again, the EU system applies on the side of the EU Member States, though so far it has rarely led to investigations by the Commission and even more rarely to proceedings before the CJEU.[47] On the Swiss side, with the exception of the Public Procurement Agreement there is no particular supervision (national or supranational) authority and there is no equivalent to the infringement procedures of EU and EEA law. Here, everything depends on private enforcement (where, however, there is no preliminary ruling system on the Swiss side, as already noted).

---

[44] Namely through the addition of the new Chapter 3a to the Federal Law of 6 October 1995 on technical trade barriers (SR 946.51) and through the adoption of implementing legislation.

[45] There is also Art 259 TFEU, which allows such proceedings to be initiated by one Member State against another. However, this is extremely rare. A comparatively recent example is provided by Case C-364/10 *Hungary v Slovak Republic*, judgment of 16 October 2012, ECLI:EU:C:2012:630.

[46] Though note the refusal of the Norwegian Supreme Court in its judgment of 5 March 2013 in the case *STX Norway Offshore AS m.fl v Staten v/Tariffnemnda* to follow the EFTA Court's judgment in Case E-2/11 *STX Norway Offshore AS m.fl v Staten v/Tariffnemnda* [2012] EFTA Ct Rep I-3.

[47] See Case C-360/95 *Commission v Spain* [1997] ECR I-7337.

With respect to a future system, the Swiss Government is keen on avoiding any direct supervision through a supranational body or court and to maintain what has been termed 'autonomous self-control'.[48] It is therefore suggesting that the supervision of the bilateral market access agreements remains the task of the Joint Committees, and that a kind of substitute for a supranational mechanism be established through a new element in the dispute resolution mechanism, as discussed below.

E. Dispute Resolution

According to Article 111 EEA, the first instance for the settlement of disputes between parties to the EEA Agreement is the EEA Joint Committee. Where this is not successful and where the dispute concerns the interpretation of EEA provisions identical in substance to corresponding EU rules, the parties may agree to request the CJEU to give a ruling on the interpretation of the relevant rules. If the dispute concerns the scope or duration of safeguard measures (Articles 111(3) or 112 EEA) or the proportionality of rebalancing measures (Article 114 EEA), any party may refer the dispute to arbitration under the procedures laid down in Protocol 33. Though these procedures have never been used so far, it remains that they provide for judicial means of resolving disputes that cannot be solved by the EEA Joint Committee. The fact that the CJEU is the last instance in charge of the authoritative interpretation of EEA law reflects the character of the EEA Agreement as an association of the EEA EFTA states to the EU's internal market.[49]

Again, it would appear that the EU is envisaging a similar approach for the bilateral market access agreements with Switzerland. At present, dispute resolution is essentially a matter for the Joint Committees. As in most agreements there is no other mechanism on the side of Switzerland, there is no means of solving disputes such as that already mentioned concerning corporate taxation[50] through a judicial mechanism. Two market access agreements provide for the possibility of arbitration, though only one of them solely for matters concerning the proportionality of rebalancing measures (namely the Customs Agreement; the Insurance Agreement makes this possible for all types of disputes, which is in fact not acceptable under subsequent CJEU case law).[51] Further, for some issues the Air Transport Agreement provides for the EU mechanism even if a matter is brought up by Switzerland.

---

[48] In the original German, 'autonome Selbstkontrolle'; see A Glaser and L Langer, 'Die Institutionalisierung der Bilateralen Verträge: Eine Herausforderung für die schweizerische Demokratie', SZIER 2013, 563–583, at 581.

[49] See in particular Opinion 1/91 (EEA I) [1991] ECR I-6079 and Opinion 1/92 (EEA II) [1992] ECR I-2821.

[50] See above n 42.

[51] A third agreement with a similar clause does not concern market access, namely the Cooperation Agreement between the European Atomic Energy Community and the Swiss Confederation in the field of controlled thermonuclear fusion and plasma physics, OJ 1978 L 242/2. See further C Tobler, 'Schiedsgerichte im bilateralen Recht?' (2012) *Schweizerische Zeitschrift für internationales und europäisches Recht* 1–6.

An example is the dispute over German rules on the use of its air space by aeroplanes flying to or from Zurich Airport, which, upon a complaint of Switzerland, led to decisions by the European Commission,[52] the (then) Court of First Instance[53] and finally, the Court of Justice.[54] Compared to the mechanism under EEA law, this approach has the disadvantage that Switzerland has to accept judgments by the Court of an international organisation of which it is not a member.

In terms of a future institutional system, the Swiss Federal Government is prepared to accept a system similar to that of the EEA, though with the important difference that, failing a solution in the Joint Committee, it would be possible for one party *alone* to bring the matter to the CJEU for a ruling on the interpretation of the relevant rules. In fact, such a model implies that the European Commission is informally given the role of supervisor on the EU side. To that extent, it is easily conceivable that the EU might be prepared to accept such a model, which goes considerably further than EEA law. However, it must be added that the Swiss Government takes the view that in such a system the actual resolution of the dispute would remain with the Joint Committee, which would have to discuss what to do with the Court's interpretation. It has been suggested that giving the CJEU the decisive role with respect to the interpretation of the bilateral market access agreements would be acceptable for Switzerland provided that the country succeeds in negotiating a 'freely available veto' right with respect to CJEU case law.[55] However, to the present writer it seems unlikely that the EU is willing to agree to such a clause, which plainly makes it impossible to reach the homogeneity aimed at by the EU. Unsurprisingly, it is clear from the perspective of the EU that any ruling of the CJEU would have to be fully binding on the parties.[56]

III. THE PRESENT SITUATION: IMPACT OF THE INITIATIVE ON MASS IMMIGRATION

In principle negotiations on the points discussed above can begin as soon as the EU has adopted its mandate. This was temporarily halted by political developments in

---

[52] Commission Decision of 5 December 2003 on a procedure relating to the application of Art 18(2), first sentence, of the Agreement between the European Community and the Swiss Confederation on air transport and Council Regulation (EEC) No 2408/92 (Case TREN/AMA/11/03—German measures relating to the approaches to Zurich airport), OJ 2004 L 4/13.

[53] Case T-319/05 *Switzerland v Commission* [2010] ECR II-4265.

[54] Case C-547/10 P *Switzerland v Commission*, judgment of 7 March 2013, ECLI:EU:C:2013:139. On this judgment see, eg, V Michel, 'Accord CE/Suisse. La Cour avalise la démarche du Tribunal en rejétant au fond les prétentions de la Suisse et en occultant son statut contentieux' (2013) *Europe* 2013 Mai Comm 5, p 36; PJ Slot, 'Slot, PJ: Zwitserland t. Commissie' (2013) *Ars aequi* 853–859; G van der Loo (Case note), (2013) *Sociaal-economische wetgeving* 335–336, and C Tobler, 'Luftverkehrsrecht: Auslegung des Luftverkehrsabkommens EU-Schweiz. Keine Anwendbarkeit der Dienstleistungsfreiheit' (2013) *Europäische Zeitschrift für Wirtschaftsrecht* 432–434.

[55] In the original German 'ein frei ausübbares Vetorecht'; Glaser and Langer, above n 48, at 582.

[56] See to that effect the interview with CJEU President Skouris in the Swiss press: 'Ich weiss, worauf Sie hinauswollen', *Tages-Anzeiger*, 17 October 2013.

Switzerland. On 9 February 2014, the popular initiative on mass immigration was accepted, introducing into the Swiss Federal Constitution new rules concerning immigration and imposing on the Swiss Federal Government a number of obligations that are also relevant for the bilateral law with the EU. These include, first, the obligation to draft Federal legislation that caps immigration into Switzerland and that gives precedence to Swiss citizens when concluding contracts of employment. Second, there is the obligation to renegotiate and amend existing international treaties contrary to the new immigration system. Further, there is also a prohibition, namely that of refraining from concluding new international agreements, that would conflict with the new immigration regime.

As a first legal consequence of the vote, the Swiss Federal Government found itself unable to sign the Protocol extending the Agreement on the Free Movement of Persons to Croatia as planned. With respect to this latter Agreement, it is obvious that the new regime envisaged by the Federal Constitution is contrary to it.[57] The Agreement should therefore be renegotiated, though the EU has indicated repeatedly (even before the vote was taken) that it is not prepared to do so.

As a first political consequence of the vote of 9 February 2014, the EU is suspended all on-going negotiations on bilateral agreements or participation of Switzerland in EU programmes based on such agreements (which is particularly painful for Switzerland in the field of education and research, namely Erasmus+ and Horizon 2020) and it also refrained from proceeding with the adoption of its mandate for negotiations on the institutional issues discussed in this contribution. The EU has stated that it wishes to assess the overall situation in the light of the Swiss vote and in the light of the concrete suggestions to be made by the Swiss Government.[58] It is therefore at present not clear whether and when the process with respect to the renewal of the institutional aspects of the bilateral market access law will be continued. At the time of writing, it seemed possible that negotiations might commence if a pragmatic solution can be found with respect to Croatia (possibly a solution to be adopted by the Swiss Federal Government on an informal level). This is actually what happened. Negotiations are now ongoing.

---

[57] See in particular J Hänni and S Heselhaus, 'Die eidgenössische Volksinitiative "Gegen Masseneinwanderung" (Zuwanderungsinitiative) im Lichte des Freizügigkeitsabkommens und der bilateralen Zusammenarbeit mit der EU' (2013) *Schweizerische Zeitschrift für internationales und europäisches Recht* 19–64, and C Kaddous, 'Rechtsgutachten über die Vereinbarkeit der Initiative "gegen Masseneinwanderung" und der ECOPOP-Initiative "Stopp der Überbevölkerung—ja zur Sicherung der natürlichen Lebensgrundlagen" mit dem Personenfreizügigkeitsabkommen zwischen der Schweiz und der Europäischen Union (FZA), die Anwendung der "Guillotine"-Klausel und einer allfälligen Neuverhandlung des FZA' (Genf, 2013) http://www.economiesuisse.ch/de/SiteCollectionDocuments/Gutachten-_Kaddous_20132111.pdf.

[58] Declaration of the European Commission following the popular vote in Switzerland on the 'mass immigration' initiative, 9 February 2014, http://europa.eu/rapid/press-release_MEMO-14-96_en.htm.

IV. IN CONCLUSION: THE EEA—DIRECTLY OR INDIRECTLY AN OPTION FOR SWITZERLAND?

According to Schwok and Levrat,[59] the bilateral agreements between the EU and Switzerland are 'substitutes for the European Economic Area'. Łazowski[60] goes even further, calling the development of the bilateral law 'a process of steady progress towards accession to the EEA through the back door'. However, the fact remains that the bilateral law provides for a considerably lower degree of access to the EU's internal market than does EEA law. Further, the institutional rules on amendments to the bilateral agreements as well as their interpretation, supervision and enforcement are also markedly different, and the matter is further complicated by the fact that different agreements provide for different approaches.

It has been noted above that with respect to these institutional issues, the EU is in fact suggesting an indirect *rapprochement* by Switzerland to the EEA, within the formal framework of the bilateral law. However, the question remains whether a more direct route should not also be (re-)considered.[61] After all, it is obvious that the system of the EEA is simpler and from an institutional perspective also more effective than that of the present bilateral law. Further, the EEA Agreement gives full access to the EU's internal market, lifting these countries beyond the status of third states vis-à-vis the EU,[62] whilst leaving them freedom of action in the fields of agriculture, foreign relations and monetary policy in particular—freedom that is much treasured in Switzerland precisely in these fields.

Article 128 EEA states explicitly that Switzerland is entitled to EEA membership, should it wish it. For reasons that are not convincing to the present writer (that is, arguments linked to sovereignty understood as the freedom to make one's own decisions formally independent of others), the Swiss Federal Government appears to be set against making the case for a second attempt at Swiss EEA membership, and against even just considering it seriously. It is submitted that given the benefits that EEA membership have brought to the EEA EFTA states,[63]

---

[59] R Schwok and N Levrat, 'Switzerland's Relations with the EU after the Adoption of the Seven Bilateral Agreements' (2001) *European Foreign Affairs Review* 335–354, at 335.

[60] A Łazowski, 'Chapter 5: Switzerland' in S Blockmans and A Łazowski (eds), *The European Union and Its Neighbours. A Legal Appraisal of the EU's Policies of Stabilisation, Partnership and Integration* (The Hague, TMC Asser Press, 2006) 147–184, at 167.

[61] See, eg, F Blankart, 'EWR und bilaterale Verträge' in G Baur (ed), *Europäer—Botschafter—Mensch: Liber Amicorum für Prinz Nikolaus von Liechtenstein* (Vaduz, Liechtenstein Verlag, 2007) 43–49; C Baudenbacher, 'Der Bilateralismus ist am Ende—Wie könnte ein EWR II aussehen?' in Freiburghaus and Kreis, above n 6, 153–168, and, in the same volume, D Freiburghaus, 'Die schweizerische Europapolitik nach dem EWR-Trauma', 127–137.

[62] See C Baudenbacher, 'Liechtensteiners Can Buy Secondary Homes in Austria Because Liechtenstein is No Third Country' (2011) *European Law Reporter* 182–185.

[63] Regarding the position of Liechtenstein in the EEA, see, eg, G Baur, 'Liechtenstein im EWR—die genutzte Chance' in Freiburghaus and Kreis, above n 6, 81–94, and J Pelkmans and P Böhler (eds), *The EEA Review and Liechtenstein's Integration Strategy* (Brussels, Centre for European Policy Studies, 2013), in particular the conclusions at 143. Regarding Norway see, eg, K Børde, 'The European Economic Area, Norway and the European Union' in P-C Müller-Graff and E Selvig (eds), *The European Economic Area—Norway's basic status in the legal construction of Europe* (Berlin, Berlin

reconsidering EEA membership would be a promising path also for Switzerland, not least given that the EEA itself may evolve. In fact, such membership would not only give Switzerland full access to the EU market, but it would also at a stroke solve the institutional issues with respect to the bilateral law that present so many difficulties at this point in time.

Finally, it is not entirely inconceivable that in such a context the EU might be willing to discuss certain cautious limits to immigration. In the EEA framework, Switzerland's neighbour Liechtenstein continues to benefit from a (formally transitional) regime set up when it joined the EEA. That regime limits the possibility of EU citizens and their families to take up residence (though not employment) in the country.[64] Clearly, Switzerland cannot be compared to the microstate of Liechtenstein. However, talks about EEA membership might open up space for discussing difficult issues in a generally more positive context.

Verlag A Spitz and Oslo, Tano Aschehoug, 1997) 9–15; C Hillion, *Integrating an outsider. An EU perspective on relations with Norway, European Report No 16* (Oslo, Europautredningen, 2011); and H Bull, 'Norwegen im EWR—ein nationaler Kompromiss' in Freiburghaus and Kreis, above n 6, 37–69. Regarding Iceland, see, eg, J Jonsdottir, *Europeanization and the European Economic Area—Iceland's participation in the EU's policy process* (London/New York, Routledge, 2013); M Elvira Méndez-Pinedo and I Domurath, 'Island und Europa: 2012 am Scheideweg?' in Freiburghaus and Kreis, above n 6, 71–80. It should be added that in Iceland, EU membership is at present no longer on the political agenda.

[64] See the explanation given on this matter by the assistant secretary general of the EFTA, Dr Georges Baur, in the Swiss press (*Neue Zürcher Zeitung* of 11 February 2014).

Index